T0213864

Lecture Notes in Artificial Intelligence   12187

Subseries of Lecture Notes in Computer Science

More information about this series at http://www.springer.com/series/1244

Don Harris · Wen-Chin Li (Eds.)

Engineering Psychology and Cognitive Ergonomics

Cognition and Design

17th International Conference, EPCE 2020
Held as Part of the 22nd HCI International Conference, HCII 2020
Copenhagen, Denmark, July 19–24, 2020
Proceedings, Part II

 Springer

Editors
Don Harris
Coventry University
Coventry, UK

Wen-Chin Li
Cranfield University
Cranfield, UK

ISSN 0302-9743   ISSN 1611-3349 (electronic)
Lecture Notes in Artificial Intelligence
ISBN 978-3-030-49182-6   ISBN 978-3-030-49183-3 (eBook)
https://doi.org/10.1007/978-3-030-49183-3

LNCS Sublibrary: SL7 – Artificial Intelligence

This Springer imprint is published by the registered company Springer Nature Switzerland AG
The registered company address is: Gewerbestrasse 11, 6330 Cham, Switzerland

Foreword

The 22nd International Conference on Human-Computer Interaction, HCI International 2020 (HCII 2020), was planned to be held at the AC Bella Sky Hotel and Bella Center, Copenhagen, Denmark, during July 19–24, 2020. Due to the COVID-19 coronavirus pandemic and the resolution of the Danish government not to allow events larger than 500 people to be hosted until September 1, 2020, HCII 2020 had to be held virtually. It incorporated the 21 thematic areas and affiliated conferences listed on the following page.

A total of 6,326 individuals from academia, research institutes, industry, and governmental agencies from 97 countries submitted contributions, and 1,439 papers and 238 posters were included in the conference proceedings. These contributions address the latest research and development efforts and highlight the human aspects of design and use of computing systems. The contributions thoroughly cover the entire field of human-computer interaction, addressing major advances in knowledge and effective use of computers in a variety of application areas. The volumes constituting the full set of the conference proceedings are listed in the following pages.

The HCI International (HCII) conference also offers the option of "late-breaking work" which applies both for papers and posters and the corresponding volume(s) of the proceedings will be published just after the conference. Full papers will be included in the "HCII 2020 - Late Breaking Papers" volume of the proceedings to be published in the Springer LNCS series, while poster extended abstracts will be included as short papers in the "HCII 2020 - Late Breaking Posters" volume to be published in the Springer CCIS series.

I would like to thank the program board chairs and the members of the program boards of all thematic areas and affiliated conferences for their contribution to the highest scientific quality and the overall success of the HCI International 2020 conference.

This conference would not have been possible without the continuous and unwavering support and advice of the founder, Conference General Chair Emeritus and Conference Scientific Advisor Prof. Gavriel Salvendy. For his outstanding efforts, I would like to express my appreciation to the communications chair and editor of HCI International News, Dr. Abbas Moallem.

July 2020   Constantine Stephanidis

HCI International 2020 Thematic Areas and Affiliated Conferences

Thematic areas:

- HCI 2020: Human-Computer Interaction
- HIMI 2020: Human Interface and the Management of Information

Affiliated conferences:

- EPCE: 17th International Conference on Engineering Psychology and Cognitive Ergonomics
- UAHCI: 14th International Conference on Universal Access in Human-Computer Interaction
- VAMR: 12th International Conference on Virtual, Augmented and Mixed Reality
- CCD: 12th International Conference on Cross-Cultural Design
- SCSM: 12th International Conference on Social Computing and Social Media
- AC: 14th International Conference on Augmented Cognition
- DHM: 11th International Conference on Digital Human Modeling and Applications in Health, Safety, Ergonomics and Risk Management
- DUXU: 9th International Conference on Design, User Experience and Usability
- DAPI: 8th International Conference on Distributed, Ambient and Pervasive Interactions
- HCIBGO: 7th International Conference on HCI in Business, Government and Organizations
- LCT: 7th International Conference on Learning and Collaboration Technologies
- ITAP: 6th International Conference on Human Aspects of IT for the Aged Population
- HCI-CPT: Second International Conference on HCI for Cybersecurity, Privacy and Trust
- HCI-Games: Second International Conference on HCI in Games
- MobiTAS: Second International Conference on HCI in Mobility, Transport and Automotive Systems
- AIS: Second International Conference on Adaptive Instructional Systems
- C&C: 8th International Conference on Culture and Computing
- MOBILE: First International Conference on Design, Operation and Evaluation of Mobile Communications
- AI-HCI: First International Conference on Artificial Intelligence in HCI

Conference Proceedings Volumes Full List

38. CCIS 1224, HCI International 2020 Posters - Part I, edited by Constantine Stephanidis and Margherita Antona
39. CCIS 1225, HCI International 2020 Posters - Part II, edited by Constantine Stephanidis and Margherita Antona
40. CCIS 1226, HCI International 2020 Posters - Part III, edited by Constantine Stephanidis and Margherita Antona

http://2020.hci.international/proceedings

17th International Conference on Engineering Psychology and Cognitive Ergonomics (EPCE 2020)

Program Board Chairs: **Don Harris, Coventry University, UK, and Wen-Chin Li, Cranfield University, UK**

- Shan Fu, China
- Crystal Ioannou, UAE
- Peter Kearney, Ireland
- Peng Liu, China
- Heikki Mansikka, Finland

- Lothar Meyer, Sweden
- Ling Rothrock, USA
- Axel Schulte, Germany
- Lei Wang, China
- Jingyu Zhang, China

The full list with the Program Board Chairs and the members of the Program Boards of all thematic areas and affiliated conferences is available online at:

http://www.hci.international/board-members-2020.php

HCI International 2021

The 23rd International Conference on Human-Computer Interaction, HCI International 2021 (HCII 2021), will be held jointly with the affiliated conferences in Washington DC, USA, at the Washington Hilton Hotel, July 24–29, 2021. It will cover a broad spectrum of themes related to Human-Computer Interaction (HCI), including theoretical issues, methods, tools, processes, and case studies in HCI design, as well as novel interaction techniques, interfaces, and applications. The proceedings will be published by Springer. More information will be available on the conference website: http://2021.hci.international/.

General Chair
Prof. Constantine Stephanidis
University of Crete and ICS-FORTH
Heraklion, Crete, Greece
Email: general_chair@hcii2021.org

http://2021.hci.international/

Contents – Part II

Human Factors in Human Autonomy Teaming and Intelligent Systems

Cognitive Psychology in Aviation and Automotive

Contents – Part I

Human Physiology, Human Energy and Cognition

Cognition and Design of Complex and Safety Critical Systems

Measuring Situation Awareness in Control Room Teams

Carolina Barzantny[(✉)] and Carmen Bruder

German Aerospace Center (DLR), Aviation and Space Psychology,
Hamburg, Germany
Carolina.Barzantny@dlr.de

Abstract. The importance of monitoring activities in control rooms continues to increase. Teams of operators are required to monitor a system for any abnormal system behavior, and must be able to exert manual control over the system in case of automation failure. Being ready to act requires operators to be aware of the system status at all times. However, developing and maintaining high situation awareness in a highly complex and dynamic environment can be challenging. Hence, the absence of situation awareness has often been attributed as the cause of human error in the past. A better understanding of situation awareness using different methods for quantification are required in order to reduce error and enhance the training of control room teams. The following study concentrates on evaluating situation awareness in a simulated control center task. Twenty-one three-person teams ($N = 63$ participants) were tested. Performance, gaze, and communication data were integrated as individual measures of situation awareness. A relationship between the three measures was identified. Post-hoc analyses revealed differences between high and low performers with regards to their situation awareness. The development of situation awareness over time was also taken into consideration. Results reveal that when investigating situation awareness in control room teams, the use of multiple measures is a promising approach.

Keywords: Eye tracking · Control room team · Situation awareness · Automation · Communication · Human error

1 Introduction

Control rooms can be found in fields where safety is highly critical, such as aviation, traffic, health care, or power plant control. In these environments, they act as centers in which the control operations are being coordinated and constantly monitored in order to guarantee the stability and safety of the systems [1]. Due to an increase in automation, monitoring activities in the control room have gained importance. Monitoring requires the operator to visually scan the system status for any abnormal system behavior and be ready to act if a failure occurs [2]. In the control room, monitoring is often based on prior knowledge and follows certain strategies, rather than simply waiting for a failure to occur [3]. Because of the complexity of system control rooms, teams of operators monitor a system together. Collaborative monitoring requires team

© Springer Nature Switzerland AG 2020
D. Harris and W.-C. Li (Eds.): HCII 2020, LNAI 12187, pp. 3–17, 2020.
https://doi.org/10.1007/978-3-030-49183-3_1

members not only to visually scan for failures, but to interact with each other and exchange relevant information at all times in order to keep track of the system's current status [4]. Staying highly aware under such circumstances is difficult. Therefore, in order to prevent the occurrence of human error in control room teams, ways to maintain and train situation awareness in control room teams are needed [5].

The psychological concept of situation awareness is widely known and commonly used in human factors research [6, 7]. The term was first used in the context of aircraft piloting and has been extensively investigated in the field of aviation ever since [e.g. 8–10]. In recent years, it has been transferred to other domains such as driving [11], medicine [12, 13], nuclear power plant control [14, 15], and cyber security [16]. In this research, the main finding is that high situation awareness is generally linked to better performance. For example, Bell [8] found that fighter pilots with a higher situation awareness make fewer decision errors in a combat scenario than pilots with lower situation awareness. Conversely, low situation awareness is still found to be the major cause of human error. According to Jones and Endsley [17], over 70% of pilot errors that are related to situation awareness can be traced back to level one of the three levels of situation awareness, which involves the initial perception of information. At level two, the information that has been perceived is then understood and processed on a deeper level. At least 20% of pilot errors can be attributed to difficulties with level two situation awareness. With level three situation awareness, future events can be anticipated [18]. According to Endsleys' model [6, 7] it takes all three levels of information processing for an individual to make a decision in the end. In order to gain insight into an individual's level of situation awareness, appropriate measures are needed.

Measures of situation awareness mainly include task performance measures, memory probes, and subjective as well as objective rating techniques [19–21]. However, because situation awareness is a more fluid concept that is achieved over time, more process-oriented measures are needed. In this context, eye tracking has been found to be beneficial as an online indicator of situation awareness. In aviation, it has become a frequently used method [22, 23]. Furthermore, in a wide range of domains, such as problem solving and reasoning [24, 25], driving [26, 27], medicine [28], education [29], music [30] and chess [31], various studies have integrated eye tracking in order to understand and compare visual attention processing [32, 33]. Little research has been done on this topic in the context of control rooms. For example, Sharma and colleagues [5] used eye tracking in a chemical plant environment and were able to find differences among operators concerning their fixation patterns.

Another process-oriented measure of situation awareness is communication [34, 35]. Authors have stressed the importance of effective teamwork and communication at work [36]. Specifically in the control room, communication is crucial for teams to be successful [4]. Here, it is not only critical that operators become aware of their own situation, but the situation of their team members as well. By exchanging relevant information, they can ultimately achieve higher situation awareness [37]. In other words, communication not only allows one's own situation awareness to be modified and enhanced, but it also promotes sharing it, ultimately affecting the situation awareness of the whole team [38]. Therefore, measuring the level and quality of communication between team members can help assess the level of achieved SA [39] and contribute as an additional measure for evaluating situation awareness in control room teams.

Taking previous research into account, studies have mostly focused on not one, but multiple measures for investigating situation awareness, thus demonstrating the necessity of using multiple measures when investigating teams, specifically in a complex environment such as the control room. As this study concentrates on examining teams in a simulated control center task, it therefore uses a variety of measures of situation awareness. We assumed that the measures of performance, gaze, and communication behavior would be related, and that they could be used to help gain insight into the situation awareness of the operators:

Hypothesis I: There is a relationship between performance, gaze, and communication behavior.

By examining the link between different situation awareness measures, we further assumed that operators who are better at detecting failures while monitoring should differ from low performers with regards to their situation awareness:

Hypothesis II: High performers differ from low performers with regard to their gaze and communication behavior.

Continuous measures such as eye tracking and verbal communication are beneficial when it comes to investigating situation awareness over time. They allow tracking the state of situation awareness at all times. Taking multiple measures into account should further help investigate if and how situation awareness was achieved:

Hypothesis III: The increase of situation awareness over time can be observed in different measures.

2 Method

The reported study was part of the DLR project COCO (*Collaborative Operations in Control Rooms*). The overall aim of COCO was to evaluate different psychological and physiological factors that influence control room teams. The study was conducted using ConCenT (*generic Control Center Task Environment*), a simulation in which control center activity was simulated [40].

2.1 Simulation

In ConCenT, teams of three have to supervise several distributed production facilities and monitor the environment to determine whether or not a failure has occurred (monitoring task). If there is a failure, they have to determine the cause of the failure (diagnosis task) and find a solution to the problem (remedy task). In order to complete all three tasks, operators are required to collaborate and exchange information at all times. Because only the monitoring task was taken into consideration for the analysis, the diagnosis and remedy tasks will not be described here further.

In order to understand how the collaborative monitoring task was conducted, the structure of ConCenT is illustrated in Fig. 1. The control center that needs to be supervised consists of nine production plants which are distributed over three different sites: Alpha, Bravo, and Charlie. Each plant comprises three overlapping assembly lines, adding up to a total of 27 lines. Joint power stations supply their corresponding sites with energy. Operators A, B, and C are each in charge of monitoring the status of nine of the 27 assembly lines. Their status is indicated by individual gauges on their associated control panel (Fig. 2). Failures are indicated by a gauge's actual value falling below or exceeding the limits of its associated tolerance range, indicating a failure in the associated plant. A failure was the consequence of a critical situation that the team members could only anticipate by exchanging information about the system status. Rules on how to anticipate a critical situation were given to the team members beforehand. This enabled team members to gather expectations about critical situations and possible failures within the system. Whenever a failure occurred, all operators had to report it within a time interval of four seconds.

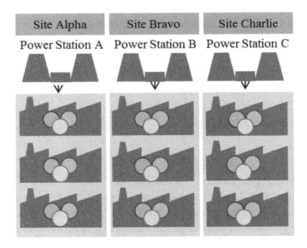

Fig. 1. Structure of ConCenT. Three sites with three plants ▟▟▟. Each plant comprises three overlapping assembly lines ◖◗. Every site is supplied with energy by one power station ▟▖▟.

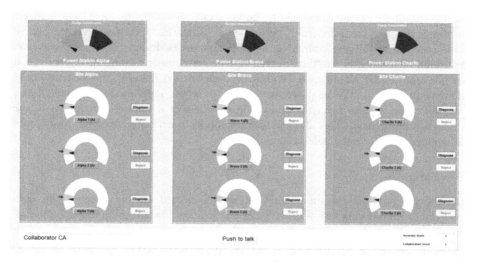

Fig. 2. Control Panel. Each operator must monitor 12 gauges. The top three gauges represent the energy levels of the joint power stations. The nine gauges below indicate the status of the assigned assembly lines. Next to each gauge, there is a button for reporting failures in case the associated black arrow exceeds or falls below the tolerance area.

2.2 Eye Tracker

Eye movements were recorded with the Eye Follower System manufactured by LC Technologies, Inc. Management of raw data was conducted using NYAN software. Subjects were seated in front of a 24-inch LCD computer display at a distance of approximately 60 cm. The system operated at 120 Hz and was combined with the simulation tool ConCenT to ensure that both systems used the same timestamp. The fixation-detection algorithm was set to require a minimum of six gazes on a particular point on the screen (within a deviation threshold of 25 pixels). All successive fixations falling on an AOI (area of interest) were categorized as *gaze duration*.

2.3 Participants

Twenty-one teams (total $N = 63$ participants), were tested. Participant age ranged between 18 and 34 years ($M = 21.57$, $SD = 3.39$). 47.6% of the participants were female and 52.4% male. 41 individuals were applicants for air traffic control training at DFS (German Air Navigation Service Provider), 22 individuals were students and graduates from various universities. Participants were compensated €25 for participating in the 2.5-h test.

2.4 Procedure

Three participants were seated next to each other. Room dividers prevented direct eye contact between the participants. Each operator position included a separate computer and eye-tracking system. After reading comprehensive instructions and completing a ten-minute practice scenario, teams performed a 72-min test scenario. Over the course of the scenario, a failure occurred at six different times during the monitoring task. Each failure had to be reported by every single team member within four seconds. If it was not reported by all members within the four-second interval, the system would automatically switch into the diagnosis task and it would individually be counted as a miss. Rules on system behavior and on how to detect a failure were given to the participants beforehand. This allowed team members to exchange relevant information and enabled them to anticipate failures in time.

2.5 Variables

Performance, gaze, and communication data were collected. For the present study, only data from the monitoring task was analyzed. Performance measures included number of failures detected and response time in seconds. The analysis of gaze was based on four distinct monitoring phases, which were predefined as taking place before and during the occurrence of a failure. These phases were derived based on the normative model on how to identify operators monitoring appropriately that was used in previous research on monitoring tasks [22, 41]. During the first two phases, operators had to identify the relevant information [identification phase] and verify this information within the team [verification phase]. During the third phase, a failure could be anticipated by the team [anticipation phase]. During the fourth and final phase, the failure was visible [detection phase]. For each phase, the information that was needed to be perceived and shared was marked as relevant. This information also represented the relevant areas of interests (AOIs) for eye movement analysis. In order to conduct the gaze analysis, fixation-based eye-movement parameters were used. These included relative fixation count (ratio between number of fixations on relevant AOIs and all fixations within a given time span) and relative gaze duration (ratio between gaze duration on relevant AOIs and total gaze duration within a given time span). The time to first fixation was used only during the anticipation and detection phases. Verbal communication was analyzed with respect to the accuracy of information that was shared by each team member in order to anticipate and detect each of the six failures. In order to define an individual's quality of communication, participants could score on a scale from 0 (no or false communication of relevant information) to 1 (correct communication of relevant information) within each of the four monitoring phases.

3 Results

The data gathered from 52 participants were used for analysis. Eleven data sets were excluded due to missing data or failed manipulation checks. Analysis was conducted on the individual level and focused on the time before and during the occurrence of each of the six failures (monitoring phases). The six failures were referred to as items. On a scale from 0 to 6, an average of 4.33 ($SD = 1.37$) failures were detected. The average response time was 2.17 s $(SD = 0.56)$. On a scale from 0 (no gaze on relevant information) to 1 (all fixations on relevant information) relative fixation count and relative gaze duration varied between $M = .41$ and $M = .50$ $(SD = 0.09\text{-}0.19)$ within each of the four monitoring phases. On a scale from 0 to 6, the average communication quality was 3.30 $(SD = 0.89)$. The level of communication varied between the four monitoring phases (see Fig. 3).

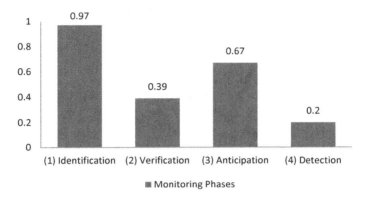

Fig. 3. Mean communication quality from 0 to 1 for each monitoring phase over all six failures.

3.1   Linking Performance, Gaze and Communication

Multiple correlations between detection performance, gaze data, and communication quality were calculated. Figure 4 shows the overall results in a simplified manner. A statistically significant relationship between all eye movement parameters (relative gaze duration, relative fixation count, and time to first fixation) and the number of detected failures was revealed, $F(10,41) = 3.34$, $p < .01$, $R = .67$. In particular, eye movement parameters in the anticipation and detection phases were correlated to detection performance $(p < .01)$. In order to investigate the relationship between detection performance (in terms of numbers of failures detected) and communication quality, a non-parametric correlation of Kendall's tau-b was run. A positive relationship was identified, $r_T(51) = .26$, $p < .05$. For response time, this relationship turned out to be negative, $r_T(48) = -.35$, $p = .001$. Multiple correlations between gaze data and communication quality revealed no statistically significant relationship $F(10,38) = 1.78$, $p > .05$, $R = .57$. However, non-parametric rank correlations of Kendall's tau-b showed a significant relationship between eye movement parameters and communication quality during the anticipation phase $(p < .05)$.

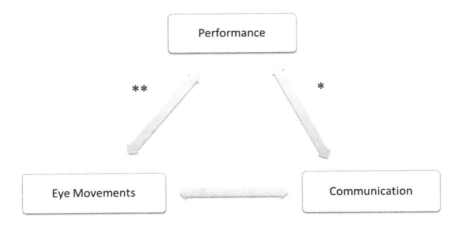

Fig. 4. Simplified illustration of the link between the three measures of situation awareness. * $p < .05$, ** $p < .01$.

3.2 High Vs. Low Performers

Participants were split post-hoc into two groups, high and low performers, based on their total number of detected failures using a median split (*Mdn* = 4.4). Two groups were created, one with 26 high performers and the other with 26 low performers. High performers detected a significantly higher number of failures than low performers ($U = 0$, $z = -6.40$, $p = < .001$) and their mean response time was significantly lower than that of low performers, $t(49) = 2.39$, $p < .05$ (Fig. 5). In order to test whether high and low performers differed with regard to their eye movement data, a one-way multivariate analysis of variance (MANOVA) was conducted. A statistically significant MANOVA effect was obtained, Wilks-λ = .63, $F(10,41) = 2.44$, $p < .05$, partial η^2 = .37. High performers had a higher relative fixation count and higher relative gaze duration than low performers in the last three monitoring phases [verification, anticipation, detection] and a lower time to first fixation in the last phase [detection]. In terms of their overall communication quality, high performers (*Mdn* = 3.25, n = 24) did not significantly differ from low performers (*Mdn* = 2.75, n = 25), $U = 207$, $z = -1.88$, $p > .05$.

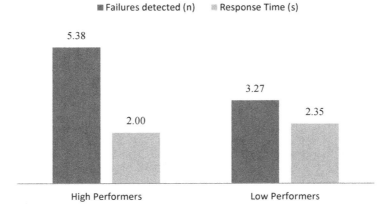

Fig. 5. Descriptive performance results of high and low performers.

3.3 Performance and Communication Over Time

In addition to linking the different measures and comparing them for the two groups of high and low performers, consideration was also given to the development of performance measures and communication quality over time. Figures 6 show the descriptive results. A Cochran's Q test determined a statistically significant difference over time in the proportion of participants who detected a deviation successfully, $p < .001$. This applied both to high and low performers, $p < .001$. Pairwise comparisons using continuity-corrected McNemar's tests with Bonferroni correction revealed that significantly more high performers detected failures two to six than failure one, $p < .01$. Correspondingly, it was shown that low performers detected failures three to six significantly more often than failures one and two ($p < .001$). High and low performers differed significantly in their mean response times as determined by independent-samples t-tests when detecting failure three, $t(42) = 3.28$, $p < .01$, and five, $t(40) = 2.55$, $p < .05$. In terms of the communication quality of individual participants, statistically significant deviations were displayed between the six items (Friedman test: $\chi^2(5) = 15.15$, $p = .01$, $n = 47$). This applied to low performers, $\chi^2(5) = 20.48$, $p = .001$, $n = 23$, but not to high performers, $\chi^2(5) = 0.10$, $p > .05$, $n = 24$. Post-hoc analysis of low performers revealed a statistically significant difference between items two and five, $z = -3.63$, $p < .01$, as well as two and six, $z = -3.00$, $p < .05$, as item two had the lowest communication quality, whereas five and six had the highest. Mann-Whitney U tests revealed that high and low performers differed significantly with regard to item two, $U = 187$, $z = -2.24$, $p < .05$ and four, $U = 198$, $z = 2.28$, $p < .05$.

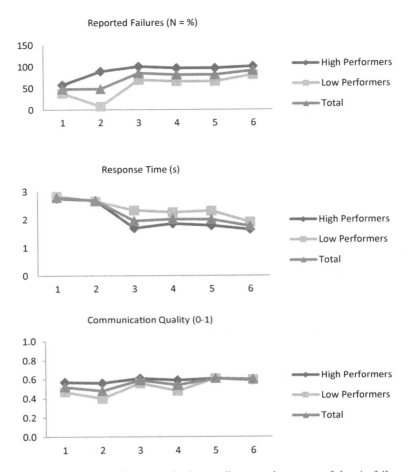

Fig. 6. Performance and communication quality over the course of the six failures.

4 Discussion

The present study addressed the benefit of using multiple measures of situation awareness in control room teams. In a simulated control center task, teams of three were asked to monitor different production facilities and detect failures. Information was distributed among team members in a way that made communication necessary within the team. Performance was measured by counting the number of failures detected and collecting the associated response times. Eye tracking was integrated to examine where individuals directed their gaze before and during the occurrence of each of the six failures. Additionally, communication was recorded for the same time intervals and analyzed based on the previously defined information that needed to be shared with the team members in order to anticipate and detect failures.

4.1 Linking Multiple Situation Awareness Measures

The results of this study show that both gaze and communication behavior is linked to monitoring performance. It was found that when the gaze was directed towards the relevant information during each monitoring phase more, failures were detected and reported faster and more consistently. This entailed longer and more frequent fixations on relevant information during time intervals before and during the occurrence of a failure. Therefore, relevant information was processed more intensively and more often than irrelevant information [42, 43]. Further, participants that fixated a failure earlier were able to report it more accurately and much faster. This shows that by following certain strategies, and ultimately being more aware of the situation, operators are able to anticipate and detect failures in time during control room monitoring [3, 5, 41].

Besides investigating situation awareness by means of performance and gaze measures, the quality of information exchange within the team was analyzed as well. When more relevant information was communicated accurately and at the appropriate time, system failures were detected earlier and more consistently. Therefore, this work supports previous results that showed communication is strongly linked to performance [44, 45]. It indicates that the more aware someone is, the more accurate his or her communication will be, which ultimately affects the final outcome.

Lastly, it was assumed that there would be a link between gaze and communication behavior. No overall relationship was found except for a link between the two measures for the distinct monitoring phase of anticipation, supporting the proposed importance of anticipatory processes in complex fields where safety is critical [46]. Right before the occurrence of a failure, the words being spoken by the participants concerned where they were looking, emphasizing the need to share task-relevant information immediately before a system failure occurred. If no communication had occurred at this point, it would have made it impossible for team members ultimately to detect a failure. The fact that no relationship was found for the other three distinct monitoring phases might be explained by consistently high communication quality among participants during the first phase. Moreover, the detection phase was only a few seconds long, so it was nearly impossible for all team members to share and confirm the detection of a failure. Furthermore, communication analysis was based on assumptions on what kind of information had to be shared in order to anticipate and detect a failure, but not on what kind of information needed to be received. Taking this into account when analyzing communication on the team level might result in finding a relationship between gaze and communication behavior.

4.2 High and Low Situation Awareness

Post-hoc analysis showed significant differences between high and low performers in terms of their eye movements. Overall, high performers were better at directing their gaze toward relevant information at the right time [cf. 32]. In three out of four monitoring phases, they focused longer and more frequently on relevant information. Also, they directed their gaze at the failures earlier. Having more fixations on task-relevant areas and shorter times to first fixate relevant information is consistent with previous findings on expertise in eye tracking research [22, 33, 47]. Results showed that high performers were more efficient and knew how to anticipate and detect a failure better, indicating they had higher situation awareness than low performers. However, with regard to their communication quality, high and low performers did not differ significantly. Though, for two failures communication was found to differ between high and low performers, indicating that there must have been some difference between the two groups at some point. For future research it would be of interest to consider analyzing not only the quality but also the quantity of communication, allowing a more objective approach to analyzing communication in control room teams.

4.3   The Development of Situation Awareness

Results show an increase in performance and communication quality over time. Teams were able to improve when and what kind of information was exchanged while their performance improved as well. This is in line with Cooke [48], who found that command-and-control teams improve their interactions over time, accompanied by improvements in team performance. With regards to this study, the increase in communication quality can be attributed to the group of low performers. High performers started off the simulation with a better quality in their communication and therefore started off the scenario with higher situation awareness. Both groups improved their performance, which is likely to happen with participants who did not have any previous experience with the simulation. In this context, the first ten minutes of the task were mostly needed to adapt to the task. This is consistent with previous research showing that performance increases early in the team development stages [48]. However, it must be said that high performers adapted to the situation more quickly than low performers. They started off the simulation with a higher performance and were better at detecting failures throughout the scenario. They performed better and communicated more effectively in the early stages of the scenario than low performers. This indicates that they had higher situation awareness right from the beginning and were able to maintain it over time.

4.4   Conclusion and Outlook

Our findings provide important implications for the integration of different measures of situation awareness in control room teams and the development of situation awareness in complex teamwork scenarios. Performance, gaze, and communication behavior were found to be useful when investigating situation awareness in team-based monitoring. Efficient gaze behavior and the quality of communication are closely linked to the amount of system failures detected and the speed of detection. High situation awareness is demonstrated by directing one's gaze toward relevant information faster and more frequently, and by sharing information accordingly when having to anticipate a failure. While an increase in situation awareness could be seen in overall performance and communication behavior, high performers started off with higher situation awareness than low performers. The noticeable increase of situation awareness at the beginning of the task suggests the need for knowledge enhancement and training for control room teams right before and at the start of their cooperation. Since the analysis was conducted on an individual level, analyses must also be carried out on a team level by using advanced methods in order to investigate team cognition patterns and draw conclusions about team situation awareness [39]. Current and future research focuses on applying reported single team outcomes to multi-team situations, in which individuals of not one but several organizations work together in a collaborative manner.

References

1. Suchman, L.: Centers of coordination: a case and some themes. In: Resnick, L.B., Säljö, R., Pontecorvo, C., Burge, B. (eds.) Discourse, Tools and Reasoning: Essays on Situated Cognition, pp. 41–62. Springer, Heidelberg (1997). https://doi.org/10.1007/978-3-662-03362-3_3
2. Eißfeldt, H., et al.: Aviator 2030 – Ability requirements in future ATM systems II: Simulations and Experiments (28). DLR, Köln (2009)
3. Vicente, K.J., Roth, E.M., Mumaw, R.J.: How do operators monitor a complex, dynamic work domain? the impact of control room technology. Int. J. Hum Comput Stud. **54**(6), 831–856 (2001)
4. Carvalho, P.V.R., Vidal, M.C.R., de Carvalho, E.F.: Nuclear power plant communications in normative and actual practice: a field study of control room operators' communications. Hum. Factors Ergon. Manuf. **17**(1), 43–78 (2007)
5. Sharma, C., Bhavsar, P., Srinivasan, B., Srinivasan, R.: Eye gaze movement studies of control room operators: a novel approach to improve process safety. Comput. Chem. Eng. **85**, 43–57 (2016)
6. Endsley, M.R.: Design and evaluation for situation awareness enhancement. In: Proceedings of the Human Factors Society 32nd Annual Meeting, pp. 97–101. Human Factors Society, Santa Monica (1988)
7. Endsley, M.R.: Toward a theory of situation awareness in dynamic systems. Hum. Factors **37**(1), 32–64 (1995)
8. Bell, H.H., Lyon, D.R.: Using observer ratings to access situation awareness. In: Endsley, M. R., Garland, D.J. (eds.) Situation Awareness Analaysis and Measurement, pp. 129–146 (2000)
9. Cak, S., Say, B., Misirlisoy, M.: Effects of working memory, attention, and expertise on pilots' situation awareness. Cogn. Technol. Work **22**, 1–10 (2019). https://doi.org/10.1007/s10111-019-00551-w
10. Hauland, G.: Measuring individual and team situation awareness during planning tasks in training of en route air traffic control. Int. J. Aviat. Psychol. **18**(3), 290–304 (2008)
11. Ma, R., Kaber, D.B.: Situation awareness and driving performance in a simulated navigation task. Ergonomics **50**(8), 1351–1364 (2007)
12. Zhang, Y., et al.: Effects of integrated graphical displays on situation awareness in anaesthesiology. Cogn. Technol. Work **4**(2), 82–90 (2002)
13. Gillespie, B.M., Gwinner, K., Fairweather, N., Chaboyer, W.: Building shared situational awareness in surgery through distributed dialog. J. Multidisc. Healthc. **6**, 109–118 (2013)
14. Burns, C.M., et al.: Evaluation of ecological interface design for nuclear process control: situation awareness effects. Hum. Factors **50**(4), 663–679 (2008)
15. Hogg, D.N., FOLLESØ, K., Strand-Volden, F., Torralba, B.: Development of a situation awareness measure to evaluate advanced alarm systems in nuclear power plant control rooms. Ergonomics **38**(11), 2394–2413 (1995)

16. Lif, P., Granåsen, M., Sommestad, T.: Development and validation of technique to measure cyber situation awareness. In: 2017 International Conference on Cyber Situational Awareness, Data Analytics And Assessment (Cyber SA), pp. 1–8. IEEE (2017)
17. Jones, D.G., Endsley, M.R.: Sources of situation awareness errors in aviation. Aviat. Space Eviron. Med. **67**(6), 507–512 (1996)
18. Endsley, M.R., Garland, D.J.: Theoretical underpinnings of situation awareness: a critical review. Situat. Aware. Anal. Meas. **1**, 24 (2000)
19. Fang, Y., Cho, Y.K., Durso, F., Seo, J.: Assessment of operator's situation awareness for smart operation of mobile cranes. Autom. Constr. **85**, 65–75 (2018)
20. Gutzwiller, R.S., Clegg, B.A.: The role of working memory in levels of situation awareness. J. Cogn. Eng. Decis. Making **7**(2), 141–154 (2013)
21. Gardner, A.K., Kosemund, M., Martinez, J.: Examining the feasibility and predictive validity of the SAGAT tool to assess situation awareness among medical trainees. Simul. Healthc. **12**(1), 17–21 (2017)
22. Hasse, C., Bruder, C.: Eye-tracking measurements and their link to a normative model of monitoring behaviour. Ergonomics **58**(3), 355–367 (2015)
23. Peißl, S., Wickens, C.D., Baruah, R.: Eye-tracking measures in aviation: a selective literature review. Int. J. Aerosp. Psychol. **28**(3–4), 98–112 (2018)
24. Ball, L.J., Phillips, P., Wade, C.N., Quayle, J.D.: Effects of belief and logic on syllogistic reasoning: Eye-movement evidence for selective processing models. Exp. Psychol. **53**, 77–86 (2006)
25. Tsai, M.J., Hou, H.T., Lai, M.L., Liu, W.Y., Yang, F.Y.: Visual attention for solving multiple-choice science problem: an eye-tracking analysis. Comput. Educ. **58**(1), 375–385 (2012)
26. Merat, N., Jamson, A.H., Lai, F.C.H., Carsten, O.: Highly automated driving, secondary task performance, and driver state. Hum. Factors **54**(5), 762–771 (2012)
27. Underwood, G., Chapman, P., Brocklehurst, N., Underwood, J., Crundall, D.: Visual attention while driving: sequences of eye fixations made by experienced and novice drivers. Ergonomics **46**(6), 629–646 (2003)
28. Law, B., Atkins, M.S., Kirkpatrick, A.E., Lomax, A.J.: Eye gaze patterns differentiate novice and experts in a virtual laparoscopic surgery training environment. In: Proceedings of the 2004 symposium on Eye tracking research & applications, pp. 41–48 (2004)
29. Jarodzka, H., Scheiter, K., Gerjets, P., Van Gog, T.: In the eyes of the beholder: how experts and novices interpret dynamic stimuli. Learn. Instr. **20**(2), 146–154 (2010)
30. Fink, L.K., Lange, E.B., Groner, R.: The application of eye-tracking in music research. J. Eye Mov. Res. **11**(2) (2018)
31. Charness, N., Reingold, E.M., Pomplun, M., Stampe, D.M.: The perceptual aspect of skilled performance in chess: evidence from eye movements. Mem. Cogn. **29**(8), 1146–1152 (2001)
32. Bruder, C., Hasse, C.: Differences between experts and novices in the monitoring of automated systems. Int. J. Ind. Ergon. **72**, 1–11 (2019)
33. Gegenfurtner, A., Lehtinen, E., Säljö, R.: Expertise differences in the comprehension of visualizations: a meta-analysis of eye-tracking research in professional domains. Educ. Psychol. Rev. **23**(4), 523–552 (2011)
34. Garbis, C., Artman, H.: Team Situation Awareness as Communicative Practices. A Cognitive Approach to Situation Awareness: Theory and Application. Ashgate, Aldershot (2004)
35. Wright, M.C., Endsley, M.R.: Building shared situation awareness in healthcare settings. In: Improving healthcare team communication, pp. 97–114. CRC Press, Boca Raton (2017)
36. Leonard, M., Graham, S., Bonacum, D.: The human factor: the critical importance of effective teamwork and communication in providing safe care. BMJ Qual. Saf. **13**(suppl 1), i85–i90 (2004)

37. Salas, E., Prince, C., Baker, D.P., Shrestha, L.: Situation awareness in team performance: implications for measurement and training. Hum. Factors **37**(1), 123–136 (1995)
38. Gorman, J.C., Cooke, N.J., Winner, J.L.: Measuring team situation awareness in decentralized command and control environments. Ergonomics **49**(12–13), 1312–1325 (2006)
39. Cooke, N.J., Gorman, J.C., Myers, C.W., Duran, J.L.: Interactive team cognition. Cogn. Sci. **37**, 255–285 (2013)
40. Schulze-Kissing, D., Bruder, C.: Der Einsatz synthetischer Aufgabenumgebungen zur Untersuchung kollaborativer Prozesse in Leitzentralen am Beispiel der "Generic Control Center Task Environnment" (ConCenT). In: Proceedings of the Workshop Cognitive Systems, Bochum (2016)
41. Bruder, C., Eißfeldt, H., Maschke, P., Hasse, C.: A model for future aviation: operators monitoring appropriately. Aviat. Psychol. Appl. Hum. Factors **4**(1), 13–22 (2014)
42. Jacob, R.J.K., Karn, K.S.: Eye tracking in human-computer interaction and usability research: Ready to deliver the promises. In: Hyönä, J., Radach, R., Deubel, H. (eds.) The Mind's Eye: Cognitive and Applied Aspects of Eye Movement Research, pp. 573–605 (2003)
43. Pannasch, S.: Ereignisbezogene Veränderungen der visuellen Fixationsdauer (Unpublished doctoral dissertation). Technische Universität Dresden, Dresden (2003)
44. Stout, R.J., Cannon-Bowers, J.A., Salas, E., Milanovich, D.M.: Planning, shared mental models, and coordinated performance: an empirical link is established. Hum. Factors **41**(1), 61–71 (1999)
45. Chang, S., Waid, E., Martinec, D.V., Zheng, B., Swanstrom, L.L.: Verbal communication improves laparoscopic team performance. Surg. Innov. **15**(2), 143–147 (2008)
46. Kallus, K.: Anticipatory processes in critical flight situations. In: Mechanisms in the Chain of Safety, pp. 113–122. CRC Press, Boca Raton (2017)
47. Poole, A., Ball, L.J.: Eye tracking in HCI and usability research: current status and future prospects. In: Ghaoui, C. (ed.) Encyclopedia of Human Computer Interaction, pp. 211–219. Idea Group, Pennsylvania (2006)
48. Cooke, N.J., Gorman, J.C., Duran, J.L., Taylor, A.R.: Team cognition in experienced command and-control teams. J. Exp. Psychol. Appl. **13**, 146–157 (2007)

Exploring the Effects of Large Screen Overview Displays in a Nuclear Control Room Setting

Alexandra Fernandes[(✉)], Alf Ove Braseth, Robert McDonald, and Maren Eitrheim

Institute for Energy Technology, Digital Systems, Halden, Norway
alexandraf@ife.no

Abstract. This paper explores the impact that large screen overview displays have on human performance in a nuclear power plant control room. We collected direct performance measures (accuracy and response time) in a full scope, digital research simulator, using a simplified task method. The participants were licensed operators who were asked to answer questions regarding process state. They provided answers in four types of trials combining two variables with two conditions each: individual or teamwork set-ups; and using the large screen display or the workstation displays to assess information. The results show that the operators were more accurate when the workstation displays were available than when the large screen display was available; there was a trend for quicker response times when the operators had the large screen available instead of the workstation displays; and finally, the operators were both most accurate and quicker responding in team conditions than individual conditions. We found an impact of the type of display on both the accuracy of the operators' response (better in the workstation displays) and the response times (better in the large screen display). The results do not provide conclusive evidence in favor of any type of display. Performing the tasks in a team condition, however, seemed to have a systematic effect both on response time and accuracy. We close by discussing the contributions of this and describing future steps.

Keywords: Large screen displays · Overview displays · Nuclear control room · Task performance

1 Introduction

The first chapter frames the need for performing research on the effect on large-screen overview displays (LSOD) on human performance. Then, a framework for the assessment of LSOD is presented. Lastly, research questions for the current study are presented. Although the research is focusing on the nuclear domain, the contributions are relevant for other industries where centralized control of processes in present (such as chemical and petroleum).

© Springer Nature Switzerland AG 2020
D. Harris and W.-C. Li (Eds.): HCII 2020, LNAI 12187, pp. 18–29, 2020.
https://doi.org/10.1007/978-3-030-49183-3_2

1.1   Motivation

Advances in technology development lead to digitalization of modern control rooms, as found in nuclear industries. These technologies have the potential of reducing costs and improve flexibility in both new builds and in modernizing existing control rooms. One such technology is large-screen overview displays (LSODs). Governing nuclear standards and guidelines suggest LSODs have the potential of enhancing the crew's situation awareness (SA) and to improve communication, leading to better control room performance [1]. Furthermore, it is described in literature [2] that operating complex plants using only smaller personal workstations can result in keyhole effects, where the crew can miss the bigger picture of the plant state by being over focused in selected aspects of the process [3].

These suggestions are supported by earlier field studies of conventional nuclear power plant control rooms, describing unfortunate effects by moving from larger analogue panels – where all actions were visible to the whole crew – to desktop-displays – where it is difficult to see what each crew member is doing [4]. The reduced transparency in crew actions as also shown that rapid process overview from personal workstations is worse compared to the larger analogue panels from the past [5]. There is, however, few conclusive evidences, based on empirical work, exploring the effects of using LSOD to mitigate these challenges [6].

To assess the effect of LSOD on human performance, a framework was developed [7] defining what a LSOD is and how it could be assessed. Figure 1 illustrates the concept of LSOD in the current work. It suggests that: i) the LSOD should be centrally placed in the control room, being visible for the whole crew from their normal seated positions; and ii) it needs to be designed for its purpose from the ground up, focusing on key process components for overview purposes. In this approach, detailed interaction is enabled at the personal workstations only, with the LSOD being used exclusively for monitoring.

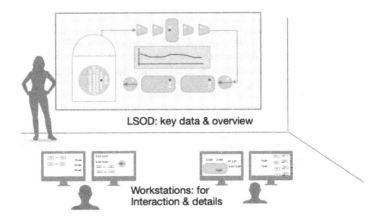

Fig. 1. LSOD concept used in the current work

Further, this framework proposed to use the following dimensions for assessment of LSOD: i) Team performance; ii) Individual performance; iii) Top-down structured problem solving (where the work is goal-oriented, and the operators attempt to solve a generic task); and iv) Bottom-up reactive actions (where warnings and/or alarms inform the operators). The current work is one study of an incremental series of several studies that are deemed needed to understand the effects of LSOD on operator performance. The contribution of this paper is to explore bottom-up, data driven scenarios, for both individual and team performance. This is done by prompting operators to search for specific process information in difference trials, comparing the effects of using LSOD or smaller workstation displays (WSD). The next section presents the questions used to guide the research process.

1.2   Research Questions

In this work, three core research questions guided the design of the data collections. The first research question is linked with the assumption that the LSOD would support maintenance of awareness of plant status. The second question is linked with the assumption that the LSOD would make information more quickly accessible to the operators. The third question is exploring the way LSOD might be differentially affecting operator performance. The questions were formulated as:

1. Does the use of LSOD, when compared to WSDs, have an impact on accuracy rates?
2. Does the use of LSOD, when compared to WSDs, have an impact on response times?
3. Are there different impacts of the use of LSOD, for individual and crew performance?

2   Method

In this chapter we describe the study design, participants, presented displays, materials and equipment used in the data collection, as well as the procedure for implementation. We close the sessions presenting a few relevant limitations of the current study that are important to understand the findings.

2.1   Design

The study had a within-subject design where all operators participated in all the test conditions. Two main variables were studied: the type of displays (LSOD/WSD) and way of working (Individual/Team). For the type of displays, the operators had access to either the LSOD or the WSD. For the way of working, the operators would perform the task individually, independently of other crew members, or simultaneously as a team, discussing the answers. This meant that on individual trials the operators were performing the task alone, not being allowed to talk with other crew members, while in the team conditions, the shift supervisor would hold a tablet computer with the questions, read them out loud, and then record the answer that all team members agreed upon. The participants were requested to answer 32 questions in each trial.

Two different scenarios representing snapshots of the plant status were presented to the participants. Each participant went through the tasks four times, two in individual trials and two in crew trials. As shown in Table 1, the participants saw each scenario two times, but in two different displays, to avoid exact repetition of the tasks.

Table 1. Example of a study run for one team

Instructions (5 min)		
Practice run (5 min)		
Individual	LSOD	Trial 1 (5 min)
	WSD	Trial 2 (5 min)
Break (5 min)		
Instructions (5 min)		
Team	LSOD	Trial 3 (5 min)
	WSD	Trial 4 (5 min)

The conditions in this study do not map to what it expected in a nuclear control room, where the LSOD is presented jointly with the WSDs. Since the goal in this study was to amplify potential effects of LSOD on human performance it seemed more likely to differentiate results when the two types of displays did not overlap (only LSOD versus only WSD).

In the condition where only the WSD were available, the operators had the required displays open in the screens and were not allowed to navigate the interface.

2.2 Participants

Ten licensed operators (based in the United States) participated in the study in three independent occasions in 2018 and 2019. The operators represented two different power plants: two crews of three operators from one plant; and a crew of four operators from a different plant. All participants were male and had an average age of 44.7 years old ($SD = 6.5$). Their experience with computerized interfaces was on average of 6.5 years ($SD = 5.2$) and they reported using it for some or most tasks at the home plant. All the participants were experienced operators, with more than six years of experience in control room context.

2.3 Displays

The operators were presented with a frozen simulator in a predefined status. In the trials they had access to the WSDs, only two screens were available, one showing the Safety Injection System/Residual Heat Remover (SIS/RHR), and another showing the Steam Generator/Auxiliary Feed Water (SG/AFW). Figure 2 shows the targeted displays during the data collection. The operators were not allowed to navigate in the system. An example of the LSOD and WSDs for the same plant status is shown below.

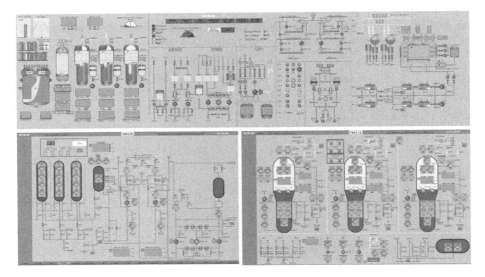

Fig. 2. Example of the simulator interface: LSOD (on top), SIS/RHR (bottom left) and SG/AFW (bottom right).

2.4 Materials and Equipment

The study was conducted in the Halden Man-Machine Laboratory (HAMMLAB). Here, a full-scale nuclear reactor simulator is available, and the facilities emulate a fully digital main control room, with dedicated stations for reactor operator, turbine operator and shift supervisor. Figure 3 shows and overview of the simulator facilities.

Fig. 3. HAMMLAB facilities

Questions. A set of 32 questions were selected for this pilot study from a pre-existing database and considering their applicability to the current test conditions in HAMMLAB.

The questions focused on detection of process parameters (example: *What is SG B NR level?*); comparison of different parameters (example: *Which SG has the highest AFW flow?*); calculations (example: *What is the SG C feed flow - steam flow differential?*); and knowledge-based questions (example: *Is the RHR system line-up correct for this condition?*). The questions presented different response options: insertion of numerical values, "yes/no" or "open/closed" questions, and "multiple-choice" questions.

Data Collection Application. The tasks in this study were presented in a tablet through an application developed specifically for this purpose [8]. Figure 4 shows an example of how the questions are presented in the data collection app. There are different ways to answer the questions, such as inserting numbers or selecting one of the available options (as illustrated in the figure). The participants can also use the "Don't know" button on the bottom right to skip a question they are not sure how to respond or where they are spending too much time. It is possible to edit the answer while on the page, but once the participants submit the answer (by swiping to the next question) it is not possible to go back to previous answers.

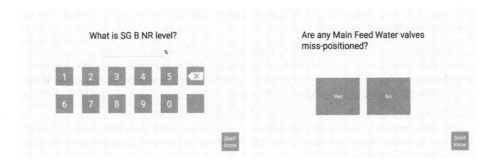

Fig. 4. Example from two screens in the Microtask data collection application.

2.5   Procedure

The data collection occurred in the fourth day of interaction with the interface, following a separate study where the operators were handling full scope simulation scenarios for two days, after a day of training and familiarization with the interface.

The operators were informed that they would be performing simplified tasks, without interaction with the system, and that we would collect data on response accuracy and time.

Before the study the participants performed trials in order to familiarize with the data collection application by answering eight practice questions that illustrated all possible response possibilities in the study (yes/no; insert numbers; and multiple choice).

All participants answered the same questions in the four trials, but the order of the 32 questions was randomized every time. Also, the correct answers to the same questions were different for the two scenarios and could also variate between the LSOD and the WSD due to the format of the parameters (e.g. rounded or not rounded decimals).

For the individual trials, each participant sat at a specific workstation and answered the questions without interaction with the system or communication with the rest of the team. In the team trials, the shift supervisor had the tablet with the questions, read them out loud, and inserted the answer the team agreed upon.

2.6   Limitations

Here we describe limitations of the current study that should be considered. Microtasks are designed to address interface assessment, obtaining objective accuracy and response time data. They do not recreate realistic control room operation procedures and are focused on information gathering assignments (in opposition to control/execution). However, we argue that these tasks are seamless for interface evaluation, focusing on the impact that specific interface features (such as visualizations strategies and formats) can have in human performance and as such making them very relevant for the research problem we are addressing in this project.

For this data collection we were conducting a preliminary and exploratory pilot where the scientific rigor was not enforced – there were limitations we were aware of already before the data collection:

- *Narrow non-standardized question database*, only 32 questions were available for the pilot study, after a selection of questions from previous studies that were applicable to the existing interface. This led to the need to repeat questions with the participants answering the same 32 questions 4 times, one in each trial. The questions had the same answers twice, one with each type of interface.
- *Restricted scenarios/plant status*, only two scenarios were developed for the pilot study, meaning that the participants answered to the same questions with similar answers twice during the trials.

3   Results and Discussion

In this chapter we present the main findings and interpretations regarding the main studied variables: accuracy and response time variation according to the type of display used and the work condition the team was presented with.

3.1   Accuracy

There was a global accuracy rate of 0.90 ($SD = 0.09$). The average accuracy for the trials with the LSOD was of 0.87 ($SD = 0.10$) and for the WSD was of 0.94 ($SD = 0.03$). Comparing the two ways of working, performance in the individual trials ($M = 0.88$, $SD = 0.09$) was lower than on the team trials ($M = 0.95$, $SD = 0.01$). Table 2 shows descriptive statistics for time and accuracy in each condition and display.

Table 2. Breakdown of descriptive statistics per condition and display

Display	Condition	Time (Average)	Time (N)	Time (SD)	Accuracy (Average)	Accuracy (N)	Accuracy (SD)
LSOD	Individual	10.5	10	2.7	0.85	10	0.11
LSOD	Team	8.2	3	1.9	0.94	3	0.00
WSD	Individual	11.6	6	3.6	0.93	6	0.04
WSD	Team	10.9	3	1.0	0.96	3	0.02
Total		10.6	22	2.8	0.90	22	0.09

Figure 5 illustrates the accuracy ratings for each display (LSOD *versus* WSD) in each condition (individual *versus* team). The results show that performance was high in both conditions and for both types of displays (error rate was below 20%). This error rate is equivalent to the ones found in previous implementations of the Microtask method [8, 9]. It is possible to see that the team trials had higher accuracy rates than the individual trials and the performance was slightly better on the WSD than on the LSOD – this was particularly noticeable for the individual trials.

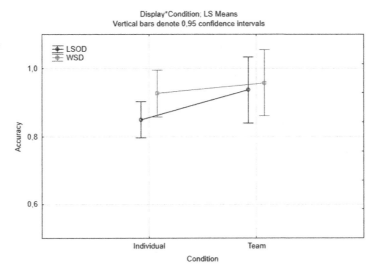

Fig. 5. Accuracy ratings for each display type, according to condition

3.2   Response Time

The average response time was of 10.6 s per question ($SD = 2.8$). In the trials with the LSOD, the response time was of 10 s ($SD = 2.7$) and for the WSD was of 11.36 s ($SD = 2.92$). Regarding the two test conditions, the participants were faster in the team trials ($M = 9.5$, $SD = 2.0$) than on the individual trials ($M = 11.0$, $SD = 3.0$). Figure 6 shows the average response time for each display, according to the condition. It is possible to observe that the LSOD seemed to introduce and advantage in the response times with shorter response times than the WSD.

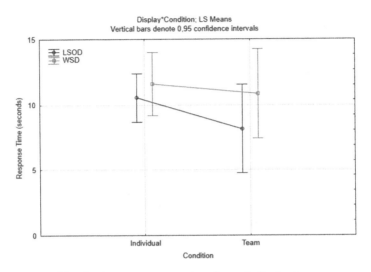

Fig. 6. Average response time for each display type

3.3   Speed-Accuracy Trade-off

The speed-accuracy trade-off is a phenomenon well described in the literature that refers to the phenomenon of slow responses with high accuracy rates and/or quick responses with low accuracy rates [10, 11]. This is a consistent behavioral phenomenon often reported in cognitive science. The absence of a speed-accuracy trade-off is seen as an indicator that the participants were able to follow the instructions of responding "as quickly and accurately as possible", indicating that the participants were engaged and focused in the task.

In the current study there was not a significant correlation between response time and accuracy for neither displays ($p > 0.05$). As shown in the trend in Fig. 7, for the LSOD the participants were quicker when answering correctly, while for the WSD no trend is visible (possibly due to the very high accuracy rates in this condition). This is an indicator that the operators were able to complete the requested task and shows an expected variability in the responses mediated by the difficulty of the task.

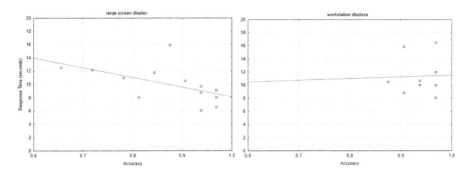

Fig. 7. Plot of accuracy against response time in LSOD (left) and WSD (right)

4   Conclusions

This chapter presents a summary of the findings of the study and highlights its contribution for understanding the effects of large screen overview displays on operators' performance in nuclear control rooms. We end with references to future work.

4.1   Findings and Contributions

The impact of LSOD on human performance was explored, both on the individual and the team levels. These were our findings:

1. Does the use of LSOD, when compared to WSD, have an impact on accuracy rates?

   Combining the results from the individual and the team trials, we observed a trend that the participants were more accurate when using the WSDs than the LSOD. As such, for this study we found an impact of the type of display on the accuracy of the participants' responses.

2. Does the use of LSOD, when compared to WSD, have an impact on response times?

   Combining the results from the individual and the team trials we found a trend for quicker response times when the participants had the LSOD available instead of the WSD. As such, we can infer that for this study, the response times were impacted by the type of display available.

3. Are there different impacts of the use of LSOD, at the individual and the team operating levels?

   It was possible to observe that the operators were more accurate and quicker when responding in the team conditions versus the individual condition. This variable seems to be a relevant variable mediating both response time and accuracy in control room performance. This is a relevant finding since the team condition brings more context to the proposed tasks, making it closer to real work conditions where communication, peer checking, and verification are part of the work processes. Nonetheless, other methods will be required to understand these results such as tools for assessing communication, teamwork and work processes.

The main contribution of this study is an assessment of differential impact of LSOD and WSD on individual and crews' performance. We were able to identify advantages and disadvantages of each type of display. Considering that the data was collected only in one context (digital research simulator), no conclusive evidence of the advantages of LSOD versus WSD can be drawn from this pilot study. However, it was visible that team performance was consistently superior than individual performance, confirming the relevance of crew work for plant safety.

4.2   Further Work

Next steps in the project will involve a new study to further explore the impact of LSOD on human performance. This study will require a more complex design in order to tackle the identified relevant variables and overcome the limitations of the current study.

It will be required to generate a larger question database to avoid repetition between trials. In the current pilot we selected only 32 questions from previous studies which resulted in a high repetition rate. Ideally, we would develop a large database of questions (grouped by characteristics such as response type and/or nature of the task) and randomly extract between 30 to 40 questions to present in each trial. Such a database, where the questions are clearly categorized would support the comparison of results when using the same question category in different trials (e.g. *What is the flow in pump x?* could be asked about several different pumps without the need of repetition).

Further explorations of the individual versus team conditions will also be interesting, especially considering the potential benefits of team conditions/teamwork as a mitigating factor for response accuracy, contributing to overall plant safety and performance.

References

1. O'Hara, J.M., Brown, W.S., Lewis, P.M., Persensky, J.J.: Human-system interface design review guidelines. (NUREG-0700, Rev. 2). U.S. Nuclear Regulatory Commission, Washington, USA (2002)
2. IEC 61772 International standard, Nuclear power plants – Control rooms – Application of visual display units (VDUs), Edition 2.0, International Electrotechnical Commission, Geneva, Switzerland, p. 22 (2009)
3. Woods, D.D.: Toward a theoretical base for representation design in the computer medium: ecological perception and aiding human-cognition. In: Flach, J., Hancock, P., Caird, J., Vicente, K. (eds.) Global Perspectives on the Ecology of Human-Machine Systems, vol. 1, pp. 157–188. Lawrence Erlbaum Associates Inc., Hillsdale (1995)
4. Vicente, K.J., Roth, E.M., Mumaw, R.J.: How do operators monitor a complex, dynamic work domain? The impact of control room technology. Int. J. Hum. Comput. Stud. **54**(6), 831–856 (2001). https://doi.org/10.1006/ijhc.2001.0463
5. Salo, L., Laarni, J., Savioja, P.: Operator experiences on working in screen-based control rooms. In: Proceedings of the NPIC & HMIT Conference, Albuquerque, USA (2006)

6. Kortschot, S., Jamieson, G.A., Wheeler, C.: Efficacy of group view displays in nuclear control rooms. IEEE Trans. Hum.-Mach. Syst. **48**(4), 408–414 (2018)
7. Braseth, A.O., Eitrheim, M.H.R., Fernandes, A.: A Theoretical Framework for Assessment of Large-Screen Displays in Nuclear Control Rooms (HWR-1245). OECD Halden Reactor Project, Halden (2019)
8. Hildebrandt, M., Fernandes, A.: Micro Task Evaluation of Innovative and Conventional Process Display Elements at a PWR Training Simulator (HWR-1169). OECD Halden Reactor Project, Halden (2016)
9. Hildebrandt, M., Eitrheim, M.H.R., Fernandes, A.: Pilot Test of a Micro Task method for Evaluating Control Room Interfaces (HWR-1130). OECD Halden Reactor Project, Halden (2016)
10. Bruyer, R., Brysbaert, M.: Combining speed and accuracy in cognitive psychology: is the inverse efficiency score (IES) a better dependent variable than the mean reaction time (RT) and the percentage of errors (PE)? Psychol. Belg. **51**(1), 5–13 (2011). https://doi.org/10.5334/pb-51-1-5
11. Townsend, J.T., Ashby, F.G.: Methods of modeling capacity in simple processing systems. In: Castellan, J., Restle, F. (eds.) Cognitive Theory, vol. 3, pp. 200–239. Erlbaum, Hillsdale (1978)

Operator Actions Outside the Control Room: A Field Study

Alexandra Fernandes[(✉)], Rossella Bisio, and Claire Blackett

Institute for Energy Technology, Humans and Automation, 1777 Halden, Norway
alexandraf@ife.no

Abstract. In the nuclear industry, while there exists a growing body of knowledge on human reliability data for actions inside the main control room, there is a lack of empirical data for field operator tasks. In this paper we present an initial study to verify a new framework for collecting reliability data for actions outside the control room. The study focuses on verifying the applicability and relevance of this framework in real world contexts, specifically regarding performance shaping factors. We have conducted a data collection at the Halden Boiling Water Reactor in Norway with six crews during normal operation. The preparation included: 1) selection of a target scenario where actions outside the control room were relevant; 2) conducting a walkthrough at the site with an experienced operator; 3) performing a task analysis based on the walkthrough; 4) creating a checklist for observation and data collection at the plant; 5) making a questionnaire to assess operators' perception and understanding of the task; and 6) developing a semi-structured guide for a debriefing interview. During the study the researchers shadowed the two involved operators both in the field and in the control room. The findings confirmed the framework assumptions that performance shaping factors such as communication, background knowledge and situation understanding play a crucial role in actions outside the control room. Other findings from the study highlight the relevance of: a) trust in the team; and b) procedures for standardized task performance, as well as to reduce variability in operators' actions.

Keywords: Human reliability · Field operators · Nuclear power plant

1 Introduction

Within the nuclear industry, a significant amount of effort has been dedicated to the study of human reliability, with important implications for training, human-machine interfaces, procedural support, and safety culture [1, 2]. Those studies have primarily focused on operations in the main control room, where human actions are considered to be particularly critical for the safety of the plant.

The human factors and ergonomics (HFES) community has questioned whether traditional Human Reliability Analysis (HRA) methods derived from operation of analogue control rooms can successfully accommodate the modified and new types of tasks and actions that characterize digital and/or hybrid control rooms. Human reliability has traditionally focused on obtaining empirical data from complex, full scope studies

© Springer Nature Switzerland AG 2020
D. Harris and W.-C. Li (Eds.): HCII 2020, LNAI 12187, pp. 30–41, 2020.
https://doi.org/10.1007/978-3-030-49183-3_3

where realistic simulations of control room operations are conducted. As a consequence of the growing digitalization in control rooms, it is possible to observe a renewed claim for empirical data on operator actions and especially the likelihood of errors in the new settings [3]. This has led to a growing body of data regarding control room actions, generated in simulator experiments, where the difficulty of the tasks is experimentally manipulated to increase the chances of observing human performance errors.

Simultaneously, operations outside the control room have come to attract more attention, as a more integrated view on safety surfaced in the HFES literature [4]. The contextual aspects of work in the field such as physical demands or the impact of fatigue or noise levels, have been vastly described in the classical ergonomics literature [5]. On the other hand, the cognitive aspects of operator performance outside the control room and cooperation with the main control room have deserved a lot less consideration. With this work we intend to explore these aspects and attempt to both describe and empirically explore the performance shaping factors more relevant for field operations. These are factors that can affect human performance and can be behavioral and/or contextual [6].

A central aim of our ongoing work on operator reliability for actions outside the control room, consists on the mapping of the most relevant performance shaping factors for field work. The literature on this topic is very scarce and there are very few instances where empirical data on field operator actions was collected [7], making it difficult to understand and estimate the impact of actions outside the control room for overall plant safety.

One of the core challenges regarding empirical data collections outside the control room relates to the available methods [8]. Quite often the methods used inside the control room are not directly applicable to actions outside the control room. The nature of the tasks inside and outside the control room can be clearly distinguished: the space where field operators work is a lot more vast than the control room, allowing free movement of the operators and limiting observation possibilities; environmental conditions such as noise, temperature, humidity or radiation are more likely to vary, affecting tasks planning and execution; the physical demands on the field operators are significantly different which can impact their performance; and planning of the tasks outside the control room might be of particular relevance, since the field operators often walk long distances in the plant and need to make sure they have the correct procedures and tools before they leave the job briefings and head to the rounds. As such, collecting data inside and outside the control room presents significantly different challenges that require different methods and strategies.

1.1 Framework

The framework that supports the work on this paper can be found in [9]. This framework proposes a classification and methodology to collect empirical data for actions outside the control room and covers: 1) task identification and characterization; 2) performance shaping factors; 3) scenario characteristics; 4) data collection environments; and 5) methods for empirical data collection. Table 1 summarizes the components of this framework's first draft. We intend to elaborate and improve the framework based on iterations resulting from empirical data collections and its findings.

Table 1. Components of the framework supporting this work

Framework topic	Characteristics/Examples
1) Task identification and characterization	Frequency; Complexity; Existing support; Collaboration; Organizational context; Safety implications; Environmental conditions; Available time
2) Performance shaping factors	Training and experience; Procedures and administrative control; Ergonomics and Human-Machine Interaction; Time pressure; Complexity; Environment; Fitness at work; Work processes
3) Scenario characteristics	Targeted variables; Normal operation; Maintenance tasks; Disturbance scenarios; Emergency scenarios
4) Data collection environments	Real-world; Training centers; Virtual reality simulation
5) Methods for empirical data collection	Observations; Audio and video recordings; Interviews and Debriefs; Walkthrough and Talk-through; Task analysis; Questionnaires; Role playing; Response accuracy; Response time; Biometric data; Eye-tracking; Report analysis

Outside the control room, there is a considerable diversification of tasks which often reflects the specificity of the plants. This can lead to very sparse data, that cannot be generalized. To overcome these aspects we suggest grouping tasks, by classifying them based on their complexity and cognitive demand rather than single steps or other plant specific details. Contextual circumstances and time pressure are also taken into consideration.

The second item in the framework – performance shaping factors – is the focus of the current work. Some performance shaping factors cannot be easily controlled in studies outside the control room. For instance, training and experience, or existing procedures and administrative control. Those are as such discarded in our work (attending to the final aim of manipulating variables in data collections). Likewise, contextual factors and fitness to work are also out of scope since their implications are well described in the literature. We will then focus on ergonomics and human machine interfaces, complexity, time pressure, and the work processes surrounding the task execution.

The scenarios refer to the context provided to the operators. They involve a description of the status of the plant and/or of the task the operators are asked to fulfil. The scenarios can cover when a task is executed in the expected conditions without additional disturbance, or it can involve situations where unexpected events occur or where significant incidents/accidents are presented. In the presented field study normal operative conditions has been considered to verify the hypothesized relevance of the selected performance factors at least in this condition.

Regarding data collection environments we present three alternatives: i) real-world context, where the data can be collected directly at the plant; ii) training centers, where simulations of events and scenarios can be used with the operators performing actions on mock-ups or decommissioned components; and iii) virtual reality simulations, where we are able to present all levels of scenarios, but where realism and generalizability are compromised. In this study we used the real-world approach.

The final item refers to methods to collect data. After screening existing methods within the nuclear context, we have identified as more promising: interviews, debriefings, task analysis, questionnaires, biometric data, and eye tracking. Other methods that can support the data collection are observation, audio/video recording, walkthrough, talk-through, response accuracy, response time, role playing, report analysis.

1.2 Study Objectives

This is an initial exploratory study in a real-world setting, where a routine task is being performed. The focus of the study will be on the identification of performance shaping factors. The objectives for this study are:

1. Assess whether *communication*, *situation awareness*, and *background knowledge* are relevant factors shaping field operations, this will be measured through the feedback of the operators through interviews and questionnaires
2. Evaluate the efficacy of using *talk-through*, *walkthrough*, and *task analysis* as tools to prepare data collection in the field, measured through qualitative assessment by the research team, considering the obtained information before the data collection and its usefulness to understand the work processes
3. Explore the applicability of *direct observation* as a data collection method in real world settings, measured by the research team, assessing the value of observations compared with other possible methods (process expert assessment, biometric data, etc.)

1.3 Halden Research Nuclear Reactor Operational Characteristics

The Halden Boiling Water Reactor (HBWR) is a small (25 MW) boiling water reactor used for research on fuel properties and material corrosion. The reactor was initiated in 1958 and was operated by the Institute for Energy Technology until 2018. The reactor is currently on permanent shutdown, and daily operations are reduced, consisting of maintaining reactor stability and safety.

The control room is operated by a crew of two operators in three shifts (morning, evening, and night). In the control room, besides the operators there is a reactor engineer that supports operations and is involved in task planning. In the control room the operators have workstations with digital interfaces, as well as analogue wall panels, and a large screen display to support process overview.

Unlike commercial nuclear power plants where the roles of control room and field operators are separate, at the Halden Reactor the same operators perform actions and monitoring both inside and outside the control room. This implies that all tasks are planned and executed by the same two operators, one being at the control room at all times and the other acting as field operator as necessary, leaving the main control room when required. Contact with the control room when the operator is on the field is maintained through telephone (most common) or noise cancelling headphones with transmission to the control room.

2 Method

The study was conducted together with another experiment where the effects of large screen displays on operator performance were being tested. As such, for half the crews, the large screen display was not available at the control room for the tested scenario. This was not deemed relevant for the purposes of the study, since we were mostly interested on the observations performed outside the control room. Nonetheless, in the debrief interviews, some of the control room operators mentioned that the large screen display was missed either during planning or execution stages for process overview inside the control room.

2.1 Task Classification

To prepare the data collection, we contacted a process expert with several years of experience at the Halden Reactor. The preparation was done in three consecutive phases over a period of two weeks: 1) initial interview: the process expert was initially interviewed by the research team to gather information about work processes and operational characteristics at the plant; 2) walkthrough: the process expert guided the research team through a walkthrough at the plant, focusing on the target scenario tasks; 3) talk-through: was conducted after the visit with the support of Piping & Instrumentation Diagrams (P&IDs) and procedures to clarify aspects of task performance that came up to the research team while performing task analysis.

A result of the walkthrough with the process expert was a task analysis of the targeted scenario which identified the main characteristics of the actions outside the control room and allowed us to better understand the nature of the task and explore possible paths for solving it.

2.2 Participants

Six crews of two operators, took part in the study, with six operators acting as field operators and six as control room operators. The participants were all male, Norwegian, had an average age of 47.6 years (SD = 7.9) and had on average 13.9 years of experience has nuclear operators (SD = 8.1; Median = 14.5).

2.3 Tools

Observation Checklist. The observation checklist was used by two researchers – one at the control room and one shadowing the field operator outside the control room. The observation checklist was constructed based on the task analysis that preceded the data collection and was discussed with a process expert. It included four main moments:

1. *Preparation activities*: such as retrieving documentation, discussing, and checking pre-conditions for the test;
2. *Going to target components*: included getting necessary equipment (protection clothing, hat, telephone, documentation), leaving control room and reaching the target components for the test;

3. *Performing test*: preparing local conditions, executing accorded plan and perform test, restore local conditions;
4. *Return and wrap-up*: getting back to main control room and closing task.

Operator Assessment. At the end of the scenario the operators were asked to individually respond to a questionnaire evaluating the relevance of specific factors in the task they had just performed. The questionnaire included 14 items to be rated in a Likert scale from 1 (completely disagree) to 5 (completely agree) and a final section for open comments. The items included the following factors: importance of communication with control room; there as a lot to do; the noise level on the telephone was high; there was a time pressure; external factors such as noise, temperature, humidity and vibrations are relevant; you need to be an experienced operator; you are dependent on existing procedures; you had a predefined plan in the current task; there was a lot to think about; it was a complicated task; you need to have a lot of knowledge; it was a difficult task to perform; communication between the inside and outside control room was appropriate; planning was important; overall it was a difficult task.

Interviews. The operators were interviewed jointly at the end of the scenario. The interview was initiated by a comparison of the answers the two operators provided to the questionnaire, and then exploring any comments they added to it. A semi-structured interview was used that focused on the relevance of performance shaping factors (as formulated in the questionnaire), the specificities of task execution, and feedback on the study experience.

2.4 Scenario

A process expert was responsible for designing the test scenarios and providing the instructions to the crews. The task used for the data collection consisted on the test of a pump, running it for 5 min. The pump is part of the tertiary cooling system at the reactor. The operators needed to be aware of the need to close a parallel circuit used for chemical samples before the test is initiated. At the end the operators need to restore the initial conditions. The scenario did not foresee additional disturbances and was presented as a work order in standard daily activity.

2.5 Procedure

Before the data collection started the operators were briefed on the focus and goals of the data collection, as well as the plan for the data collection. They were then presented with an informed consent form. After this, the operators and researchers went into the control room were the task would take place.

   The operators were briefed on the core task to be performed in a normal day scenario and then could initiate the work. Two researchers were at the back of the main control room observing the planning stage. When the field operator left the room, one researcher would shadow him, while another stayed with the control room operator.

The researchers used pen and paper during the data collection and recorded notes in a pre-defined observation checklist, taking note of time stamps, communication characteristics and any other information on the duration of the task.

At the end of the scenario the operators were invited to a room adjacent to the main control room, where they filled in the questionnaire individually and then were interviewed together.

3   Results and Discussion

3.1   Planning Phase

In this study we were able to have access to a process expert who could guide us through the initial preparations for the data collection. We performed interviews and a tour to the power plant facilities. The process expert was questioned about possible alternatives to perform the tasks, potential errors, possible implications, required background knowledge on the actions, and requirements on communication.

Even though we were analyzing a relatively simple and short task, that is close to routine tasks at the plant, the preparation required several resources in order to be able to map all the steps and understand the nature of the actions outside the control room. This emphasizes the challenges regarding data collections in the field, in a space that is less familiar to researchers and analysts.

3.2   Observations

The scenario had a duration between 16 and 37 min across the six crews (*Median* = 29 min). We organized the findings according to the different stages in the scenario: planning, moving to the field, execution, and debriefing.

Planning. All the crews planned the task together. To understand the current status of the plant all crews used the workstations, in most cases also the analog panel. When the Large Screen Display was available it was used significantly only by one crew.

In all cases the P&IDs were the main support on which to reason cooperatively to formulate a plan. Four crews retrieved also a procedure describing how to operate the pump object of the test.

The communication style varied, in two cases, the crew members were sitting close to each other from the beginning of the planning, other crews started with separately checking the status of the loops at different workstations, with limited verbal communication. The details of the plan had some variations, but all operators agreed to operate the main tasks (open/closing pumps) under continuous communication. The time spent on planning varied from three to 21 min.

Moving into the Field. In five out of six cases, the field operator brought the P&ID to the field, only one case he picked the procedure for operating the pump. In all cases they chose the mobile phone as communication device. This choice was justified by the small size of the task and the fact that the noise level in the hall was low, especially compared to when the reactor was active and the cooling loops functioning at regime. The distance between the control room and the operating area was very short (200 m or a 1-min walk).

During a scenario an extra loop, the chemical analysis circuit (CAC) was supposed to be isolated, in order to avoid spurious results influenced by the increased pressure generated by the tested pump. No crews considered this step in their plans, but all recognized immediately the need as reminded by the process expert and/or the reactor engineer. Most crews isolated the CAC from the control room, two crews let the operation to the field operator, in one case the field operator checked the status of CAC even if the control room was responsible to operate it. It is important to mention that the operating crew is usually not responsible for task planning and as such this can be seen as an extra requirement on them for the current study. The engineering team would normally prepare and plan the tasks that would be delivered to the operators for execution.

Execution. All crews communicated to the control room while operating the pumps. Some operators relied mainly on sensorial input like noise, vibrations rather than on local instrumentation for monitoring the effects of the actions, others used also the displayed values of pressure gauges. Only in two cases the field operator had to operate in addition valves in adjacent circuits, on request from the control room. During the five minutes wait, while PB2 was operating, two field operators went back to the control room, one performed a short inspection of other areas, and the others waited by the pumps. In average, the complete operation took 16 min, with small variance among the crews.

Debriefing. The scenario did not explicitly require a debrief after the field operator returned to the control rooms, but three crews did it, checking if the situation was correctly restored in the control room interfaces and with the field operator shortly reporting technical details.

3.3   Questionnaire

The operators were very congruent in the ratings they attributed for each item in the questionnaire. A central difference relates to the rating regarding the noise levels during the phone calls, which showed a tendentially higher rating by the field operation in comparison with the control room operation. A similar trend was visible for the item "there was a lot to do" that was often rated higher by the field operators.

Three factors were consistently signaled by all participants as very relevant in field work: communication with control room, its clarity, and planning of the work before leaving to the field (Fig. 1).

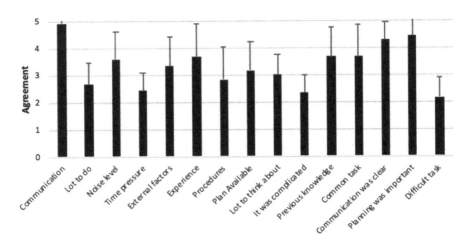

Fig. 1. Ratings of agreement on importance of performance shaping factors

The task was not seen as difficult or complicated, and the operators did not think they were under time pressure to complete it.

A common comment from the operators referred to the fact that noise canceling headphones with communication capabilities were available, but still not taken into the field.

3.4   Debriefing Interview

The interviews with the crew focused on the actions performed outside the control room and were initiated with an analysis of the responses to the questionnaire items.

The fact that there was not a specific procedure for this scenario contributed to increase the difficulty level of a task that was considered otherwise common. The lack of procedure required more planning and reasoning before performing the necessary steps to complete the pump test. Another factor highlighted by some of the operators relates to the differences in operation now that the reactor is in permanent shutdown, mentioning that some tasks are now more difficult because it is harder to "know what reference values are expected for the current reactor status", however, other operators mentioned that they felt "less stress" performing this task since the reactor is in shutdown.

In the interview the operators stressed the importance of communication in the current task. They mentioned that maintaining a phone conversion where they share the ongoing actions inside and outside the control room helped them to maintain good collaboration and a shared understanding of the task. The noise levels outside the control room were often noted by the operators, but it did not seem to disturb the conversation. On the other hand, holding the phone and operating some of the valves in the field was not compatible and required the operators to put the phone down while manipulating valves with two hands – and alternative is available with the use of noise cancelling headphones with a transmitter, but none of the crews took them to the field.

Another recurrent topic in the interview was the need for planning in the current task. Being able to set up a plan for task execution was crucial in this scenario since there was not a specific procedure that could be implemented. For planning, aspects such as background knowledge and experience were mentioned as relevant by the operators. Likewise, planning using the P&IDs drawing and/or partially applicable procedures contributed to the creation of a shared understanding of the task goals and steps that was reckoned important by the operators.

3.5   Methodological Insights

Observing operation in the field requires a good understanding of the task and knowledge of the components, even if superficial. An important aspect missing from the current data collection is process expert expertise assessing the crew performance in the field. This could be achieved through post-hoc analysis, collecting video and/or audio recordings, but ideally could be done online, with an expert on site.

Observation has anyway an impact on task performance, not being the observer behind the scene, as it could be in a simulator set up, but rather close in normally small area with restricted possibility of movement. The intrusiveness of the observer has been commented in the interviews.

Regardless of the alternative data collection methods, interviews and debriefs are crucial qualitative data necessary to understand the observations and interpret other types of data collected (e.g. errors performing the tasks, response time, biometric data).

4   Conclusions and Further Work

4.1   Findings and Contributions

We were able to successfully conduct a data collection in a real world setting and obtain relevant input and information towards the verification of the anticipated framework. We mapped typical ways of working, main tasks characteristics, developed a study design, selected tools, and collected data based on the theoretical hypothesis and classifications proposed beforehand.

The opportunity to prepare the data collection with support from a process expert was valuable in the current setting. The quality of the observations and the understanding of the events during the scenario would not have been possible without some degree of guidance from a process expert.

The pre-identified performance shaping factors *communication*, *situation aware-ness*, and *background knowledge* were verified as relevant in the current study. Moreover, the operators highlighted the relevance of *trust* as well due to the need of close collaboration. In the current study context, awareness and understanding of the task and plant status was achieved through joint planning of actions and frequent communication during task execution. It was facilitated by the fact that both operators need to work closely together and have the same background (both are control room and field operators at this plant). Considering this, we believe that situation awareness can be a key relevant performance shaping factor affecting operator's performance in commercial plants, where the field operators is often less involved in the planning stages and has a different background from the control room operator.

In the current study we performed close direct observations while the operators performed the tasks. However, the application of this technique in real world data collections will be limited due to safety/security reasons at the plants. It can be useful in simulations at training centers, especially if the observer is a trained operator who can recognize components and better understand the actions being performed. Although useful for the research purposes, this type of observation was considered intrusive and might generate additional stress to the operators, especially if they are not used to being observed (for instance in training context).

The questionnaires were a quick way to register the operators' individual assessment of the task and served well their purpose as a discussion topic in the debrief interview. The interviews were a central aspect of the data collection and are essential to obtain an overview of the tasks as well as understand how and why the crew implemented the work.

4.2   Limitations

We would like to present three core limitations with the current work that we plan to mitigate in future data collections:

- *Generalization of findings*

The setting of the HBWR is quite different from the commercial power plant settings. The reactor is currently in shutdown mode, is small, and was used exclusively for research purposes. It has a different organization, team composition and conduct of operations when compared to commercial power plants. As we seen before, only two operators composed the shift and both have an equivalent role and can perform control actions inside and outside the control room. This implies that they always plan and discuss all tasks together and are both aware of the specificities of both types of work – this is not necessarily the case in commercial power plants where the roles of field operator and control room operator are well demarked.

- *Selected task*

In the current work we were unable to control variables in the study and restricted the data collection to observations and descriptions of the events as performed in a routine task. This was useful as an initial technique to explore performance outside the control room. However, we expect that incident/accident scenarios will be the most relevant since they present extreme situations where the performance shaping factors can become more visible/observable. Also, controlling variables within the data collections will enable us to compare performance in situations where specific parameters are stressed. This will not be possible, of course, in real world data collections, and as such simulations (e.g. in training centers), become more attractive as data collection environments.

- *Assessing performance – process expertise*

Regarding the methods and tools, we consider that the process expertise when evaluating performance (online or after the scenarios) will be an important component in the understanding and accurate evaluation of the operators' performance, especially when we focus on aspects such as situation awareness and background knowledge. In the current study, the human factors researcher were the only ones assessing performance based on the checklist developed with the support of the process expert. In a simple task such as the one presented here this is doable, but in more complex scenarios, we expect that process knowledge will be decisive in understanding the crews' actions and decisions online.

4.3   Further Work

We are planning further studies for verification of the presented framework. These will take place in training centers and/or real-world contexts (focusing on commercial power plants). We will further explore the role and relevance of different performance shaping factors for different scenarios (e.g. in routine *versus* incident situations) and emphasize the study of other aspects of the framework, namely the methods for data collection. In the near future we also aim at testing the feasibility and usefulness of new tools for data collection in training centers, involving quick responses to simplified tasks and use of eye-tracking in realistic contexts.

Acknowledgements. The authors would like to thank Ronny Sandbaek for his support in planning and performing the data collection with crucial process expertise.

References

1. Swain, A.D., Guttmann, H.E.: Handbook of Human Reliability Analysis with Emphasis on Nuclear Power Plant Applications: Final Report (NUREG/CR-1278). Nuclear Regulatory Commission of the United States of America, Washington, USA (1983)
2. Oliveira, L.N., Santos, J.A.L., Carvalho, P.V.R.: A review of the evolution of human reliability analysis methods at nuclear industry. In: International Nuclear Atlantic Conference – INAC 2017, Belo Horizonte, MG, Brazil, 22–27 October 2017 (2017)
3. Zou, Y., Zhang, L., Dai, L., Li, P., Qing, T.: Human reliability analysis for digitized nuclear power plants: case study on the LingAo II nuclear power plant. Nucl. Eng. Technol. **49**(2), 335–341 (2017)
4. Huber, S., van Wijgerden, I., de Witt, A., Dekker, S.W.A.: Learning from organizational incidents: resilience engineering for high-risk process environments. Process Saf. Prog. **28**(1), 90–95 (2009)
5. Kantowitz, B.H., Sorkin, R.D.: Human Factors: Understanding People-System Relationships. Wiley, Hoboken (1983)
6. Boring, R.: How many performance shaping factors are necessary for human reliability analysis? In: Proceedings of the 10th International Conference on Probabilistic Safety Assessment and Management (2010)
7. Skjerve, A.B., Nihwiling, C., Nystad, E.: Lessons learned from the extended teamwork study (HWR-867). The OECD Halden Reactor Project, Halden (2008)
8. Blackett, C.: Operator Reliability for Actions Outside the Control Room: Scope and Research Direction (HWhP-070). OECD Halden Reactor Project, Halden (2019)
9. Bisio, R., Fernandes, A., Blackett, C.: A Framework to Analyse Human Performance Outside the Control Room (HWR-1277). OECD Halden Reactor Project (2020)

Promoting Operational Readiness Through Procedures in Nuclear Domain

Jari Laarni[1(✉)], Jatta Tomminen[1], Marja Liinasuo[1], Satu Pakarinen[2], and Kristian Lukander[2]

[1] VTT Technical Research Centre of Finland Ltd., Espoo, Finland
jari.laarni@vtt.fi
[2] Finnish Institute of Occupational Health, Helsinki, Finland

Abstract. Operating procedures provide a description of the actions that are needed to operate a particular system in a safe and efficient manner. We developed an analysis framework for the identification of resilience skills that enable intelligent use of procedures. An analysis of critical functions and their interaction was carried out by using the Functional Resonance Analysis Method (FRAM; [4]). The basic idea behind the FRAM is to develop questions that are discussed with those who will use the procedure in their work. According to our results, the FRAM methodology was successfully applied to the analysis of the selected proceduralized activity. It was found that one fruitful approach is to first create an overview FRAM model describing the main activities of the task from the perspective of the nuclear process, and after that, create a more detailed description, looking at the task from the control room operators' perspective. Some potential variability of the functions was identified – mainly related to the communication and collaboration between operators and between operators and personnel in the field. Implications of our results to procedure design and operator training will be discussed.

Keywords: Functional Resonance Analysis Method · Procedure design · Nuclear power · Control room operator

1 Introduction

1.1 Operating Procedures in Nuclear Domain

Operating procedures provide a description of the actions that are needed to operate a particular system in a safe and efficient manner. According to some estimates, approximately 70% of the incidents in the nuclear domain have been associated with failures in procedure usage [6]. Procedures can be presented in different formats such as step-by-step text-based instructions, decision trees and flowcharts [12]. Traditionally, operating procedures have been presented in paper format, but today procedures are presented to a larger extent on a computer [8]. Procedures guide operator behavior and set constraints of what is acceptable and what is not. There is a trade-off between too strong level of guidance and too weak guidance: Too strong guidance restricts adaptive way of working, needed in varying situations, but too weak guidance may have detrimental effects on a crew's performance and shared understanding of the situation [13].

D. Harris and W.-C. Li (Eds.): HCII 2020, LNAI 12187, pp. 42–51, 2020.
https://doi.org/10.1007/978-3-030-49183-3_4

Traditionally, it has been thought that in safety-critical domains, human-system interfaces and procedures are designed with the aim of ensuring safe practice, and the aim of training is to provide to the personnel enough knowledge and ensure that tools are used as planned (see Fig. 1). However, when designing human-system interfaces for complex domains, it is not possible to anticipate all possible work situations, procedures and training. Instead, arriving to the optimal solution requires flexible thinking and problem solving. There is always a tension and gap between work-as-imagined and work-as-done [5]. Human-system interfaces (HSIs) and procedures are designed based on the designers' view of the work of operative personnel - which is only partly grounded on the work-as-done. Since human-system interfaces and procedures are designed from the perspective of work as designed, personnel must make continuous adaptations in order to manage and accomplish their work tasks. To succeed in this, they need resources for actions provided by their skills and by organizational support. Regarding skills, resilience is especially needed for enabling intelligent use of procedures [7]. The organization, in turn, can support the crew by, e.g., providing technical backup from other workers and professionals, when additional expertise is needed. Even though HSIs and procedures are used in daily work, the larger the gap between work-as-imagined and work-as-done the more problems there may emerge in their usage and a larger role the resources for action plays. Normally, training plays a key role in the pursuit of reconciling the gap between work-as-designed and work-as-done.

Fig. 1. A traditional view according to which training has an important role in aligning the work-as-imagined and work-as-done.

The aim of our study was to explore the applicability of the Functional Resonance Analysis Method (FRAM) method for procedure development [4]. The FRAM method can be used as a tool for understanding the reasons behind the gap between work-as-imagined and work-as-done, from the perspective according to which procedures represent work-as-imagined, and the actual crew activities represent work-as-done.

A FRAM model was developed by a free software tool called the FRAM Model Visualizer [3]. The basic idea behind the FRAM is to develop questions that are discussed with those who will use the procedure in their work. The objective of these questions is to identify the critical functions related to nuclear process control and the interactions of these functions. The model was further developed, and its level of appropriateness was tested by analyzing video recordings of simulator tests in which actual operator performance (work-as-done) could be observed. In the future, we will also experimentally evaluate the framework in simulator tests in which two different versions of the procedure are compared in a quasi-experimental set-up.

In this paper, we first present 1) the results of single-person interviews in which a number of key issues related to procedure development were discussed and 2) the results of two focus group meetings in which a FRAM model for one proceduralized activity was developed. The model describes the potential variability of the system in terms of functions. Each function has been defined using six aspects: Input, Output, Time, Resource, Control and Precondition [4]. Second, we present the preliminary results of observations about a simulator study at one of Finnish nuclear power plants, in which the analyzed procedure was used. Video-recordings from thirteen simulator runs were analyzed. The aim of these observations was to verify the conclusions made on the grounds of FRAM modelling.

2   Methods

2.1   Data Collection

Data was collected by focus groups, single-person interviews and video-based observations. Two focus group sessions were arranged with ten participants. Most of the participants were procedure developers and simulator trainers in one Finnish nuclear power plant. The aim of the focus groups was to develop a FRAM model for a particular incident situation and to analyze the procedure designed for managing this situation. In addition, we carried out four single-person interviews by interviewing four experts from three different organizations (from two Finnish NPPs and from the Finnish Nuclear Regulatory Authority).

In order to compare work-as-designed and work-as-done, video-based structured observations were conducted, in which video recordings of simulator test sessions were observed. Simulator runs of thirteen operator crews were analyzed.

2.2   Data Analysis

Interviews were transcribed, and the notes were analyzed in order to explore the debates conducted around the critical functions and their couplings. Notes were made during observations of simulator test sessions, and answers to key research questions were tabulated on an observation table. Audio recordings were first transcribed, and then analyzed by using the grounded theory approach by one researcher.

3   Results

3.1   Description of the Procedure

The target procedure (i.e., triggering of the boron chain) consists of about twenty procedural steps in each of which a particular action is associated. The goal of the procedure is to drive the plant to a safe end state. Most of the operator tasks are inspections of correct functioning of automation systems.

3.2   Interview Results

According to single-person interviews, power companies are responsible for their own procedure development, and STUK, the Finnish nuclear authority, plays a supervisory role. Practices and processes of procedure development somewhat differ from one power plant to another.

According to the experts' interviews, methods and tools they are using nowadays are quite good and sufficient for their purposes. However, they also felt that that more formal methods and tools for procedure development could be beneficial. Typically, task analysis has been thought as an important method in procedure design. However, according to the interviewees, formal task analysis methods are not systematically used in nuclear power plants. Instead, designers use safety analysis reports and their own less systematic notes as a starting point for their design work. Some of them, however, thought that a systematic application of task analysis might be useful for determining whether the tasks can be performed or not.

The FRAM method was first briefly described to the interviewees. Some of the interviewees were familiar with FRAM, but none of them had ever used it. Differing opinions were expressed regarding the utility of the FRAM method in procedure development: while some were skeptical, others thought that the method may be helpful. For instance, FRAM was seen as potentially useful in the training of new procedures. By using FRAM one could go through all the functions and their justifications, and at the same time, evaluate how these justifications were derived.

3.3   Building a FRAM Model

Incident Scenario Modelled in FRAM. The scenario starts out as routine testing, that is then interrupted by a sudden, unexpected launch of an emergency shutdown following a control rod drop -failure, leading to a launch of chemical shin (boric acid) to bring the reactor to zero power level and sub-critical state.

The first focus group considered the target scenario from the process point of view. In the first round, fourteen functions for either the Reactor Operator (RO) or the Turbine Operator (TO) were identified. A failed reactor shutdown is the trigger for all the subsequent events in the scenario run. Three partial conditions can lead to the triggering of the boron chain. After the boron release, the operators' main aim is to bring the reactor to a sub-critical state. SIRM measurements provide critical information for this interpretation.

To build the FRAM model, the main functions and their interrelations were first identified and presented by the FRAM notation (see Fig. 2). Second, the couplings between functions were defined and illustrated by thin lines connecting the functions.

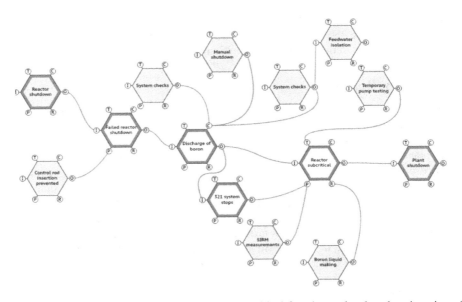

Fig. 2. A simplified FRAM model, describing the critical functions related to the triggering of the boron chain, designed on the basis of the first focus group meeting. The model was developed by a free software tool named the FRAM Model Visualizer [3].

The FRAM model was evaluated with regard to the number of couplings (antecedents and consequences), since according to [4], their number is associated with the variability of a particular function, and the variability increases with the number of couplings. Table 1 shows the number of couplings for some functions. Only the most critical upstream and downstream functions are presented. Upstream functions belong to those functions, which have already been completed, and downstream functions belong to those, which follow a particular function.

Table 1. Summary of the variability associated with some key functions.

Function	Upstream functions	Downstream functions
Initiating reactor shutdown	0	1
Failed reactor shutdown	2	1
Triggering of the boron chain	4	2
Cooling system stops	1	1
Reactor sub-critical	5	1
Reactor shutdown	1	0

As can be seen, the number of upstream couplings is largest for the functions of triggering of the boron chain and reactor sub-criticality. This means that the variability and adjustments of upstream functions have a quite large effect on these two functions.

Operator's Perspective. In the second focus group meeting, the scenario was analyzed from the operators' perspective. The model became more detailed in this phase, and a larger number of functions were identified and described (see Fig. 3). Most of the functions were allocated to the RO or TO, who perform a majority of the operations, but there were also functions allocated to the shift supervisor (SS), who has an important role as a superior.

All in all, the variability was more pronounced at the beginning of the emergency situation than in its later phases. The participants emphasized that it is particularly important to complete actions correctly immediately once the failure is detected.

Based on the discussions, the participants recommended some improvements to the target procedure, which can be considered as the main benefit of the modelling work. For example, it was found that a description of the end-state of a procedural action was missing from two procedure steps.

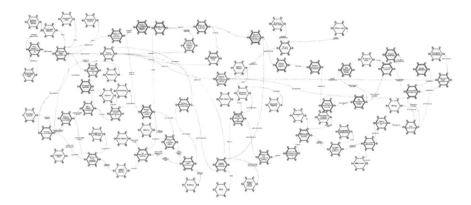

Fig. 3. A more complex FRAM model that was designed on the basis of the second focus group meeting, to clarify the operator perspective (operations). The text is not intended to be readable - the aim is only to illustrate the complexity of the model when the number of functions is higher (cf. Fig. 2). The model was developed by the FRAM Model Visualizer [3].

3.4   Observations of Simulator Training Exercises

The main goal of the observations of simulator runs was to verify the conclusions made on the grounds of FRAM models.

In the simulator runs, triggering of the boron chain was caused by a failure in the insertion of control rods, requiring the cessation of reactor activity chemically. Once the boron was launched, the RO and TO confirmed the stability of the processes and also followed the decrease of nuclear activity, and finally on the basis of SIRM measurements confirmed that the plant has been brought to a sub-critical state.

All crews applied the failed reactor shutdown procedure in the simulator run. However, contrary to our expectations, only six crews applied the triggering of the boron chain -procedure, which has been particularly developed for this incident. The failed reactor shutdown procedure was used instead, mainly because it is more familiar to the operators, and it includes the major part of the operator tasks found in the triggering of the boron chain procedure. In addition to these two, operators used several other procedures in the simulator run.

The crews performed the functions allocated to them in accordance with the procedures. The Shift Supervisor (SS) accomplished his/her own procedure and supervised the RO's and TO's task execution. He/she could also share additional tasks with the other operators, and declare Site Emergency. The SS typically coordinated the use of procedures and checked that all tasks were adequately completed. Some proceduralized tasks were not completed in a chronological order. It was also found that the operators did not accomplish their tasks completely independently, but some of the actions were performed in collaboration with other operators.

All the crews achieved the main goals of the situation. The overall variability of performance time between crews was moderate: the average completion time was 31 min (range 27 to 33 min). However, within the scenario, there was considerable variability in the time of observation for certain critical activities (Fig. 4). For example, the triggering of the boron chain was observed at fastest in 30 s and at slowest in 9 min 10 s after the start of the simulator run. The average duration was 5 min 10 s.

We analyzed the amount of variability between crews regarding some critical functions.

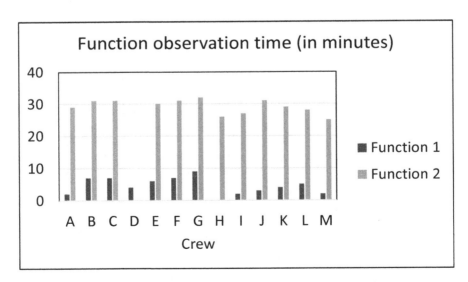

Fig. 4. Elapsed time until observing two critical functions in minutes for thirteen crews. Two crews (i.e., D and H) did not observe one of the two functions. Function 1: Triggering of the boron chain. Function 2: Reactor sub-criticality.

The amount of variability seemed to be largest for two functions, identification of triggering of the boron chain and verification of pumping of boron. Other functions for which some variability was observed were time for attainment of reactor sub-criticality (see Fig. 4), performing a reactor shutdown and stopping manually in-pumping.

With regard to the identification of boron release, there were quite big differences between the crews in the time they needed to observe the release. With regard to the verification of pumping of boron, the differences between crews were mainly associated with the adjustment of the water level of the reactor. Some TOs considered it a failure, if the level exceeded 5 m. There were also some variability in initiating reactor shutdown: while some crews tried to drive the control rods into the core several times, some crews did it only once or twice.

Basically, the same sources of variability were identified with both methods (i.e., with observation or modelling). However, it was also found that FRAM modelling identified variability in some functions for which little variability was observed during the simulator runs.

4 Discussion

4.1 FRAM Method in the Analysis of EOPs

We were able to demonstrate the gap between the work-as-design and the work-as-done with regard to one particular procedure/operational condition. We were also able to identify the most critical functions and sources of variance in procedure execution. The results are thus in line with some earlier studies, in which the FRAM model was able to identify the most critical functions and their couplings [9, 14].

In addition, one concrete suggestion for improvement emerged in the focus groups, and the change was planned to be implemented in the proposed procedure step. It was also found that the SS's role has not been identified in a sufficient degree in existing job descriptions.

FRAM could be especially helpful in the analysis of novel situations for which there is no existing procedures available. The method could also be helpful in safety analysis to provide information on potential successes and failures. The method seems to be quite sensitive, and it is able to identify less obvious, hidden couplings and low variability in functions, which may be difficult to identify by other means. On the negative side, it can also identify couplings, which are less relevant and meaningful. In order to prevent identification of this kind of 'imagined variability' [11], it is important to discuss with operators whether they consider the variability real or not - indicating that the results should be always verified against an independent method, preferably with a party with complementary knowledge than those having created the model.

The presentation of the model becomes easily quite complex as the number of functions increases. If the number of functions is quite big, it is quite difficult to present the results in a simple way, and visualizations based on the FRAM Model Visualizer become quite difficult to interpret. A model's value may thus deteriorate, if modelling is conducted in too detailed level. Overall, there is an urge for more illustrative ways to present the modelling results [9].

One problem is that a hierarchical structure is missing from FRAM models, and therefore it is difficult to zoom in or out on a model. To find the optimal level of detail, it would be necessary to conduct the modelling work at different levels of detail as we did in our work. Also, it should be more explicitly specified the type of a coupling between functions, i.e. what is transferred between functions, matter, energy, information or something else. One possibility would be to use colors to specify different types of couplings.

It was found that the application of the method was quite laborious, and it takes time to learn to apply the method in an efficient manner. Therefore, it is important to allow the personnel participating in FRAM workshops enough time for familiarization and training with the method. These observations are in line with some previous studies on FRAM [8, 14].

Overall, as compared to some earlier studies in other domains in which the method has been used in procedure design, the findings seem to be quite modest [2, 10]. One reason for these unremarkable findings is that the role of procedures is different in nuclear domain: there is more rigor in the development of procedures in nuclear field, and strict adherence to procedures is more or less a norm [1].

5   Conclusions

FRAM models were able to describe operator work as it is done through functions and links between these functions. When comparing the variability in performance, predicted by the FRAM and observed in simulator runs, it was found that the method was able to identify main sources of variability, those small adjustments in a daily work characteristic of Safety-II. Also, the experts thought that FRAM might be useful especially in the early stages of procedure design.

Some areas for development were identified, and it was thought that the method may be more useful for work analysis method than as a means to develop procedures. Yet, the FRAM method has some potential for use in procedure design, especially in designing procedures for novel situations. One of the most favorable feature is its versatility: the method can be applied for many purposes.

Overall, formal methods are able to tighten up the development of procedures, and FRAM, as one example of these methods, may provide added value to the development of procedures also in nuclear domain.

Acknowledgments. The authors would like to thank the procedure designers, the simulator trainers and other personnel involved in this study.

References

1. Carvalho, P.V.R., de Oliveira, M.V., dos Santos, I.J.L.: A computerized tool to evaluate the cognitive compatibility of the emergency operational procedures task flow. Prog. Nucl. Energy 51(3), 409–419 (2009)
2. Clay-Williams, R.: Where the rubber meets the road: using FRAM to align work-as-imagined with work-as-done when implementing clinical guidelines. Implementation Sci. 10 (1), 125 (2015)
3. FRAM Homepage. http://functionalresonance.com/FMV/index.html. Accessed 31 Jan 2020
4. Hollnagel, E.: FRAM, the functional resonance analysis method: modelling complex socio-technical systems. Ashgate, Farnham (2012)
5. Hollnagel, E.: Why is work-as-imaged different from Work-as-done? In: Wears, R.L., Hollnagel, E., Braithwaite, J. (eds.) Resilient health care, volume 2: The resilience of everyday clinical work. Ashgate, Abingdon (2015)
6. Marsden, P.: Procedures in the nuclear industry. In: Stanton, N. (ed.) Human Factors in Nuclear Safety, pp. 99–116. Taylor & Francis, London (1996)
7. Norros, L., Savioja, P., Liinasuo, M., Wahlström, M.: Can proceduralization support coping with the unexpected? Int. Electron. J. Nucl. Saf. Simul. 5(3), 213–221 (2014)
8. Patriarca, R., Bergström, J.: Modelling complexity in everyday operations: functional resonance in maritime mooring at quay. Cogn. Technol. Work 19(4), 711–729 (2017)
9. Patriarca, R., Bergström, J., Di Gravio, G.: Defining the functional resonance analysis space: combining abstraction hierarchy and FRAM. Reliab. Eng. Syst. Saf. 165, 34–46 (2017)
10. Saurin, T.A., Wachs, P.: Modelling interactions between procedures and resilience skills. Appl. Ergon. 68, 328–337 (2018)
11. Smith, D., Veitch, B., Khan, F., Taylor, R.: Understanding industrial safety: comparing fault tree, bayesian network, and FRAM approaches. J. Loss Prev. Process Ind. 45, 88–101 (2017)
12. Stanton, N.A., Salmon, P., Jenkins, D., Walker, G.: Human Factors in the Design and Evaluation of Central Control Room Operations. CRC Press, Boca Raton (2010)
13. Suchman, L.A.: Plans and Situated Actions: The Problem of Human-Machine Communication. Cambridge University Press, Cambridge (1987)
14. de Vries, L.: Work as done? understanding the practice of sociotechnical work in the maritime domain. J. Cogn. Eng. Decis. Mak. 11(3), 270–295 (2017)

Research on BIM and Mobile Equipment in Substation Construction Schedule Management

Rui Liu$^{(\boxtimes)}$ (iD) and Fan Liu$^{(\boxtimes)}$ (iD)

North China Electric Power University, Beijing, China
liuruibeijing@163.com, sailliu@126.com

Abstract. Large-scale buildings have been leading the application of BIM technology for progress management. However, the progress management of the substation is still relying on manual handwritten records, which will delay the owner's understanding of the construction schedule from the actual date. Delay of the construction project progress phenomenon is common. This study reviewed for BIM and schedule management information collection technology, cited schedule management platform of Glodon. The platform use mobile devices to collect information on construction site, and then the platform could reflect the progress of each subdivisional work, eventually the information can be integrated into BIM platform + wisdom site, managers can not only distinguish real time schedule of the construction site in different colors in the BIM model, but also can see the data analysis, progress of the warning, the reasons of the sluggish progress, and decide what remedial measures should be taken and so on.

Keywords: BIM · Mobile equipment · Substation · Construction · Schedule management

1 Introduction

With the national promotion of digital China, the big data strategy has also been implemented in the construction industry, which manifested the application of engineering technology in the direction of digitalization. In response to the national policy, the state grid proposed the concept of digital state grid, and took advantage of the situation by issuing specifications and opinions on three-dimensional design in the field of power transmission and transformation engineering at the parent company level and the provincial company level. The strategy of the digital state grid conforms to the development trend of the state grid and meet the power transmission and transformation project management needs of state grid, such as non-intuitive technical disclosure, inaccurate information transmission of various stakeholders, manual recording of communication in each link, lagging information understood by managers compared with the construction site, and scattered distribution of engineering information in various departments. The three-dimensional, real-time, automatic and integrated management mode, as well as the project collaborative management platform based on

© Springer Nature Switzerland AG 2020
D. Harris and W.-C. Li (Eds.): HCII 2020, LNAI 12187, pp. 52–67, 2020.
https://doi.org/10.1007/978-3-030-49183-3_5

three-dimensional design, which runs through every link of substation construction, have become the eagerly anticipated platform of state grid. The purpose of this paper is to study the progress management of substation. Through the combination of 3d digital technology and other advanced technologies, real-time control of construction site progress is realized and reflected in the 3d digital collaborative management platform.

3D design in the construction industry mainly refers to BIM (Building Information management). Building information model (BIM), which is put forward by Dr Chuck Eastman, means that the building contain all the geometry, building components, properties, functional properties, quantity and all the information in the other elements, and brings together engineering data and information from different stages. Such as: construction phase, construction schedule and operation information in the process of maintenance, etc. [1] the application of BIM in all stages not only reduces the communication cost of participants in the construction industry, but also makes the transmission of construction information more accurate, which is conducive to the accumulation of engineering data.

3D design has been gradually applied in the construction industry due to its features of direct model display, accurate and comprehensive data transmission, and real field simulation. In the application of large-scale construction projects, 3d design is not only widely used in the design stage, but also has important applications in the construction stage, such as progress management, quality management, safety management, etc. by combining platform construction with advanced information acquisition technology. However, these applications in substation projects are lagging behind, such as Three-dimensional information is rarely used during construction, For example, 3d informatization is rarely used in the construction stage, and field data are often recorded manually. When the data is submitted to the management department, the progress information that the manager has learned is delayed compared with the actual progress of the construction site. In order to understand the construction progress of the sub-station in real time, it is necessary for the owners to select the information acquisition technology to collect the construction site data.

Information collection technology includes mobile phone, RFID, bar code, photography, etc. Different collection technology has its characteristics and applicable conditions. Through reading the literature, this paper makes a literature review on the information collection technology that can realize progress management. Finally, Glodon 5DBIM management platform is applied to the progress management of the substation, so that the progress information of the substation can be distinguished by color in the three-dimensional model between completed and unfinished tasks, and the statistics and progress information can be reflected on the platform.

2   Literature Review

2.1   An Overview of BIM in Progress Management

Xue Li et al. [2] studied the application of BIM in construction progress management, summarized the problems encountered in the implementation of construction progress and the advantages of BIM over traditional technology. By associating the Project with

BIM, the construction simulation is realized, and then how the engineering data provided by BIM assists the construction to achieve progress management is elaborated. Zheng haoyu [3] studied the process management of steel structure by using Tekla software in BIM technology, such as model establishment, collision checking, calculation of engineering quantity, drawing of components and sorting, classification and numbering of component information in the design stage. The application of BIM in the machining of machine components. The application of construction simulation and schedule management in construction stage. At the same time, the application of BIM and RFID in construction progress is introduced.

2.2 A Review of Progress Management Information Collection Techniques

According to the classification of building types, buildings are basically divided into traditional buildings and prefabricated buildings. The two types of buildings have their own characteristics. Traditional buildings have high requirements for information acquisition technology due to their complicated structures such as steel bars and cement, while prefabricated buildings have relatively simple requirements for information acquisition technology due to their high quantifiable components. To provide appropriate technologies for different types of buildings, the following Table 1 sorts out the current progress information collection technologies.

Table 1. Comparison of different progress management techniques

	Technical name	How to implement progress management	Characteristic
1	Multimedia tools	Use photos, video, audio, audio and other media as attachments to calendar events to collect data for progress analysis [4]	Advantages: It makes progress management more intuitive Disadvantages: It need manual operation, and need to consume the time and energy of staff to input information [5]
2	Email-services	Through the application, field personnel fill out e-forms and send emails to the system, which automatically updates the calendar and generates a complete progress report. Finally, all messages are stored in the corresponding dates in the bar chart [6]	Advantages: users can check questions and answers, have enough time to check answers before answering, and can get photos, videos and other files [5] Disadvantages: some users have no access to the Internet, and it is not convenient to use mobile phones at the construction site

(continued)

Table 1. (*continued*)

	Technical name	How to implement progress management	Characteristic
3	Voice-based tools	The user enters the construction site information into the system by voice and can access the information effectively in the computer system [7]	Advantages: quick response, quick forwarding of emergency information, time-saving, efficient, convenient, recorded information can record the scene events Disadvantages: There is not enough time to think and respond, it is difficult to back up previous files, and the user is prone to error when choosing the answer [5]
4	Smartphones, tablets, laptops	These devices strengthen project control by providing managers with field information, including resource data, project delivery information, and progress information. These devices can handle spreadsheets or industry-specific applications and have the ability to use cameras, GPS, voice, email, and access the Internet. It can be combined with other technologies such as bar codes [8]	Advantages: small device size, excellent mobility, many functions, it can be combined with RFID reader and other technologies, Disadvantages: high cost, limited portability, need to develop professional applications [5]
5	Barcoding	The barcoding is scanned by bar code reader or scanner, which is used to capture and read the information related to items in the bar code. This method can collect real-time data. The main application fields of progress management are material tracking, inventory statistics, construction progress tracking and manual tracking [9]	Advantages: low cost, large capacity for content and type of data. High reliability, easy to produce, easy to identify by mobile devices, can be read in any direction [5] Disadvantages: easy to damage

(*continued*)

Table 1. (*continued*)

	Technical name	How to implement progress management	Characteristic
6	RFID	RFID is a kind of automatic identification technology, which collects and statistics the progress information of the construction site through radio frequency acquisition and transmission of construction site data. It is mainly applied to view component properties, material statistics, positioning, etc. [10]	Advantages: wide reading range, no line-of-sight handling, and durability in built environments in different weather conditions Disadvantages: relatively high initial and maintenance costs, weak signal strength, limited service life, Active RFID requires regular battery changes. RFID tags are susceptible to interference from metallic materials [5]
7	UWB	UWB is a network of receivers and tags that communicate with each other over large broadband lines. The tags emit ultra-wideband radio pulses that allow the system to find their 3D coordinates even if there are multiple paths. This method is suitable not only for physical entity related activities, such as delivery of installation, but also for other non-structural activities such as welding and inspection [11]	Advantages: longer reading range than laser scanning. indoor and outdoor working capabilities, Low pulse rate results in low average power demand. Compared to RFID systems, UWB provides accurate 3D location information without integration with other technologies [5]
8	GPS	GPS works by receiving signals from satellites in order to locate specific objects attached to tags. It is mainly used to track steel structure materials from component manufacturing to storage, installation and maintenance. so as to reflect the progress. In terms of progress management, such as using a robotic total station and sensors to automate the data collection and positioning process of the tunneling machines used to construct sewer and storm water municipal pipelines [12]	Disadvantages: multipath error in crowded environments. It's not economical when you need to link GPS to every site object [5]

(*continued*)

Table 1. (*continued*)

	Technical name	How to implement progress management	Characteristic
9	Photogrammetry	A 3D model of the project in progress is generated from the photos, and then the completed 3D model is compared with the 3D CAD model to automatically calculate the percentage of completion of each component to measure progress [13]	Advantages: high degree of automation, accurate measurement progress Disadvantages: The sensitivity of the target area and detector to the lighting conditions is high. In the case of shadow, the lighting conditions affect the image processing. Progress can only be monitored on the structural frame of the component closest to the camera. The statistical process requires manual intervention, resulting in time-consuming and laborious work [5]
10	3D laser scanning	The distance to the target is calculated by firing a laser pulse at the target and counting the return time of the time pulse. A laser scan can send millions of 3D dots in minutes. Progress on the construction site can be tracked by identifying the built components in the 3D point cloud and comparing them with the 3D BIM model [14]	Disadvantages: high cost; Need clear line of sight, crowded space is difficult to get widely used; The sensor needs to be calibrated regularly and the preheating time is long. Moving machinery or personnel may create noise in the point cloud, resulting in additional time for users to manually modify; As the distance increases, the level of detail that can be captured decreases. The scanner is not easy to carry and is not suitable for indoor environment. The value in the construction project is not high [5]
11	Videogrammetry	The technology extracts features from the video and reconstructs the pixels of each frame according to the video to form a 3D point cloud, which is compared with the 3D BIM model to reflect the progress [15]	Advantages: not subject to field temperature changes or edge deflection, Medium in accuracy and quality, low cost compared to laser scanning [5]

(*continued*)

Table 1. (*continued*)

	Technical name	How to implement progress management	Characteristic
12	Range images	Through the distance sensor (distance camera), the construction object is digitized into a 3D model, which is compared with the known model to achieve progress management. It can be used to track moving objects, construction equipment and materials [15–18]	Features: suitable for short range applications, cheaper than laser scanners and more expensive than photogrammetry cameras [5]
13	AR	AR is a combination of technologies, hardware including head-mounted displays, GPS, data gloves and smart boards. The software includes 3D studio Max and BIM. Through photography, camera measurement, laser scanning and other methods to collect field data. Overlap the collected field data with 4D BIM or other software models to reflect the construction progress [19–22]	Features: AR faces the following challenges: user comfort, power limitations, ability to function in harsh environments, robust image registration for outdoor uncontrolled conditions. Filtering ambient noise and data interferences, and adding more interactivity the AR interface [5, 23]

You can see through the literature review, although progress acquisition technology has developed rapidly, but most of the technology exist barriers on the accuracy or the feasibility. This paper takes feasibility as the starting point, USES the Glodon progress management platform, realizes the substation progress management based on the owner's perspective. The specific thinking is: firstly, mobile phone is selected as the collection technology of construction site progress information, which is combined with BIM and Project to achieve project-level progress management. Then, the appropriate information is extracted to achieve project group progress management. In the process of project-level progress management, by associating the progress with the BIM model, the construction and the demand for labor, materials and capital of the project can be simulated. If there is an unreasonable schedule, the schedule can be optimized to provide resource prediction for the owner to ensure the schedule.

3   The Basic Situation of Substation

In this paper, 110 kV substation is taken as an example. The general layout of the substation is rectangular (the fence is 81.0 m long and 40.2 m wide), covering a total area of 3555.6 m^2, and an area of 3256.2 m^2 within the center line of the fence. There are two buildings in the station area: power distribution unit building and water pump room. The power distribution unit building is a steel frame structure with two floors above ground and one underground. The first underground floor is the interlayer of cables. The first floor is arranged with the main transformer room, 10 kV power distribution unit room, 110 kV power distribution unit room, duty room, living room, safety tool room, toilet, etc. The second floor is arranged with capacitor room, secondary equipment room and water tank room. The outdoor ancillary works include: the inbound road, the in-station road, the fence, the cable trench, the accident oil pool and the reservoir.

In the construction of the substation, the schedule management mainly faces the following problems: insufficient personnel and mechanical equipment, construction materials organization report is not timely, procurement is not timely, construction management is not appropriate, power outages plan arrangement is not appropriate, coordination management work is not in place and other reasons caused by the delay. BIM5D is dedicated to solving these problems.

4   Software Systems: BIM5D

BIM5D integrates field systems and hardware into a unified platform that aggregates and models the resulting data into a data center. The platform presents data of sub-application systems such as production planning, schedule management, quality management and safety management in a unified way, forming an interconnection. Key indicators of the project are presented in the form of intuitive charts, helping the project to achieve digitalization, systematization and intelligence. This paper take the transformer substation in BIM5D schedule management platform for case study. Through the progress of platform, Managers can understand the construction progress by looking at the progress management platform, and can dynamically control and adjust the project, which will make the project schedule more controllable. By comparing and analyzing the data, monitoring and alarming, managers can timely understand the progress problems and ensure the project delivery as scheduled.

5   Application Steps

This paper describes the functions of the platform in meeting the owner's schedule management needs from the project level and the project group level respectively.

5.1   Project Level Management

Project-level management mainly solves the problem of integrating data collected on site, 3d model and Project progress plan into the platform, where the Project progress can be reflected in real time. To achieve such a function, key problems need to be solved as follows: First, the BIM should be associated with the Project through the platform, so as to match the progress plan with the information in the model (such as materials, costs and other information). Second, collect the construction site progress information. Third, relate the collected information to the BIM model, and calculate the progress report. Forth, Display statistical models and reports on APP, computer and WEB. The specific implementation method is shown in Table 2:

Table 2. Implementation steps for the progress management platform

Create a project	Add projects,open new products,add members,select roles
Data preparation	Type of work,cooperative units,materials dictionary,mechanical equipment dictionary,construction task structure
Planning system construction	Master plan,period plan,weekly plan
Production activity tracking	Progress tracking,custom photo tracking.
Production information application	Production homepage,production weekly meeting,big data analysis
Production information output	Weekly plan report,construction log,photo album

5.2   Create Project Information

Create the basic information of the substation so that the staff can retrieve the relevant information when compiling the progress plan. How to do it: add the project name, the name of the new substation, and the members that can use the BIM5D platform. Create the basic information of the type of work, cooperative units, materials dictionary, mechanical equipment dictionary, construction task structure and so on.

5.3   Associate the Project with the Platform

The prepared Project plan is associated with the platform, and the progress plan is displayed on the platform to facilitate the later association with the BIM model. The specific operation is as follows: click the function key "select Project" on the BIM5D platform page, select the Project to be associated with, select the corresponding WBS function, and click "generate plan" (as shown in Fig. 1). After compiling the plan content, the Project will be associated with the platform after uploading. The status of successful uploads is shown in Fig. 2.

Fig. 1. Upload the production plan to the cloud

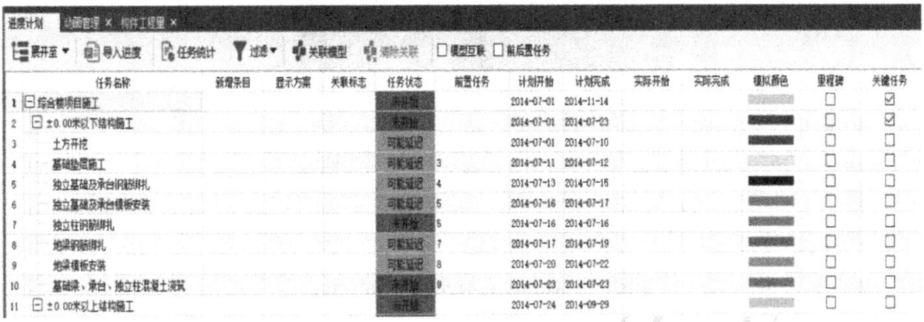

Fig. 2. Successfully tie the production plan to the platform

6 Associate BIM with the Platform

By associating BIM with the progress plan of the platform, the construction progress can not only be vividly displayed in the model, but also in the early stage of construction, the project amount can be extracted and the funds can be calculated to judge whether the materials, funds and other resources can meet the supply demand of the progress. The specific way of association can be related according to the single floor or flow section of the substation, but also according to the profession(such as, beam, column, wall, etc.).

Here's how to do it: schedule list in the BIM5D platform has an "associated model" function that can associates the schedule with the BIM model. The specific methods are as follows: select the specific schedule to be associated, click "associated model" and jump to the interface of the model association (as is shown in Fig. 3). There are two types of associated model: "single floor mode" and "flow section linkage mode". After selecting "single mode", select the target floor and component type, and then select them in the model view on the right. Click "select the associated element" to make the association successful. At this point, return to the main interface of construction simulation to check whether it is successful. See Fig. 4 for the status after success. The site is displayed with the monomer and can be associated simultaneously. Based on this, the schedule plan is associated with the BIM model on the platform, and then the schedule changes on the construction site are updated on the model.

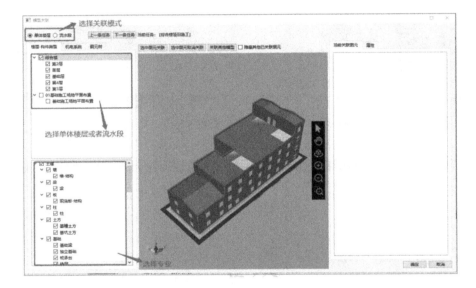

Fig. 3. Model correlation interface

Fig. 4. The schedule plan is associated with the model

7 Upload the Information Collected on Site to the Platform

7.1 Set Control Points and Track Items

Substation engineering consists of construction engineering and electrical equipment installation engineering. Construction engineering mainly includes construction of buildings and structures, while electrical equipment installation engineering mainly includes primary equipment installation and secondary equipment installation, experiment and debugging, etc.. First, according to the specific situation of the substation, the composition of the substation is divided, forming a process. Then, in the WEB side, according to the composition of the substation, control points and tracking matters are set. The tracking matters can refer to the control points, and the items and stages can be linked to the process, which is composed of components. The new tracking plan on the PC side should refer to the tracking plan on the WEB side. The App side can edit the components under the plan and the processes to be completed under the components (such as start and end, etc.). The edited construction can be viewed on PC, WEB and App. Through the setting of control points and tracking items, the construction progress of the substation is divided into nodes and processes. By submitting the completion of nodes and processes at the mobile terminal, the construction progress can be clearly displayed in the platform statistical function.

7.2 Set Control Points and Track Items

When the construction personnel complete a process on site, they can use the mobile APP to track the progress by submitting the state of the process and components, and send the completed process to the APP in the form of taking photos. The specific filling process is as follows:

Click "component tracking" in the APP to enter the process list interface. The process list interface displays the track plan uploaded by the PC side, as well as items planed to be hooked up. The right side shows the number of artifacts associated with this plan and the number is completed. The principle of defining the process state is as follows: according to the process state, the process is divided into [not started], [in progress] and [completed]. If all components in the process are not started, the process state is [not started]. If there is one component in the process that has not been started and not all of them have been completed, then the process state is [in progress]; If all components in the process are completed, the state of the process is [completed]. The three states are shown in different colors. The process list interface is shown in Fig. 5. At this point, the build status is submitted to the App.

Fig. 5. The process list interface

8   Distinguish Progress by Color on the BIM Model

Use 'trace model view' function on the web to display the completed process on a WEB page. The specific operation is as follows: filter trees control the model's visibility in the view. When selecting [state filtering], by associating the filter tree with the intersection of all the primitives, the associated components in the view are displayed according to [color setting], and [color setting] can set the color of component state. Select the primitive in the view to view the attribute of the primitive. If the component of the primitive have tracking data. you can view the process of data in [process details], including time, description, picture and control point. At this point, the construction schedule is color-coded in the BIM model. The WEB trace model view is shown in Fig. 6.

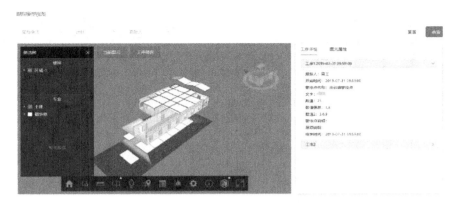

Fig. 6. The WEB trace model view

9 Statistics Displayed on PC, WEB, and APP Platforms

All the information statistics are on the production page. The owner manager can see the progress of each item, whether it is delayed or advanced. The total number of tasks in a week, completion rate, completion rate of each sub-project, advance or delay and other information, construction units complete the task on time, All of this provides the basis for the owner to make a better decision.

10 Progress Management Platform Based on Project Group

The progress management platform based on project group means that when the owner has multiple projects under construction, the platform interface can be used to check the overview of each project, so as to directly reflect whether the project funds, materials and other resources can meet the schedule. The project group platform can be drilled down to each project level. Grid has been widely used in ERP system, which can calculate the quantity and time of materials from purchase to storage. And the progress management system can calculate the work amount of components, required capital and labor force in terms of flow section and working procedure. the statistics of quantity compared with data on ERP system, we can see weather resources can meet the requirements of schedule on time.

11 Technical Key Points

The progress management platform mainly faces the following technical key points:

(1) Power grid companies usually have the original progress management system, They want the new platform to be a successor to the original. How to combine the new progress management system with the original system is a key technical point.

Business data can be retrieved from the application platform through RESTful API or embedded directly into the WEB page of the application platform.

(2) How to realize that you can view the BIM model on the web without installing BIM software is also a technical difficulty that needs to be overcome. The BIMFACE development platform can be used to realize this function.

(3) How to undertake the results of various design software, so that these results can be displayed on the PC side is another difficulty to be overcome. The GGP graphics platform independently developed by Glodon can solve this problem.

12 Conclusion

This paper summarized information acquisition technology used for schedule management, and put forward the feasible scheme for the Power grid as a starting point, select phone as schedule collection technology, combine information collected by phone, Project and BIM model, with the progress information management platform as the medium, and make managers understand construction schedule in real time. The system can realize the following economic benefits:

(1) The system can automatically export daily and weekly statistical statements, which greatly simplifies the workload of managers and makes the construction process information traceable. The BIM 3D model is introduced into the substation construction management, so that the progress management can be visualized in 3d, and the 3d digital information management of progress information can be realized.

(2) Prior to construction, unreasonable working procedure and construction arrangement can be found through construction simulation. This can avoid the problem that situation found in the construction site lead to reschedule the process problem. Which can save the time limit and ensure the progress of the project.

(3) The project quantity of each stage can be extracted by BIM, and the required resources of each stage can be calculated. Compared with the data of ERP system, it can judge whether the resource arrangement of materials, labor and other resources meets the schedule.

References

1. Guo, Y.: Research on ontology-based BIM and IOT integrated system to assist green construction. 郭妍, 基于本体的 BIM 与 IOT 集成系统辅助绿色施工研究
2. Li, X., Jing, X., Zhang, Q.: Research on construction schedule management based on BIM stechnology. Procedia Eng. **174**, 657–667 (2017)
3. Zheng, H.: Application of BIM technology in steel structure construction process. 郑皓予, BIM 技术在钢结构施工进程中的应用
4. Abdelrehim, M.: Interactive voice-visual tracking of construction as-built information. Ph.D. thesis, University of Waterloo, 168 p. (2013)

5. El-Omari, S., Moselhi, O.: Integrating automated data acquisition technologies for progress reporting of construction projects. Atomation Constr. **20**(6), 699–705 (2011)
6. Hegazy, T., Abedl-Monem, M.: Email-based system for documenting construction as-built details. Automation Constr. **24**, 130–137 (2012)
7. Schexnayder, C., Jaselskis, E.J., Fiori, C.: Tele-engineering from the Inka road. In: 9th LACCEI Latin American and Caribbean Conference, Engineering for a Smart Planet, Innovation, Information Technology and Computational Tools for Sustainable Development, Medellin, Colombia, 3–5 August, pp. WE1-1-WE1-10 (2011)
8. Ghanem, A.A.: Real-time construction project progress tracking: a hybrid model for wireless technologies selection, assessment, and implementation. Ph.D. thesis, The Florida State University, 217 p. (2007)
9. Navom, R., Sacks, R.: Assessing research issues in automated project performance control (APPC). Automation Constr. **16**(4), 474–484 (2007)
10. Jiménez, A.R., Seco, F., Zampella, F., Prieto, J.C., Guevara, J.: Indoor localization of persons in AAL scenarios using an inertial measurement unit (IMU) and the signal strength (SS) from RFID tags. In: Chessa, S., Knauth, S. (eds.) EvAAL 2012. CCIS, vol. 362, pp. 32–51. Springer, Heidelberg (2013). https://doi.org/10.1007/978-3-642-37419-7_4
11. Cho, Y.K., Youn, J.H., Martinez, D.: Error modeling for an untethered ultra-wideband system for construction indoor asset tracking. Automation Constr. **19**(1), 43–54 (2010)
12. El-Omari, S., Moselhi, O.: Integrating automated data acquisition technologies for progress reporting of construction projects. Automation Constr. **20**(6), 699–705 (2011)
13. Memon, Z.A., Majid, M.Z.A., Mustaffar, M.: An automatic project progress monitoring model by integrating auto CAD and digital photos. In: Computing in Civil Engineering, June 2005
14. Turkan, Y., Bosché, F., Haas, C.T.: Toward automated earned value tracking using 3D imaging tools. J Constr. Eng. Manag. **139**(4), 423–433 (2013)
15. Omar, T., Nehdi, M.L.: Data acquisition technologies for construction progress tracking. Automation Constr. **70**, 143–155 (2016)
16. Teizer, J., Bosche, F., Caldas, C.H.: Real-time, three-dimensional object detection and modeling in construction. In: Proceedings of the 22nd International Symposium on Automation and Robotics in Construction, September 2005
17. Teizer, J.: 3D range imaging camera sensing for active safety in construction. J. Inf. Technol. Constr. **13**, 103–117 (2008)
18. Zhu, Z., Brilakis, I.: Comparison of optical sensor-based spatial data collection techniques for civil infrastructure modeling. J. Comput. Civil Eng. **23**(3), 170–177 (2009)
19. Rankohi, S., Waugh, L.: Review and analysis of augmented reality literature for construction industry. Vis. Eng. **1**(1) (2013)
20. Brilakis, I., Fathi, H., Rashidi, A.: Progressive 3D reconstruction of infrastructure with videogrammetry. Automation Constr. **20**(7), 884–895 (2011)
21. Ibrahim, Y.M., Kaka, A.P., Aouad, G.: As-built documentation of construction sequence by integrating virtual reality with time-lapse movies. Architectural Eng. Des. Manag. **4**(2), 73–84 (2008)
22. Golparvar-Fard, M., Pena-Mora, F., Savarese, S.: D4AR-a4-dimensional augmented reality model for automating construction progress monitoring data collection processing and communication. J. Inf. Technol. Constr. **14**, 129–153 (2009)
23. Arashpour, M., Wakefield, R., Blismas, N.: Autonomous production tracking for augmenting output in off-site construction. Automation Constr. **53**, 13–21 (2015)

Modeling Distributed Situational Awareness to Improve Handling Emergency Calls in Operation Centres

Marcel Saager[✉] and Marie-Christin Harre

Humatects GmbH, Oldenburg, Marie-Curie Str. 1, 26129 Oldenburg, Germany
{saager,harre}@humatects.de

Abstract. In todays control centres such as traffic control centres, police control centres or in emergency control centres more and more messages arrive. The control centre personnel has to understand the messages and initiate measures to handle the situation fast e.g. by delegating steps to field workers. To handle the situation efficiently, correctly and avoid errors a good distributed situational awareness is needed. The underlying paper provides a model about distributed situational awareness for handling emergency calls (DSA-HEC Model). This model serves as a basis for the development of a supportive human-machine interaction, which is optimally adapted to the tasks of the control center personnel.

Keywords: Distributed situation awareness · Operation centre · Model

1 Introduction

Nowadays, more and more messages and phone calls arrive in german control centres such as traffic control centres, police control centres or in emergency call centres [3]. The main task of the personnel in the control centre is to understand the messages, prioritise, initiate necessary measures to handle the situation and delegate important steps to field workers. Considering the increasing number of messages and phone calls, more personnel is needed to manage the occurring work in these operation centres. To handle the situation efficiently, correctly and avoid errors a good distributed situational awareness is needed. This becomes especially important in german emergency call centres, where the correct planning of operations can quickly decide about life and death.

To offer support for the personnel via optimized processes or efficiently designed Human Machine Interfaces (HMI), a deeper understanding of the distributed situational awareness in operation centres is needed.

Currently, there exist no models specifically about the distributed situational awareness of control centres handling emergency calls in research. The underlying paper fills this gap by providing a model about distributed situational awareness for handling emergency calls (DSA-HEC Model). The DSA-HEC model was derived by applying a combination of the EAST method and the D3COS approach. The methodology and the model are described in detail in the underlying paper.

© Springer Nature Switzerland AG 2020
D. Harris and W.-C. Li (Eds.): HCII 2020, LNAI 12187, pp. 68–78, 2020.
https://doi.org/10.1007/978-3-030-49183-3_6

The paper starts by presenting related work including existing studies and models addressing the workflow in control centres as well as common approaches to assess the distributed situational awareness. After this introduction of the context the paper is situated in, a detailed description of the methodology and the study that was applied to derive the DSA-HEC model is described in Sect. 3. The model and its validation is described in detail in Sect. 3.3. The paper closes with a discussion and a conclusion.

2 Related Work

The underlying paper focuses on operation centres handling emergency calls. This kind of control centres are responsible for receiving, processing and forwarding information. They mainly act regional and help citizens in emergency situations who contact the control room operators by telephone calls or automatic alarm systems [10]. Baumann structures the tasks of control centres in individual operations and higher-level system tasks. Individual operations are often processed according to protocols. During a call, dispatching is already processed and, if necessary, further instructions are given to the caller. Superordinate system tasks can be divided into three areas. Firstly, the steering of the operation from a bird's eye view. On the other hand, the holistic documentation and statistical monitoring of the operation. In addition, the control center is responsible for an active quality management [2].

To handle such situation, the control room operators need situation awareness (SA). Roughly described, situation awareness, viewed individually, is a kind of state in which the individual is aware of the environment and the current situation he or she is engaged in. SA focuses on "how operators develop and maintain a sufficient understanding of 'what is going on' in order to achieve success in task performance" [12]. For this, Endsley defined a model which explains situation awareness in three layers. Layer one is a general perception of all elements surrounding the individual. Layer two is the understanding of the current situation. For this purpose, all information from step one is considered. In layer three the individual projects future states. All three layers allow the individual to assess the current situation and make appropriate decisions for handling. Finally, the individual can take and evaluate decisions in the situation [6]. Situation awareness in control rooms is well studied e.g. for air traffic control [7], power grid systems [8, 5] or for petrochemical industry [9].

The underlying paper does not focus on the individual situation awareness. The handling of emergency calls is rather a team task - for example, the employee in the control room has to accept the call, understand and assess the situation and then send a suitable employee to the specified location as help, who in turn has to make a quick assessment of the emergency situation in order to solve it. This requires distributed situation awareness (DSA) [12]. Currently, there exist no model that handles the distributed situational awareness for handling emergency calls in control centres. Related Work has been conducted to analyze and model distributed situational awareness in other domains such as the energy distribution sector by Salmon et al. [13], for ship bridges by Denker et al. [4] or for future road transportation systems by Banks et al. [1]. Currently, there exist no models about the distributed situational awareness of such control centres in research. The underlying paper fills this gap and provides a model about distributed situational awareness in german control centres that handle emergency calls: To gain a deeper understanding of the underlying principles for the distributed situational awareness, an analysis was conducted for a traffic control centre. For this purpose, a combination of the EAST method and the D3COS approach was applied:

EAST stands for Event Analysis of Systemic Teamwork (EAST) and is a method to model distributed cognition in systems [16]. The method comprises three network models (task, social and information) and their combination. To get the full amount of information of the given models, they have to be combined in an appropriate way. One method to structure the models of these information is offered by the D3COS approach.

The D3COS approach was developed in a european project having the same name. D3COS stands for Designing Dynamic Distributed Cooperative Human-Machine Systems and had the aim to develop affordable methods, techniques and tools which go beyond assistance systems and address the design, development and evaluation of cooperative systems from a multi-agent perspective where human and machine agents are in charge of common tasks [11]. The model offers similar specifications as the EAST models, starting with a specification of tasks, the human operators have to conduct, the social network of agents that fulfil the tasks and the resources needed for successful task completion.

In the underlying paper a combination of both methods has been applied to analyze distributed situational awareness to handle emergency calls and messages in a traffic control centre.

3 Derivation of the DSA-HEC Model

The method to derive the DSA-HEC model is described in detail in the upcoming sections. Section 3.1 presents the methodology in general, Sect. 3.2. the results of its application for the traffic control centre and in Sect. 3.3 the generalization and validation is depicted.

3.1 Methodology

In the underlying paper a combination of both methods (EAST and D3COS) has been applied to analyze distributed situational awareness to handle emergency calls and messages in a traffic control centre. For this purpose an interview was conducted with traffic control centre personnel. The interview led to a detailed specification of tasks that are executed by the traffic centres employees in case there occurs a problem with the traffic lights. In addition, the network of agents as well as the resources were specified. The details of the methodology are described in the following section.

The original version of the EAST method comprises 12 steps that aim to create three network models [4]. These network models are divided into task network, information network and social network. In addition, the combinations of the individual networks are considered. In addition, the EAST method can be used to determine a hierarchical classification with regard to system levels. A distinction is made between the micro level (the individual human-machine interaction), the meso level (the operations in the automated systems) and the macro level (the system of networks). Stanton et al. [14] reduces EAST's previously introduced 12-step method to a five-step method. These five steps limit the EAST method to the elementary diagram types. Briefly broken down, the steps are as follows:

1. **Determine scenario:** In a first step, the scenario that is subject of the analysis is specified. This first step is important to ensure that the limits of the analysis are clearly defined and that the tasks and cooperation of different involved agents can be investigated in a targeted manner for clearly defined use cases.
2. **Plan observation for the scenario:** The observation to investigate the tasks, communication and social networks has to be planned in the second step. This includes determining the location, the persons participating in the observation and the type of information collection. The latter can be carried out by empirical observation as well as by an interview to concretize analysis results in a higher level of detail.
3. **Carry out observation:** The observation is carried out in the third step following the detailed planning that was defined in step 2. During the observation, the results have to be documented in detail to ensure that they can be used for the creation of network models in step 4.
4. **Create network models based on observation:** As previously stated, EAST involves three network models (task, social and information). These network models are created in a fourth step based on the results achieved during the previous steps.
5. **Combination and analysis of the networks:** The combination of the networks specified in step 4 is combined in the last step. In the underlying paper, this step was done by applying the D3COS approach [11].

The previously described steps were carried out for analyzing the distributed situational awareness for handling emergency calls in a traffic control centre. The results of the analysis for the different steps are described in the upcoming section.

3.2   Result for the Traffic Control Centre Personnel

In the following sections, the analysis results for the traffic control centre use case are described in detail.

Scenario. The scenario considered here concerns the control centre for the traffic lights, which is intended to ensure a smooth flow of traffic. Three employees monitor the traffic lights around the clock for this purpose. They are supported by a specially developed software system which displays the status of the traffic lights. The employees encounter different use cases: Construction measures and modifications of traffic lights, traffic light signal is lost/failed (this refers especially to the acoustic signal, which is important for blind road users), damage to traffic lights, communication disturbance or technical defect at a traffic light or there can be the case that an urgent problem has to be solved, e.g. repairing a burst pipe located underneath a traffic light.

Observation (planning). The investigation was conducted at the Oldenburg (Germany) traffic control centre. For this purpose, two employees have been involved in the analysis - a civil engineer specialized in traffic and a traffic engineer, who is responsible for the management of the control center. Both are assigned to the expert group of control center employees. Due to the high workload, it was not possible to include field personnel (e.g. technicians working in the field to repair traffic lights). Nevertheless, both experts assured that they know this perspective in detail, although it does not concern their daily work environment.

The analysis was conducted on two separate appointments. At the first appointment the objectives of the analysis were discussed with the test persons. Furthermore, during this first session, the working environment of the test persons was examined, and the interviewers were familiarized with the domain. This was relevant for the preparation of the second appointment. For the second appointment, an interview guide was created to ensure that all information needed for the next steps was collected.

Observation. As described before, two appointments take place to gain the information required for step 4. The first appointment mainly supported in preparing the second session, that was necessary to collect all information needed to derive the network models. The second session lasted 3 h and the tasks, communication and social networks were discussed intensively on the basis of the interview guide.

Networks Based on Observation. The interview led to the network models shown in Fig. 1, 2 and 3. Figure 1 describes the task model, Fig. 2 the information and communication model and Fig. 3 visualizes the social network.

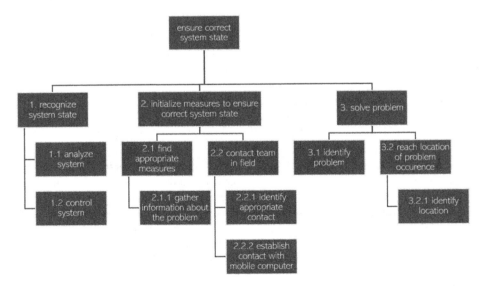

Fig. 1. Task model.

The task model shown in Fig. 1 visualizes the tasks, the traffic centre personnel carries out. The task model is done as hierarchical task model (HTA). A HTA starts with the main task of the operator on top. This task is then broken down into subtasks and thus specified in more detail [15]. In case of the traffic centre, the main task is to ensure a correct system state in which e.g. all traffic lights are working properly. As a first step, the personnel has to recognize the current system state (1. recognize system state). For this purpose, the personnel analyzes the system (1.1) and controls it continuously with the help of a specially developed software system supporting this task. Furthermore, citizens report incidents at traffic lights that require rapid intervention (e.g. via emergency calls). In case a problem occurs (e.g. a traffic light is not working), the personnel has to initialize measures to ensure a correct system state (2.). For this purpose, the personnel has to find appropriate measures to solve the problem (2.1) and therefore gather information about the problem (2.1.1). In most cases it is necessary that field operators support the control room team e.g. investigating the situation on site and carry out repairs. Therefore, the control room operator has to identify an appropriate contact (e.g. a contact who has the necessary expertise, is close by and can reach the scene of the incident as quickly as possible) (2.2.1) and establish the contact via mobile computer (2.2.2). The field operator will then solve the problem (3.). Therefore, he or she has to identify and understand the problem (3.1), identify the location of the problem (3.2.1) and reach the location of problem occurrence (3.2).

Figure 2 depicts the information and communication diagram as EPC. EPC (event driven process chain) is a modelling language to visualize processes in companies. A legend is provided in Fig. 2 on the bottom. Therefore, it is well suited to represent the information flow in the system. Starting from the compromised system state (top left in Fig. 2), the control room personnel analyzes the current system state to further specify the problem. Based on this, the control room personnel determines the methods to solve the problem situation. The chosen methods are followed by controlling the situation with the help of the central computer, which monitors the traffic lights and calls the appropriate field personnel to handle the incident. In the underlying use case, "appropriate" means that the suitable field personnel based on skills and distance to the location of the problem is ordered for the respective situation. For this purpose, a list of responsibilities exists. When the field personnel is contacted and on site, it corresponds continuously with the control room personnel to solve the problem. In case the problem seems to be solved, the control room personnel performs an acceptance test. If the system is working correctly, the solution is accepted and a proper system status is finally restored.

The social network diagram shown in Fig. 3 is built with UML use case diagram elements. The social network diagram is intended to show the interdependence between the individual actors. In this regard three actors are important: The control room operator or control room personnel, the field personnel and in some cases the police. The police might be involved e.g. when a citizen notices a problem with the traffic light system and calls them; if there occur already subsequent problems (e.g. accidents) or if the police recognizes a problem with the traffic lights on their traditional patrol. In case a problem occurs, the police and the control room personnel are in constant contact with each other.

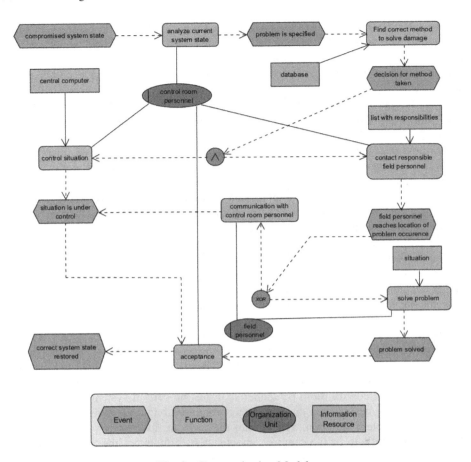

Fig. 2. Communication Model.

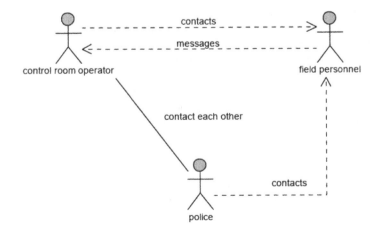

Fig. 3. Social network.

The field personnel is only contacted directly by the police, if the control room operators is not available. Nevertheless, the field personnel communicates solely with the control room and report information on the current status.

Combination of Networks. As described before, the combination of the network models was done on the basis of the D3COS approach. The D3COS model is shown in Fig. 4. On the highest level, the tasks are shown. The second level shows the relevant actors (control room personnel, police, field personnel) and the involved technical equipment (control room computer, mobile computer). On the lowest level, the resources are visualized. These include lists of relevant information (e.g. a list of appropriate field personnel), a database e.g. containing relevant information about the actual state and find appropriate countermeasures, information about the problem situation and entities that endanger the proper state of the system and the actual state of the traffic light that might e.g. repaired by the field personnel.

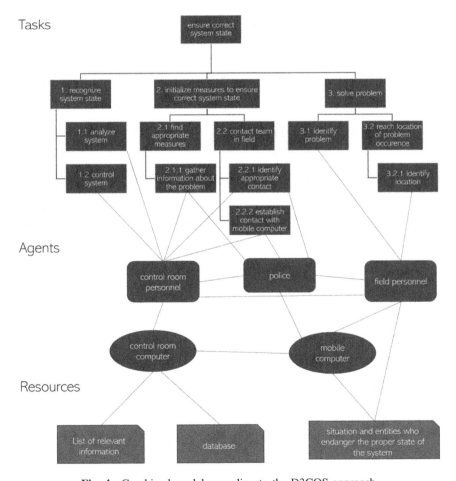

Fig. 4. Combined model according to the D3COS approach.

3.3   Generalization and Validation

To explore and evaluate the general validity of the resulting model for operations centres, the model obtained via the analysis in the traffic control centres was evaluated by an investigation in an police operations centre. This control centre is referred to as a cooperative control centre, i.e. the fire brigade, rescue service and police are coordinated jointly. The subject chosen for the interview was an employee at the control centre who answers calls according to the duty schedule. To do this, the employee logs on to a telephone computer and assumes a role. Depending on the role, he or she then receives the calls intended for that role. For example, if an employee has to deal with the emergency services, they log on in the role provided. The employee is both a firefighter and an emergency medical technician, which is the minimum requirement for this job. For each call, the employee has to check and evaluate the emergency situation so that the appropriate emergency services can be alerted.

Based on this validation, a generalized model was derived. This model is the DSA-HEC model and is shown in Fig. 5. In both control centres considered (police operations centre, traffic control centre) the tasks were essentially equal. For this

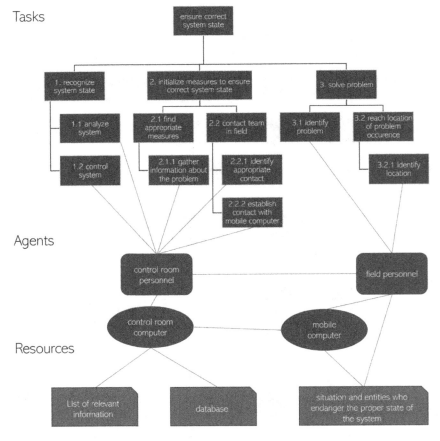

Fig. 5. The DSA-HEC model.

reason, the basic tasks shown in the diagram above have remained the same. The actors also have a lot in common: Both consider the control room personnel and the field personnel. The police as an actor seems to have been especially relevant for the traffic control centre. This does not necessarily apply to the police operations centre. Thus, the police is excluded in the generalized model. The resources are also quite similar: Both work with a list of relevant information to determine the relevant personnel to resolve a situation and have a database with information about the global system state and possible countermeasures. In addition, both centres also need the information about the situation that has to be resolved as well as about involved entities.

4 Discussion

The DSA-HEC model presented in the underlying paper is helpful to understand the situation in today's control centers. Such understanding is urgently needed to improve the current situation: The control center personnel who answer emergency calls need good support through appropriate software in combination with mobile technologies. To be able to create such software in a targeted way, the knowledge of today's processes, the information needed by different agents to have a good situation awareness is urgently needed.

However, it must be noted that the model also has its limitations: It refers solely to the task of accepting emergency calls in control centers. This was investigated for two control centers in different areas (police/main control center, traffic control center), so that a generalized model could be derived, which especially emphasizes the similarities of the work in such centers. Since two control centres are relatively few, the transferability and validity should be checked in further studies in other domains. It should also be taken into account that specifically german control centres with regional proximity were studied. Transferability to other cities and countries should therefore be verified thoroughly.

It is therefore recommended that the DSA-HEC model should be used as a reference point for initial studies in case a support system for handling emergency calls should be developed. The model should then be specifically adapted to the existing conditions of the centre under consideration in order to develop a software-based support system perfectly tailored to the needs and tasks of the regarded control room operators.

5 Conclusion

The overall result of the underlying paper is the DSA-HEC model - a model that provides deeper insight about distributed situational awareness to handle emergency calls in control centres. On the basis of this model, requirements can be systematically derived how to optimize actual processes and improve actual HMIs to better support situation awareness and the tasks of control centre personnel. This is absolutely necessary to efficiently handle the increasing number of messages in future HCI design in control centres.

Acknowledgments. The authors acknowledge the financial support by the Federal Ministry for Economic Affairs and Energy of Germany in the project Intellimar (project number 03SX469D).

References

1. Banks, V., Stanton, N., Burnett, G., Hermawati, S.: Distributed cognition on the road: using EAST to explore future road transportation systems. Appl. Ergon. **68** (2017)
2. Bauman, A., Sellin, S., Breckwoldt, J.: Standardisierte Notruf-Abfragesysteme für die Leitstelle. Georg Thieme Verlag Kg, Stuttgart (2009)
3. Beckhoff, O., Hoffmann, A.: 110 und 112 - Missbrauch von Notrufen nimmt zu (2019). https://www.spiegel.de/panorama/110-und-112-missbrauch-von-notrufen-nimmt-zu-a-1164711.html. Accessed 24 Oct 2019
4. Denker, C.: Assessing the spatio-temporal fitness of information supply and demand on ship bridges. Ph.D. dissertation, Carl von Ossietzky Universität Oldenburg (2016)
5. Endsley, M.R., Connors, E.S.: Situation awareness: state of the art. In: 2008 IEEE Power and Energy Society General Meeting-Conversion and Delivery of Electrical Energy in the 21st Century, pp. 1–4. IEEE, July 2008
6. Endsley, M.R., Garland, D.J. (eds.): Situation Awareness Analysis and Measurement. CRC Press, Boca Raton (2000)
7. Endsley, M.R., Rodgers, M.D.: Attention distribution and situation awareness in air traffic control. In: Proceedings of the Human Factors and Ergonomics Society Annual Meeting, vol. 40, no. 2, pp. 82–85. SAGE Publications, Los Angeles, October 1996
8. Giri, J., Parashar, M., Trehern, J., Madani, V.: The situation room: control center analytics for enhanced situational awareness. IEEE Power Energy Mag. **10**(5), 24–39 (2012)
9. Ikuma, L.H., Harvey, C., Taylor, C.F., Handal, C.: A guide for assessing control room operator performance using speed and accuracy, perceived workload, situation awareness, and eye tracking. J. Loss Prevention Process Ind. **32**, 454–465 (2014)
10. Marks, J.: Masterplan Leitstelle 2020. Ruksaldruck GmbH, Berlin (2013)
11. Osterloh, J., Bracker, H., Müller, H., Kelsch, J., Schneider, B., Lüdtke, A.: DCoS-XML: a modelling language for dynamic distributed cooperative systems. In: 2013 11th IEEE International Conference on Industrial Informatics (INDIN), Bochum, pp. 774–779 (2013)
12. Salmon, P.M., Stanton, N.A., Jenkins, D.P.: Distributed Situation Awareness: Theory, Measurement and Application to Teamwork. CRC Press, London (2017)
13. Salmon, P.M., et al.: Distributed situation awareness in command and control: a case study in the energy distribution domain. In: Proceedings of the Human Factors and Ergonomics Society Annual Meeting, vol. 50, no. 3, pp. 260–264. SAGE Publications, Los Angeles (2006)
14. Stanton, N.A.: Representing distributed cognition in complex systems: how a submarine returns to periscope depth. Ergonomics **57**(3), 403–418 (2014)
15. Stanton, N.A.: Hierarchical task analysis: Developments, applications, and extensions. Appl. Ergon. **37**(1), 55–79 (2006)
16. Stanton, N.A.: EAST: a method for investigating social, information and task networks. In: Contemporary Ergonomics and Human Factors 2014: Proceedings of the International Conference on Ergonomics & Human Factors, Southampton, UK, 7–10 April 2014

Multidimensional Risk Dynamics Modeling on Operator Errors of Nuclear Power Plant

Guanyin Wu[1], Yi Lu[2(✉)], Ming Jia[1], Zhen Wang[2], Caifang Peng[2],
Yanyu Lu[2], and Shan Fu[2]

[1] State Key Laboratory of Nuclear Power Safety Monitoring Technology
and Equipment, China Nuclear Power Engineering Co., Ltd.,
Shenzhen 518172, China
[2] Department of Automation, School of Electronic Information
and Electrical Engineering, Shanghai Jiao Tong University,
800 Dongchuan Road, Shanghai 200240, China
luyil@sjtu.edu.cn

Abstract. In the operation of nuclear power plant and especially when the digital human-machine interactive system is adopted, the cognitive decision and acts of operator play more and more important role in determine the plant's safe operation. In order to analysis the risk mechanism of human error and control the risk transmission, this study proposes a framework to conceptually model the performance shaping factor (PSF) interaction that involve the interactions of organizational, operator and technical system factors. Using the method of engineering psychology, the operator workload is adopted to be the central risk indicator and multiple levels of resource channel are considered in a quantitative manner. To reflect the dependency between PSFs, the system dynamics based modeling approach is adopted to identify the interactions between PSFs and the overall risk boundary. It helps to establish a dynamic model for human reliability assessment and human-machine interface design. Although this paper is focused on the method application on nuclear field, it has the potential to be extended to other industrial sectors.

Keywords: Human error · Operator behavior · Risk boundary · Performance shaping factors · System dynamics

1 Introduction

The safety operation of the nuclear power plant (NPP) is critical issues for public safety, when considering the sustainable growth of and guaranteeing people's normal life order. With the development of the technologies in NPP, increasingly sophisticated human computer interaction has been introduced into the I&C system, especially in its main control room (MCR). There is increasing evidence that human error is a major contributor to system risk: approximately 50%–80% of the incidents and the accidents in these safety-critical systems have been associated with human error, such as in the field of high-risk organizations, such as aviation, chemical processing, and nuclear plants [1].

© Springer Nature Switzerland AG 2020
D. Harris and W.-C. Li (Eds.): HCII 2020, LNAI 12187, pp. 79–89, 2020.
https://doi.org/10.1007/978-3-030-49183-3_7

Human reliability analysis (HRA) methods are a means of addressing this problem by identifying, modeling, quantifying, and reducing human error and risk [2, 3].

Human error risk identification method were widely studied in complex systems and the analysis of human error accidents provided useful information for system design and safety assessment. For example, the Human Error Assessment and Reduction Technique (HEART) is employed to determine the probability of human error occurring during each of the maintenance tasks, while fault tree analysis is used to define the potential errors throughout the maintenance process [4]. The system's human error reduction and prediction method (SHERPA) was developed for the nuclear reprocessing industry and was defined as a classification method to identify potential errors related to human activities [5]. A human error template method (HET) was raised for civil flight deck to detect the human error incidents [6]. The hazard and operation ability study (HAZOP) method was originally developed for the safety of power plant or operation [7, 8]. The cognitive reliability and error analysis method (CREAM) was identified as a human reliability analysis method, which can be used to predict potential human errors and analyze errors [9]. Based on the "Swiss Cheese" accident cause model of accident causation raised by Reason, the human factor analysis and classification system (HFACS) was developed to investigate and analyze human error in the aviation industry [10, 11].

However, when considering the application of HRA methods in the field of NPP especially facing the human error risk mechanism in digital main control rooms (MCRs), The suitability of existing HRA methods in digital MCRs is often questioned. As indicated by Liu et al. HRA research needs to revise the model and data in HRA based on the current knowledge of human performance for HRA applications in digital MCRs [12].

In this study, properly understanding the risk interactions in nuclear power plant operation process requires first understanding how the performance shaping factors (PSF) behave towards states of increasing risk in a dynamic and systematic way. In order to analysis the risk mechanism of human error and control the risk transmission, this study proposes a framework to conceptually model the risk dynamics that involve the interactions of organizational, operator and technical system factors. As a data base, the operator workload is adopted to be the central risk indicator and multiple levels of resource channel are considered in a quantitative manner. Moreover, a system dynamics approach based conceptual model is established to provide a framework for operator risk boundary identification, especially for the design and safety assessment of digital MCRs in nuclear power plant.

2   Framework for Human Error Assessment

2.1   Factor Interaction Category

For informing HRA, simulators, investigation reports, cognitive experiment literature and experts judgments were all used to provide potential data and strengthen the database. For many PSF-based HRA methods, human error probability (HEP) of a human failure event is obtained by modifying its nominal HEP with multipliers for

PSFs [26]. Some researcher has attempt to fill the gaps in determine the PSF multiplier design in SPAR-H and its successors [12]. SPAR-H model combines stimulus response and information processing methods, and names tasks in different stages of information processing as "diagnosis" and "action". HRA analysts need to be able to consider all aspects of diagnosis and action, as well as the potential for NPP operator to success-fully perform required operations. In order to illustrate the PSFs interaction focusing on the NPP operation, the proposed new classification is based on the risk interaction dynamics to reflect the NPP operator's duties and defines the dependencies among enhanced PSFs.

Considering the characteristic of the digital main control rooms in NPP, the enhanced PSF categories are describes as following:

(1) Organization Management factors: in this study, we focus on the teamwork (also identified as working processes), experience/training and the procedure.
(2) Human Behavior factors: in this study, we focus on the fatigue (also identified as the fitness for duty), and working condition (also identified as the stress/stressors).
(3) Task Executor factors: it is also know as local factor and it describes the object operated by NPP operator to execute intended task, such as technical system and its related interfaces. In this study, we focus on the task complexity, human-system interface (also identified as ergonomics), and time pressure (also identified as available time).

Considering the factor interactions, the relationships between three categories can be illustrated as shown in Fig. 1. As an emergency property, the human error proba-bility is highlighted by grey block.

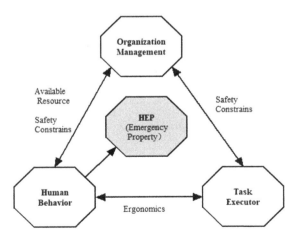

Fig. 1. PSF categories aiming for NPP operator HEP.

2.2   System Dynamics Approach

The System Dynamics (SD) model is a methodology to recognize and solve the system problems by analyzing the information feedback, dealing with the dynamic structure and feedback mechanism between the qualitative and quantitative factors of the complex system, so as to obtain the overall cognition and problem solving of the system. It provides a framework for dealing with dynamic complexity. In the field of system safety, system dynamics has been used as an important supplement to analyze organizational accidents and proposed safety policy in the field of aviation, astronautics and chemical industries [13, 14].

For the causal loop diagram (CLD) modeling phase, there are three basic building blocks: the reinforcing loop, the balancing loop, and the delay. For the stock-flow simulation phase, the interested reader is referred to the author's earlier publication for basic elements used in modeling, such as [15]. In order to help understand the dependency and dynamic relationship between the HEP and enhanced PSFs, the system dynamics approach is adopted to model the risk dynamics systematically. The data supporting risk analysis include:

(1) Engineering assumptions grounded in practical experience of digital MCRs and NPP accident investigation.
(2) Organization behavior modes and safety features proposed in literatures reviews, such as the systems theories based accident models.
(3) Accessible NPP operating data, such as human error categories identified by accident statistics.

Based on the factor interaction category mentioned in Sect. 2.1, a framework for SD modeling for PSF interaction is proposed as Table 1 shows. It identified relevant SD properties/function types used in modeling for each enhanced elements of three PSF categories.

Table 1. Factors Identification Framework for SD modeling for PSF interaction.

PSF categories	PSFs	SD properties	Function types
Organization Management	Teamwork	Predetermined	Constant
	Experience/training		Initial Value
	Procedure		Constant
Human Behavior	Fatigue	Partial time-varying	Stock
	Working condition	Time-varying	Flow/Auxiliary
Task Executor	Task complexity	Predetermined	Constant
	Human-system interface	Predetermined	Constant
	Time pressure	Partial time-varying	Flow

3 Human Error Probability Identification

3.1 Multi-resource Occupancy Channel Data

In this paper, the proposed method called multidimensional risk dynamics modeling on operator errors mainly includes:

(1) Update the PSF multiplier design for HEP calculation based on enhanced PSF categories which has been described in Sect. 2.
(2) Use the multidimensional workload assessment method as referred to the reference [15, 16] and adopting the physiological factors measurement method to work out the workload value to represent critical time-varying human behavior PSF elements which play an important role in determine the human error risk boundary of the digital MCR operator in NNPs.
(3) Adopt metrics for identifying the human error probability referring to the standardized plant analysis of risk-human reliability analysis (SPAR-H) method [17].
(4) Model the internal mechanism and dynamic relationships between enhanced PSFs and HEP using the system dynamics modeling method.

As the critical time-varying PSF factors, in this study, using the working condition (i.e. stress/stressors) as an example for method application, the mental pressure also known as work load is measure as an input data to initiate the improved calculation of HEP.

The common methods of stress measurement include skin electrical response, heart rate, blood volume pulse, etc. This study adopted the physiological factors measurement method to measure the factors of heart rate, voice and action volume to calculate the comprehensive workload of operator. The multidimensional data sources were divided into the following parts:

(1) Voice acquisition equipment obtains the audio information (i.e., speech).
(2) Wearable heart rate meter measures the heart rate.
(3) Video monitor obtains the action amount; relevant data sources and one sample window in test are shown in Fig. 2.

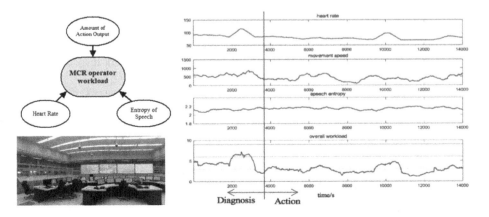

Fig. 2. Multi-resource channel measurement of work load and one sample window in test

3.2   HEP Calculation Metrics

According to the data consistency processing, the collected data was calculated, and the calculation formula of workload was obtained as follows:

$$Work\,load(t) = 0.7M(t) + 0.14H(t) + 0.16S(t) \tag{1}$$

In it, $W(t)$ means the work load of MCR operator in task, $M(t)$ represents the amount of action output, $H(t)$ represents the heart rate, and $S(t)$ represents the entropy of speech. Data collection and calculation were carried out for the whole process of MCR operation task, and one sample window data measured is shown in Fig. 2 (right). It can be seen that the average workload value of the dispatcher is 6 in the diagnosis period, while in the action period, it is 3. In this metrics the value range of workload is [0,10], and the value range of working conditions is [1,5] (referring to [12]), so the grade of stress in the diagnosis period can be obtained by the mapping equation as follows:

$$Work\,Condition(t) = k \cdot \frac{Work\,Load(t)}{2} \tag{2}$$

Table 2. PSF score assignment for action process case: emergency relief valve opening.

PSFs	Status	Multiplier value
Teamwork	Deficiency in communication	7
Experience/training	High	0.5
Procedure	Normal	1
Working condition	TBD	Auxiliary variable
Task complexity	Quite	10
Human-system interface	Nominal	1
Time pressure	Work load $\begin{bmatrix} M(t) \\ H(t) \end{bmatrix}$	Auxiliary variable

This study takes the actual NPP MCR task as an example: in one emergency relief valve opening task, which involves both the diagnosis and action types. It is necessary to analyze the PSF and its level division in the two task types of work respectively for calculation, and then add up to get the final HEP.

As an example, in the process of diagnosis task, PSF such as teamwork, experience, procedure, fatigue, working condition, task complexity, and HMI etc. can be involved. For the process of action task, PSF such as teamwork, experience, procedure, working condition, and task complexity etc. can be involved. Combined with the operator's own situation and the overall organization conditions, each PSF factor can be valued, and the HEP value was calculated by the above formula. The assignment of the PSF composite and associated multipliers for two task types are shown in Table 2 and 3 as following. Therefore, the actual PSF(t) can be calculated, and the calculation of HEP for action process above should be determined as following:

$$HEP(t) = \frac{\text{NHEP} \cdot E - PSF_{composite}(t)}{\text{NHEP} \cdot \left(E - PSF_{composite}(t) - 1\right) + 1} \tag{3}$$

Where the NHEP is the nominal HEP and it equals 0.01 for diagnosis and equals 0.001 for action. The $E\text{-}PSF_{composite}(t)$ equals the involved enhanced PSF scores. Compared with the static PSF calculation, the improved HEP is updated by the multi-resource occupancy channel data which provide a efficient way to evaluate the HEP in real time and more accurate metrics to predict the operator's reliability level.

Table 3. A Sample: PSF score assignment for diagnosis process

PSFs	Status		Multiplier value
Teamwork	Deficiency in communication		7
Experience/training	Nominal		1
Procedure	Normal		1
Fatigue	TBD		Stock variable
Working condition	Work load	$\begin{bmatrix} M(t) \\ H(t) \\ S(t) \end{bmatrix}$	Flow variable
Task complexity	Moderately		4
Human-system interface	Nominal		1
Time pressure	Work load	$\begin{bmatrix} M(t) \\ H(t) \end{bmatrix}$	Flow variable

4   System Dynamics Modeling for Operator Error Assessment

4.1   Conceptual Model for PSF Interaction

In this paper, the dependences among these PSFs were considered. For traditional method calculating HEPs, such as the SPAR-H method focuses on an isolate-point, which could produce overly optimistic or overly pessimistic results. In order to solve the correlation problem and reduce the repeated calculation when allocating the PSF threshold in HEP quantification, a system dynamic approach based model was introduced to describe the PSF interactions, as Fig. 3 shows.

In Fig. 3, the different color of variables indicate their PSF categories. The polarity note A marked at the causal link means this link can be enabled in the task involving the action process (such as *Working condition* → *HEP*). Meanwhile, the polarity note D marked at the causal link means this link can be enabled in the task involving the diagnosis process (such as *Fatigue* → *HEP*).

From the figure, the relationship between PSFs and the direct and latent impact on HEP were all illustrated. As shown by this PSF interaction dynamics, some PSFs play a role as initiator and its SD property is constant or initial value and other PSF such as the Fatigue is a stock variable which experience a accumulative process and introduce a dynamic characteristics on the HEP value, especially in a medium and long-time view.

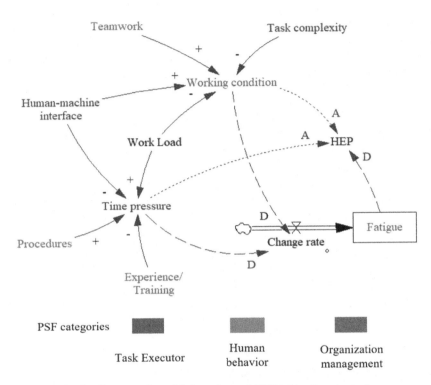

Fig. 3. Conceptual model for enhanced PSF interaction dynamics

4.2   Simulation Test and Results

In the process of establishing the SD model for quantitative simulation, in combination with the empirical operation data of the NNP digital MCR, the variable function definition should be evaluated by expert judgments and referring to relevant human performance and reliability literatures. Moreover, the SD model should experience relevant credibility and sensitivity tests for model structure and parameter setting check, which helps to ensure the consistency with the propose conceptual model in Sect. 2.1.

In order to investigate the stability of the model and the simulation precision, according to the complexity and nature of the digital MCR, this study introduced a medium term simulation experiments for 100 weeks by selecting different simulation step length (i.e., DT = 0.25, 0.5 and 1). The emergency relief valve opening task is also chosen as the test case which involves both diagnosis and action processes. The simulation results is shown in Fig. 4.

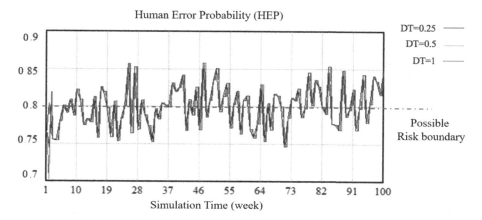

Fig. 4. Simulation results for case study: emergency relief valve opening task

In this study, the possible human error risk boundary is setting as 0.8, and the oscillations characteristics of HEP can be observed, which reflects the dynamics pattern of time-varying enhanced PSF interaction such as work condition and time press. The model can be used to establish the simulation experiment of strategy scenario. By setting different PSF scores under relevant task types, the simulated model behaviors can be compared and analyzed, and it can help to establish a decision-making tools for producing human reliability improving measures under a systematic way and a dynamic version. Moreover, the benefit of safety investment can also be evaluated under time-domain simulation.

In this model, the feedback loops may exist in the PSF interactions and the loop-domain analysis can be introduced to identify the critical risk factors including cognitive decision-making ability, technical system reliability and organizational management. Especially, the human reliability level can be improved from individual accident learning ability and workload control [18, 19]. The sufficient training also should be emphasized to make the training intervals and types consistent with task characteristics.

5   Conclusion

In summary, this paper provided a systemic and dynamic view for nuclear power plant human error risk analysis, guided the digital MCR human-machine interface design for mitigation and proactive control of human errors and promoted the concept of risk boundary for enhancing of SPAR-H method. The multidimensional workload assessment based method can calculate the comprehensive workload of MCR operator from the two aspects: physiology and psychology and map the workload value to the critical time-varying PSF factors. The proposed conceptual system dynamics model to illustrate the dynamic relationships between PSF and HEP can make the safety vision in traditional NPP human reliability analysis move from the isolated-point calculation to time-domain monitoring. Some improvements to avoid empirical and structured analysis framework has also be verified here and the feasibility of proposed approach can be also seen. The detailed modeling for comprehensive PSF factor coverage is being under our further research.

Acknowledgments. This research was sponsored by the National Science Foundation of China (No. 61803263) and the Startup Fund for Youngman Research at SJTU of China (SFYR at SJTU).

References

1. Griffith, C.D., Mahadevan, S.: Inclusion of fatigue effects in human reliability analysis. Reliab. Eng. Syst. Saf. **96**(11), 1437–1447 (2011)
2. Hollnagel, E.: Cognitive Reliability and Error Analysis Method. Elsevier Science Ltd, Oxford (1998)
3. Spurgin, A.J.: Human Reliability Assessment Theory and Practice. CRC Press, London (2010)
4. Singh, S., Majumdar, A., Kyriakidis, M.: Incorporating human reliability analysis to enhance maintenance audits: the case of Rail Bogie maintenance. Int. J. Progn. Health Manage. **8**(1), 1–10 (2018)
5. Stanton, N.A., Salmon, P.M., Rafferty, L.A., Walker, G.H., Baber, C.: Human Factors Methods: A Practical Guide for Engineering and Design. Ashgate Publishing Limited, Farnham (2013)
6. Marshall, A., et al.: Development of the human error template–a new methodology for assessing design induced errors on aircraft flight decks
7. Kletz, T.A.: HAZOP and HAZAN: notes on the identification and assessment of hazards. J. Hazard. Mater. **8**(4), 385–386 (1984)
8. Swann, C.D., Preston, M.L.: Twenty-five years of HAZOPs. J. Loss Prev. Process Ind. **8**(6), 349–353 (1995)
9. Hollnagel, E.: Cognitive Reliability and Error Analysis Method (CREAM). Elsevier, Oxford (1998)
10. Shappell, S.A., Wiegmann, D.A.: A human error approach to accident investigation: the taxonomy of unsafe operations. Int. J. Aviat. Psychol. **7**(4), 269–291 (1997)
11. Shappell, S.A., Wiegmann, D.A.: The human factors analysis and classification system-HFACS. Am. Libr. **1**(1), 20–46 (2000)
12. Liu, P., Qiu, Y.P., Hu, J.T., Tong, J.J., Zhao, J., Li, Z.Z.: Expert judgments for performance shaping factors' multiplier design in human reliability analysis. Reliab. Eng. Syst. Saf. (2020, in press)
13. Dulac, N., Owens, B., Leveson, N.G.: Demonstration of a new dynamic approach to risk analysis for nasa's constellation program. MIT CSRL Final report to the NASA ESMD Associate Administrator (2007)
14. Bouloiz, H., Garbolino, E., Tkiouat, M., Guarnieri, F.: A system dynamics model of behavioral analysis of safety conditions in a chemical storage unit. Saf. Sci. **58**(1), 32–40 (2013)

15. Song, B., et al.: A multidimensional workload assessment method for power grid dispatcher. In: Harris, D. (ed.) EPCE 2018. LNCS (LNAI), vol. 10906, pp. 55–68. Springer, Cham (2018). https://doi.org/10.1007/978-3-319-91122-9_5

16. Wang, Z., Fu, S.: Evaluation of a strapless heart rate monitor during simulated flight tasks. J. Occup. Environ. Hyg. **13**(3), 185–192 (2016)

17. Gertman, D.I., Blackman, H., Marble, J., Byers, J., Smith, C.: The SPAR-H human reliability analysis method. Washington, D.C.: U.S. Nuclear Regulatory Commission, NUREG/CR-6883 (2005)

18. Ryu, K., Myung, R.: Evaluation of mental workload with a combined measure based on physiological indices during a dual task of tracking and mental arithmetic. Int. J. Ind. Ergon. **35**(11), 991–1009 (2005)

19. Teng, X., et al.: The identification of human errors in the power dispatching based on the TRACEr method. In: Harris, D. (ed.) EPCE 2018. LNCS (LNAI), vol. 10906, pp. 80–89. Springer, Cham (2018). https://doi.org/10.1007/978-3-319-91122-9_7

Using IDHEAS to Analyze Incident Reports in Nuclear Power Plant Commissioning: A Case Study

Zijian Yin[1,2], Zhaopeng Liu[1], Dongfang Yang[1], and Zhizhong Li[2(✉)]

[1] State Key Laboratory of Nuclear Power Safety Monitoring Technology
and Equipment, China Nuclear Power Engineering Co., Ltd, Shenzhen 518172,
Guangdong Province, People's Republic of China
zijianyin.cn@gmail.com,
{liuzhaopeng, yangdongfang}@cgnpc.com.cn
[2] Department of Industrial Engineering, Tsinghua University,
Beijing 100084, People's Republic of China
zzli@tsinghua.edu.cn

Abstract. In the lifecycle of a nuclear power plant (NPP), commissioning is the last stage before commercial operation. To understand the nature of human errors in NPP commissioning tasks, the IDHEAS (Integrated Human Event Analysis System) method was adopted in this study to analyze 311 incident reports of NPP commissioning tasks, i.e. identifying the human errors as well as macrocognitive functions, proximate causes and cognitive mechanisms behind them. Results indicate that, in NPP commissioning tasks, individual failures of high-level mental processing had the highest occurrence frequency (59% of human errors with macrocognitive functions identified clearly), which should be specially concerned in risk management. As for human errors related with teamwork, failures of team communication were common in all categories of commissioning. The ratio of U1 items (reports didn't provide sufficient information to analyze, 44% in total) emphasizes the necessity of a standardized format for incident reports to support HRA research. In this case study, analysis results presented an unsatisfactory between-analyst reliability of IDHEAS, and as a side product, four usability problems of IDHEAS were identified, indicating that some modifications are in need to improve the method.

Keywords: HRA · IDHEAS · NPP · Commissioning · Incident reports

1 Introduction

Safety-critical systems, such as nuclear power plants (NPPs) and air-traffic control systems, have high requirements on the safety and robustness, as failures in these systems can lead to catastrophic results on people and the environment. Among various causes of system failures, a major one is the human performance related problem, termed "human error". In practice, human reliability analysis (HRA) is conducted to evaluate the risk brought by human errors. The first published HRA method was THERP (Technique for Human Error Rate Prediction) (Swain and Guttmann 1983),

© Springer Nature Switzerland AG 2020
D. Harris and W.-C. Li (Eds.): HCII 2020, LNAI 12187, pp. 90–103, 2020.
https://doi.org/10.1007/978-3-030-49183-3_8

after which a diversity of HRA methods has been developed and used (Boring et al. 2010). In recent years, NRC (US. Nuclear Regulatory Commission) published a newly developed HRA method, namely IDHEAS (Integrated Human Event Analysis System) (Whaley et al. 2016), as well as one application report (NUREG-2199, Xing et al. 2017), aiming at construct a more scientific framework based on cognitive psychology theories and reduce variability of HRA results (Liao 2015).

Yet, one critical difficulty in conducting HRA has been identified as the scarcity of experience data (Park and Jung 2007). To deal with this problem, existing HRA methods use data collected in some other ways like simulator experiments and expert judgements. Though these alternatives provide quantitative data somehow, all of them have biases and thus will affect the accuracy of quantitative HRA results. Operator performance in a simulator experiment can deviate from that in real scenario, even though the experiment design is perfect. Similarly, expert judgements depend on the expert's subjective knowledge and experience, which is argued over the past decades. This means that if the data from real situations are available, we should try our best to make use of this resource. Many human performance databases have been established to collect such data in order to support quantitative HRA. Examples of such databases include NUCLARR (Nuclear Computerized Library for Assessing Reactor Reliability) (Gertman et al. 1990), CORE-DATA (Kirwan et al. 1997), HERA (Human Event Repository and Analysis System) (Hallbert et al. 2006), and so on.

Current HRA researches in the NPP domain mainly focus on the actions in main control rooms, with some for test and maintenance activities, while little work has been done for commissioning tasks. The owner and government authority often care much on the safe operation of a NPP and thus set up corresponding standards and regulations, but would think human performance problems under construction stage mainly the vendor's own issues only if a plan meeting design requirements is finally delivered. Actually human errors in the commissioning stage has both safety and economic importance. They may cause harms to workers, facility damage, bad delay of the project, and even latent problems inside the system that may cause accidents in the later operation.

The main objective of commissioning is to find out any potential problems in all devices and sub-systems of a NPP, and to guarantee that all functions of the NPP can work well in commercial operation stage. The commissioning work can be divided into five categories: NI (Nuclear Island) commissioning, CI&BOP (Conventional Island & Balance of Plant) commissioning, electric commissioning, I&C (Instrumentation & Control) commissioning, and technical management. To achieve the objective, the main work of commissioning teams is to conduct various tests on devices and sub-systems, and clear any faults found. Considering the differences between commissioning tasks and traditional HRA applications, it is necessary to test the usability of the existing HRA methods for application in the context of commissioning tasks.

In this study, hundreds of incident reports from NPP commissioning work were analyzed using the framework of the IDHEAS method. As the only real experience data source, incident reports are of great importance for HRA study, because these reports contain many human errors occurred in the past decade in the CNPEC (China Nuclear Power Engineering Co., Ltd.) commissioning division. The aim of this study mainly consists of two parts. Firstly, analysis of these reports can show us the nature of human errors in commissioning; this can not only help us to extract useful information for

HRA, but also provide basic knowledge for structuring these records into a database. Secondly, the usability of the selected HRA method can be tested when applied to analyze incident reports of commissioning. Potential usability problems can be found and some improvement suggestions may arise during this process.

The remainder of this article is organized as follows. Section 2 gives an introduction to the HRA method used in this study. Section 3 describes our methodology to organize this analysis process. Section 4 reports the results of data analysis. Section 5 discusses the results as well as some problems met. Section 6 concludes this study.

2   The IDHEAS Framework

Up to date, more than one hundred HRA methods have been developed. Earlier HRA methods are lack of the basis of psychology and cognitive science. An obvious issue is that error mechanisms and cognitive process are not clearly analyzed in these methods. The newly developed method by NRC, IDHEAS, seems to overcome these shortcomings to some extent.

IDHEAS uses a macrocognitive model as its cognitive basis, as reflected in its framework (Fig. 1). In this model, human activities are divided into five macrocognitive functions: detecting & noticing, understanding & sensemaking, decision-making, action, and teamwork. The relationship between these macrocognitive functions is parallel and cyclical, as shown in Fig. 2. The specific working process of a macrocognitive function is driven by cognitive mechanisms. In the macrocognitive model of IDHEAS, the functioning of a cognitive mechanism is affected by performance influencing factors (PIFs), which refers to all potential contextual factors that contribute to human performance related to the cognitive mechanism. Failures of a cognitive mechanism become proximate causes, and result in the failure of a macrocognitive function finally (Whaley et al. 2016). This framework is the technical basis of IDHEAS. By using this framework, we can analyze the failure modes and mechanisms of various kinds of human errors.

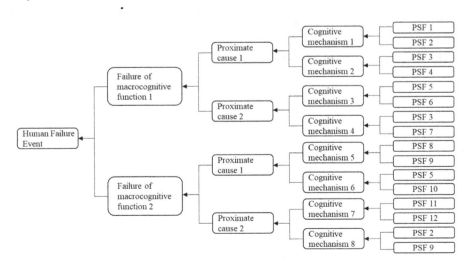

Fig. 1. The IDHEAS framework (Whaley et al. 2016)

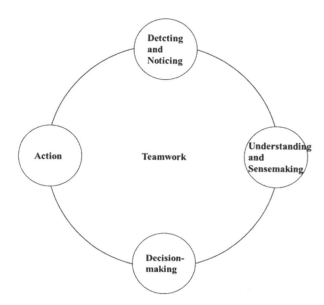

Fig. 2. Relationships between macrocognitive functions (Whaley et al. 2016)

A set of publications on IDHEAS are now available. NUREG-2114 provides the cognitive basis of IDHEAS (Whaley et al. 2016). Chang and Xing (2016) and Xing and Chang (2018) provide the general analyzing framework of this method. NUREG-2199 provides an example of IDHEAS application for NPP internal at-power events (Xing et al. 2017). Even though, the method is still under development and finalizing, and the application of this method is limited. A few studies have tried to use IDHEAS. In qualitative analysis, Liu et al. (2017) has used the framework of IDHEAS to analyze 103 investigation reports of incidents and accidents from a petrochemical plant in China. They found that 35% of incidents and accidents were caused by human errors while errors of commission are more than errors of omission. Some usability problems of IDHEAS were also found during the analysis. With regard to quantitative analysis, Liao et al. (2015) collected human performance data to estimate human error probabilities (HEPs) for 14 crew failure modes (CFMs) in IDHEAS, and identified five major technical challenges when applying these data for HEP quantification. Zwirglmaier et al. (2016) adopted Bayesian networks to build a cognitive causal framework of the CFM "critical data misperceived" in IDHEAS. The quantification process combined both expert elicitations and observed data, which was an available strategy for estimating human error probabilities (Zwirglmaier et al. 2016). A pilot testing for IDHEAS was conducted by Liao in 2015. This testing chose three scenarios and five human failure events developed in the US HRA Empirical Study, and gave some insights from the pilot testing. Overall, IDHEAS had several strengths like structured qualitative analysis framework, consideration of cognitive activities, development of detailed timelines, formal self-consistent quantification approach, traceability and insights for error reduction, which indicated that this newly developed HRA method made sense

(Liao 2015). However, the method also had some weaknesses, which needed improving. For example, the qualitative analysis needed fairly extensive resources, and the binary decision trees of PIFs would contribute to inter-analyst variability (Liao 2015).

3   Methodology

The incident reports were collected from the database of experience reports in CNPEC. The reports in the database were first screened by several commissioning subject-matter experts (SMEs) to find out events that were related to human failures. Totally 311 incident records were identified. Based on these reports, our study was carried out following the six steps as shown in Fig. 3.

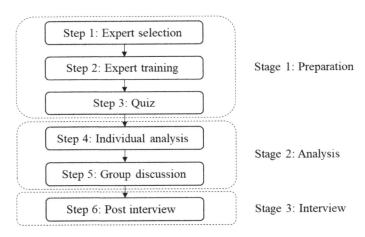

Fig. 3.   Main steps of this study

3.1   Step 1: Expert Selection

In this study, we chose experienced SMEs in commissioning as analysts. There were two reasons for doing so. First, SMEs were very familiar with the daily work in commissioning as well as potential human errors, while some experts even join the investigation of some analyzed incidents. Many incident reports were prepared by commissioning staff but not HRA experts, so some reports might not include some details that could be common knowledge of commissioning but essential for HRA. For this consideration, SMEs could be more powerful than experts in HRA and other fields as they had a better knowledge about these incidents. Second, it was a CNPEC's requirement that the HRA method needed to be comprehensible enough for commissioning experts and easily used in their daily work. The analysis process and results by SMEs could reflect potential usability problems in practice well.

Totally 12 SMEs were selected, 3 from NI commissioning teams, 2 from CI & BOP commissioning teams, 2 from electric commissioning teams, 3 from I & C commissioning teams, and 2 from technical management commissioning teams. All SMEs were very familiar with commissioning and none of them learned about IDHEAS before.

3.2   Step 2: Expert Training

As SMEs had little knowledge on IDHEAS, it was important to provide training so that every SME could understand the IDHEAS framework and use it to analyze incident reports. The training mainly included two parts: (1) the cognitive basis and macrocognitive model in IDHEAS and (2) the detailed content and meaning of items in IDHEAS framework. All training materials were translated into Chinese from NUREG-2114.

3.3   Step 3: Quiz

After all SMEs were trained, a quiz was conducted in order to guarantee that they had learned IDHEAS adequately. The quiz consisted of ten simple scenarios, for which macrocognitive functions, proximate causes, and cognitive mechanisms were to be identified. Results of the first quiz are shown in Table 1. More than half of SMEs had correct rates less than 70%, indicating that some SMEs hadn't learnt IDHEAS well. Therefore, we explained each scenario wrongly answered for each SME. All SMEs were required to review the training materials, and SMEs with correction rates lower than 80% were asked to take one more quiz. Results of the second quiz are shown in Table 2, which indicates the improvement of training. After that, all SMEs started to analyze. Scenarios in two quizzes were chosen from NUREG-2114 and translated into Chinese.

Table 1. Results of 1st quiz

Correct rate	100%	90%	70%	60%	40%	30%	Total
# of SMEs	1	1	3	3	3	1	12

Table 2. Results of 2nd quiz

Correct rate	80%	70%	60%	Not finished	Total
# of SMEs	6	2	1	1	10

3.4   Step 4: Individually Analyzing

The incident reports were classified into five categories according to associated job types (NI commissioning, CI & BOP commissioning, electric commissioning, I & C commissioning, and the others). Every SME only needed to analyze reports in his own category. Each SME needed to identify the human errors recorded in every report, as well as the macrocognitive function, proximate cause, and cognitive mechanism behind each human error.

3.5   Step 5: Group Discussion

Since variability among the results existed across experts, several group discussion sessions were organized to reach a consensus on the analysis after all SMEs had finished their own work. During each group discussion session, SMEs within the same group and one Ph.D. student majored in human factors sit together and reviewed the incident process. First identified were human errors occurred in this incident. After that, the error mechanism (how this human error occurred) was discussed. Then the related macrocognitive function, proximate cause, and cognitive mechanism were determined. Finally, if no one held counterview on the results, one report was finished and the discussion continued to the next one.

3.6   Step 6: Post Interview

Post interview aimed at finding out potential usability problems and the cause of variability during the analysis process using IDHEAS. After the group discussion, each SME was interviewed about the reasons why differences existed between his own judgement and the shared results after discussion, what usability problems he had met during the analysis, and his attitudes towards this analysis process and the IDHEAS framework.

4   Results

Four types of incident reports were abandoned during the analysis: (1) incidents in which no human errors occurred, (2) incidents in which human errors had no relationship with commissioning at all, (3) reports that didn't provide sufficient information about the incidents to identify what human errors occurred, and (4) repeated reports. Except these abandoned reports, for NI commissioning there were totally 68 reports analyzed, and 76 human errors were identified. For CI & BOP commissioning there were totally 46 reports analyzed, and 52 human errors were identified. For electric commissioning there were totally 16 reports analyzed, and 19 human errors were identified. For I & C commissioning there were totally 34 reports analyzed, and 36 human errors were identified. For technical management there were totally 14 reports analyzed, and 14 human errors were identified. Note that the amount of human errors was larger than (or equal to) that of reports, because some incidents included more than one human error. Tables 3, 4, 5, 6 and 7 shows the results of the five commissioning job types after group discussion, respectively. Table 8 shows the variability of the results in NI commissioning by comparing results of individual analysis and group discussion.

Table 3. Counts of human errors in NI commissioning (68 reports, 76 human errors)

Macrocognitive function failure	Proximate cause	Cognitive mechanism
Detecting and Noticing (n = 3)	Cue/Information not perceived (n = 2)	Attention: missing a change in cues (n = 1)
		U1 (n = 1)
	Cue/Information misperceived (n = 1)	U1 (n = 1)
Understanding and Sensemaking (n = 26)	Incorrect data used to understand the situation (n = 2)	Information available in the environment is not complete, correct, accurate, or otherwise sufficient to create understanding of the situation (n = 1)
		Data not properly recognized, classified, or distinguished (n = 1)
	Incorrect frame used to understand the situation (n = 19)	Incorrect or inadequate frame/mental model used to interpret/integrate information (n = 18)
		U1 (n = 1)
	Incorrect integration of data, frames, or data with a frame (n = 1)	Improper integration of information or frames (n = 1)
	U1 (n = 4)	
Decision-making (n = 13)	Incorrect goals or priorities set (n = 2)	Incorrect goals selected (n = 2)
	Incorrect internal pattern matching (n = 1)	Failure to retrieve previous experiences (n = 1)
	Incorrect mental simulation or evaluation of options (n = 3)	Inaccurate portrayal of the system response to the proposed action (n = 2)
		Cognitive biases (n = 1)
	U1 (n = 7)	
Action (n = 12)	Failure to execute desired action (n = 5)	U1 (n = 5)
	Execute desired action incorrectly (n = 7)	Recognition errors (n = 2)
		U1 (n = 5)
Teamwork (n = 8)	Failure of team communication (n = 7)	Source error of omission (n = 1)
		Source error of commission (n = 2)
		Target error of omission (n = 1)
		Target error of commission (n = 3)
	U2 (n = 1)	
U1 (n = 12)		
U2 (n = 2)		

(Note: U1: The reports didn't provide sufficient information to analyze human errors. U2: Issues were not covered in IDHEAS.)

Table 4. Results of CI & BOP commissioning (46 reports, 52 human errors)

Macrocognitive function failure	Proximate cause	Cognitive mechanism
Understanding and Sensemaking (n = 13)	Incorrect frame used to understand the situation (n = 10)	Incorrect or inadequate frame/mental model used to interpret/integrate information (n = 9)
		U1 (n = 1)
	U1 (n = 3)	
Decision-making (n = 11)	Incorrect goals or priorities set (n = 8)	Incorrect goals selected (n = 8)
	Incorrect mental simulation or evaluation of options (n = 2)	Inaccurate portrayal of the system response to the proposed action (n = 2)
	U1 (n = 1)	
Action (n = 4)	Execute desired action incorrectly (n = 3)	Task switching interference (n = 1)
		Manual control issues (n = 1)
		U1 (n = 1)
	U2 (n = 1)	
Teamwork (n = 9)	Failure of team communication (n = 7)	Source error of omission (n = 4)
		Target error of omission (n = 1)
		Target error of commission (n = 1)
		U1 (n = 1)
	Error in leadership/supervision (n = 1)	Failure to verify that other operator(s) or staff has correctly performed their responsibilities (n = 1)
	U2 (n = 1)	
U1 (n = 15)		

Table 5. Results of electric commissioning (16 reports, 19 human errors)

Macrocognitive function failure	Proximate cause	Cognitive mechanism
Detecting and Noticing (n = 3)	Cue/Information not perceived (n = 3)	U1 (n = 3)
Understanding and Sensemaking (n = 2)	Incorrect frame used to understand the situation (n = 1)	U2 (n = 1)
	U1 (n = 1)	
Decision-making (n = 6)	Incorrect goals or priorities set (n = 2)	Incorrect goals selected (n = 2)
	Incorrect internal pattern matching (n = 3)	Not updating the mental model to reflect the changing state of the system (n = 3)

(*continued*)

Table 5. (*continued*)

Macrocognitive function failure	Proximate cause	Cognitive mechanism
	Incorrect mental simulation or evaluation of options (n = 1)	Inaccurate portrayal of the system response to the proposed action (n = 1)
Action (n = 2)	Failure to execute desired action (n = 1)	U1 (n = 1)
	Execute desired action incorrectly (n = 1)	U1 (n = 1)
Teamwork (n = 5)	Failure of team communication (n = 5)	Source error of omission (n = 2)
		Incorrect timing of communication (n = 1)
		U1 (n = 2)
U1 (n = 1)		

Table 6. Results of I & C commissioning (34 reports, 36 human errors)

Macrocognitive function failure	Proximate cause	Cognitive mechanism
Detection and Noticing (n = 1)	Cue/Information not attended to (n = 1)	U1 (n = 1)
Understanding and Sensemaking (n = 14)	Incorrect frame used to understand the situation (n = 13)	Incorrect or inadequate frame/mental model used to interpret/integrate information (n = 13)
	Incorrect integration of data, frames, or data with a frame (n = 1)	Improper integration of information or frames (n = 1)
Decision-making (n = 5)	Incorrect internal pattern matching (n = 2)	Not updating the mental model to reflect the changing state of the system (n = 1)
		Cognitive biases (n = 1)
	Incorrect mental simulation or evaluation of options (n = 3)	Inaccurate portrayal of the system response to the proposed action (n = 2)
		Cognitive biases (n = 1)
Action (n = 12)	Failure to execute desired action (n = 3)	U1 (n = 3)
	Execute desired action incorrectly (n = 9)	Mode confusion (n = 1)
		Recognition errors (n = 4)
		Manual control issues (n = 1)
		U1 (n = 3)
Teamwork (n = 2)	Failure of team communication (n = 1)	Source error of omission (n = 1)
	U2 (n = 1)	
U1 (n = 2)		

Table 7. Results of technical management commissioning (14 reports, 14 human errors)

Macrocognitive function failure	Proximate cause	Cognitive mechanism
Detecting and Noticing (n = 3)	Cue/Information not perceived (n = 3)	U1 (n = 3)
Understanding and Sensemaking (n = 3)	Incorrect frame used to understand the situation (n = 1)	U1 (n = 1)
	U1 (n = 2)	
Decision-making (n = 3)	Incorrect mental simulation or evaluation of options (n = 3)	Inaccurate portrayal of the system response to the proposed action (n = 3)
Action (n = 3)	Execute desired action incorrectly (n = 3)	U1 (n = 3)
Teamwork (n = 1)	Failure of team communication (n = 1)	U1 (n = 1)
U2 (n = 1)		

Table 8. Variability of the results for NI commissioning

Convergence*	Macrocognitive function	Proximate cause	Cognitive mechanism
0	47.4% (n = 36)	65.8% (n = 50)	77.6% (n = 59)
1	30.3% (n = 23)	18.4% (n = 14)	13.2% (n = 10)
2	15.8% (n = 12)	13.2% (n = 10)	9.2% (n = 7)
3	6.5% (n = 5)	2.6% (n = 2)	0

(*Note: convergence means the number of SMEs whose result was the same with that after group discussion. For example, the third row means there were 12 (15.8%) macrocognitive functions having two SMEs holding the same results with that after group discussion.)

5   Discussion

There were 197 human errors identified in total considering all commissioning job types. As for the causes, 5.1% (10) were due to failures of detecting and noticing, and 29.4% (58) due to failures of understanding and sensemaking, 19.3% (38) due to failures of decision-making, 16.8% (33) due to failures of action, 12.7% (25) due to teamwork, 16.7% (33) due to unclear reasons. These results reflect the characteristics of human errors in NPP commissioning. Among the four individual-related macrocognitive functions, the amount of failures of high-level mental processing (understanding & decision-making) is about twice as much as that of the others (detecting & action). This may be attributed to the fact that the involved devices or systems in commissioning were very complex themselves or had complicated inter-relationships. One typical human error was that the tester conducted a test on his target system and caused the malfunction of another system, since he failed to consider the relationship between the two systems. The complexity within individual systems as well as the relationships among systems would bring up high requirements on commissioning staff's knowledge, mental models, and decision-making skill. Risk management and staff training should consider such a nature of NPP commissioning work.

The fifth macrocognitive function "teamwork" represents human activities related to communication and collaboration. In the results, the proximate cause "failure of team communication" was found to appear in all categories of commissioning tasks. This reflects a common problem in commissioning. As the commissioning of an entire NPP system was arranged into various crews in five commissioning categories, the communication among different crews was quite important in order to avoid unexpected influence caused by tests on each other. At the same time, the communication within members in one crew could also fail due to an unreliable communication system or other problems. Failures in teamwork should also be cared much in risk management.

Among 197 analysis results of human errors, 44% include "U1" items in different detail levels (macrocognitive function level, proximate cause level and cognitive mechanism level). In other words, nearly half of human errors couldn't be analyzed into the level of cognitive mechanism, and some human errors couldn't even be analyzed into the first level macrocognitive function. This exposes an obvious problem of incident reporting. The reporting format was not compatible with the IDHEAS framework, especially the absence of detailed information about cognitive process. As a result, the provided information was not enough to support deep analysis. A guideline for writing reports is in need so as to guarantee that human errors in an incident are reported with enough details.

As shown in Table 8, analysis results present an unsatisfactory between-analyst reliability. Considering the 3-analyst group of NI commissioning, only 6.5% macrocognitive functions of human errors were analyzed correctly by all the three SMEs, and nearly half macrocognitive functions of human errors were analyzed correctly by no one. The post interview helped reveal the reasons why SMEs' individual-analysis results were so different from the final results of group discussion. Six main reasons are summarized: (1) The SMEs misunderstood some items in the framework of IDHEAS, and thus selected inappropriate items. For example, a tester forgot to do something he should have done, and some SMEs thought about this as the failure of "working memory". However, not all such examples were within the scope of working memory. (2) The SMEs had an inaccurate analysis of the human errors and cognitive process. For example, there was a case that one tester left the work place and thus did not monitored some important information. Some SMEs held the opinion that the human error was not monitoring and selected "failure of detecting and noticing". However, the root of this human error was about the wrong decision to leave. (3) Some items were hard to distinguish in the context of commissioning. For instance, a tester went into an incorrect room and operated the device (devices in two rooms were nearly the same). Some SMEs attributes this to the function "detecting and noticing" as the tester didn't recognize the room number, while other SMEs attributed this to the function "action" (mechanism "recognition errors"). (4) Some reports did not provide enough information, and the SMEs made a selection by mere guesswork. (5) Several human errors occurred in one incident, and the SMEs only analyzed one of them. (6) The SMEs did not analyze some incidents. This unsatisfactory between-analyst reliability emphasizes the necessity of group discussion, and demonstrates the need for fairly extensive resources (Liao 2015).

At least four usability problems of IDHEAS were found. Firstly, the expressions in IDHEAS are not easily understandable for SMEs. There are many terms from cognitive psychology, such as "frame", "mental model", "schema", "situation awareness", "prospective memory", "compatibility", which are hard to understand for some SMEs who have less knowledge on psychology and cognitive science. Second, some items in the framework are confusing. For example, the cognitive mechanism "recognition errors" has similar meaning with mechanisms in "detecting and noticing". Third, some issues in commissioning are not covered in the IDHEAS framework (labeled as "U2" in analysis). For example, the manual teamwork (e.g. two people lift a device together) is not covered in macrocognitive function "teamwork" which only includes two proximate causes "failure of team communication" and "error in leadership/supervision". Last but not least, analysis using IDHEAS is a resource-consuming process. Identification of cognitive mechanism is very difficult from common incident reports, and it is suggested to interview those people involved in the incidents. At the same time, the variability of results is large, which means that several SMEs need to work together to reach at a reliable analysis result.

6   Conclusion

In this study, 12 SMEs were organized to analyze 311 incident reports of NPP commissioning using a newly developed HRA method IDHEAS. The results reveal current human reliability problems in commissioning. More than two-thirds individual human errors were due to failures of high-level mental processing. In teamwork-related items, failures of communication were very common in all commissioning teams. Unsatisfactory between-analyst reliability was found, and group discussion seems very essential. High ratio of "U1" indicated that a guideline for reports writing was in need to provide detailed information for HRA. Finally, some usability problems of IDHEAS were identified in this case study, suggesting some modifications in need.

Acknowledgments. This study was partly supported by China Nuclear Power Engineering Co., Ltd (CNPEC) Science and Technology Innovation Project (Project No. K-A2017.401).

References

Boring, R.L., Hendrickson, S.M.L., Forester, J.A., Tran, T.Q., Lois, E.: Issues in benchmarking human reliability analysis methods: a literature review. Reliab. Eng. Syst. Saf. **95**(6), 591–605 (2010)

Chang, Y.J., Xing, J.: The general methodology of an integrated human event analysis system (IDHEAS) for human reliability analysis method development. In: 13th International Conference on Probabilistic Safety Assessment and Management (PSAM 13), Seoul, Korea, 2–7 October 2016 (2016)

Gertman, D., et al.: Nuclear Computerized Library for Assessing Reactor Reliability (NUCLARR): Summary Description (NUREG/CR-4639). U.S. Nuclear Regulatory Commission, Washington DC (1990)

Hallbert, B., et al.: Human Event Repository and Analysis (HERA) System, Overview. Idaho National Laboratory (2006)

Kirwan, B., Basra, G., Tayloradam, S.E.: CORE-DATA: a computerised human error database for human reliability support. In: IEEE Sixth Conference on Human Factors & Power Plants Global Perspectives of Human Factors in Power Generation, 9/7-912, Orlando, FL, US, 8–13 June 1997 (1997)

Liao, H.: Insights from pilot testing of the IDHEAS HRA method. Procedia Manuf. **3**, 1350–1357 (2015)

Liao, H., Groth, K., Stevens-Adams, S.: Challenges in leveraging existing human performance data for quantifying the IDHEAS HRA method. Reliab. Eng. Syst. Saf. **144**, 159–169 (2015)

Liu, P., Lyu, X., Qiu, Y., Hu, J., Li, Z.: Identifying macrocognitive function failures from accident reports: a case study. In: Cetiner, S.M., et al. (eds.) Advances in Human Factors in Energy: Oil, Gas, Nuclear and Electric Power Industries, Advances in Intelligent Systems and Computing, 495, 29–40. Proceedings of the AHFE International Conference on Human Factors in Energy: Oil, Gas, Nuclear and Electric Power Industries, 27–31 July 2016, Florida, USA (2017)

Park, J., Jung, W.: OPERA—a human performance database under simulated emergencies of nuclear power plants. Nucl. Eng. Technol. **92**(4), 503–519 (2007)

Swain, A.D., Guttmann, H.E.: Handbook of Human Reliability Analysis with Emphasis on Nuclear Power Plant Applications (NUREG/CR-1278). U.S. Nuclear Regulatory Commission, Washington DC (1983)

Whaley, A.M., et al.: Cognitive Basis for Human Reliability Analysis (NUREG-2114). U.S. Nuclear Regulatory Commission, Washington DC (2016)

Xing, J., Chang, Y.J.: Use of IDHEAS general methodology to incorporate human performance data for estimation of human error probabilities. In: 14th International Conference on Probabilistic Safety Assessment and Management (PSAM 14), Los Angeles, CA, US, 16–21 September 2018 (2018)

Xing, J., Parry, G., Presley, M., Forester, J., Hendrickson, S., Dang, V.: An Integrated Human Event Analysis System (IDHEAS) for Nuclear Power Plant Internal Events At-Power Application (NUREG-2199). U.S. Nuclear Regulatory Commission, Washington DC (2017)

Zwirglmaier, K., Straub, D., Groth, K.M.: Capturing cognitive causal paths in human reliability analysis with Bayesian network models. Reliab. Eng. Syst. Saf. **158**, 117–129 (2016)

Cognitive-Based Severe Accident Information System Development in a Human Factors Project

Zheng Zhi[✉], Qiuyu Wang, Haitao Lian, Yufan Wang, Fei Song,
and Shuhui Zhang

Shanghai Nuclear Engineering Research and Design Institute, Shanghai, China
{zhizheng, wangqy, lianhaitao, wangyufan, songfei,
zhangsh}@snerdi.com.cn

Abstract. The peaceful use of nuclear energy has been attractive around the world due to its advantages of high energy density, reliability and cleanliness. Although nuclear energy has the bright prospect of eventually becoming the vital approach to reduce the global carbon emission, considering its catastrophic damage, study of severe accidents in nuclear power plant is thorny issue. Severe accidents refer to accident conditions that exceed the design basis and cause significant fuel degradation. The tasks in severe accidents have particular characteristics different from other operating conditions, such as high uncertainty of task objects, high cognitive requirements of task responses, and duty conversion in task executions. All of these characteristics interact intimately and bring great challenges to existing HFE analysis and HCI design. This paper analyzes thorough requirements of the severe accident information system from existing human computer interface design and human factors engineering, and develops the computerized severe accident management guidance system and the severe accident specific displays. Together, these elements comprise the cognitive-based severe accident information system. In the severe accident conditions, the severe accident information system will support the MCR and TSC to perform fault diagnosis and accident mitigation operations, which can tremendously alleviate the psychological pressure and workload, increase the accident response efficiency and accuracy, and improve the situation awareness of relevant personnel.

Keywords: Severe accidents · Human factors engineering · Cognitive · Information system design

1 Introduction

The peaceful use of nuclear energy has been attractive around the world due to its advantages of high energy density, reliability and cleanliness. Although nuclear energy has the bright prospect of eventually becoming the vital approach to reduce the global carbon emission, in the event of severe accidents, like the Three Mile Island accident, the Chernobyl accident, and the Fukushima nuclear accident, the integrity of the pressure vessel was destroyed, which resulted in the massive release of radioactive

D. Harris and W.-C. Li (Eds.): HCII 2020, LNAI 12187, pp. 104–113, 2020.
https://doi.org/10.1007/978-3-030-49183-3_9

materials and catastrophic influence on human society. Figure 1 illustrates the classification of nuclear power plant operation states of International Atomic Energy Agency (IAEA) [1]. Severe accidents are design extension conditions with significant fuel degradation. Mitigation measures of severe accidents are open issues because of the complexity and unpredictability. Therefore, the study of severe accidents has always been a key issue in the field of nuclear power.

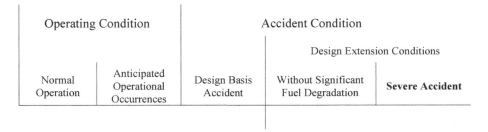

Operating Condition		Accident Condition		
			Design Extension Conditions	
Normal Operation	Anticipated Operational Occurrences	Design Basis Accident	Without Significant Fuel Degradation	**Severe Accident**

Fig. 1. Nuclear power plant operation states

This paper will start with requirements analysis of severe accidents and introduce severe accident information system (SAIS), which consists of the computerized severe accident management guidelines (CSAMG) and the severe accident specific displays (SASD). The SASI, whose general architecture is illustrated in Fig. 2, is being developed by the author's organization. The workstations based on SAIS severs, contain CSAMG and SASD, cooperating with each other to support operators to mitigate severe accidents.

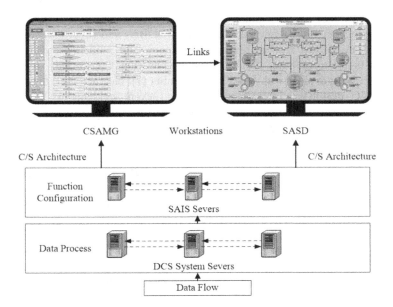

Fig. 2. General architecture of MCR and TSC servers and workstations

The Data flow is from the bottom up in Fig. 2. Distribute control system (DCS) servers are able to collect and process the original plant operation data. SAIS severs access to the data from DCS, which can configurate them into required functions. CSAMG supports real-time data monitoring and computer-aided judgment of power plants and SASD is able to display real-time plant states and control relevant instruments, both of which are connected with SAIS severs through Client/Server (C/S) architecture. CSAMG and SASD will be used by main control room (MCR), technical support centre (TSC), and even emergency operations facility (EOF) to monitor the plant data, diagnose the accident status, make mitigation strategies, and in some cases authorize the MCR to conduct the mitigation operations.

2 Requirement Analysis

In the past, severe accident researches mainly focused on the physics mechanism of accidents [2] and the reliability of equipments, but the consideration of human factors and the human computer interfaces (HCIs) were limited [3]. Compared with normal, transient and emergency conditions, systematic human factors engineering (HFE) analysis process was not fully applied in severe accidents and dedicated human system interface resource was not designed. Consequently, HCIs designed for normal conditions may not adequately support the operators to monitor the plant state and make appropriate decisions for the accident mitigation [4].

After the Fukushima accident, the priority of human factors research on severe accidents has been increased as the update of NUREG-0711 by Nuclear Regulatory Commission (NRC) in the United States, which explicitly provides severe accidents for the scope of human factors engineering [5]. According to Nuclear Safety Act (NSA) by Nuclear Safety and Security Commission (NSSC) in Korea, accident management plan (AMP) covering beyond design basis accidents (BDBA) and severe accidents in the aspect of organizational responsibilities, equipment, and guidelines, is required to submit [6]. In the meantime, the Inclusive Engineering Consortium standard IEC 60964, which is equivalent with GB 13630 in China [7], has increased the instrument & control (I&C) design requirements of BDBA and severe accidents [8]. Therefore, the completeness and suitability of current designs to support the performance of operators and technical experts in the condition of severe accidents require thorough estimation, and potential design improvements need to be identified.

From the perspective of human factors, the tasks in severe accidents ought to utilize mitigation methods and equipments whatever is available. And severe accidents have particular characteristics different from other operating conditions, which can be classified into three types as illustrated in Fig. 3. Degradation operation makes high uncertainty of instrumentation and equipment usability, which means MCR and TSC have high cognitive requirements to evaluate and balance the actual plant state and the appropriate mitigation path. Meanwhile, decision duty conversion from MCR to TSC and multi-center cooperation produce a new communication pattern. All of these characteristics interact intimately and bring great challenges to existing HFE analysis and HCI design.

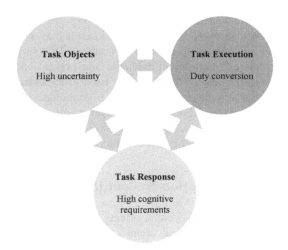

Fig. 3. Severe accidents characteristics

Currently, the optimization of HCI design focuses on the computerized procedures system and the operation monitoring screen system, both of which can be designed with the way of optimizing the existing system partially or developing a new system independently [9]. Given the design requirements and particular characteristics of severe accidents, this paper decides to develop the computerized severe accident management guidelines independently and increase some specific displays of severe accidents to the existing screen system to provide a new way for accident mitigation. In this research, the input data sources are mainly from the analysis results of CAP1400 severe accident management guideline (SAMG), utilizing cognitive work analysis (CWA) [10] and goal-directed task analysis (GDTA) [11] methodology (See Fig. 4).

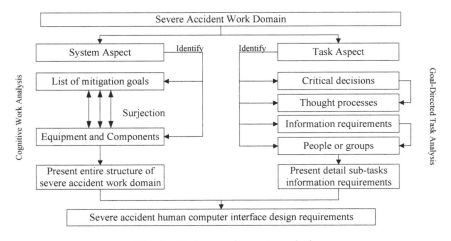

Fig. 4. Design requirements analysis

CWA and GDTA are task analysis methods based on work domains to identify the system architecture, information requirements, and situational awareness systematically from the work domain and task perspective. CWA analyzes the surjection relationship between mitigation goals and equipment available and present entire architecture of severe accidents system, the results of which are used to structure the CSAMG and SASD. While GDTA analyzes the severe accidents from the task aspect to identify the concrete sub-tasks information requirements, whose results are able to support the detail design of SAIS. Consequently, the task analysis provides effective requirement inputs for the severe accident human computer interface (HCI) design.

3   Severe Accident Information System (SAIS)

Based on the requirement analysis, severe accidents information system architecture is illustrated in Fig. 5. The detail general architecture of MCR and TSC server and workstation has mentioned in Fig. 2. CSAMG in MCR and TSC perform different guidelines of SAMG. In the meantime, because of the consideration of the nuclear power plant instrument & control (I&C) safety, the gateway of DCS is unidirectional, which means there should be two layers to guarantee the normal function of SAIS.

The plant I&C network layer consists of MCR workstation, MCR server, and DCS server, which mainly achieves the MCR plant monitoring and process control function. The plant management layer consists of MCR/EOF/TSC workstation, TSC server, and plant data management server, which mainly supports the TSC guidelines execution and plant status identification. All of the workstations based on the SAIS sever, contain CSAMG and SASD. CSAMG is designed to support the MCR and TSC to implement SAMG and make mitigation strategies through computer, while SASD is aimed to provide functions for MCR to control the equipments and soft controllers. They are combined to mitigate nuclear power plant severe accidents.

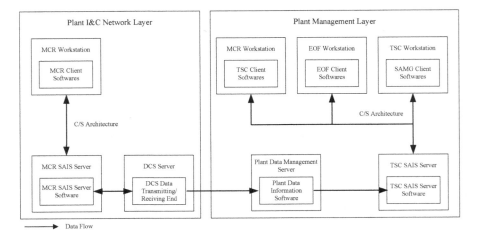

Fig. 5. Severe accidents information system architecture

CSAMG takes the paper version of SAMG as the framework input, whose design makes full use of flowcharts, logic diagrams, interactive tables and other easy-to-understand graphical ways. CSAMG supports real-time data monitoring and computer-aided judgment of power plants, and shares them in TSC and MCR to facilitate the communication and exchanges of decision makers and executors.

SASD based on DCS is able to display real-time plant states and control relevant equipment. This paper optimizes the information selection, display and organization form which makes full use of the design of the existing displays, reduces the sub-task requirements of displays navigation and improves the situational awareness of operators.

CSAMG and SASD are integrated into existing design of MCR and TSC, which can coordinate with each other. When nuclear power plant severe accident happens, on the one hand, plant data management server collects the plant status data from DCS server unidirectionally, and sends them to TSC server software, which supports the TSC workstation to diagnose severe accidents status and establish mitigation measures, the EOF workstation to review and authorize the TSC mitigation strategy, the MCR workstation to display and guide the mitigation operation of MCR. On the other hand, MCR server is able to exchange the plant status data with DCS server bidirectionally, and supports MCR workstation to control instrument and conduct mitigation operations.

3.1   CSAMG

The current measures for severe accidents are mainly based on paper version guidelines, which guide MCR and TSC in data acquisition, accident diagnosis, and decision making. For the use of paper version SAMG, the entrance conditions and guidelines mutual jumps need to be judged and reviewed manually, which means when MCR and TSC implement the SAMG, they should perform parameter acquisition and calculation at the same time. The current measure is inefficient and time-consuming and brings high psychological pressure and workload on the MCR and TSC operators.

Given the different team responsibility in accident mitigation, the computerized severe accident management guidelines is of two types, which includes MCR portion and TSC portion. MCR is mainly in charge of three guidelines to monitor the current plant state, support the TSC decision-making, and conduct the TSC mitigation strategy. TSC mainly takes charge of 23 guidelines to diagnose the accident plant state, make mitigation strategy, and evaluate the effectiveness of the strategy. Figure 6 illustrates the general layout and TSC portion interface of CSAMG. The general layout is divided into five areas, including:

- Page navigation area: this area provides normal page functions, like the guidelines entrance condition, operation, attachment, log and display link.
- DFC & SCST monitoring area: this area monitors the seven conditions of DFC and five conditions of SCST automatically based on the plant real time data. There are three alarm types, including orange for DFC alarm, red for SCST alarm, and magenta for bad data quality.
- SAMG navigation area: this area takes the paper version of SAMG as the framework.

- Detail steps display area: this area details the SAMG navigation area as mentioned in plain text, which contains concrete pumps, valves, etc. Keeping the highly consistency with paper version is able to maintain high situation awareness of MCR and TSC in accident mitigation.
- Decision-making area: this area is highly interactive and provides particularly functions to support the decision-making, such as equipment usability analysis, mitigation path active/negative effects analysis and mitigation strategy making.

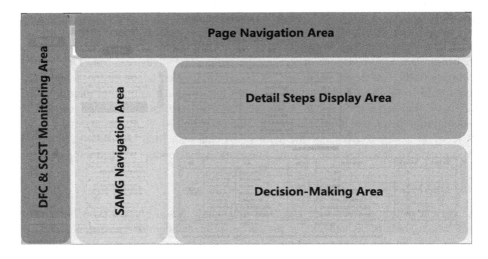

Fig. 6. The general layout and TSC interface of CSAMG (Color figure online)

CSAMG is driven by real time data from the power plant operation. Utilized the strength of the computer system in rule-based response, this system presents MCR and TSC with a friendly and easy to understand interactive interface to support users to monitor the operation status, provide parallel information deserving attention in time, make accident decisions, and implement mitigation strategies. Consequently, the accuracy and efficiency of MCR and TSC in performing SAMG will be greatly improved and psychological pressure in severe accidents will be relieved. Meantime, CSAMG design also considers other nonfunctional design as:

- Hardware and software performance requirements
- Nuclear power plant information security
- Maintainable and extendible
- Human-machine interface optimization

3.2   SASD

The existing HCI displays of the nuclear power plant provide current plant accident status to support operators in monitoring the accident progress. From the perspective of the integrity of HCIs, the existing displays contain all the information and soft controllers required to perform mitigation tasks. However, there are two aspects that are inadequate to supporting the severe accident mitigation:

1) Frequent displays changes

   Due to the complexity of severe accidents tasks, operators often need to switch between multiple displays frequently. Multi-displays switching tasks have a contribution to the psychological load of MCR and TSC, leading to longer accident response time and key information missing.

2) Mismatch with task cognitive model and requirements

   The non-deterministic task characteristics bring new challenges and requirements for information organization and presentation. The structure and hierarchy of the existing displays cannot well match the cognitive models and requirements of operating personnel.

Therefore, in this research, severe accident specific displays are developed according to the SAMG structures and information organization forms, to reduce the displays switching and improve the ability of monitoring the plant status, which could enhance the situation awareness and tasks implementation efficiency. There are mainly four hierarchies of the severe accident specific displays:

- Navigation level: this level contains one display, providing navigation links to severe accident displays at all hierarchies.
- Goal monitoring level: this level consists of two displays, which are DFC and SCST displays, for monitoring the high-level functional status and key parameters.
- Process level: this level includes multiple displays, grouped by the high-level functions, to present the mitigation process status, provide relevant control equipments for MCR and static equipment labels for TSC, which is for the sake of nuclear power plant I&C safety.
- Auxiliary calculation level: this level provides support for TSC to perform specific calculation tasks in severe accidents, such as calculation tasks that support the hydrogen flammability in the containment.

Utilized the results of severe accident task analysis, the structures and information have been composed organically, which demonstrates no more than two steps are used to switch different displays. Figure 7 is illustrated to introduce the main layout of passive injection path to reactor coolant system process displays. The general layout is divided into five areas, including:

- Goal monitoring area: this area contains the mitigation goals from seven conditions of DFC and five conditions of SCST based on the plant real time data. It is convenient for MCR and TSC to acquire the current plant status and effectiveness of mitigation strategies.

- Important parameter monitoring area: this area monitors important parameters required in the mitigation operations, such as containment pressure and hydrogen concentration.
- Internal navigation area: this area provides internal navigations in the same functional group, which are designed for the identical mitigation goals.
- External navigation area: this area provides external navigation links to other hierarchies' displays needed in current mitigation process.
- Main process area: this area shows all equipment and control measures in main mitigation process according to the different authority of MCR and TSC.

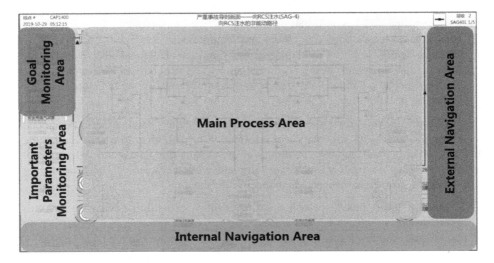

Fig. 7. The general layout and MCR interface of SASD

The whole layout of the process displays keep consistent [12], which adopts the order from left to right and top to bottom, fully considering the physical location of equipments. For the sake of reducing displays switching, certain equipments can repeat in multiple displays of different mitigation process, whose design principle is to make sure mitigation process completeness in every display. For example, the passive injection path to reactor coolant system display contains all passive core cooling system water sources, valves, and related parameters required by SAMG.

4   Conclusion

Cognitive-based severe accident information system, which consists of the computerized severe accident management guidelines and the severe accident specific displays, contributes to the plant state monitoring, critical cognitive decision making, and accident mitigation operation in the conditions of severe accidents. It can observably reduce the mitigation tasks response time, relieve the psychological pressure of operators, enhance the situation awareness in accident conditions, and improve the nuclear power plant safety eventually. This research describes requirements and the prototype design of the SAIS. Future works will continue to develop the cognitive-based severe accident information system and carry out a human factors experiment for whole system validation and verification.

References

1. IAEA: No. SSR-2/1 (Rev. 1). Safety of nuclear power plants: design. International Atomic Energy Agency (IAEA), Vienna (2017)
2. Asmolova, V., Ponomarev-Stepnoyb, N.N., Strizhov, V., et al.: Challenges left in the area of in-vessel melt retention. Nucl. Eng. Des. **209**(1–3), 87–96 (2001)
3. Johnson, G.L.: Instrumentation, control, and human system interface contributions to historical severe accidents. In: Nuclear Plant Instrumentation, Control and Human-Machine Interface Technologies (NPIC & HMIT), San Francisco, CA (2017)
4. Johnson, G.L.: Severe nuclear accidents: lessons learned for instrumentation, control, and human factors. Electric Power Research Institute (EPRI), Palo Alto, CA (2015)
5. O'Hara, J.M., Higgins, J., Fleger, S.: Human factors engineering program review model (NUREG-0711) revision 3: update methodology and key revisions. Office of Scientific & Technical Information Technical Reports (2012)
6. Etc. Regulation of the NSSC No. 12. Regulations on technical standards for radiation safety control. Nuclear Safety and Security Commission, Republic of Korea (2014)
7. GB 13630. 核电厂控制室设计. 中国国家标准化管理委员会 (2015)
8. IEC 60964 (Rev. 3): Nuclear power plant – control rooms – design. Inclusive Engineering Consortium (2018)
9. Gilmore, W.E.: Human factors guidance for building a computer-based procedures system: how to give the users something they actually want. In: Yamamoto, S., Mori, H. (eds.) HCII 2019. LNCS, vol. 11569, pp. 303–316. Springer, Cham (2019). https://doi.org/10.1007/978-3-030-22660-2_21
10. Naikar, N., Hocroft, R., Moylan, A.: Work domain analysis: theoretical concepts and methodology (2005)
11. Kaber, D.B., Segall, N., Green, R.S., et al.: Using multiple cognitive task analysis methods for supervisory control interface design in high-throughput biological screening processes. Cogn. Technol. Work **8**(4), 237–252 (2006). https://doi.org/10.1007/s10111-006-0029-9
12. Rasmussen, J.: Skills, rules, and knowledge; signals, signs, and symbols, and other distinctions in human performance models. IEEE Trans. Syst. Man Cybern. **SMC-13**(3), 257–266 (2012)

Human Factors in Human Autonomy Teaming and Intelligent Systems

Mixed-Initiative Human-Automated Agents Teaming: Towards a Flexible Cooperation Framework

Caroline P. C. Chanel$^{(\boxtimes)}$, Raphaëlle N. Roy, Nicolas Drougard,
and Frédéric Dehais

ISAE-SUPAERO, Université de Toulouse, Toulouse, France
{caroline.chanel,raphaelle.roy,nicolas.drougard,
frederic.dehais}@isae-supaero.fr

Abstract. The recent progress in robotics and artificial intelligence raises the question of the efficient artificial agents interaction with humans. For instance, artificial intelligence has achieved technical advances in perception and decision making in several domains ranging from games to a variety of operational situations, (e.g. face recognition [51] and firefighting missions [23]). Such advanced automated systems still depend on human operators as far as complex tactical, legal or ethical decisions are concerned. Usually the human is considered as an ideal agent, that is able to take control in case of automated (artificial) agent's limit range of action or even failure (e.g embedded sensor failures or low confidence in identification tasks). However, this approach needs to be revised as revealed by several critical industrial events (e.g. aviation and nuclear powerplant) that were due to conflicts between humans and complex automated system [13]. In this context, this paper reviews some of our previous works related to human-automated agents interaction driving systems. More specifically, a mixed-initiative cooperation framework that considers agents' non-deterministic actions effects and inaccuracies about the human operator state estimation. This framework has demonstrated convincing results being a promising venue for enhancing human-automated agent(s) teaming.

Keywords: Mixed-initiative interaction · Shared-autonomy · Human operator monitoring · Sequential decision making under uncertainty and partial observability · POMDP

1 Introduction

Recent advances in coupling robotics and artificial intelligence have generated a large number of applications of multi-UAV or multi-robot systems to deal with 3D (Dirty, Dull, Dangerous) missions in industry and in research. Surveillance [39,40], search and rescue missions [32,48], exploration [5], or inspection missions [30] are a few examples of the potential power of those automated systems.

© Springer Nature Switzerland AG 2020
D. Harris and W.-C. Li (Eds.): HCII 2020, LNAI 12187, pp. 117–133, 2020.
https://doi.org/10.1007/978-3-030-49183-3_10

Thereby, these automated systems still rely on human agents for the tricky tactical, ethical and moral decisions. Usually, the human is considered as an ideal agent in charge of taking over when the automated agent fails [44], or when the artificial agent is not able/suitable to make the decision. However, the capacity of human agents to take over when the automated system fails can be strongly affected, for instance, by a poor user interface design, the complexity of automated agents operation, a high operational pressure, or emotional commitment. Those factors could diminish the human operator performance and judgment during interaction leading to the need of careful design of authority sharing [12].

Indeed, the question of human-automated agent(s) interaction has mainly been studied in the literature through the concept of autonomy levels [24,36]. Sliding autonomy design [4,17], adaptive automation [43,45] or the shared autonomy design [26] are examples of this concept. Related with the latter, the mixed-initiative (MI) framework is particularly interesting because it establishes a coordination strategy that defines the role of the humans and the automated agents according to their recognized skills [1,2], considering them as teammates rather than master-slave agents. The main idea is that each agent might seize the initiative - it chooses to contribute to the task that it does best. That is to say if an agent (human or automated agent) controls the interaction, the other agents work to assist him [2,27]. In a more general framework, tasks should not be determined in advance, but rather they should be negotiated between agents [6].

Following the classical MI concept [2], the recognized skills of the involved agents may define their role during mission execution. In our view, the role of a given agent (e.g. the tasks to perform) would not only be defined by its skills. A special attention should also be given to the current capabilities of such an agent. Artificial agents such as mobile robots, autonomous cars, or aircraft still have limitations concerning their embedded sensors in real-life environments (e.g. limited camera field of view, or bias in image processing algorithms, poor GPS signal confidence) that potentially limit their performance. It may bring, for instance, low confidence when they are performing identification tasks [20,30,48] or execution errors during autonomous navigation [16]. Similarly, human agents that interact with such automated agents may also be confronted to difficulties, such as physical and/or cognitive limitations. This crucial point is addressed in the following section.

1.1   Human Skills *versus* Human Capabilities

In spite of the advantages of using autonomous (artificial) agents in several operational contexts, the human operators are still vital for the successful completion of a wide variety of missions. If it is not for assuming responsibility issues, the human operator is the agent that still produces tactical, moral, social and ethical decisions, while being flexible and creative, and able to handle complex and unknown situations [34]. These abilities are not (yet) embedded in artificial (automated) agents.

Interestingly, de Winter and Dodou (2014) [53] highlighted that the well-known Fitts' list (1951), *a list of 11 statements about whether a human or a machine performs a certain function better* still remains an interesting support - at least a starting point - for agent task allocation purposes. Yet this high-level concept does not take into account the capabilities of the agents during mission execution. Indeed, during mission execution, human operators may be subject to pressure, emotional commitment [50], task complexity [19] or long task duration [10], causing them to suffer from cognitive load or fatigue, and consequently, generating degraded mental states [13, 41]. These various events can lead human operators to perform poorly by taking potentially poor decisions [13, 50].

For instance, a technical report from the U.S. Army, Navy, and Air Force [52] suggested the percentage of involvement of human factors in UAVs operations varied across aircraft models from 21% to 68%. It has also been shown in [31] that 50% of the terminal failures in disaster robotics are due to human error. To sum up, just like artificial agents, it must be accepted that human operators are not ideal agents either. Those examples show that, when mission efficiency is the goal, allocating tasks during mission execution to a non-performing agent, even if this agent is generally the most capable of executing the task, would not be the best solution. However, from the human operator's point of view, it is not always bearable or acceptable that artificial (automated) agents could seize the initiative, except if human cognitive capabilities or performance are degraded.

The mixed-initiative framework then proposes a reasonable design to deal with non-performing agents as it enables to the other ones to seize the initiative during mission execution.

2   A New Mixed-Initiative Interaction Paradigm

In our view, in order to cope with non-ideal agents, including the human operator, the mixed-initiative framework should be redefined as: *a cooperation strategy that defines the role of involved agents according to their recognized skills and current capabilities*.

Such a novel framework definition requires to monitor the capabilities of all involved agents (human and automated agents). Fortunately, monitoring the states and actions of automated agents is supported by a recognized field of research. For instance, works related to execution monitoring can be found in the spacecraft [21] or robotics [37] literature.

Besides, monitoring the state and actions of a human operator (e.g. mental resources and performance) when interacting with automated systems is not a trivial task. Research in the Human Factors and Neuroergonomics fields is globally focused on the study and evaluation of the conditions in which the human reaches her/his limits of engagement during task operation [10, 14, 38, 41]. Neuroergonomics contributes to the development of human agents monitoring tools in ecological settings [15, 42] to avoid such degraded states.

However, the evaluation of the generality and the robustness of such algorithms still remains to be proved, given that the human-related features are usually operator-dependent, task-dependent and session-dependent. Thus, it is necessary to consider such monitoring system inaccuracies. In addition to that, the involved agents may also present non-deterministic behavior, what could result in different outcome states during mission execution. As example, these uncertainties may relate to the mission in question or its progression, the automated agent and the cognitive states of the human agent. Thus, it is necessary to cope with those uncertainties while ensuring efficient mission completion through the use of an adequate decision-making framework.

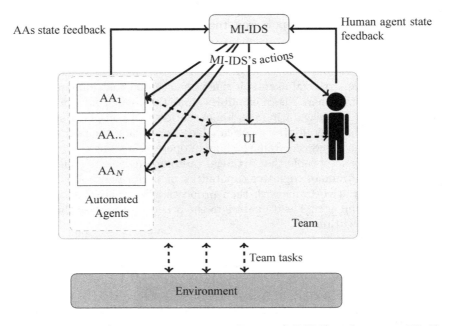

Fig. 1. Mixed-Initiative Interaction Driving System (MI-IDS) architecture. UI: User Interface.

Therefore, supposing that both automated agents and human monitoring tools are available, a Mixed-Initiative Interaction Driving System (MI-IDS) could explicitly define the tasks (role) of agents for maximizing mission performance (see Fig. 1). In other words, the MI-IDS estimates if an agent is able to seize the initiative from the other(s), while predicting if it is profitable for the long-term mission performance. Such a mixed-initiative concept has been applied to human-robot interaction [20,49], and in assistive systems [22,33], based on Partially Observable Markov Decision Processes (POMDPs) [28].

The POMDP framework takes into consideration uncertainties related to the partial observability of states (e.g. mental states) or the potentially non-deterministic behavior of the human operator [9,20]. The POMDP solution can launch actions to mitigate the decline of the human agent's performance [49], or deliberately, can take the initiative to assign a given task to an automated agent [20] to ensure the proper accomplishment of the mission. The POMDP framework is detailed in the following part. Then, some of our previous works based on this framework are reviewed.

3   POMDP - Theoretical Background

The works presented in the following are built upon Partially Observable Markov Decision Processes (POMDPs), which offer a sound mathematical model for sequential decision-making under probabilistic uncertainty and partial observability.

A POMDP [29,47] is a tuple $\langle \mathcal{S}, \mathcal{A}, \Omega, T, O, R, b_0 \rangle$, where: $\mathcal{S}$ is the set of states; $\mathcal{A}$ is the set of actions; Ω is the set of observations; $T : \mathcal{S} \times \mathcal{A} \times \mathcal{S} \to [0,1]$ is the transition function, such that: $T(s,a,s') = p(s_{t+1} = s' | s_t = s, a_t = a)$ where $t \in \mathbb{N}$ is the time step of the process and s_t (resp. a_t) is the random variable representing the state (resp. action) at time step t; $O : \Omega \times \mathcal{A} \times \mathcal{S} \to [0,1]$ is the observation function such that: $O(o,a,s') = p(o_{t+1} = o | s_{t+1} = s', a_t = a)$ where o_{t+1} is the random variable representing the observation at time step $t + 1$; $R : \mathcal{S} \times \mathcal{A} \to \mathbb{R}$ is the reward function, that defines the gain that a process going through a given state and executing a given action will add to its previous and future gains to define its total value; b_0 is the initial probability distribution over states. We denote by $\Delta_{\mathcal{S}} \subset [0,1]^{\mathcal{S}}$ the (continuous) set of probability distributions over states, named *belief state space*. Figure 2 depicts the dynamic influence diagram of a POMDP to drive human-automated agent interaction. The actions in this figure, the sequential choice of which must be optimised, are those of MI-IDS. Thus, these actions may relate to supervision actions, to launch alarms in order to mitigate the decline of the human agent's performance [49], or directly to assign a given task to an automated (artificial) agent [9,20].

At each time step, the MI-IDS updates its current *belief state* b about the complete state of the system including human, artificial agents, their environment, mission, etc. This belief update is implemented by applying the Bayes' rule thanks to the information given by the action performed $a \in \mathcal{A}$ and the observation received $o \in \mathcal{O}$:

$$b_a^o(s') = \frac{p(o, s' \mid a, b)}{p(o \mid a, b)} \tag{1}$$

where

$$p(o, s' \mid a, b) = O(o,a,s') \sum_{s \in S} T(s,a,s')b(s)$$

and

$$p(o \mid a, b) = \sum_{s' \in \mathcal{S}} p(o, s' \mid a, b). \tag{2}$$

Solving a POMDP consists in finding a policy function $\pi : \Delta_{\mathcal{S}} \to \mathcal{A}$ that maximizes a performance criterion. The expected discounted reward from any initial belief state

$$V^\pi(b) = E_\pi \left[\sum_{t=0}^{\infty} \gamma^t r(b_t, \pi(b_t)) \,\middle|\, b_0 = b \right] \tag{3}$$

is usually the performance criterion optimized for an infinite horizon. In this criterion, $0 < \gamma < 1$ is called the *discount factor* and represents the probability that the process will stop at each time step. The optimal policy π^* is the policy that maximizes the value function (Eq. 3). The resulting value function, called the *optimal value function* and denoted by V^*, satisfies the Bellman equation:

$$V^*(b) = \max_{a \in A} \left[r(b,a) + \gamma \sum_{o \in \Omega} p(o \mid a, b) V^*(b_a^o) \right] \tag{4}$$

where $r(b,a) = \sum_{s \in S} R(s,a)b(s)$ and $p(o \mid a, b)$ is defined in Eq. 2.

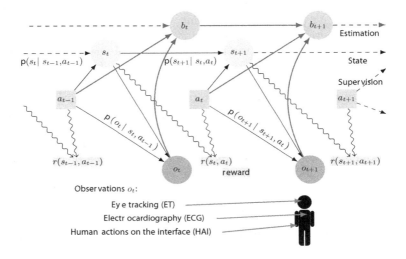

Fig. 2. Graphical representation of a POMDP for driving the human-automated agent interaction.

It has been proven that iterating the equation, starting with a value function which is piecewise linear and convex (PWLC), creates a sequence of PWLC value functions that converge to the optimal value function V^* [47]. Therefore, in the nth stage of the optimization, the value function V_n can be parameterized as a set of hyperplanes over Δ_S named α-*vectors* denoted by $\alpha_n \in \mathcal{V}_n \subset \mathbb{R}^S$. Indeed, the value of a belief b can be defined as:

$$V_n(b) = \max_{\alpha_n \in \mathcal{V}_n} \sum_{s \in S} \alpha_n(s)b(s).$$

Each α-vector is associated with an action $a(\alpha_n)$, e.g. $\forall a \in \mathcal{A}$, $R(.,a) \in \mathbb{R}^S$ is an α-vector of V_0 such that:

$$V_0 = \max_{a \in \mathcal{A}} r(b,a) = \max_{a \in \mathcal{A}} \sum_{s \in S} R(s,a)b(s) = \max_{\alpha_0 \in \mathcal{V}_0} \sum_{s \in S} \alpha_0(s)b(s).$$

In the region of the belief space where α_n maximizes V_n, $a(\alpha_n)$ is the optimal action (at the nth optimization stage). The optimal policy at this step is then: $\pi_n(b) = a^*(\alpha_n^*)$ such that $\alpha_n^* = \arg\max\limits_{\alpha_n \in \mathcal{V}_n} \sum\limits_{s \in \mathcal{S}} \alpha_n(s)b(s)$.

Recently, researchers proposed a structured POMDP model, named Mixed Observability Markov Decision Processes (MOMDPs, see [3,35]), which factorizes the state space $\mathcal{S}$ in fully and partially observable parts: $\mathcal{S} = \mathcal{S}_v \times \mathcal{S}_h$. MOMDPs exploit the specific structure of the state set to reduce the dimension of the belief state space, resulting in a significant gain in policy computation time [35]. The principle of MOMDP solving is the same as POMDPs, it consists in finding a set of policies $\pi_{s_v} : \Delta_{\mathcal{S}_h} \to \mathcal{A}$, $\forall s_v \in \mathcal{S}_v$, which maximize the criterion:

$$\pi_{s_v}^* \in \arg\max\limits_{\pi_{s_v}:\Delta_{\mathcal{S}_h} \to \mathcal{A}} E_{\pi_{s_v}} \left[\sum_{t=0}^{\infty} \gamma^t r_{s_v^t}\left(b_h^t, \pi_{s_v^t}(b_h^t)\right) \middle| b_0 = (s_v^0, b_h^0) \right] \qquad (5)$$

where $b_h \in \Delta_{\mathcal{S}_h}$ and $r_{s_v}\left(b_h, \pi_{s_v}(b_h)\right) = \sum_{s_h \in \mathcal{S}_h} r(s_v, s_h, a)b_h(s_h)$.

As for the POMDP, the value function at a time step $n < \infty$ can also be represented by a set of α-vectors $\forall s_v \in \mathcal{S}_v$:

$$V_n(s_v, b_h) = \max\limits_{\alpha \in \mathcal{V}_n(s_v)} \sum_{s_h \in \mathcal{S}_h} \alpha(s_h)b_h(s_h) \qquad (6)$$

where, α is a hyperplan over the sub-space $\Delta_{\mathcal{S}_h}$. In this way, the value function over the complete state space is parametrized by the set $\mathcal{V}_n$ that in turn is composed by the sets $\mathcal{V}_n(s_v)$, i.e. $\mathcal{V}_n = \{\mathcal{V}_n(s_v), \forall s_v \in \mathcal{S}_v\}$. So, given a belief state (s_v, b_h) the optimal action $a^*(\alpha^*)$ is defined by the α^*-vector, such as:

$$\alpha^* \in \arg\max\limits_{\alpha \in \mathcal{V}_n(s_v)} \sum_{s_h \in \mathcal{S}_h} \alpha(s_h)b_h(s_h). \qquad (7)$$

For more details about MOMDP resolution and algorithms, please refer to [3,35].

This efficient model framework has been used in our laboratory to drive the human-automated agents interaction with promising results as detailed in the following section.

4   Proof-of-Concept Systems

4.1   MOMDP Implementations to Drive the Human-Autonomous Agents Interaction

Search and Rescue Scenario. Humans are generally confronted with concurrent tasks while performing an automated system supervision. Gateau et al. (2016) [20] have addressed a dual-task paradigm in a search and rescue scenario. In the primary-task the human operator had to collaborate with autonomous artificial agents to perform target identifications by means of a user interface. In his/her secondary-task, the human operator had to memorize a series of digits (Short-Term Item Memorization task) and report it via the user interface. It was shown the volunteers had a lower performance when achieving both tasks simultaneously than when achieving each of them separately. Thus, special attention could be given to when a request should be launched to the human operator to perform target identification.

The main point in this work was to implement an integrated MOMDP-based system that would consider the *availability* of the human operator and her/his non-deterministic behavior based on the average time-to-answer a given request [20]. The *availability* of the human operator was measured by means of an eye-tracking (ET) device. The online processing of the gaze data acquired with such a device made possible to associate it to a region of the screen (or area of interest) where the human operator might be paying attention at a given time step t (visual attention estimation). The Fig. 3, taken from [20], illustrates the proposed architecture.

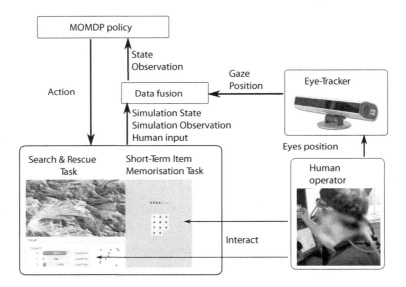

Fig. 3. MOMDP-based supervision architecture for the search and rescue scenario (from [20]).

The use of such information in the MOMDP model allowed to compute a policy that performs requests to the human operator respecting his/her supposed *availability*, while allocating tasks to the automated (artificial) agents such as *go to target i, send request, proceed identification*. It was shown that applying a MOMDP policy that integrates the *availability* estimation (with gaze monitoring condition) improved the human operator's performance on the secondary-task, compared to a driving policy that does not consider it (without gaze monitoring condition). Moreover, it was also shown the performance of the automated agents in the search and rescue mission had not been penalized. The average expected rewards had the same order of magnitude in both studied conditions (with and without gaze monitoring). It means that even when the human operator was not available to help the autonomous agents in identifying targets (by answering a request), the system could achieve the target recognition task alone (but with more risk of error).

However, several mission parameters used to define the MOMDP model transition and observation functions were roughly estimated. For instance, the average time-to-answer a request given the stimuli used (yellow bounding box visual effect) was taken from [25], and fake values concerning the accuracy performance of the human operator or of the automated agents in the target identification task were used. And finally, beside the good results obtained with this dual-task paradigm, the mission performance metric (the one optimized by the policy) did not include the scores obtained by the human operator in the short-term memorization task (secondary-task). This score was not directly considered by the model. It means the policy was not taking it into account for the maximization of the expected sum of rewards problem. The performance improvement of the operator in this secondary-task was only a consequence of the fact that the policy chose to achieve the recognition task without help of the human operator, that, at a given moment was estimated as *not available* to the automated agents. So, the policy indirectly favored the secondary-task performance improvement.

Cognitive State Estimation During a Target Search Mission. As highlighted in Sect. 1.1, the human operator should not be considered as a providential agent always capable to take over when the automated (artificial) agent fails. In this sense, the originality of the work proposed in [49] relies on the fact that a MOMDP model, approached by experimental data [41], was defined to supervise the interaction between a mobile teleoperated robot and a human operator, this last, supposed to be monitored thanks to eye-tracking (ET) and electrocardiogram (ECG) devices.

In the proposed MOMDP model, the robot operation mode (autonomous or manual mode) and mission states (e.g. going to zone, searching the target, handling the target, returning to base, on base and failed) could be considered as fully observable state variables, while the operator's cognitive ability, considered as *Cognitive Availability*, was modeled as a partially observable state variable. The *Cognitive Availability* was defined as the opposite of *Attentional Tunneling* [11], a degraded mental state in which the human operator fails in detecting changes in the environment because his/her attention is focused on another specific task.

The estimation of this partially observable state variable, ensured by the *belief state update*, was based on the output of the ANFIS classifier proposed in [41]. This classifier demonstrated a good performance, being able to detect the *Attentional Tunneling* state based on eye-tracking (ET) and electrocardiogram (ECG) features. Technically, the confusion matrix of the ANFIS classifier was used to approximate the $p(o_{t+1}|s_{t+1}, a_t)$ probability function used in the MOMDP model.

The actions considered in the model were related with high-level instructions such as: *go to zone, search target, handle target, return to base, get attention* and *countermeasure launching.* The first four actions could be performed by the policy only if the robot was in autonomous mode. For instance, it was assumed the mobile robot was able to autonomously navigate and avoid obstacles, but if the policy chooses *go to zone* and the ultrasound embedded sensor fails, the robot mode turns to manual mode. Interestingly, the *get attention* action, supposed to be implemented in the user interface, should be used when the robot needed help and the operator's Cognitive Availability was estimated as *not available*. The *countermeasure launching* action, also supposed to be implemented in the user interface, should be executed when an important event arrives during a manual operation and the operator was considered as *not available* (e.g his attention was focused on handling the robot and he would not notice the alerts on the user interface).

In spite of the interesting methodology described in [49] to approach the MOMDP model based on experimental data and on the classifier accuracy [41], the obtained policy was only evaluated in simulation. Statistical analysis about mission states visitation, and *get attention* or *countermeasure* actions launching were discussed. Moreover, the transition function of several state variables where roughly approximated given that the previous experiments [41] had not provided enough data concerning all mission states transitions.

The Firefighter Robot Game. A more recent project, based on a firefighter robotic mission [7, 9, 18] has been addressed in our lab in order to mitigate the drawbacks of our previous approaches: (i) the need for sufficient data to feed (MO)MDP models; (ii) the definition of a global common score reflecting mission performance, and being dependent of the efficiency of all involved agents; (iii) the implementation of a monitoring system to estimate the cognitive state of the human-operator during the interaction; and finally (iv) the evaluation in situ of the resulting (MO)MDP policy to drive such an interaction system.

The Firefight Robot game is a human-robot mission [18] that immerses the human-operator in a scenario where she/he plays a fireman who must cooperate with a robot that is present in a small area with few trees. The goal of the mission is to fight as many fires as possible in a limited amount of time (ten minutes). Through the user interface (UI), shown in Fig. 4(a), the human operator can supervise all robot parameters (position, temperature, battery, embedded water tank level, operation mode) and can receive the video streaming from its camera.

In this mission scenario, the battery charge level of the robot decreases with time, then needing probably to be recharged several times during the mission. If the battery is empty the mission fails and is finished. The volume of water contained by the robot is not unlimited: to recharge in water, the robot has to reach the a water tank that in turn should dispose of enough water. For that, the human operator has to continuously fill this ground tank using dedicated buttons in the UI. Unfortunately, leaks may appear on the ground tank during the mission, and the human-operator needs to fix them using the dedicated buttons for that. The temperature of the robot can increase when it is too

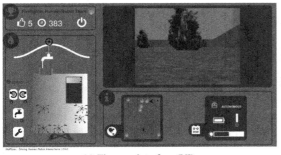
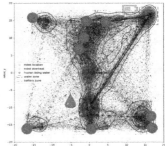

| (a) The user interface (UI). | (b) Crowdsourcing data plot example. |

Fig. 4. The Firefighter Robot game. Figure (a) shows the human operator control interface. On the left of this interface is shown the current score and remaining mission time. The ground tank sub-task is bellow it. On the right of this interface the robot video stream is displayed, and below it, the map locating the robot in the arena and robot parameters. Figure (b) plots several robot trajectories illustrating the amount of data acquired thanks to the crowdsourcing platform.

close to flames and the mission terminates when it is too hot. The robot has two modes of operation: a manual mode, in which it is directed piloted by the human operator; and an mode, in which the robot drives itself with a hard-coded strategy, including shooting water and the recharge of water or battery when necessary.

In this mission the presence of fires is supposed to be felt as a danger by the operator. The limited time for mission accomplishment would induce pressure. The temperature and battery risk would require human operator to monitor robot parameters all the time. Moreover, the ground tank filling sub-task, only performed by the human operator is demanding and requires a constant attention. All these elements are suppose to lead to a high engagement from the human-operator during the mission, and may favor the appearance of degraded cognitive states (e.g. performance decline).

This robotic mission is still available on an opened crowdsourcing platform[1]. Since the website launch, advertising was done in the authors' (professional and social) networks to encourage Internet users to carry out the mission in order to collect as much anonymous data as possible. During mission realization, the robot operation mode can change randomly, as well as, the appearance of alarms related to the robot parameters. These random mode changes and alarm launches were implemented with the aim of obtaining a representative and balanced dataset. Currently, we have collected more than a thousand mission realizations (see Fig. 4(b) where those data is illustrated).

In a first work [9] based on those data, we proposed the application of machine learning techniques, namely classification and Markov Chain learning, to define the parameters of a Markov Decision Process (MDP) model - it consists in the

---

[1] http://robot-isae.isae.fr/welcome.

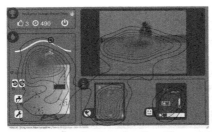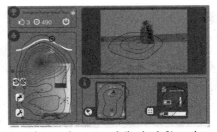

(a) Eye gaze fixations density with respect to operation modes: manual (in the left), and autonomous (in the right).

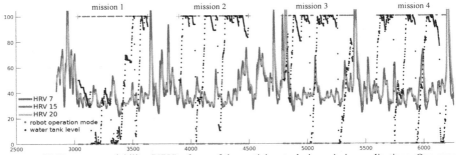

(b) Heart rate variability (HRV) of one of the participants during mission realisations. One may note that as the ground tank level increases HRV decreases. It may relates to an increase of the cognitive load [8, 7] of the human operator.

Fig. 5. Examples of physiological data acquired during Firefighter Robot mission realizations. The figure (a) illustrates the eye gaze density of participants with respect to the robot operation mode. The figure (b) plots the heart rate variability (HRV) for one of the participants among missions. The HRV feature have been online computed [8] and than recorded for further analysis.

same principle as the MOMDP with only fully observable states. The suggested MDP model has explored behavioral data (mouse clicks and keystrokes) from users. Until today, the evaluation of the obtained MDP policy was only performed in simulation [9]. In any case, the proposed methodology for the model learning and the obtained simulation results suggested the approach is promising.

In complement of the data acquired thanks to the crowdsourcing platform, experiments have been done in ISAE-SUPAERO facilities. During these experiments several volunteers equipped with eye-tracking (ET) and electrocardiogram (ECG) have played the Firefighter Robot game following an experimental protocol including 4 mission realizations per participant. The acquired physiological and behavioral data were studied and allowed us to reveal interesting results concerning performance prediction [7].

The participants performed differently so that we could identify high and low score mission groups that also exhibited different behavioral, cardiac (e.g heart rate, heart rate variability) and ocular patterns (e.g. number of fixations in the areas of interest). The Fig. 5 shows some ET and ECG features collected during experiments. More specifically, our results, recently published in [7], indicated that the higher level of automation could be beneficial to low-scoring participants but detrimental to high-scoring ones and vice versa. In addition, inter-subject single-trial classification results showed that the studied behavioral and physiological features were relevant to predict mission performance. The highest average balanced accuracy (74%) was reached using the features extracted from all input devices (ET, ECG, mouse clicks and keystrokes). We believe these features, computed on sliding 10-s time windows, and the achieved classification accuracy will allow us to approach an observation function (i.e. O). This observation function will be explored to maintaining a *belief state* on the human-operator engagement during mission.

The combination of the methods suggested in [9] and in [7] is under study. The aim will be to proceed to a MOMDP model learning (with all experimental and crowdsourcing data acquired) followed by the policy computation. We expect the achieved policy will choose the operation mode of the robot, or to launch alarms, depending on the current human-operator engagement (or performance), in order to maximize the overall mission performance.

5   Conclusion and Perspectives

The research concerning human-autonomous agents interaction still is an actual field. Among authority sharing approaches, the mixed-initiative interaction design has been shown to be a promising framework to drive such interactions, as it considers all involved agents (human and artificial) as teammates rather than master-slave agents. In this paper we suggested a redefinition of the mixed-initiative interaction concept in order to integrate the notion of *agents' current capabilities*, assuming that performance of the involved agents - including the human agent - may not be forthcoming. This new definition implicitly relies on the development of agent monitoring systems.

Our current contributions on this topic propose to rely on the POMDP model, or on the (MO)MDP model following state variables observability assumptions. The POMDP framework allows to model non-deterministic (probabilistic) action effects of the human-automated agents system and observation uncertainties (inaccuracies) related to the human operator monitoring systems. This decision-making framework enables, on the one hand, to maintain a *belief state* on human operator cognitive state, and on the other hand, to compute an interaction driving policy able to adapt the automated agents' behavior in function of such an estimation.

The presented proof-of-concept missions have shown promising results, as those systems have demonstrated: to increase the human performance during mission accomplishment [20] and to be able to launch countermeasures [49] when the interaction driving system estimates it necessary. However, as discussed, in order to perform well the POMDP framework needs an accurate modelling of the human-automated agent interaction, which in turn depends on huge data acquisition and confident human monitoring means based on human performance-related features.

In this vein, a crowdsourcing platform was developed [18], and the collected data have been explored [9] to approximate the state variables transition function - it allows to model non-deterministic (probabilistic) action effects. Lab experiments with volunteer participants have also been done, based on the same platform [7]. The aim of this study was to identify behavioral (mouse clicks, keystrokes, eye gaze fixations) and physiological (cardiac activity) features useful to predict performance using classifiers. Thus, a possible solution to approximate an observation function of the cognitive state of the human operator could be based on such classifier outputs.

Future work will address the problem of merging crowdsourcing and lab experiments datasets extending [7,9] works. A special attention will be given to an automated way to learn which are the relevant state variables, as well as their granularity in order to attain a sufficient faithful model that can be processed and solved by existing POMDP (MOMDP) algorithms. It specially relates to the trade-off between a fair model and a solvable model. On another hand, one can question the confidence of the human operator monitoring system in detecting degraded mental states. Ongoing work is searching for online solutions that exploits, in addition of the ET and ECG features, electroencephalogram (EEG) features [46] in order to increase confidence of the monitoring system. And finally, the *in situ* evaluation with a real robot, of the resulting POMDP policy is planned to be done.

Acknowledgments. Many thanks to all undergraduate, graduate master and PhD students, technical employees, and research colleagues that have contributed to the development of these works. These works were financially supported by the Direction Générale de l'Armement (DGA) nowadays Agence de l'Innovation de Défense (AID), the Conselho Nacional de Desenvolvimento Científico e Tecnológico do Brazil (CNPq), and the Dassault Aviation Chair (CASAC 2016–2021, see https://www.isae-supaero.fr/fr/isae-supaero/mecenat-relations-avec-la-fondation-isae-supaero/chaire-dassault-aviation-casac).

References

1. Adams, J.A., Rani, P., Sarkar, N.: Mixed initiative interaction and robotic systems. In: AAAI Workshop on Supervisory Control of Learning and Adaptive Systems, pp. 6–13 (2004)
2. Allen, J., Guinn, C.I., Horvtz, E.: Mixed-initiative interaction. IEEE Intell. Syst. Their Appl. **14**(5), 14–23 (1999)
3. Araya-Lopez, M., Thomas, V., Buffet, O., Charpillet, F.: A closer look at MOMDPs. In: Proceedings of the 22nd IEEE International Conference on Tools with Artificial Intelligence - Volume 02, ICTAI 2010, pp. 197–204. IEEE Computer Society, Washington, DC (2010)
4. Beer, J.M., Fisk, A.D., Rogers, W.A.: Toward a framework for levels of robot autonomy in human-robot interaction. J. Hum. Rob. Interact. **3**(2), 74–99 (2014)
5. Benavides, F., Carvalho Chanel, C.P., Monzón, P., Grampín, E.: An auto-adaptive multi-objective strategy for multi-robot exploration of constrained-communication environments. Appl. Sci. **9**(3), 573 (2019)

6. Carneiro, J., Martinho, D., Marreiros, G., Novais, P.: Intelligent negotiation model for ubiquitous group decision scenarios. Frontiers Inf. Technol. Electron. Eng. **17**(4), 296–308 (2016)
7. Chanel, C.P.C., Roy, R.N., Dehais, F., Drougard, N.: Towards mixed-initiative human-robot interaction: assessment of discriminative physiological and behavioral features for performance prediction. Sensors **20**(1), 296 (2020)
8. Chanel, C.P.C., Wilson, M.D., Scannella, S.: Online ECG-based features for cognitive load assessment. In: 2019 IEEE International Conference on Systems, Man and Cybernetics (SMC), pp. 3710–3717. IEEE (2019)
9. Charles, J.A., Chanel, C.P.C., Chauffaut, C., Chauvin, P., Drougard, N.: Human-agent interaction model learning based on crowdsourcing. In: Proceedings of the 6th International Conference on Human-Agent Interaction, pp. 20–28. ACM (2018)
10. Cummings, M.L., Mastracchio, C., Thornburg, K.M., Mkrtchyan, A.: Boredom and distraction in multiple unmanned vehicle supervisory control. Interact. Comput. **25**(1), 34–47 (2013)
11. Dehais, F., Causse, M., Tremblay, S.: Mitigation of conflicts with automation: use of cognitive countermeasures. Hum. Factors **53**(5), 448–460 (2011)
12. Dehais, F., Causse, M., Vachon, F., Tremblay, S.: Cognitive conflict in human-automation interactions: a psychophysiological study. Appl. Ergon. **43**(3), 588–595 (2012)
13. Dehais, F., Hodgetts, H.M., Causse, M., Behrend, J., Durantin, G., Tremblay, S.: Momentary lapse of control: a cognitive continuum approach to understanding and mitigating perseveration in human error. Neurosci. Biobehav. Rev. (2019)
14. Dehais, F., Peysakhovich, V., Scannella, S., Fongue, J., Gateau, T.: Automation surprise in aviation: real-time solutions. In: Proceedings of the 33rd Annual ACM Conference on Human Factors in Computing Systems, pp. 2525–2534. ACM (2015)
15. Dehais, F., Rida, I., Roy, R.N., Iversen, J., Mullen, T., Callan, D.E.: A pBCI to predict attentional error before it happens in real flight conditions. In: International Conference on Systems, Man, and Cybernetics, 9th Workshop on Brain-Machine Interface Systems. IEEE (2019)
16. Delamer, J.A., Watanabe, Y., Chanel, C.P.C.: Solving path planning problems in urban environments based on a priori sensors availabilities and execution error propagation. In: AIAA Scitech 2019 Forum, p. 2202 (2019)
17. Desai, M.: Sliding scale autonomy and trust in human-robot interaction. Ph.D. thesis, University of Massachusetts, Lowell (2007)
18. Drougard, N., Chanel, C.P.C., Roy, R.N., Dehais, F.: Mixed-initiative mission planning considering human operator state estimation based on physiological sensors. In: IROS workshop on Human-Robot Interaction in Collaborative Manufacturing Environments (HRI-CME) (2017)
19. Durantin, G., Gagnon, J.F., Tremblay, S., Dehais, F.: Using near infrared spectroscopy and heart rate variability to detect mental overload. Behav. Brain Res. **259**, 16–23 (2014)
20. Gateau, T., Chanel, C.P.C., Le, M.H., Dehais, F.: Considering human's non-deterministic behavior and his availability state when designing a collaborative human-robots system. In: 2016 IEEE/RSJ International Conference on Intelligent Robots and Systems (IROS), pp. 4391–4397. IEEE (2016)
21. Georgeff, M.P., Ingrand, F.F.: Real-time reasoning: the monitoring and control of spacecraft systems. In: Sixth Conference on Artificial Intelligence for Applications, pp. 198–204. IEEE (1990)

22. Hoey, J., Von Bertoldi, A., Poupart, P., Mihailidis, A.: Assisting persons with dementia during handwashing using a partially observable Markov decision process. In: International Conference on Computer Vision Systems: Proceedings (2007)
23. Hrabia, C.E., Hessler, A., Xu, Y., Seibert, J., Brehmer, J., Albayrak, S.: Efffeu project: towards mission-guided application of drones in safety and security environments. Sensors **19**(4), 973 (2019)
24. Huang, H.M., Pavek, K., Novak, B., Albus, J., Messin, E.: A framework for autonomy levels for unmanned systems (ALFUS). In: Proceedings of the AUVSI's Unmanned Systems North America, pp. 849–863 (2005)
25. Imbert, J.P., Hodgetts, H.M., Parise, R., Vachon, F., Dehais, F., Tremblay, S.: Attentional costs and failures in air traffic control notifications. Ergonomics **57**(12), 1817–1832 (2014)
26. Javdani, S., Admoni, H., Pellegrinelli, S., Srinivasa, S.S., Bagnell, J.A.: Shared autonomy via hindsight optimization for teleoperation and teaming. Int. J. Rob. Res. **37**(7), 717–742 (2018)
27. Jiang, S., Arkin, R.C.: Mixed-initiative human-robot interaction: definition, taxonomy, and survey. In: 2015 IEEE International Conference on Systems, Man, and Cybernetics, pp. 954–961. IEEE (2015)
28. Kaelbling, L.P., Littman, M.L., Cassandra, A.R.: Planning and acting in partially observable stochastic domains. Artif. Intell. **101**(1–2), 99–134 (1998)
29. Kaelbling, L., Littman, M., Cassandra, A.: Planning and acting in partially observable stochastic domains. AIJ **101**(1–2) (1998)
30. Liu, C., Kroll, A.: A centralized multi-robot task allocation for industrial plant inspection by using A* and genetic algorithms. In: Rutkowski, L., Korytkowski, M., Scherer, R., Tadeusiewicz, R., Zadeh, L.A., Zurada, J.M. (eds.) ICAISC 2012. LNCS (LNAI), vol. 7268, pp. 466–474. Springer, Heidelberg (2012). https://doi.org/10.1007/978-3-642-29350-4_56
31. Murphy, R.R.: Disaster Robotics. MIT Press, Cambridge (2014)
32. Murphy, R.R., et al.: Search and rescue robotics. In: Siciliano, B., Khatib, O. (eds.) Springer Handbook of Robotics, pp. 1151–1173. Springer, Heidelberg (2008). https://doi.org/10.1007/978-3-540-30301-5_51
33. Nikolaidis, S., Ramakrishnan, R., Gu, K., Shah, J.: Efficient model learning from joint-action demonstrations for human-robot collaborative tasks. In: 2015 10th ACM/IEEE International Conference on Human-Robot Interaction (HRI), pp. 189–196. IEEE (2015)
34. Nothwang, W.D., McCourt, M.J., Robinson, R.M., Burden, S.A., Curtis, J.W.: The human should be part of the control loop? In: 2016 Resilience Week (RWS), pp. 214–220. IEEE (2016)
35. Ong, S.C.W., Png, S.W., Hsu, D., Lee, W.S.: Planning under uncertainty for robotic tasks with mixed observability. Int. J. Rob. Res. **29**(8), 1053–1068 (2010)
36. Parasuraman, R., Sheridan, T.B., Wickens, C.D.: A model for types and levels of human interaction with automation. IEEE Trans. Syst. Man Cybern. Part A Syst. Hum. **30**(3), 286–297 (2000)
37. Pettersson, O.: Execution monitoring in robotics: a survey. Rob. Auton. Syst. **53**(2), 73–88 (2005)
38. Pope, A.T., Bogart, E.H., Bartolome, D.S.: Biocybernetic system evaluates indices of operator engagement in automated task. Biol. Psychol. **40**(1–2), 187–195 (1995)
39. Portugal, D., Rocha, R.P.: Distributed multi-robot patrol: a scalable and fault-tolerant framework. Rob. Auton. Syst. **61**(12), 1572–1587 (2013)
40. Portugal, D., Rocha, R.P.: Cooperative multi-robot patrol with bayesian learning. Auton. Rob. **40**(5), 929–953 (2016)

41. Régis, N., et al.: Formal detection of attentional tunneling in human operator-automation interactions. IEEE Trans. Hum. Mach. Syst. **44**(3), 326–336 (2014)

42. Roy, R.N., Charbonnier, S., Campagne, A., Bonnet, S.: Efficient mental work-load estimation using task-independent eeg features. J. Neural Eng. **13**(2), 026019 (2016)

43. Scerbo, M.W.: Adaptive automation. In: Neuroergonomics: The Brain at Work, pp. 239–252 (2008)

44. Schurr, N., Marecki, J., Tambe, M.: Improving adjustable autonomy strategies for time-critical domains. In: Proceedings of The 8th International Conference on Autonomous Agents and Multiagent Systems-Volume 1, pp. 353–360. International Foundation for Autonomous Agents and Multiagent Systems (2009)

45. Sheridan, T.B.: Adaptive automation, level of automation, allocation authority, supervisory control, and adaptive control: distinctions and modes of adaptation. IEEE Trans. Syst. Man Cybern. Part A Syst. Hum. **41**(4), 662–667 (2011)

46. Singh, G., Roy, R.N., Carvalho Chanel, C.P.: Towards multi-UAV and human inter-action driving system exploiting human mental state estimation. In: 10th International Conference on Bioinformatics Models, Methods and Algorithms (2019)

47. Sondik, E.J.: The Optimal Control of Partially Observable Markov Processes. Electronics Labs, Stanford University, California (1971)

48. Ubaldino de Souza, P.E.: Towards mixed-initiative human-robot interaction: a cooperative human-droneteam framework. Ph.D. thesis, Institut Supérieur de l'Aéronautique et de l'Espace, Université de Toulouse (2017). https://depozit.isae.fr/theses/2017/2017_Ubaldino_de_Souza_Paulo-Eduardo_D.pdf

49. de Souza, P.E.U., Chanel, C.P.C., Dehais, F.: MOMDP-based target search mission taking into account the human operator's cognitive state. In: 2015 IEEE 27th International Conference on Tools with Artificial Intelligence (ICTAI), pp. 729–736. IEEE (2015)

50. Souza, P.E., Chanel, C.P.C., Dehais, F., Givigi, S.: Towards human-robot inter-action: a framing effect experiment. In: 2016 IEEE International Conference on Systems, Man, and Cybernetics (SMC), pp. 001929–001934. IEEE (2016)

51. Sun, X., Wu, P., Hoi, S.C.: Face detection using deep learning: an improved faster rcnn approach. Neurocomputing **299**, 42–50 (2018)

52. Williams, K.W.: A summary of unmanned aircraft accident/incident data: human factors implications. Technical report, Federal Aviation Administration Oklahoma City, Civil Aeromedical Institute (2004)

53. de Winter, J.C., Dodou, D.: Why the fitts list has persisted throughout the history of function allocation. Cogn. Technol. Work **16**(1), 1–11 (2014)

A Framework for Human-Autonomy Team Research

Nancy Cooke[⊠], Mustafa Demir, and Lixiao Huang

Arizona State University, Mesa, AZ 85212, USA
{NCooke,MDemir,Lixiao.Huang}@asu.edu

Abstract. On a team, autonomy must be able to work alongside human counterparts and carry out the fundamentals of teamwork and taskwork. In this paper we refer to these machine teammates as autonomy. These Human-Autonomy Teams (HATs) need to be assembled to have the appropriate roles and responsibilities and to interact in an interdependent manner. One challenge in assembling an effective Human-Autonomy Team involves doing research on human-autonomy teaming that can provide input to autonomy development BEFORE the autonomy is developed. We propose here a five-step process to doing HAT research and provide four examples of the application of this process. The five steps involve 1) knowledge elicitation to determine the essential aspects of HAT in a given domain, 2) development of a synthetic task environment with Wizard of Oz capability, 3) development of measurement strategies, 4) human subject experimentation, and 5) translation to the developers of artificial intelligence and robots that will serve as teammates.

Keywords: Human-robot interaction · Teaming with AI · Human-centered AI

1 Challenges for Human-Autonomy Teaming Research

A couple of decades ago, Moravec, one of the leaders in Artificial Intelligence (AI), indicated that "we are very near to the time when virtually no essential human function, physical or mental, will lack an artificial counterpart. The embodiment of this convergence of cultural developments will be the intelligent robot, a machine that can think and act as a human" [1; p. 1]. This seemed like a very bold statement at that time, but presently, team science on human-autonomy teaming (HAT) is playing a vital role in guiding the development of highly interactive AI and robots in complex task environments in which humans and autonomy jointly accomplish a common goal or task. There are many applications in which humans and autonomy need to team at a cognitive level to accomplish a task too risky for all-human teams. For instance, robots can be used to speed rapid repair of bombed runways to maintain forward base operations or can serve as an unmanned wingman to a manned F-35 [23].

In general, autonomy is "a system in which has a set of intelligence-based capabilities that allow it to respond to situations that was not programmed or anticipated in the design (i.e., decision-based responses)" [7:3]. On a team, autonomy must be able to work alongside human counterparts and carry out the fundamentals of teamwork and taskwork. In this paper we refer to these machine teammates as autonomy, recognizing

© Springer Nature Switzerland AG 2020
D. Harris and W.-C. Li (Eds.): HCII 2020, LNAI 12187, pp. 134–146, 2020.
https://doi.org/10.1007/978-3-030-49183-3_11

that this is a broad category of machines often made up of components of varying levels of autonomy. More important than level of autonomy for serving as a teammate is the degree to which the teammates are interdependent and that the teamwork toward a common goal requires team members to interact.

Thus, HAT can be defined as a sociotechnical system in which at least one human and one autonomous system interact interdependently over time in order to complete a common goal or task [15]. Research on human-autonomy teaming (HAT) plays a vital role in guiding the development of highly interactive Artificial Intelligence (AI) and robots in complex task environments to help humans accomplish common goals. However, there are challenges involved in conducting research that can produce results that can serve as input for the development of autonomy. Most importantly research on HAT cannot wait until the autonomy is developed, as then it is too late to provide meaningful input. Instead, a research environment or testbed is needed to "get ahead of the curve" and conduct research that can guide autonomy development. Specifically, effective HAT research needs: a realistic task environment, a challenging team environment with unexpected events, ways of testing different autonomy concepts, and measures of team performance and process metrics. In this paper we first describe a five-step process for systematic HAT research. Then, we briefly summarize four HAT research projects that exemplify the five-step framework and discuss their respective contributions.

2   A Systematic Approach to HAT Research

What are the essential requirements for a testbed in which to conduct HAT research? We view the establishment of a testbed as a process. The first step is understanding the problem space through *knowledge elicitation methods*. Knowledge elicitation is "the process of collecting from a human source of knowledge, information that is thought to be relevant to that knowledge" [1, p.802]. Knowledge elicitation includes three types of methods: (a) observations and interviews, (b) process tracing techniques, and (c) conceptual techniques. These methods can also help better understand team cognition through both individual aggregation of knowledge elicited and understanding team-level cognitive processes [4, 21, 22].

The second step involves developing a *synthetic task environment* in the lab [12] using the *Wizard of Oz* (WoZ; [19, 25]) paradigm that simulates the real-world task environment and autonomy. The idea comes from the iconic movie [3], and it is similar to a reverse Turing test [24]. The WoZ paradigm allows researchers to get ahead of the design curve and test capabilities of intelligent autonomy that is not easily implemented today. This step is probably the most difficult and least specified as it involves abstracting essential elements of the envisioned task and representing them in the testbed scenarios. It also involves abstracting capabilities of an agent and representing alternatives in the scenario.

The third step is *measurement* which is drawing from literature on all-human teaming and adapting theories and measures to HAT. The current literature on team cognition and teamwork in all-human teams posits that team cognition is not only the sum of individual knowledge of team members [26], but that team cognition evolves over time [6]. The theory of Interactive Team Cognition (ITC) considers the coordination of information across team members as team cognition. ITC underlines three assumptions: team cognition (a) is a process; (b) must be measured at the system level; and (c) is context-dependent. Team cognition therefore needs to be measured through team interactions (e.g., communication and coordination) [12, 13]. These recent publications regarding all-human teams provide important input in setting directions for future research on the development of effective HATs in various task contexts and have the advantage of being amenable to real-time interactions.

The fourth step is to conduct *human subject experimentation* using unobtrusive and real-time measures to model and measure the effectiveness of HAT. Effectiveness of HAT includes more than a single outcome, but multi-criteria outcomes, team states (e.g., team trust, team workload, team situation awareness), team interaction processes, and team inputs. The whole HAT functions as a cognitive system [5]. Considering teams as systems, ITC measures are primarily interaction-based real-time measures of team cognition [6].

The final step is *translation* that involves applying the findings from the human subjects' experiments to program real robotic agents for HAT studies. This step involves transdisciplinary knowledge exchange between those who are developing the autonomy and those conducting the human subjects research. Although difficult, this step is essential to close the loop on the applied research process.

3   Contributions from This Approach

By applying this five-step process, we have learned several lessons about HAT that can be useful in guiding the design of future autonomy. First and foremost we have learned the importance of considering HAT as a system, with all the features of a system. The system must be well-integrated from the beginning with appropriate roles assigned to human and autonomy teammates. The teammates need to be interdependent and need to be assigned roles most appropriate for their capabilities and limitations. Also, the system needs to be assessed at the system level. Finally, interdependence means that interaction among teammates is central to a well-functioning system. In the remainder of this paper we provide examples of projects that have adopted this framework to study HAT.

3.1   Human-Synthetic Team Research in a Remotely Piloted Aircraft System Synthetic Task Environment

Research in our Remotely Piloted Aircraft System (RPAS) synthetic task environment has been ongoing for over 20 years [2]. Research was initially done with teams of all humans, but more recently the project incorporated a synthetic teammate as the pilot. The main goal of this project is replacing one of the human team members with a synthetic agent which is an Adaptive Control of Thought-Rational (ACT-R [1]) based cognitive model. In the past decade, we conducted various experiments in a simulated RPAS task environment in which we compared human-synthetic teams with all-human teams or with WoZ human-synthetic teams over a series of 40-min missions.

In the RPAS synthetic task environment, three heterogeneous and interdependent team members are required to take good photographs of critical target waypoints which were part of five 40-min missions (each consisting of 11–40 targets). To accomplish this goal, the team members communicated by interacting with each other through a text-based communication system (see Fig. 1a) [7]. The team is comprised of: (1) the *navigator* who provides a dynamic flight plan with information regarding speed and altitude restrictions of the waypoints to the pilot; (2) the *pilot* who controls the Remotely Piloted Aircraft (RPA) by controlling its fuel and adjusting altitude and airspeed, and negotiates with the photographer about the correct altitude in order to take a good photo; and (3) the *photographer* who takes photos of each target waypoint, adjusts camera settings, and sends feedback to the other team members. Therefore, the basic goal of the team is to take good photographs of ground targets during the missions. Teams must also maintain all Remotely Piloted Aircraft (RPA) flight and sensor systems and observe any restrictions associated with particular waypoints. The experimental manipulation is applied to the pilot role which is isolated in one room, while the navigator and photographer are together in another room and separated from each other by a partition (Fig. 1b).

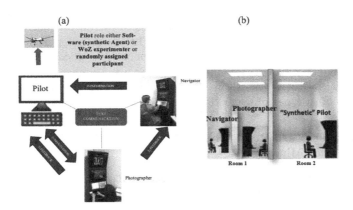

Fig. 1. (a) RPAS simulated testbed and (b) distribution of participants location.

In one of our studies, we compared three conditions based on manipulating the pilot role: (1) **control**—the pilot was a randomly assigned participant and the other two team members knew that the pilot was human; (2) **synthetic**—the pilot was an ACT-R based synthetic agent and the other team member knew that it was a software agent; or (3) **experimenter**—*the* pilot was a WoZ "synthetic" agent and the other two human team members were told that it was a software agent [11]. In the study we focused on how team interaction and effectiveness (team situation awareness and performance) differ across these three conditions, and how team interaction is associated with team effectiveness. Because the ACT-R based synthetic agent was still under development, its interaction abilities were insufficient for the RPAS task. In order to demonstrate expert teaming behavior, we designed the experimenter condition by applying a WoZ paradigm on the pilot role. The WoZ "synthetic" pilot (the experimenter) coordinated effectively with the other two roles while using limited vocabulary like an ACT-R based synthetic agent. It pushed and pulled the information to the other two team members in a timely manner and used a coordination script. In the study, we used various team performance and process measures as well as a measure of trust. Additionally, we used several dynamical systems measures based on different types of interactions, including system stability (Lyapunov [8]), system predictability (determinism [8]), and system order and disorder (entropy [14]).

From the findings associated with communication behavior, we concluded that experimenter teams pushed more information than teams in the other two conditions. Additionally, there was a positive correlation between pushing information and both team situation awareness and team performance. Through this study, we saw that anticipation of other team members' behaviors as well as information requirements are important for team effectiveness. Developing mechanisms to enhance the anticipatory pushing of information with HATs is necessary in order to increase the efficacy of teamwork in such teams [10]. Another finding from this study was that the experimenter condition demonstrated metastable coordination (not rigid nor unstable) and performed better than the control and synthetic teams that demonstrated unstable and rigid coordination, respectively. Even though the experimenter condition used limited vocabulary like the synthetic teams, the timeliness of the interactions overcame that limitation and helped their team effectiveness [9]. Later on, an approach similar to the experimenter condition in which a coordination model was applied in a medical setting by the leader of a code blue resuscitation trials, there was a similar benefit to enhancing team effectiveness [16]. Thus, in this case, the WoZ paradigm produced results that generalized to other types of teams (e.g. code blue).

3.2 Urban Search and Rescue Human-Robot Team Research in Simulated Minecraft Task Environment

Using robots in Urban Search and Rescue (USAR) is a challenging but also promising field that has significant potentials as it has appeared during recent disasters, including the 2001 World Trade Center collapse [21], the 2004 Mid Niigata [20], the 2011 Tohoku earthquakes in Japan [11], and the hurricane season in the Southeast of North America, to include Katerina, Wilma, Rita in 2005 [20], as well as hurricane Harvey in 2018 [8]. In these novel events, the USAR-with-robots overall goal is to explore a chaotic disaster task environment while searching for and rescuing victims [14].

In this study, we consider a USAR robot as "a physically situated intelligent agent" [22:7] and also as a team member that interacts with the operator via text chat communication. One of the key aspects of being on a team is interacting with other team members. In human teams a lot of this is done by communicating in natural language, but this is a bit of a sticking point for current AI/robots. The robot must be able to explain to the human teammates and both must be able to recognize the intentions of the other and interact in a way that makes sense. An explanation from a robot should provide an expected outcome in a manner understandable to a human [16]. Our aim in the USAR study is to identify which interaction and explanation strategies support team effectiveness. Communication behaviors (i.e., pushing and pulling information) are the basis of different explanation strategies. Thus, we had four conditions: (1) *always explain*—the robot proactively explains plan deviations, (2) *explain if asked*—the robot explains plan deviations only when asked, (3) *pull prime*—the robot explains only when asked and the participant is primed in initial social exchanges to request information, and (4) *never explain*—the robot provides no explanations. Our research question in this study is what type of explanation strategy is associated with the highest levels of team effectiveness (i.e., team situation awareness, calibrated trust, and performance)? Explanations are seen as a mechanism for facilitating team situation awareness and trust calibration. When observed behaviors do not fit the human's mental model, they may infer or attribute causes that explain the observed behavior. This attribution may be related to the agent's intention or to general causes of the unexpected behavior, either of which may diminish trust in the agent. In these situations, if the agent behaving unexpectedly explains their behavior to the human, situation awareness may improve, and teamwork goals will be achieved.

For the simulated task environment, we used the computer game Minecraft (version 1.11.2), which supports simulation of complex tasks, because the task environment is highly dynamic, diverse, and complex. Applying different novel conditions in Minecraft allows the user to be flexible in terms of changing the complexity of the task, such as adding fire, floating, and structural collapses. Figure 2a shows a view of Minecraft task environment. Two computers with Windows OS were used for this experiment. One computer was a desktop computer that was used to view the PowerPoint, record missions using Snagit, and complete the missions in the Minecraft game. This computer included two monitors with mirrored screens as well as two keyboards. The monitors were connected through a small wall opening, allowing for the participant and confederate (WoZ) workstations to be in a different room. The participant's monitor was overlaid with a laser-cut wood frame, allowing a small circle in the center of the screen as a limited view. Additionally, the robot's monitor was overlaid with a laser-cut acrylic (i.e., transparent) frame that designates the area of the screen the participant can see. The other computer was a laptop used to record Minecraft game data with Snagit.

Fig. 2. (a) A screen view of simulated Minecraft task environment and (b) team members' location (the randomly assigned participant on the left and the WoZ robot on the right).

Situational model discrepancy explanations were operationalized as behaviors that, due to the human teammate's task or environmental constraints may result in differences between the robot and the human's understanding. Two types of situational model discrepancy explanations occur over the course of the two missions: when the robot encounters an unplanned opening to another room, they use it to access and search that room. Additionally, the robot will encounter areas that are blocked by debris and will move on. For unplanned openings, the robot will explain that they found a route to the target room through an opening. For blockages, the robot with explain that they cannot access the target room because it is blocked. The team's goal in this task is to produce an accurate map of a collapsed building with the location of victims and structural changes, i.e. collapses and openings. Participants were told that the map would be provided to rescuers who would extract these victims from a building. The actual building contained inconsistencies from the starting map and had several environmental dynamics (e.g., fire, collapses, and contact with victims).

Team situation awareness was measured by the participant's map accuracy across missions. Performance was measured by proportion of collected victims. Trust was measured using Jian et al. (2000) [17] 's trust in automation scale. Additionally, measures of workload (NASA-TLX; [15]), communication behavior (pushing and pulling information), communication flow, task-related experience and demographics were obtained.

In this study, the WoZ paradigm allowed us to execute our main experimental manipulation, i.e., adjustment of robot's explainable behavior across the four conditions. The WoZ provided explanations as scripted depending on the condition. This avoided the need to implement four different robot explanation conditions in software. Our initial findings indicate that moderate levels of explanation are positively and significantly related to team situation awareness, whereas moderate levels of pushing information are positively related with team performance. Overall, we find that in novel conditions, some explanations are good but too many can impair performance. Without applying WoZ paradigm, we could not obtain this finding using the current technology. Thus, this finding can guide the design of the future USAR robot behavior.

3.3   Human-Driverless Car Research in CHARTopolis Task Environment

Soon when self-driving cars become increasingly popular, yet do not replace all human-driven cars, there will be a transition period in which both types of cars share the road. The intent of the self-driving car should be made easy to understand by pedestrians, cyclists, and other drivers through displays and other drivers on the road through signal lights and other mechanisms. How human drivers interact with self-driving cars to improve safety and efficiency is a critical question to be studied before that era arrives. The name of the testbed, CHARTopolis, comes from Center for Human-AI-Robot Teaming (CHART) at Arizona State University. It is a testbed for studying interactions between human-driven and self-driving cars that is capable of simulating conditions and challenges like those experienced by full-size autonomous vehicles when on the road with human-driven vehicles.

Many considerations went into the development of this testbed. First, our focus is on human interactions and communications, so the resolution or fidelity of full-size real cars are less important. Second, for safety concerns, running the experiment on the real road involves many safety issues, including human subject's safety considerations and the logistics of controlling weather and pedestrians. Third, using full-size cars are very expensive. To make the approach accessible to other researchers, we aim to build a low-cost testbed that can be replicated by other research teams and organizations. Fourth, we need technology that has an autonomous mode, and some autonomous functions are not technologically ready. WoZ can fill the gap of technology by having hidden humans remotely controlling the vehicles. Fifth, design of the road may resemble many different environments, and we chose an urban setting to start. To accomplish our goal, we worked with a multidisciplinary team, including a team from Mechanical Engineering and Computer Science, a team from Design and Theater, and a team from Human Factors and Human System Engineering.

The Go-CHART car used in CHARTopolis testbed is a self-made four-wheel vehicle, resembling a standard autonomous sedan, running on a mini testbed (see Fig. 3) [18].

Fig. 3. Go-CHART car and mini testbed (Picture credit: Shenbagaraj Kannapiran)

The enlarged testbed uses a dynamic media environment in an urban setting, where the buildings are projected to white 3D models and the scenes are subject to change with the rotating shadow of sunrise and sunset (see Fig. 4).

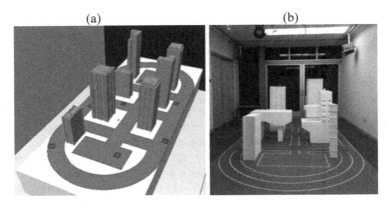

Fig. 4. CHARTpolis building and roads: (a) technical 3D view of the model and (b) incomplete model still in process (Picture credit left: Lance Gharavi)

The human subject interface includes a Logitech steering wheel, a PC monitor with camera feed and input boxes (see Fig. 5).

Fig. 5. (a) Human subject experiment participant station and (b) participant screen view of the testbed (Pictures credit: Shenbagaraj Kannapiran)

Using the HAT framework described here enables us to use a low-cost controllable testbed to study the following research questions for the future of transportation:

- Do the driving behaviors of autonomous vehicles cause a shift in the driving behaviors of human drivers?
- Does identifying the cars as driverless impact driver behavior?
- Will driverless vehicles lead to increased distraction while driving?
- Will driverless vehicles increase driver stress?

Without the use of WoZ method, research on human–agent teaming in such a context would lag behind system development.

3.4 Next Generation Combat Vehicles-Human Team Research

To protect the lives of soldiers and maximize the success of missions on the battlefield, Next Generation Combat Vehicles (NGCVs) are a family of future military vehicles, aiming to develop mobile protected firepower using modern technology for battlefield usage. In one version, a section of NGCVs includes a Manned Combat Vehicle (MCV) with seven crew members and two unmanned Robotic Combat Vehicles (RCVs). The RCVs are used as wingmen to improve crew survivability and increase lethality. However, remotely controlling an unmanned vehicle when sitting in a moving manned vehicle changes the nature of many current tasks, which requires appropriately reallocating functions and providing effective interfaces to support human decision making and team performance. Communications and coordination among the crew members and the artificial agents (i.e., MCVs, and RCVs) is especially challenging when uncertainty and possibilities abound in the problem space. The goal of this project is to study human–agent teaming effectiveness, especially using unobtrusive real-time team interaction processes (i.e., communications) to measure team states (e.g., team trust, team workload, team resilience, and team situation awareness).

Using testbed accessibility, face validity of constructs, and modification effort as filtering criteria, we filtered many options (e.g., video games, army testbed simulations) and decided to develop two versions of our own testbeds. The first one is a physical world testbed. We modified CHARTopolis (described above) by including incrementally up to seven seats for crew members, three vehicles each controlled by two crew members, and the seventh person being the vehicle commander. We will also use military vehicles to decorate the roads and manipulate perturbations to enhance the context (see Fig. 6).

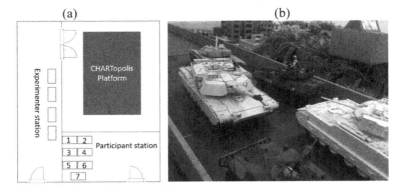

Fig. 6. NGCVs testbed modification: (a) floor plan of the testbed and (b) decorative military vehicles and figures)

With the WoZ method, we can use RCVs as remote control vehicles and focus on humans' interactions when each pair of operators controlling a vehicle for mobility and target identification, as well as their responses to task-related perturbations. Moreover, the Go-CHART cars have some autonomous vehicle functions (e.g., lane following and target recognition), and we can also have hidden experimenters drive the RCVs to achieve additional autonomous functions to study crew members' interactions and coordination with higher level of automation in the context of NGCVs.

The second one uses the virtual world of Minecraft (see Fig. 7). Its advantages include the following aspects:

- Malmo/Minecraft can address the key requirements of diverse experiments, by providing the capability or control required.
- Team size: One or many participants (human or computational) can perform tasks in the same Minecraft environment, and participants can be geographically distributed.
- Team structure: Asset control structure can be constrained by specifying the tools and information available to each player. Communication structure can be controlled by revising the source code for the chat capability from broadcast to narrowcast. Adherence to command structure can be measured behaviorally, and thus managed through rewards and feedback.
- Environmental complexity: The virtual environment can be arbitrarily complex and large, incorporate high fidelity web displays, and can be dynamically manipulated.
- Measurement: Key data can be extracted from the environment through the API.
- Easy availability: Malmo is an open-source tool that comes with a free Minecraft license. It is programmable by children and most adults.

(a)   (b)

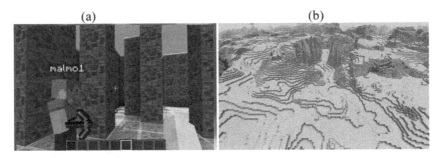

Fig. 7. NGCVs simulation in Minecraft: (a) participant view and (b) a topologic view of the simulated task environment (Picture credit: Glenn Lematta)

Without the WoZ method, the topic of human-agent teaming on the future battlefield would be impossible to study in a short term. Many organizations are currently working on the NGCV project, focusing on different aspects of the vehicle capabilities, and the vehicles currently in development. If we wait for the vehicles, then it will be too late to study human-agent teaming effectiveness. By that time, the financial cost and time to modify the vehicles and training of crew members will be too expensive. This HAT framework provides the ideal solution to address research needs early in the development cycle.

4 Conclusions

The five-step framework described here is essential for studying HAT. Without it is impossible to provide input to AI and robotic systems under development. The approach has applications for addressing real-world HAT problems. It allows for research that compares alternative concepts of operations of technology that is yet to be realized. Moreover, the resulting interaction-based measures and models may guide the development of future intelligent agents. Finally, the results derived from this framework have been shown to generalize to other domains outside of those tested.

References

1. Anderson, J.R.: How Can the Human Mind Occur in the Physical Universe?. Oxford University Press, Oxford (2007)
2. Ball, J., Myers, C., Heiberg, A., et al.: The synthetic teammate project. Comput. Math. Organ. Theor. **16**(3), 271–299 (2010)
3. Frank Baum, L.: The Wonderful Wizard of Oz. George M. Hill Company (1900)
4. Cooke, N.J.: Varieties of knowledge elicitation techniques. Int. J. Hum Comput Stud. **41**(6), 801–849 (1994)
5. Cooke, N.J., Gorman, J.C.: Interaction-based measures of cognitive systems. J. Cogn. Eng. Decis. Making **3**(1), 27–46 (2009)
6. Cooke, N.J., Gorman, J.C., Myers, C.W., Duran, J.L.: Interactive team cognition. Cogn. Sci. **37**(2), 255–285 (2013)
7. Cooke, N.J., Shope, S.M.: Designing a synthetic task environment. In: Schiflett, L.R.E., Salas, E., Coovert, M.D. (eds.) Scaled Worlds: Development, Validation, and Application, pp. 263–278. Ashgate Publishing, Surrey (2004)
8. Demir, M., Likens, A.D., Cooke, N.J., Amazeen, P.G., McNeese, N.J.: Team Coordination and Effectiveness in Human-Autonomy Teaming. IEEE Trans. Hum. Mach. Syst. **49**(2), 1–10 (2019)
9. Demir, M., Cooke, N.J., Amazeen, P.G.: A conceptual model of team dynamical behaviors and performance in human-autonomy teaming. Cogn. Syst. Res. **52**, 497–507 (2018)
10. Demir, M., McNeese, N.J., Cooke, N.J.: Team situation awareness within the context of human-autonomy teaming. Cogn. Syst. Res. **46**, 3–12 (2017)
11. Demir, M., McNeese, N.J., Cooke, N.J.: The evolution of human-autonomy teams in remotely piloted aircraft systems operations. Front. Commun. **4**, 50 (2019)
12. Gorman, J.C.: Team coordination and dynamics two central issues. Curr. Dir. Psychol. Sci. **23**(5), 355–360 (2014)
13. Gorman, J.C., Amazeen, P.G., Cooke, N.J.: Team coordination dynamics. Nonlinear Dyn. Psychol. Life Sci. **14**(3), 265–289 (2010)
14. Gorman, J.C., Grimm, D.A., Stevens, R.H., Galloway, T., Willemsen-Dunlap, A.M., Halpin, D.J.: Measuring real-time team cognition during team training. Hum. Factors (2019). https://doi.org/10.1177/0018720819852791
15. Hart, S.G., Staveland, L.E.: Development of NASA-TLX (Task Load Index): Results of empirical and theoretical research. In: Hancock, P.A., Mashkati, N. (eds.) Human Mental Workload, pp. 139–183. North Holland Press, Amsterdam (1988)

16. Hinski, S.T.: Training the code team leader as a forcing function to improve overall team performance during simulated code blue events (2017). http://hdl.handle.net/2286/R.I.46236. Accessed 27 Jan 2020

17. Jian, J.-Y., Bisantz, A.M., Drury, C.G.: Foundations for an empirically determined scale of trust in automated systems. Int. J. Cogn. Ergon. **4**(1), 53–71 (2000)

18. Kannapiran, S., Berman, S.: Go-CHART: A miniature remotely accessible self-driving car robot (2020).

19. Kelley, J.F.: An iterative design methodology for user-friendly natural language office information applications. ACM Trans. Inf. Syst. **2**(1), 26–41 (1984)

20. Liu, Y., Nejat, G.: Robotic urban search and rescue: a survey from the control perspective. J. Intell. Robot. Syst. **72**(2), 147–165 (2013)

21. McNeese, M.D., Ayoub, P.J.: Concept mapping in the analysis and design of cognitive systems: a historical review. Applied Concept Mapping. https://www.taylorfrancis.com/. Accessed 24 Nov 2019

22. Moon, B.M., Hoffman, R.R., Novak, J.D., Cañas, A.J. (eds.): Applied Concept Mapping: Capturing, Analyzing, and Organizing Knowledge. CRC Press, Boca Raton (2011)

23. Moravec, H.: Mind Children: The Future of Robot and Human Intelligence. Harvard University Press (1990)

24. Oppy, G., Dowe, D.: The turing test. In: Zalta, E.N. (ed.) The Stanford Encyclopedia of Philosophy. Metaphysics Research Lab, Stanford University (2019)

25. Riek, L.D.: Wizard of Oz studies in HRI: a systematic review and new reporting guidelines. J. Hum. Robot Interact. **1**(1), 119–136 (2012)

26. Salas, E., Cannon-Bowers, J., Church-Payne, S., Smith-Jentsch, K.: Teams and teamwork in the military. In: Cronin, C. (ed.) Military Psychology: An Introduction. Simon & Schuster, Needham Heights (1998)

Safety Challenges of AI in Autonomous Systems Design – Solutions from Human Factors Perspective Emphasizing AI Awareness

Hannu Karvonen[(✉)], Eetu Heikkilä, and Mikael Wahlström

VTT Technical Research Centre of Finland Ltd., P.O. Box 1000,
02044 VTT Espoo, Finland
{hannu.karvonen, eetu.heikkila, mikael.wahlstrom}@vtt.fi

Abstract. Artificial intelligence (AI) is a key technology that is utilized in autonomous systems. However, using AI in such systems introduces also several safety challenges, many of which are related to complex human-AI interactions. In general, these challenges relate to the changing roles of the people who interact with the increasingly autonomous systems in various ways. In this paper, we consider a set of practical safety challenges related to applying advanced AI to autonomous machine systems and present solutions from the perspective of human factors. We apply the novel concept of AI awareness (AIA) to discuss the challenges in detail, and based on this, provide suggestions and guidelines for mitigating the AI safety risks with autonomous systems. In addition, we briefly consider the system design process to identify the actions that should be taken to ensure AIA throughout the different systems engineering design phases. The theoretical research presented in this paper aims to provide the first steps towards considering AIA in autonomous systems and understanding the human factors perspective viewpoint on AI safety for autonomous systems.

Keywords: Artificial intelligence · Autonomous systems · Human factors · Safety · Systems engineering

1 Introduction

Autonomous systems (AS) are expected to change profoundly several of their application domains, including the mobility of people, logistics of goods, and industrial environments. There is no single agreed definition for the concept of autonomy or autonomous systems. On a general level, autonomy has been defined by NASA as the "system's ability to achieve goals and operate independently from external control" [1]. Autonomy is not the same as automation or artificial intelligence (AI), but often relies on automation as a building block and may make use of AI methods [2]. Autonomous systems, on the other hand, have been defined in NASA's recent 2020 Technology Taxonomy as the "cross-domain capability that enables the system to operate in a dynamic environment independent of external control" [3].

© Springer Nature Switzerland AG 2020
D. Harris and W.-C. Li (Eds.): HCII 2020, LNAI 12187, pp. 147–160, 2020.
https://doi.org/10.1007/978-3-030-49183-3_12

Typical features of an autonomous system include the ability to perceive its environment using various sensors, plan relevant actions based on the situational awareness created by the sensor data fusion, as well as to make decisions and act accordingly [4]. In many industries, categorizations have been developed to describe the levels of autonomy, and to clarify the differences of traditional industrial automation and autonomous systems. In practice, many of the definitions are used interchangeably. For example, SAE International [5] presents six levels of driving automation for road vehicles, ranging from manually driven to fully autonomous.

In this paper, we consider specifically machine systems with high levels of autonomy (i.e., with the capability to perform a major portion of the operative tasks) that are used by humans who are in a supervisory or co-operative role in relation to the system. In detail, we focus on the safety challenges within the intended functionality of the machine system. Therefore, considerations regarding intended adversarial attacks against the AS (e.g., cyber-security attacks) are excluded from this paper, although in practical system design adversarial attacks need also to be considered [6].

More specifically, we will consider the interaction between the human user and AS with a focus on how the human may keep track of the autonomous system's decision-making. To describe this generic process, we use the term 'artificial intelligence awareness' (AIA). Given that the robustness of autonomous machine systems' decision-making has not yet reached a level in which human monitoring and intervention is not needed, AIA can be seen as a relevant design aim in developing these systems. Based on earlier literature, generic guidelines for supporting AIA in the design of autonomous systems are also presented in this paper.

2 Background

To present the background concepts and literature, we next go through a review about AI with autonomous systems, the key concepts of situation, automation and artificial awareness (and related concepts), as well as safety challenges of AI in autonomous systems.

2.1 Artificial Intelligence with Autonomous Systems

With autonomous systems, a technology that is needed to enable increasing levels of autonomy falls under the label 'artificial intelligence'. In this paper, by AI we mean techniques that are used for the following two purposes with autonomous machine systems: firstly, for handling the data collected by sensor systems to form a technical situation awareness, and secondly, to interpret this situation awareness to make decisions on future actions. It is therefore AI that allows, for example, obstacle detection, classification, collision avoidance and path planning, which are essential for autonomous machine system operations.

AI does not have a generally accepted definition. However, it has been defined, for example, as the "science and engineering of making computers behave in ways that, until recently, we thought required human intelligence" [7]. In general, artificial intelligence (e.g., machine/deep learning or natural language processing in specific) supports both the technical and human decision-making with complex autonomous machine systems (e.g., in cars, ships, unmanned aerial vehicles, and work machines with high levels of autonomy). In this paper, we mostly refer to machine learning when discussing about AI. Gradually, as the autonomy level increases, it is typical that the support provided by the system for detailed human decision-making transforms into a more technical and automated decision-making process made by the system where the human is only accepting or rejecting the suggested decisions.

Currently, a plethora of data from various heterogeneous sensor sources need to be combined and interpreted by the system in a sensor data fusion process to make an appropriate proposal for a user for further actions or an independent decision for the autonomous system. It can be very hard for humans to gain useful knowledge out of this vast array of data as such and currently only specialized analysts can do that. The optimum situation would be that humans and AI work in seamless co-operation by utilizing each other's best capabilities.

2.2 Situation Awareness, Automation Awareness, and AI Awareness

To structure user awareness-related issues in technology-mediated environments, the concepts of situation awareness (SA) and automation awareness (AA) have been discussed in previous literature. A widely cited definition of SA is by Endsley [8, 9] who describes it as "the perception of elements in the environment within a volume of time and space, the comprehension of their meaning, and the projection of their status in the near future". AA, on the other hand, is not yet an equally established concept. Generally, it can be seen as a part of SA, which focuses specifically on automation and comprises of perceiving the current status of the automation, comprehending the status and its meaning to the system behavior, as well as projecting its future status and meaning [10, 11].

When designing complex systems that apply AI and involve human-machine collaboration, a set of unsolved issues exist. To concretize the various dimensions of these issues, the concept of artificial intelligence awareness (AIA) has been proposed to represent a taxonomy for the awareness-related phenomena of AI-enabled systems [12]. AIA in work environments has been defined by Karvonen, Heikkilä, and Wahlström [12] as the worker's perception of the current decision made by the AI system, his or her comprehension of this decision, and his or her estimate (i.e. projection) of the decision(s) by the AI system in the future. A visual description of the relationship between SA, AA, and AIA is presented in Fig. 1 and can be found with their detailed descriptions in [12].

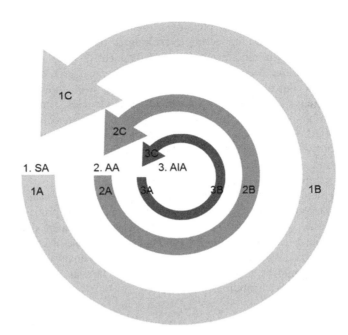

Fig. 1. The Awareness Circles of SA, AA and AIA from [12]. The figure is meant to reflect the relationships between 1. Situation awareness, 2. Automation awareness, and 3. AI awareness. Explanations for the used codes are, 1A: *Perception of the current situation*, 1B: *Comprehension of the current situation*, 1C: *Projection of the future situation*; 2A: *Perception of the current status of the automation*, 2B: *Comprehension of the current status of the automation*, 2C: *Projection of the future status of the automation*; 3A: *Perception of the current AI-based decision (s) by the system*, 3B: *Comprehension of the current AI-based decision(s) of the system and their basis*, 3C: *Projection of the system's AI-based decision(s) in the future and their basis.*

2.3   Key Concepts of AI Awareness

Previously, we [12] have identified three key concepts related to AI awareness: transparency, communication, and appropriate trust. Firstly, transparency refers to how transparent the functioning of the AI is (see, e.g., [13]). The aim is to make the typical black box of AI processes more transparent and clear for the user to comprehend. This is often referred to as 'explainable AI' in the literature (see, e.g., [14]). What is needed for the user to understand these processes are, for example, the presentation of reasons behind the decisions, simplifications of the used algorithms, and illustrative visualizations of the AI's processes.

Secondly, communication refers both to the way in which the AI system communicates its functioning, intentions, capabilities, and limitations to the user and also to the possibilities of the AI to understand human communication. Therefore, the above-mentioned transparency of the system is a concept that is also closely related to communication. However, they are not the same as features of AI: for example, transparency can be enhanced by the traceability of the decision-making of the AI while communication refers to the *way* this enhanced transparency of the system is communicated to the user. In practice, good communication of the system can mean the utilization of interaction technologies that are natural for the human users. Therefore, multimodal output user interfaces, for example, can be beneficial. On the other hand, the communication of humans understood by the AI system is essential. To enable more natural ways of humans to communicate (e.g., voice or gestures) to be utilized, the AI-enabled system needs vast human factors and input user interface research and design efforts.

Third, appropriate trust refers to the aim that the human operator can trust the AI on an appropriate level, based on the knowledge about, for example, 1) the capabilities of the AI-based system, 2) the quality and relevancy of the used data, or 3) has the system learned the required skills without becoming biased. In order to calibrate trust into an appropriate level, the user has to have a clear idea of the capabilities of the used algorithms as well as what kind of data has been used in teaching the AI system. This concept also includes the consideration of the mitigation of the problematic effects of overtrust or distrust in automation, which has previously been a major contributing factor to accidents with highly automated solutions (e.g., in case of the grounding of the Royal Majesty in 1995).

2.4   Safety Challenges of AI in Autonomous Systems

The use of AI in different safety-critical systems (e.g., in land transport, maritime, or drone systems) is increasing rapidly and the implications of this phenomenon have been the focus of scientific publications recently (see e.g., [15–17]). However, the safety of AI is a relatively new and unexplored field of study [18]. Generally, the discussion on AI and safety is intertwined with the debate revolving around the questions of ethics, legal or regulatory aspects, and the acceptability of AI. In the literature, several fundamental safety challenges of AI applications have been identified, for example, by Yampolskiy [18–20]. Nevertheless, when considering AI in autonomous systems, numerous concrete safety problems hinder the introduction of the systems in wider use.

In this paper, we focus on the specific AI safety challenges adopted from the widely cited work of Amodei, Olah, Steinhardt, Christiano, Schulman, and Mané [21]. In the literature, several other AI challenges have also been introduced, but the ones described by Amodei et al. are among the most crucial when developing safety-critical autonomous systems. These challenges, with our short interpretation of their meaning in case of an autonomous system, are defined here based on Amodei et al. [21] as follows:

1) Avoiding Negative Side Effects

   - How to ensure that the system does not disturb its environment in negative ways while pursuing its goal?

2) Avoiding Reward Hacking

   - How to ensure that there are no loopholes in the system that allow unintended rewards?

3) Scalable Oversight

- How to ensure that the system performs reasonably with limited information?

4) Safe Exploration

- How to ensure that exploratory moves do not lead to bad repercussions?

5) Robustness to Distributional Shift

- How to ensure that the system does not make bad decisions in a setting that is different from the one that was used for training?

A detailed account of these challenges with an example case of a cleaning robot is provided in [21]. In the literature citing the Amodei et al. [21] paper, these challenges have been analyzed mostly from technical perspectives (see, e.g., in [22, 23]). In addition to designing the technical system, however, a wider systemic perspective is required to be able to apply AI in autonomous systems safely. One systemic perspective to safety challenges is that of human factors, which we will discuss in detail in the next chapter.

3   AI Awareness Perspective to AI's Human Factors and Safety Challenges

The safety challenges of AI need to be solved in order to deploy it in practical use cases of safety-critical environments. In the following, we review each of the above-presented safety challenges of Amodei et al. [21] from the perspective of human factors and, particularly, from the viewpoint of AI awareness. Additionally, some examples of these challenges and proposed solutions with autonomous systems are provided. In the end of each subsection, the AI safety challenge is also gone through from the perspective of the three different situation awareness stages proposed by Endsley [8, 9] to show what AIA specific to that challenge means. Finally, a summary table of these findings is presented.

3.1   Avoiding Negative Side Effects

Avoiding negative side effects is a major challenge for the design of autonomous systems [21]. For example, an autonomous cargo-handling machine (e.g., an automated container crane) might be designed to optimize the amount of container moves. In such case, examples of negative side effects might include damage to the cargo due to extreme maneuvers when pursuing the speed targets or even causing safety-related problems for the manual machine operators working in the same area.

This negative side effects problem can be approached from the human factors perspective, for example, by performing a comprehensive domain and task analyses (e.g., core-task [24] or cognitive work analysis [25]) to ensure that the autonomous systems' AI's decision-making goals are not contradicting with the goals of the other entities in the same environment. Naturally, these goas should not either be in contradiction with the priorities of the safety, productivity, and health [25] goals of entire socio-technical and safety-critical system at hand.

Additionally, in case of a semi-autonomous system under remote supervision and operation, it is important to provide sufficient information of the autonomous systems' decision-making rationale for the remote operator as well as the other stakeholders when needed. Furthermore, a possibility to intervene safely to the system operation is required when undesired behavior is noticed. All this necessitates an appropriate level of AI awareness for the remote operators of the autonomous system.

In the context of this safety challenge, AI awareness of the human operator of the system can be in specific said to be referring to 1) perceiving the effects of the autonomous system in question to its environment, 2) contrasting the perceived effects of the autonomous system with the tasks and aims of the operation, and 3) projecting the trend effects of the operation in relation to potential future operations.

3.2 Reward Hacking

Reward hacking [21] is another challenging issue in autonomous system development from the human factors perspective. With an autonomous system, this challenge may appear in several ways through misspecified reward functions, causing the system to operate in a way unintended by the system designers. For example, if a cargo-handling machine would be rewarded based on the speed of movements, an undesired result could be that the system actually carries less cargo to reduce its weight only to increase its speed.

For the operators of the autonomous system, this is also an AI awareness issue, as in many cases the decision-making rationale behind the AI's decisions may not be intuitive or easy to understand. Therefore, it is important to enforce AI transparency for the user to be able to see the rationale behind the decisions by the AI system.

In the literature, several approaches have been presented regarding the questions of AI transparency [13], explainability [14], and interpretability [26]. Typically, these approaches utilize simplifications and visualizations to enhance transparency and the system's understandability. Additionally, the system can be designed to require approval by a human operator before rewarding the system, for example, after performing new types of actions.

In the context of this safety challenge, AI awareness of the human operator can be in specific said to be referring to 1) perceiving the elements influencing the autonomous system's or AI's reward system, 2) understanding the autonomous system's or AI's reward system in relation to the tasks and aims of the operation, and 3) projecting trends within the AI's potential machine learning processes.

3.3 Scalable Oversight

Scalable oversight [21] becomes important when autonomous systems are placed in highly dynamic environments. A simple example would be an autonomous harvester encountering a new type of obstacle that was not included in its training data. The system needs to be able determine whether the obstacle is something that it can try to avoid on its own, or whether it should request assistance from a human operator (who is typically in a remote location).

From the AI awareness perspective, it is important to consider how the monitoring of the system by the user(s) from a supervisory perspective is implemented. In system design, it is crucial to create clear definitions about how the system should be supervised and define the scenarios where the human user should be asked to intervene and take over. Additionally, it is crucial to give the user the appropriate information about the current situation before taking over the machine.

In the context of this safety challenge, AI awareness of the human operator can be in specific said to be referring to 1) perceiving the autonomous system in an appropriate manner, depending on the autonomous system's situation in the field, 2) comprehending the meaning of oversight levels vis-à-vis the autonomous system's situation in the field, and 3) projecting the changes in the level of oversight within the monitored autonomous system or systems.

3.4   Safe Exploration

Highly efficient autonomy is likely to require some extent of exploration capabilities. This means that the system is allowed to perform exploratory moves within defined limits [21]. For example, a semi-autonomous rubber-tired container crane may be allowed to experiment various route options for optimal performance. However, this is likely to be a challenging issue, partly because it potentially makes the system more unpredictable for remote operators and for other people working in the same area with the crane.

Therefore, in system design, it is important to ensure that all the people who interact with the system have sufficient knowledge of the system capabilities and its limitations, as well as about the extent the system is allowed to explore. The capabilities of the system must be communicated in the user interface design solutions, which should also demonstrate the limits of the system understandably.

One approach to AI awareness in this context is to simulate exploration scenarios to design means for human supervision related to exploratory moves. In this approach, appropriate simulation systems are an essential and cost-effective tool in design work.

In the context of this safety challenge, AI awareness of the human operator can be in specific said to be referring to 1) perceiving the autonomous system's exploration, 2) understanding the limits of safe exploration in contrast to the autonomous system's current operation, and 3) projecting trajectories and anticipating the autonomous system's exploration positions.

3.5   Robustness to Distributional Shift

Robustness to distributional shift [21] becomes important especially when an autonomous system is introduced to a new or modified environment or when the environmental conditions drastically change. For example, an autonomous system operating in an outside environment may encounter weather changes. For such situations, it is important to develop means for human-system interaction and supervision to support the adaptation to the new environment.

From the AI awareness perspective, system designers should ensure that people interacting with the system are aware of the system's limitations also when the environment changes. In order to make the capabilities of the AI more understandable, the system should communicate about its performance, process, and purpose (see [27] for details) to the user.

In the context of this safety challenge, AI awareness of the human operator can be in specific said to be referring to 1) perceiving the autonomous system's environment, 2) understanding the impact of the environment for the autonomous system, and 3) projecting the environmental change around the autonomous system.

3.6   Synthesis on Autonomous Systems and AIs Safety Challenges

To synthesize the results of this chapter regarding AIA and its implications of Amodei et al.'s [21] safety challenges, Table 1 is presented. In Table 1, we have included the three SA elements originally introduced by Endsley [8, 9] from the definition of situation awareness: the *perception* of elements in the environment within a volume of time and space, the *comprehension* of their meaning, and the *projection* of their status in the near future. In later literature [12], *estimation* has also been used instead of *projection*.

Table 1. AI awareness implications of Amodei et al.'s [21] AI safety challenges (including the three SA elements originally introduced by Endsley [8, 9]). AS: autonomous system.

AI safety challenge	Perception	Comprehension	Projection
1. Avoiding negative side effects	Perceiving the effects of the AS to its environment	Contrasting the perceived effects of the AS with the tasks and aims of the operation	Projecting the trend effects of the operation
2. Reward hacking	Perceiving the elements influencing the AS's/AI's reward system	Understanding the AS's/AI's reward system in relation to the tasks and aims of the operation	Projecting trends within the AI's machine learning
3. Scalable oversight	Perceiving the AS in an appropriate manner, depending on the AS's situation in the field	Comprehending the meaning of oversight levels vis-á-vis the AS's situation in the field	Projecting the changes in the level of oversight within the monitored AS or ASs
4. Safe exploration	Perceiving the AS's exploration	Understanding the limits of safe exploration in contrast to the AS's current operation	Projecting trajectories and anticipating the AS's exploration positions
5. Robustness to distributional shift	Perceiving the AS's environment	Understanding the impact of the environment for the AS	Projecting the environmental change around the AS

4   Implications for the Systems Engineering of AI-Enabled Autonomous Systems

In the previous sections, we provided an overview of the AI safety challenges, their implications for human-AI interaction with autonomous systems, and suggestions for solutions to these challenges from the human factors perspective. In the following, we discuss further these aspects from the perspective of the design process of autonomous systems that employ AI. We have divided the system design process to generic systems engineering phases (see e.g., [28]) of 1) concept design, 2) architecture design, 3) detailed design, implementation and integration, 4) system verification and validation, as well as 5) operation and maintenance. Each of these phases, and how AIA should be considered in them, will be discussed in next paragraphs separately.

Firstly, in the concept design phase, the potential scenarios for human-AI collaboration should be defined and documented, and taken into account when writing the user and system requirements. These descriptions need to be broad enough, in order to incorporate all potential stakeholders that may interact with the system, as well as define the types of these interactions. One example of a systematic approach in this phase is to define a detailed Concept of Operations (ConOps, see e.g., [29]) for the designed system.

Secondly, in the architecture design phase, the collected data plays a crucial role. The collection, use, and handling of potentially large masses of data needs to be carefully planned. The data-related procedures must be documented to be able to provide the user sufficient information regarding the amount and quality of the data that is used to train the AI system, and to help select the potential machine learning methods best suitable for the application.

Thirdly, in detailed design, implementation, and integration phases, the main issues include the design and implementation of the AI system for transparency and communication, which were discussed also earlier in this paper. Careful user interface design is required to provide the user with relevant information of the AI system's operation to enable an appropriate level of transparency, and for the AI to be able to understand communication that is intuitive for humans.

Fourthly, system verification and validation (V&V) of AIA-related functions from the human factors perspective is a challenging task, as currently the standardization for AI-enabled machine systems is only starting to develop. It is likely that extensive simulator-based V&V involving the actual users of the systems will be needed. These will not only provide a safe way of trying different scenarios with the autonomous system, but also cut down development costs, as a physical prototype will not be needed to be developed at least in the beginning phases of the development. The actual environment of use should be modelled in V&V, to take into account also the various other tasks the users may need to handle simultaneously while interacting with the AI system.

When the system is implemented into production and made operational, it is important to ensure that the users have the sufficient skills to operate and maintain the system safely. This can be achieved through proper design of operation and maintenance processes. In work-related environments, this design is partly an organizational issue, which calls for AI-specific training of the users at an appropriate level. Additionally, change management procedures need to be in place to handle maintenance of AI systems, for example to adapt the systems to changing environments of use.

As a summary, as discussed in detail also in [12], AIA is based on the ways for the human user to gain understanding about the AI's functioning. These ways include, for example, 1) the system's user interfaces, 2) the provided AI-specific training of the users, 3) the users' general knowledge of the principles of computer systems and AI, 4) the momentary high level of cognitive workload of the user, and 5) the user's subjectively experienced level of complexity of the AI system. All of these human factors engineering related topics should be deeply considered also in the different systems engineering phases of AI-enabled autonomous machine systems.

5   Discussion

Autonomous systems are a major application area for AI technologies. AI is applied, for example, in the implementation of object detection and collision avoidance of autonomous cars. Although the level of autonomy with different safety-critical systems gradually increases, the systems will still be in interaction with human users. Regarding the use of AI with these systems, several concrete safety issues have been raised in literature.

The technical assurance and reliability evaluation of AI systems is important, but also a broader systemic view is needed. Human factors is one part of this consideration and the key safety issues of AI should be addressed from a human factors point of view to ensure the safety of users and other people interacting with autonomous machine systems that employ AI.

We have argued that one key human factors concept related to AI is artificial intelligence awareness. Similar issues as interacting with a human counterpart influence AI awareness: for example, you have to understand the logic and functioning of the AI, be able to communicate with it in a fluent manner, and trust in its actions at an appropriate level, considering the system's capabilities.

The transparency and intelligibility of AI's decision-making logic can be improved in practice, for example, by means of simplifications and visualisations. In a decision scenario that is presented by the system to the user, he or she can be shown alternative possibilities for the decision with grounds for choosing exactly these decision alternatives to be presented as well as estimations of possible effects of each decision. To clarify the AI system's reasons for choosing each decision that is presented, in some cases, it may be useful to visually illustrate the chain of reasoning that led to a particular outcome. Therefore, from the human factors perspective, in AI-enabled decision-making it is essential to enable the traceability of the decision-making. Traceability makes it possible for the human user to assess on what basis the decision has been made, i.e., pointers on what are the data and the processes used in the AI system's decision-making.

AI awareness also includes functional communication between the user and the AI system. AI must be able to tell the user what the system is and is not capable of, what its current status is, and what it plans to do next. In addition, it must be able to "listen" to the user: for example, it should adaptively consider the instructions given by the user. AI's ability for discourse is improving all the time as the techniques for processing natural language develop. It is also possible to utilise more and more versatile multimodal user interfaces in the future with these systems.

Transparency, intelligibility, and communication are also the foundation for the building of an appropriate level of human trust (see e.g., [27]) in AI. Reaching an appropriate level of trust in an automated system is not a trivial challenge: the user cannot trust the system if it does not clearly communicate its intentions to the user or if its actions are difficult to understand. In this kind of a situation, distrust or mistrust may occur. On the other hand, a system simplified to the extreme can be mistaken for being more capable than it is. Therefore, overtrust may occur. An appropriate level of trust in AI can be built in stages as more and more demanding tasks are gradually assigned to the AI system.

To support the development of an appropriate level of trust, measures for the correctness of the presented information are needed. In other words, the calibration of trust to an appropriate level [27] requires the development of measures for the correctness of the presented information for the human user. These measures may include, for example, probabilities or confidence levels calculated by the system regarding the presented information's correctness.

6   Conclusions

Increasing the level of autonomy and usage of AI in a system have significant effects to the human-technology interaction. This change will introduce new types of risks related to human's awareness of the AI functionality that need to be considered in design. One of these related issues is AI awareness, which is based on the concepts of situation awareness and automation awareness. In addition to a sufficient level of situational awareness, humans interacting with and being near the machine system need to achieve also a sufficient level of automation and AI awareness. In this paper, we have argued that AIA is a key concept to be considered when studying and designing future sociotechnical systems with high levels of autonomy realized with AI. Considering during design how to support the AIA of the users of a safety-critical system when the system is in use contributes to the safety of the entire joint intelligent system formed by the human-technology entity.

In the future design of AI-enabled autonomous systems, answering questions, such as how to best support human AIA through design choices or how to increase the system transparency, better the computer-human communication, and the calibration of trust to an appropriate level, become crucial. This paper has taken the first steps to address these questions and provided some initial answers. For example, the system's user interfaces and the provided training in case of work systems provide some key ways to support an appropriate level of AIA. In order to answer these questions fully, both theory and practice lizing AI. Finally, empirical R&D case studies both in naturalistic and experimental settings are needed in future research.

References

1. National Aeronautics and Space Administration.: NASA technology roadmaps – TA 4: robotics and autonomous systems (2015). https://www.nasa.gov/sites/default/files/atoms/files/2015_nasa_technology_roadmaps_ta_4_robotics_and_autonomous_systems_final.pdf. Accessed 23 Feb 2020

2. Fong, T.: Autonomous systems – NASA capability overview (2018). https://ntrs.nasa.gov/archive/nasa/casi.ntrs.nasa.gov/20180007804.pdf. Accessed 23 Feb 2020

3. Miranda, D.: 2020 NASA technology taxonomy – TX10: autonomous systems (2020). https://ntrs.nasa.gov/archive/nasa/casi.ntrs.nasa.gov/20200000399.pdf. Accessed 23 Feb 2020

4. Pendleton, S., et al.: Perception, planning, control, and coordination for autonomous vehicles. Machines **5**(1), 6 (2017)

5. SAE International: SAE-J3016 Taxonomy and definitions for terms related to driving automation systems for on-road motor vehicles (2014)

6. Papernot, N., Mcdaniel, P., Jha, S., Fredrikson, M., Celik, Z.B., Swami, A.: The limitations of deep learning in adversarial settings. In: IEEE European Symposium on Security and Privacy (EuroS&P), pp. 372–387. IEEE (2016)

7. Moore, A.: Carnegie Mellon Dean Of Computer Science On The Future Of AI. Forbes (2017). https://www.forbes.com/sites/peterhigh/2017/10/30/carnegie-mellon-dean-of-computer-science-on-the-future-of-ai/#3d4124e72197. Accessed 23 Feb 2020

8. Endsley, M.R.: Situation awareness global assessment technique (SAGAT). In: Proceedings of the National Aerospace and Electronics Conference (NAECON), pp. 789–795. IEEE, New York (1988)

9. Endsley, M.R.: Measurement of situation awareness in dynamic systems. Hum. Factors **37** (1), 65–84 (1995)

10. Karvonen, H., Liinasuo, M., Lappalainen, J.: Assessment of automation awareness. In: Automaatio XXI Conference, vol. 44 (2015)

11. Karvonen, H., Liinasuo, M., Lappalainen, J.: Assessment of situation and automation awareness, SAFIR2014 research report, VTT Research Report VTT-R-05997-14 (2014)

12. Karvonen, H., Heikkilä, E., Wahlström, M.: Artificial intelligence awareness in work environments. In: Barricelli, B.R., et al. (eds.) HWID 2018. IAICT, vol. 544, pp. 175–185. Springer, Cham (2019). https://doi.org/10.1007/978-3-030-05297-3_12

13. Theodorou, A., Wortham, R.H., Bryson, J.J.: Designing and implementing transparency for real time inspection of autonomous robots. Conn. Sci. **29**(3), 230–241 (2017)

14. Doran, D., Schulz, S., Besold, T.R.: What does explainable AI really mean? A new conceptualization of perspectives. arXiv preprint arXiv:1710.00794 (2017)

15. Kurd, Z., Kelly, T., Austin, J.: Developing artificial neural networks for safety critical systems. Neural Comput. Appl. **16**(1), 11–19 (2007). https://doi.org/10.1007/s00521-006-0039-9

16. Fournaris, A.P., Lalos, A.S., Serpanos, D.: Generative adversarial networks in AI-enabled safety-critical systems: friend or foe? Computer **52**(9), 78–81 (2019)

17. Cummings, M.L., Britton, D.: Regulating safety-critical autonomous systems: past, present, and future perspectives. In: Living with Robots, pp. 119–140. Academic Press (2020)

18. Yampolskiy, R.V.: Artificial Intelligence Safety and Security. Chapman and Hall/CRC, Boca Raton (2018)

19. Yampolskiy, R.V.: Artificial intelligence safety engineering: Why machine ethics is a wrong approach. In: Müller, V. (ed.) Philosophy and Theory of Artificial Intelligence. Studies in Applied Philosophy, Epistemology and Rational Ethics, vol. 5, pp. 389–396. Springer, Heidelberg (2013). https://doi.org/10.1007/978-3-642-31674-6_29

20. Yampolskiy, R.V.: Taxonomy of pathways to dangerous artificial intelligence. In: Workshops at the Thirtieth AAAI Conference on Artificial Intelligence (2016)
21. Amodei, D., Olah, C., Steinhardt, J., Christiano, P., Schulman, J., Mané, D.: Concrete problems in AI safety. arXiv preprint arXiv:1606.06565 (2016)
22. Mohseni, S., Pitale, M., Singh, V., Wang, Z.: Practical solutions for machine learning safety in autonomous vehicles. arXiv preprint arXiv:1912.09630, (2019)
23. Alexander, R.D., Ashmore, R., Banks, A.: The state of solutions for autonomous systems safety (2018). http://eprints.whiterose.ac.uk/127573/1/02_ALEXANDER_ASHMORE_AND_BANKS_THE_STATE_OF_SOLUTIONS_FOR_AUTONOMOUS_SYSTEM_SAFETY.PDF. Accessed 23 Feb 2020
24. Norros, L.: Acting Under Uncertainty – The Core-Task Analysis in Naturalistic Study of Work and Expertise. VTT, Espoo (2004)
25. Vicente, K.J.: Cognitive Work Analysis: Toward Safe, Productive, and Healthy Computer-Based Work. CRC Press, Mahwah (1999)
26. Rudin, C.: Stop explaining black box machine learning models for high stakes decisions and use interpretable models instead. Nat. Mach. Intell. **1**(5), 206–215 (2019)
27. Lee, J.D., See, K.A.: Trust in automation: designing for appropriate reliance. Hum. Factors J. Hum. Factors Ergon. Soc. **46**(1), 50–80 (2004)
28. Forsberg, K., Mooz, H.: The relationship of systems engineering to the project cycle. Eng. Manage. J. **4**(3), 36–43 (1992)
29. Fairley, R., Thayer, R.: The concept of operations: the bridge from operational requirements to technical specifications. Ann. Soft. Eng. **3**(1), 417–432 (1997). https://doi.org/10.1023/A:1018985904689

Human-Autonomy Teaming and Explainable AI Capabilities in RTS Games

Crisrael Lucero[(✉)], Christianne Izumigawa, Kurt Frederiksen, Lena Nans, Rebecca Iden, and Douglas S. Lange

Naval Information Warfare Center Pacific, San Diego, USA
crisrael.lucero@navy.mil

Abstract. Real-time strategy games often times mimic the appearance and feel of military-like command and control systems. Artificial intelligence and machine learning research enjoys utilizing the environments produced by these games and are often focused on creating intelligent agents to beat them or accomplish high scores. Instead of creating these agents, or bots, to beat real-time strategy games, this work instead focuses on creating machine learning-driven agents to work with human players. However, due to the advancements in the deep learning field, machine learning models have become harder to understand, and are called 'black-box models' due to the inability to see the inner workings of such algorithms. To remedy this, we describe how we take human-autonomy teaming and explainable artificial intelligence techniques to shed light and provide inside for players to understand recommendations by the system.

Keywords: Human-Autonomy Teaming · Artificial intelligence · Explainable AI · StarCraft II · Wargaming

1   Introduction

Games are a common research environment for artificial intelligence (AI) and machine learning (ML) and often times used in education material such as creating a Tic-Tac-Toe playing AI agent using the alpha-beta pruning algorithm. Real-time strategy (RTS) games are sub-genre of strategy video games that serve as a popular frontier for deep learning research. One such RTS game, StarCraft II (SC2) by Blizzard Entertainment, has received a lot of attention due to recent success in defeating professional SC2 players[1] with a few caveats. Research has had a heavy focus on building AI bots to master these RTS games and several AI competitions are held for different game environments such as MicroRTS[2] and

---

[1] https://deepmind.com/blog/article/alphastar-mastering-real-time-strategy-game-starcraft-ii.

[2] https://sites.google.com/site/micrortsaicompetition/home.

This is a U.S. government work and not under copyright protection in the U.S.;
foreign copyright protection may apply 2020
D. Harris and W.-C. Li (Eds.): HCII 2020, LNAI 12187, pp. 161–171, 2020.
https://doi.org/10.1007/978-3-030-49183-3_13

Bot Bowl[3]. There has been little focus on building Human-Autonomy Teaming (HAT) and battle management aids that are driven by AI and ML models within the RTS genre, despite the natural relationship to Command and Control (C2) systems. Furthermore, the emergence of the need for eXplainable AI (XAI), or AI models that can explain actions at a human-understandable level, has not made much of an emergence within the AI in RTS literature.

The focus of this paper is to discuss our initial work done with tackling the problems and incorporating principles of XAI and HAT by creating an AI agent that interacts with human players to provide recommendations, assist in tasks, and teach someone to play the game more efficiently and at a higher level.

2   Background and Related Work

Human-Autonomy Teaming and Explainable AI are research areas that have very similar goals with regards to transparency and trust. HAT is based on advances in providing automation transparency, a method for giving insight into the reasoning behind automated recommendations and actions, along with advances in human automation communications [1]. Systems of humans and AI agents working together to provide significant mission performance improvements that surpasses what humans or AI can do alone is one of the fundamentals of HAT [2]. This work was heavily inspired by shared autonomy research conducted that teamed humans and deep reinforcement-learned agents to solve a spaceship landing game [3]. The work showcased autonomous pilots having strong mechanical precision and navigational control but took too long to land the spaceship in the designated landing zone. The human pilots were able to understand the goal and get the spaceship to the landing zone quickly, but lacked mechanical skills to prevent crash landings. Together, the human-machine team vastly outperformed the other two.

To goal for XAI, as defined by the DARPA XAI program [4], is to create a suite of new or modified ML techniques that produce explainable models that, when combined with effective explanation techniques, enable users to understand, appropriately trust, and effectively manage the emerging generation of AI system [2].

2.1   Black Box Models and Issues Within XAI

Deep neural networks have revolutionized industries with their ability to process large amount of high-dimensional data while providing high accuracy at a fast rate. They can classify faces and objects, provide better user interaction with recommendations, translate languages, self-drive a car, and beat the best humans at their own games. However, these *black-box* models pick up patterns and create representations of the data that we do not fully understand, but need to. Black box models are systems that take some input, perform some processing, and

---

[3] https://bot-bowl.com/.

give output with no real way to observe the processes that occurred. The term spans across several applications, but within the context of machine learning, usually deep learning algorithms are considered to be black box models due to the inability for humans to understand and difficulty to decipher.

A position paper has advised not to use black box machine learning models for high stakes decisions [5], it is often difficult to use a more interpretable model over a deep learning model for complex problems and unstructured sources of data. The work describes how, under certain circumstances, you can continue to use more human-interpretable ML models without a hit in accuracy or precision. With the rising trend of using AI/ML within healthcare and criminal justice, it has become strongly advocated against using black box models that make predictions that deeply impact human life [5,6]. Organizations such as the European Union with their General Data Protection Regulation[4] or the US ACM[5] have come out with statements for increasing transparency within black box models. As these systems are slowly being integrated into our lives, we must start questioning their decisions and demand more transparency from them. The decisions they make must be judged on whether it was made "for the right reason" or else we will encounter unintended consequences.

There has been progress in this area as we are seeing frameworks such as LIME [7] and DeepLIFT [8] used to explain multi-layer perceptron meanwhile GuidedBackprop [9] and Grad-CAM [10] apply to convolutional neural networks.

The work we performed is simply for a video game, so players are not making decisions that deeply impact human life based on AI-driven recommendations. However, we did imply the natural relationship to C2 systems, and SC2 is a warfare-like video game, so we still explore the XAI space. We believe that providing explanations behind recommendations, or at least interpretable decisions, it can help build trust in the system.

3 Learning Agent Teammate for Collaborating with Humans

The Learning Agent Teammate for Collaborating with Humans (LATCH) system is a suite of Human-Autonomy Teaming aids that are driven by ML models trained on different aspects of wargaming. The system is currently built to solve different aspects of SC2 due to Blizzard Entertainment's release of large amounts of in-game, human replay data and the creation of the StarCraft II Learning Environment (SC2LE) [11]. The SC2LE was originally created to allow researchers to deploy deep reinforcement learning agents into SC2 for training; additionally, it provides a set of libraries that allows us to build our HAT aids to communicate with the game.

LATCH uses a modular architecture in which each module focuses on one area of an RTS game. Work on a modular architecture was proposed for an

---

[4] Regulation (EU) 2016/679.

[5] https://www.acm.org/articles/bulletins/2017/january/usacm-statement-algorithmic-accountability.

ensemble of different algorithms in SC2 [12], but the work focused on beating the in-game bots rather than building HAT tools. For example, in SC2 there is a concept of a player's Build Order, which is the sequence of logistics-oriented actions that a player must undergo in order to achieve a certain army composition. The Build Order AI agent is housed in one of the modules discussed in this paper.

Table 1. Differences between the modular architecture components from Lee, D. et al. and our components and the type of machine learning technique was used for each module. NN = neural network, CNN = convolutional neural network, LSTM = Long Short-Term Memory.

Module	Lee et al. [12]	Our work
Build order	Fully connected NN	Fully connected NN w/soft-max output
Tactics	CNN	LSTM/CNN, Converted as a visualization agent
Micromanagement	Scripted	Scripted
Worker management	Scripted	Scripted
Scouting	Scripted + LSTM	None

Table 1 shows the differences between the original modular architectural work and how we've either chosen a similar route for solving the problem or experimented with other solutions. Because the nature of each problem was different, some modules were either not done or converted to a different problem type. For example, the Tactics module originally was used for choosing where to send the army. To incorporate this as a HAT tool, we instead use a heatmapping approach discussed the in "Tactical Visualization Agent" section. The goal of the LATCH HMI is for a user to be able to glance at the screen and immediately understand what needs to be done. Each modular component should be able to convey it's information in an easily digestible method (Fig. 1).

A centralized hub manages the communication between the SC2 game environment, data from each of the modules, and inputs from the human player via the human-machine interface (HMI). The HMI is built on a Flask[6] web application and serves as the medium of displaying information from each of the agents/modules (Fig. 2).

This work takes principles of HAT found in literature and how they've been applied within the LATCH system to create a suite of tools to aid human player performance. Alongside the creation of these tools, we seek to explore XAI techniques in order to build trust between human players and the ML-driven HAT tools.

---

[6] https://palletsprojects.com/p/flask.

Fig. 1. The human-machine interface is represented as a web-based GUI on a second monitor that interacts with human input, game environment data, and data from the agent-based modules.

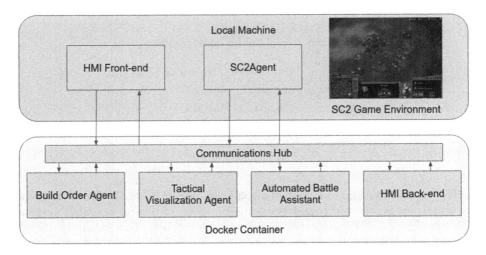

Fig. 2. The modules, HMI back-end, and communications hub reside in a Docker container whereas an SC2Agent and the SC2 game environment are on the local machine. The SC2Agent reads information from the game environment to send back to the hub so that the different modules can obtain the environment data. The SC2Agent also reads data sent by each module and HMI from the hub in order to interact directly with the game. The HMI back-end reads from the hub information sent by each module and displays information on the local machine's web browser.

3.1 Build Order Agent

As stated above, the build order in SC2 is the pattern of production aimed at achieving a certain goal. Build orders, also called macromanagement, are akin to starting formations in Chess, where a player has a general strategy for their unit formation/placements but adapts based on how the game progresses and actions/reactions from the opponent. The Build Order Agent housed inside that module uses a fully connected deep neural network that is trained on what should be built based on a player's current resources and capabilities, enemy units/buildings the player has seen, and the time of the game. Other RTS games might not necessarily have a build order or resource gathering component, but this type of agent and approach can be used in many logistics-oriented sequence problems.

Our Build Order Agent uses a supervised deep learning technique similar to work done on build order agents for a predecessor game, StarCraft: BroodWar [13] with similar results shown in Table 2. The training data was obtained by Blizzard Entertainment's corpus of game replay data. The input vector consisted of the game environment data, as seen by the current player, such as game time, allied units, enemy units seen, and resources.

Table 2. Build order agent results

Metric	Our results	Justesen and Risi [13]
Pairs trained on	623,215	631,657
Pairs tested on	155,804	157,914
Top-1 error rate	38.35%	54.60%
Top-3 error rate	19.86%	22.92%

The machine learning model had a soft-max output layer; this not only gives you an output action and confidence level, but a set of several potential actions with confidence levels represented as percentages for each. This naturally moved into the Build Recommendation component of our HMI. The highest recommended action was represented at the top and the other recommendations followed in descending order. We limit the HMI to representing the top four recommendations in order to not overload players with several options and update the choices every five seconds. SC2 is a very fast-paced game that requires quick decision making; originally the agent was updating the choices and their corresponding percentages every time the game state changed which only introduced more things to look at. Studies have shown that users typically prefer having choices [14]. Suppose you have System A which gives you a highly accurate, singular answer and System B which gives you several answers with confidence levels that may not be as accurate as System A but close enough. Users would prefer System B because of the availability of choice.

3.2   Tactical Visualization Agent

SC2 is played with the *Fog of War* mechanic, which makes the game environment partially observable. This limits the player's information on what the enemy is doing and the movements they make unless they send scouting and reconnaissance units. During our explanation of the modules, we stated that we replaced the original work's Tactics module with a Tactical Visualization agent. The problem was changed from determining "where to send your units" to "how do we convince the player to send their units?"

Work towards using a "defogging" capability [15] has been done, also in StarCraft: Brood War, and we borrow techniques used for SC2. The approach uses an LSTM autoencoder architecture that takes the player's observations as inputs and produces a heatmap as output. We experiment with three different encoder-decoder architectures within the Keras machine learning API: LSTM, convolutional neural networks, and ConvLSTM2D (a combination of convolutional networks and LSTMs). Figure 3 showcases an example heatmap produced by these ML models.

Fig. 3. An example of how the Tactical Visualization module would update the heatmap on the HMI. Red squares represent predicted locations of enemy army units. Blue squares represent predicted locations of enemy stationary structural units. Green squares represent predicted locations of enemy worker and scouting units. (Color figure online)

The color theory behind the heatmap representations was based off a work done showcasing that certain colors do not mean the same across every culture [16]. The experimentation for our study focuses on US-based participants, so we associate the colors in both the HMI and heatmap to fit the findings of this paper. The color red represent locations of enemy army units, which are typically noted as "Danger." This is to have the player avoid sending scouting units in that general direction or exercise caution when doing so in the event the player wants to gain knowledge of the enemy army composition. The color blue is mostly recognized as "Cold" and followed by "Safe". Stationary structural units in SC2 are typically buildings and generally don't represent great threat towards a player. The color green is mostly recognized as "Go" and also "Safe," and since they represent worker/scouting units, it is not a threat to the player at all.

3.3   Automated Battle Assistant

The Automated Battle Assistant encompasses the micromanagement, scouting, and worker management aspect of the modular architecture. This module is mostly scripted and is represented as switch buttons under the "Tools" component of the HMI. This allows the user to automate certain tasks and alleviate some of the workload. Automating the workers would have the module continue producing worker agents, have them gather resources, and distribute them across different bases for optimal resource gathering. Automating the scouting would have the module send worker units to scout the enemy base or areas of interest. A future component would be to have the scouts observe areas of the heatmaps provided by the Tactical Visualization Agent. The two modules can work well with each other, as the Tactical Visualization Agent performs better the more the player scouts and the Automated Battle Assistant can showcase the power of scouting and information gathering to the user. Automating the defense would have the module actively have units on standby and reserve counter-attack any attacks on allied bases.

Due to the current simplicity of the module and need for additional future work, it has very little HAT capabilities incorporated. This module manages 3 different problems in the game, so this can potentially split into new modules that use AI/ML-driven approaches for solutions. However, the issue we try to continue pushing forward is to not overload the operator with several tools and take there attention away from playing the actual game.

4   Discussion and Future Work

When it comes to designing a system that is supposed to work in tandem with a human to form a "team," many designers fail to understand the essence of what a "teammate" is. Many systems that provide general concepts of HAT tend to lean towards intelligent decision support tools, where capability developed is seen as just a tool. When comparing teammates from a field like sports, there's a lot more than just seeing your teammates as tools. Having a mindset that your teammates are just tools or systems typically deteriorates performance as it instills distrust and lack of empathy. The goal of the LATCH tool is to eventually use lifelong machine learning techniques to grow with the human. Other modules developed would be designed to specifically understand the player's preferred play-styles, weaknesses, and strengths. Some of these capabilities and modules may not be represented in the HMI, but in other ways such as pre- and post-game briefs. Athletes in team sports understand the importance of team cohesion, trust, and practice. The level of communication between humans occur before the game, during the game, and after the game. The HMI serves as mechanism for during-the-game communication for on-the-fly decisions and corrections that need to be made to assist the player. A pre-game brief could discuss weaknesses with the players and help adjust their play-style by surveying what they want to practice. A post-game brief could provide an analysis of how well the player did, if they met their goals determined in the pre-game survey, and overall progress tracking. Kulesza et al. [18] introduce 3 principals when creating explainable AI systems: be sound, be complete, and don't overwhelm. However, other studies have shown that every user has different preferences with regards to the types of explanations they want from AI agents [19].

One component of the HMI that was not discussed was the "Hint" section. Presumably, textual hints would appear based on the game state. It is optimal for players to spend resources to continue building their army, advance technology, and create infrastructure instead of having the resource grow and be idle. Hints could provide a way to notify a user to spend resources when they stockpile a large amount, or if the human is optimally gathering as much resources as their infrastructure is capable of supporting. We don't want to overwhelm the user with many suggestions and notifications, as it can ruin the immersion within the game itself and distract the player from more urgent events.

4.1 Experimentation

To evaluate LATCH in this study format, the target sample size is 52 participants. Assuming $\alpha = 0.05$, power $(1 - \beta) = 0.80$, and a medium-to-small effect size $= 0.35$, a minimum of 52 participants are required for a within-subjects, or repeated-measures, design.

The participants for our experiment will be civilian personnel with no prior experience playing SC2, but can have experience playing other RTS games. Recruitment will be through an open call for participants from NIWC Pacific. All participation will be voluntary and participants can withdraw from the study at any time.

Participants will be asked to complete a 20–30 min tutorial and training session that is already built into SC2. They will then complete a total of four SC2 games: two with the LATCH tool and two without. Each game will be played in the in-game map, *Ascension to Aiur*, which is a smaller map in which much of the training data for the machine learning agents learned over. Experimenters will observe participants and collect data from the SC2 environment as well as calculate their performance using the built-in scoring system. A NASA Task Load Index workload questionnaire[7] will be administered after each game and a system usability survey will be administered after each game with the LATCH tool. At the end of the session, the Situation Awareness Global Assessment

---

[7] https://humansystems.arc.nasa.gov/groups/tlx/downloads/TLXScale.pdf.

Technique [17] questionnaire will be administered alongside a trust evaluation questionnaire.

5 Summary

In this paper we presented the Learning Agent Teammate for Collaborating with Humans human-machine interface and how we've incorporated aspects of human-autonomy teaming within our modules and presented methods of explainable AI capabilities. There's still more development of recommendation system modules and experimentation to be done for this tool, but the initial first steps have been taken. Further experimentation is still to be conducted to determine if the tool can help players understand and perform better in real-time strategy games and if the tools can be transferred to more realistic C2-like systems.

References

1. Shively, R.J., Lachter, J., Brandt, S.L., Matessa, M., Battiste, V., Johnson, W.W.: Why human-autonomy teaming? In: Baldwin, C. (ed.) AHFE 2017. AISC, vol. 586, pp. 3–11. Springer, Cham (2018). https://doi.org/10.1007/978-3-319-60642-2_1
2. Ezer, N., Bruni, S., Cai, Y., Hepenstal, S.J., Miller, C.A., Schmorrow, D.D.: Trust engineering for Human-AI teams. In: Proceedings of the Human Factors and Ergonomics Society Annual Meeting, vol. 63, no. 1, pp. 322–362 (2019)
3. Reddy, S., Dragan, A.D., Levine, S.: Shared autonomy via deep reinforcement learning. arXiv preprint arXiv:1802.01744 (2018)
4. Explainable Artificial Intelligence (XAI): DARPA Broad Agency Announcement, DARPA-BAA-16-53 (2016)
5. Rudin, C.: Stop explaining black box machine learning models for high stakes decisions and use interpretable models instead. Nature Mach. Intell. **1**, 206–215 (2019)
6. Goodman, B., Flaxman, S.: European union regulations on algorithmic decision-making and a 'Right to Explain'. AI Magazine **38**(3), 50–57 (2017)
7. Ribeiro, M.T., Singh, S., Guestrin, C.: Why should i trust you?: explaining the predictions of any classifier. CoRR, abs/1602.04938 (2016)
8. Shrikumar, A., Greenside, P., Kundaje, A.: Learning important features through propagating activation differences. CoRR, abs/1704.02685 (2017)
9. Zeiler, M.D., Fergus, R.: Visualizing and understanding convolutional networks. CoRR, abs/1311.2901 (2013)
10. Selvaraju, R.R., Das, A., Vedantam, R., Cogswell, M., Parikh, D., Batra, D.: Grad-CAM: why did you say that? visual explanations from deep networks via gradiant-based localization. CoRR, abs/1610.02391 (2016)
11. Vinyals, O., et al.: StarCraft II: a new challenge for reinforcement learning. arXiv preprint:1708.04782
12. Lee, D., Tang, H., Zhang, J.O., Xu, H., Darrell, T., Abbeel, P.: Modular architecture for StarCraft II with deep reinforcement learning. In: AAAI Fourteenth Artificial Intelligence and Interactive Digital Entertainment Conference (2018)
13. Justesen, N., Risi, S.: Learning macromanagement in StarCraft from replays using deep learning. In: IEEE Conference on Computational Intelligence in Games, pp. 162–169 (2017)

14. Reed, A.E., Mikels, J.A., Lockenhoff, C.E.: Choosing with confidence: self-efficacy and preferences for choice. Judgm. Decis. Mak. **7**(2), 173–180 (2012)
15. Synnaeve, G. et al.: Forward modeling for partial observation strategy games - a StarCraft defogger. In: Proceedings of the 32nd International Conference on Neural Information Processing Systems, pp. 10761–10771 (2018)
16. Sun, Y., Vu, K.-P.L.: Population stereotypes for color associations. In: Harris, D. (ed.) EPCE 2018. LNCS (LNAI), vol. 10906, pp. 480–489. Springer, Cham (2018). https://doi.org/10.1007/978-3-319-91122-9_39
17. Endsley, M.R.: Situation awareness global assessment technique (SAGAT). In: Proceedings of the IEEE 1988 National Aerospace and Electronics Conference (1988)
18. Kulesza, T., Burnett, M., Wong, W.-K., Stumph, S.: Principles of explanatory debugging to personalize interactive machine learning. In: Proceedings of the 20th International Conference on Intelligent User Interfaces, pp. 126–137 (2015)
19. Anderson, A., et al: Explaining reinforcement learning to mere mortals: an empirical study. CoRR, abs/1903.09708 (2019)

Rationality, Cognitive Bias, and Artificial Intelligence: A Structural Perspective on Quantum Cognitive Science

Yoshihiro Maruyama[✉]

Research School of Computer Science, College of Engineering and Computer Science,
The Australian National University, Canberra, Australia
`yoshihiro.maruyama@anu.edu.au`

Abstract. Human beings are not completely rational; there is some irrationality, as well as bounded rationality, involved in the nature of human thinking. It has been shown through recent advances in quantum cognitive science that certain aspects of human irrationality, such as cognitive biases in the Kahneman-Tversky tradition, can be explained via mathematical models borrowed from quantum physics. It has also been shown in quantum cognitive science that human rationality exhibits a special sort of non-classical phenomenon as observed in quantum physics as well, namely the phenomenon of contextuality, which extends the notion of non-locality, what Einstein called "spooky action at a distance". In the present paper we elucidate and articulate the nature of human rationality and irrationality as observed in cognitive bias experiments and cognitive contextuality experiments. And we address the question whether non-human agents, such as animals and robots, can exhibit the same sort of cognitive biases and cognitive contextuality. Technically, we shed new light on these (quantum) cognitive experiments from the viewpoint of logic and category theory. We argue, inter alia, that the logic of cognition is substructural or monoidal, rather than Cartesian (which encompasses classical, intuitionistic, etc.), just as the logic of quantum mechanics and information is substructural or monoidal. The logic of reality is thus intertwined with the logic of cognition; the logical link between physical reality and the conscious mind would possibly allow us to go beyond the Cartesian dualism separating matter and mind as intrinsically different entities.

Keywords: Human rationality · Machine rationality · Animal rationality · Cognitive bias · Artificial intelligence · Substructural logic · Quantum cognitive science

1 Introduction

Rationality has been discussed in various fields of science and humanities, leading us to highly transdisciplinary studies, which are arguably inescapable in light of

D. Harris and W.-C. Li (Eds.): HCII 2020, LNAI 12187, pp. 172–188, 2020.
https://doi.org/10.1007/978-3-030-49183-3_14

the very nature of rationality. There are different traditions of rationality studies, and one of them is the cognitive science of rationality, which is concerned with different cognitive experiments to test the nature of rationality.

In the present paper we discuss cognitive bias experiments in the Kahneman-Tversky tradition (see, e.g., [14,25]) and cognitive contextuality experiments as conceived in recent developments of quantum cognitive science (see, e.g., [4,9,19,22,27]); cognitive bias experiments are also elucidated in a novel manner within the emerging paradigm of quantum modelling of cognition.

It is debatable whether rationality is necessarily of human nature or it can be possessed by other non-human entities. At least primitive forms of rationality can be observed in non-human animals. At the end of the day, rationality could be conceived as the trait of cognition that helps us to survive in different environments; in this conception of rationality, many other animals, or all the existing animals that have indeed survived until now, could be argued to have rationality in one way or another.

It is highly controversial whether cognitive biases are really biases. Quantum modelling of cognition has enabled us to give mathematical models of cognitive biases (see, e.g., [4,9,22,27]), and so there are surely formal rationales for cognitive biases. Human deviations from the principles of classical rationality, such as the ones rational decision theory presupposes, may just mean that human rationality is intrinsically different from classical rationality theoretically posited. It may just be that human rationality is non-classical rationality, such as quantum rationality or of any other non-classical sort.

Concerning the nature of human rationality, Amartya Sen, a Nobel Prize winner in Economics, says as follows [23]:

> [T]he puzzle from the point of view of rational behavior lies in the fact that in actual situations people often do not follow the selfish strategy. Real life examples of this type of behavior in complex circumstances are well known, but even in controlled experiments in laboratory conditions people playing the Prisoners' Dilemma frequently do the unselfish thing.

Classical rationality is arguably selfish. And yet human rationality is (occasionally) not. Deviations from classical rationality as in the Prisoners' Dilemma (which shall be discussed below as well) are systematically unselfish or at least not random phenomena. There is some sort of logic or mechanism underlying the unselfish nature of human rationality, which could be explicated and articulated in different ways. Quantum cognitive science may be regarded as one of such attempts to shed new light on the unselfish and other natures of human rationality.

The rest of the paper is organised as follows. In Sect. 2, we discuss three kinds of cognitive biases in human rationality, and elucidate the nature of rationality in relation to cognitive bias experiments. In the last part of the section we argue that both the logic of reality and the logic of cognition are substructural or monoidal; in contrast to the Cartesian dualist theory, there are certain commonalities between the world of matter and the world of mind (cf. the Chalmers' double aspect theory of information [7]). In Sect. 3, we discuss cognitive contextuality in human rationality, and elucidate the nature of rationality in relation to recent contextuality experiments and violations of Bell-type inequalities in them. In both Sects. 2 and 3, we discuss what happens when human agents are replaced by animal agents or by artificially intelligent agents such as robots. Some cognitive traits still hold whereas others disappear; such considerations on non-human rationality would lead us to a deeper understanding of the nature of human rationality. We finally conclude with brief remarks and outlooks.

2   Cognitive Bias and the Nature of Rationality

In this section we focus upon three kinds of cognitive biases, namely the order bias, the conjunction bias, and the disjunction bias, each of which shall be analyzed in detail in the following. In the last part of the section, we discuss the relationships between the logic of cognition and the logic of reality, both of which are arguably substructural in logical terms or monoidal in category-theoretical terms.

2.1   The Order Effect: Cognitive Non-Commutativity

Non-commutativity is a fundamental property in quantum theory; if all operators are commutative, then all systems must be classical, and there is no such thing as quantum theory at all. A similar phenomenon has been observed in psychology as well, and it is called the order effect or the order bias, a case of cognitive non-commutativity. Most typically, it is the question order bias in particular. A subject's answer to a given question can be affected by the past questions the subject was asked; this is also a case of contextuality, since past questions are contexts for present questions.

A well-known experiment on the question order effect in cognitive science is as follows [21]:

- Q_1: Clinton is honest and trustworthy.
- Q_2: Al Gore is honest and trustworthy.
- If Q_1 was asked first and then Q_2, $\text{Prob}(Q_1) = 50\%$ and $\text{Prob}(Q_2) = 60\%$.
- If Q_2 was asked first and then Q_1, $\text{Prob}(Q_1) = 57\%$, and $\text{Prob}(Q_2) = 68\%$.

This shows that probabilities, $\text{Prob}(Q_1)$ and $\text{Prob}(Q2)$, are affected by the question order. A possible interpretation of the experimental results is that Clinton is less trusted than Al Gore.

Quantum cognitive science gives a mathematical model of the order effect in terms of non-commuting observables A_1, A_2 such that $[A_1, A_2] \neq 0$ (see, e.g., [4]). In terms of substructural logic (see, e.g., [10]), non-commutativity can be modelled by monoidal conjunction $\otimes$, which is non-commutative in the absence of the exchange rule. Quantum-logically, we would have the cognitive violation of distributivity:

$$\text{Prob}(Q_1 \wedge (Q_2 \vee \neg Q_2)) = \text{Prob}(Q_1)$$

does not equal

$$\text{Prob}((Q_1 \wedge Q_2) \vee (Q_1 \wedge \neg Q_2)) = \text{Prob}(Q_1 \wedge Q_2) + \text{Prob}(Q_1 \wedge \neg Q_2).$$

They must be equal in classical probability theory; the laws of classical probabilities are already violated in such a simple case.

Do this sort of biases exist in non-human agents such as robots and animals? Animals would easily be affected by order contexts; for example, dogs would change their answers (or outputs) after they have been given suitable treats, which can be expressed in the form of questions (or inputs). How about robots? If they are solely based upon classical logic and probability theory, they may not change their answers according to the change of question order. However, they would change their answers if they are based upon statistical methods taking contextual information into account, such as the standard vector space model of meaning in natural language processing, which relies, in particular, upon the distributional hypothesis saying that words appearing in similar contexts have similar meanings.

Another question is whether it is rational to be order-sensitive or it is irrational. From an evolutionary point of view, order-sensitivity could be an advantage for survival in certain situations, and in that particular sense, it would be rational to be order-sensitive. If we, however, take logic and truth to be context-independent, then, our logical answer must not be order-sensitive because that means the universal nature of logic and truth is eroded by some contaminated information in actual reality. This conception of rationality may be called absolute rationality. Rationality allowing for context-sensitivity may be called contextual rationality. It would be a matter of philosophical debate whether one of them is more rational than the other. Overall, human rationality is contextual in many respects, and the contextuality of human rationality is linked with the bounded nature of it (for bounded rationality, see [24]).

2.2   The Conjunction Effect: The Linda Experiment

Cognitive biases make the logic of human cognition deviate from the standard classical logic; this happens to be the case for different logical constants. Here we discuss conjunction. The Linda experiment is a notable case of this, exhibiting a pathological behaviour of conjunction in actual human thinking [25]. In the Linda experiment, subjects are given the following description about Linda:

> Linda is 31 years old, single, outspoken, and very bright. She majored in philosophy. As a student, she was deeply concerned with issues of discrimination and social justice, and also participated in anti-nuclear demonstrations.

Then, they are asked to judge which of the following two propositions is more probable than the other:

(i) Linda is a bank teller.
(ii) Linda is a bank teller and is active in the feminist movement.

It is known that most people robustly choose (ii), regardless of their ethnic, geographical, intellectual, and other sorts of background. Why is that? The given description makes Linda look like a feminist, and thus subjects choose (ii) stating that Linda is active in the feminist movement.

In classical psychology, this is understood as the phenomenon of what is called the conjunction effect or the conjunction bias: $\text{Prob}(\varphi \wedge \psi)$, the probability of φ and ψ (φ conjuncted with ψ), should be less than or equal to $\text{Prob}(\psi)$, the probability of ψ, i.e., it must hold that

$$\text{Prob}(\varphi \wedge \psi) \leq \text{Prob}(\varphi)$$

but, in actual Linda-type experiments, to be paradoxical, humans tend to judge that $\text{Prob}(\varphi \wedge \psi)$ is higher than $\text{Prob}(\psi)$. So something is wrong with human thinking in light of classical probability theory.

In classical psychology, the Linda problem is understood as an instance of representativeness biases [14,25]; human cognition takes the probability of a representative case to be higher than the probabilities of other cases (cf. prototype theory in cognitive science [20]). Representativeness biases are also called as representativeness heuristics. Cognitive heuristics give outputs faster than purely logical thinking methods whilst taking the risk of occasional errors; still it works in many typical situations, and thus of practical value in ordinary life, in which there is not necessarily enough time for precise logical thinking. Heuristics are arguably the "mental shortcuts" that human beings have learned in the process of evolution to make their lives easier and increase the probability of survival. Because human beings can be killed by thinking too much in certain situations even if thinking too much eventually leads to correct answers. Put another way, being correct does not necessarily serve the purpose of survival with the limitation of time; speed can be more strongly correlated with the probability of survival.

In such an argument, however, it is presupposed that it is wrong to violate classical probability theory or classical decision theory; in the standard conception of the Linda problem, it is presupposed that it is incorrect to choose (ii). Quantum psychology gives a mathematical model of human judgments in the Linda problem, thereby explicating the underlying logic of human judgments in the Linda problem (see, e.g., [4]). Logically, quantum logic does not really help because $\varphi \wedge \psi \leq \varphi$ holds in quantum logic (most typically, in the algebraic logic of projection operators in a Hilbert space). Substructural logic without weakening (see, e.g., [10]) allows us to invalidate $\varphi \wedge \psi \leq \varphi$; intuitively, this may be understood as saying that having two resources φ and ψ can be more than (not less than or equal to; not $\leq$) having just one resource φ. Substructural probability theory (i.e., probability theory over substructural logic) thus allows us to account for the Linda problem or the conjunction effect. $\text{Prob}(\varphi \wedge \psi) \leq \text{Prob}(\varphi)$ is not necessarily valid in substructural probability theory. The logical meaning of the Linda problem is that conjunction follows the laws of substructural logic rather than classical logic.

Does such a bias exist in non-human agents? It may be difficult, if not impossible, to make animals understand logical constants such as conjunction; even if it is feasible it would still be difficult to make them understand more complex linguistic descriptions. Yet some sort of associations between symbols and judgments may be learnable to relatively intelligent animals, and in such a way, something like the Linda problem may be observed in animal experiments. How about robots? It depends. If the robot reasons based upon formal logic, the Linda problem would never arise. If it rather infers based upon statistical machine learning, then statistical associations between the characteristics of feminists and the description about Linda could reproduce the conjunction effect.

Is the conjunction effect a bias at all? Is it irrational? As we discussed above, the Linda problem is considered to be a case of representativeness heuristics in human judgments, which do have certain advantages over strictly precise algorithms (just as heuristic algorithms do in computer science and artificial intelligence). There is surely some rationale for the conjunction effect, and it is also possible to account for it in terms of non-classical logic such as substructural logic. It, therefore, is not necessarily illogical. If logicality with respect to one conception of logic implies rationality, then the conjunction effect may be regarded as rational. If rationality, however, requires logicality with respect to some absolutist conception of logic, it may not be rational. Put another way, logical pluralism would allow us to consider the conjunction effect rational, whilst logical monism would not (since substructural logic could not be the only possible logic).

2.3   The Disjunction Effect: The Prisoners' Dilemma

There is yet another case of deviation from classical logic in human cognition; let us here discuss the so-called disjunction effect or disjunction bias in the Prisoners' Dilemma. The Prisoners' Dilemma is given by the following, game-theoretical table:

	Confess	Lie
Confess	$(-8, -8)$	$(0, -10)$
Lie	$(-10, 0)$	$(-1, -1)$

The story is as follows: there are two prisoners who committed some crime together and were both arrested; they are interrogated by police officers; if both of them confess then both of them are sentenced to the eight years imprisonment; if both of them lie then they are sentenced to the one year imprisonment; if only one of them confesses then the person who confessed is released and the person who did not is sentenced to the ten years imprisonment. It is assumed that they are causally separated and cannot communicate with each other. Should they confess or lie in such a situation? A prisoner should confess when the other prisoner confesses; this is just because -8 is greater than -10. A prisoner should confess when the other prisoner lies; this is just because 0 is greater than -1. We can thus conclude that a prisoner should confess whether the other prisoner confesses or not. This reasoning leads us to the conclusion that they both confess, and as a consequence, they are sentenced to the eight years imprisonment. This is however not a happy ending; obviously, the total amount of utilities are maximised when both of them lie rather than confess. Classically, the Prisoners' Dilemma may be regarded as indicating that Adam Smith's idea of *laissez-faire*, or his classical free market economic theory, is misconceived. If each agent just pursues its own interest, the greatest amount of total happiness is not necessarily achieved. Classically, this suggests that there should be some intervention in the market as in Keynesian economics.

Yet human beings are not completely rational; they only have bounded rationality. As a result, their behaviour deviates from classical economics or classical decision theory. That is, the rational strategy, in classical theory, is to confess rather than lie, whether an agent knows about the other's choice or not; in practice, more people come to confess when they are told about the other's choice. This is the disjunction effect in the Prisoner's Dilemma. This exhibits violation of Savage's sure thing principle or the so-called law of total probability, that is, it violates:

$$\text{Prob}(\varphi|\psi \vee \neg\psi) = \text{Prob}(\psi)\text{Prob}(\varphi|\psi) + \text{Prob}(\neg\psi)\text{Prob}(\varphi|\neg\psi).$$

What happens in actual human experiments is the following [26]: taking φ as meaning to lie,

$$\text{Prob}(\varphi|\psi \vee \neg\psi) > \text{Prob}(\psi)\text{Prob}(\varphi|\psi) + \text{Prob}(\neg\psi)\text{Prob}(\varphi|\neg\psi).$$

Quantum cognitive science gives a (quantum) mathematical model of this deviation (see, e.g., [4]). Logically, we can again rely upon substructural logic. In (probability theory over) substructural logic without contraction (see, e.g., [10]; also discussed in more detail in the next subsection), we can have the following in a consistent manner ($\wp$ below denotes substructural disjunction in the absence of contraction):

$$\text{Prob}(\varphi|\psi \wp \neg\psi) \neq \text{Prob}(\varphi|\psi \vee \neg\psi).$$

For example,

$$\text{Prob}(\varphi|\psi \wp \neg\psi) > \text{Prob}(\varphi|\psi \vee \neg\psi)$$

can indeed hold in Łukasiewicz logic (in the Łukasiewicz case, $\wp$ is often written as $\oplus$). That is to say, if disjunction is substructural, the invalidity of the law of total probability is no contradiction or paradox, and can happen in a totally consistent manner.

Can the disjunction bias be observed in non-human cognitive systems such as animals and robots? Animals could readily be affected by contextual information about other animals' behaviour. If they are highly rational (in the classical sense), then they may follow the law of total probabilities; yet this is not probable. Animals could even exhibit more strange correlations than human beings. How about robots? If they strictly follow the laws of classical logic and probability theory over them, then they do not deviate from the law of total probabilities, thus exhibiting no disjunction effect. If not, robots could exhibit some disjunction effect as well as human beings. In general, Statistical AI as opposed to Symbolic AI would show some disjunction effect, since they make inferences based upon contextual information in a bottom-up manner rather than upon purely logical principles in a top-down manner.

Is the disjunction effect a case of irrationality? The classical probabilistic rationality does not apply in the disjunction effect as in the Prisoners' Dilemma, but nonetheless the substructural probabilistic rationality does. If it must hold that either we humans are irrational or classical probability theory is wrong, it may be more rational to argue for the latter rather than the former. As to the nature of human rational behavior, Amartya Sen, the first Asian Nobel Prize winner in Economics, says as follows [23]:

> [T]he puzzle from the point of view of rational behavior lies in the fact that in actual situations people often do not follow the selfish strategy. Real life examples of this type of behavior in complex circumstances are well known, but even in controlled experiments in laboratory conditions people playing the Prisoners' Dilemma frequently do the unselfish thing.

Classical rationality is selfish; yet human rationality is occasionally unselfish. If only one of selfish rationality and unselfish rationality is truly rational, the true conception of rationality would be unselfish rationality, for unselfish rationality seems to have contributed much to the human survival. If human rationality is totally selfish, that could possibly extinguish the human race entirely (and it might possibly happen at the end of the day; yet it seems unlikely). The classical conception of rationality does not make room for unselfish rationality, and this is the reason why the non-classical conception of rationality is required in order to elucidate the nature of rationality.

2.4 Logic of Cognition and Logic of Reality

From a logical point of view, the order effect is about the invalidity of the exchange rule, the conjunction effect about the invalidity of the contraction rule, and the disjunction effect about the invalidity of the weakening rule. All this is the major features of substructural rules; they are called structural rules in symbolic logic. The cognitive experiments above may thus be interpreted as saying that the logic of cognition is occasionally substructural.

The cognitive experiments above have also been major concerns in quantum cognitive science, and there are a number of quantum models developed for them (see, e.g., [4]). Here, from a logical point of view, we address the substructural nature of quantum theory or quantum reality. The invalidity of the exchange rule just means non-commutativity, which is a well-known property of quantum theory. In relation to quantum physics, the invalidity of the weakening and contraction rules manifests in what are called the No-Deleting No-Cloning properties of quantum states or quantum information in particular. We can clarify the substructural correspondence between the logic of cognition and the logic of reality in terms of (monoidal) category theory (for monoidal categories, see, e.g., [13]):

- The No-Cloning and No-Deleting theorems state that quantum information (or quantum states in general) can neither be (uniformly) copied nor deleted (see any standard textbook on quantum foundations or quantum computing).
- Categorically, this means that there are no diagonals

$$\delta : H \to H \otimes H$$

and no projections

$$p : H \otimes H \to H$$

in monoidal categories in general, instances of which are categories of Hilbert spaces and dagger-compact categories as in categorical quantum mechanics [2]; in general they do not have diagonals or projections. Note that $\delta : H \to H \otimes H$ and $p : H \otimes H \to H$ are operations to copy (duplicate) and delete states in H, respectively. This is a special property of tensor product, and for direct product, $\delta : H \to H \times H$ and $p : H \times H \to H$ do exist. Note also that entanglement, non-locality, and Bell's theorem (refuting the Einsteinian classical realism) all come from the special property of tensor product.

- The logical meaning can then be explicated as follows. Replacing an arrow $\to$ in categories by deducibility $\vdash$ in logic (they correspond to each other via the so-called Curry-Howard-Lambek correspondence),

$$\varphi \leq \varphi \otimes \varphi$$

is contraction, and

$$\varphi \otimes \varphi \leq \varphi$$

is weakening in terms of substructural logic (note further that δ and p correspond to proofs of these). A principal idea underlying categorical quantum mechanics is that the logic (or type theory) of quantum mechanics is substructural (cf. the traditional Birkhoff-von Neumann's quantum logic is Cartesian, that is, validates both contraction and weakening, even though distributivity is invalid in it; note also that the substructural logic of quantum mechanics is much stronger than what is called linear logic in theoretical computer science). Categorically, monoidal product $\otimes$ coincides with cartesian product $\times$ if and only if $\otimes$ allows both diagonals and projections (under the assumption of exchange or commutativity). Substructural logic (or substructural type theory) is monoidal category theory in disguise.

In terms of No-Cloning and No-Deleting, the conjunction effect is about No-Deleting, and the disjunction effect about either No-Cloning or No-Deleting. The logic of cognitive biases arguably follows the (substructural) logic of quantum information; or at least there is something in common between the logic of cognition and the logic of quantum information, which can be explicated and articulated in terms of monoidal category theory.

3   Cognitive Contextuality and the Nature of Rationality

All of the above cases may arguably be understood in terms of contextuality. In the question order effect, past questions are contexts for present questions, causing cognitive non-commutativity. In the Linda problem, the description about Linda gives a specific context to enable the conjunction effect. The problem per se can be answered without any description, and the description gives rise to a contextual effect, a particular form of which is the conjunction effect. In the disjunction effect in the Prisoners' Dilemma, a prisoner's judgment is affected by contextual information about the other prisoner's judgment. The nature of cognitive contextuality can be studied in a more systematic manner via the theory of Bell-type inequalities as developed in in quantum physics, which per se is a purely statistical theory, and thus, in principle, applies to any statistical correlations, whether they come from physical experiments or cognitive experiments (or whatever else).

The life scientist says, "Life is wet, warm, and noisy". Cognitive systems are sensitive to environments or contexts in general, just as quantum systems are. In a sense, both physics and cognition are sensitive to contextual information. The theory of contextuality is one way to elucidate such an analogy between cognitive science and quantum physics. It has also been experimentally verified that there are certain violations of Bell-type inequalities in cognitive experiments. Let us discuss these in the following.

The classic Bell contextuality (non-locality) correlations can be given in the following manner:

	$(0,0)$	$(0,1)$	$(1,0)$	$(1,1)$
(a_1, b_1)	$1/2$	0	0	$1/2$
(a_1, b_2)	$3/8$	$1/8$	$1/8$	$3/8$
(a_2, b_1)	$3/8$	$1/8$	$1/8$	$3/8$
(a_2, b_2)	$1/8$	$3/8$	$3/8$	$1/8$

Here a_1 and a_2 denote Alice's measurements, and b_1 and b_2 Bob's measurements, Tuples of numbers denote tuples of measurement results of Alice and Bob. Numbers, such as $1/2$, $1/8$, and $3/8$, denote probabilities. For example, when Alice and Bob perform (a_1, b_1) respectively, they get $(0,0)$ respectively with probability $1/2$. The table may look like an ordinary collection of probabilities; however it is actually impossible to realise this probability table via classical physics. There is a quantum realisation, and the table is physically implementable in an actual experiment. Note that Bell-type theorems and Bell-type inequalities about contextuality and non-locality (what Einstein called "a spooky action at a distance") are just concerned with such statistical correlations, which may come from physical experiments, but may come from cognitive experiments just as well (or from any other sort of experiments). From such a perspective, contextuality and non-locality are purely about statistical correlations.

There are different theories of contextuality, such as the theory of logical Bell inequalities (see [1,3]) and the contextuality-by-default theory (see [6,9]). Here we briefly explain logical Bell inequalities, which characterise contextuality as local consistency plus global inconsistency (the contextuality-by-default theory even considers local inconsistency, which can be important in certain cognitive experiments). Abramsky-Hardy's logical Bell inequalities basically look like the following.

- Logical Bell inequalities: $\sum_i \text{Prob}(\varphi_i) \leq N - 1$.
- Logical CHSH inequalities: $|\sum_i E_i| \leq N - 2$ where $E_i = 2\text{Prob}(\varphi_i) - 1$.
- In the Bell table case as above the formulas in the logical Bell inequalities are as follows: $\varphi_1 := a_1 \leftrightarrow b_1$; $\varphi_2 := a_1 \leftrightarrow b_2$; $\varphi_3 := a_2 \leftrightarrow b_1$; $\varphi_4 := a_2 \oplus b_2$.
- Then both of the above logical Bell inequalities are violated; the above inequalities must classically hold.

Abramsky et al. [1] has first given a sheaf theory of contextuality and non-locality, but logical Bell inequalities themselves may be understood in an elementary manner without any knowledge of sheaf theory. Abramsky-Hardy's logical Bell inequalities, in principle, are applicable beyond physics and so to cognitive experiments in particular.

The so-called PR Box is as follows:

	$(0,0)$	$(0,1)$	$(1,0)$	$(1,1)$
(a_1,b_1)	1/2	0	0	1/2
(a_1,b_2)	1/2	0	0	1/2
(a_2,b_1)	1/2	0	0	1/2
(a_2,b_2)	0	1/2	1/2	0

This is known to be super-quantum (i.e., strictly stronger than any quantum correlations, which are strictly stronger than any classical correlations; note that strength is measured by degrees of violation of Bell inequalities) and yet it does not go beyond the no-signalling principle. In the present case the formulas in the logical Bell inequalities are as follows: $\varphi_1 := a_1 \leftrightarrow b_1$; $\varphi_2 := a_1 \leftrightarrow b_2$; $\varphi_3 := a_2 \leftrightarrow b_1$; $\varphi_4 := a_2 \leftrightarrow \neg b_2$. Then the above logical Bell inequalities are violated.

A cognitive experiment by Cervantes-Dzhafarov [6] has yielded super-classical correlations, which are approximately (not exactly) like this:

	$(0,0)$	$(0,1)$	$(1,0)$	$(1,1)$
(a_1^1, b_1^1)	9/10	0	0	1/10
(a_1^2, b_2^1)	8/10	0	0	2/10
(a_2^1, b_1^2)	8/10	0	0	2/10
(a_2^2, b_2^2)	0	6/10	4/10	0

Note that a_i^j means a_i in context b_j; this is the idea of contextuality-by-default. The table above looks very similar to the PR Box; probably the experiment was designed to simulate the PR Box correlations within a cognitive experiment set-up. Since no-signalling is actually violated, Bell inequalities must be extended so as to separate the effect of violation of no-signalling (or what is called direct influence) from the effect of (non-direct and proper) contextuality. Let

$$\tau = \sum_{i \in \{1,2\}} |E[a_i^1] - E[a_i^2]| + \sum_{j \in \{1,2\}} |E[b_j^1] - E[b_j^2]|.$$

Note that τ represents how no signalling (aka. marginal selectivity) is violated. The extended CHSH inequality

$$\text{CHSH} - \tau \le 2$$

is violated in the above cognitive experiment [6], where

$$\text{CHSH} = \max_{k,l \in \{1,2\}} | \sum_{i,j \in \{1,2\}} E[a_i^j b_j^i] - 2E[a_k^l b_l^k] |.$$

Cognitive systems, therefore, exhibit contextuality (in the mathematically rigorous sense) as well as physical (quantum) systems.

Note that logical CHSH inequalities can be extended likewise:

$$|\sum_i E_i| - \tau \le N - 2.$$

Logical Bell inequalities can be extended in the same way:

$$\sum_i \text{Prob}(\varphi_i) - \sigma \le N - 1.$$

In the Cervantes-Dzhafarov case:

$$\sigma = \sum_{i \in \{1,2\}} |\text{Prob}(a_i^1) - \text{Prob}(a_i^2)| + \sum_{j \in \{1,2\}} |\text{Prob}(b_j^1) - \text{Prob}(b_j^2)|.$$

This represents the degree to which no-signalling (aka. marginal selectivity) is violated. Note that no signalling or marginal selectivity makes $\tau = \sigma = 0$; this could hold in a Cervantes-Dzhafarov-type experiment with its question order symmetric, since the asymmetry of probabilities in the original Cervantes-Dzhafarov experiment is arguably caused by the asymmetry of question order. And they are violated in the Cervantes-Dzhafarov experiment (since $|\sum_i E_i| = 4 = \sum_i \mathrm{Prob}(\varphi_i); \tau < 2; \sigma < 1$).

Can non-human agents, such as animals and robots, show cognitive contextuality? The experimental structure of the Cervantes-Dzhafarov set-up is actually quite simple, and as long as a certain sort of associations can be learnable, any primitive animal (possibly even nematodes or roundworms) could simulate the results of the Cervantes-Dzhafarov experiment to the extent that allows for the violation of Bell-type inequalities. The same applies to artificial intelligence, which could learn associations as required in the Cervantes-Dzhafarov experiment in an almost perfect manner, and could even yield the super-quantum experimental results that are equivalent to those of the PR Box; note that the original results were not super-quantum. All this Gedanken experiment indicates that quantum or even super-quantum contextuality can be shown in primitive intelligent agents and the full capacities of human intelligence are not really required to that end. It is an interesting question whether there is any sort of contextuality (or other related phenomena) that can exist in human agents but cannot in animal agents. Even in such a case, probably, artificial intelligence could simulate any of such human and animal agents. Yet such a separation between human and animal intelligence would nevertheless lead to a deeper understanding of what human intelligence really is (or what the intrinsic nature of human intelligence consists in).

There are several remarks to be made about related work. Another perspective on cognitive contextuality is developed in [19], which makes a distinction between erasable contextuality and unerasable contextuality in order to account for a fundamental difference between physical contextuality and cognitive contextuality. Quantum cognitive science is essentially different from Penrose's quantum brain science; the difference is explicated and articulated in [17, 19]. Contextuality studies make sense beyond physics and cognitive science, for example, in linguistic science as well [18]. There are moreover rich conceptual implications at the interface of artificial intelligence, cognitive science, and quantum physics, in particular quantum information [15–17].

4   Concluding Remarks

We finally give several remarks and outlooks as well as the summary of the discussion so far.

Caliskan et al. [5] have shown, in their well-known *Science* article, that the standard machine learning model of natural language processing replicates those human-like biases that implicitly exist in human linguistic practice. Such machine biases, arguably, reflect human biases. While some machine biases come from characteristics of machines themselves, others are results of human biases, that is, machine learning systems learn human-like biases from data containing, whether explicitly or implicitly, human biases. This is a phenomenon in natural language processing. There is another case in vision research; Watanabe et al. [28] have shown that their deep learning model of object recognition replicates the motion-induced illusions that the human agent experience. There is yet another case in information retrieval. It would already be well known that Google's image search engine replicates certain biased associations; for example, the search results with the term *Joshikosei* in Japanese (meaning a female high school student in English) include a number of sexual images (due to a biased association in the Japanese society). Such biased associations surely originate from human biases.

In the present paper we have focused upon cognitive biases in the tradition of Kahneman and Tversky [14], exploring the relationships between human biases and machine biases in terms of cognitive biases in particular. Humans are known to have cognitive biases. Do machines have cognitive biases then? Some even argue that "to be human is to have cognitive biases" [12]. Rather than sticking to giving a single answer to such a question, we have conceived of different possible answers based upon different paradigms of artificial intelligence (i.e., Symbolic AI, Statistical AI, etc.). These considerations would allow us to develop different methods to prevent cognitive biases in AI agents such as robots. Especially, those bottom-up statistical machine learning biases that come from human biases in data could be overcome with the help of top-down symbolic methods; solving Statistical AI bias problems via the methods of Symbolic AI would lead us to a fruitful integration of Statistical and Symbolic AI. In general, disadvantages in bottom-up statistical machine learning methods can be overcome via top-down symbolic methods. It would even result in a novel paradigm of artificial intelligence which could be called Integrated AI as opposed to Statistical AI and Symbolic AI (cf. [8,11] as early instances of Integrated AI for natural language processing); the killer application of Integrated AI may possibly be a solution to machine bias problems.

At the same time we have also discussed the nature of human rationality in contrast with the nature of non-human rationality, such as machine rationality and animal rationality of more primitive form. Cognitive biases are associated with human heuristics, which give fallible and yet more efficient decision making methods than logically rigorous and so infallible ones. We have not presupposed that biases are about irrational aspects of the human mind, and we have explored certain logic or rationales lurking behind cognitive bias phenomena in the human mind.

In general, human rationality or intelligence, at least at the present time, appears quite different from machine rationality or intelligence; for example, the machine can compute much faster than the human, while creativity is lower in the machine than in the human. Yet statistical machine learning allows the machine to get closer to the human, and even enables the simulation of various human biases. In the Linda problem, it is usually considered irrational to choose (ii), that is, "Linda is a bank teller and active in the feminist movement". Machine learning models, however, tell us the mathematical mechanism of human decision making that accounts for why quite some humans tend to choose (ii). Put another way, there is a rationale (or mathematical account) for choosing (ii) rather than (i);

in light of this, choosing (ii) is, arguably, not necessarily irrational. We can thus argue that what is rational is not that obvious in cognitive bias issues. Having said this, it is possible to prevent cognitive biases in AI agents by combining symbolic logical methods with statistical machine learning methods in a suitable way as discussed above.

From a broader perspective, all this helps us to understand the nature of human rationality in relation to non-human rationality such as machine rationality and animal rationality, and it would be fruitful to seek further interactions between cognitive psychology and artificial intelligence. As artificial intelligence is developed further, the psychology of artificial intelligence would become more and more important.

In the present paper we have argued that the logic of cognition is substructural as well as the logic of reality. The Cartesian dualism has long separated the realm of matter and the realm of mind. Yet there are at least certain logical commonalities between the two realms, which could be some sort of meta-laws governing different realms of entities at once. In general, quantum cognitive science tells us different laws shared by microscopic quantum reality and macroscopic human mind, which might be superficial coincidences, and yet might not be. At least it allows us to undermine the presuppositions of the Cartesian dualism, which greatly influenced the practice of science (perhaps in both good and bad ways). As quantum cognitive science advances, we could lead to an entirely new perspective on the relationships between the realm of matter and the realm of mind.

Acknowledgements. The author would like to thank his colleagues (in the JST PRESTO project and others) for the substantial and pleasant discussions that have inspired the present work in many ways. The author hereby acknowledges that the present work was financially supported by JST PRESTO (grant code: JPMJPR17G9) and JSPS Kakenhi (grant code: 17K14231).

References

1. Abramsky, S., Brandenburger, A.: The sheaf-theoretic structure of non-locality and contextuality. New J. Phys. **13**, 113036 (2011)
2. Abramsky, S., Coecke, B.: A categorical semantics of quantum protocols. In: Proceedings of the 19th Annual IEEE Symposium on Logic in Computer Science, pp. 415–425 (2004)
3. Abramsky, S., Hardy, L.: Logical bell inequalities. Phys. Rev. A **85**, 062114 (2012)
4. Busemeyer, J., Bruza, P.: Quantum Models of Cognition and Decision. Cambridge University Press, Cambridge (2014)
5. Caliskan, A., et al.: Semantics derived automatically from language corpora contain human-like biases. Science **356**, 183–186 (2017)
6. Cervantes, V., Dzhafarov, E.: Snow queen is evil and beautiful: experimental evidence for probabilistic contextuality in human choices. Decision **5**, 193–204 (2018)
7. Chalmers, D.: The Conscious Mind: In Search of a Fundamental Theory. Oxford University Press, Oxford (1996)

8. Coecke, B., Sadrzadeh, M., Clark, S.: Mathematical foundations for a compositional distributional model of meaning. Linguist. Anal. **36**, 345–384 (2010)
9. Dzhafarov, E., et al.: On contextuality in behavioural data. Philos. Trans. A Math. Phys. Eng. Sci. **374**, 20150234 (2016)
10. Galatos, N., et al.: Residuated Lattices: An Algebraic Glimpse at Substructural Logics. Elsevier Science, San Diego (2007)
11. Grefenstette, E., Sadrzadeh, M.: Experimental support for a categorical compositional distributional model of meaning. In: Proceedings of EMNLP 2011, pp. 1394–1404 (2011)
12. Hansen, A.: Outsmart Your Instincts. Forness Press, Minneapolis (2017)
13. Heunen, C., Vicary, J.: Categories for Quantum Theory. OUP, Oxford (2019)
14. Kahneman, D., Tversky, A.: Subjective probability: a judgment of representativeness. Cogn. Psychol. **3**, 430–454 (1972)
15. Maruyama, Y.: AI, quantum information, and external semantic realism: Searle's observer-relativity and chinese room, revisited. In: Müller, V.C. (ed.) Fundamental Issues of Artificial Intelligence. SL, vol. 376, pp. 115–126. Springer, Cham (2016). https://doi.org/10.1007/978-3-319-26485-1_8
16. Maruyama, Y.: Quantum pancomputationalism and statistical data science: from symbolic to statistical AI, and to quantum AI. In: Müller, V.C. (ed.) PT-AI 2017. SAPERE, vol. 44, pp. 207–211. Springer, Cham (2018). https://doi.org/10.1007/978-3-319-96448-5_20
17. Maruyama, Y.: The frame problem, Gödelian incompleteness, and the Lucas-Penrose argument: a structural analysis of arguments about limits of AI, and its physical and metaphysical consequences. In: Müller, V.C. (ed.) PT-AI 2017. SAPERE, vol. 44, pp. 194–206. Springer, Cham (2018). https://doi.org/10.1007/978-3-319-96448-5_19
18. Maruyama, Y.: Compositionality and contextuality: the symbolic and statistical theories of meaning. In: Bella, G., Bouquet, P. (eds.) CONTEXT 2019. LNCS (LNAI), vol. 11939, pp. 161–174. Springer, Cham (2019). https://doi.org/10.1007/978-3-030-34974-5_14
19. Maruyama, Y.: Contextuality across the sciences: Bell-type theorems in physics and cognitive science. In: Bella, G., Bouquet, P. (eds.) CONTEXT 2019. LNCS (LNAI), vol. 11939, pp. 147–160. Springer, Cham (2019). https://doi.org/10.1007/978-3-030-34974-5_13
20. Medin, D., Altom, M., Murphy, T.: Given versus induced category representations: Use of prototype and exemplar information in classification. J. Exp. Psychol. Learn. Mem. Cognit. **10**, 333–352 (1984)
21. Moore, D.: Measuring new types of question-order effects: additive and subtractive. Public Opin. Q. **66**, 80–91 (2002)
22. Pothos, E., Busemeyer, J.: A quantum probability explanation for violations of 'rational' decision theory. Proc. Biol Sci. **276**(1665), 2171–2178 (2009)
23. Sen, A.: Rational fools: a critique of the behavioral foundations of economic theory. Philos. Public Aff. **6**, 317–344 (1977)
24. Simon, H.: Bounded rationality and organizational learning. Organ. Sci. **2**, 125–134 (1991)
25. Tversky, A., Kahneman, D.: Judgments of and by representativeness. In: Judgment Under Uncertainty: Heuristics and Biases. Cambridge University Press, Cambridge (1982)
26. Tversky, A., Shafir, E.: Choice under conflict: the dynamics of deferred decision. Psychol. Sci. **3**, 358–361 (1992)

27. Wang, Z., Solloway, T., Shiffrin, R., Busemeyer, J.: Context effects produced by question orders reveal quantum nature of human judgments. Proc. Nac. Acad. Sci. **111**, 9431–9436 (2014)
28. Watanabe, E., et al.: Illusory motion reproduced by deep neural networks trained for prediction. Front. Psychol. **9**, 345 (2018)

A Concept on the Shared Use of Unmanned Assets by Multiple Users in a Manned-Unmanned-Teaming Application

Gunar Roth[(✉)] and Axel Schulte

Institute of Flight Systems, University of the Bundeswehr Munich,
Werner-Heisenberg-Weg 39, 85577 Neubiberg, Germany
{gunar.roth,axel.schulte}@unibw.de

Abstract. In this work, we describe a concept of how multiple users can be given coordinated access to a limited number of unmanned assets. Previous research efforts studied concepts of controlling multiple unmanned vehicles in manned-unmanned-teams. However, these studies imply that the unmanned assets are at one user's exclusive command. Due to their utility however, it is plausible that additional users will have interest in using these assets. To this end, we assign the users to different roles with associated access rights. Derived from established definitions in computer science, we use the terms "host" and "client." To meet variable requirements of users, we define multiple levels of resource sharing that can be requested by the client. Over these levels, control is increasingly transferred from host to client. We then applied this concept to our application and identified additional requirements for the request and the provision of unmanned assets. We furthermore discuss the integration of an assistant system to support the host's decision-making concerning the processing of requests. Mission-planning capabilities allow the assistant system to generate suitable implementations. Based on our concept and the identified requirements, we present our approaches to enable the interaction between host, client, and the assistant system in our application.

Keywords: Human-Machine interaction · Manned-Unmanned teaming · Human-Agent teaming · Assistant system

1 Introduction

1.1 Manned-Unmanned-Teaming

Manned-unmanned-teaming (MUM-T) describes the process of teaming the crew of a manned command vehicle with one or more unmanned vehicles in order to increase mission efficiency and effectiveness [1, 2]. The unmanned assets can support with capabilities such as reconnaissance, surveillance, engagement, or electronic warfare to achieve a given mission goal.

The overall idea with MUM-T is to combine manned and unmanned vehicles to increase mission efficiency by merging their advantages and compensating each other for their respective disadvantages [2]. In these teams, humans contribute most

© Springer Nature Switzerland AG 2020
D. Harris and W.-C. Li (Eds.): HCII 2020, LNAI 12187, pp. 189–202, 2020.
https://doi.org/10.1007/978-3-030-49183-3_15

significantly with their cognitive abilities, such as problem solving, mission planning, the recognition of interconnections and their individual experience [3]. These qualities as well as the authority to decide about potential weapon use make the human vital in such a team. Unmanned vehicles on the other hand, can contribute to mission success with support in reconnaissance by automated sensing and perception, the increase of the sensor range of the manned system and the automated task execution. In particular, remaining distant to potential enemies or potentially hazardous areas can reduce the risk for the manned command vehicle.

1.2   Multiple Users in a Manned-Unmanned-Teaming Application

Previous work studied concepts of controlling multiple unmanned vehicles in manned-unmanned-teams [1, 4–6]. However, these studies imply that the unmanned vehicles are at one user's exclusive command. Due to their utility however, it is plausible that additional users will have need in using these assets. Such a secondary user might be acting cooperatively with the primary user on the joint mission, or be acting independently requesting the unmanned vehicles for their unique purposes.

Besides the advantages of making limited resources available to other users in a MUM-T application, we also expect disadvantageous effects on the primary user's workflow and situational awareness (SA). The user's mental picture of availability, location and planning of resources can be adversely affected by uncoordinated foreign access. Such SA issues are most likely associated with an additional loss of performance, especially when resource capacity is insufficient to cover the additional demand. We aim to reduce SA and performance issues and increase the effective use of the unmanned vehicles by supporting a coordinated use between the users.

2   Concept

In this section, we describe our concept of how multiple users can be given coordinated access to a limited number of unmanned assets. For simplification, we initially consider only two users and a single unmanned vehicle. However, the concept can be applied to multiple unmanned vehicles and multiple users. To develop this concept, we have oriented ourselves on applications of third-party services, such as artillery [7], medical evacuation [8], search and rescue [9], close air support [10], and unmanned aircraft system handover [11].

2.1   Distribution of Roles

When different users access and control an unmanned vehicle, it is crucial that there is a defined role distribution including continuous accountability for the asset. To this end, we define different roles with associated rights that are assigned to the individual users. Derived from already established definitions in computer science, we will use the terms "host" and "client."

The host is responsible for an unmanned asset, makes it available to other users and coordinates its use. The host can either benefit from the asset or only take on a coordinating role. The client represents the external user who wants to use the capabilities of the host's asset. To this end, a request can be directed to the host that specifies the desired use. Depending on the urgency, capabilities and availability of the resources, the host has the ability to accept, reject, modify or offer an alternative to the request. Depending on the requirements, the host can grant the client access to the unmanned asset. However, the host will always be responsible for the asset and also has the necessary authority to revoke the client's access when and if desired. Whereas only one user can be host of an unmanned asset, multiple users can request its use as clients.

2.2   Levels of Shared Use

To meet the variable requirements of both the client and the host, we define multiple levels of resource sharing depicted in Fig. 1. The access by the client ranges over different levels from a purely passive use over an indirect use by means of a request, up to the exclusive active use. Depending on the respective level, the use of the asset by the host is reduced accordingly. It is thereby presupposed that the client holds the necessary competence to access and control the asset.

Level 0. This level serves as a reference as the client is not granted any use of the unmanned vehicle. The host has exclusive usage rights over the asset whereas the client cannot take any advantage of it.

Level 1. On this level, the client is granted passive use of the asset. The client receives results emerging from the host's current use, but cannot actively influence the generation of results. Although the client has no means of using the unmanned vehicle based on own demands, this level offers the opportunity to share the sensor outcomes of an unmanned vehicle without interfering with its control. Thus, this level can support a shared situational picture of the environment.

Level 2. This level enables the client to make unmanned vehicles related task requests to the host and thereby grants indirect control of the asset. The host is required to implement the task and can therefore decide whether to execute it as requested, modify, or reject it. Although this form of shared use increases the coordination effort for the host, it allows them to adapt the requests to their own needs and intentions.

Level 3. While the host was actively using the resource on the previous levels and had sole direct control over it, control is relinquished to the client on level 3. Accordingly, the client is no longer subject to the host's approval of tasks as on level 2. Once the host grants active use, the client can control the asset at their own discretion. However, the host still has the responsibility over the unmanned asset and the authority to revoke the client's usage rights. Consequently, the client can use the resource widely without restriction at this level, yet the host can regain full control of the asset at any time, e.g. because of own demand or due to safety reasons. This level may require less coordination effort for the host because only the unmanned vehicle and the time period have to be assigned to the request, however the corresponding asset is then temporarily unavailable to the host.

Handover. Levels 1 to 3 represent different possibilities for the shared use of an unmanned vehicle, with control continuously shifting from host to client as levels increase. However, the responsibility and authority over the resource remains unaffected and lies always with the host. The remaining option is to transfer responsibility and authority from the host to the client in a handover. This process changes the role distribution in that the client becomes the new host of the asset. The former host becomes a client who is required to make a request to use the asset again.

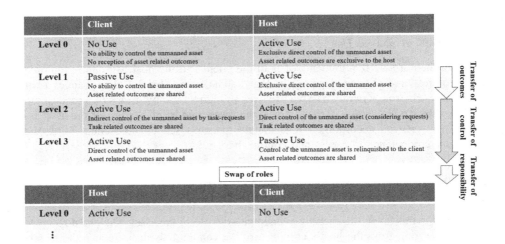

Fig. 1. Levels of shared use.

2.3   Strategies for the Distribution of Resources

Based on the levels 2 and 3 of shared use, various strategies result for structuring a network of several users and several unmanned vehicles. The examples (a)–(c) in Fig. 2 illustrate the distribution of several assets between two users, with one of them hosting all assets. Example (d) presents a configuration with multiple clients and distributed responsibility.

Distributed Shared Use. The unmanned vehicles in example (a) are distributed in such a way that each is used exclusively by one user. Accordingly, the client is either not allowed to have any use (level 0) or shared active use (level 3). Since they are each used exclusively, coordinating their use between multiple users is not required. However, the allocation of the unmanned vehicles to the respective user must be coordinated. Apart from a change in the available resources, host and client are not influenced by each other. It is not necessary that the host has control over at least one unmanned vehicle. It is conceivable that all unmanned vehicles are used exclusively by a client.

Mixed Shared Use. In example (b), some of the unmanned vehicles are used exclusively and some are shared to be used by task-requests. The usage of shared assets must therefore be coordinated so that host and client can make optimal use of them. At the same time, however, assets can be reserved for exclusive use so that conflicts arising from shared use can be cushioned. In addition to the allocation of the users to the unmanned vehicles, the coordination effort is increased accordingly by the coordination of shared use.

Collective Shared Use. In the configuration of (c), none of the unmanned vehicles are used exclusively by a single user. Instead, all assets are shared to be used by client task requests. This requires a very high coordination of their use, yet it provides the possibility to make maximum use of free capacities.

Multiple Clients and Distributed Responsibilities. Until now, we described the distribution of unmanned vehicles between two users, where one acted as host and the other as client. However, responsibility for multiple assets as well as their use is not limited to two parties. Example (d) shows a configuration with three users in which responsibility for the unmanned vehicles is distributed among two of the users, each of whom acts as host, and one acts purely as a client. There is a distributed shared use between host A and client A. Host A, however, is also a client to host B and accordingly supporting user and supported user (client B) at the same time. Host B does not use the own asset, but has a purely providing function. However, the asset is not available to a single client, but is shared by two clients.

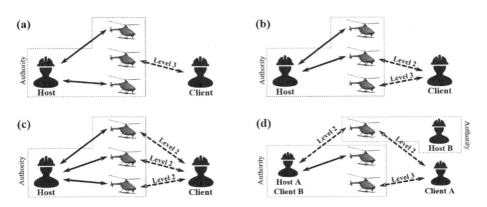

Fig. 2. Strategies for the distribution of unmanned vehicles

3   Application

Our specific research focuses on the teaming of a manned two-seated helicopter and unmanned aerial vehicles (UAVs) to accomplish dynamic and complex military missions [12]. In our scenario, the helicopter crew has multiple UAVs at their command that support the reconnaissance of mission-relevant areas and serve to increase the helicopter's sensing range. They are controlled according to a task-based guidance approach [13, 14]. This approach provides that the UAVs do not have to be controlled manually, but can carry out high-level mission tasks given by the helicopter crew.

Using automation on board the UAV, this complex task is broken down into executable sub-tasks that can be processed in sequence.

In addition to the helicopter crew, a further user is integrated into the mission scenario, who also requires the capabilities of the UAVs to accomplish their own mission. This role will initially be assigned to a ground-based unit such as a forward air controller or a convoy leader. However, this secondary user is not limited to be ground-based, but could also be an airborne unit like another helicopter or a jet fighter.

3.1   Identified Role Distribution

Within our application, we define that the helicopter crew is responsible for the UAVs and therefore acts as host. The additional ground unit serves as client and is authorized to make requests for the temporary use of the UAV services. As host, the helicopter crew is required to decide whether to accept, modify, reject or cancel requests made by the client.

3.2   Identified Levels of Shared Use

In order to interfere as little as possible with the helicopter mission and pilot's use of the UAVs, the scope of usage by the client should be flexibly oriented to its minimum requirements. By applying the levels of shared use to our application, we identified three types of client requests. The transfer of authority is not considered in the following because it is currently not intended to be applied to our application.

Level 1. The client is permitted to receive the UAV's live sensor data and the results from its automated sensor perception. However, no control over the sensor or the UAV is granted. The client cannot actively manipulate the generation of results and is therefore merely a passive recipient. Since only the sensory output is shared with the client, there is no interference with the pilots' use of the UAVs or their mission plan.

Level 2. By requesting specific reconnaissance tasks, the client is enabled to influence the tasking of the UAVs. The requested tasks have to be integrated by the helicopter crew into their own mission plan by assigning them to the schedule of a specific UAV and are therefore subject to their approval. Modifications or rejections of requests have to be tolerated by the client.

Level 3. The client is temporarily given control of the UAV and can thus use it independently to accomplish the individual goal. During this period, the helicopter crew cannot use the UAV for their own needs. However, the responsibility and authority over the UAV remains with the helicopter crew, who can withdraw control from the client at any time.

3.3   Requirements for the Effective Shared Use of Unmanned Vehicles

To enable the effective shared use of unmanned vehicles, it is necessary to identify the requirements for each user. However, we will not discuss technological aspects, such as means of data transmission, but functional aspects of the interaction between host and client. In this context, it is important to consider the relationship between host and client and their specific requirements, depending on whether both users act in a common mission space, require similar situation information or pursue a common mission goal.

Networked Distribution of Tactical Information. According to our defined levels of shared use, the exchange of tactical information concerns only such data that was generated by the respective shared unmanned vehicle. However, tactical information with an origin other than the asset can be essential for an effective sharing of unmanned vehicles. The demand for third-party tactical information is bidirectional. For example, the host requires information from the client to verify how the unmanned vehicle is used in order to wield authority. Additionally, information distribution between cooperating units that operate in a common battlefield is important for overall information superiority and efficient cooperation. After all, it seems contradictory to provide support through the exchange of resources while withholding tactical information in this matter.

However, information distribution between two users is highly dependent on their degree of cooperation. Exchange may include general tactical information (such as positions and attitudes of forces or other kinds of threats), vehicle specific tactical information (such as airspaces, flight corridors or no-fly zones for airborne systems), or mission specific tactical information (such as flight or march routes, mission objectives, points of interest or time over targets).

Request of Resources. Requesting the use of an unmanned vehicle requires information about the availability of the asset and a specified form of the request. A well-defined form of requests can be found in many applications of operational support, such as the artillery, medical evacuation, search and rescue, or close air support [7–10].

Information about the availability of resources and the associated host is crucial to enable the client to make a directed request. The extent to which information on resource availability is shared is again subject to the cooperation between client and host. Information distribution can range from a simple notification that an unspecified number of assets is available to the provision of asset-specific information such as number, capabilities, and scheduled tasks.

A well-defined form and content of the request should ensure that the request is complete. Moreover, uniformity and conciseness should contribute to quick perception and comprehension by the host. Thereby, we have to differentiate between mandatory and optional parameters. Mandatory parameters define the minimal content of a request and thus guarantee that the request is complete. They must also always be defined by the client and should not be modified by the host. If only the mandatory parameters are defined, the host has the greatest possible flexibility to implement the request. Optionally defined parameters allow the client to specify the request more precisely, but in return limit the host's flexibility in implementing the request. The client should therefore be able to indicate whether an optional parameter represents a condition or a preference.

Mandatory parameters are the requested level of shared use, a priority, and, if applicable, the requested UAV task in a level 2 request or the duration of use in level 1 and level 3 requests. If an explicit task is requested, the duration is automatically derived from the duration of the task. Optional parameters are, for example, a specific start time or a specific UAV.

The priority describes the urgency of the request and its importance for the client's mission. The choice of priority should aim to minimize interference with the host's mission plan. For our application, we have defined the three following priorities:

High: The request is time- and mission-critical (e.g. due to a threat to the client).
Medium: The request is mission-critical but not time-critical.
Low: The request is not mission critical, but contributes to mission efficiency.

Provision of Resources. To provide the service of an unmanned vehicle, the host has to verify the request for its general feasibility and then assign a start time and a UAV if these were not specified in the request. Thereby, the host should orient on the priority and the specifications of the client and check whether parameters need to be changed or defined. Since the helicopter crew has to integrate the client requests into their own mission plan, it may happen that they can only approve requests under adjustments. In general, these should be made manually. Alternatively, it should be possible to delegate the modification of these parameters back to the client by indicating the parameters that need to be changed. This should help to reduce the task load of the host and allows the client to choose an alternative at own discretion.

4 Support by an Assistant System

We presume that the workload of the helicopter crew is increased in MUM-T applications, because in addition to controlling the own helicopter they are also responsible for the management of the UAVs [2]. Therefore, our institute has been working on different approaches to support the crew by an assistant system. One approach pursues the support in mission planning and re-planning by applying a mixed-initiative approach. More information on our application can be found in [15, 16].

We expect that the manual processing of the requests will result in an increased task load and workload of the helicopter crew. Therefore, we aim to extend the support by the assistant system to the processing of requests. Assistance shall be provided by verifying the general feasibility of a request and by suggesting a suitable implementation.

4.1 Pre-processing

In order to generate effective responses to requests, the assistant system needs to access additional knowledge from a mission planner. This planner has already been developed to assist in the field of mission planning and re-planning and has knowledge of the current mission plan, including the planned tasks for helicopters and UAVs [15, 17]. Since the mission planner also has knowledge of the mission objective, it can identify tasks that have not yet been planned by the helicopter crew but are important for the completion of the mission. With this knowledge, the assistant system should be able to check the general feasibility of a request and generate a suitable implementation, i.e. to determine which UAV to assign and the start time for an associated request. The basis for this is an optimization considering both the current mission plan and the parameters defined by the client.

4.2 Post-processing

Within the pre-processing, the assistant system determines the best solution in terms of its optimization metrics for implementing the request, although other solutions may also exist. In this way, the host will be supported with the automated generation of alternatives to the initial solution proposal in a post-processing. The assistant system should provide a selection of solutions if several possibilities for implementing a request are identified.

Alternatives can be generated by the assistant system either based on constraints imposed by the host or by free variation. In both cases, this will result in either the assigned UAV, the start time or both being changed. The assistant system then generates a new optimized solution proposal under consideration of the additional constraints. Thus, the generated alternatives may be worse than the initial solution proposal in terms of the assistant system's optimization metrics or they may violate the specifications selected by the client. However, for reasons that are not available to either the client or the assistant system, such as a tactical preference by the pilot crew, it may be necessary to select an alternative.

4.3 Integration

Whereas the automation on board the UAVs is controlled in a hierarchical manner, the assistant system is intended to be in a cooperative relationship with the users. In order to support the processing of client requests, the assistant system should serve as a central gateway for all communication and interaction between host and client. Under this premise, requests can be pre-processed by the assistant system before the pilot is confronted with them. Thus, a generated solution proposal can be presented simultaneously to the corresponding request. Figure 3 shows our application in work-system notation [18]. Visible are the two work processes of the client and the host. They are linked through the interactions of the request and the provision of UAV services. Within a work process, a distinction is made between the workers and the tools. A worker knows and pursues the work objective by own initiative. To achieve it, the worker uses tools in a hierarchically degraded manner. Depending on the automation, it can be located either on the side of the tools or on the side of the workers. The process of mission planning takes place by hierarchically using the planning tools for helicopters and UAVs (green arrows) and can be performed actively by the pilot or passively by the assistant system. Pilot and assistant system are linked cooperatively through the interaction to implementation proposals (blue line).

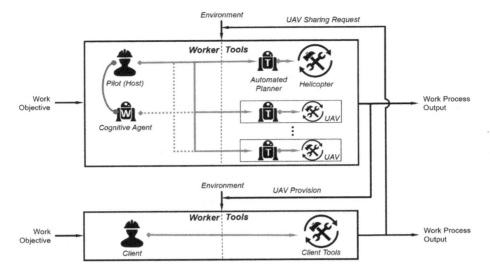

Fig. 3. Our MUM-T application in work-system notation (Color figure online)

5   Implementation

In order to investigate automation and pilot assistance in the scope of MUM-T applications, our institute operates a helicopter research simulator. A generic helicopter cockpit serves to simulate the conduct of military transport missions in combination with three UAVs. The workstation of the ground unit is simulated using a handheld device, which can be used to formulate UAV access requests.

Based on our concept and the application-specific considerations, we have developed a prototype of an assistant system and integrated it into our research simulator. Furthermore, we have implemented interfaces for host and client and the interaction between them and the assistant system. These interfaces are, however, prototypical and subject to continuous development.

In the following sections, we will illustrate the interaction between a helicopter crew and a convoy operating in a common mission area. Thereby, we discuss the request of a reconnaissance task by the convoy and the subsequent interaction between the assistant system and the helicopter crew.

5.1   Interface Client

With the handheld device, the client has access to an interactive tactical map of the simulated operation area with all provided tactical situation information. This map also provides information about the host and available UAVs and serves to initiate and specify UAV access requests.

The requests initially contain the priority, the requested level and, if applicable, the specific task. Using an adjustment menu, the client can then specify the requests by various factors, such as the duration or an explicit start time of the requested service.

In case that the appropriate information about available UAVs (especially their capabilities, positions, and tasks) is provided, the client can also specify the particular UAV.

Figure 4 shows aspects of the client interface. To the left, the tactical symbol of the own unit is shown (blue circle) as well as the planned route (black line). By selecting the upper section of the route, the depicted context menu opens and offers different actions for the referenced object (green bordered). Among other actions, a level 2 request for a recon task can be made here. The right side shows the specification menu after selecting the recon request. The request and the associated reference object are already defined by the general context menu. The priority is preset, but can be adjusted. The UAV and the start time can be selected as optional parameters. After confirmation, the request is forwarded to the host.

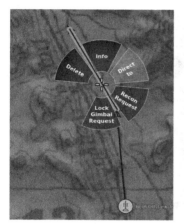

Fig. 4. Parts of the client interface (left: context menu, right: specification menu) (Color figure online)

5.2   Interface Host

The helicopter crew is provided with an interactive map in their displays, which is similar to the client's map but with an extended functionality. It serves, among other things, for overviewing the tactical situation, for tasking the UAVs and for processing client requests. Figure 5 shows the presentation of the request and the corresponding solution proposal that the assistant system has determined during the pre-processing phase. A dialogue box is used to present the request in text form. The yellow exclamation mark indicates that the request has a medium priority.

Below this, also in textual form, is a summary of the proposed solution, which proposes the immediate assignment to UAV1 (orange). In addition, the proposed solution is shown on the tactical map (in the middle of the illustration). Embedded in the mission's situation picture, the proposed solution is displayed as a blue-framed mission arrow, which connects the selected UAV with the location of the requested mission.

Using the dialog box, the host can decide whether to accept the proposed solution, decline the request, or have an alternative generated by initiating the assistant system's post-processing.

Fig. 5. An illustration of the host interface (top: dialog box, middle: visualization of proposed task) (Color figure online)

6   Conclusion and Outlook

We described our concept for sharing unmanned vehicles in a MUM-T application, which aims at allowing multiple users coordinated access to unmanned vehicles. To this end, we defined two different roles with associated rights and responsibilities. The host is the supporting user who provides access to an unmanned vehicle. The client is the supported user who can request respective services. To enable a variable provision of the unmanned vehicles, we defined three different levels of shared use. These levels allow to flexibly transfer control from host to client. We then applied this concept to our application and identified further specific requirements for requesting and providing unmanned vehicles. We furthermore described an assistant system to support the host's decision-making by proposing suitable implementations of requests. Finally, we presented our approaches to the implementation in a helicopter research simulator, in particular the corresponding human-machine interfaces. As an example, we demonstrated and described the process of filing a task request and the associated interaction between the assistant system and the host.

In our application, only a single request was handled at a time. Future efforts aim to enable the processing of several simultaneous requests from one or multiple clients. This is associated with additional requirements for the request and provision of the unmanned vehicles, such as the definition of time dependencies between multiple requests from a single client. Enhancements to the assistant system include the development of different methods to implement requests, adaptive intervention behavior and variable levels of support, based on the crew's workload.

References

1. Uhrmann, J., Strenzke, R., Rauschert, A., Meitinger, C., Schulte, A.: Manned-unmanned teaming: artificial cognition applied to multiple UAV guidance. In: NATO RTO SCI-202 Symposium on Intelligent Uninhabited Vehicle Guidance Systems, Neubiberg (2009)
2. Strenzke, R., Uhrmann, J., Benzler, A., Maiwald, F., Rauschert, A., Schulte, A.: Managing cockpit crew excess task load in military manned-unmanned teaming missions by dual-mode cognitive automation approaches. In: AIAA Guidance, Navigation, and Control Conference, Portland, pp. 6237–6260 (2011)
3. Schulte, A., Donath, D.: Cognitive engineering approach to human-autonomy teaming (HAT). In: 20th International Symposium on Aviation Psychology, Dayton (2019)
4. Wickens, C.D., Dixon, S.R., Ambinder, M.S.: Workload and automation reliability in unmanned air vehicles. Hum. Factors Remot. Oper. Veh. **7**, 209–222 (2006)
5. Parasuraman, R., Barnes, M., Cosenzo, K., Mulgund, S.: Adaptive automation for human-robot teaming in future command and control systems. In: Army Research Lab Aberdeen Proving Ground Md Human Research and Engineering Directorate (2007)
6. Chen, J.Y., Barnes, M.J., Harper-Sciarini, M.: Supervisory control of multiple robots: human-performance issues and user-interface design. IEEE Trans. Syst. Man Cybern. Part C (Appl. Rev.) **41**(4), 435–454 (2010)
7. Field Manual 6-135 – Field Artillery, 10 August 1944
8. Field Manual 4-02.2 – Medical Evacuation, May 2007
9. Joint Publication 3-50 – National Search and Rescue Manual Volume I: National Search and Rescue System, 1 February 1991
10. Joint Publication 3-09.3 – Close Air Support, 25 November 2014
11. Field Manual 3-04.155 – Army Unmanned Aircraft System Operations, April 2006
12. Uhrmann, J., Schulte, A.: Concept, design and evaluation of cognitive task-based UAV guidance. Int. J. Adv. Intell. Syst. **5**(1), 145–158 (2012)
13. Uhrmann, J., Strenzke, R., Schulte, A.: Task-based guidance of multiple detached unmanned sensor platforms in military helicopter operations. In: Cognitive Systems with Interactive Sensors, Crawley (2010)
14. Uhrmann, J., Schulte, A.: Task-based guidance of multiple UAV using cognitive automation. In: The Third International Conference on Advanced Cognitive Technologies and Applications, COGNITIVE 2011, Rome, pp. 47–52. (2011)

15. Schmitt, F., Schulte, A.: Experimental evaluation of a scalable mixed-initiative planning associate for future military helicopter missions. In: Harris, D. (ed.) EPCE 2018. LNCS (LNAI), vol. 10906, pp. 649–663. Springer, Cham (2018). https://doi.org/10.1007/978-3-319-91122-9_52

16. Brand, Y., Schulte, A.: Design and evaluation of a workload-adaptive associate system for cockpit crews. In: Harris, D. (ed.) EPCE 2018. LNCS (LNAI), vol. 10906, pp. 3–18. Springer, Cham (2018). https://doi.org/10.1007/978-3-319-91122-9_1

17. Schmitt, F., Roth, G., Schulte, A.: Design and evaluation of a mixed-initiative planner for multi-vehicle missions. In: Harris, D. (ed.) EPCE 2017. LNCS (LNAI), vol. 10276, pp. 375–392. Springer, Cham (2017). https://doi.org/10.1007/978-3-319-58475-1_28

18. Schulte, A., Donath, D., Lange, D.S.: Design patterns for human-cognitive agent teaming. In: Harris, D. (ed.) EPCE 2016. LNCS (LNAI), vol. 9736, pp. 231–243. Springer, Cham (2016). https://doi.org/10.1007/978-3-319-40030-3_24

Allocation of Moral Decision-Making in Human-Agent Teams: A Pattern Approach

Jasper van der Waa[1,2]($\boxtimes$) (ID), Jurriaan van Diggelen[1],
Luciano Cavalcante Siebert[2], Mark Neerincx[1,2], and Catholijn Jonker[2]

[1] TNO, Perceptual and Cognitive Systems, Soesterberg, The Netherlands
{jasper.vanderwaa,jurriaan.vandiggelen,mark.neerincx}@tno.nl
[2] Interactive Intelligence Group/AiTech, Delft University of Technology,
Delft, The Netherlands
{l.cavalcantesiebert,c.m.jonker}@tudelft.nl

Abstract. Artificially intelligent agents will deal with more morally sensitive situations as the field of AI progresses. Research efforts are made to regulate, design and build Artificial Moral Agents (AMAs) capable of making moral decisions. This research is highly multidisciplinary with each their own jargon and vision, and so far it is unclear whether a fully autonomous AMA can be achieved. To specify currently available solutions and structure an accessible discussion around them, we propose to apply Team Design Patterns (TDPs). The language of TDPs describe (visually, textually and formally) a dynamic allocation of tasks for moral decision making in a human-agent team context. A task decomposition is proposed on moral decision-making and AMA capabilities to help define such TDPs. Four TDPs are given as examples to illustrate the versatility of the approach. Two problem scenarios (surgical robots and drone surveillance) are used to illustrate these patterns. Finally, we discuss in detail the advantages and disadvantages of a TDP approach to moral decision making.

Keywords: Team Design Patterns · Dynamic task allocation · Moral decision-making · Human-Agent Teaming · Machine Ethics · Human Factors · Meaningful human control

1 Introduction

As the field of Artificial Intelligence (AI) progresses, agents will be endowed with far-reaching autonomous capabilities, making them particularly suited for dull, dirty and dangerous complex tasks. Inevitably, such systems must be capable of dealing with morally sensitive situations. The field of Machine Ethics aims to create artificial moral agents (AMAs) that follow a given set of ethical principles [2,21]. Such agents could be developed by constraining their actions or operational environment, by incorporating ethical principles in their decision-making

© Springer Nature Switzerland AG 2020
D. Harris and W.-C. Li (Eds.): HCII 2020, LNAI 12187, pp. 203–220, 2020.
https://doi.org/10.1007/978-3-030-49183-3_16

processes [17], or by making them learn morality from humans [8]. Whereas some authors have speculated about the possibility of obtaining AMAs with human-, or super-human level moral decision making, we believe that this is likely not achievable in the short term [17], if ever.

In the foreseeable future practice, AMAs must collaborate with humans and ensure that humans always remain in control, and thus responsible, over any morally sensitive decision (also referred to as meaningful human control [24]). In this way, the moral decision making takes place at the team level. Different tasks, such as identifying a morally sensitive situation, making the actual decision and explaining this decision, can be allocated at run-time to different team members depending on the current circumstances. This is known as dynamic task allocation [16].

By regarding AMAs as part of a larger human-agent team, the ideas, concepts and theories from Human Factors literature can be used to complement the relative new field of Machine Ethics. This paper aims to structure and propose potential solution directions by proposing the use of team design patterns (TDPs) that capture reusable, and proven solutions to a common problem in a HAT [29].

The purpose of this paper is twofold. First, we show how moral decision-making can be construed as a team task. This allows meaningful human control to be achieved by dynamically allocating tasks to humans and agents depending on properties such as the moral sensitivity, available information and time criticality. Depending on which task allocation strategy is chosen, different levels of moral competences are required from each agent. Our second contribution lies in utilizing the concept of TDPs to describe these options in a structured way. Four patterns are provided and will be discussed within two problem scenarios, namely drone surveillance and robotic medical surgery. Our approach helps to structure current and future research in the application of AMAs and allows for a precise specification of human-AMA collaboration.

In the following sections we briefly discuss possible approaches to develop AMAs and the field of Human-Agent Teaming. This is followed by a description of two scenarios in which moral decision-making plays an important role. We continue with the identification of a set of tasks in moral decision making, including relevant stakeholders. Next, we describe four illustrative TDPs and mention for each requirements for both humans and AMAs and the (dis)advantages of that pattern. The final sections contain a discussion and conclusion on how the concept of task-allocation defined through TDPs offers a novel perspective to deal with morally sensitive situations in human-agent teams.

2   Background

2.1   Artificial Moral Agents

The field of Machine Ethics aims to create AMAs that follow a given set of ethical principles [2,21]. Such agents can be developed by implicitly constraining their action set or the context in which they operate, or by explicitly incorporating ethical principles and theories in their decision-making processes [17]. The former method could improve morality because internal functions can be developed in a manner that avoids unethical behavior, e.g. by properly shifting the responsibility of such decisions to a human or by designing the environment in a manner that such decisions are not necessary. The latter approach allows agents themselves to be intrinsically moral. However, it may be difficult to reach consensus on a moral standard due to cultural, philosophical, and individual differences [32]. In both approaches, it is important to properly identify all relevant stakeholders and elicit their value-requirements for the AMA using approaches such as Value-Sensitive Design [11].

Wallach, Allen, and Smit [32] classify the architectures for explicit AMAs in the *top-down* imposition of ethical theories, and the *bottom-up* building of systems which aim at goals or standards. Top-down approaches must deal with the difficulty of reaching consensus on which ethical theories such a system should follow, and with uncertainty on the world regarding the reasons or impacts of a given action. If such theories are defined too abstract their real-world application might not be possible, but if they are defined too statically, they probably will fail to accommodate new conditions [2,32]. In bottom-up approaches the system builds up through experience what is to be considered morally correct in certain situations [13], for example by analyzing dilemmas and interacting with ethicists [3] or by learning (moral) preferences from human behavior [8,12,20]. Finally, AMAs may also be developed with a hybrid approach (top-down and bottom-up), e.g. [4,15].

The benefits of developing AMAs and whether we should develop such agents is controversial [31]. There are two main lines of arguments supporting the development of AMAs: to avoid negative moral consequences of AI or to better understand moral decision making. We will be focusing on the first one, which relates to a myriad of factors such as which moral values to include, the risks of moral decisions, the complexity of human-agent interaction, the time criticality of moral decisions, and the automation level of the system [9]. Since the development of full AMAs (agents which are capable of autonomously making a "proper" moral decision in any situation) is not achievable in the short term [17], if ever, it is fundamental to understand the limitation of AMAs and research how such agents might be combined in complex human-agent teams.

2.2 Human-Agent Teaming and Design Patterns

The behavior of AI systems should not be studied in isolation [23]. Contextual factors have a major impact on its performance. Furthermore, humans are involved in various ways, e.g. for providing instructions, for correcting the agent if needed, or for interpreting the agent's outcomes. A recent article [14] summarizes this as "no AI is an island", and argues that AI agents should be endowed with intelligence that allows them to team up with humans.

Whereas teaming skills come naturally to humans, coding them into an agent has proven challenging. Some first attempts have been made in [19]. It involves (among others) making the agent decide which information to share with team-mates, which actions to undertake to complement those of its teammates, when to switch tasks, and how to explain its behavior to others that depend on it. Such team behaviors change over time, and depend on the context, competencies and performance of the involved actors, risks, and the state of others.

Despite the intricacies involved, we can observe patterns in team behavior which allow us to describe at a general level how AI systems are to collaborate with humans [18,25]. A team design pattern (TDP) is defined as a description of generic reusable behaviors of actors for supporting effective and resilient team-work [30]. In [29], a simple graphical language is defined to describe team pat-terns, providing an intuitive way to facilitate discussions about human-machine teamwork solutions among a wide range of stakeholders including non-experts. The language includes ways to represent different types of work, different degrees of engagement, and different environmental constraints. The graphical language can be used to capture both time and nesting, which are critical aspects to under-standing teamwork. It enables a holistic view of the larger context of teamwork.

This paper aims to provide TDPs for incorporating AMAs in morally sensi-tive tasks.

3   Problem Scenarios

3.1   Surgical Robots

Medical surgery may benefit from the accuracy and precision of robotic devices. Nevertheless, it is not trivial how to use surgical robots in critically constrained situations involving delicate surrounding tissues, and intricate anatomical struc-tures around which to maneuver [1]. Current surgical robots operate under no autonomy (master-slave teleoperation). Future surgical robot autonomy can be achieved by constraining or correcting human action, carrying out specific tasks, or even operating without any human supervision. Scenarios in which robots perform entire medical procedures (with or without human supervision) are not likely in the foreseeable technological future [10].

From a moral standpoint, it must be possible to hold someone responsible when surgery fails, avoiding a so-called *responsibility gap* [10]. Moral implica-tions on the development and use of surgical robots are largely depending on its autonomy [22]. If a surgical robot is not autonomous at all, moral issues are mostly related to the surgeons' fitness, or training. With increasing autonomy the system might be confronted with moral dilemmas that arise during surgery. Depending on the time that is available to make a decision, the robot or the surgeon must make that decision (assuming that passing the decision making task to the human requires more time). Surgical robots must align with best practices in codes of conduct in the medical domain [28] as well as different val-ues and best practices among surgeons. The surgical robot problem scenario can be characterized as follows:

– **Moral values**, e.g. human welfare (curing the patient, performing safe surgery), autonomy (surgical robots should respect a patient's decision).

- **Moral dilemmas**, e.g. choosing between performing a critical task in brain surgery with risk of brain damage (conflicts with safe surgery), or aborting the surgery with the consequence of greatly reduced life expectancy (conflicting with curing the patient).
- **Risks**: Improper actions during the surgery may impose long term risks (e.g. incomplete recovery), or short-term risks (e.g. acute medical complications). The severity of these risks may be small (leading to minor inconveniences or temporary light pain), to severe (leading to severe life long handicaps, or death).
- **Time criticality**: Some decisions (such as stopping a bleeding) require high decision speed. Other tasks (such as disinfecting a wound) may be less urgent.

3.2 Drone Surveillance

Unmanned aerial vehicles are aircraft that can fly without an onboard human operator. Such vehicles are attractive for military applications, e.g. for surveillance and even delivering airstrikes [5]. However, these applications come with moral implications, especially for autonomous aircraft which might select and engage targets autonomously [24]. It is also within this context that the term *meaningful human control* has been coined.

The use of unmanned aerial vehicles (commonly known as drones) is not exclusive to military applications. Surveillance applications of drones include environmental monitoring, tracking of livestock and wildlife, observing large infrastructures such as electricity networks, and the surveillance of people and the spaces they pass through [7].

One of the most widely discussed moral implications of drone surveillance is related to privacy, which is not unique to the application of drones but is heightened by technology [27]. We can identify three sub-tasks for surveillance drones (adapted from [5]): *search* an area to find a person with suspicious behavior or that matches given criteria, *profile* the person by classifying appearance and movement, and *warn* the person. One example of a moral implication is to *profile* a person in an open space. This task may require a drone to harm people's behavioral privacy and freedom. Such systems should be properly designed to account for an individual's rights and potential moral implications. This drone surveillance problem scenario can be characterized as follows:

- **Moral values**, e.g. privacy, safety, physical integrity [7].
- **Moral dilemmas**: Profiling (which compromises privacy) versus not profiling a person (which compromises safety).
- **Risks**: Risks can be low (such as a minor invasion of privacy through video recording during profiling, or failing to prevent shoplifting), or high (such as warning innocent people with force, or failing to prevent a terrorist attack).
- **Time criticality**: Some decisions (such as stopping a person that is about to attack someone) require high decision speed. Other decisions (such as deciding where to do surveillance in a peaceful situation) require low decision speed.

4   Tasks and Actors

This section outlines a set of common abstract tasks and actors that are relevant in teamwork within morally sensitive environments.

Figure 1 shows a decomposition of team work in general and work required for moral decision making in specific. In this paper, we refer to a task as *work* to stress that it need not be ordered by someone.

Work can be divided in direct and indirect work. As defined in [29], *direct work* is any type of work that aims at reducing the distance to the team goal, whereas *indirect work* aims at making the team more effective or efficient at achieving the team goal, but does not move the team closer to its goal. Direct work includes, but not limited to, *sensing, decision making* and *acting*. A special type of decision making, particularly relevant for this paper, is *moral decision making*. We define this as making decisions that have a moral dimension; that is, 'right' or 'wrong', or something in between [6].

Indirect work includes *standing by, work handover*, and *work supervision*. An agent on *standby* is receptive to requests from other agents to intervene work. *Supervision* means that the agent is not doing the work by itself, but is monitoring other agents for events that require intervention. One of the resulting interventions could be a reallocation of tasks, which are often facilitated by a *work handover* activity. During *handover*, agents share information (or lack thereof) about task progress, present threats and opportunities, relevant contextual factors, etc. to allow for a fluid transition.

Indirect work related to moral decision making are *moral supervision, value elicitation* and *explaining the moral context*. This follows in part the model of ethical reasoning from [26]. This model identifies the need for *moral supervising*: The identification of a situation as being morally sensitive. A morally sensitive situation involves moral dimensions sufficiently important to warrant the more involved moral decision-making as opposed to regular decision-making. Hence, *moral supervision* consists of *recognizing situations, identifying moral dimensions*, and *decide on dimension significance* [26]. *Value elicitation* is the work in which human moral values are made explicit and transferred to an artificial agent. This can be done once, iteratively or continuously. Finally, agents might require to *explain the moral context* to allow other agents to take part in the moral decision-making work.

For this paper, we distinguish between four types of agents relevant in moral decision-making as depicted in Fig. 2. These play a role in our illustrative TDPs. This list can be extended with more agents when relevant and required for a pattern (e.g. with clients, designers, developers, etc.). The four agent types are *Human Agent, Artificial Agent, Partial AMA* and *Full AMA*. Each differ in their competence with moral decision-making and related indirect work. The *Human Agent* is capable of performing moral decision-making due to a human's (assumed) innate ability in moral supervision and decision-making. The *Artificial Agent* is only competent in work not related to moral decision-making. Most current AI systems fall under this type of agent. The *Partial AMA* cannot autonomously perform moral supervision, moral decision-making or both.

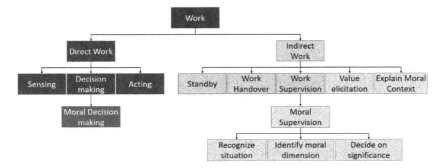

Fig. 1. An overview of several important kinds of work for moral decision-making in a human-agent team context. Solid colors denote work directly related or contributing to the main task, whereas a pattern fill denotes indirectly related or supportive work. Blue denotes regular work, as opposed to red that denotes work related to moral decision-making. (Color figure online)

However, it can support a more competent agent (e.g. a *Human Agent* with such work. The *Full AMA* is able to make human or super-human moral decisions independently. These examples of agent types serve as an exemplar decomposition of competencies in agents to construct TDPs on moral decision-making as we do below.

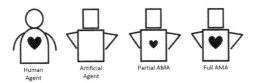

Fig. 2. An overview of several important tasks and their related actors for moral decision-making in a human-agent team context.

5   Team Design Patterns for Moral Decision-Making

This section illustrates four patterns that dynamically assign moral decision-making work to different agents. A pattern is described in a single table, containing its name, both a textual and visual description, requirements for both humans and agents, and potential advantages and disadvantages. For the visual description, we adopt the graphical language proposed by [29], which also allows direct translation to a formal language. In addition to a table, the scenarios described in Sect. 3 function as examples on how each pattern could function.

The visual pattern language is intended to be intuitive and serves to quickly explain an approach to a multi-disciplinary group of researchers and facilitate focused discussions. Task allocation is expressed in a single frame where certain agents lift certain blocks, signifying that they are (jointly) performing that work. Dynamic task allocation is represented by a temporal succession of such frames, separated by arrows. A dashed arrow from an agent to a temporal arrow denote that agent takes the initiative to switch between an alternative task allocation.

5.1 TDP1: Human Moral Decision Maker

In this first pattern, all work related to moral decision-making are allocated to *Human Agents*. All work that is not morally sensitive is assigned to *Artificial Agents*. The *Human Agents* need to perform *moral supervision* and *work supervision* to obtain sufficient situation awareness to halt relevant *Artificial Agents* and make the moral decisions in time. The pattern's effectiveness relies heavily on a sufficient cognitive workload for the *Human Agents*. An overload might result in reduced moral decision performance as the human lacks important situation awareness. An underload might result in distractions or drowsiness which is detrimental to *moral supervision*, resulting in missed moral decisions that end up being implicitly made by the *Artificial Agents*.

In the surveillance problem scenario, the drones can perform largely autonomously as *moral decision-making* applies only to the less frequent decisions of profiling and warning. Human operators are supervising the intentions and information streams from drones. Their task is to monitor the progression of work to sufficiently understand situations relative to the task at hand, while also processing drone intentions to intervene when a drone decision is morally sensitive. As the number of drones increases, operators will lack the required situational understanding due to cognitive overload. Decisions to profile or warn might be made too often or too little, affecting task performance. Similar issues will play a role in the surgical robot problem scenario.

This pattern allows *Artificial Agents* to behave autonomously while moral responsibility lies fully at the human. However, this pattern is unsuited when constant task and moral supervision demands a too high of a cognitive workload on the available *Human Agents* (Table 1).

5.2 TDP2: Supported Moral Decision-Making

This pattern is similar to TDP1 but does not require *Human Agents* to *supervise work*. A major disadvantage of the previous pattern, TDP1, was that both *work* and *moral supervision* could result in the cognitive overload of *Human Agents*. The omission of *task supervision* from *Human Agents* alleviates this but would lead to an insufficient situational understanding for *moral decision making*. To remedy this, the interrupted agent explains the situational context in such a way that supports *Human Agents* in their *moral decision-making*. Hence, an *Artificial Agent* with no knowledge about morality is insufficient, and a *Partial AMA* is required with enough knowledge about morality to identify what to explain and do so sufficiently.

Under this pattern, the surgical robot would provide relevant information when interrupted by a doctor. This relevance should be based on a combination

Table 1. TDP1: human moral decision maker.

Name:	**Human moral decision maker**

Description:	An *Artificial Agent* performs autonomously the main task, while a *Human Agent* supervises for sufficient situational awareness and to assess a situation's moral sensitivity. When the human perceives the need for a moral decision, the human takes over decision-making.
Structure:	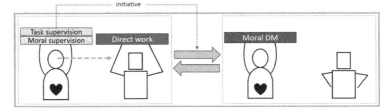
Requirements:	1. The *Human Agent* must predict morally sensitive decisions in time. 2. The *Human Agent* must have a sufficient understanding of the moral implications. 3. The *Artificial Agent* must be capable of halting and resuming its work at any time.
Advantages:	+ The *Human Agent* is responsible for any made or missed moral decisions. + *Artificial Agents* do not require any moral competencies.
Disadvantages:	– The *Human Agent* may suffer from cognitive under- or overload when performing both *task* and *moral supervision*, preventing the perception of morally sensitive decisions and/or to make them in time. – The *Human Agent* may become an ethical scapegoat if this pattern is wrongly applied.

between context and a model of moral values. For example, the robot is aware of a complication that comprises the patient's welfare. At this point a doctor interrupts and intents to remedy this complication. However, the robot is aware that remedying this complication could reduce the patient's quality of life to such an extent that conflicts with the patient's previously communicated decision regarding quality of life. This is a clear dilemma caused by conflicting moral values (human welfare and human autonomy). As such, the robot reiterates the patient's decision and explains how the available decisions reduce the quality of life. This allows the doctor to make this moral decision with more information, as opposed to acting instinctively and remedy the complication.

Table 2. TDP2: supported moral decision-making.

Name:	**Supported moral decision making**

Description: An *Artificial Agent* performs autonomously the main task, while a *Human Agent* only supervises for the situation's moral sensitivity. When the human perceives the need for a moral decision, the human takes over decision-making. The *Partial AMA* supports the *Human Agent* through explanations about the situation relevant for the current moral decision.

Structure:

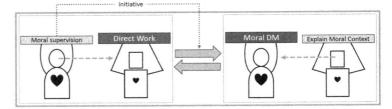

Requirements:

1. The *Human Agent* must predict morally sensitive decisions in time.
2. The *Human Agent* must have a sufficient understanding of the moral implications.
3. The *Artificial Agent* must explain the moral context sufficiently to allow a *Human Agent* to make moral decisions.
4. The *Artificial Agent* must be capable of halting and resuming its work at any time.

Advantages:

+ The *Human Agent* may suffer from less cognitive overload as the need for sufficient situational understanding is reduced.
+ The *Human Agent* is responsible for any made or missed moral decisions.

Disadvantages:

− The *Human Agent* may suffer from cognitive underload when performing *moral supervision*, preventing the perception of morally sensitive decisions and/or to make them in time.
− The explanation may bias the *Human Agent* unintentionally, creating a responsibility gap.

The main advantage of this pattern is that it still attributes moral decision-making to a *Human Agent* while omitting the need for constant *task supervision*. However, the explanations from a *Partial AMA* could potentially bias the *Human Agent* in a decision, causing a potential responsibility gap. Furthermore, *moral supervision* may prove to strain cognitive workload just as much as *task* and *moral supervision* combined. Both would severely reduce the use of this pattern.

This pattern is an example on how the disadvantage of one pattern (TDP1) can lead to another pattern (TDP2) and introduce an additional multi-disciplinary research challenge (how to sufficiently explain a moral context). In addition, the pattern description directly supports multi-disciplinary research. In this case, researchers from Human Factors can provide explanation requirements to allow unbiased and effective *moral decision-making*. These requirements can then be used by researchers from Machine Ethics to research how a *Partial AMA* can fulfil these requirements. Throughout, the TDP offers a common ground (Table 2).

5.3   TDP3: Coactive Moral Decision Making

This third pattern alleviates humans even further compared to TDP2. This pattern sets *Human Agents* on *stand by*, meaning that they are free to perform other unrelated work. However, it requires from *Partial AMAs* to also perform *moral supervision* to warn *Human Agents* when a moral decision has to be made. Furthermore, since *Human Agents* are not at all involved a *work handover* is required. This is a sufficient period of time to update *Human Agents* with the current task at hand, progression, situational context and more. In addition, as *Partial AMAs* identify the need for a moral decision in this pattern, they are obliged to also *explain the moral context*. Finally, to further ensure *Human Agents* to be capable of making a moral decision, the *Partial AMA* is involved directly in *moral decision making*. Here, the *Partial AMAs* function as a decision-support systems. They might analyze boundaries based on their computational moral model to rule out certain decisions, or take a data-driven approach and suggest decisions in line with past desirable outcomes. These approaches all require *Partial AMAs*, as they require a broad sense of morality but not sufficiently detailed enough to allow them to make moral decision autonomously.

Using this pattern both the surveillance drones and surgical robot would play a vital role in *moral decision-making*. The drones are allowed to identify civilians that should be profiled or warned, and to provide their human operator with an overview of the situation, followed with a decision supported directly by their input. The surgical robot performs its work autonomously but when it needs to make a decision that could affect the patient's (quality of) life in an unexpected way, the surgeon will be involved through tele-operation where the surgical robot provides an information feed, reasoning and potential limitations on the surgeon's decisions.

The main advantage of this pattern is that it allows *Partial AMAs* to fully act autonomously until a moral sensitive situation. In such a case, the *Human Agent* is involved, updated and supported in making the moral decision. The

Table 3. TDP3: coactive moral decision-making.

Name:	**Coactive moral decision making**

Description: A *Human Agent* is on *stand by*, potentially doing unrelated work, while an *Partial AMA* performs *direct work* and *moral supervision* to detect moral sensitive situations. When this occurs, the *Partial AMA* initiates a *work handover* and *explanation of moral context* to involve the human sufficiently in the work. This is followed with the *Human Agent* and *Partial AMA* jointly making the moral decision.

Structure:

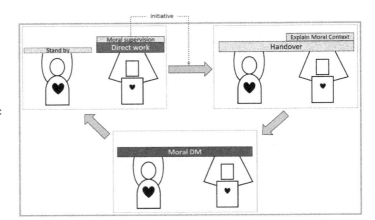

Requirements:
1. *Human Agent* needs to be on *standby*.
2. The *Human Agent* and *Partial AMA* must have a sufficient understanding of moral implications.
3. The *Artificial Agent* must explain the moral context sufficiently to involve a *Human Agent* in a moral decision.
4. The *Partial AMA* must support the *Human Agent* in *moral decision-making*.

Advantages:
+ The *Human Agent* does not need to *supervise work* or perform *moral supervision*.
+ The *Human Agent* still makes moral decisions and is supported to do so with a *Partial AMA*.
+ The *Partial AMA* do not make moral decisions autonomously.

Disadvantages:
− The *Human Agent* cannot intervene in the *Partial AMA's* work.
− The *work handover*, *explanation of moral context* and co-active *moral decision-making* may bias the *Human Agent*.
− The handover may introduce too much overhead for agents and humans to make a moral decision in time.

main disadvantage is that this pattern could widen the responsibility gap as the *Human Agent* relies almost fully on the *Partial AMA* for *moral decision-making*, except for making the actual decision.

This third pattern illustrates how TDPs can be used to describe complex ideas, while making potential flaws more transparent that would require future research. In addition, this pattern illustrates how TDPs can have complex intricacies, dependencies and effects, which all require extensive evaluation in experiments (Table 3).

5.4 TDP4: Autonomous Moral Decision Making

This final pattern makes use of *Full AMAs* to fully automate both *direct work* as well as *moral decision-making*. This pattern illustrates how such a *Full AMA*, and a *Partial AMA* for that matter, can be obtained and maintained. It introduces *value elicitation* to explicitly elicit the moral values from *Human Agents* and reliably transfer these in *Full AMAs*. This process can be repeated after a predetermined time (e.g. after a single decision or a longer period of time) to warrant for inadequacies, moral drift and other factors. This elicitation process allows *Full AMAs* not only to perform the *direct work* autonomously, but also to perform *moral supervision* and independently *make moral decisions*. The explicit work of *moral supervision* allows humans to check when, and even if, the *Full AMA* identifies morally sensitive situations adequately.

Within the surveillance scenario, drones will act as the *Full AMAs* and require a decision-model that follows the set of relevant human values elicited beforehand. The drones will be activated and no human will be further involved in the *direct work* or *moral decision-making*, up until a new *value elicitation* is deemed necessary. The same occurs for the surgical robot scenario, where the doctor will only activate the surgical robot after some elicitation process.

A major advantage is that any moral decisions can be traced back to a controlled elicitation process. However, this is only true when the method with which human values are elicited is adequate and their incorporation into the agent is faithful to those elicited. Also, human values are subject to change hence new iterations of *value elicitation* should be determined.

This final pattern illustrates how TDPs may look seemingly simple, but may require a substantial effort from the research community to achieve. Furthermore, this pattern illustrates the idea that patterns can regard any abstraction and temporal level. Finally, this shows that patterns can be combined. A *value elicitation* can be deemed necessary to obtain a *Partial AMA* as well. As such, this pattern may find a place in any of the previous three TDPs (Table 4).

Table 4. TDP4: autonomous moral decision-making.

Name:	**Autonomous moral decision making**

Description:	Values are being elicited from the *Human Agent* and incorporated in the *Full AMA's* decision model. The agent performs the *direct work*, *moral supervision* and *moral decision-making* autonomously leaving the *Human Agent* free.

Structure:	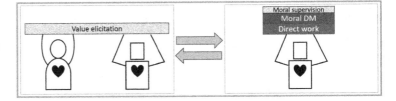

Requirements:	1. Moral values need to be adequately elicited from the *Human Agent*. 2. The *Full AMA* must adequately incorporate human values in a decision model. 3. The *Full AMA* must predict morally sensitive decisions in time. 4. The *Full AMA* must have a sufficient understanding of the moral implications.

Advantages:	+ No *Human Agent* required after value elicitation. + All relevant work except for *value elicitation* is done autonomously. + Autonomous moral decisions can be traced back to a controlled *value elicitation*.

Disadvantages:	− Impossible with the current state of the art to effectively implement this pattern. − Human values may prove to be impossible to elicit adequately. − Difficult to determine when to repeat *value elicitation*.

6   Discussion

The above four TDPs illustrated our proposed approach on a dynamic task allocation perspective to moral decision-making. In this section we discuss the versatility of this approach, as well as its drawbacks, in more detail.

Each TDP proposes a solution on an abstract level, which can then be made concrete with more detailed sub patterns. A sub-TDP describes an aspect of its super-TDP in more detail. For example, *value elicitation* can be done through forced choice experiments and discrete choice modelling [6], inverse reward design [12], but also methods from value-sensitive design [11]. Each of these could be used as a sub-TDP to realize *value elicitation* in TDP4. This varying level of abstraction in TDPs and the capability to nest and/or link them, shows the versatility of a TDP approach to dynamic task allocation for moral decision-making.

However, a difficulty of the TDP approach could arise from the potential combinatorial explosion of TDPs than can be nested and linked. This can be handled by two approaches on how to define and construct a TDP. The first approach is top-down, where all possible combinations in nesting and linking a set of TDPs is viewed as a complete description of the solution space. Next, the space will be pruned by scientific theories, the current state of what is possible, and rigorous evaluations over different scenarios. The advantage of this approach is that it can be done systematically and is scenario independent. The disadvantage lies in how the initial set of sub-TDPs should be defined. The second approach is bottom-up and is more scenario-driven. Given a specific problem within a scenario, a solution is found, generalized to a TDP, and followed by evaluations over scenarios. The advantage is that this approach is driven by a current problem and its solution is generalized to apply for other scenarios as well. However, a disadvantage is that the complete solution space is never fully acknowledged and certain solutions may be overlooked.

As discussed earlier, the TDP approach enables a dynamic task allocation and teaming perspective to moral decision making. However, when there is disagreement around this perspective, the TDP approach is not suited to structure that discussion as it assumes it by default. Furthermore, TDPs assign responsibility to humans and agents but they are not meant to define responsibility in a legal way. A TDP defines a generic solution to an often occurring problem over different scenarios, it does not define regulation or policy on responsibility. TDPs can however, structure the discussion around policy on task allocation strategies. For example, policies on meaningful human control and if TDPs should allow for it directly (e.g. TDP1 and 2), indirectly (e.g. TDP3 and 4), or prevents it.

The clear visual language, structured description and formalisation of a TDP invites different disciplines and parties to discuss and share research, ideas and arguments. This is a clear advantage in the multi-disciplinary and -party research on moral decision-making. The risk lies in that TDPs can become simplifications of a problem. This risk arises when a TDP be to generic and loses a connection to a reoccurring problem, but it may also arise when TDPs are only used to structure discussions instead of also evaluating and implementing them over a variety of scenarios.

7   Conclusion

We proposed the concept of team design patterns (TDPs) to unify ideas from Machine Ethics on artificial moral agents (AMAs) with ideas from Human Factors on dynamic task allocation in human-agent teams (HATs). Such patterns describe how and when AMAs can be applied to perform moral decision-making within a HAT. These patterns offer a way to structure and specify generic solutions, and the discussion around them, on issues related to responsibility gaps, meaningful human control and co-active moral decision-making. We identified a limited set of tasks relevant to moral decision-making, specifically moral supervision and (co-active) moral decision-making. A similarly set of actors were identified, where we defined an AMA as either being a Partial AMA that supports only specific elements of moral decision-making, and a Full AMA that has the capabilities to perform moral decision-making fully autonomously. These tasks and actors were then used in four illustrative TDPs. These patterns ranged from the human performing all morally sensitive tasks, towards the AMA performing them all, with two patterns to illustrate that a Full AMA is not required to aid moral decision-making with an intelligent agent. With these, we showed how TDPs can help define requirements on moral decision-making, how the difficulties on implementing AMAs can be bypassed by an appropriate TDP, and how one TDP can lead to another to improve or extend the former or to explore a different approach. Although none of the four illustrative TDPs offer the golden solution to moral decision-making, we believe that a TDP approach stimulates structured discussions and design when it comes to morally sensitive AI applications.

We offered the TDP approach to structure the multi-disciplinary field of researching moral decision-making from a dynamic task allocation and HAT perspective. Future research will focus on evaluating these patterns, ultimately aiming at the construction of a library of TDPs for this field.

References

1. Abbink, D.A., et al.: A topology of shared control systems-finding common ground in diversity. IEEE Trans. Hum.-Mach. Syst. **48**(5), 509–525 (2018)
2. Anderson, M., Anderson, S.L.: Machine ethics: creating an ethical intelligent agent. AI Mag. **28**(4), 15–15 (2007)
3. Anderson, M., Anderson, S.L.: GenEth: a general ethical dilemma analyzer. Paladyn J. Behav. Robot. **9**(1), 337–357 (2018)
4. Arnold, T., Kasenberg, D., Scheutz, M.: Value alignment or misalignment-what will keep systems accountable? In: Workshops at the Thirty-First AAAI Conference on Artificial Intelligence (2017)
5. Beckers, G., et al.: Intelligent autonomous vehicles with an extendable knowledge base and meaningful human control. In: Counterterrorism, Crime Fighting, Forensics, and Surveillance Technologies III, vol. 11166, p. 111660C. International Society for Optics and Photonics (2019)
6. Chorus, C.G.: Models of moral decision making: literature review and research agenda for discrete choice analysis. J. Choice Model. **16**, 69–85 (2015)
7. Clarke, R.: The regulation of civilian drones' impacts on behavioural privacy. Comput. Law Secur. Rev. **30**(3), 286–305 (2014)
8. Conitzer, V., Sinnott-Armstrong, W., Borg, J.S., Deng, Y., Kramer, M.: Moral decision making frameworks for artificial intelligence. In: Thirty-First AAAI Conference on Artificial Intelligence (2017)

9. Dignum, V.: Responsible Artificial Intelligence: How to Develop and Use AI in a Responsible Way. Springer, Cham (2019). https://doi.org/10.1007/978-3-030-30371-6

10. Ficuciello, F., Tamburrini, G., Arezzo, A., Villani, L., Siciliano, B.: Autonomy in surgical robots and its meaningful human control. Paladyn J. Behav. Robot. **10**(1), 30–43 (2019)

11. Friedman, B., Hendry, D.G.: Value Sensitive Design: Shaping Technology with Moral Imagination. MIT Press, Cambridge (2019)

12. Hadfield-Menell, D., Milli, S., Abbeel, P., Russell, S.J., Dragan, A.: Inverse reward design. In: Advances in Neural Information Processing Systems, pp. 6765–6774 (2017)

13. IEEE Global Initiative, et al.: Ethically aligned design: a vision for prioritizing human well-being with autonomous and intelligent systems (2018)

14. Johnson, M., Vera, A.: No AI is an Island: the case for teaming intelligence. AI Mag. **40**(1), 16–28 (2019)

15. Kim, T.W., Donaldson, T., Hooker, J.: Grounding value alignment with ethical principles. arXiv preprint arXiv:1907.05447 (2019)

16. Lerman, K., Jones, C., Galstyan, A., Matarić, M.J.: Analysis of dynamic task allocation in multi-robot systems. Int. J. Robot. Res. **25**(3), 225–241 (2006)

17. Moor, J.H.: The nature, importance, and difficulty of machine ethics. IEEE Intell. Syst. **21**(4), 18–21 (2006)

18. Neerincx, M.A., van Diggelen, J., van Breda, L.: Interaction design patterns for adaptive human-agent-robot teamwork in high-risk domains. In: Harris, D. (ed.) EPCE 2016. LNCS (LNAI), vol. 9736, pp. 211–220. Springer, Cham (2016). https://doi.org/10.1007/978-3-319-40030-3_22

19. Neerincx, M.A., et al.: Socio-cognitive engineering of a robotic partner for child's diabetes self-management. Front. Robot. AI **6**, 118 (2019). https://doi.org/10.3389/frobt.2019.00118

20. Noothigattu, R., et al.: A voting-based system for ethical decision making. In: Thirty-Second AAAI Conference on Artificial Intelligence (2018)

21. High level expert group on artificial intelligence. Ethics guidelines for trustworthy AI (2019). https://ec.europa.eu/futurium/en/ai-alliance-consultation. Accessed 12 May 2020

22. O'Sullivan, S., et al.: Legal, regulatory, and ethical frameworks for development of standards in artificial intelligence (AI) and autonomous robotic surgery. Int. J. Med. Robot. Comput. Assist. Surg. **15**(1), e1968 (2019)

23. Rahwan, I., et al.: Machine behaviour. Nature **568**(7753), 477–486 (2019)

24. de Sio, F.S., Van den Hoven, J.: Meaningful human control over autonomous systems: a philosophical account. Front. Robot. AI **5**, 15 (2018)

25. Schulte, A., Donath, D., Lange, D.S.: Design patterns for human-cognitive agent teaming. In: Harris, D. (ed.) EPCE 2016. LNCS (LNAI), vol. 9736, pp. 231–243. Springer, Cham (2016). https://doi.org/10.1007/978-3-319-40030-3_24

26. Sternberg, R.J.: A model for ethical reasoning. Rev. Gen. Psychol. **16**(4), 319–326 (2012)

27. Thompson, R.M.: Drones in domestic surveillance operations: fourth amendment implications and legislative responses. Congressional Research Service, Library of Congress (2012)

28. Tung, T., Organ, C.H.: Ethics in surgery: historical perspective. Arch. Surg. **135**(1), 10–13 (2000)

29. van Diggelen, J., Johnson, M.: Team design patterns. In: Proceedings of the 7th International Conference on Human-Agent Interaction, pp. 118–126. ACM (2019)

30. van Diggelen, J., Neerincx, M., Peeters, M., Schraagen, J.M.: Developing effective and resilient human-agent teamwork using team design patterns. IEEE Intell. Syst. **34**(2), 15–24 (2018)
31. van Wynsberghe, A., Robbins, S.: Critiquing the reasons for making artificial moral agents. Sci. Eng. Ethics **25**(3), 719–735 (2019). https://doi.org/10.1007/s11948-018-0030-8
32. Wallach, W., Allen, C., Smit, I.: Machine morality: bottom-up and top-down approaches for modelling human moral faculties. AI Soc. **22**(4), 565–582 (2008). https://doi.org/10.1007/s00146-007-0099-0

The Cueing Effect in Retrieval of Expertise: Designing for Future Intelligent Knowledge Management System

Liang Zhang[1,2], Xiaoqin Li[3], Ting Xiong[4], Xiaoyue Pang[5], and Jingyu Zhang[1,2(✉)]

[1] Key Laboratory of Behavioral Science, Institute of Psychology, Chinese Academy of Sciences, Beijing 100101, China
zhangjingyu@psych.ac.cn
[2] University of Chinese Academy of Sciences, Beijing 100049, China
[3] School of Psychology, Beijing Sport University, Beijing 100084, China
[4] Department of Psychiatry, Dalhousie University, Halifax, NS B3H 4R2, Canada
[5] Siemens Ltd. China, Beijing 100102, China

Abstract. Along with the rapid technological developments in the past few decades, human work is becoming more knowledge-based, and professional expertise is becoming even more important. In this way, effective methods to retrieve and transfer such expertise are greatly needed. Prior research has found that pictures can be used as visual cues for supporting general memory retrieval, but whether this effect can be used to support professional expertise retrieval is not fully understood. The aim of the present study is to explore whether the picture cues can support the retrieval of professional expertise in a typical mechanical fault diagnosis task. Sixteen postgraduates who majored in mechanics with vehicle repair experience took part in the study. On the first day, they were trained for 1.5 h on a simulated vehicle maintenance and repair task. After that, they were asked to accomplish three fault diagnosis tasks. On the next day, they participated in a 30-min expertise retrieval test. In the test, they were presented with or without picture cues (i.e., key-picture-cue, random-picture-cue, and without cues) and then answered questions to measure their memory over yesterday's operations. The results showed that participants retrieved more accurately with picture-cues compared to the scenario without the cues, and the accuracy in the key-picture-cues scenario was higher than the random-picture-cues scenario. These results show a robust cueing effect in the retrieval of expertise in fault diagnosis operations and indicated a potential application of expertise retrieval and transfer when designing an intelligent knowledge management system in the future.

Keywords: Memory retrieval · Cueing effect · Fault diagnosis · Professional expertise · Knowledge management

D. Harris and W.-C. Li (Eds.): HCII 2020, LNAI 12187, pp. 221–230, 2020.
https://doi.org/10.1007/978-3-030-49183-3_17

1 Introduction

Information explosion, along with the fast development of manufacturing technology, is reforming world industries. Whereas automation is widely used, human decision making is still vital. This is especially the case for performing complex technical tasks that require a great deal of expertise, for example, diagnosing a fault in a complex system [1]. To solve such a problem, the operators need to retrieve the most critical information from the vast amount of professional knowledge store in their memory. Given the fast increasing of knowledge, it is becoming more and more challenging.

The intelligent knowledge management system is believed to resolve such a challenge as it can store, manage, and present the key knowledge in an organization [2]. When proper information is provided to operators at the right time, the problem solving and decision-making process can be enhanced. However, building a system that can directly providing the solutions also relies heavily on operators' knowledge and experience, which is not only time consuming but returns to the chicken-and-egg problem as well [3].

One possible solution is to take a swarm intelligence perspective to build a self-growing system. In such a system, some easily accessible information of the individual level operations (e.g., the video or photos of performing certain tasks) can be collected in an unobtrusive manner, evaluated by their peers for further synthesis, and then presented to operators to promote the retrieval of their already-had knowledge. Whereas the first two steps can be achieved by modern technologies, e.g., the wide-spread cameras in nowadays factories, and the very familiar online comment system, a key question should be answered first: whether presenting this easily accessed information can enhance operators' memory retrieval?

Previous psychological studies have shown that pictures can be used as visual cues to support memory retrieval [4, 5]. It is proposed that generative retrieval is a cue generating process in which additional cues that provide contextual information, including the target event, are produced [6]. Moreover, memories are retrieved faster in response to the concrete cues compared with the abstract cues [7].

Such an effect has been tested out of the laboratories in daily contexts with the help of new photographic technology. Many life-logging systems have been developed both in research laboratories and as commercial products [8, 9], and studies have used these products to investigate whether these systems can help people retrieving their auto-biographical memories. They found that some kinds of picture cues captured by life-logging technologies, e.g., SenseCam images, can provide effective links to events in people's personal past. Interestingly, the cues automatically captured by the system were as effective in triggering memory as images that people captured on their own initiative [5].

The pictures captured randomly can induce the cueing effect of memory retrieval provides an important basis for the proposed new intelligent knowledge management system. If such an effect holds true, the pictures captured by the cameras in factories could be used as the cues for supporting expertise retrieval. However, whether this kind of cueing effect also exists in performing a complex task in the factory environment is not fully understood yet. Therefore, in this study, we used different types of picture cues to investigate the cueing effects on memory retrieval for the fault diagnosis tasks. Based on the previous evidence, we hypothesized that: compared with the cue-free condition, participants would retrieve more memories with cues.

2 Methods

2.1 Participants

Sixteen postgraduates (all male, mean age = 23.53 ± 1.06 years, ranged from 22 to 26 years, majored in mechanics) voluntarily participated in this study. All of them had learned mechanics-related knowledge for more than 4 years. One participant's data was excluded because he had less experience and could not remember the experimental process after training. Thus, 15 participants' data were included in the analysis. Before starting the experiment, the participants were briefed about the experimental protocols and signed informed consent forms voluntarily. The experiment took two days to accomplish. Afterward, participants got their compensation for participation.

2.2 Experimental Platform and Tasks

In the experiment, a computerized simulation calling "Car Mechanic Simulator (CMS)" was used as the experiment platform. CMS is designed to simulate automobile maintenance and repairing, which is highly detailed and realistic. It displays the interfaces as same as the scenes in the auto repair plant. Users in CMS play the role of car mechanics and repair cars for clients. Participants were required to complete three tasks, namely, fault diagnosis tasks. In each task, they received a description of the condition and faults of the car, and then they had to fix up the problem according to the description. To this end, they needed to remove the faulty parts, purchase new parts, and replace the new one. In the experiment, each participant needed to complete all of the three diagnostic tasks, and the orders were counterbalanced.

The six items of NASA-TLX were used to collect the ratings of mental workload right after the task was accomplished. Also, the participant was required to evaluate the task difficulty by answering a 7-point item, "how difficult do you think the task is?" (1 represents very easy to 7 very difficult.).

The retrieval performance was measured with a 16-item questionnaire. The questionnaire consists of two kinds of operations, i.e., effective operations and ineffective operations. Effective operations were defined as the operations of detecting, removing, purchasing, and replacing faulty parts, while ineffective operations were defined as the operations of detecting, removing, purchasing, and replacing non-faulty parts. Furthermore, the retrieval performance was evaluated by three dimensions (namely retrieval type, see Table 1), i.e., integrity, specificity, and operation order. Integrity referred that participants' recall of the main operational steps during the diagnosis task, including both operations directly related and not directly related to the task, such as the number and the name of the failure auto parts; the specificity referred that participants' recall of some more detailed information, such as the inspections and operations performed during the troubleshooting. More detailed information about the retrieval task was shown in the following "procedure" session.

Table 1. Dimensions of the retrieval questionnaire.

Operations	Retrieval type
Effective operations	Integrity
	Specificity
	Operation order
Ineffective operations	Integrity
	Specificity

2.3 Experiment Design

The cue type was varied as a within-subjects variable at three levels. In the cue-free condition, there were no pictures as a cue in the retrieval task. In the key-cue condition, the picture cues were selected by experimenters from the scene closely related to task completion. In the random-cue condition, picture cues were captured automatically by computer at a fixed time interval.

2.4 Procedure

The experiment took two days to accomplish. On the first day, the experiment consisted of a training session and a formal session (Fig. 1 presents the experimental procedure). In the training period, the participants were offered a brief training on the mechanics of the automobile. Then the participants completed three practice diagnostic tasks with a guidebook describing the detailed steps of fault diagnosis. The total training time was approximately 1.5 h, including three 5-min breaks.

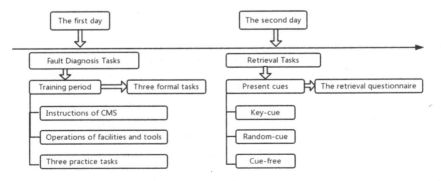

Fig. 1. The experiment procedure.

In the official session, the participants were asked to accomplish three tasks without any guidance. The three tasks were evaluated by experts beforehand so that the difficulty and complexity were similar. In each task, there was a description briefly describing the car's condition and problems, and then participants were asked to diagnose the faults and to find three faulty parts according to the description with a time limit (30 min). The operation process of each task was automatically recorded by screen recording software. After accomplishing each task, the participants were asked to complete the NASA-TLX questionnaire and evaluate the task difficulty, and then had a 2–5 min break.

The next day, the participants came to the laboratory again. They were asked to retrieve memories about the operating process of three diagnostic tasks accomplished yesterday in three scenarios (with key-cue, with random-cue and no cue). Participants were given a brief description of each task, and then Picture cues (10 key-cue pictures, 10 random-cue pictures, and, without pictures) were presented to help the participants recall their completion process one day before. Each picture was presented for 10 s and approximately 25 cm × 14 cm in size as key cues or random cues. Finally, the participants completed the retrieval questionnaire as well as the NASA-TLX questionnaire and task difficulty question. The diagnosis tasks, the types of the cue, and the retrieval tasks were all presented randomly to balance the potential influences (Fig. 2) .

Fig. 2. The scenarios of the experimental platform.

2.5 Data Analysis

The results were analyzed using repeated measured ANOVAs in this article.

3 Results

3.1 Task Difficulty and Workload

In both fault diagnosis tasks and retrieval tasks, participants were required to report their subjective workload and evaluate the task difficulty. In order to control the potential influence of task difficulty and workload, these two were manipulated as control variables. In order to test whether there were differences between differences in task difficulty and subjective workload among the three fault diagnosis tasks and three retrieval tasks, repeated measured ANOVAs were conducted. The average score of task difficulty and the subjective workload was shown in Table 2.

Table 2. The descriptive statistics of task difficulty and workload

Cue type	Task difficulty mean (SD)	Workload mean (SD)
Fault diagnosis task		
Key-cue	3.53 (1.51)	56.73 (17.06)
Random-cue	3.40 (1.30)	57.93 (15.05)
Cue-free	4.00 (1.31)	61.33 (14.52)
Retrieval task		
Key-cue	4.20 (1.08)	56.00 (12.43)
Random-cue	4.87 (1.06)	59.93 (14.13)
Cue-free	4.67 (1.23)	58.67 (12.38)

The results showed that there are no significant differences in task difficulty ($F(2,15) = 1.470$, p = 0.247) and subjective workload ($F(2,15) = 0.844$, p = 0.441) among the three fault diagnosis tasks. Moreover, participants did not self-report significant differences in task difficulty ($F(2,15) = 1.856$, p = 0.175) and workload ($F(2,15) = 2.086$, p = 0.143) among three retrieval tasks.

3.2 Retrieval of Effective Operations

Retrieval Integrity and Specificity Under Different Cue Scenarios. Conditions. In order to test the effect of the cue type on retrieval integrity and specificity, a 3 (cue type: key-cue, random-cue, cue-free) × 2 (retrieval type: integrity, specificity) repeated measure ANOVA was performed. Figure 1 presents the retrieval accuracy of effective operations for all types of cues (namely key-cue, random-cue, and cue-free), and both types of retrievals (namely integrity and specificity). For the effective operations, there was a main effect of retrieval type such that accuracy for integrity was significantly higher than for specificity ($F(1,15) = 12.68, p < 0.05, \eta^2 = 0.48$, see Fig. 3). No effect of cue type ($F(2,15) = 1.88, p = 0.172$) nor interaction were detected.

One-way ANOVA was tested for the integrity accuracy and specificity accuracy, separately. The results showed that the main effect of cue type was not significant for Integrity ($F(2,15) = 0.390$, p = 0.680, $\eta^2 = 0.027$). But a significant main effect of cue type was found for the specificity in the effective operations ($F(2,15) = 3.369$, p < 0.05, $\eta^2 = 0.194$). The post hoc analysis showed that participants retrieved more accurate with the key-cue (0.87 ± 0.11) compared to the cue-free (0.72 ± 0.21) (p < 0.05) and random-cue (0.87 ± 0.11, marginally significant, p = 0.084). There was no significant difference between the random-cue and the cue-free condition (p > 0.1).

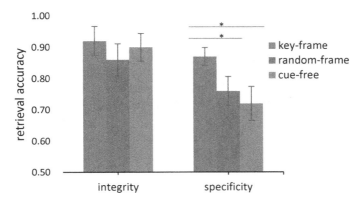

Fig. 3. The retrieval accuracies for effective operations.

Retrieval for Operation Order. We were also interested in determining whether there was a cueing effect in retrieving the operation order. Therefore, a repeated-measures ANOVA was conducted to examine the effect of cue type (key-cue, random-cue, and cue-free) on retrieval for the integrity of operation order. We found a marginally significant main effect of cue type ($F(2,15) = 2.523$, $p = 0.098$, $\eta^2 = 0.153$ see Fig. 4.). The post hoc analysis showed that the retrieval accuracy was significantly higher in the key-cue scenario (0.67 ± 0.28) than the cue-free scenario (0.46 ± 0.24) ($p < 0.05$). And there was no significant difference between key-cue and random-cue (0.51 ± 0.27).

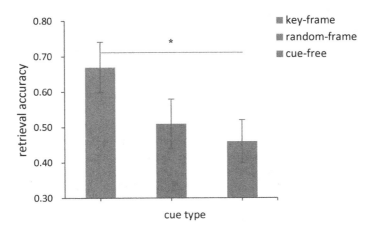

Fig. 4. The accuracies for the operation order among different cue types.

3.3   Retrieval of Ineffective Operations

For ineffective operations, a 3 (cue type: key-cue, random-cue, cue-free) × 2 (retrieval type: integrity, specificity) repeated measures ANOVA was conducted. The results showed that there was a significant main effect of retrieval type ($F(1,15) = 133.14$, $p < 0.0001$, $\eta^2 = 0.905$, see Fig. 4.) on retrieval accuracy, whereas the main effect of cue type ($F(2,15) = 1.03$, $p = 0.371$) and interaction ($F(2,15) = 0.80$, $p = 0.46$) were not significant (Fig. 5).

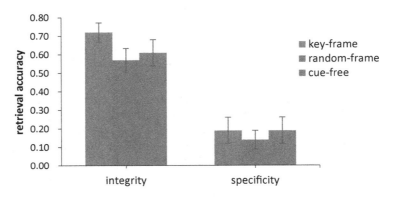

Fig. 5. The retrieval accuracies for ineffective operations.

4   Discussion

The present study investigated the cueing effect on memory retrieval during simulated vehicle maintenance and repair operation. Participants who majored in mechanics took part in the study, and all of them were trained ahead to be familiar with the fault diagnosis tasks. They were asked to retrieve the operating process of fault diagnosis they performed one day before. The results showed that: firstly, there was no difference in perceived task difficulty and subjective workload among the three fault diagnosis tasks. Thus, the retrieval differences between the tasks were not caused by task difficulty or workload. Secondly, there was a main effect on the retrieval type (integrate vs. specific memory). The accuracy of integrity was higher than that for specificity. This is in line with the real situation. It is easier to recall the main operational steps than detailed information. But sometimes details are the key to solve problems. Intelligent knowledge management systems are also designed to help with coping with imprecise information.

Thirdly, as to the cueing effect, a significant cueing effect was found for the specificity in the effective operations. Participants retrieved more accurately with the key-cue compared with the cue-free and random-cue scenarios. In the key-cue scenario, the accuracy rate of operation orders retrieval is higher than the other two scenarios. This suggests the key-cue has positive effects on memorizing the operational sequence. In our study, the key-cue pictures were selected from the steps closely related to task completion. According to previous studies [5], these visual cues may provide contextual information and facilitate target retrieval. While the random-cue pictures were captured from the participant's operation scene at a fixed time interval. We did not find a cueing effect in the random-cue scenario. This result is different from the previous studies with SenseCam, in which the automatically captured cues were found to be as effective in triggering memory as images captured by the participants [6]. One possible reason is that the interval in Sellen's study was much longer (3 versus 10 days) than the present study (1 day). As the interval increases, the retrieval increases, and difficult, thus increasing the magnitude of the cueing effect.

Another possible reason is that the participants in this study were relatively homogeneous. They all have studied mechanical related knowledge for more than four years, and have a good understanding of automobile mechanics. Thus, they could be regarded as "experts" to solve car-repairing problems because they were able to master the operation process after the training. Therefore, both the problem-solving tasks and samples in this study are very similar to scenarios in real factories.

In the present study, the simulated vehicle maintenance and repair operation tasks that we chose are very similar to the factory maintenance task. The approaches and the processes to solve the problems have great uncertainty. In this type of problem-solving task, it requires participants to put up hypotheses through the problem, and then verify or eliminate these hypotheses one by one, then finally solve the problem through their own knowledge and practical experience. To help users to complete this kind of problem-solving task is the main focus that intelligent knowledge management systems are designed for. Therefore, the cueing effect we found shows a new approach to help with the expertise retrieval and transfer in the industry. However, it is worth noting that the number of participants in the study is limited, and the test interval is relatively short. Further studies are needed to verify whether the cueing effect exits for the other demography over a longer period of time.

Acknowledgment. This research was supported by the National Key Research and Development Plan (Grant No. 2016YFB1001201, 2018YFC0831001 and 2018YFC0831101), and the National Science Foundation of China (U1736220). We are particularly grateful to the support of the Siemens-CAS program "Research in Human-Autonomous System Incorporating with Knowledge."

References

1. Holsapple, C. (ed.): Handbook on Knowledge Management 1: Knowledge Matters, vol. 1. Springer, Berlin (2013). https://doi.org/10.1007/978-3-540-24746-3
2. Maier, R., Hadrich, T.: Knowledge management systems. In: Schwartz, D., Te'eni, D. (eds.) Encyclopedia of Knowledge Management, 2nd edn, pp. 779–790. IGI Global, Hershey (2011)
3. Szczerbicki, E. (ed.): Intelligent Systems for Knowledge Management, vol. 252. Springer, Berlin (2009). https://doi.org/10.1007/978-3-642-04170-9
4. Gennip van, D., Hoven van den, E., Markopoulos, P.: Things that make us reminisce: everyday memory cues as opportunities for interaction design. In: Digital Collections, Practice and Legacy, pp. 3443–3452 (2015)

5. Sellen, A., Fogg, A., Aitken, M., Hodges, S., Rother, C., Wood, K.: Do life-logging technologies support memory for the past? An experimental study using SenseCam. In: Rosson, M.B., Gilmore, D. (eds.) Proceedings of the ACM CHI 2007 Human Factors in Computing Systems Conference, 2nd edn, pp. 81–90. ACM Press, New York (2007)
6. Uzer, T.: Retrieving autobiographical memories: how different retrieval strategies associated with different cues explain reaction time differences. Acta Physiol. **164**, 144–150 (2016)
7. Uzer, T., Brown, N.R.: The effect of cue content on retrieval from autobiographical memory. Acta Physiol. **172**, 84–91 (2017)
8. Jalal, A., Kamal, S., Kim, D.: A depth video sensor-based life-logging human activity recognition system for elderly care in smart indoor environments. Sensors **14**(7), 11735–11759 (2014)
9. Sellen, A.J., Whittaker, S.: Beyond total capture: a constructive critique of lifelogging. Commun. ACM **53**(5), 70–77 (2010)

The Effect of Group Membership, System Reliability and Anthropomorphic Appearance on User's Trust in Intelligent Decision Support System

Xiangying Zou[1,2,3], Chunhui Lv[1,2], and Jingyu Zhang[1,2(✉)]

[1] CAS Key Laboratory of Behavioral Science, Institute of Psychology,
Beijing 100101, China
zhangjingyu@psych.ac.cn
[2] Department of Psychology, University of Chinese Academy of Sciences,
Beijing 100049, China
[3] Department of Industrial Engineering, Tsinghua University,
Beijing 100084, China

Abstract. Past studies have found that the in-group membership of an intelligent agent can improve users' trust. We explored whether such an effect depends on system reliability levels and anthropomorphic appearance. We manipulated reliability levels (95%, 70%, 45%) and anthropomorphic appearance (human-like vs. computer-like appearance) of an intelligent decision support system in our study. The minimum group paradigm was adopted to manipulate the group membership of the intelligent system (in-group vs out-group). We measured trust by using both subjective rating and compliant behaviors toward the system recommendations. The results showed that the intelligent system with an in-group membership resulted in higher trust as compared to the system with an out-group membership. The magnitude of these effects did not differ across different reliability levels and anthropomorphic appearances. We discussed such findings in light of human-robot interaction theories and potential implications for designing trustworthy decision support system.

Keywords: Intelligent decision support system · Group membership · Trust · Anthropomorphism · Human-robot interaction

1 Introduction

With the fast development of artificial intelligence, intelligent systems have become increasingly popular in our daily life from offering health services to supporting important technical decisions. Although it is widely believed that the use of artificial intelligence can liberate users from demanding work, the proper usage of intelligent system is still a problem for both researchers and practitioners. While overuse or overreliance can result in loss of situational awareness and degrade alertness, underuse can result in a less effective human-in-the-loop system.

© Springer Nature Switzerland AG 2020
D. Harris and W.-C. Li (Eds.): HCII 2020, LNAI 12187, pp. 231–242, 2020.
https://doi.org/10.1007/978-3-030-49183-3_18

Trust toward intelligent system has been found to be the key variable that underlies human usage of the intelligent system. As an important concept in human-robot interaction, trust could be defined as an attitude towards an intelligent agent believing it can help achieve the user's goal under uncertainty and vulnerability [1]. Trust affects people's decision making in uncertain or risky environments [2] and influences system effectiveness relates to safety, performance, and frequency of use [1]. Specifically, trust influences people's willingness to accepting information from intelligent agencies and adopting advice provided by them [3].

The reliability of the system is the foundation of trust. Many studies have suggested that operators' trust increases as the system reliability increases [4, 5] and distrust occurs when the intelligent agent makes an obvious error [6, 7]. Generally speaking, when the interaction persists and the system performance feedback is adequate, the users' trust will match with the system's overall reliability in the long run [4, 5, 8, 9].

However, users' trust is not always compatible with system reliability. When users put more trust in a system that has inadequate reliability, overtrust occurs and it leads to overuse of the system. For example, when human operators believe the automated system to be very reliable, they would reduce their monitoring behavior and have undermined situational awareness which will make them less capable to takeover the system when a certain failure occurs [10]. On the other hand, when users do not trust a reliable system, undertrust occurs and it leads to reluctance to use a certain system. For example, when people do not trust the system's recommendation, they would devote more attention to monitor the system or even refuse to use the system, which can reduce the overall efficiency and increase the workload of the operator. Figure 1 provides an illustration of the relationship [1].

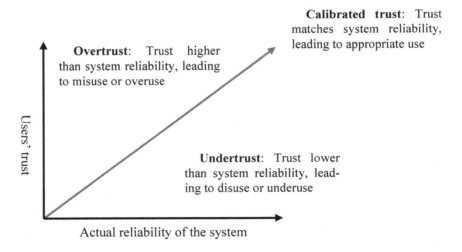

Fig. 1. Relationships between trust and reliability.

The mismatch between trust and system reliability happens for different reasons. First, when individuals have no contact history with a new system, their trust are largely determined by the obtained information that can vary significantly to induce different expectations [7]. It has been found that advertisements, designers' descriptions, training materials, etc., can all influence the initial trust of users. Second, without adequate feedback about system performance, it is hard to adjust one's trust to match the system reliability. However, in many cases, the system performance is not revealed to its operators. For example, it is very hard to perceive the performance of the X-ray screening system since the actual occurrence rate is too low to be encountered. As a result, the trust toward system may often deviate from the system reliability and can not be self-corrected.

To reduce such deviation, researchers have been exploring factors other than reliability to understand and calibrate users' trust [8, 11]. Among many factors, anthropomorphic features have received a lot of research attention. Anthropomorphism refers to the attributes that make nonhuman objects such as robots, computers, and animals to be like human, in appearance, voices, behaviors, etc. [12]. There is a very fundamental reason that the humanness attribute is important for human-system trust: people have a well-established mindset that while machine errors are inherent, human behaviors can change and improve [13]. But when anthropomorphic features are given to a machine, people may generate more human-related expectations toward the machine. In this way, users may be more likely to adjust their trust when the system seems to be more human.

Previous studies have also suggested that anthropomorphic features along could significantly increase participants' trust toward intelligent agents [14–17]. For example, an interactive interface with human appearance and human sound could significantly increase the social presence, pleasure, and trust in decision-making assistant agents of participants [15]. In another study, researchers have found that a decision supportive device with anthropomorphic appearance received more trust as compared to a system without [16].

While most studies focus on individual level anthropomorphic features, recently, a new type of anthropomorphic features, group membership, has been brought into attention. As an important factor in interpersonal and intergroup relationships, group membership generally leads to in-group preference and out-group bias [18]. The effect of group membership not only appears in human relationships but also in human-robot interaction, especially in the era when human-robot teaming is more emphasized.

Previous studies have found that after inducing the group membership of robots, humans could treat robots as in-group members and showed a preference for them [19–22]. Specially, some researchers conducted experiments using the minimum group paradigm. In their experiment, participants were told to participate in a study of language-learning training, and they would conduct this study with robot NAO or other participants. After that, participants were randomly divided into blue and green groups, and the participants in the blue group were in the same group with NAO. After the experimenter introduced participants to NAO, participants completed a pretend language-learning training task on the computer (actually evaluating NAO) without further interaction with NAO. They found that participants expressed a significantly higher acceptance and willingness to interact with the robots in the same group, even considered them are more anthropomorphic [20, 22]. Others also conducted experiments using the minimum group paradigm. But in their study, they grouped participants by asked them four questions about computers and robots (in effect, randomly grouped). Some of them were grouped with a robot NAO, others were grouped with a computer. Then, participants performed the Shell Game Task with NAO. In the Shell Game Task, a ball was placed under one of the three cups, and then the cups were shuffled, and the participants had to say which cup the ball was under. After the participant gave his/her answer, NAO would have a 50% probability of disagreeing with the participant's choice and gave it an answer, and then asked the participant if he wanted to change the answer. They found that in-group participants sat closer to NAO, but found no difference in trust levels [19]. Besides, some researchers used true groups (nationality) in their experiment. Participants play a card game in a tablet PC with two NAO robots. Participants were informed that the in-group robot was developed by students of the same nationality and that the robot had a name in their national style. They found that participants evaluated robots of the same nationality more positively and more human-like [21].

However, previous studies only have examined the influence of group membership using simple tasks based on one-shot interaction or several primitive interactions. Whether this effect can also be applied to the performing of complex task in a repeated manner, i.e., a continuous interaction with a typical decision support system (DSS), is not fully understood yet. Also, the effects of preference may not apply to trust situations.

In addition, it is not fully understood whether such an effect depends on reliability levels or other anthropomorphic features (e.g., appearance). It is useful to first make a distinction between superficial and deep-level anthropomorphic features. We defined the obvious, primary, biological features as superficial anthropomorphic features (such as appearance, sound), and advanced, social features as deep-level anthropomorphic features (such as personality, intelligence). Compared with superficial features, deep-level features may more likely to influence people's trustworthiness judgement. We treated group membership to be a deep-level anthropomorphic feature because the favoring of the ingroup member has been found to be a very strong and prompt reaction of human beings. In human-robot interaction, studies have pointed out that individuals use human social categories such as gender, race, and group to intelligent agents, and show social behavior toward intelligent agents [23]. Nonetheless, they didn't think that anthropomorphism is the reason why people ascribe social characteristics to intelligent agents.

Moreover, we would postulate that such a feature may have a different effect as compared to other superficial features (e.g., appearance). In the first place, we would argue that the effect of group membership would not depend on its appearance. This is because when the group membership is elicited, users can judge it to be human-like without paying attention to its outlook. As a result, there will be no interaction between group membership and appearance. Moreover, since a deep-level feature can overwhelm the effect of a superficial level feature, we would argue the effect of appearance might be reduced or even not significant in our study.

Second, while previous studies have pointed out that reliability is the foundation of trust, we would argue that group membership may not depends on it. Some researches had found that participants' trust toward systems with different appearances (male or female appearance) was not different in high-reliability conditions, but in low and medium conditions, participants' trust toward systems was affected by appearances. When the reliability of the system is insufficient, participants will use other clues to help judge whether the system is trustworthy [24]. In contrast, since the group membership is an intrinsic trait of the system, it may have a universal influence on user's trust regardless of its reliability.

To summarize, we sought to explore the influence of group membership on user's trust toward a complex DSS in performing a continuous task. We would predict that this effect is significant and would not depends on system reliability and superficial anthropomorphic features such as appearance.

2 Method

2.1 Participant

A total of 40 participants were recruited in this study, including 14 male and 24 female students from Beijing Forestry University. The age of participants was ranging from 18 to 25 (M = 20.0, SD = 2.06). All participants had a normal or corrected-to-normal vision, and never participated in similar experiments before. They received ¥60 as a reward after the experiment.

2.2 Experiment Design

A 2 × 2 × 3 within-subject design was used in this study. The first factor was group membership of the intelligent systems which had two levels: in-group and out-group. The second factor was the anthropomorphic appearance of the intelligent systems, which had two levels: an avatar-look and a computer-look. The third factor was the system reliability, which was manipulated using the accuracy of the system recommendation. Three levels were set by using the configuration of a previous study [24]: 95% (high), 70% (medium) and 45% (low). The sequence of group membership and anthropomorphic appearance in the experiment were counterbalanced, and the sequence of reliability level was all in a descending trend, 95%-70%-45%.

The dependent variables were subjective trust and behavioral trust. The measurements were provided in the following section.

2.3 Experimental Manipulation

We used the artistic preference task (i.e. a widely used variation of the minimum group paradigm) to manipulate the group membership [25]. Twelve modern paintings were used in this task (see Fig. 2). In performing the task, participants were told to choose one preferred painting from a pair shown on the screen for six times. After that, they saw a feedback which categorized them as either a member of constructionists or transformationists (the category was actually given in a random manner). Afterwards, they would see the names and images of four agents that will interact with them in the following task. Two agents named Andi and Dave had human-like appearance, another two agents with machine-like appearance were named TS17 and LCH5 (see Fig. 3).

Every participant was told that one human-look agent and one machine-look agent were in the same preference group (in-group), while the other two agents were in another group with a different artistic preference (out-group).

After that, the participants answered three manipulation testing questions, including "Which preference group do you belong to?", "Which intelligent systems are in the same preference group as you are?" and "What are the names of the intelligent system that are in the same preference group as you are?". Participants who correctly answered all three questions were kept for further analyses.

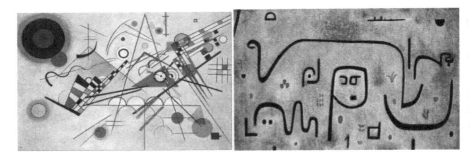

Fig. 2. Examples of paintings used in the experiment

Fig. 3. Agents used in the experiment (Dave on the upper left and Andi on the upper right).

2.4 Decision Support System

We used an adapted TNO trust task as our main task [17]. This experimental paradigm was used to examine human reliance of decision support systems [26], in which the system features can be easily manipulated.

Participants would see a series of numbers and were asked to make predictions one at a time. The original number sequence were recurring 1-2-3-1-2, but each number in the entire series had a 20% chance to become another two numbers in a random manner (e.g. the number 1 may become the number 2 or 3) [17].

At the start of each trial, participants were required to select his/her answer from 1, 2, and 3. Afterwards, they were told that the intelligent system made a suggestion. Next, the participants decided whether to keep their original choice or comply with the system's recommendation (if the two were different). Finally, they reported to what extent they trusted the recommendation on a single 9-point Likert item (1 representing the lowest level of trust and 9 representing the highest level of trust). The whole process in a trial was shown in Fig. 4.

After every 5 trials (which is called a block), participants would see overall performance feedback for the past 5 trials. The exact wording was "You have correctly predicted n times with the help of (the name of the intelligent system) in the previous five trials." After that, they reported an overall trust toward the system on the same subjective trust item.

In total, there were 240 trials in this experiment. Each block contains 5 trials and each condition contains 4 blocks. Subjective trust of each condition was created by averaging the mean of all 20 trial-level trust ratings and the mean of all 4 block-level trust ratings. Behavioral trust was the total compliance rate of each condition. Compliance was defined as the behavior when system recommendation was inconsistent with the initial choice of the participants, the participants changed their original option by following the system recommendation [17].

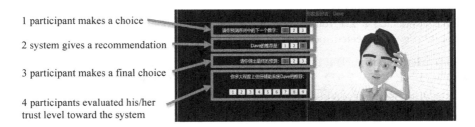

Fig. 4. Procedure of TNO trust task.

2.5 Procedure

After participants arrived in the laboratory, they signed the informed consent form and the experimental confidentiality agreement. Then, they were asked to perform two tasks, including painting preference selection task and numerical sequences prediction task. Then, the experiment was started according to the instruction of the experimenter.

First, participants performed painting preference selection task. At the end of the task, the experiment program would tell participants his/her group with a type of anthropomorphic appearances (avatar or computer). Then, they performed numerical sequences prediction task with these two appearances. After 120 trials, the experiment program would tell participants to take a break. After one minute, the experiment program would tell participants his/her group with another type of anthropomorphic appearances. Then, they performed numerical sequences prediction task with another two appearances.

Finally, participants reported some demographic information, then they were paid, thanked and debriefed.

3 Results

3.1 Subjective Trust

The average scores of subjective trust in each condition were shown in Table 1. There was no significant effect on the sequence of variables, so the sequence of variables was removed from further analyses.

Table 1. The descriptive statistics of subjective trust.

		Avatar		Computer	
		In-group	Out-group	In-group	Out-group
Reliability	95%	6.54 (1.50)	6.23 (1.41)	6.48 (1.35)	6.25 (1.38)
	70%	6.46 (1.48)	6.43 (1.47)	6.39 (1.62)	6.26 (1.52)
	45%	6.13 (1.34)	5.88 (1.32)	5.86 (1.35)	5.80 (1.24)

The values in the table are Mean (SD)

We conducted a 2 (group membership) × 2 (anthropomorphic appearance) × 3 (reliability level) repeated measures of ANOVA on subjective trust.

Group Membership. The result revealed a significant main effect of group membership, F (1, 39) = 7.972, p < 0.01, η^2 = 0.170. Subjective trust in the in-group intelligent system was significantly higher than the out-group intelligent system.

System Reliability. The main effect of system reliability of intelligent system was significant, F (2, 78) = 10.805, p < 0.001, η^2 = 0.217. Post hoc analysis showed that subjective trust was not significantly different between 95% and 70% conditions, but trust in 95% and 70% conditions were both significantly higher than that in 45% condition, p < 0.01 and p < 0.001, respectively.

Anthropomorphic Appearance. There was no significant main effect of anthropomorphic appearance, F (1, 39) = 0.450, p = 0.506, η^2 = 0.011.

No significant 2-way or 3-way interactions were found.

3.2   Behavioral Trust

The average scores of behavioral trust in each factor were shown in Table 2. There was no significant effect on the sequence of variables, so the sequence of variables was removed from further analyses.

Table 2. The descriptive statistics of behavioral trust.

		Avatar		Computer	
		In-group	Out-group	In-group	Out-group
Reliability	95%	0.65 (0.26)	0.56 (0.28)	0.67 (0.34)	0.63 (0.32)
	70%	0.68 (0.31)	0.61 (0.35)	0.65 (0.31)	0.64 (0.32)
	45%	0.62 (0.30)	0.57 (0.33)	0.60 (0.33)	0.63 (0.35)

The values in the table are Mean (SD)

We conducted a 2 (group membership) $\times$ 2 (anthropomorphic appearance) $\times$ 3 (reliability level) repeated measures of ANOVA on behavioral trust.

Group Membership. The main effect of group membership was approaching significance, F (1, 39) = 3.741, p = 0.060, η^2 = 0.088. Behavioral trust in the in-group intelligent system was marginally higher than the out-group intelligent system.

System Reliability. There was no significant main effect of system reliability, F (1.343, 78) = 1.013, p = 0.368, η^2 = 0.025.

Anthropomorphic Appearance. There was no significant main effect of anthropomorphic appearance, F (1, 39) = 0.438, p = 0.512, η^2 = 0.011.

No significant 2-way or 3-way interactions were found between the variables.

4   Discussion

The present study examined whether the effect of group membership on human trust toward intelligent system exists and depends on reliability levels and other anthropomorphic features (i.e., appearance). We found that the in-group membership can promote subjective trust and, to a lesser extent, behavioral trust. When the in-group identity was elicited by a seemingly irrelevant categorization task, the participants showed more trust toward the agent of the same group membership. Consistent with previous studies on human-to-human trust [27–29] and general preferences with robot [19], this study provides new evidence that this effect could also be applied to trust toward system recommendation in dealing with complex problems. The difference between subjective and behavioral trust may be due to the influence of self-confidence. It has been found that people with high self-confidence are more likely to persist in their choices and less likely to take advice from others [30]. As a result, although in-group membership can result in more trust intentions, such intention may not be fully transferred to behavioral choices. In future research, self-confidence can be manipulated or measured to examine whether it the cause of such discrepancy between subjective and behavior trust.

In addition, similar to previous studies, our results showed that system reliability had a significant positive influence on subjective trust [4, 5, 8, 9], but it did not moderate the effect of group membership. This finding suggests that the effect of group membership is rather robust regardless of the actual reliability levels. This is a very important feature since it implies that such an effect can be used to gauge users' trust in systems of different reliability levels. This is particularly important to improve users' trust toward the system that is effective but enjoyed a recent failure.

We did not find that anthropomorphic appearance could influence users' trust, nor it interacted with group membership to influence users' trust. This result is quite interesting since appearance was generally found in previous studies to influence users' preference and trust. It at least implies that the appearance of the agent may not be a prerequisite for the effect of group membership on users' trust. A more bold claim is that group membership is a much stronger and deep-level anthropomorphic feature when it is elicited, it is not important whether the agent has a human-like or machine-like appearance (a superficial feature). Future studies may further explore whether this finding can be replicated and whether the elicitation of the group-membership reduces the effect of other superficial features.

The findings of the present paper may have some implications for system design. The group membership can be elicited to gauge human trust as it seems to be a very powerful effect. However, it seems that this effect is too strong that it must be carefully used. When the system's performance was perceived to be inferior to its actual performance (undertrust), elicitation of the in-group membership can be useful. On the contrary, out-group membership can be elicited to reduce over-trust toward certain systems.

Several limitations of the study must be mentioned. First, we only examined college students using a laboratory experiment of which they have no previous knowledge. However, for real-world DSS users, they generally have quite profound knowledge of certain domains. Future studies may benefit from examining how real experts may respond to this effect. Second, in our study, we offered the system performance feedback every 5 trials, but in real world, the feedback can be vaguer. Theoretically, it might increase the effect size of the group membership because such a cue might be more relied upon when actual performance can not be evaluated. Finally, we only used a particular type of minimum group paradigm to elicit the group membership, whether other methods, such as using real world group categorization, can result in same effects, is worth further exploration.

In conclusion, the current study investigates the effect of group membership on trust toward intelligent agent of a decision support system and found that such an effect exists and depends not on reliability levels and anthropomorphic appearance. This study may serve as a guide for further studies and new design features for robots, intelligent system and smart applications.

References

1. Lee, J.D., See, K.A.: Trust in automation: designing for appropriate reliance. Hum. Factors **46**(1), 50–80 (2004)
2. Park, E., Jenkins, Q., Jiang, X.: Measuring trust of human operators in new generation rescue robots. Paper presented at the proceedings of the JFPS international symposium on fluid power (2008)
3. Freedy, A., DeVisser, E., Weltman, G., Coeyman, N.: Measurement of trust in human-robot collaboration. In: 2007 International Symposium on Collaborative Technologies and Systems, pp. 106–114. IEEE, May 2007
4. Chavaillaz, A., Wastell, D., Sauer, J.: System reliability, performance and trust in adaptable automation. Appl. Ergon. **52**, 333–342 (2016)
5. Ross, J.M., Szalma, J.L., Hancock, P.A., Barnett, J.S., Taylor, G.: The effect of automation reliability on user automation trust and reliance in a search-and-rescue scenario. Paper presented at the proceedings of the human factors and ergonomics society annual meeting (2008)
6. de Vries, P., Midden, C., Bouwhuis, D.: The effects of errors on system trust, self-confidence, and the allocation of control in route planning. Int. J. Hum. Comput. Stud. **58**(6), 719–735 (2003)
7. Dzindolet, M.T., Peterson, S.A., Pomranky, R.A., Pierce, L.G., Beck, H.P.: The role of trust in automation reliance. Int. J. Hum. Comput. Stud. **58**(6), 697–718 (2003)
8. Schaefer, K.E., Chen, J.Y., Szalma, J.L., Hancock, P.A.: A meta-analysis of factors influencing the development of trust in automation: implications for understanding autonomy in future systems. Hum. Factors **58**(3), 377–400 (2016)
9. Sanchez, J., Fisk, A.D., Rogers, W.A.: Reliability and age-related effects on trust and reliance of a decision support aid. Paper presented at the proceedings of the human factors and ergonomics society annual meeting (2004)
10. Farrell, S., Lewandowsky, S.: A connectionist model of complacency and adaptive recovery under automation. J. Exp. Psychol. Learn. Mem. Cogn. **26**(2), 395 (2000)
11. Hancock, P.A., Billings, D.R., Schaefer, K.E., Chen, J.Y., De Visser, E.J., Parasuraman, R.: A meta-analysis of factors affecting trust in human-robot interaction. Hum. Factors **53**(5), 517–527 (2011)
12. Bartneck, C., Kulić, D., Croft, E., Zoghbi, S.: Measurement instruments for the anthropomorphism, animacy, likeability, perceived intelligence, and perceived safety of robots. Int. J. Soc. Robot. **1**(1), 71–81 (2009)
13. Madhavan, P., Wiegmann, D.A.: Effects of information source, pedigree, and reliability on operator interaction with decision support systems. Hum. Factors **49**(5), 773–785 (2007)
14. Qiu, L., Benbasat, I.: Evaluating anthropomorphic product recommendation agents: a social relationship perspective to designing information systems. J. Manag. Inf. Syst. **25**(4), 145–182 (2008)
15. Nass, C., Steuer, J., Tauber, E.R.: Computer are social actors. In: Conference on Human Factors in Computing Systems, CHI 1994, Boston, Massachusetts, USA, April 24–28, p. 204 (1994). Conference Companion
16. Pak, R., Fink, N., Price, M., Bass, B., Sturre, L.: Decision support aids with anthropomorphic characteristics influence trust and performance in younger and older adults. Ergonomics **55**(9), 1059 (2012)
17. de Visser, E.J., et al.: Almost human: anthropomorphism increases trust resilience in cognitive agents. J. Exp. Psychol. Appl. **22**(3), 331 (2016)

18. Messick, D.M., Mackie, D.M.: Intergroup relations. Annu. Rev. Psychol. **40**(1), 45–81 (1989)
19. Deligianis, C., Stanton, C.J., McGarty, C., Stevens, C.J.: The impact of intergroup bias on trust and approach behaviour towards a humanoid robot. J. Hum.-Robot Interact. **6**(3), 4–20 (2017)
20. Kuchenbrandt, D., Eyssel, F., Bobinger, S., Neufeld, M.: Minimal group - maximal effect? Evaluation and anthropomorphization of the humanoid robot NAO. In: Mutlu, B., Bartneck, C., Ham, J., Evers, V., Kanda, T. (eds.) ICSR 2011. LNCS (LNAI), vol. 7072, pp. 104–113. Springer, Heidelberg (2011). https://doi.org/10.1007/978-3-642-25504-5_11
21. Häring, M., Kuchenbrandt, D., André, E.: Would you like to play with me?: how robots' group membership and task features influence human-robot interaction. Paper presented at the proceedings of the 2014 ACM/IEEE international conference on human-robot interaction (2014)
22. Kuchenbrandt, D., Eyssel, F., Bobinger, S., Neufeld, M.: When a robot's group membership matters. Int. J. Soc. Robot. **5**(3), 409–417 (2013)
23. Nass, C., Moon, Y.: Machines and mindlessness: social responses to computers. J. Soc. Issues **56**(1), 81–103 (2000)
24. Pak, R., Mclaughlin, A.C., Bass, B.: A multi-level analysis of the effects of age and gender stereotypes on trust in anthropomorphic technology by younger and older adults. Ergonomics **57**(9), 1277–1289 (2014)
25. Tajfel, H., Billig, M.G., Bundy, R.P., Flament, C.: Social categorization and intergroup behaviour. Eur. J. Soc. Psychol. **1**(2), 149–178 (1971)
26. Van Dongen, K., van Maanen, P.P.: Under-reliance on the decision aid: a difference in calibration and attribution between self and aid. In: Proceedings of the Human Factors and Ergonomics Society Annual Meeting, vol. 50, no. 3, pp. 225–229. SAGE Publications, Los Angeles, October 2006
27. Brewer, M.B.: In-group bias in the minimal intergroup situation: a cognitive-motivational analysis. Psychol. Bull. **86**(2), 307 (1979)
28. Brewer, M.B., Kramer, R.M.: The psychology of intergroup attitudes and behavior. Annu. Rev. Psychol. **36**(1), 219–243 (1985)
29. Kramer, R.M., Brewer, M.B.: Effects of group identity on resource use in a simulated commons dilemma. J. Pers. Soc. Psychol. **46**(5), 1044 (1984)
30. Sun, L., Chen, L., Duan, J.: Advice taking in decision-making: strategies, influences and feature research. Adv. Psychol. Sci. **25**(1), 169–179 (2017)

Cognitive Psychology in Aviation and Automotive

Assessing Professional Cultural Differences Between Airline Pilots and Air Traffic Controllers

Wesley Tsz-Kin Chan[1]([⊠]) and Wen-Chin Li[2]

[1] Cranfield University, Cranfield, UK
wesley.chan@cranfield.ac.uk
[2] Safety and Accident Investigation Centre, Cranfield University, Cranfield, UK
wenchin.li@cranfield.ac.uk

Abstract. Past studies have found that values and attitudes influenced by national culture remain detectable in airline pilots, even after equalisation by training and organisational exposure. There is however insufficient research to ascertain if this relative strength of nationally-determined traits is because national culture is in itself change-resistant, or if it is because professional pilot training and international airline environments lack the power to impel shifts in cultural behaviour. Using a survey with items imported from the Flight Management Attitudes Questionnaire and the ATC Safety Questionnaires, this study compares the non-technical values and attitudes of pilots (n = 21) and air traffic controllers (n = 13) from the same national cultural background to examine whether the dissimilar pilot and ATC professional and organisational experiences bring about detectable changes in nationally-determined traits. It was discovered that professional and organisational exposure affected hierarchical relations between superiors and subordinates, levels of concern towards automation usage, and the desire for high earnings and career advancement. An understanding of how certain non-technical skills are changed by professional and organisational exposure has the potential to change training, influence equipment designs, and highlight issues in cross-cultural and cross-profession communications.

Keywords: Cultural behaviours · Training · Aviation training

1 Introduction

1.1 The Relative Influence of Different Cultures

Individuals' attitudes and behaviours at work are influenced by the three cultural concepts of *national, organisational,* and *professional* cultures [1, 2]. *National culture* is "developed during adolescence when a person's sensibilities to rules and conceptions, interpersonal relations, and moral and religious ideals are formed" [3]. *Organisational culture*, often known as 'company culture', is determined by conventions of 'the way things are done' within a work environment. *Professional culture* involves the values and attitudes shared amongst people of functionally similar occupations through socialisation and occupational training [2].

© Springer Nature Switzerland AG 2020
D. Harris and W.-C. Li (Eds.): HCII 2020, LNAI 12187, pp. 245–252, 2020.
https://doi.org/10.1007/978-3-030-49183-3_19

Studies conducted in multi-cultural airlines have demonstrated that traits of national culture, which are deeply ingrained in individuals' personalities as its values and attitudes are established during adolescence [4], remain detectable in airline pilots' values and attitudes on the flight deck even after equalisation by common pilot training and company culture [3]. There however remains insufficient conclusions as to whether this observed precedence of national culture over organisational and professional impacts is because national culture is change-resistant, or if on the contrary it is because pilot training and air crew recruitment selection processes which are globally similar [2] do not provide enough impetus for a significant cultural-shift in nationally moulded values and attitudes.

Humans function more effectively when operating within acquainted cultural contexts as they provide social constructs for individuals to know what to expect of others, and of what others expect of them [5]. In the pilot-air traffic control (ATC) interactive environment, a mismatch between the different players' expectations can lead to a failure to understand and comprehend what has been communicated. The Tenerife accident involving the collision of two Boeing 747s in 1977 provides a relevant example of cross-cultural, cross-context communicative issues. First, the flight crew misunderstood a *route clearance* of a "right turn after take-off", as provided by ATC, as an immediate *take-off clearance* and inappropriately initiated their acceleration for take-off. This was compounded when the flight crew's radio transmission of "we are now at take-off" (as in currently accelerating on the *take-off roll*) was misunderstood by the air traffic controller as that the aircraft was holding in position at the *take-off initiation point*. This series of events eventually caused the aircraft to catastrophically collide with another B747 aircraft that was also on the runway [6].

Contemporary studies confirm that pilot-ATC communicative issues remain unresolved. In a 2018 study, *pilot-ATC communications*, as an explanatory factor, was found to be responsible for 17% of safety performance indicator events in an European air navigation service provider [7]. Further investigation of how cultural traits are affected by professional and organisational training can provide opportunities to improve pilot-ATC mental model sharing by providing indications of both parties' contextual expectations and how these are influenced by occupational exposure.

1.2   Comparing Airline Pilots and Air Traffic Controllers

In this study, a consistent methodology was used to assess and compare the non-technical values and attitudes of airline pilots and air traffic control officers (ATCOs) from an identical national cultural background (East Asian).

Pilots and controllers are a good match for comparative assessment of organisational and professional influences. The two groups operate in the same environment and share functionally similar non-technical skills which are directly influenced by cultural traits [8, 9]. Safety management systems (SMS) and safety culture concepts also apply to both airline pilots and air traffic controllers [10], with Team Resource Management (TRM) and Normal Oversight Safety Survey (NOSS) principles used by ATC directly derived from airline based Crew Resource Management (CRM) and Line Operations Safety Audit (LOSA) techniques [11].

The anticipated outcome of this project is to identify particular traits and non-technical skills which are influenced by professional and organisational exposure. For training design, the identification of content areas where values and attitudes have been discovered to be amenable by organisational and professional cultures provides clues for which content areas to focus on to enable efficient and cost effective training transfer, and which non-technical skill deficiencies (the ones that are not amenable by training) are better catered for through other systemic changes. In relation to human-systems integration, the results can assist in the strategic application of adaptive equipment and procedure designs to compensate for cross-cultural teamwork.

2   Method

2.1   Participants

Thirty-four responses were included in this analysis, of which 21 were from pilots and 13 from air traffic controllers (ATCOs). Participants were recruited with the assistance of the Hong Kong Airline Pilots' Association and Hong Kong Air Traffic Control Association, who distributed through email to their own members and associated groups in the East Asian region a hyperlink to a survey which was hosted online.

2.2   Instrument

The survey distributed to airline pilot participants consists of relevant items imported from the established Flight Management Attitudes Questionnaire (FMAQ) [9], which measures respondents' work values, as well as their attitudes towards *command, communications, stress*, and *automation*. ATC data was collected using questions drawn from the Air Traffic Control Safety Questionnaire (ATCSQ) [11]. As the ATCSQ was developed by adapting FMAQ items with ATC terminologies and for the ATC work environment, the items in the two surveys are conceptually equivalent. Responses were rated on a 5-point Likert scale, with higher scores representing stronger agreement and greater desire for the item statement.

2.3   Research Design

Responses included in this analysis were collected over two time periods. The air pilot data was collected over an eight-month period from April to December 2018, whilst ATC data was collected over a four-month period from August to December 2019.

The survey was digitally hosted on the Jisc *Online Surveys* (pilot dataset) and *Qualtrics* (ATC dataset) platforms. Relevant groups were sent an email containing a hyperlink which redirected the participants onto a web-based interface through which the survey was completed online.

Ethical approval was provided by the Cranfield University Research Ethics System (CURES/9367/2019). Participation was voluntary with no identifying information collected.

Results were analysed using Microsoft Excel. Negatively worded items were reverse coded to ensure directionality, and survey items were consolidated into corresponding composite scales representing different content areas, following FMAQ and ATCSQ groupings, to generate content area scores (see Table 1). One-way Analyses of Variance (ANOVAs) were run for these content area scales to statistically establish whether there were significant differences between air pilot and ATC groups.

3   Results and Discussion

Survey items were compiled into composite scales representing various work values and attitudinal content areas. The results for content areas where significant differences were found between pilots and ATCOs are presented in Table 1. On a 5-point scale, higher scores represent an inclination for autocratic command, greater awareness of automation induced communications effects and higher concern for automation, and greater desire for work values items.

Table 1. Significant results by content area and profession

Content area	ATCOs		Pilots		Effect size for differences
	Mean	SD	Mean	SD	(*small; **moderate; ***large)
Command	2.84	1.63	2.41	1.41	0.018*
Recognition of communications effects when using automation	2.85	1.39	4.05	0.91	0.171***
Automation concern	4.00	0.95	3.32	1.27	0.083**
Work values - rewards	3.70	0.66	4.29	0.67	0.104**

3.1   Hierarchical Behaviour

Significant differences between pilots and ATCOs were found on the scale assessing attitudes toward *command* ($F(1,236) = 4.24$, $p < 0.05$, $\eta^2 = 0.02$, see Table 2). Indicative of the effect of hierarchy and command gradients between superiors and subordinates, the results show that ATCOs (M = 2.84, SD = 1.63) had a preference for steeper, more hierarchical command gradients in comparison to pilots (M = 2.41, SD = 1.41). As the subjects tested in both airline pilot and ATC groups were of the same national cultural background, and hence the 'starting point' should be the same, the finding of significant differences between the two groups provides evidence to show that that attitudes toward command and hierarchy are feasibly shaped by organisational and professional exposure.

Table 2. Items assessing attitudes toward command

Survey version	Items
ATCOs	1. The executive controller should always take control in an emergency 2. Controllers should not disagree with their supervisors except when flight safety is threatened 3. Leadership of the team comes from the sector supervisor 4. Trainees should not question senior team members' decisions 5. In abnormal situations, I rely on my superiors to tell me what to do 6. Supervisors who encourage suggestions from team members are ineffective 7. In your work environment, subordinates are afraid to express disagreement with their superiors
Pilots	1. The Captain should take physical control and fly the aircraft in emergency and non-standard situation 2. Crew members should not question the decisions or actions of the Captain except when they threaten the safety of the flight 3. Successful flight deck management is primarily a function of the Captain's flying proficiency 4. Junior crew members should not question the Captain's or senior crew members' decisions 5. In abnormal situations, I rely on my superiors to tell me what to do 6. Captains who encourage suggestions from crew members are weak leaders 7. In your work environment, subordinates are afraid to express disagreement with their superiors

3.2 Attitudes Toward Automation

In relation to the usage of automation, there were significant differences between pilots and ATCOs on the content areas of *recognition of communication effects* when using automation ($F(1,60) = 16.55$, $p < 0.01$, $\eta^2 = 0.22$, see Fig. 1) and *automation concern* ($F(1,91) = 6.86$, $p < 0.05$, $\eta^2 = 0.07$, see Fig. 1). Pilots (M = 4.05, SD = 0.91) were of greater agreement that the use of automation generates a requirement for more communications between team members than ATCOs (M = 2.85, SD = 1.39), whilst air traffic controllers (M = 4.00, SD = 0.95) were more concerned about the negative impacts of automation than pilots (M = 3.32, SD = 1.27).

The opposing findings of respondents' attitudes in the two content areas is possibly reflective of risk mitigation strategies acquired through organisational and professional training. Automation in ATC generally do not require nor permit direct human participation [12], whereas the use of automation on the flight deck heightens the importance of intra-crew communication as pilot-computer interactions need to be coordinated between crew members [13]. This may explain the finding of pilots' greater awareness of the importance of communication when using automation. Greater awareness leads to heightened communications on the flight deck, and as communication is a criterion for safe flight [13], it provides an explanation for the finding of pilots' significantly lower level of concern in relation to the negative impacts of automation.

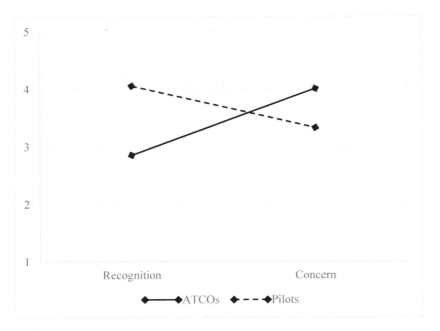

Fig. 1. *Recognition of communications effects when using automation*, and *automation concern* content area scores for ATCOs (solid line) and pilots (dashed line). Notice that the two content areas produced contrasting results.

The aforementioned finding of ATCOs' more hierarchical attitudes toward command may also explain the findings of automation attitudes. High scores on the command scale reflect less team communication and more unquestioned reliance on the person in charge. With modern automation technologies often considered as an additional crew member [14], it is therefore probable in consequence that ATC controllers will be less recognisant for communications requirements when interacting with this "silent crew-member", and be more concerned about its ability and possible negative impacts.

3.3   Rewards

ATCOs and pilots differed significantly on the work values scale of *rewards*, which consists of items assessing respondents' desire for high earnings and opportunities for advancement to higher-level jobs ($F(1,60) = 10.42$, $p < 0.01$, $\eta^2 = 0.15$). Pilots were found to be more reward driven ($M = 4.29$, $SD = 0.67$) than ATCOs ($M = 3.70$, $SD = 0.66$).

The differences between the two groups in this content area are highly likely to be due to influences of both professional and organisational cultures. Professional influences are reflected by the stereotypical "pilot persona [of] boats, cars, motorcycles, big watches, etc." [2]. Organisational factors, on the other hand, are best understood by considering the different work environments. As pilots work in aircraft and are therefore predominantly isolated from the corporate office environment, they are less exposed to symbolic communication and shared experiences (e.g. seasonal parties, award ceremonies, etc.) [2]. In contrast, ATCOs who work in fixed locations would be more exposed to the communication of organisational cultures and hence may be more susceptible to resulting behavioural changes.

4   Further Research

Although the results provide probable deduction of specific behaviours and attitudes which may be influenced by organisational and professional cultures, they are in no way conclusive. When determining changes in nationally-determined traits, it is difficult to separate the effects of industry-wide training syllabi which are similar for both pilots and ATCOs (such as CRM and Team Resource Management), with the effects of a wider range of organisational and professional factors that, to the contrary, are occupationally varied. The use of national cultural background as a control variable in this study may also fail to capture intra-culture discrepancies, such as participants' previous education, employment, or cross-cultural experiences.

Nevertheless, the interaction between national, organisational, and professional cultures and how it affects behavioural changes in CRM dependent industries merits further investigation. For example, longitudinal studies based on training evaluations can paint a clearer picture of how individuals' values and attitudes, from a known starting point, changes through professional training and exposure to organisational, company cultures. The use of objective measures of individual traits (such as cognitive attention [15]) to categorise respondent groups can also enhance future studies by taking into account and providing an objective control for intra-culture variations in values and attitudes.

5   Conclusion

Previous research on the effect of national cultural traits on air pilots' values and attitudes are insufficient in revealing whether detected cultural differences between pilots of different cultural backgrounds are due to relative strengths in their nationally-determined traits, or if it is because organisational and professional exposure, such as pilot training, are ineffective in creating behavioural changes. By complementing air pilot data with equivalent data from air traffic controllers, survey results from pilots and controllers from the same national background were compared to assess how exposure to different organisational and professional cultures can affect individuals' non-technical values and attitudes.

Pilots and ATCOs differed in hierarchical behaviours of individualism and command, as well as in attitudes toward automation, suggesting that these content areas can be influenced by organisational and professional cultures. Professional motivations and organisational environments have also been discussed as a likely cause for differences in desire for rewards and advancement opportunities.

The results can inform training, equipment, and procedure designs. In content areas where values and attitudes have been discovered to be amenable by organisational and professional cultures, the use of national background as the criterion for equipment and procedural changes to 'fit the task to the human', as is often the case in culturally responsive designs, may not be entirely ideal. Suggestions for further research include expanding the study to other vocational positions to evaluate inaccuracies arising from pilot and ATC similarities, and to introduce objective assessments of culturally influenced traits to take into account intra-cultural variations.

References

1. Helmreich, R.L.: Building safety on the three cultures of aviation. In: Proceedings of the IATA Human Factors Seminar (1998)
2. Dahlstrom, N., Heemstra, L.R.: Beyond multi-culture: when increasing diversity dissolves differences. In: Strohschneider, S., Heimann, R. (eds.) Kultur and sicheres handeln, pp. 79–95. Verlag fur Polizeiwissenschaft (2009)
3. Chan, W.T.-K., Harris, D.: Third-culture kid pilots and multi-cultural identity effects on pilots attitudes. Aerosp. Med. Hum. Perform. **90**(12), 1026–1033 (2019). https://doi.org/10.3357/AMHP.5397.2019
4. Tanu, D.: Global Nomads: towards a study of "Asian" third culture kids. In: Proceedings of the 17th Biennial Conference of the Asian Studies Association of Australia, Melbourne, Australia (2008)
5. Merritt, A., Maurino, D.: Cross-cultural factors in aviation safety. Adv. Hum. Perform. Cogn. Eng. Res. (2004). https://doi.org/10.1016/S1479-3601(03)04005-0
6. Roitsch, P.A., Babcock, G.L., Edmunds, W.W.: Human Factors Report on the Tenerife Accident. Air Line Pilots Association, Washington, D.C. (1977)
7. Li, W.-C.: Safety Presentation: Top Five ANSP Risks and Associated Mitigations. Safety and Accident Investigation Centre, Cranfield University, Bedford (2019)
8. Knecht, C., Muehlethaler, C., Elfering, A.: Nontechnical skills training in air traffic management including computer-based simulation methods: from scientific analyses to prototype training. Aviat. Psychol. Appl. Hum. Factors (2016). https://doi.org/10.1027/2192-0923/a000103
9. Helmreich, R.L., Merritt, A.C.: Culture at Work in Aviation and Medicine. Routledge, New York (1998)
10. ICAO: Doc 9859, Safety Management Manual (SMM), Doc 9859 AN/474 (2013)
11. Bunjevac, S., Seychell, A.F.: Eurocontrol Guidelines for TRM Good Practices, Brusseels (2015)
12. Hopkin, V.: Air-traffic control automation. In: Handbook of Aviation Human Factors, 2nd edn. (2009) https://doi.org/10.1201/b10401-27
13. Sherman, P.J., Helmreich, R.L., Merritt, A.C.: National culture and flight deck automation. results of a multination survey. Int. J. Aviat. Psychol. (1997). https://doi.org/10.1207/s15327108ijap0704_4
14. Chialastri, A.: Automation in aviation. In: Kongoli, F. (ed.) Automation, 1st edn., pp. 79–102. InTech, Rijeka (2012). https://doi.org/10.5772/49949
15. Nisbett, R.E., Choi, I., Peng, K., Norenzayan, A.: Culture and systems of thought: holistic versus analytic cognition. Psychol. Rev. (2001). https://doi.org/10.1037/0033-295X.108.2.291

Comparison of Pedestrians' Gap Acceptance Behavior Towards Automated and Human-Driven Vehicles

Wenxiang Chen, Qianni Jiang, Xiangling Zhuang[✉], and Guojie Ma

Shaanxi Key Laboratory of Behavior and Cognitive Neuroscience,
School of Psychology, Shaanxi Normal University, Xi'an, China
zhuangxl@snnu.edu.cn

Abstract. To protect pedestrian safety, automated vehicles can adopt a conservative strategy by yielding to pedestrians in all interactions and external human-machine interface was suggested to convey vehicle intentions to pedestrians. However, automated vehicles also could convey messages to assist existing pedestrians' road-crossing decision-making, which is another way to ensure pedestrian safety but has generally been neglected. The current study explored the effect of assistance information on pedestrian gap acceptance behavior by presenting three colors similar to a traffic light to indicate the instant safety to cross road. Forty-eight participants completed the gap acceptance task in a virtual reality environment when interacting with human-driven vehicles or automated vehicles in a mixed or non-mixed traffic environment. The results showed that generally pedestrians had similar gap acceptance trends in rejecting small gaps towards two types of vehicles, but are more likely to accepted a large gap when they interacted with automated vehicles. The assistance information helped pedestrians to make safer road-crossing decisions, but whether the two types of vehicles drove in separately or in mixed condition did not affect pedestrian behavior. The null effect of driving context indicates that pedestrians may rely on their legacy strategy of gap acceptance regardless of vehicle type and the assistance information just only had minor effects.

Keywords: Gap acceptance · Time to arrival · Pedestrian safety · Automated vehicles

1 Introduction

Pedestrians are the most vulnerable road users that accounting for 22% of the fatalities in traffic accidents (World Health Organization 2013). The conflicts between vehicles and pedestrians often occur as a result of unsafe interaction (Kaparias et al. 2015; Ni et al. 2016), especially when drivers do not yield on time or pedestrians inappropriately accept a small gap to cross. To solve the former issue, the desire for deploying automated vehicles to increase crossing safety has surged up these years (Köhler et al. 2013; Schneemann and Heinemann 2016). And for the later issue, researchers suppose pedestrians should be partially responsible for their safety without any help from the drivers, thus previous studies attempted to identify pedestrian perceptual and cognitive

© Springer Nature Switzerland AG 2020
D. Harris and W.-C. Li (Eds.): HCII 2020, LNAI 12187, pp. 253–261, 2020.
https://doi.org/10.1007/978-3-030-49183-3_20

failures that may lead to unsafe road-crossing decision-making (Koh and Wong 2014; Pawar and Patil 2015).

Automated vehicles were expected to adopt a conservative strategy, where once the automated system recognizes pedestrians' intention to cross, they should give way to pedestrians (Schneemann and Heinemann 2016). In order to help pedestrians to recognize and accept vehicles' yielding, automated vehicles were suggested to equip the external human-machine interface (eHMI) to convey vehicle intentions. The eHMI was expected to establish a new interaction mode with other road users, to compensate for the absence of common human-human interactions (Rasouli and Tsotsos 2019; Schieben et al. 2019). Following this line of research, many studies have evaluated the effect of different types of messages (texts, symbol, lights, animations, etc.) on pedestrian stated feeling of safety and crossing behavior, especially when automated vehicles would decelerate or yield to pedestrians (Holländer et al. 2019; Lee et al. 2019a, b; Nuñez Velasco et al. 2019). For example, pedestrians were found to cross more often when they encountered a yielding vehicle with the eHMI, which was thought to increase the efficiency of interaction between pedestrians and automated vehicles (de Clercq et al. 2019; Song et al. 2018). In another study, researchers added eyes on the car to establish an eye-contact communication between automated vehicles and pedestrians (Chang et al. 2017). When the automated vehicles equipped with this "eyes on a car" interface, pedestrians could make road-crossing decisions more quickly and feel safer.

However, in contrast, some studies implied the limited effect of such communication information. In a video-based road-crossing task, Nuñez Velasco et al. (2019) suggested that automated vehicles equipped with interfaces to communicate with pedestrians could only increase their perceived risk, but pedestrians' crossing intentions were not affected. Some researchers reckoned that pedestrian may rely on their legacy strategy to make decisions (e.g., estimating time-to-arrival, vehicle speeds or distance to make decisions), instead of the communication information (Clamann et al. 2017). Another possible explanation is that vehicle deceleration rate could also serve as informal communication information to help pedestrians understand the intentions of automated vehicles, which then could support pedestrians to detect yield behavior and cross immediately (Ackermann et al. 2019; Fuest et al. 2018). Besides, pedestrians' understanding of the automated vehicles' intentions may vary for different designs of the message (Lee et al. 2019a) or the level of familiarity (i.e., learning effect) (Lee et al. 2019b). Judging from the above studies, pedestrians could recognize intentions of automated vehicles by communication information, but it is still not determined that to what extent such information affects pedestrians' road-crossing decision-making.

Compared with the conservative strategy, the current study suggests a strategy to assist pedestrians' gap selection decision-making rather than consistent yielding. In this strategy, automated vehicles would not yield to pedestrians when pedestrians do not have road rights. Instead, automated vehicles just send assistance information to pedestrians to support the existing gap selection strategy to increase safety. This strategy is necessary to ensure efficient vehicle flow, especially at places where pedestrians do not have road rights. Besides, considering pedestrians' decision-making is easy to be affected by several factors (e.g., vehicle size, vehicle speeds, traffic environment) (Kaparias et al. 2015; Pawar and Patil 2015; Petzoldt 2016), this strategy is expected to reduce errors in pedestrians' gap selection decision-making. By this strategy, automated vehicles behave similarly to human-driven vehicles except for the assistance information. Will pedestrians make gap acceptance decisions based on assistance information or will they treat the automated vehicles just as human-driven vehicles? It is necessary to compare pedestrians' road-crossing behavior when inter-acting with these two types of vehicles and identify pedestrian strategies. Moreover, if the pedestrians had different crossing strategy towards the two types of vehicles, then whether automated vehicles driven in traffic that were surrounded by human-driven vehicles may be another concern to address. We expect that pedestrians may need to transit strategies constantly if the two types of vehicles driven in mixed traffic condi-tions, which causing additional cognitive load.

2   Methods

2.1   Participants

Participants were recruited with rewards from Shaanxi Normal University. A sample of 48 students (mean age = 18.78 years, SD = 1.08 years, 17 males and 31 females) took part in the experiment. All participants had normal or corrected to normal visions.

2.2   Apparatus

A custom program was used to carry out the experiment. The program was developed based on the jMonkeyEngine, which is a 3-D game engine developed by Java language. The program ran on a high-performance computer and render the virtual environment to an HTC VIVE Pro headset. The headset refreshed at 90 Hz with a resolution of 2880 * 1600 pixels (1440 × 1600 pixels per eye) and with a field of view of 110°.

The model of road environment (as shown in Fig. 1.) was developed by Esri CityEngine and Blender software. A four-lane, two-way road was used and the lane

Fig. 1. The traffic scene from pedestrians' perspective (human-driven vehicles were presented)

width was 3.5 m. The sidewalks, street trees, and road lamps were also included in order to provide a realistic experience of the traffic environment.

2.3 Stimulus and Design

Two types of vehicles were designed to simulate human-driven vehicles and automated vehicles. Compared to the appearances of human-driven vehicles, the simulated automated vehicles were equipped with a signal on top to distinguish itself with human-driven vehicles and a frontal display conveying the assistance information to pedestrians. Vehicles could either drive at a mixed traffic environment (human-driven and automated vehicles shared a lane and were presented randomly) or not (only human-driven vehicles or automated vehicles were present). Therefore, there are four kinds of interaction situations between pedestrians and vehicles as follows:

(1) pedestrians interact with human-driven vehicles only (HUM-only);
(2) pedestrians interact with automated vehicles only (AV-only);
(3) pedestrians interact with human-driven vehicles in a mixed traffic environment (HUM-mixed);
(4) pedestrians interact with automated vehicles in a mixed traffic environment (AV-mixed).

Vehicles approached pedestrians at a constant speed of 30 km/h. When the vehicle interacted with pedestrians, the time gap ranged from 1.4 s to 6.4 s (at 1.0 s intervals). For automated vehicles, the assistance information was designed to reflect the risk of crossing, according to the time-to-arrival (TTA) between vehicles and pedestrians. The signal simulated the common traffic light with three states in red (TTA < 3.4 s), yellow (3.4 s < TTA < 4.8 s) and green color (TTA > 4.8 s). At the beginning of each trial, participants always required to stand 0.5 m away to the curb. Therefore, they had to walk 4 meters to complete the crossing task during the experiment.

2.4 Procedure

At first, participants were explained about the task and procedure of the experiment. They were told that the vehicle would not yield or decelerate, and they had to accept an appropriate time gap to cross safely. In addition, they were explained about the meaning of assistance information: the red state means that it may be dangerous if they chose to cross, even they crossed in a hurry; the green state means it would be safe to cross, even they crossed at leisure; and the yellow state is a situation between the red state and green state, whereas it is not recommended to cross for the reason of safety.

Then they had to cross the lane for at least three times, in order to get familiar with the environment and adapt themselves to walk with the headset in the virtual reality environment. After that, they had to complete eight blocks of crossing task. The order of blocks was balanced. There were two blocks for only human-driven vehicles (HUM-only) or only automated vehicles (AV-only) respectively and four blocks for mixed traffic environment (HUM-mixed and AV-mixed). In each block, participants would cross the road for 15 times (i.e., 15 trials).

For each trial, a sequence of vehicles approached the pedestrian from left to right. The first vehicle always appeared very close to the pedestrian with the time-to-arrival of 1 s (excluded for the analysis), in order to present an ecological perception for the following vehicles. And the following vehicles provide a randomized gap from 1.4 to 6.4 s (at 1.0 s intervals). Participants could walk to cross the road at any time at any walking pace and then go back to the starting position to prepare for the next trial. The experiment lasted about 45 to 60 min.

3   Results

For each trial, pedestrians could either accept or reject the current time gap. Therefore, trials were labeled as "accepted" or "rejected" respectively according to the movement of the VR headset. Because of the limitation of the program, if pedestrians started to cross when a vehicle was passing by, it would record a response with an incorrect timestamp (13 trials were excluded from all analyses). To sum up, a total of 12218 decisions (6471 waiting decision and 5747 crossing decision) were used for the following analyses.

Considering the binary nature of crossing decisions, a Generalized Linear Mixed Model (GLMM, using glmer function from lme4 package 1.1-21 for R 3.6.1) with a logit link function was used for modeling pedestrians' decisions. Specifically, the independent variables (interaction conditions and gap size) and their interactions were modeled as the fixed effects, with a random effect of individual difference (i.e., the difference of individual from the overall participants), by maximum likelihood method. The linear mixed model (LMM) was also used to estimate the reaction time of pedestrians. Continuous variables were scaled (M = 0, SD = 1) to fit the model.

The summary of the model is shown in Table 1. The predicted probability was calculated according to the model and was plotted in Fig. 2. Both the main effects of situations and gap size are significant (ps < 0.02), as well as the interaction effect (p < 0.001).

Table 1. Result of the generalized linear mixed model for pedestrians' road-crossing decisions.

Predictors	Log-odds	Std. error	CI	p
(Intercept)	−0.15	0.26	−0.66–0.35	0.549
Gap size	3.93	0.12	3.70–4.16	**<0.001**
Situation (AV)	0.23	0.10	0.04–0.43	**0.020**
Situation (M-HUM)	0.13	0.10	−0.06–0.32	0.173
Situation (M-AV)	0.20	0.10	0.00–0.40	**0.046**
Gap size * situation (AV)	0.38	0.16	0.07–0.69	**0.017**
Gap size * situation (M-HUM)	0.04	0.15	−0.25–0.33	0.795
Gap size * situation (M-AV)	0.57	0.17	0.24–0.89	**0.001**
Observations	12218			
Marginal R^2/conditional R^2	0.736/0.862			
AIC	5715.020			

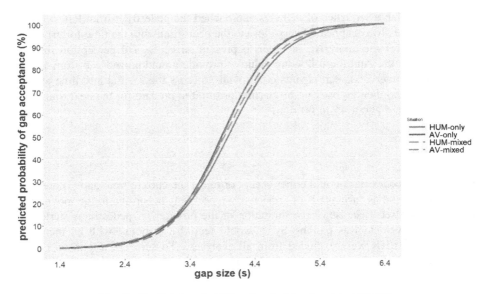

Fig. 2. Predicted probability of pedestrians' gap acceptance

The results indicate that, in general, the likelihood of pedestrians accepting a specific gap increased with gap size ($p < 0.001$). More importantly, pedestrians crossed more often when interacting with automated vehicles, regardless of whether in a mixed traffic condition (ps < 0.05). The significant effect of interaction between gap size and interaction situation means that the transition from rejecting to accepting was more abruptly when pedestrians interacted with automated vehicles, regardless of the traffic environment (ps < 0.02). No significant difference was found between HUM-only and HUM-mixed conditions, or between AV-only and AV-mixed (all ps > 0.17). As shown in Fig. 2, for larger gaps, pedestrians crossed more often in front of automated vehicles than human-driven vehicles.

4   Discussion

The current study compared pedestrians' gap acceptance behavior when interacting with human-driven vehicles and automated vehicles in the different traffic environments. For both two types of vehicles, pedestrians showed a general tendency to cross at larger gaps. In addition, pedestrians' road-crossing decision-making was proved to be affected by assistance information when interacting with automated vehicles. Pedestrians accepted more large gaps in front of automated vehicles. And when automated vehicles and human-driven vehicles shared a lane, the effect of assistance information remained the same as they drive separately.

When pedestrians interact with human-driven vehicles, especially when human-driven vehicles drive on a separate lane, pedestrians' gap acceptance behavior reflected the legacy strategy. For automated vehicles, the assistance information showed the objective and unbiased estimated risk of crossing, which should be more reliable than pedestrians' estimation of the crossing risk. Compared with human-driven vehicles, pedestrians accepted more larger gaps when interacting with automated vehicles. And pedestrians' gap acceptance behavior was more sensitive to object time-to-arrival with the help of assistance information. This result suggested that the proposed strategy which just conveys information to support existing gap acceptance behavior was feasible.

Pedestrians' gap acceptance behavior also indicated that pedestrians inclined to make decisions based on their legacy strategy. For example, when gap size smaller than 3.4 s, the automated vehicles reminded pedestrians a higher level of risk to cross for smaller gaps. If pedestrians take a strategy to follow the signals conveyed by automated vehicles, they would not cross for small gaps. However, pedestrians still crossed in such cases (TTA <= 3.4 s) from time to time as they do when interacting with human-driven vehicles.

Studies have proved that the accuracy of time-to-arrival estimation is affected by several factors in traffic, such as vehicle size (Petzoldt 2016), approaching speed (Petzoldt 2016, 2014), driving experience (DeLucia and Mather 2006), age of perceivers (Rusch et al. 2016). Estimation of time-to-arrival was reckoned as a main source of information for pedestrians' gap acceptance decisions (Petzoldt 2014). In the current study, the vehicle size, vehicle speeds remained unchanged, which then helped pedestrian estimate time-to-arrival more accurately. Even so, assistance information still played a role in pedestrians' decision-making. It is expected that in a more complex traffic environment where different kinds of vehicles present with changed vehicle speeds, automated vehicles with assistance information would further increase crossing safety.

As to the traffic environment, no difference was found for human-driven vehicles in mixed or non-mixed traffic, nor the automated vehicles. One reason may be that in the current study, assistance information only had a minor effect on pedestrians' decision. Considering unchanged vehicle speeds, reduced uncertainty of time-to-arrival estimation may serve as the main source of information, even when assistance information was conveyed by automated vehicles. Therefore, similar strategies were employed for all four kinds of interaction situations. A further step is to introduce the variability of vehicle speeds and compare pedestrians' strategies of decision-making when their estimation of time-to-arrival became more inaccurate.

5 Conclusions

In the current study, automated vehicles just send messages to assist pedestrians' gap acceptance decisions, whereas vehicles did not yield as usually do. Assistance information conveyed by automated vehicles was found to help pedestrians make safer road-crossing decisions. No difference for the traffic environment reflected pedestrians rely on their legacy gap acceptance strategy to cross and assistance information had a minor effect.

Acknowledgments. This work is supported by the National Natural Science Foundation of China (31970998).

References

Ackermann, C., Beggiato, M., Bluhm, L.-F., Löw, A., Krems, J.F.: Deceleration parameters and their applicability as informal communication signal between pedestrians and automated vehicles. Transp. Res. Part F Traffic Psychol. Behav. **62**, 757–768 (2019). https://doi.org/10.1016/j.trf.2019.03.006

Chang, C.-M., Toda, K., Sakamoto, D., Igarashi, T.: Eyes on a car: an interface design for communication between an autonomous car and a pedestrian. In: Proceedings of the 9th International Conference on Automotive User Interfaces and Interactive Vehicular Applications, AutomotiveUI 2017, pp. 65–73. ACM, New York (2017). https://doi.org/10.1145/3122986.3122989

Clamann, M., Aubert, M., Cummings, M.: Evaluation of vehicle-to-pedestrian communication displays for autonomous vehicles. In: Transportation Research Board Meeting (2017)

de Clercq, K., Dietrich, A., Núñez Velasco, J.P., de Winter, J., Happee, R.: External human-machine interfaces on automated vehicles: effects on pedestrian crossing decisions. Hum. Factors (2019). https://doi.org/10.1177/0018720819836343

DeLucia, P.R., Mather, R.D.: Motion extrapolation of car-following scenes in younger and older drivers. Hum. Factors **48**(4), 666–674 (2006). https://doi.org/10.1518/001872006779166352

Fuest, T., Sorokin, L., Bellem, H., Bengler, K.: Taxonomy of traffic situations for the interaction between automated vehicles and human road users. In: Stanton, N.A. (ed.) Advances in Human Aspects of Transportation. AISC, vol. 597, pp. 708–719. Springer, Cham (2018). https://doi.org/10.1007/978-3-319-60441-1_68

Holländer, K., Colley, A., Mai, C., Häkkilä, J., Alt, F., Pfleging, B.: Investigating the influence of external car displays on pedestrians' crossing behavior in virtual reality. In: Proceedings of the 21st International Conference on Human-Computer Interaction with Mobile Devices and Services - MobileHCI 2019. Presented at the 21st International Conference, Taipei, Taiwan, pp. 1–11. ACM Press (2019). https://doi.org/10.1145/3338286.3340138

Kaparias, I., Bell, M.G.H., Biagioli, T., Bellezza, L., Mount, B.: Behavioural analysis of interactions between pedestrians and vehicles in street designs with elements of shared space. Transp. Res. Part F Traffic Psychol. Behav. **30**, 115–127 (2015). https://doi.org/10.1016/j.trf.2015.02.009

Koh, P.P., Wong, Y.D.: Gap acceptance of violators at signalised pedestrian crossings. Accid. Anal. Prev. **62**, 178–185 (2014). https://doi.org/10.1016/j.aap.2013.09.020

Köhler, S., Schreiner, B., Ronalter, S., Doll, K., Brunsmann, U., Zindler, K.: Autonomous evasive maneuvers triggered by infrastructure-based detection of pedestrian intentions. In: Intelligent Vehicles Symposium (IV), 2013 IEEE, pp. 519–526. IEEE (2013)

Lee, Y.M., et al.: Understanding the messages conveyed by automated vehicles. In: Proceedings of the 11th International Conference on Automotive User Interfaces and Interactive Vehicular Applications - AutomotiveUI 2019. Presented at the 11th International Conference, Utrecht, Netherlands, pp. 134–143. ACM Press (2019a). https://doi.org/10.1145/3342197.3344546

Lee, Y.M., et al.: Investigating pedestrians' crossing behaviour during car deceleration using wireless head mounted display: an application towards the evaluation of eHMI of automated vehicles. In: Proceedings of the Tenth International Driving Symposium on Human Factors in Driving Assessment, Training and Vehicle Design, pp. 252–258. University of Iowa (2019b)

Ni, Y., Wang, M., Sun, J., Li, K.: Evaluation of pedestrian safety at intersections: a theoretical framework based on pedestrian-vehicle interaction patterns. Accid. Anal. Prev. **96**, 118–129 (2016). https://doi.org/10.1016/j.aap.2016.07.030

Nuñez Velasco, J.P., Farah, H., van Arem, B., Hagenzieker, M.P.: Studying pedestrians' crossing behavior when interacting with automated vehicles using virtual reality. Transp. Res. Part F Traffic Psychol. Behav. **66**, 1–14 (2019). https://doi.org/10.1016/j.trf.2019.08.015

Pawar, D.S., Patil, G.R.: Pedestrian temporal and spatial gap acceptance at mid-block street crossing in developing world. J. Saf. Res. **52**, 39–46 (2015). https://doi.org/10.1016/j.jsr.2014.12.006

Petzoldt, T.: Size speed bias or size arrival effect—How judgments of vehicles' approach speed and time to arrival are influenced by the vehicles' size. Accid. Anal. Prev. **95**(Part A), 132–137 (2016). https://doi.org/10.1016/j.aap.2016.07.010

Petzoldt, T.: On the relationship between pedestrian gap acceptance and time to arrival estimates. Accid. Anal. Prev. **72**(Supp C), 127–133 (2014). https://doi.org/10.1016/j.aap.2014.06.019

Rasouli, A., Tsotsos, J.K.: Autonomous vehicles that interact with pedestrians: a survey of theory and practice. IEEE Trans. Intell. Transp. Syst. 1–19 (2019). https://doi.org/10.1109/tits.2019.2901817

Rusch, M.L., Schall Jr., M.C., Lee, J.D., Dawson, J.D., Edwards, S.V., Rizzo, M.: Time-to-contact estimation errors among older drivers with useful field of view impairments. Accid. Anal. Prev. **95**, 284–291 (2016). https://doi.org/10.1016/j.aap.2016.07.008

Schieben, A., Wilbrink, M., Kettwich, C., Madigan, R., Louw, T., Merat, N.: Designing the interaction of automated vehicles with other traffic participants: design considerations based on human needs and expectations. Cogn. Tech. Work **21**(1), 69–85 (2019). https://doi.org/10.1007/s10111-018-0521-z

Schneemann, F., Heinemann, P.: Context-based detection of pedestrian crossing intention for autonomous driving in urban environments. In: 2016 IEEE/RSJ International Conference on Intelligent Robots and Systems (IROS). IEEE, pp. 2243–2248 (2016)

Song, Y.E., Lehsing, C., Fuest, T., Bengler, K.: External HMIs and their effect on the interaction between pedestrians and automated vehicles. In: Karwowski, W., Ahram, T. (eds.) Intelligent Human Systems Integration. AISC, vol. 722, pp. 13–18. Springer, Cham. (2018) https://doi.org/10.1007/978-3-319-73888-8_3

World Health Organization: Pedestrian safety: a road safety manual for decision-makers and practitioners (2013)

An Eye Catcher in the ATC Domain: Influence of Multiple Remote Tower Operations on Distribution of Eye Movements

Maik Friedrich$^{(\boxtimes)}$ ⬤, Anneke Hamann, and Jörn Jakobi

German Aerospace Center, 38108 Brunswick, Germany
Maik.Friedrich@dlr.de

Abstract. The future of Remote Tower Operations is focusing on the development and implementation of the Multiple Remote Tower Operations (MRTO) which allows for monitoring and controlling several aerodromes in parallel. While Single Remote Tower Operations have already become reality, the implementation of MRTO poses a significant change in Air Traffic Control Officers' (ATCOs) workflow, especially in terms of work situations, responsibilities and challenges. Even though MRTO brings along the potential to reduce the risk for human error due to boredom and also helps financially stabilize smaller airports, it might increase workload. Yet the changes to workload of an ATCO have to be carefully addressed and analyzed. The ATCOs' mental workload is connected to the ability to maintain a stable "picture" of the situation. This picture is generated from all the information gathered in monitoring the MRTO workstation. In order to analyze the influence that MRTO has on ATCOs' process of gathering information, we collected eye-tracking data from different experiments that varied in traffic and workplace designs. In addition to the eye-tracking we used the subjective rating scale ISA to measure the perceived workload. Only professional ATCOs participated in our real time simulation study. This paper focuses on the analysis of gaze distribution and gaze pattern while handling simulated traffic.

The analysis concentrated on, first, the influence of the workplace design on the information gathering process and second, the measurements of workload by eye-tracking and subjective rating. The results present eye-tracking behavior of the participants in a descriptive manner because statistical conditions for inferential statistics are not met. The discussion shows the impact of MRTO on the ATCOs' workflow in comparison to single remote or conventional tower environments.

Keywords: Training · Multiple Remote Tower Operation · Eye-tracking · Workload

1 Introduction

In 2017, the number of people traveling by aircraft increased to a new high of almost 4 billion [1]. Due to this increase, it becomes necessary to explore methodologies that increase efficiency while ensuring the same safety in air traffic control (ATC).

© Springer Nature Switzerland AG 2020
D. Harris and W.-C. Li (Eds.): HCII 2020, LNAI 12187, pp. 262–277, 2020.
https://doi.org/10.1007/978-3-030-49183-3_21

A technology that supports this process is the remote surveillance for airports, also called remote tower operations (RTO) [2]. Research began on the basis of single remote tower operations and is driven by an optimal distribution of workload for the Air Traffic Control Officers (ATCOs) of smaller airports, and economic advantages. The low amount of traffic at some smaller airports can lead to under-utilized ATCOs and is, at the same time, non-profitable. Single Remote Tower, is a solution that centralizes the provision of air traffic service for several aerodromes in one center, as already implemented at Leipzig airport [3]. Multiple Remote Tower Operations (MRTO) take this approach even a step further by combining several aerodromes in one workstation.

The concept of MRTO is not only a more efficient way of managing the costly time resources of an ATCO but also reduces the danger of boredom [4] and sleepiness by providing a continuous workload [5]. In the context of this paper, MRTO is defined as an ATCO controlling several aerodromes at the same time, in contrast to controlling several aerodromes after each other. The workplace, described in detail below, allows for monitoring and managing up to three aerodromes via live video, radar, planning tool, and radio communication.

From a human factors perspective, the particular MRTO challenge is to maintain a separate mental picture for each aerodrome and quickly change between them [6]. As described above, this concept can reduce the risk of boredom but at the same time workload has to stay on a manageable level. Since workload has a connection to performance, see summary [7], the identification of methodologies that support the estimation of workload are important.

Workload is the strain or impact of stressors on the ATCO, depending on his/her abilities, resources etc. [8, 9]. An ATCO's workload is expected to be of a cognitive quality [10] and is therefore specified in this paper as mental workload [11]. Studies [12–14] in the area of measuring mental workload in ATC use subjective measurements for assessment. A common online measurement is the Instantaneous Self-Assessment (ISA) Scale [15], that evaluates the mental workload in real-time simulations using a five-point rating scale [16, 17]. Besides its subjectivity, the disadvantage of the ISA scale is the intrusiveness that will repeatedly interrupt ATCO during the task performance.

Promising alternatives that use objective measurements are the recording of electrophysiological activities (EEG) [e.g., 18–20], the structured analysis of the traffic situation [e.g., 21] or the application of an eye-tracking metric (dwell time, fixation duration, pupil dilation) [e.g., 22, 23]. Even though the most common connection between workload and eye-tracking metrics is pupil dilation [24–26], the focus of this paper is on dwell time, fixation duration, and transition frequency, because the pupillary response can also be influenced by external stimuli (e.g., lighting conditions) [24] that cannot be controlled in the out-the-window view of a tower or in this case panoramic view (PV) of a remote tower. Dwell time, fixation duration, and transition frequency could been shown as indicators for workload in other domains [26, 27]. Therefore, a priority of this paper is examining the application of the existing metrics to the MRTO environment. If successful this could provide a basis for future developments.

With the increase of automation in the ATC domain the ATCO's behavior might be the only direct input into the system that can be measured in the future. In consideration of the research presented above, the authors believe that, at present, the evaluation of eye-tracking metrics as an indicator for mental workload is the most promising approach. However, to the authors' knowledge, there is no study that correlates the subjective and objective measurements in a realistic scenario and in the context of MRTO. Therefore, the application of selected eye-tracking metrics as an objective measurement for mental workload as extension or replacement of the subjective workload ratings would provide a good foundation for future MRTO.

Research on the connection between mental workload and eye-tracking metrics has already been conducted in other ATM domains such as cockpit [28], or weather displays [29]. Previous studies in MRTO [5] explored the ATCO performance in relation to Traffic Volume and Traffic Complexity in a real-time simulation environment. The present study focuses on eye-tracking metrics as possible objective indicators for mental workload during MRTO. It is part of an exploratory research with different interface designs and workload configurations with the aim to identify possible influences of the workplace and evaluate subjective against objective measurements. In connection to workload, the three eye tracking metrics, fixation frequency and average duration and average transition frequency were selected [27] to extend the result to the MRTO environment. In collaboration with the air navigation service providers Hungaro Control (HC), Oro Navigacija (ON), and Frequentis, an ATC system manufacturer, the German Aerospace Center (DLR) conducted this study [30].

2   Research Questions

Based on the existing literature and the eye-tracking metrics applied and evaluated in different domains, the following research questions (RQ) are proposed. RQ1: Is the amount of traffic connected to the subjective mental workload? RQ2: How does the arrangement of information influence the dwell time on the different Areas of Interest (AoI)? RQ3: Is the subjective rating of mental workload correlated with the selected eye-tracking metrics?

With regards to RQ1 we hypothesize that more traffic leads to an increase in subjective workload, similar to the model assumption of [21]. We also hypothesize that the information gathering process is changed [17], especially the distribution of dwell time onto the workplace (RQ2) by a rearrangement of information. As extension to RQ2 it is also important to see how the shift in information gathering is connected to the rearrangement, which could provide valuable insights into the general gathering of information during MRTO. With regards to RQ3 we assume that the selected metric will show a connection to the subjective measurement.

3   Method

A study including eye-tracking measurement was conducted on a prototype workplace for MRTO in a simulated real-time environment. Two groups of participants had to control three aerodromes at the same time and manage the traffic in different scenarios designed to induce workload. Eye-tracking data was collected and analyzed using the selected metrics. In the following section the details of the study are presented.

3.1   Participants

For this study two groups of participants were recruited. The first group consisted of 6 ATCOs (4 male/2 female) from HC. The first group participated in the study from 12th to the 22nd of November 2018. Their age was between 29 and 59 years (M = 42.6, SD = 9.55) and their working experience between 7 and 36 years (M = 17.7, SD = 9.6). The second group consisted of 6 ATCOs (all male) from ON. The second group participated in the study from 4th to the 11th of December 2018. Their age was between 25 and 37 years (M = 29.6, SD = 3.9) and their working experience between 1.5 and 8 years (M = 3.9, SD = 2.4). All participants in each group were active ATCOs and none had previously participated in a multiple RTO study. The ATCOs participated voluntarily during their working hours of their respective company. The study was performed in accordance with the General Data Protection Regulation (EU) 2016/679.

3.2   Design and Material

The study was conducted in the TowerLab [5] at the Institute of Flight Guidance, DLR. Figure 1 presents the workplace with the necessary screens and their names. The simulation, including traffic and realistic flight information, is provided by the traffic simulator NARSIM [31] and was supported by the planning tool (FlightStrip) for MRTO developed by Frequentis. The PV (208° horizontal and 32° vertical) was separated into three rows with one medium sized airport (Main) and two small airports (Second and Third). On the right side of each PV view were the pan-tilt-zoom (PTZ) cameras of the particular airport. Between PV view and FlightStrip, the radar screens for each airport (RADAR) were positioned. To increase the distinctiveness, the interfaces (PV, PTZ, RADAR and strip bay on FlightStrip screen) of each airport were color coded with a specific airport color. Radio communication was performed via headset and the frequencies for all airports were coupled.

A between-subject design was used with the factors "arrangement of information" and "traffic amount". To reduce learning effects, each scenario had slightly different scheduled traffic and a special event. The events were selected with regards to expected similar workload, and designed using feedback from experts from HC and ON. The traffic distribution was 50% for the main and 25% for each of the second and third airport. In two cases the event included variation in the traffic distribution.

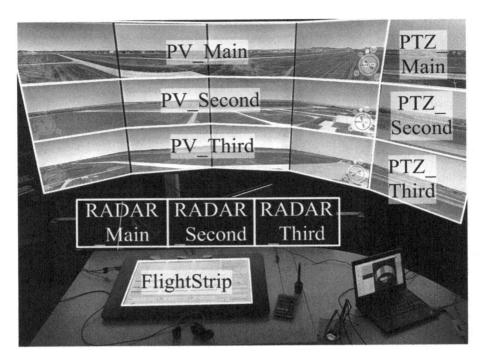

Fig. 1. MRTO real-time simulation platform with planning tool and defined AoIs (yellow frames) for group one (Color figure online)

Two events included the handover of one airport to another ATCO. The data after the handover was not used for the analysis. Each participant had to control a minimum of 4 scenarios with 3 active aerodromes in parallel. The operational modes were normal (no degraded modes or special procedures) and it was always day time at each aerodrome. None of the scenario had clouds and always visual meteorological conditions (VMC).

The participants were divided into two traffic groups with an average amount of 20 and 28 aircrafts per hour (90% traffic with instrument flight rules, IFR). The traffic groups' names (20 and 28) are derived from the amount of traffic. The arrangement of information for traffic group 20 is presented in Fig. 1. For traffic group 28 PV_Main and PV_Third were interchanged and also were PTZ_Main and PTZ_Third.

3.3 Procedure

The participants of the two groups were scheduled each for two days and in pairs. After arrival, the participants received a briefing concerning the MRTO workplace, the procedures and their task. The participants also gave written consent to the recording of personal data. Each participant performed a training session of approximately 40 min, to familiarize themselves with the arrangement of information and especially with the FlightStrip interface. The duration of each run varied between 40 and 45 min, depending on the participant. Each participant controlled three aerodromes at the same time. Before each run, the eye-tracking glasses were calibrated to record the eye movement of the ATCO in charge. During each run the participants answered the ISA scale every five minutes. One participant was selected randomly to start with the first scenario while the other completed questionnaires. After the first run the participants switched places. This alternating procedure was repeated until each participant had finished 4 scenarios. The group 20 additionally completed a 5th emergency scenario that is not part of this paper. Each pair of participants was debriefed together.

3.4   Data Analysis

We focus our analysis on descriptive data rather than inferential statists between the groups. This is due to the small sample size and the explorative experimental design that varies two factors between the two groups The influence between the two factors cannot be distinguished and therefore the results section has to account for the influence of both. The same applies to our interpretation of the results in the Discussion and Conclusion sections.

The eye-tracking data was analyzed with the Eye-Tracking Analyzer Software by DLR [32] that uses a velocity-based fixation detection algorithm [33] to separate fixations and saccades. This was necessary to reduce the misclassification in the raw data due to the large number of AoIs and possible intertwining scan paths. The velocity threshold was defined individually as the fastest five percent movements within each run. The selected AoI are presented in Fig. 1. Eye-tracking data was only valid within these AoIs. Due to the different durations of runs, only the first 40 min of each run were used for data analysis.

The ISA scale is a 5 value scale (1 = underutilized, 2 = relaxed, 3 = comfortable, 4 = high, 5 = excessive) to indicate the level of workload for the past 5 min. As a general interpretation of the ISA scale, all values below the average can be described as underload whereas values above the average are considered as overload, but both are leading to performance decrements [34, 35]. The Yerkes-Dodson-Law [36] states that there is an inverted U relationship between arousal and performance with the general goal of moderate levels, hence their optimal performance level. The two ends of the ISA scale represent extreme values (boredom and overstrain) that are not preferable for longer periods. The optimal value is in the center of the scale. The participants received an audio signal that indicated that they had to complete the questionnaire and were instructed to do so within 30 s. The ISA was presented on the left upper side on the FlightStrip screen.

4   Results

The following sub sections are derived from the research questions. Due to technical issues, participant one from group 20 and participants one and two from group 28 were not recorded. Moreover, one run from participant two of group 20 was not recorded. Due to a relative small number of observations for the ISA category "excessive" (20 N = 10 and 28 N = 25 in relation to an average of 140 observations per ISA Value), value 5 is not further analyzed

Traffic Amount and Workload

The first analysis concerned the amount of traffic in connection to workload (RQ1). Figure 2 presents the descriptive data that supports RQ1. The analysis shows that participants in group 28 on average classify the workload as higher and closer to the optimum of "comfortably busy" than the participants in group 20. The value underutilized was selected in 15.9% (25 in group 20 and 14 in group 28) of all 245 situations. In total 2.8% (2 in 20 and 5 in 28) of the participants classified the situation as excessive.

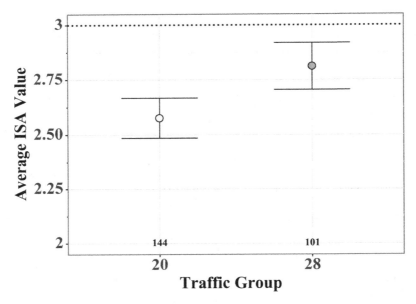

Fig. 2. Average ISA score per traffic group. The number on the bottom represents amount of observations for each group. Error bars show the standard error of the mean. The dotted line indicates the scale average.

4.1   Distribution of the Areas of Interest

The second analysis concerns the influence of the arrangement of information onto the dwell time on the different AoIs (RQ2). Figure 3 shows the distribution of dwell times onto the defined AoIs (see Fig. 1). The invalid eye data of each participant was removed and the dwell times were calculated in percentage for each participant to allow comparability.

The results indicate two different scanning behaviors, with the biggest difference on the PV AoIs. The dwell times for traffic group 20 show almost the same ratio in attention distribution between PV_Main ($M = 9.34$, $SD = 9.6$), PV_Second ($M = 9.77$, $SD = 4.63$), and PV_Third ($M = 11.12$, $SD = 3.87$). By contrast, the dwell times for traffic group 28 show that the attention is distributed in connection to the traffic handled on PV_Main ($M = 31.76$, $SD = 7.53$), PV_Second ($M = 5.25$, $SD = 3.42$), and PV_Third ($M = 2.68$, $SD = 2.05$).

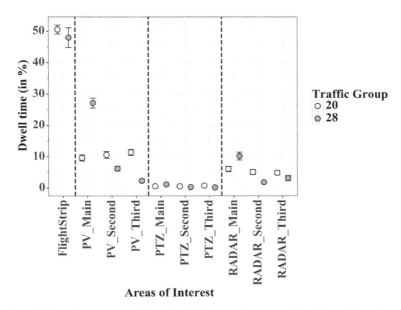

Fig. 3. Dwell time in percentage for each AoI per traffic group. Error bars show the standard error of the mean.

Table 1 Mean dwell times percentages separated by Traffic group static mask and ISA value shows the mean dwell time percentages for AoI FlightStrip and PV_Main. The results show that in traffic group 28 the subjective workload has an influence on the distribution between FlightStrip and PV_Main whereas in traffic group 20 the dwell time percentage seams stable.

Table 1. Mean dwell times percentages separated by traffic group static mask and ISA value.

Traffic group	Static mask	ISA	Mean	SD
20	FlightStrip	1	49.05	10.58
20		2	50.41	10.63
20		3	53.6	12.93
20		4	48.49	7.44
20	PV_Main	1	9.65	5.91
20		2	12.1	7.73
20		3	8.72	6.12
20		4	7.71	5.7
28	FlightStrip	1	59.22	16.69
28		2	43.05	15.32
28		3	36.78	14.12
28		4	47.08	14.74
28	PV_Main	1	19.06	8.22
28		2	35.69	16.24
28		3	32.9	11.14
28		4	30.04	13.36

4.2   Fixation Frequency and Average Duration

The third analysis concerns the eye-tracking metrics average number of fixations per minute and average duration of fixation per minute in connection to the subjective perceived workload. With respect to RQ3 the amount of fixation and average duration were selected as metrics to compare against the ISA scale. Because ISA is applied every five minutes (to evaluate the past five minutes), the time before a valid answer was separated into 5 one-minute segments. For these segments the average number of fixations was calculated. The same procedure was applied for the average duration of the fixation and in the subsection transition frequency.

Figure 4 shows the results of the analysis on average number of fixations per traffic group and ISA Value. The values indicate that on average traffic group 20 fixated more often than traffic group 28 if they were underutilized or relaxed (ISA Values 1 and 2). The same pattern is visible for high (ISA Value 4) subjective workload.

Figure 5 complements the results from Fig. 4. As for Fig. 4, the excessive value was excluded from the analysis due to the same small number of observations. The average duration of a fixation per minute is longer for the traffic group 28 for underutilized, relaxed or high subjective workload compared to traffic group 20. For the comfortable ISA value, the average number of fixations is similar and so is the average duration of fixations. The results from Fig. 4 and Fig. 5 indicate that reduced workload leads to a higher number of shorter fixations.

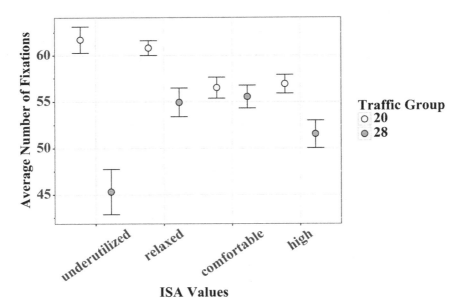

Fig. 4. Average number of fixations per ISA values and separated by traffic group. Error bars show the standard error of the mean.

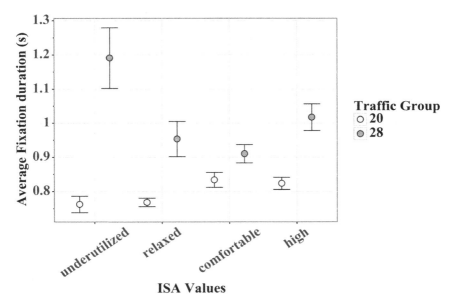

Fig. 5. Average duration of fixations per ISA values and traffic group. Error bars show the standard error of the mean.

4.3   Transition Frequency

The final analysis extends the previous analyses by incorporation of AoIs and therefore the task of MRTO (RQ3). The task of MRTO is strongly connected to the order in which the ATCO gathers information from the workplace. By assuming that one AoI represents one possible source of information, the order in which information is gathered provides information on the strategy. Therefore, fixations are combined to macro fixations (all fixations on the same AoI).

The workload of the task should influence the macro fixations and therefore extends the search for possible eye-tracking metrics that could help, as proposed by RQ3, to determine the workload via eye-tracking metrics. The number of transitions between AoIs and the average transition duration was selected as possible metric for the following analysis. The transition and duration are measured if the fixation changes between AoIs. The results in Fig. 6 show the number of transitions per minute decrease for the traffic group 20 with increased subjective workload. Traffic group 28, has a low number of transitions while underutilized. With increased subjective workload the number of transitions seem to increase. Figure 7 presents the average duration in seconds from the last fixation on an AoI to the first fixation on a different AoI. Traffic group 20 has higher values than 28 for the subjective workload that is below comfortable.

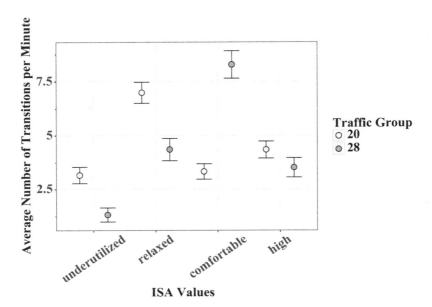

Fig. 6. Average number of transitions per ISA values, separated by traffic group. Error bars show the standard error of the mean.

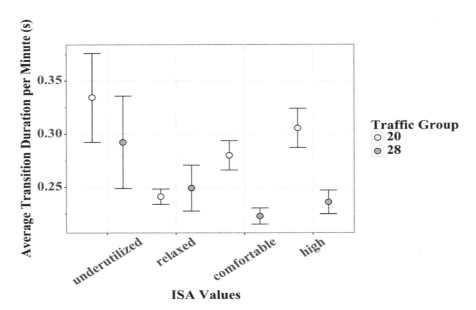

Fig. 7. Average transition duration of fixations per ISA values and separated by traffic group. Error bars show the standard error of the mean.

5   Discussion

The results need to be summed up and interpreted for each research question individually. As mentioned above, as conditions for inferential statistical analysis have not been met, the analysis was restricted to descriptive data only. Therefore the results as we found them are open to discussion and need to be interpreted in this section. The explorative means of the experiment is reflected in the expert sample, the relative small sample size, and the experimental design that varied two factors at the same time. The development of additional metrics was also not pursued due to the small sample size. Since the influence between the arrangement of information and the amount of traffic cannot be distinguished definably, this section has to take both into account.

5.1   Amount of Traffic Connected to Subjective Workload

As we expected for RQ1, the results show that the amount of traffic increases the subjective workload. For both traffic groups and therefore also for both arrangements of information the subjective workload is below the scale average which means that the participants were more often insufficiently challenged.

5.2   Arrangement of Information

RQ2 predicted an influence of the arrangement of information onto the dwell time distribution on the MRTO workplace, as it was shown in different domains already [e.g., 26, 37]. The distribution of dwell time per AoI seems to vary for each traffic group. The dwell time distribution of traffic group 20 suggests an equal monitoring of the PV view for each airport. Due to the order of the PV, the participants in traffic group 20 had to visually cross PV_Second and PV_Third while switching between PV_Main and FlightStrip. On the contrary, traffic group 28 could switch between PV_Main and FlightStrip without crossing any other PV.

Considering that the increased amount of traffic was distributed equally among the traffic groups, the dwell time distribution should be similar for each group. Even though [17] showed that workload influences the strategies for information gathering and can lead to a shift in the sources of information gathering, the sum for the PV areas is comparable for both traffic groups. This rather indicates a different distribution of dwell time on the PV and not a shift of attention to a different system, e.g. the radar, as source of information. A possible explanation could be the increased probability of aircraft movements at the same time on the main airport. This could also lead to an exponential increase of attention in traffic group 28 rather than a linear as expected.

5.3   Subjective Rating in Connection to Eye-Tracking Metric

The results in relation to RQ3 are separated into the analysis of 4 metrics that are complementary in two pairs. The first pair counts the fixation frequency and the average duration of the fixations. The second pair looks at the task related transitions between AoIs and the duration between them.

The results of the first metric pair corresponded with the arrangement of information, because the participants in traffic group 28 pay more attention to the PV_Main. Literature [e.g., 27, 28] suggest that an increase in fixation frequency and a decrease in average duration is connected to an increase in workload. The connection is similar for the transition frequency that should increase and the transition duration that should decrease with an increase in workload.

Especially at low subjective workload their number of fixations and the duration of fixation indicate that they monitor less AoIs for a longer period. Dwell time percentage for the category underutilized support this when traffic group 28 has almost 80% of its attention on only FlightStrip and PV_Main. The effect is reduced when workload increases to a medium level, assuming that this kind of workload is only reached if traffic on all three aerodromes must be handled in parallel, which then forces the ATCO to observe all PV AoIs.

Our interpretation of the results of the second metric pair is that the transition frequency per minute is increased with increasing subjective workload for traffic group 28, while the transition frequency per minute decreases for traffic group 20 until ISA Scale "comfortable" is reached. Concordantly, the average transition duration per minute is lower for traffic group 28 until the ISA scale average is reached. As the first metric pair, this indicates that during underutilized phases, traffic group 28 only concentrates on two AoIs that are close together in the workplace arrangement.

The selected metric for RQ3 seems to indicate subjective workload in a relative narrow window. This extends the work of eye metric as workload metric from [26, 27], but also draws attention to the information arrangement as an important factor that has to be considered in advance to the application of the selected eye metrics.

6   Conclusions

In summary, this explorative study aimed at the evaluation of three RQ in relation to the MRTO workplace. The study analyzed the subjective workload and the eye movement of two traffic groups with different arrangements of information. In order to induce a wide spectrum of subjective workload, the number of movements in both traffic groups was higher than generally aimed for in the concept for MRTO. The results of this study cannot be used to identify a limit of movements for one ATCO operating MRTO. The same applies for the determination that MRTO are only valid for 3 aerodromes at the same time. Safety and efficiency in ATC are dependent on a variety of factors (e.g. flight operation modes, traffic situation, weather conditions, etc.) that we did not systematically alter for the extent of this study.

A conclusion in terms of the subjective workload is a careful interpretation of the ISA scale, especially below and above the average. Underload, moderate, and overload seam to influence the eye movement quite differently and have to be evaluated stepwise.

The authors believe that the most suitable dwell time distribution for the MRTO concept should be similar to traffic group 20. Even if traffic also influences the dwell time distribution, an arrangement of the most important AoI with the less important AoIs in between seems more promising with this study. This provides indication in terms of the best workplace design. Furthermore, the study could provide valuable indications for eye metrics as objective workload measuring. In summary, the successful application of eye metrics depends on the scan path and on the arrangement of information, but seems predictable for a fixed set-up.

Future work should concentrate on an experimental design that allows for inferential static analysis of the single factors that are described in this paper. This should be followed by a structured analysis of additional factors for safe and efficient ATC and their detailed analysis in a systematic manner.

Acknowledgements. The authors thank SESAR Joint Undertaking for funding this project as well as their project partners Hungaro Control, Oro Navigacija and Frequentis for their collaboration. This project has received funding from the SESAR Joint Undertaking under the European Union's Horizon 2020 research and innovation programme under grant agreement No 730195.

References

1. International Civil Aviation Organization. Air transport, passengers carried in 2017. Civil Aviation Statistics of the World and ICAO staff estimates (2019). https://data.worldbank.org/indicator/IS.AIR.PSGR
2. Fürstenau, N. (ed.): Virtual and Remote Control Tower. RTA. Springer, Cham (2016). https://doi.org/10.1007/978-3-319-28719-5
3. DFS. Die ersten Starts und Landungen im Remote Tower Center, 7th October 2018. https://www.dfs.de/dfs_homepage/de/Presse/Pressemitteilungen/2018/04.12.2018.-%20Die%20ersten%20Starts%20und%20Landungen%20im%20Remote%20Tower%20Center/
4. Fisherl, C.D.: Boredom at work: a neglected concept. Hum. Relat. **46**(3), 395–417 (1993)
5. Hagl, M., et al.: Impact of simultaneous movements on the perception of safety, workload and task difficulty in a multiple remote tower environment. In: 2019 IEEE Aerospace Conference. IEEE (2019)
6. Möhlenbrink, C., Friedrich, M., Papenfuss, A.: RemoteCenter: Eine Mikrowelt zur Analyse der mentalen Repräsentation von zwei Flughäfen während einer Lotsentätigkeitsaufgabe [RemoteCenter: A microworld for analysing the mental representation of two airports during the air traffic control task.]. In: Tagungsband 8. Berliner Werkstatt Mensch-Maschine-Systeme. Berlin-Brandenburgische Akademie der Wissenschaften, Berlin (2009)
7. Young, M.S., et al.: State of science: mental workload in ergonomics. Ergonomics **58**(1), 1–17 (2015)
8. Edwards, T.: Human performance in air traffic control. Dissertation, University of Nottingham (2013)
9. International Organization for Standardization: Ergonomic principles related to mental workload. General terms and definitions (1991). ISO 10075:1991
10. Hadley, G.A., Guttman, J.A., Stringer, P.G.: Air traffic control specialist performance measurement database (1999). (DOT/FAA/CT-TN99/17)
11. Hancock, P.A., Chignell, M.H.: Mental workload dynamics in adaptive interface design. IEEE Trans. Syst. Man Cybern. **18**, 647–658 (1988)
12. Lamoureux, T.: The influence of aircraft proximity data on the subjective mental workload of controllers in the air traffic control task. Ergonomics **42**(11), 1482–1491 (1999)

13. Mercado-Velasco, G., Mulder, M., Van Paassen, M.: Analysis of air traffic controller workload reduction based on the solution space for the merging task. In: AIAA Guidance, Navigation, and Control Conference (2010)
14. Ahlstrom, U.: Work domain analysis for air traffic controller weather displays. J. Saf. Res. **36** (2), 159–169 (2005)
15. Kirwan, B., et al.: Human factors in the ATM system design life cycle. In: FAA/Eurocontrol ATM R&D Seminar (1997)
16. EUROCONTROL. Instantaneous Self Assessment of workload (ISA). HP repository (2012). https://ext.eurocontrol.int/ehp/?q=node/1585
17. Friedrich, M., et al.: The influence of task load on situation awareness and control strategy at the ATC tower environment. Cogn. Technol. Work **20**, 205–217 (2018)
18. Aricò, P., et al.: A passive brain–computer interface application for the mental workload assessment on professional air traffic controllers during realistic air traffic control tasks. Prog. Brain Res. **228**, 295–328 (2016)
19. Brookings, J.B., Wilson, G.F., Swain, C.R.: Psychophysiological responses to changes in workload during simulated air traffic control. Biol. Psychol. **42**(3), 361–377 (1996)
20. Abbass, H.A., et al.: Augmented cognition using real-time EEG-based adaptive strategies for air traffic control. In: Proceedings of the Human Factors and Ergonomics Society Annual Meeting. SAGE Publications, Los Angeles (2014)
21. Averty, P., et al.: Mental workload in air traffic control: an index constructed from field tests. Aviat. Space Environ. Med. **75**(4), 333–341 (2004)
22. Peißl, S., Wickens, C.D., Baruah, R.: Eye-tracking measures in aviation: a selective literature review. Int. J. Aerosp. Psychol. **28**(3–4), 98–112 (2018)
23. Ziv, G.: Gaze behavior and visual attention: a review of eye tracking studies in aviation. Int. J. Aviat. Psychol. **26**(3–4), 75–104 (2016)
24. Beatty, J., Lucero-Wagoner, B.: The pupillary system. In: Handbook of Psychophysiology, vol. 2, pp. 142–162 (2000)
25. Klingner, J.M., Measuring cognitive load during visual tasks by combining pupillometry and eye tracking. Stanford University Palo Alto, CA (2010)
26. Holmqvist, K., et al.: Eye Tracking: A Comprehensive Guide to Methods and Measures. Oxford University Press, Oxford (2011)
27. Faulhaber, A.K., Friedrich, M.: Eye-tracking metrics as an indicator of workload in commercial single-pilot operations. In: Longo, L., Leva, M.C. (eds.) H-WORKLOAD 2019. CCIS, vol. 1107, pp. 213–225. Springer, Cham (2019). https://doi.org/10.1007/978-3-030-32423-0_14
28. Ellis, K.K.E.: Eye tracking metrics for workload estimation in flight deck operations. Theses and Dissertations, p. 288 (2009)
29. Ahlstrom, U., Friedman-Berg, F.J.: Using eye movement activity as a correlate of cognitive workload. Int. J. Ind. Ergon. **36**, 623–636 (2006)
30. GRANT AGREEMENT - PJ05 Remote Tower - H2020-SESAR-2015-2/H2020-SESAR-2015-2, in 730195, p. 317. Single European Sky ATM Research Joint Undertaking, Europa (2016)
31. Teutsch, J., Postma-Kurlanc, A.: Enhanced virtual block control for Milan Malpensa airport in low visibility. In: Integrated Communications, Navigation and Surveillance Conference (ICNS) 2014. IEEE (2014)
32. Friedrich, M., Rußwinkel, N., Möhlenbrink, C.: A guideline for integrating dynamic areas of interests in existing set-up for capturing eye movement: looking at moving aircraft. Behav. Res. Methods **49**(3), 822–834 (2016). https://doi.org/10.3758/s13428-016-0745-x

33. Salvucci, D.D., Goldberg, J.H.: Identifying fixations and saccades in eye-tracking protocols. In: Eye Tracking Research and Applications Symposium, pp. 71–78. ACM Press, New York (2000)
34. Mracek, D.L., et al.: A multilevel approach to relating subjective workload to performance after shifts in task demand. Hum. Factors **56**(8), 1401–1413 (2014)
35. Vu, K.-P.L., et al.: Pilot and controller workload and situation awareness with three traffic management concepts. In: 29th Digital Avionics Systems Conference. IEEE (2010)
36. Yerkes, R.M., Dodson, J.D.: The relation of strength of stimulus to rapidity of habit formation. J. Comp. Neurol. Psychol. **18**, 459–482 (1908)
37. Hong, W., Thong, J.Y., Tam, K.Y.: The effects of information format and shopping task on consumers' online shopping behavior: a cognitive fit perspective. J. Manag. Inf. Syst. **21**(3), 149–184 (2004)

Effects of Mental Workload and Risk Perception on Pilots' Safety Performance in Adverse Weather Contexts

Shan Gao and Lei Wang[✉]

College of Flying Technology, Civil Aviation University of China,
Tianjin, China
wanglei0564@hotmail.com

Abstract. Many air crashes are related to pilots' mental workload and their risk perception when they meet adverse weather. The ability to manage weather risk is critical for pilots' performance. However, it is difficult to reflect variations in psychological parameters using scales in hazardous scenarios, and previous results have therefore been subjective and inaccurate. To grasp the subjective variation in psychological parameters and propose effective severe-weather training for pilots, this study examined heart-rate variation (HRV) and electrodermal activity (EDA) variables under hazardous scenarios. Nineteen participants were recruited to complete a flying task where the flight was divided into different segments according to the weather. Participants were divided into normal and abnormal groups according to their safety performance; the results showed that the two groups performed similarly during good weather and landing. Compared to the abnormal group, the normal group had a more stable inter-beat intervals (IBI) and higher skin conductivity level (SCL) during hazardous scenarios. The normal group also showed rapid increases in SCL after the weather worsened. These findings indicate that unstable HRV and lower activated EDA are associated with safety performance under hazardous scenarios. On that basis, a method based on physiological parameters is proposed to evaluate pilots' mental workload and risk perception without too much interference. Finally, some specific suggestions for training are made to ensure flight safety.

Keywords: Heart-rate variation · Electrodermal activity · Flight safety

1 Introduction

Mental workload is typically characterized by the level of mental activity for a subject [1], like monitoring and decision-making. It reflects the relationship between the resources needed to finish a specific task and our limited available resources. In relation to traffic, mental workload is defined as the level of effort required to maintain safety; in this way, it is the same as flight tasks [2]. Driving conditions occupy the space between safety and danger due to potential errors in subjective evaluation and compensation behaviors, which account for many accidents [3, 4]. According to the safety report of the CAAC (Civil Aviation Administration of China) [5], the main cause of flight accidents is

D. Harris and W.-C. Li (Eds.): HCII 2020, LNAI 12187, pp. 278–291, 2020.
https://doi.org/10.1007/978-3-030-49183-3_22

the crew, accounting for 69.77% between 2014 and 2018. Regarding fatal aircraft accidents, the IATA (International Air Transport Association) [6] noted that the main causes are related to SOP (standard operation procedure) adherence and SOP cross-verification, accounting for 61% of accidents during the same period. To address flight crew errors, the IATA mainly suggested developing crew performance and monitoring or cross-verification. Pilots may take risks because of inconsistencies between the risk they perceive and their internal threshold [7]. For the same level of risk, risk-prone pilots will adopt more risk-taking behaviors, although it is not their intention. Hence, mental workload has become an important indicator for measuring and evaluating performance in risk situations. Some pilots may perform more nervously than others, increasing the likelihood of accidents. Meanwhile, the lack of adjusting and adapting ability may broke the balance of risk and then errors happen. Thus, keeping the level of mental workload within a suitable range is helpful for maintaining safety. Moreover, identifying risky pilots and proposing specific training is also crucial for flight safety [8].

Risk perception and risk management are essential skills for pilots, and they affect safety performance by adjusting operations in a risk environment [9, 10]. Deteriorated or inaccurate subjective evaluations of potential risks can give rise to accidents [11]. In the risk homeostasis theory [3], accidents happen because of inconsistent risk states between the environment and subjective perception. Risk perception, as the first step of situational awareness, can reflect the ability to identify environmental risks. Many studies have focused on the subjective measuring of risk perception using question-naires [12, 13]. However, the ability to adapt and adjust is more important than risk perception when pilots face risks since it involves adjusting the relationship between the human and the environment. When pilots sense pressure during a task, they focus their attention on that task [14], which can destabilize safety and cause accidents. Although pilots receive training and preparation for bad weather, extreme weather changes can nevertheless threaten safety. Many studies have suggested that flying visual flight rules (VFR) into instrument meteorological conditions (IMC) causes accidents, and sensitivity to environmental risks are closely related to flight safety performance [15–17].

Accidents and unsafe events related to weather are common. Despite useful solutions for bad weather, like preflight preparations and adherence to minimum standards for weather conditions, pilots still face great challenges meeting safety demands. An excellent pilot should be able to correctly evaluate and manage risks. Thus, risk sensitivity is vital for pilots, and it is helpful to maintain an appropriate level of mental workload. O'Hare [17] suggested that pilots who are more likely to continue flying in bad weather have a poor ability to evaluate risks and decide to tolerate them. Many studies have used subjective measurement scales and behavioral observation to estimate mental workload and risk perception [18, 19]. However, the results are often inconsistent due to subjective methods. Recently, wearable and portable wireless equipment have attracted attention from researchers, with an increasing focus on mental health. While the physiological method in psychology may be unstable for measurement, researchers are increasingly accepting this objective approach to investigating human intention [20–22]. Given the high costs of pilot training, it is essential to estimate variations in physiology indicators and identify risk-prone trainees before their admission to reduce airlines' cultivation costs. This method can also help identify pilots' shortcomings and develop specific training. Therefore, the present study aimed to explore mental workload variations and risk perception ability in risk scenarios.

The main parameters of physiological measurement include heart rate, heart-rate variability, skin electrical activity, and brain electrical response. At present, we can continuously measure variations in physiological indicators under working conditions given the portability of wearable devices. These have been widely used in research on risk perception and psychological change in driving, flying, and other areas [23, 24]. For risk perception during flying, heart-rate variability and electrodermal analysis have been widely used. For physiological indicators, heart rate (HR) and heart-rate variation (HRV), reflecting the stability of heart movement, are widely used to represent mental workload, which is closely related to the sympathetic nervous system [25, 26]. The most-used indicators are IBI (inter-beat intervals) [27], which reflects the interval between two successive heartbeats, and SDNN (standard deviation of NN intervals) [28], which captures the levels of sympathetic and parasympathetic nervous system activity, which are associated with mental workload.

This study investigated pilots' mental workload and risk perception in risk operations based on physiological indicators using wearable and portable wireless physiological equipment to minimize the extent of interruption during operations. A hazard scenario was designed, and participants were recruited to accomplish the flying task. We focused on the effects of mental workload and risk perception on safety performance. Risk-prone pilots and their dynamic physiological parameters are discussed, and some useful recommendations are made to enhance the effects of training.

2   Methods

2.1   Participants

First, an experiment recruitment letter was distributed both online and offline. Then, we selected 19 flying cadets (see Fig. 1) who were skilled at using flight simulators at the Flight Technology College of the Civil Aviation University of China (CAUC). They were aged 18–33 (M = 20.47, SD = 3.405); data were collected from November to December in 2019. All of the subjects reported that they had not participated in any flight simulation experiments like this one and were fit to perform the flight tasks. Before the experiment started, all provided signed informed consent allowing us to collect their physiological parameters during the simulation.

Fig. 1. Flying simulation platform

2.2   Equipment

The experiment was based on the flying simulation platform at the Operation Safety and Human Factors Engineering Laboratory in Flight Technology College of the CAUC. The simulation flight was performed on a high-performance computer equipped with an Intel Core i7 CPU and an NVIDIA GeForce GTX 1060 6 GB graphics card. Three 27 in liquid crystal displays covering a 180° visual angle were used for the visual presentation. The flight simulator was controlled by a set of flight control equipment (Logitech, USA), including a flight control column with a 1.8 m USB interface, a throttle controller with a 1.5 m PS/2 cable, and a pair of rudder pedals. An iPad 2018 was used as the pilot instructor station (Apple, USA).

PPG uses an ear clip sensor, which is clamped on the earlobe and fixed on the collar with another clip. The relationship between the optical signal and blood flow was calculated using the transmission and reflection principle of the wavelength beam. Then, the conversions from optical signals to electrical signals were amplified to obtain the changes in volume, pulse, and blood flow. EDA was attached to the tips of the index and ring fingers by electrodes; it mainly depends on changes in electrical conductivity between two points to reflect the skin's electrical activity. The wearable physiological signal sensors were all 43*25*12 mm in size, with a resolution of 24 bit and a sampling frequency of 64 Hz (see Fig. 2). Data transformation used radio frequency and Bluetooth transmission technology. After proper wearing and normal data transmission were confirmed, the subjects began the simulation.

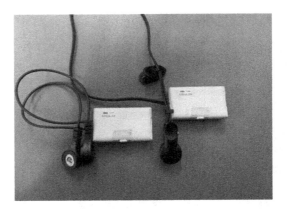

Fig. 2. Wearable physiological signal sensors

2.3   Scenarios Design

A cruising and landing flying task (Cessna SP-G1000) was performed using the flight simulator and X-plane 11. The whole flight procedure had two weather changes. The starting point was above RW16R Tianjin/Binhai airport, 3000 ft, with 110 knots and heading 80°. The marginal scattered cloud ceiling was 5000 ft, and visibility was 20 statute miles (about 32 km). The first change happened when they reached the TJK point; the marginal broken cloud ceiling descended to 3000 ft, and ground visibility was 12 statute miles (about 19 km) with mild rain and storm. The second change happened six miles from the CI1RZ waypoint. The weather got worse, and marginal ground visibility was just seven statute miles (about 11 km) with heavy rain and storm. Sometimes, lightning and turbulence would make the conditions more adverse. Pilots faced a dilemma of turning back or staying on the route. The experiment ended when the participants landed on runway 16R (or crashed) at Tianjin airport. The whole task took about 30 min and the description of variables used in this study was presented (see Table 1).

Table 1. Description of flying segments and physiological variation

Flying segments	Description
Segment	
Baseline	3 min before the simulation started
Segment 1	3 min after the simulation started
Segment 2	3 min after the first change in weather
Segment 3	3 min after the second change in weather
Segment 4	3 min before the aircraft touched down on the runway
Variation in physiological parameters (weather contributed)	
IBI1-2	IBI variation after the first change in weather
IBI1-3	IBI variation after the second change in weather
IBI1-4	IBI variation during the approach and landing
SCL2-1	SCL variation after the first change in weather
SCL3-1	SCL variation after the second change in weather
SCL4-1	SCL variation during the approach and landing

The experiment had a 2 × 4 mixed factorial design. All of the subjects were divided into two groups according to their safety performance, and each experienced different weather conditions during the whole flying task (weather conditions were controlled by a Control Pad, an app on the iPad 2018). Hence, there were two independent variables, including weather conditions (4 levels) within groups and safety performance (2 levels) between groups. HRV and EDA were the dependent variables reflecting their mental workload and risk perception.

2.4   Experiment Procedure

All of the participants provided signed informed consent and read the flight information covered weather report carefully (see Table 2).

Table 2. Brief flight information

Aircraft weights	
Aircraft empty	1721 lbs
Payload	624 lbs
Fuel remaining	36.3 lbs (about 45 min)
Total	2381.3 lbs (max 2558)
Flight plan	
Departure airport RW16R	16R TIANJIN/Binhai
TJK	
TJK-13	
CI1RZ	
FF16R	
Destination	RW16R 16R TIANJIN/Binhai
Weather report: TIANJIN/Binhai	
09:00 h	
Scattered at 5000 ft AMSL	
Ground visibility 20 SM (32 km)	
Atmospheric pressure 1025.25 mb	
Temperature 53.6°F	
Dewpoint 47°	
Almost no wind	
Barometric pressure 29.92	

First, they had 20 min to become acquainted with the simulator. Second, all of the participants were asked to carefully read information about the flying task before beginning. The information included the route, remaining fuel, and a brief weather report. Finally, the subjects needed to put on the physiological signal sensors, and data transformation was adjusted. After that, they performed the simulation. The flight task and brief information were provided, and the participants just needed to follow the route displayed on the Navigation Display (see Fig. 3).

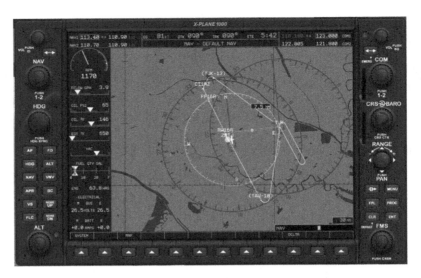

Fig. 3. Flight route displayed on the Navigation Display

2.5   Data Collection and Analysis

Data Collection. After the subjects learned about the experiment and provided informed consent, they were asked to clean their fingers on their left hand as well as the lobes of their left ears to avoid any sweat or dirt that could affect the sensors. To accurately obtain the changes in parameters during the flight and avoid the effects of adaptation on physiological variation in the simulation, we selected the segments for

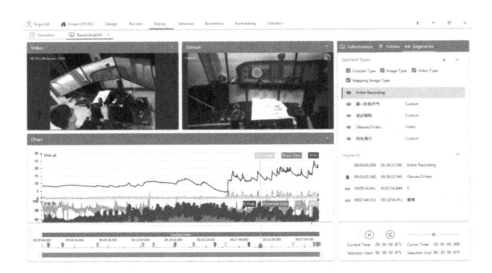

Fig. 4. ErgoLAB Human-Machine-Environment platform

approximately three minutes after every weather change. We took a rest period for about three minutes before starting the simulation as the baseline. After the experiment, the measurement data were imported into the ErgoLAB Human-Machine-Environment platform for data processing (see Fig. 4).

Data Preprocessing. Although the experimental conditions were strictly controlled, there was still a large amount of noise in the data. Thus, the data needed to have artifacts removed and be further analyzed. Therefore, the ErgoLAB Human-Machine-Environment platform was used to further smooth the data, and PPG and EDA indicators were extracted (see Fig. 5). The mean values of IBI, SDNN, LF/HF, SCL, and SCR were mainly obtained as dependent variables.

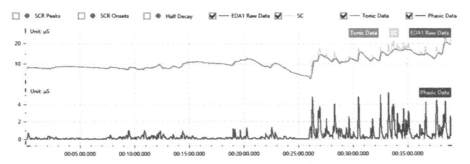

Fig. 5. Pre-treatment of EDA data

Analysis Methods. First, the dependent variable index in the baseline was tested, and the results showed that there were no differences between the two groups. A scatterplot and the Shapiro–Wilk method were used to test the trends and normality of the physiological data. To avoid individual differences, the variety in the physiological data relative to the baseline was also calculated, and changes in IBI and SCL were analyzed. A t test or the Mann-Whitney U test is used to judge differences between groups; the correct method depends on the type of data. For data normality, repeated-measures ANOVA was used to analyze weather changes and safety performance. Violations of the spherical hypothesis were corrected using Greenhouse-Geisser correction. The results were the outcomes of the MANOVA, with the unitary analysis of variance as a reference. If the data satisfied the spherical hypothesis, the results of the unitary analysis of variance would be accepted.

3 Results

3.1 Statistics of Physiological Parameters Between Groups in the Segments

After reviewing flying performance, the participants were divided into normal and abnormal groups. The abnormal subjects had several unsafe performances, including stall warnings, runway overshoot, bounced landing, overspeed landing, wrong runway landing, and crashed.

Table 3. Summary statistics for physiological parameters in each segment

Variables	Segments	Normal		Abnormal		t test
		Mean	Std.	Mean	Std.	p-value
IBI (ms)	Baseline	851.77	125.01	817.66	165.56	0.615
	Segment 1	781.49	73.11	798.86	164.90	0.787
	Segment 2	794.09	62.84	782.61	157.34	0.850
	Segment 3	792.96	70.25	742.38	118.94	0.260
	Segment 4	711.86	69.37	689.55	102.17	0.577
SCL (µs)	Baseline	–	–	–	–	–
	Segment 1	–	–	–	–	–
	Segment 2	13.82	7.72	6.10	4.71	**0.023**
	Segment 3	14.49	8.34	6.17	4.72	**0.022**
	Segment 4	16.14	7.86	7.11	4.72	**0.010**
SCR (µs)	Baseline	–	–	–	–	–
	Segment 1	0.40	0.22	0.22	0.21	0.102
	Segment 2	0.29	0.19	0.15	0.16	0.100
	Segment 3	0.41	0.24	0.20	0.18	**0.049**
	Segment 4	0.51	0.24	0.36	0.21	0.172

The results showed that the mean values and standard deviations for IBI in the normal group were lower than in the abnormal group, indicating a stable heart rate. For SCL and SCR, the normal group was higher than the abnormal group, meaning the responses of the normal group were more obvious (see Fig. 6).

3.2 Effects of Mental Workload on Safety Performance

The results showed that the mean value of IBI in each segment met normality. Thus, t tests were used to test the differences between the two groups. Because of the small sample size, the parameters of HRV were not normally distributed except IBI. Mann-Whitney U was used to examine the differences. The results showed that there were no significant differences in heart-rate variability between the two groups.

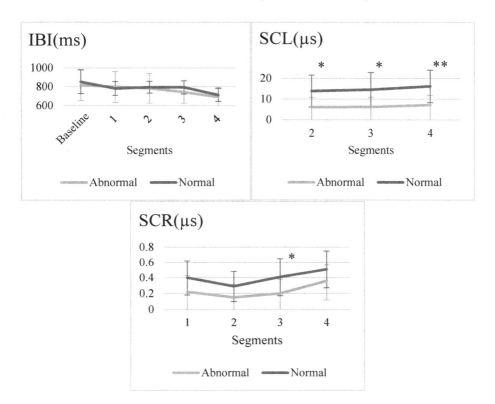

Fig. 6. Mean values and standard deviations of IBI/SCL/SCR between different groups

The mean IBI value in the abnormal group showed a continual downward trend, which declined faster (with a higher slope) after the weather changed. The normal group showed a decrease after starting the experiment and before landing; it was basically flat and slightly increased when severe weather occurred (see Fig. 6).

Furthermore, the variation in IBI after the occurrence of severe weather was analyzed (see Table 4), and the data all met the normal distribution. The t test showed that there was a significant difference in IBI1-4 ($p = 0.031$).

Table 4. Comparison of IBI variation between groups

Variation in IBI	Normal		Abnormal		t test
	Mean	Std.	Mean	Std.	p-value
IBI1-2 (ms)	−12.59	38.29	16.25	23.54	0.077
IBI1-3 (ms)	−11.46	59.01	56.48	66.48	**0.031**
IBI1-4 (ms)	69.63	48.65	109.31	87.22	0.272

The mean IBI values were further analyzed by repeated-measures ANOVA. The experimental data did not meet the spherical hypothesis, and the MANOVA results were taken as the criterion. We found a statistical difference in IBI between segments but not in safety performance or interaction between groups (see Table 5).

Table 5. ANOVA of physiological parameters

Variables	Group			Segment			Group × Segment		
	F	df	p	F	df	p	F	df	p
IBI	0.185	1	0.672	10.929	4.000	**0.000**	1.423	4.000	0.278
Variation in IBI	4.287	1	0.054	27.994	1.597	**0.000**	1.359	1.597	0.270
SCL	7.004	1	**0.017**	38.109	2.000	**0.000**	7.280	2.000	**0.006**
Variation in SCL	13.188	1	**0.002**	38.109	2.000	**0.000**	7.280	2.000	**0.006**

3.3 Effects of Risk Perception on Safety Performance

The SCLs of the baseline and Segment 1 showed that there was no statistical difference between the two groups according to the Mann–Whitney U test. The SCL of Segments 2–4 was normality with homogeneous variance. The t test showed that there were statistical differences between the two groups. The normal group had a higher skin electricity level than the abnormal group. The SCR only showed statistical differences in Segment 3; the normal group was higher than the abnormal group (see Table 3).

Table 6. Comparison of SCL variation between the groups

Variation in SCL	Normal		Abnormal		t test
	Mean	Std.	Mean	Std.	p-value
SCL2-1 (ms)	2.24	1.06	0.72	1.76	**0.031**
SCL3-1 (ms)	2.91	1.32	0.78	1.84	**0.009**
SCL4-1 (ms)	4.56	1.31	1.73	1.39	**0.000**

We further analyzed the effects of SCL variation during the flight; all differences met normal distribution with homogeneous variance. The t test showed that SCL variation after the appearance of bad weather in the two groups had statistical significance (see Table 6); SCL variation in the normal group was higher than in the abnormal group. Repeated-measures ANOVA was used to analyze the interaction between safety performance and risk segment. The data did not meet the spherical hypothesis. MANOVA showed that safety performance, segments, and the interaction between them were statistically significant (see Table 5). The normal group had a significantly greater change of SCL in the risk scenario, and the change was more pronounced (with a higher slope) when the weather got worse.

4   Discussion

This study aimed to explore the effects of mental workload and risk perception on safety performance in risk scenarios. Previous studies have shown that a proper level of mental workload is helpful for performance [29, 30]. In this study, there is a relationship between mental workload and safety performance [31, 32]. Figure 6 showed that pilots in the normal group had a small change in IBI after the occurrence of severe weather, which means their heart rates were more stable. It's can be seen a helpful element to their greater performance. Table 4 showed that the variation of IBI in segment 3 has a significant difference between two groups (same as SCR in Table 3). Therefore, the causes of different safety performance are not the periods in good weather or landing, but those with severe weather. It's same as the study mentioned that the flying from VFR into IMC contribute a vital cause to crash [15–17].

Otherwise, pilots showed obviously different in SCL. The results in Tables 3 and 5 showed that the SCL and changes in the normal group were significantly greater than those in the abnormal group, indicating that the pilots in normal group had greater risk perception ability and more sweat. It might be beneficial to adjust their heart rate and reduce their mental workload to perform better. As mentioned in Picard's study [33], EDA is the only physiological indicator without the contamination of parasympathetic branch. This indicated that good pilots owned a rapidly adjusting and adapting ability when flying into bad weather. On the contrary, some pilots just showed nervous and stay in that dilemma without any compensation behaviors, which contribute to the inconsistence of risk and their poor safety performance. The repeated-measures ANOVA also showed a significant change of SCL in the risk scenarios. Therefore, stable psychological state is necessary for a safe flight, and we should put forward a higher requirement for risk perception and adjusting ability.

Unfortunately, other parameters of HRV showed no significant differences. There could be two reasons for this. First, the degree of mission involvement might not be related to HRV. Some studies have suggested that complex situations in flight simulation do not affect changes in HRV since respiration can effectively regulate changes in heart rate, which leads to decreased HRV sensitivity [34]. The slight increase in the mean IBI value in the normal group could support this. They owned a greater risk perception and adjusting ability with higher SCL, which partly offset fluctuations in this change; the same holds for the other parameters. Therefore, the self-regulating effect of individuals should be considered at the same time. Another reason is the effects of parasympathetic nerve we mentioned above, potentially balancing the variation of HRV parameters.

5   Conclusion

This study investigates the relationships between mental workload, risk perception and safety performance by using HRV and EDA. 19 flying cadets were recruited to perform a flying task and we collected their physiological data during flight. The results indicate that: (1) Mental workload and risk perception affected safety performance in adverse weather conditions, and risk perception is more obvious. (2) The causes, which lead to the changes of physiological parameters, are not related to their flying skills, but their risk perception and adjusting ability. They play a key role in perception response. Good pilots have greater risk perception and adjusting ability to keep a stability psychological state when they are facing risks. More importantly, the contribution of this study is to measure the variation of pilots' mental workload and risk perception without interruption. It's helpful to understand their performance in risks and propose specific training advices. Besides, the physiological measurement using wearable devices could be used in the selection of flying cadets and lower the airline costs.

Acknowledgments. We appreciate the support this work received from the National Natural Science Foundation of China (grant no. U1733117) and the Postgraduate Research and Innovation Project of Tianjin (grant no. 2019YJSS068).

References

1. Wickens, C.D.: Multiple resources and mental workload. Hum. Factors **50**, 449–455 (2008)
2. Boer, E.R.: Behavioural entropy as a measure of driving performance. In: Proceedings of the Third International Driving Symposium on Human Factors in Driver Assessment, Training and Vehicle Design, Rockport, Maine, pp. 225–229 (2005)
3. Wilde, G.J.: The theory of risk homeostasis: implications for safety and health. Risk Anal. **2**(4), 209–225 (1982)
4. Wilde, G.J.: Accident countermeasures and behavioural compensation: the position of risk homeostasis theory. J. Occup. Accid. **10**(4), 267–292 (1989)
5. Civil Aviation Administration of China: China aviation safety annual report 2018. CAAC, Beijing (2019)
6. International Air Transport Association: Safety report 2018. IATA, Montreal (2019)
7. Fuller, R.: Towards a general theory of driver behaviour. Accid. Anal. Prev. **37**(3), 461–472 (2005)
8. Guzek, M., Jurecki, R., Lozia, Z., Stanczyk, T.L.: Comparative analyses of driver behaviour on the track and in virtual environment. In: Proceedings of the Driving Simulation Conference, Paris, France, pp. 221–232 (2006)
9. Williges, R.C., Wierwille, W.W.: Behavioral measures of aircrew mental workload. Hum. Factors **21**(5), 549–574 (1979)
10. Gopher, D., Donchin, E.: Workload: an examination of the concept (1986)
11. Mansikka, H., Virtanen, K., Harris, D.: Comparison of NASA-TLX scale, modified Cooper-Harper scale and mean inter-beat interval as measures of pilot mental workload during simulated flight tasks. Ergonomics **62**(2), 246–254 (2019)
12. Annett, J.: Subjective rating scales: science or art? Ergonomics **45**(14), 966–987 (2002)
13. O'Hare, D.: Pilots' perception of risks and hazards in general aviation. Aviat. Space Environ. Med. **61**(7), 599–603 (1990)
14. Mulder, G.: The concept and measurement of mental effort. In: Hockey, G.R.J., Gaillard, A.W.K., Coles, M.G.H. (eds.) Energetics and Human Information Processing. NATO ASI Series (Series D: Behavioural and Social Sciences), vol. 31, pp. 175–198. Springer, Dordrecht (1986). https://doi.org/10.1007/978-94-009-4448-0_12
15. Pauley, K., O'Hare, D., Wiggins, M.: Risk tolerance and pilot involvement in hazardous events and flight into adverse weather. J. Safety Res. **39**(4), 403–411 (2008)

16. Goh, J., Wiegmann, D.A.: Visual flight rules (VFR) flight into instrument meteorological conditions (IMC): a review of the accident data (2001)
17. O'Hare, D., Owen, D.: Continued VFR into IMC: an empirical investigation of the possible causes (1999)
18. Lansdown, T.C., Brook-Carter, N., Kersloot, T.: Distraction from multiple in-vehicle secondary tasks: vehicle performance and mental workload implications. Ergonomics 47(1), 91–104 (2004)
19. Fooken, J., Schaffner, M.: The role of psychological and physiological factors in decision making under risk and in a dilemma. Front. Behav. Neurosci. 10, 2 (2016)
20. Hwang, S., Jebelli, H., Choi, B., Choi, M., Lee, S.: Measuring workers' emotional state during construction tasks using wearable EEG. J. Constr. Eng. Manag. 144(7) (2018). https://doi.org/10.1061/(ASCE)CO.1943-7862.0001506. Article number: 04018050
21. Wang, D., Chen, J., Zhao, D., Dai, F., Zheng, C., Wu, X.: Monitoring workers' attention and vigilance in construction activities through a wireless and wearable electroencephalography system. Autom. Constr. 82, 122–137 (2017)
22. Kinnear, N., Kelly, S.W., Stradling, S., Thomson, J.: Understanding how drivers learn to anticipate risk on the road: a laboratory experiment of affective anticipation of road hazards. Accid. Anal. Prev. 50, 1025–1033 (2013)
23. Allsop, J., Gray, R.: Flying under pressure: effects of anxiety on attention and gaze behavior in aviation. J. Appl. Res. Memory Cogn. 3(2), 63–71 (2014)
24. Veltman, J.A., Gaillard, A.W.K.: Indices of mental workload in a complex task environment. Neuropsychobiology 28(1–2), 72–75 (1993)
25. Vicente, K.J., Thornton, D.C., Moray, N.: Spectral analysis of sinus arrhythmia: a measure of mental effort. Hum. Factors 29(2), 171–182 (1987)
26. Metalis, S.A.: Heart period as a useful index of pilot workload in commercial transport aircraft. Int. J. Aviat. Psychol. 1(2), 107–116 (1991)
27. Mansikka, H., Simola, P., Virtanen, K., Harris, D., Oksama, L.: Fighter pilots' heart rate, heart rate variation and performance during instrument approaches. Ergonomics 59(10), 1344–1352 (2016)
28. Weinschenk, S.W., Beise, R.D., Lorenz, J.: Heart rate variability (HRV) in deep breathing tests and 5-min short-term recordings: agreement of ear photoplethysmography with ECG measurements, in 343 subjects. Eur. J. Appl. Physiol. 116(8), 1527–1535 (2016). https://doi.org/10.1007/s00421-016-3401-3
29. Vitense, H.S., Jacko, J.A., Emery, V.K.: Multimodal feedback: an assessment of performance and mental workload. Ergonomics 46, 68–87 (2003)
30. Morris, C.H., Leung, Y.K.: Pilot mental workload: how well do pilots really perform? Ergonomics 49(15), 1581–1596 (2006)
31. Lassiter, D.L., Morrow, D.G., Hinson, G.E., Miller, M., Hambrick, D.Z.: Expertise and age effects on pilot mental workload in a simulated aviation task. In: Proceedings of the Human Factors and Ergonomics Society Annual Meeting, vol. 40, no. 3, pp. 133–137. SAGE Publications, Los Angeles, October 1996
32. Thomas, M.I., Russo, M.B.: Neurocognitive monitors: toward the prevention of cognitive performance decrements and catastrophic failures in the operational environment. Aviat. Space Environ. Med. 78(5), 144–152 (2007)
33. Picard, R.W., Fedor, S., Ayzenberg, Y.: Multiple arousal theory and daily-life electrodermal activity asymmetry. Emot. Rev. 8(1), 62–75 (2016)
34. Shakouri, M., Ikuma, L.H., Aghazadeh, F., Nahmens, I.: Analysis of the sensitivity of heart rate variability and subjective workload measures in a driving simulator: the case of highway work zones. Int. J. Ind. Ergon. 66, 136–145 (2018)

An Object Distance Detection Method for Driving Performance Evaluation

Yang Gao⬛, Zhen Wang$^{(\boxtimes)}$, and Shan Fu

Department of Automation, Shanghai Jiao Tong University,
800 Dongchuan RD. Minhang District, Shanghai, China
b2wz@sjtu.edu.cn

Abstract. The evaluation of driving performance is a vital way to reflect the usability of in-vehicle system. Study the impact of in-vehicle interaction on driving performance can help avoiding hidden driving dangers. Speed of vehicles and distance from the vehicles ahead during driving are important indicators to reflect driving performance. In this study, Speed measurement relies on the GPS module. Conventionally, precise distance detection during driving is mostly based on radar sensors or high-resolution cameras that are both quite expensive. This paper proposed an object distance detection algorithm that relies on ordinary HD binocular camera with relatively low price to detect the distance. A new mismatch elimination method is proposed to improve the performance of the algorithm. At the same time, this paper designed a driving performance evaluation experiment. The distance is measured according to the proposed algorithm. Driving performance with primary tasks (speed maintenance and distance maintenance) and secondary tasks (touch control and voice control) on different driving scenes (straight road and curve road) are evaluated. Experimental results showed that introduction of secondary tasks dose influence the operation of the driver by distracting him. It also affects the driver's response to external changes. Both speed maintenance task and distance maintenance task have verified this conclusion. The proposed object distance detection method satisfies the accuracy required for driving performance evaluation.

Keywords: In-vehicle system · Visual-based distance detection · Driving performance evaluation

1 Introduction

With the development of industry and progress of society, the number of car ownership has increased significantly. The per capita possession of automobiles is also growing rapidly. Since the traffic scenes are getting more and more complex, requirements for driving system are higher than before.

Considering the advance of automotive industry, the emergence of the intelligent driving system is obviously the future form of transportation. Intelligent driving system can help with many traffic scenes [1]. There will be more communication and collaboration between the driver and the vehicle in the driving system. Human-machine coordinated control system will be the mainstream in the future.

© Springer Nature Switzerland AG 2020
D. Harris and W.-C. Li (Eds.): HCII 2020, LNAI 12187, pp. 292–303, 2020.
https://doi.org/10.1007/978-3-030-49183-3_23

Many factors can influence the driver, including the perception of the environment, the in-vehicle interaction and the psychological and physiological state of the driver.

Driving performance is an essential foundation of the intelligent driving system evaluation. Safe and stable driving of the vehicles is the requirement of the human-machine coordination vehicle system. Detecting vehicles that may affect the driver is an effective way to observe the traffic condition. This also serves as an indicator for driving performance evaluation.

In this article, we focus on the distance from the vehicle ahead while driving. The driver's mental status and ability of decision-making would affect the performance of distance control. Therefore, the task of keeping distance from the vehicle ahead can be the suitable reference to driving performance. On the other hand, driving speed is another indicator to reflect the driving performance. In this paper, we measured the speed by a GPS module.

Lazar-based methods and visual-based methods are two main methods for distance measurement. Traditional methods, however, cannot avoid the restriction between cost and performance. Considering the dilemma, a visual-based method was proposed in this article.

Traditional binocular visual ranging method including the following steps: calibration of the binocular camera, image rectification, stereo matching, and depth calculation. Stereo matching consumes most of the resource. In the phase of stereo matching, feature extraction and feature matching are main contents. Traditional stereo based on feature points needs a large number of calculations in view of various characteristic such as rotation invariance, scale invariance and invariance of brightness change.

2 The Object Distance Detection Method

2.1 The Visual-Based Ranging Method

Depth information calculated by visual-based ranging methods is based on pictures captured by the cameras. The binocular visual systems include two cameras with similar parameters.

Through the scheme proposed in [3], we can finish the calibration of the two cameras and obtain the internal and external parameters of the binocular camera. Those parameters reflect the hardware information of the cameras and play a role in the following processes.

Selection and Matching of the Feature Points
The selection of feature points is a key step in visual ranging. Feature points matching is the basis of parallax calculation. So far, there have been many feature points extraction methods [2]. Binary Robust Independent Elementary Features (BRIEF) is a kind of feature descriptor that simply uses binary test between pixels in a smoothed image patch [4]. With the consideration of robustness and rotation invariance, Oriented features from accelerated segment test (FAST [5]) and Rotated BRIEF (ORB) [6] were proposed. Besides, the Scale Invariant Feature Transform (SIFT) [7], the Speed Up Robust Features (SURF) [8] and the FAST methods are widely used now.

Considering our project, it is not necessary to maintain these features at the cost of computation and time. In a situation where the target object (vehicle) and the background (road) are very different, we use a calibrated binocular camera to extract feature points and target objects. Then, it is suitable to get reliable result rely on the gradient difference. We can extract feature points according to gradient differences in one-dimensional direction because of the epipolar constraints.

The feature points were selected from the peak points of the gradient in the article. At the same time, a threshold (gradient greater than 50) is set to pick out points for matching process. Each feature point will be compared with feature points on the same polar line.

Mismatching Elimination

After finishing the matching process, most of feature points have the matching point. Besides the feature points without matching points because of the camera view, there are still many mismatched point pairs.

There is no doubt that the mismatched point pairs have a large negative impact on the results. In the past, many studies have proposed solutions to eliminate it. [9, 10] and [11] used the feature of geometric consistency to eliminate feature point pairs whose parallax changes are too significant in small neighborhoods. This feature is based on the fact that the surface of objects is basically smooth in the real world, and the depth value rarely changes suddenly. When the feature points are distributed on the physical margin, it is not surprised that the depth of the feature points in the neighborhood changes suddenly. Another property called matching consistency is adopted in [12–14] and [15]. These papers believe that there should be a certain convergence between pairs of matching points in similar areas, which means that matching points of adjacent feature points are distributed in adjacent areas. The parallax change trend reflects the smoothness of the area where the matching points of the feature points are located. It is conceivable that these two characteristics also depend on the smoothness and consistency of the real world.

Further, in [16, 17] and [18], researchers put their eyes on the epipolar constraint. In simple terms, epipolar constrains describe the positional relationship of feature points on the epipolar line. A feature point and its matching point are on the same epipolar line. In the feature point matching process, the spatial ordering of feature points also plays a role. The matching point pairs in the two images of the image pair have the same ordering relationship according to the spatial position. While traversing feature points in the other image to find matching points of feature points, epipolar constraints and order constraints can greatly reduce the workload of traversal and similarity calculations.

In the matching process, mismatched point pairs are inevitable but undesired. Therefore, we screen out the mismatched pairs and discard them. This paper calculates the vector between point pairs from image pairs. In order to magnify the difference between mismatched pairs and well-matched pairs, we put the rectified image pairs in a 2*2 table. The image from the left camera was put on the upper left corner while the image from the right camera in the lower right corner. A two-dimensional Cartesian coordinate system is established. The intersection of the two images is set as the origin. The images shot by the left and right cameras are located in the third quadrant and the first quadrant, respectively. After computing the vectors between matching point pairs in the new coordinate. Mismatched pairs arrive at vectors very different from good matches because of epipolar geometry constraints.

Fig. 1. Original matches

Fig. 2. Matches after processed

Figure 1 and Figure 2 show the effect of the mismatch rejection. Because of camera calibration and image rectification, the images in a pair can be regarded as two pictures shot by the same camera at the same time. This ideal model also provides the theoretical basis for the mismatch elimination process.

The two points in the matched feature point pair are on the same polar line according to epipolar line constraints. The essential matrix was calculated in the process of calibration. It can be seen as the prior knowledge for our depth calculation. A kind of error function was defined in [11]:

$$d = p - Ep \tag{1}$$

Each feature point multiplied by the same essential matrix shows the same spatial change. Therefore, the calculation of the feature matrix can be skipped. In this paper, the slope between two points in the new coordinate system is proposed as a new feature to match point pairs.

$$k = \frac{p_y^r - p_y^l}{p_x^r - p_x^l} \tag{2}$$

In Eq. (2), k represents the slope, which is a new indicator for matching point pairs. p means the feature point. The upper corner mark indicates which camera the image is coming from, and the lower corner mark is to distinguish the horizontal and vertical coordinates.

Because of the order constraints, the mismatching point pairs have higher slope than the well-matching point pairs. Setting a threshold around the minimum slope can avoid the calculation error. Most mismatched feature point pairs are eliminated in this process.

2.2   Object Detection in 3D Space

With the process described in the previous section, we can get the three-dimensional point clouds mainly distributed on the margins of objects. This is not enough for the analysis of the target vehicle. We need do more work to extract the point clouds belong to the target vehicle.

Point Clouds Clustering

The three views of the point cloud are shown below. The outlines of vehicles were shown in Fig. 3, Fig. 5 and Fig. 7. There are still many points scattered discretely throughout the space. It is necessary to remove those discrete isolated points since they are useless for subsequent processes.

Density-based spatial clustering of applications with noise (DBSCAN) [19], as named, is a density-based clustering method. This clustering method has the advantage of not need to set the clustering method at beginning.

After applying the DBSCAN algorithm to the point cloud shown in Fig. 3, we obtain the point clouds shown in Fig. 4, Fig. 6 and Fig. 8. Different colors of point clouds represent different classes. With the application of DBSCAN, the point clouds are divided into different clusters according to the spatial density distribution. In addition, the noise marking function of DBSCAN in the clustering process also enables it to remove outlier points. By the way, we set the parameters of DBSCAN algorithm including $\mathcal{E}$ ($\mathcal{E}$ = 700 mm) and *MinPts* (*MinPts* = 15).

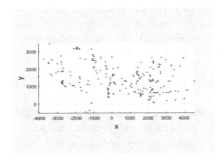

Fig. 3. Main view of original point cloud

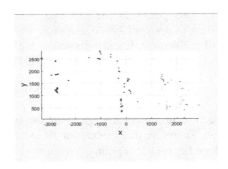

Fig. 4. Main view of point clouds after DBSCAN

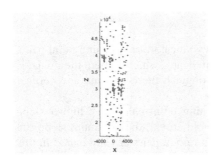

Fig. 5. Top view of original point cloud

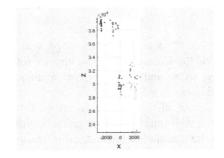

Fig. 6. Top view of point clouds after DBSCAN

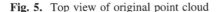

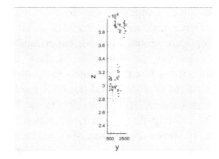

Fig. 7. Left view of original point cloud   **Fig. 8.** Left view of point clouds after DBSCAN

Target Vehicle Extraction

Point clouds located on different objects are divided into several clusters after clustering. To get the target vehicle, we need to re-integrate the clustering result.

The template matching combined with multiple frames point clouds satisfied the requirement of the experiment. It also provide the point clouds of the target vehicle. When a vehicle is running on the road, information such as the road width and the field of vision is utilized to select point clouds within the effective area in advance. Traversing and matching the point clouds classes start from the nearest point cloud class in the effective area. We get the point clouds of target vehicle by matching the combination of point clouds with a preset template.

3   Experiments

3.1   Apparatus

In this experiment, the proposed distance detection method is used to measure the distance between the vehicle and the vehicle ahead. To evaluate the driver's state during driving, physiological indicators including eye movement and heart rate were collected. Those data will be the indicators for the physical and psychological state of the driver.

Fig. 9. Driver in the cockpit   **Fig. 10.** Experimental vehicle

Distance changes in the distance maintenance task and speed changes in speed maintenance task are indicators for driving performance. Driving speed and following distance were recorded in our experiments.

To get the above-mentioned data, the following equipment is included in the experiments: a heart rate watch to record the heart rate, an eye tracker to record the driver's field of vision, and the GPS module to record the driving speed. Of course, a binocular camera (HNY-CV-002, LenaCV) for distance measurement is also included.

The participant wore a heart watch and the eye movement glasses (see Fig. 9). Figure 10 shows appearance of experimental vehicle. The binocular camera was placed on the centerline of the roof to collect images during driving.

3.2   Tasks

Following distance and the driving speed are the dependent variables in the experiment. Images captured by the binocular camera is used for the distance measurement while speed recorded by the GPS module. We set primary tasks including distance maintenance and speed maintenance. Secondary tasks (voice control and touch control) are also set in this experiment.

We asked the participant to execute the secondary tasks while perform the primary tasks. Control groups of the experiment were the primary tasks without secondary tasks. The experimental group is consist of primary tasks with different secondary tasks.

Primary Tasks
Speed Maintenance Task
In this task, we asked the participant to drive the vehicle with a preset speed (20 km/h). The change of speed during the experiment was recorded for further analysis. This task includes driving on the curve road and straight road.

Distance Maintenance Task
The participant drives on the straight road after the target vehicle and keep the following distance at a stable value. We recorded the distance from the target vehicle ahead.

Secondary Tasks
Voice Control
The participant adjusts the temperature of the vehicle air conditioner by the in-vehicle voice control system in this task.

Touch Control
The participant adjusts the temperature of the vehicle air conditioner by touching the main touchable screen in this task.

4   Results

See figures and tables.

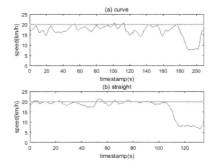

Fig. 11. Speed without secondary tasks

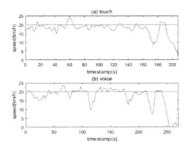

Fig. 12. Speed control with the secondary tasks (curve)

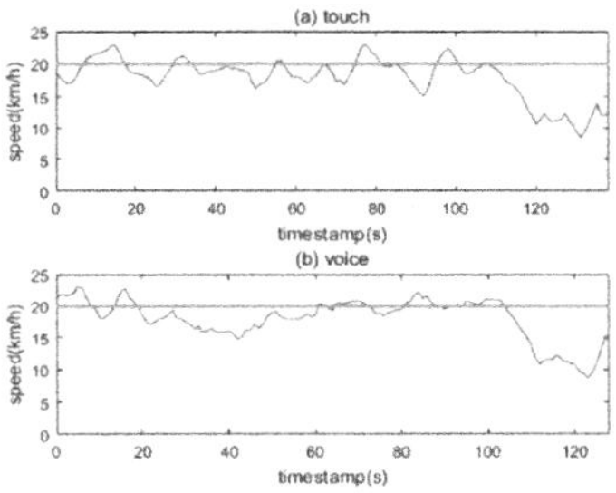

Fig. 13. Speed control with the secondary tasks (straight)

Table 1. Statistical data of speed maintenance tasks

Subtasks	No secondary tasks		Touch control		Voice control	
Type of road	Curve	Straight	Curve	Straight	Curve	Straight
Mean (km/h)	16.86	17.31	17.27	17.85	17.28	17.99
Standard deviation	4.36	3.04	5.50	3.23	3.58	3.33

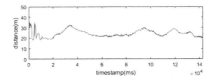

Fig. 14. Distance change without secondary tasks

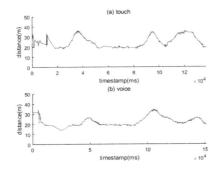

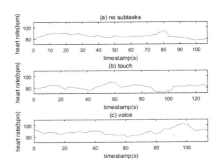

Fig. 15. Distance change with secondary tasks

Fig. 16. Heart rate during distance-maintain task

Table 2. Percentage of the time looking outside the window

Secondary tasks	First	Second	Third	Fourth	Average
Touch control	60.88%	88.53%	59.67%	81.56%	72.66%
Voice control	66.50%	90.40%	58.99%	94.02%	77.48%

Table 3. Standard deviations of distance in distance maintenance tasks

	No secondary tasks	Touch control	Voice control
Standard deviation	3.43	5.84	4.55

5 Discussion

5.1 Speed Maintenance Task

Figure 11 shows the speed changes while driving on the curve. It has a clear gap compared with the straight track without secondary task. There is no doubt that it is harder to control the direction on curve road than driving on the straight road.

After introducing the secondary tasks for air-conditioning adjustment and driving on the same route, the speed curves of driving speed are shown in Fig. 12 and Fig. 13. The former figure presents the speed changes on the curve road, while the latter one is on the straight road.

Comparing the results with and without secondary task, we find that the fluctuations of speed are more and larger with secondary tasks. Standard deviations (see Table 1) provide statistical evidence. The secondary tasks trigged the speed fluctuations. Touch control apparently caused larger and more fluctuations than voice control.

This phenomenon shows that the introduction of the secondary tasks does not only interfere with the driver's operation, but also affects his judgment of the sudden changes in the external environment. Even if the implement of the secondary tasks and changes of traffic conditions did not happen simultaneously.

Results in Table 1 validates the differences between different experiments. The mean speed is closer to the setting value while driving without secondary tasks. Primary tasks on straight road have better speed control performance than on curve road.

From timestamp 20200112165355 to 20200112165411, the speed curve has the largest change in Fig. 12. We analyze the heart rate and eye movement data during this period. The average heart rate is 80.29 bpm, while the average heart rate during the whole task is 83.53 bpm. According to the pictures captured by binocular camera, the vehicle turned around during this time and was about to go uphill.

With these recorded data, we can speculate that those secondary tasks do affect the primary task by affecting the driving operation. They also affect the driver's ability to response to changes in the external scene.

5.2   Distance Maintenance Task

Figure 14, Figure 15 and Figure 16 show the changes of the following distance during the distance maintenance task. In this task, we did not set a specific holding distance but asked the participant to maintain a stable distance. The fluctuation frequency and amplitude of the following distance curves reflect the performance of the distance maintenance task.

Standard deviations in Table 3 indicate the performance of different experiments. Since these values are arranged in descending order of voice control, touch control and no secondary tasks. This order is also the same as the order of the driving performance.

From the experimental results, we can find that the introduction of secondary tasks makes the performance of the distance-maintaining task worse. The increase of amount of peaks and troughs of the distance curve verified this conclusion. The amplitudes of distance curve is also larger in Fig. 15 than Fig. 14.

The main factor of peaks and troughs of distance curves is the sudden changes in the speed of the vehicle ahead. The introduction of secondary tasks cost the driver more time to readjust the distance. Touch control has more influence than voice control. We can speculate that the secondary tasks have affected the driver's intuitive impact on the distance-maintaining task that require continuous attention to external world.

Heart rate of the participant during the distance maintenance task is shown in Fig. 16. These figures are not significantly different between each other. In other words, the driver's psychological state is not affected too much by the secondary tasks.

Percentage of the time looking outside the window (see Table 2) shows how much the driver was distracted. While adjusting the air conditioner by the touch control, the driver took less time focusing on the road. This also shows that adjusting the air conditioner through touch control is easier to distract the driver than voice control.

6   Conclusions

From the discussion in the last section, secondary task makes negative impact on driving performance. It influences the driver by distracting him. The distraction directly influence the driving operation and makes the driver's reaction to external changes getting slow. Different in-vehicle interactions has different influence. Touch control has a greater distraction than voice control. With the analysis of the experimental results, it is clearly that distractions significantly affect driving performance. On the other hand, the proposed object distance detection method satisfies the accuracy required for performance evaluation.

References

1. Bishop, R.: Intelligent vehicle applications worldwide. IEEE Intell. Syst. Appl. **15**(1), 78–81 (2000)
2. Sun, Q.: An improved binocular visual odometry algorithm based on the random sample consensus in visual navigation systems. Ind. Robot Int. J. **44**(4), 542–551 (2017)
3. Zhang, Z.: A flexible new technique for camera calibration. IEEE Trans. Pattern Anal. Mach. Intell. **22**(11), 1330–1334 (2000)
4. Calonder, M., Lepetit, V., Strecha, C., Fua, P.: BRIEF: binary robust independent elementary features. In: Daniilidis, K., Maragos, P., Paragios, N. (eds.) ECCV 2010. LNCS, vol. 6314, pp. 778–792. Springer, Heidelberg (2010). https://doi.org/10.1007/978-3-642-15561-1_56
5. Rosten, E., Drummond, T.: Machine learning for high-speed corner detection. In: Leonardis, A., Bischof, H., Pinz, A. (eds.) ECCV 2006. LNCS, vol. 3951, pp. 430–443. Springer, Heidelberg (2006). https://doi.org/10.1007/11744023_34
6. Rublee, E., Rabaud, V., Konolige, K., et al.: ORB: an efficient alternative to SIFT or SURF. In: 2011 International Conference on Computer Vision, pp. 2564–2571 (2011)
7. Lowe, D.G.: Object recognition from local scale-invariant features. In: Proceedings of the Seventh IEEE International Conference on Computer Vision, vol. 2, pp. 1150–1157 (1999)
8. Bay, H., Tuytelaars, T., Van Gool, L.: SURF: speeded up robust features. In: Leonardis, A., Bischof, H., Pinz, A. (eds.) ECCV 2006. LNCS, vol. 3951, pp. 404–417. Springer, Heidelberg (2006). https://doi.org/10.1007/11744023_32
9. Pizarro, D., Bartoli, A.: Feature-based deformable surface detection with self-occlusion reasoning. Int. J. Comput. Vis. **97**(1), 54–70 (2012). https://doi.org/10.1007/s11263-011-0452-0
10. Lipman, Y., Yagev, S., Poranne, R., et al.: Feature matching with bounded distortion. ACM Trans. Graph. **33**(3), 1–14 (2014)
11. Lin, W.-Y.D., Cheng, M.-M., Lu, J., Yang, H., Do, M.N., Torr, P.: Bilateral functions for global motion modeling. In: Fleet, D., Pajdla, T., Schiele, B., Tuytelaars, T. (eds.) ECCV 2014. LNCS, vol. 8692, pp. 341–356. Springer, Cham (2014). https://doi.org/10.1007/978-3-319-10593-2_23
12. Lin, W.-Y., Liu, S., Jiang, N., Do, M.N., Tan, P., Lu, J.: RepMatch: robust feature matching and pose for reconstructing modern cities. In: Leibe, B., Matas, J., Sebe, N., Welling, M. (eds.) ECCV 2016. LNCS, vol. 9905, pp. 562–579. Springer, Cham (2016). https://doi.org/10.1007/978-3-319-46448-0_34
13. Wang, C., Wang, L., Liu, L.: Density maximization for improving graph matching with its applications. IEEE Trans. Image Process. **24**(7), 2110–2123 (2015)
14. Bian, J., Lin, W., Matsushita, Y., et al.: GMS: grid-based motion statistics for fast, ultra-robust feature correspondence. In: 2017 IEEE Conference on Computer Vision and Pattern Recognition (CVPR), pp. 2828–2837 (2017)
15. Maier, J., Humenberger, M., Murschitz, M., Zendel, O., Vincze, M.: Guided matching based on statistical optical flow for fast and robust correspondence analysis. In: Leibe, B., Matas,

J., Sebe, N., Welling, M. (eds.) ECCV 2016. LNCS, vol. 9911, pp. 101–117. Springer, Cham (2016). https://doi.org/10.1007/978-3-319-46478-7_7

16. Kushnir, M., Shimshoni, I.: Epipolar geometry estimation for urban scenes with repetitive structures. IEEE Trans. Pattern Anal. Mach. Intell. **36**(12), 2381–2395 (2014)

17. Talker, L., Moses, Y., Shimshoni, I.: Estimating the number of correct matches using only spatial order. IEEE Trans. Pattern Anal. Mach. Intell. **41**(12), 2846–2860 (2019)

18. Zhao, P., Ding, D., Wang, Y., et al.: An improved GMS-PROSAC algorithm for image mismatch elimination. Syst. Sci. Control Eng. **6**(1), 220–229 (2018)

19. Ester, M., Kriegel, H.-P., Sander, J., et al.: A density-based algorithm for discovering clusters a density-based algorithm for discovering clusters in large spatial databases with noise. In: Proceedings of the Second International Conference on Knowledge Discovery and Data Mining, pp. 226–231. AAAI Press, Portland (1996)

Understanding Human Behaviour in Flight Operation Using Eye-Tracking Technology

Wojciech Tomasz Korek[1,2(✉)], Arthur Mendez[2], Hafiz Ul Asad[2],
Wen-Chin Li[3], and Mudassir Lone[2]

[1] Faculty of Automatic Control, Electronics and Computer Science,
Silesian University of Technology, Gliwice, Poland
[2] Dynamics, Simulation and Control Group, Cranfield University, Cranfield, UK
{w.t.korek,a.mendez,a.ul-asad,m.m.lone}@cranfield.ac.uk
[3] Safety and Accident Investigation Centre, Cranfield University, Cranfield, UK
wenchin.li@cranfield.ac.uk

Abstract. A clear understanding of how the pilot processes the information in the cockpit while carrying out particular tasks is crucial for developing the Human-Machine Interface and inceptors that help reduce pilot workload. Eye-tracking data synchronised with aircraft dynamics data is used here to study the high-workload scenario of executing an offset landing in an engineering flight simulator. The study focused on identifying differences in behavioural patterns between line pilots and test pilots. Evidence for significant differences were found regarding the ability to multitask and monitor aircraft states. The research output will lead to reduction of the pilot's workload and, in further study, proposition of a new display setups and inceptors.

Keywords: Human behaviour · Situation awareness · Flight simulation · Eye-tracking

1 Introduction

The design of human machine interface in general and even more so in aerospace requires an in-depth understanding of the way a pilot utilises the information provided to him/her. Consequently, human behaviour has significant implications on aspects ranging from the design of individual displays and inceptors all the way to the design of flight control systems. Numerous studies exist that focus on developing an understanding of pilot's control behaviour, some of which are limited to purely mathematical representation of control action [12] while others focus on psychological aspects [5]. In [1], the author investigated the workload on an air traffic controller from the use of weather display using an eye tracker and concluded that the eye movement tracker can give a good measure of a controller workload when he was subjected to have a frequent visit of a weather display.

© Springer Nature Switzerland AG 2020
D. Harris and W.-C. Li (Eds.): HCII 2020, LNAI 12187, pp. 304–320, 2020.
https://doi.org/10.1007/978-3-030-49183-3_24

The effect of anxiety on a pilot performance during an aircraft landing has been studied in [2] where they showed, using simulated landings, that the pilot anxiety increased when encountered with difficult situation, such as landing under stressful situation. Cognitive workload of an air traffic controller has been investigated in [3] using Functional Near-Infrared spectroscopy with the findings that accuracy and speed of a pilot decreased and blood oxygenation increased with the increase in task difficulty. Eye tracking has been also used in studying different aspects of human-machine interaction [14, 15]. In this paper, the authors attempt to address some of the limitations found in mathematical models of the human pilot by using eye tracking data to provide insight into the way the pilot uses the available information. Although numerous studies have been carried out using eye-tracking for various purposes in aviation, for example recognising scan patterns of a remote air traffic control by a single controller [10], flight deck design [11], augmented reality (AR) in Primary Flight Display (PFD) [9], air traffic controller's situation awareness [7] and understanding human behaviour during aircraft-pilot coupling events [8], there has been limited transfer of this knowledge into the mathematical formulation of pilot behaviour. In this study the authors synchronise temporal and spatial eye-tracking data with aircraft data to study scenarios where the pilot is given an urgent safety critical task. The insight from this study, where pilot's attention allocation is quantified and correlated with aircraft data, enables the reconsideration of critical cockpit information for specific tasks. The overall research aim is to first understand the control behaviour and information needs of the pilot, and in doing so reduce his/her workload by proposing new display setups and inceptors. The work discussed in this paper focuses on the pilot's visual cues (situation awareness) which consists of the eye-tracker data analysis and its correlation with the aircraft data. This will help understanding and defining the whole process of the pilot's decision making within the pilot-aircraft control loop. The diagram of the control system is shown in Fig. 1. This is a part of the pilot-vehicle-system under manual control which is presented in more detail in [12]. The visual pilot cues that affect his/her decision making are directly influenced by pilot looking either on a PFD or outside the aircraft's window.

2   Task and Method

2.1   Experimental Setup

Data for the test was gathered using flight simulator and off-the-shelf eye-tracker. The eye tracker and aircraft dynamics were synchronised to provide a more complete picture of how the pilot controls the aircraft in high stress cases. Statistical analysis of experimental data was carried out to see correlations between the stick deflection levels and eye gaze positions. The tests were conducted using an engineering flight simulator called the Future Systems Simulator. The rig is a flexible aircraft systems simulator platform for the development of intelligent, integrated aerospace technologies. It is a test-bed for a wide variety technologies

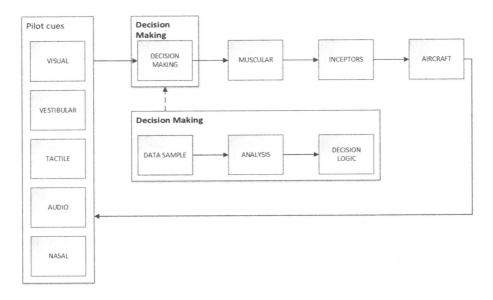

Fig. 1. Diagram showing the pilot-aircraft control loop.

impacting today's aircraft and future aircraft concepts. The tests were carried out using the mathematical model of a regular business jet.

The Pupil Labs' Pupil Core has been used for tracking eye movements. It includes a pair of glasses with a camera pointing towards where the wearer is looking and a second camera tracking the eyeball movement. Figure 2 presents the calibration process and the general eye-tracker setup. During the calibration the world frame, which is the wearer field of view, is defined. The red lines indicate the point of view of the world camera, while blue lines show the eye-camera video transmission. After calibration, a dedicated software is able to visualise the point where the test subject is looking at. Recording allows the software to create the normalised fixation positions in the world frame [13]. Fixations are a group of gaze positions focused on one point at a given time frame [6]. The Pupil Labs' Pupil Capture application allows the user to specify Areas Of Interest (AOIs). By attaching the AprilTags on the viewing range of the front-facing eye-tracker camera and defining the surface between them in the software two AOIs could be specified: PFD (marked by four AprilTags in Fig. 3) and the outside window view. These are two aspects that affect pilot's decision making [12]. With eye-tracking technology some limitations still exist regarding the collection and analysis of eye-tracking data. This is discussed in the results & analysis part.

2.2   Scenario

The test case used in this study is the offset-landing task as shown in Fig. 4. The pilot/test subject is given control of the aircraft in the final stages of the landing phase and he/she is required to correct for the lateral offset from the runway centreline and the glide path angle change that results from the manoeuvre.

Fig. 2. Eye-tracker setup.

Fig. 3. Pilot's perspective and example fixation (here: the pilot is looking on the outside of the window).

Hence, the pilot is required to make inputs in pitch, roll, and throttle to attain the desired trajectory of the aircraft. This task is classified as a high workload scenario due to the need for manoeuvring the aircraft close to the ground. Furthermore, the stress level of the task can be increased by reducing the distance from the runway, at which the pilot is allowed to execute the S-shaped manoeuvre. This task is commonly used for the handling qualities assessment of flight control systems, where the feedback from the pilot is captured on a Cooper-Harper rating scale (CHR) [4]. It should be noted that for the tests conducted in this study, the Auto-throttle functionality was enabled so as to eliminate the need for the pilot to focus on airspeed management. Hence, during the task the pilots need only focus on lateral offset distance correction and glide path angle capture and maintenance. The aircraft was also configured for landing with flaps and landing gear deployed, which eliminated the need for a pilot to get accustomed to the touch-screen based flaps and landing gear levers and any influence this might have on their behaviour. The pilots were also given a flight time in the simulator beforehand to familiarise themselves with the simulator's PFD and the sidestick sensitivity.

The experimental parameters for this offset-landing task are δ - the distance from the runway at which the pilot is allowed to execute the sidestep manoeuvre and Δ - the lateral offset distance from the runway centreline to the position of the aircraft before the manoeuvre. The initial altitude of the aircraft was determined using the longitudinal distance (δ) to the runway and a desirable glide slope angle of $3°$. Here, in these tests the offset distance from the runway centreline was fixed at 416 m which corresponds to the lateral distance between two parallel runways at the test airport. Hence, the pilot was in short conducting a switch from the right-hand side runway to the left-hand side runway. The two values of δ chosen for this study were 4 and 2 nautical miles (nm). These distances were chosen to reflect a moderate workload and a high workload scenario respectively. These distances were established through an initial handling qualities assessment of this offset landing test with varying values of δ and then capturing the feedback from the pilots on the CHR scale [4]. From these tests it was revealed that for $\delta = 4$ nm, the rating from the pilot was a "3" on the CHR scale which corresponds to the desired performance being achieved with minimal pilot compensation. For the longitudinal distance, $\delta = 2$ nm, the rating on the CHR scale was a "5" which corresponds to considerable pilot compensation being required for achieving adequate performance. Hence, $\delta = 4$ and $\delta = 2$ nm were chosen to signify a moderate and high workload scenarios respectively along with a straight-ahead landing without the S-shaped manoeuvre as the baseline.

2.3   Test Subjects

For the purpose of this test two pilots were asked to carry out the baseline and two offset landings. One of them was a line pilot who flies business jets on a regular basis with 4000 h of total flying time. The second pilot was a test pilot with significantly more experience on different types of aircraft and flight simulators: 3000 total flying hours on over 50 different aircraft types. Because of

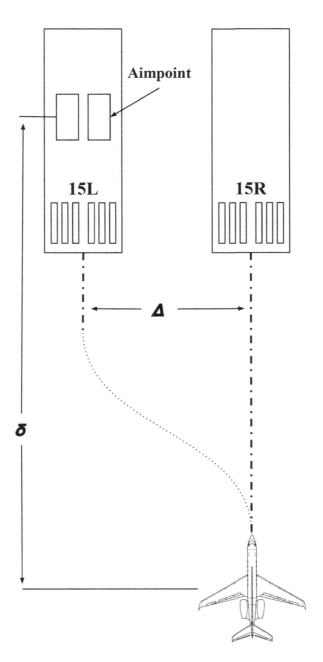

Fig. 4. Plan view of the offset-landing task.

this he was able to notice more aspects of a flight in a new environment which made his flight pattern noticeably different.

2.4   Data Curation

Two sets of data were gathered during each test: one from the eye-tracker and the other from the flight simulator. The first one, concerning the eye gaze fixations, consists of timestamp, fixations' x and y position and fixation duration. The latter includes flight dynamics data, from which the simulation time, glide angle (γ), longitudinal and lateral stick deflection (pitch and roll input) and aircraft's position and altitude are used for analysis. Two ways of data synchronisation were taken into account: distance from the airport and fixed time from the touchdown moment. The pilot's behaviour changes depend on whether the aircraft is on the ground or in the air. Because of that and since the time it takes to get from the starting point (which was identical for all the trials) to the landing point is slightly different for each flight, the second method was chosen. Thus, to synchronise the data, all recordings have been cut to end at the touchdown time t_{TD} and begin 180 s before it. This allowed for the correlation of the simulation inputs and outputs with the eye-tracker data. This time duration included the offset manoeuvre for each test/scenario. The data has been processed using MATLAB® software.

3   Results

For the initial trials the authors had a test pilot as a subject. Preliminary results of these trials have shown that during the offset landing the pilot was looking outside the cockpit for 82% of the simulation time, making it the most critical element of the pilot's field of view. In the main tests the authors decided to focus on the correlation between eye-tracking data and simulation data. Moreover, some differences of the line and test pilots' behaviour were noticed.

Figures 5 and 6 show the spatial distribution of fixation positions for line pilot and test pilot respectively. It is evident that both pilots were looking outside the aircraft's window for the majority of time for all three landings. However, the major difference is the focus of the fixations: the test pilot has a dispersed scanning pattern. He is moving his gaze more often and monitoring more elements during the flight. Figures 7 and 8 present the temporal distribution of fixation points' position in Y axis, as this was the variable used to specify the outside window/PFD threshold.

The difference in Window/PFD threshold occurs due to the eye-tracker calibration being specific to each pilot. It was evaluated by assessing the video recording and scatter plot showing the fixations' positions. Due to the limitation in the eye-tracker accuracy, both in terms of calibration and resolution, it was not possible to distinguish specific PFD elements that pilot was looking at, such as airspeed or altitude indicators. However, the gathered data provides insight into the main differences between the test subjects.

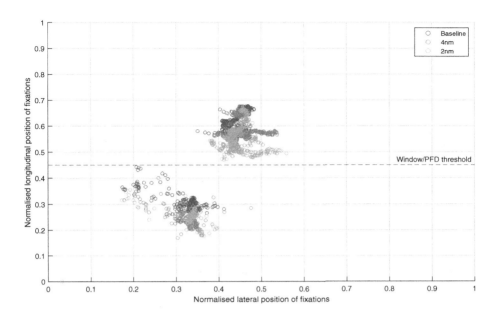

Fig. 5. Spatial distribution of fixation points for the line pilot.

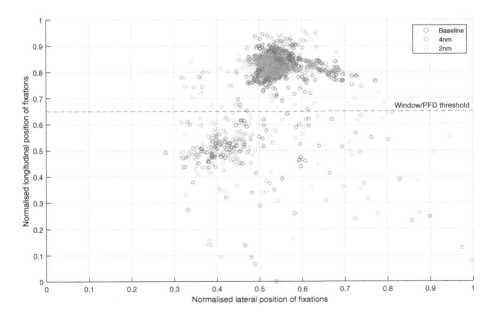

Fig. 6. Spatial distribution of fixation points for the test pilot.

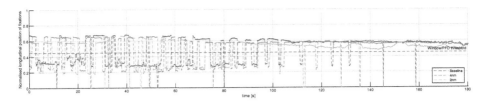

Fig. 7. Temporal distribution of fixation points' position on Y axis for the line pilot.

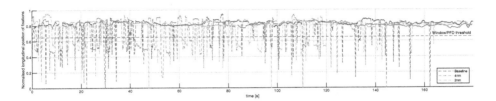

Fig. 8. Temporal distribution of fixation points' position on Y axis for the test pilot.

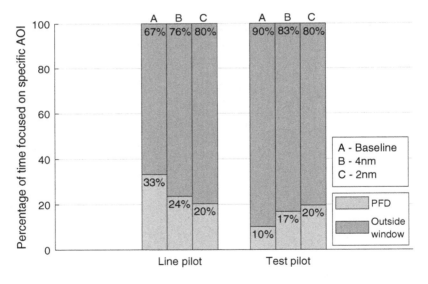

Fig. 9. Percentage arrangement of fixation focus for each pilot during each test flight.

Next difference between the pilots was that, with each landing being more stressful, behaviour of each pilot was changing differently - the line pilot preferred to look more outside the window, while the test pilot was focusing more on the PFD, although in total it was still less than the line pilot, as shown in Fig. 9.

Figures 10, 11 and 12 present the flight dynamics data from the simulator combined with pilot's AOI fixation gaze. The flight dynamic parameters consists of the aircraft's glide path angle γ (which is the landing approach angle with a $-3°$ target), longitudinal and lateral stick deflection (pitch and roll input, ranging from -1 to 1 for each axis), and Δ - the aircraft's offset distance from the runway's centreline. A fixation location above the threshold corresponds to the pilot's attention being allocated outside the cockpit and a value below the threshold corresponds to their attention fixated on the PFD.

For the baseline test (Fig. 10), it can be seen that the line pilot's pitch inputs have much higher gain/amplitude compared to the test pilot. As a consequence, the test pilot was closer to the target of $-3°$ throughout the landing unlike the line pilot who's γ had more fluctuations before the flare. Figure 10 also shows the subplot with roll inputs for both pilots. From this it can be seen that the test pilot makes more small amplitude-refining inputs compared to the line pilot and is also able to maintain a smaller offset error from the runway throughout. From the subplot of the fixation location, the test pilot makes a slightly more frequent switches between allocating attention to the PFD and outside the cockpit compared to the test pilot.

Figure 11 shows the different parameters for the 4 nm offset test. The similar observation seen in pitch inputs of baseline test can be seen here as well, i.e. the line pilot has larger amplitude inputs. In this test the roll inputs of the test pilot are much larger in amplitude compared to the line pilot. Hence, the test pilot executes the necessary manoeuvre more aggressively compared to the line pilot. The test pilot in this test, similar to the baseline test, also switches focus between PFD and outside cockpit more often than the line pilot. Figure 12 shows the same data but for the 2 nm offset test. Here pitch inputs of larger magnitude of the line pilot are observed again like in the previous tests. However, unlike the previous tests, the roll inputs of the line pilot become higher in the amplitude and the offset distance error trend for both pilots is very similar. From the fixation location subplot of Fig. 12, it can be seen that the line pilot keeps his attention fixed to the outside of the cockpit in the last minute before touchdown. As a consequence of this, his accuracy in maintaining the glide path angle is worse compared to the test pilot as observed in the γ subplot.

Table 1 shows the root mean squares (RMS) values of pitch and roll inputs made by the pilots for the different tests. The RMS value was calculated to gain an insight into how active the pilots were at the controls for each of tests. The test pilot's activity at the controls was lower compared to the line pilot for all three tests in both pitch and roll commands. It can also be observed that as the test becomes more stressful both pilots increase their activity at the controls.

This high gain nature of the line pilot is also evident in Fig. 13 which categorises the stick movements on whether the pilot was looking at the PFD or outside the window while the input was made. Figure 14 shows the same plot for the test pilot. These Figures were generated for the most stressful of the three tests, i.e. test C (2 nm offset). When the pilot is focused on the outside view while making the input it can be inferred that the pilot is looking at the

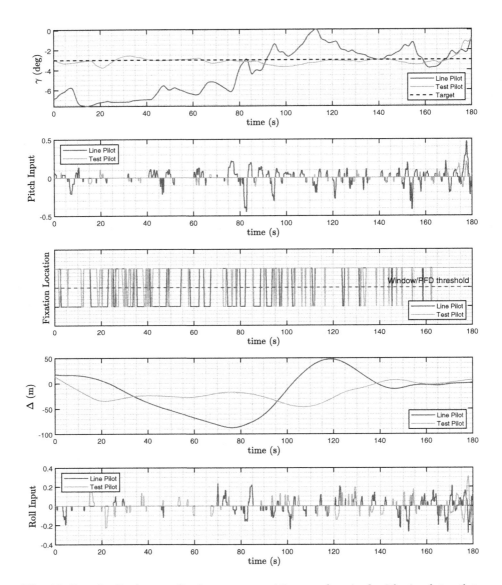

Fig. 10. Longitudinal normalised eye gaze position synchronised with simulator data for both pilots during the baseline landing.

Table 1. RMS values of pitch and roll inputs during each test for both types of pilots.

	Pitch input RMS			Roll input RMS		
	Baseline	4 nm	2 nm	Baseline	4 nm	2 nm
Line pilot	0.09	0.09	0.19	0.08	0.12	0.17
Test pilot	0.04	0.04	0.06	0.05	0.09	0.1

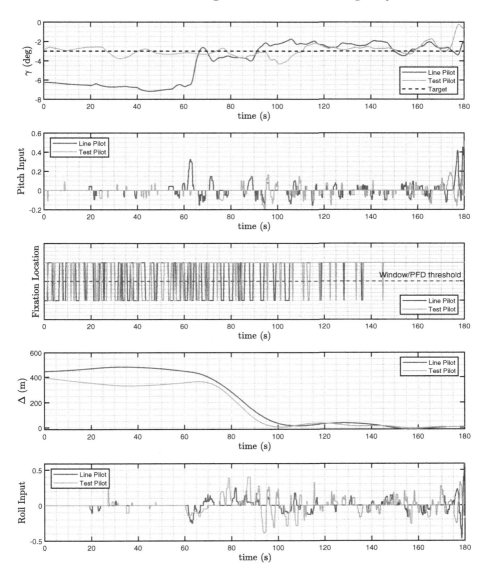

Fig. 11. Longitudinal normalised eye gaze position synchronised with simulator data for both pilots during the 4-nm offset landing.

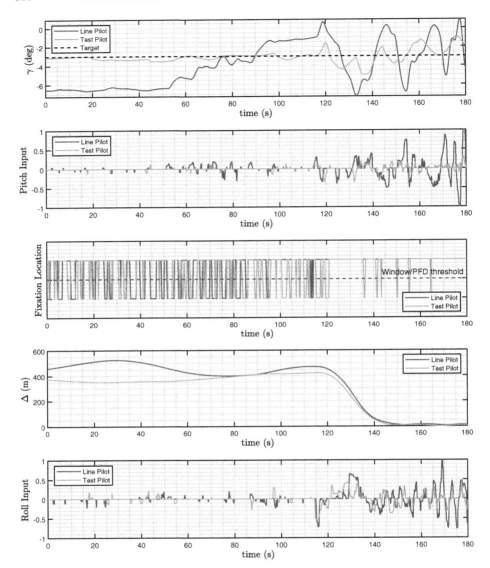

Fig. 12. Longitudinal normalised eye gaze position synchronised with simulator data for both pilots during the 2-nm offset landing.

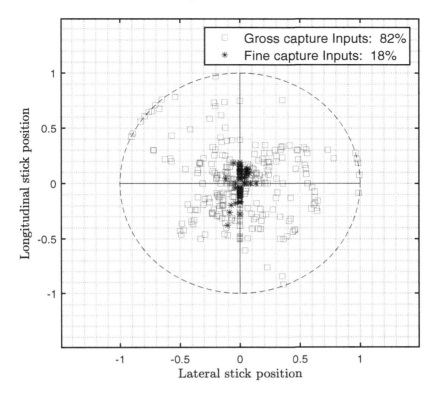

Fig. 13. Stick movements categorised according to line pilot's fixation position for the 2 nm test.

runway and aiming at touchdown point. Hence, the inputs made by the pilots in these instances are for gross capture. In contrast, when the pilots are looking at the PFD, they are trying to control and maintain their glide slope angle to an ideal value. Hence, the inputs made in these instances are for the fine/precise capture of the glide slope angle. From both these Figures it can be seen that the majority of the inputs made by both the pilots are gross capture inputs. Furthermore, the majority of their fine capture inputs are purely longitudinal. This is expected as the flight path vector and vertical speed readings on the PFD are the only cues that determine the aircraft's glide slope angle. From Fig. 14 it is also clear that the test pilot has executed high gain roll inputs while his gaze was fixed on the PFD. As the PFD doesn't give information to the pilot about the offset distance, it can be inferred that the test pilot in these instances was multi-tasking by correcting the offset through a roll input while monitoring the glide slope angle at the same time. Hence, the Figures suggest that the test pilot might be more comfortable with multi-tasking compared to the line pilot.

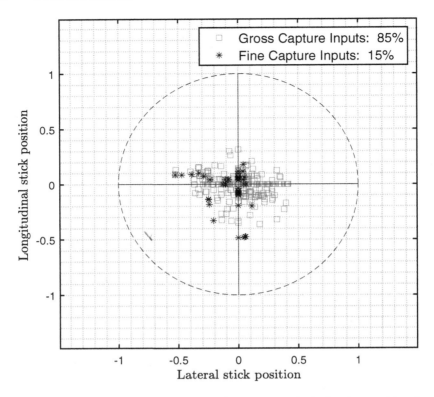

Fig. 14. Stick movements categorised according to test pilot's fixation position for the 2 nm test.

Figure 15 shows the input type distribution for both the pilots and all three of the tests conducted. It is interesting to note that as the landing scenario becomes more stressful, the line pilot tends to increase their gross capture inputs compared to their baseline landing, while the test pilot's fine capture inputs increase in the same situation.

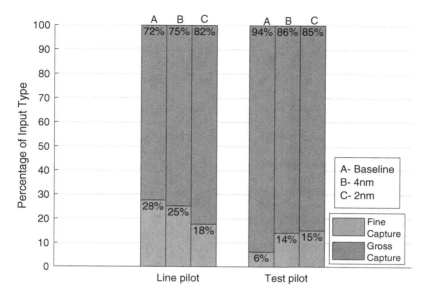

Fig. 15. Comparison of input type distribution for line pilot and test pilot for all three tests.

4   Conclusions and Further Work

In this paper the authors present a detailed analysis of the data collected over the entire test program. The analysis focuses on developing an understanding the pilot attention allocation in high workload scenarios and therefore, provides an understanding of the pilot's adopted control strategy. The Eye-tracking fixations' data gathered was correlated with the flight simulator output. The differences and similarities between the line pilot and test pilot were observed. The further analysis may use the heatmaps within AOIs to distinguish specific elements that the pilot focuses on (airspeed, altitude etc.) and develop an information usage profile. This in turn will allow the proposition of new display setups and inceptors to reduce workload. In the future more pilots may be involved as a test subjects to give more significance (and possibly variance dependable on a pilot's previous experience) to the gathered data. Moreover, different scenarios, such as air-to-air refuelling or path following will be considered along.

Acknowledgements. Co-financed by the European Union through the European Social Fund (grant POWR.03.02.00-00-I029).

References

1. Ahlstrom, U., Friedman-Berg, F.J.: Using eye movement activity as a correlate of cognitive workload. Int. J. Ind. Ergon. **36**(7), 623–636 (2006). https://doi.org/10.1016/j.ergon.2006.04.002. https://linkinghub.elsevier.com/retrieve/pii/S0169814106000771

2. Allsop, J., Gray, R.: Flying under pressure: effects of anxiety on attention and gaze behavior in aviation. J. Appl. Res. Mem. Cogn. **3**(2), 63–71 (2014). https://doi.org/10.1016/j.jarmac.2014.04.010. https://linkinghub.elsevier.com/retrieve/pii/S2211368114000333

3. Ayaz, H., et al.: Cognitive workload assessment of air traffic controllers using optical brain imaging sensors. In: Advances in Understanding Human Performance: Neuroergonomics, Human Factors Design, and Special Populations, pp. 21–31 (2010). https://doi.org/10.1201/EBK1439835012-4. http://www.crcnetbase.com/doi/abs/10.1201/EBK1439835012-4

4. Cooper, G.E., Harper Jr, R.P.: The use of pilot rating in the evaluation of aircraft handling qualities. Technical report, NASA Ames Research Center, Washington (1969). NASA-TN-D-5153

5. Demerouti, E., Veldhuis, W., Coombes, C., Hunter, R.: Burnout among pilots: psychosocial factors related to happiness and performance at simulator training. Ergonomics **62**(2), 233–245 (2019). https://doi.org/10.1080/00140139.2018.1464667. https://www.tandfonline.com/doi/full/10.1080/00140139.2018.1464667

6. IMotions: 10 Most Used Eye Tracking Metrics and Terms (2019). https://imotions.com/blog/7-terms-metrics-eye-tracking/

7. Kearney, P., Li, W.C., Yu, C.S., Braithwaite, G.: The impact of alerting designs on air traffic controller's eye movement patterns and situation awareness. Ergonomics **62**(2), 305–318 (2019). https://doi.org/10.1080/00140139.2018.1493151

8. Künzel, D.: Flight simulator assessment of pilot behaviour during aircraft-pilot-coupling events. Diploma thesis, Munich University of Applied Sciences (2016)

9. Li, W.C., Horn, A., Sun, Z., Zhang, J., Braithwaite, G.: Augmented visualization cues on primary flight display facilitating pilot's monitoring performance. Int. J. Hum.-Comput. Stud. **135** (2020). https://doi.org/10.1016/j.ijhcs.2019.102377

10. Li, W.C., Kearney, P., Braithwaite, G., Lin, J.J.: How much is too much on monitoring tasks? Visual scan patterns of single air traffic controller performing multiple remote tower operations. Int. J. Ind. Ergon. **67**, 135–144 (2018). https://doi.org/10.1016/j.ergon.2018.05.005

11. Li, W.C., Zhang, J., Le Minh, T., Cao, J., Wang, L.: Visual scan patterns reflect to human-computer interactions on processing different types of messages in the flight deck. Int. J. Ind. Ergon. **72**, 54–60 (2019). https://doi.org/10.1016/j.ergon.2019.04.003

12. Lone, M.: Pilot modelling for airframe loads analysis. Ph.D. thesis, Cranfield University (2013)

13. Pupil Labs: Pupil Labs — Core (2019). https://pupil-labs.com/products/core/

14. Saravanakumar, S., Selvaraju, N.: Eye tracking and blink detection for human computer interface. Int. J. Comput. Appl. **2**(2), 7–9 (2010). https://doi.org/10.5120/634-873

15. Shimizu, S., Tanzawa, Y., Hashizume, T.: Classification of gaze preference decision for human-machine interaction using eye tracking device. Int. J. Mechatron. Autom. **2**(2), 75 (2012). https://doi.org/10.1504/IJMA.2012.048183. http://www.inderscience.com/link.php?id=48183

Research on Eye Ellipse of Chinese Drivers

Ding Li[1,2(✉)], Ding Yi[3], and Shi Huijuan[1,2]

[1] School of Biological Science and Medical Engineering, Beihang University,
Xueyuan Road 37, Haidian District, Beijing 100083, China
dingl971316@buaa.edu.cn
[2] Beijing Advanced Innovation Centre for Biomedical Engineering,
Beihang University, Beijing 102402, China
[3] Capital Medical University School of Basic Medical Sciences, Capital Medical
University, Fengtai District, Beijing 100069, China

Abstract. Objective: Due to there is no eye ellipse for Chinese driver, this study aimed at carrying out research on the eye ellipse test of Chinese drivers. Methods: This test used camera position method (SAE) to measure the eye ellipse. 510 drivers (250 males and 260 females) participated in the test. The height ranged from 151.0 cm to 195.0 cm for males and 144.0 cm to 174.6 cm for females. The mean driving age (DA) was 6.1 years for males, and 4.7 years for females. Result: (1) The 95 percentile eye ellipse of the X-axis, Y-axis, and Z-axis were 254.9 mm, 72.3 mm, and 114.9 mm, and the 99 percentile of X-axis, Y-axis, and Z-axis were 315.4 mm, 89.6 mm, and 142.8 mm, which were fitted in the X-Z plane direction. And the X-Z plane fitted eye ellipse was tilted forward and downward with an angle of 11°. (2) The distance between the center points of the left and right eye ellipses from the Y = 0 plane was 30.3 mm, and the coordinates of the X-axis and Z-axis of the eye ellipse center point were 628 mm and 623 mm. Conclusion: Compare with SAE J941-2010 eye ellipse, the length of the eye ellipse axis in this study is larger, the center position in the car is more forward and lower. There is no significant difference in the inclination angle.

Keywords: Driver · Eye ellipse · Vehicle

1 Introduction

Nowadays, a car is one of the most common transportation. The driver's field of vision is an essential factor for driving safety, which caused a majority of traffic accidents [1]. In terms of vehicle vision design, it is crucial to ensure the drivers have a broad vehicle version. Currently, the design of car vision and seats often use the eye ellipse, which is drawn based on a large sample of driver's eye positions during simulated driving in the cabs. Because of the differences in driver's stature, weight, and driving habits, the eye point range formed by the driver in the car cab resembles an ellipse.

Early Society of Automotive Engineers (SAE) research on the eye ellipse was based on a stationary car with fixed seatback angle, fixed seat rails (that is, vertical lift and front-to-back travel are not adjustable), and no seat belts. Soon after, SAE made several modifications to the eye ellipse. In 1963, SAE change the driver's position to a

D. Harris and W.-C. Li (Eds.): HCII 2020, LNAI 12187, pp. 321–331, 2020.
https://doi.org/10.1007/978-3-030-49183-3_25

forward-looking, non-rotating head posture, and the seat had forward and backward adjustment, but the angle of seatback is still fixed. Later, SAE proposed a new factor that 5 to 40° of the angle of seatback maybe can change the eye ellipse [2–5]. In 2002, SAE tested again and considered more factors (seat position, an adjustable angle of seatback, seat belt) into simulated driving. So far, the latest SAE eye ellipse standard has been modified to the 2010 version [6]. Due to the difference of driving habits and body characteristics of different countries, the eye point of driver may not fit with the eye ellipse of European and American countries. Therefore, some researchers questioned it. Japanese researchers collected 317 drivers' eye ellipse data based on three models of car (Cedric, Corona, and Familia) in 1975. Furthermore, they compared it with the latest standard of SAE at that time. Because of the axial length of eye ellipse obtained by Japanese is bigger than the SAE eye ellipse [7], and so the principle formed [8]. The condition of driver's coordinate of the eye point to form an elliptical shape is that every coordinate obeys the normal distribution. When it fits the above conditions, the driver's coordinates of the eye point obey the two-dimensional normal distribution density function equation. Since there is no eye ellipse for Chinese drivers, the eye ellipse of the IEA has been used, resulting in some differences in the application range. Especially the visual design of 5% in crowd is quite different from the real institution of Chinese drivers. Therefore, this study aimed at carrying out research on the eye ellipse test of Chinese drivers.

2   Methods

2.1   Equipment of Experiment

The testing platform of the eye ellipse (Fig. 1) mainly included the simulation cab and the test system of eye point. To ensure the best comfort of the driver when simulated driving in the cab, the horizontal distance adjustment range between the front Seating Reference Point (SgRP) [6, 9] of the simulated seat and the Accelerator Heel Point (AHP) was 220 mm, and the horizontal distance adjustment range between the back SgRP to the AHP was 660 mm. The vertical distance adjustment range between the seat SgRP to AHP was from 250 mm to 345 mm. Meanwhile, the dashboard had 450 mm adjusting range on the X-axis and Z-axis direction, and an adjustable angle range from 0° to 40° to reduce the influence of blind spot of dashboard and make the driver be more easier to reach the position of seat when adjusting the seat. There was a rotating device connected steering wheel with steering wheel rod, which can adjust the angle of the steering wheel. The adjustable vertical swing angle of the steering wheel was from 15° to 35°, and the left and right sides' adjustable swing angle was ±5°. Due to pedal was the basic comparison point of the eye point, the design of the pedal testing platform was non-adjustable.

Fig. 1. The testing platform of the eye ellipse

The eye point position of the driver was measured using Blue enchantress M2200 camera with 1200 million pixels, a maximum resolution of 1600*1200, a photosensitive element CMOS, and connected to a computer with USB interface. The layout refers to the test method of SAE (Fig. 2). Cameras are located in the front, on the left and right sides of the driver. The left side camera, closest to the driver, was used to collect the eye point position of the driver's side view. The front camera was used to determine the coordinate of the front view of the eye. The right side camera, farthest from the driver, was used to calibrate error during measurement.

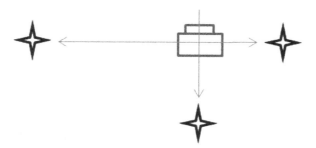

Fig. 2. Layout of cameras

The eye point recording software was independently developed by Beihang University ergonomics laboratory. Its primary function was to extract the required space point from the photo. As Fig. 3 shown, it needed to copy the photo to the "save" folder during using and then opened the "eve" folder. When the interface of Fig. 3 appeared, clicked the "punctuation system". Then, you can load the photo into the "save" folder. Click the points interested in the photo to see the corresponding "x" and "y" coordinates.

Fig. 3. The space coordinates of the eye point recording software

2.2 Participants

In terms of the eye ellipse of the driver, there were many factors, such as body height, body weight, sex, and driving habits, among which, height was the most influential factor. Therefore, this study was based on the Chinese body size standard, chose the body height as the main selection basis, used stratified sampling to recruit participants referenced to the body weight (Table 1). A total of 510 drivers (250 males and 260 females) participated in this study. The drivers with the age of 18–60 were required. Moreover, they needed to have good health and had a driving license and driving experience. The basic information of the participants was shown in Table 2.

Table 1. The reference size of sampling subjects' height and weight

Sex	Variables	The reference size							
Male	Height (m)	−1.54	1.540–1.591	1.591–1.610	1.610–1.693	1.693–1.773	1.773–1.797	1.797–1.854	1.854–
	Percentage	1%	4%	5%	40%	40%	5%	4%	1%
	Weight (kg)	−46	46–50.9	50.9–53.5	53.5–64.5	64.5–80.4	80.4–85.9	85.9–95.9	95.9–
	Percentage	1%	4%	5%	40%	40%	5%	4%	1%
Female	Height (m)	−1.451	1.451–1.482	1.482–1.501	1.501–1.574	1.574–1.65	1.650–1.673	1.673–1.719	1.719–
	Percentage	1%	4%	5%	40%	40%	5%	4%	1%
	Weight (kg)	−40.4	40.4–43.6	43.6– 45.5	45.5–55.7	55.7– 69.5	69.5–73.8	73.8–82	82–
	Percentage	1%	4%	5%	40%	40%	5%	4%	1%

Table 2. The information of subjects

	Male				Female			
	Mean	Maximum	Minimum	Standard deviation	Mean	Maximum	Minimum	Standard deviation
Height (mm)	1707.8	1880	1530	61.3	1615.1	1750	1480	57.3
Age	33.1	55.0	19.0	6.7	32.6	49.0	21.0	5.6
Driving age (year)	5.3	15.0	0.5	3.8	4.5	12.0	1.0	2.8
Weight (kg)	63.7	93.4	45.2	9.2	56.4	75.0	43.2	7.5

2.3   Protocol

1. Check and calibrate the imaging interval of the camera, during which the camera position cannot be moved. If the movement occurred, it needed to be re-calibrated.
2. After the driver adjusted the seat to his comfortable posture, the driver simulated driving in the simulated environment. The software will record the eye point three times during simulated driving.
3. After the experiment was completed, clicked the driver's eyes on the spatial eye point software to record the coordinates of the eye point (In Fig. 4, Fig. 4a was the coordinate point of the front view, Fig. 4b was the coordinate point of the side view). Besides, every driver needed to take the average of three eye points.

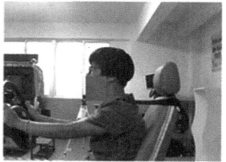

x=5.00000 y=12.63265   x=-24.20000 y=15.03265

(a) The front view   (b) The side view

Fig. 4. Collecting the coordinate of the eye point position

3   Results

3.1   Calibrate the Eye Point Position

Since the driver will move the seat that caused the proportion of actual thing to size of photo changes, and this proportion had a certain relationship with the distance between the camera and actual thing. It needed to be corrected by fitting. In this experiment, a standard piece with a length of 300 mm was selected, and seven position points were selected for fitting. Through the camera testing got the pixel distance from the standard piece to the camera and the pixel distance of standard piece. Then calculated the ratio of actual standard piece to the pixel distance, and obtained the linear equation (Fig. 5) by fitting the pixel distance from the standard piece to the camera (x) and the ratio of actual standard piece to the pixel distance (y).

$$y = 0.0284x - 0.1796 \tag{1}$$

Randomly selected position to inspect, and calculated that the pixel distance from the standard piece to the camera was 117, the pixel distance of the standard piece was 96. So the length of a standard piece was 297.3 mm and the error was less than 1%.

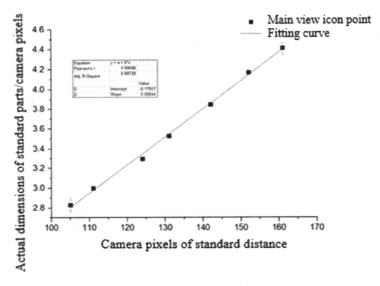

Fig. 5. Calibration point of front view fitting graph

3.2   Equipment of Experiment Distribution of Data Point

The prerequisite for the eye ellipse formed by data conformed to the normal distribution. If this condition was not be met, then it cannot calculate by the two-dimensional normal distribution. So statistical analysis needed to check first whether the collecting eye point was conformed to the normal distribution. SPSS22 software was used for the non-parametric test—KS test to analyze. The result showed the P-values of side view's X-axis and Z-axis were both bigger than 0.05 (the P-values of X-axis and Y-axis are equal, $p = 0.200$), and the data points conformed to the normal distribution.

3.3 Statistics Analysis

After checking whether the data conformed the normal distribution, the oblique ellipse equation of the eye [8, 10] was derived based on the probability density function of the two-dimensional normal distribution with SgRP as the origin. And substituted the standard deviations and the average values of the X-axis and Z-axis to obtain the size of eye ellipse. Among them, the eye ellipse of direction of the X-Z plane was tilted forward and downward with an angle of 11° (Table 3).

Table 3. The size of eye ellipse Unit: mm

Percentile	The length of X-axis	The length of Y-axis	The length of Z-axis
95th	254.9	72.3	114.9
99th	315.4	89.6	142.8

3.4 The Center Point Positions

In the coordinate system with SgRP as the origin, the driver's left and right eyes form two eye ellipses in the front view direction, which were symmetrical with respect to the $Y = 0$ plane, the distance between the center points of the left and right eye ellipses from the $Y = 0$ plane was 30.3 mm. During practical application, the left and right eye ellipses combined into one eye ellipse. At this time, the center point was the average value (the coordinates of Y-axis of mixed eye ellipse is 0), and the coordinates of X-axis and Z-axis of the center point were 628 mm and 623 mm.

4 Discussion

4.1 The Comparison of Different Country's Eye Ellipse

The axis length size of eye ellipse and location mode, which formed by SAE, has been widely used in the automobile industry. SAE has also modified a lot in the size of eye ellipse and location mode, and the modification ratio of them is relatively large. It mainly considers more practical factors. In addition, Japan and other countries have based on the research result that is obtained from their own country's drivers experiment, and it has also adopted in the SAE standard. This study selects the Japanese eye ellipse of 1975 [7] and the SAE eye ellipse of 1975 and 2010 to compare (Table 4) [6]. It can see the greater changes of the last result and measuring method from 1965 to 2010 version of SAE eye ellipse. Compare with the size and shape of 2010 version, this experiment's axis length of eye ellipse is bigger which is mainly effected by the height and standard deviation of weight; the center point position of eye ellipse is more forward and downward which probably because the height of Chinese driver is lower, and the angle has not changed a lot (Fig. 6).

When applying the eye ellipse studied by this paper to automotive design, it needs to consider these factors: (1) Observe fully about the information of a combination instrument by adjusting up the steering wheel. (2) Aim to the car model design for Chinese market, the steering wheel needs larger stroke in height adjustment or overall increase to adapt the position difference of Chinese driver's eyes. (3) The components and parts of all design-checked need to consider the position difference of Chinese driver's eyes in order to avoid customer complaints.

Currently, researchers have begun to pay attention and question whether the standard of SAE and other international eye ellipses can use well in Chinese. Automotive ergonomist also hopes to use the methods similar to SAE in order to collect the eye ellipse standard that conforms Chinese. Through the preliminary study of eye ellipse in this research, the data shows a difference when compares with different versions. This paper considers that the signification of study the size and shape of eye ellipse individual is little. Through the experiment to collect the coordinate of driver's eye point in order to explore whether the SAE standard is adapted to Chinese, and it may not be the best method at present. Many factors are the main reason, and the second reason is that every experiment collecting requires lots of manpower and material resources. Once there are problems existed in scheme, equipment, and choice of subjects, the processing procedure of subsequent data is hard to modify. Consequently, this paper think that it can be studied in several aspects: firstly, depth analysis of the relative factor formed by eye ellipse. Secondly, comparing the physical characteristics of differences in Chinese and other countries. And modify the standard constituted by European and American developed countries by methods of regression analysis. This will greatly reduce research costs and improve research efficiency.

Table 4. Comparison of eye ellipse's data[1] Unit: mm

Version	Percentile	Angle (°)	Size of eye ellipse			Distance of center point to origin[2]		
			X-axis	Y-axis	Z-axis	X-axis	Y-axis	Z-axis
SAE-1965	95th	6.5	198.0	105.0	86.0	−42.6	Left eye 4.1	640.3
	99th		267.0	149	122.0		Right eye −60.5	
SAE-2010	95th	12	206.4	60.3	93.4	664.0	Left eye 32.5	638.0
	99th		287.1	85.3	132.1		Right eye −32.5	
Japan-1975	95th	Left eye 4.3	220.0	72.0	96.0	−3.2	Left eye 31.9	632.8
	99th	Right eye 4.9	311.0	102.0	136.0		Right eye −32.8	
This paper	95th	11	254.9	72.3	114.9	628.0	Left eye 30.3	623.0
	99th		315.4	89.6	142.8		Right eye −30.3	

Remark 1: The adjustable front and back strokes of experimental car seat are greater than 133 mm.
Remark 2: In previous versions of SAE, the X-axis, Y-axis and Z-axis of eye ellipse's center centered on the H-point. In the following versions, the direction of X-axis of eye ellipse centers on the BOFRP (pedal reference point).

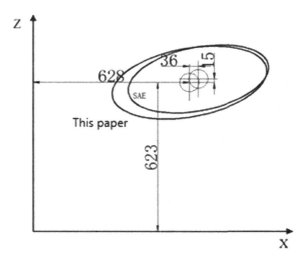

Fig. 6. The comparison of eye ellipse shape in this paper and SAE J941-2010

4.2 The Influencing Factors of Space Point of Eye Ellipse

The eye point has many influencing factors of spatial orientation, which mainly because of the driver and body two factors. Therefore, when collecting eye ellipse, selecting driver sample and body is the key point for the formation of eye ellipse. In addition to driver's height characteristics, seat height, steering wheel position and the angle of the seatback, this paper has found that the position of eye ellipse and driving experience also have a certain impact.

a) The height of the driver is an important factor. It not only influences the height of eye point (Z value, correlation coefficient with Z-axis size of eye point coordinate of side view is 0.666, $p < 0.01$), but also affects the forward and backward direction of driver (X value, correlation coefficient with Z-axis size of eye point coordinate of side view is -0.340, $p < 0.01$. The front of the driver is in the negative direction of X-axis, so the correlation coefficient is negative. It means that the lower height the driver has, the closer to the steering wheel, and the more forward the eye point is. And that is a reason for inclination formed by eye ellipse.

b) Before the survey, the assumptions have been made about the angle of seatback: the bigger angle of seatback is, the more backward the eye point is. But after the data statistics, it is found that the angle of seatback can't affect the eye point position (correlation coefficient of the angle of seatback and coordinates of X-axis is 0.056, $p > 0.05$). Through the survey and observe, possible reasons: driver adjust the seat mainly for the comfort of the back, but for each driver, the angle of the back tilt is the same. After the angle of the back tilt reaches a certain angle, driver will keep upper body upright instead of always tilting with the angle of seatback. As shown in Fig. 7, the angle of seatback on the left is 112°, the angle of seatback on the right is 104°. But the angle of seatback is larger, which can be seen from the head position of two drivers and the driver's head will not rest on the headrest, so the eye point can not be affected. The phenomenon can also explain the content mentioned before: the comfort distance of driver's eyes to the dashboard is less correlated with the driver's height.

Fig. 7. Anaylsis of driver's driving posture by the angle of seatback

c) The driving experience and orientation of eye ellipse also have a relationship. Generally speaking, the richer experience driver has, the farther distance of eye point to the steering wheel, and the elbow and knee joint will change too. Taking the driving age as the measuring standard of experience, select and compare with the driver's eye point position of two groups, which are divided into DA that over or under 5 years DA. And find that the drivers' eye point positions of more than five years' DA are more backward than the drivers' eye point positions of fewer than five years one (After statistics, the deviation is 30.3 mm).

5 Conclusion

Compare with SAE J941-2010 eye ellipse, the length of the eye ellipse axis in this study is larger, the center position in the car is more forward and lower, and there is no significant difference from the two inclination angles.

References

1. Zhu, Y., Lu, J.: Application of eye ellipse in engineering machinery dashboard design. Mach. Build. Autom. **35**(2), 31–34 (2006)
2. Meldrum, J.F.: Automobile driver eye position. SAE Trans., 599–609 (1965)
3. SAE J941—1997, Motor vehicle drivers' eye locations (1997)
4. SAE J941—2008, Motor vehicle drivers' eye locations (2008)
5. Zhang, Q., Zhao, D., Huang, Y.: Revisions and significances of different versions' SAE J941. Sci. Technol. Inf. **26**, 228–229 (2012)

6. SAE J4002—2010, H-Point Machine (HPM-II) Specifications and Procedure for H-Point Determination—Auditing Vehicle Seats (2010)
7. Ishida, T., Matsuno, M.: Study on Japanese driver eye position. In: Automotive Engineering Congress and Exposition (1975)
8. Wen, W., Du, Z.: Explanation of the two-dimensional normal distribution theory of driver's eye ellipse. Autom. Eng. (4), 223–228 (1991)
9. GB/T 11563—1995, H-point of car determines procedure (1995)
10. Ren, J., Fan, Z., Huang, J.: Statistical method suitable for different driver's eye ellipse. J. Mech. Eng. **02**, 192–197 (2006)

Evaluating Pilot's Perceived Workload on Interacting with Augmented Reality Device in Flight Operations

Wen-Chin Li[1(✉)], Zepu Yan[1], Jingyi Zhang[2], Graham Braithwaite[1], Samuel Court[1], Mudassir Lone[1], and Bikram Thapa[1]

[1] Safety and Accident Investigation Centre, Cranfield University, Bedford, UK
wenchin.li@cranfield.ac.uk
[2] Flight Technology College, Civil Aviation University of China, Tianjin, China

Abstract. Augmented Reality (AR) is a tool which can be used to improve human-computer interaction in flight operations. The application of AR can facilitate pilots integrating the information from interfaces in the flight deck to analyze various sources of messages simultaneously. There are seventeen subjects aged from 23 to 53 (M = 29.82, SD = 8.93) who have participated in this experiment. Their flight experience ranged from zero flight hours to 3000 flight hours (M = 605.00, SD = 1051.04). Two types of HCI AR design (gesture or voice control checklist) have been compared with traditional paper checklist. The results show that AR gesture control induced the highest perceived workload compared with AR voice checklist and traditional paper checklist. There are lots of complicated cognitive processes and physical movements involved in the AR gesture checklist that induced the highest level of effort and frustration based on NASA-TLX. The AR checklist application has relied on the use of the default HoloLens interactions including cursor movement linked with head movements, Air Tap gesture and Microsoft voice recognition system. The current technological features embedded in the HoloLens device are not certified to be used in the cockpit yet. The improvement in the types of interaction and displays with AR devices could lead to changes in pilot's perceived workload while interacting with an innovative device. This research demonstrated that AR integrated with voice command has potential of significant benefits to be applied in the flight deck for future flight operation.

Keywords: Augmented reality · Situation awareness · Perceived workload · Flight deck design

1 Introduction

The application of augmented reality (AR) can facilitate pilots interacting with the interfaces in the flight deck to analyze various sources of information simultaneously. System developers take the importance of human-computer interaction into account when design new operational systems to optimize pilots' situational awareness and minimize workload [1]. Augmented Reality differs from Virtual Reality (VR) as AR uses overlaid images in the real-world environment, whereas VR is based on a digital

D. Harris and W.-C. Li (Eds.): HCII 2020, LNAI 12187, pp. 332–340, 2020.
https://doi.org/10.1007/978-3-030-49183-3_26

environment where the user cannot see or interact with the real-world. Augmented Reality is a tool which can be used to improve human-computer interaction in aviation [2]. However, such innovative AR devices need to be validated before implementation in aviation.

Augmented Reality (AR) is textual, symbolic or graphical information overlaid onto the users view of the real world. In his survey of AR technology [3], defines key characteristics inherent to AR - a combination of real and virtual objects, real-time interaction and 3D registration of virtual objects. The first use of AR in aviation was during World War II with the development of head-up displays (HUDs), placing aiming gunsights into the pilots' field of view [4]. The concept was further developed during the 1960's with the inclusion of flight information. This early research in HUD technology found some utility in flight operation, but presented significant human factors issues, often with distracting and disorientating effect for pilots [5]. It was not until later standardisation effort that the full effectiveness of HUDs have been realized [6].

Helmet Mounted Displays (HMDs) offer the next evolution of HUD technology, incorporating HUD parameters (flight, weapons, navigation) and offer head-aiming off-boresight weapon delivery - improving over the compromised situational awareness inherent with traditional Cursor Control Devices (CCDs) used for this function [7]. In recent years there have been increased development of AR headsets (e.g. Google Glass, Microsoft HoloLens and Magic Leap One) that have the potential to be used in commercial aviation. Comerford and Johnson described an augmented cockpit work-space where a pilot could interact with virtual information windows, grouping data and supplanting the environment with overlaid data [8].

Over the past seventy-years there has been an increased reduction in crew complement from five person crew in the 1950s (Captain, First Officer, Navigator, Radio Operator and Flight Engineer) to two personnel (Captain and First Officer). Increased automation and reduced pilot availability may see a further reduction to single pilot operations. Studies have investigated the potential for a ground operator to assist the single pilot during high workload situations [9]. This assistance can also be offered with AR systems that guide the operator to perform flight tasks, compensating for the lack of co-pilot. Tran and his colleagues explored the use of the Microsoft HoloLens to reduce reaction time during an emergency situation [10]. By re-enacting the TransAsia Flight 235 accident, pilot performance was compared using the HoloLens to pilots using ECAM systems. For the participants using HoloLens, controls are indicated within the pilot's field of view.

In modern aviation, checklists and monitoring are considered essential for flight safety and guarding against equipment or pilot errors. Two examples of accidents where the probable cause was improper checklist procedure are that of TransAsia Flight 235, where pilots responded to an engine fire with the wrong engine [11] and Beechcraft King Air B200, where the pilot failed to identify full nose-left rudder trim prior to take-off [12]. Dismukes's study of checklist deviations highlighted the potential safety-risk where checklist procedures are not conducted [13].

The execution of a checklist may be influenced by the medium used for its representation - typically either paper format or digitised. Studies have shown that paper remains the fastest checklist medium for pilots - however they lack a pointer/memory system leading to skipped items [14]. Digitised checklists allow operation of a checklist with a pointer and colour used to indicate completed items. Studies have shown a reduction in error rate when compared to traditional paper systems [15].

The potential for AR in HCI was first explored by Weiser with his vision of "Ubiquitous Computing", where interactions with computing technology become transparent and indistinguishable from everyday life [16]. Although not all ideas presented in this paper have yet to be realised, many can now be recognised as part of modern life: mobile and wearable computing, wireless communication and the Internet-of-Things. With the combination of real and virtual objects, AR leads to concept of "Tangible Computing", a form of "Ubiquitous Computing" where everyday objects become input and output devices for computer interaction [17, 18]. The concept of "Tangible Computing" can be taken further when we consider proprioception - the sense of position and orientation of the body and limbs. This enables new HCI methods of direct manipulation via body sense; physical mnemonics to store/recall information; and gestural actions to issue commands [19].

Hand pose estimation has seen a great deal of Computer Vision (CV) research to enable gesture recognition without the use of data gloves to capture hand movements. Given the complexity of the human hand and multiple degrees of freedom for hand posture and movement, glove-based methods remain an effective method to acquire a model of hand functionality [20]. Limitations of glove-based systems (cost, restricted movement, complex calibration) has led to increased CV research into unencumbered gesture recognition, with development of methods that determine the 3D hand-pose for gesture classification, closely linked to those methods used for human body tracking. Erol and his colleagues summarised the earlier CV work for pose estimation, with techniques ranging from low degrees-of-freedom (DOF) for tracking simple gestures to complex learning methods for high DOF hand models [21]. Modern methods now employ Deep Learning techniques, with Convolutional Neural Networks proving effective at interpreting the hand from a depth map [22].

2   Method

2.1   Participants

Seventeen aviation professionals (pilots, engineers, and training pilots) aged from 23 to 53 ($M = 29.82$, $SD = 8.93$) participated in this experiment. Their flight experience ranged from zero flight hours to 3000 flight hours ($M = 605.00$, $SD = 1051.04$). The collected data was gathered from human subjects; therefore, the research proposal was submitted to the Cranfield University Research Ethics System for ethical approval. As stated in the consent form, participants have the right to terminate the experiment at any time and to withdraw their provided data at any moment even after the data collection.

2.2   Research Apparatus

Augmented Reality Device. The AR device used in the experiment is a Microsoft HoloLens headset (Fig. 1). These glasses comprise see-through holographic waveguides, two HD 16:9 light engines and built-in processors that can display holograms with a resolution of 1280×720 px per eye, a field of view of $30° \times 17.5°$ and a refresh rate of 60 Hz. Brightness and audio volume can be adjusted by 4 buttons located on top of the headset. The HoloLens comes with built-in sensors: an Inertial Measurement Unit (IMU), four environment understanding depth cameras, one 2MP photo/HD video camera, four microphones and one ambient light sensor. Its audio output consists of two speakers located near the user's ears that can emit spatial sound.

Fig. 1. Participant wearing Hololens AR device in the flight deck performing pre-landing checklist

Flight Simulator. The experiment was run on the Cranfield University Large Aircraft Flight Simulator with a representative model of the Boeing 747 simulator (Hanke, 1971). It is comprised of a realistic mock-up of a cockpit of Boeing commercial aircraft with functioning flight controls, stick-shaker stall warning, over-speed alerts, primary flight and navigation displays, and landing gear lever to name a few. The simplified overhead panel is composed of light switches, engine fire emergency levers and engine ignition switches (Fig. 2). The scenario is based on an Instrumented Landing System (ILS) in the final approach. The aircraft is set at 2000 ft and eight nautical miles (NM) from the airfield. As soon as the simulation starts, participants must execute a pre-landing checklist by interacting with the AR device and flying the aircraft for landing.

Fig. 2. B 747 Flight simulator for developing AR apps

Perceived workload measurement: NASA-TLX was applied to evaluate pilots' perceived workload among AR voice, AR gesture and paper checklist. NASA-TLX is a popular technique for measuring subjective perceived workload including Mental demand, Physical demand, Temporal demand, Performance, Effort and Frustration. The participants were required to evaluate their perceived workload among three different modes of pre-landing checklist after each trial. By analysing these six dimensions, it is possible to understand the various safety concerns on applications of AR in relation to perceived workload and HCI in flight operations.

2.3   Research Design

All participants carry out the following; (1) provide the demographical data including age, gender, qualifications, type hours and total flight hours (five minutes); (2) interacted with Hololens AR device (15 min); (3) interacted with B747 simulator to practice how to land the aircraft using a checklist (ten minutes); (4) experienced a briefing on the AR checklist app, with a detailed explanation of the item highlights by voice control and gesture control (ten minutes); (5) performed a landing by using Hololens AR device on both voice control (five minutes) and gesture control (five minutes) randomly; (6) evaluating perceived workload by NASA-TLX to three different modes of operational checklists (ten minutes).

3   Result and Discussion

There are 17 participants conducting three modes of flight operations, traditional paper checklist, gesture control AR checklist, and voice control AR checklist. One-way ANOVA was applied for data analysis. Bonferroni tests were performed to identify pairwise differences for factors with more than two levels. Partial eta-square (η^2) is a measure of effect size for ANOVA. The descriptive results of NASA-TLX scores and six dimension on three checklist modes in the pre-landing phase are shown as Table 1.

Table 1. Means and SD on NASA-TLX reflected to perceived workload on three modes of performing pre-landing procedures

Dimension	Checklist mode	N	M	SD
Mental demand	Traditional paper checklist	17	47.65	23.86
	Gesture controlled AR	17	54.12	21.01
	Voice controlled AR	17	37.94	15.72
Physical demand	Traditional paper checklist	17	47.06	22.92
	Gesture controlled AR	17	70.29	16.34
	Voice controlled AR	17	43.82	19.25
Temporal demand	Traditional paper checklist	17	52.65	22.65
	Gesture controlled AR	17	63.24	30.00
	Voice controlled AR	17	42.94	21.94
Performance	Traditional paper checklist	17	63.53	22.55
	Gesture controlled AR	17	39.71	20.80
	Voice controlled AR	17	63.24	21.21
Effort	Traditional paper checklist	17	41.47	23.70
	Gesture controlled AR	17	65.29	17.45
	Voice controlled AR	17	41.18	13.52
Frustration	Traditional paper checklist	17	42.65	30.27
	Gesture controlled AR	17	65.29	15.46
	Voice controlled AR	17	33.82	18.84
Total	Traditional paper checklist	17	49.17	15.28
	Gesture controlled AR	17	59.66	11.13
	Voice controlled AR	17	43.82	9.21

There is a significant difference of participants' perceived workload on NASA-TLX among three modes of operations for pre-landing checklist, $F(2, 48) = 7.49$, $p < .01$, $\eta^2 = 0.24$. Post-hoc comparison indicates that the AR gesture checklist induced significantly higher level of workload than traditional paper checklist and AR voice checklist. Generally, AR gesture checklist causes participants the highest level of perceived workload on flight operations (Table 1). Furthermore, there is a significant difference on physical demand among three modes of operational checklist, $F(2, 48) = 9.15$, $p < .001$, $\eta^2 = 0.28$. Post-hoc comparison shows that the physical demand of AR gesture checklist is significantly higher than traditional paper checklist and AR voice checklist. It was observed that participants have to activate a lot of checklists at pre-landing procedures by air tap gestures. Therefore, the physical demands are the highest compared with paper checklist and AR voice checklists. There is a significant difference on performance among three modes of operational checklist, $F(2, 48) = 21.34$ $p < .01$, $\eta^2 = 0.22$. Post-hoc comparison shows that performance of flight operations with AR gesture checklist is significantly lower than traditional paper checklist and AR voice checklist. Participants' have struggled to accomplish lots of physical movements and air tap gestures in additional to fly the airplane safely landing. Therefore, the performance of AR gesture checklist is the lowest compared with paper checklist and AR voice checklists.

There is a significant difference on participant's effort among three modes of checklist, $F(2, 48) = 9.31, p < .001, \eta^2 = 0.28$. Post-hoc comparison indicates that the AR gesture checklist demands participants more efforts than traditional paper checklist and AR voice checklist. It was identified that participants have to complete the pre-landing checklists by moving the focus of camera to the item in the checklist and activate by air tap simultaneously. There are lots of cognitive processes and physical efforts involved in the flight operations. The effort is the highest on the AR gesture checklist compared with paper checklist and AR voice checklists. There is a significant difference on participant's frustration among three modes of checklist, $F(2, 48) = 8.90$, $p < .01, \eta^2 = 0.24$. Post-hoc comparison indicates that the AR gesture checklist makes participants felt a significant higher level of frustration than traditional paper checklist and AR voice checklist. During the experiment a potential lack of compliance was witnessed as some participants appears to become frustrated with the physical effort and mental demand required to operate both AR device by Air Tap and the landing gear in particular. Although these instances did not result in non-compliance during the study it is likely that some may become non-compliant in a single pilot operation scenario [23]. However, the mental demand ($F(2, 48) = 2.69, p = .08$) and temporal demand ($F(2, 48) = 2.77, p = .07$) among three modes of checklist show no significant difference in the current study (Table 1). The compliance of checklist and procedures are of great interest for Human Factors research and investigations as they may be accountable for a significant number of aviation accidents. The human-cantered design of augmented visualization aids have effects on human performance and cognitive processes by increased operator's capability to manage complex checklists.

4   Conclusion

There are two types of interaction by gesture and voice controlled have been compared to traditional paper checklists. The results show that gesture control AR gives rise to unnecessary complexity and tends to be awkward to use. There are lots of complicated cognitive processes and physical movements involved in the AR gesture checklist inducing the highest level of frustration compared with paper and AR voice checklists. Therefore, participants rated the highest perceived workload to the AR gesture checklist. On the other hand, voice control AR checklists could establish the human-centered design on HCI in the flight deck for pre-landing check. It was acknowledged as the lowest workload while pilots performing pre-landing checklist. The AR checklist application has relied on the use of the default HoloLens interactions including cursor movement with head movements, Air Tap gesture, Microsoft voice recognition system. The current technological features embedded in the HoloLens device are not certified to be used in the cockpit yet. The improvement in the types of interaction and displays on AR devices could lead to changes in pilot's perceived workload while interacted with the innovative device. This research demonstrated that AR voice command has potential of significant benefits to be applied in the flight deck for future flight operation.

References

1. Dorneich, M.C., Rogers, W., Whitlow, S.D., DeMers, R.: Human performance risks and benefits of adaptive systems on the flight deck. Int. J. Aviat. Psychol. **26**(1–2), 15–35 (2016)
2. Luzik, E., Akmaldinova, A.: Psychological aspects of ensuring flight safety in civil aviation. Aviation **10**(1), 25–35 (2006)
3. Azuma, R.T.: A survey of augmented reality. Teleop. Virtual Environ. **6**(4), 355–385 (1997)
4. Prinzel, L.J, Risser, M.: Head-up displays and attention capture (NASA/TM-2004-213000). NASA Langley Research Center, Hampton, VA, United States (2004)
5. Barnette, J.F.: Role of head-up display in instrument flight (No. IFC-LR-76-2). Air Force Instrument Flight Center Randolph AFB TX, Dublin, OH, United States (1976)
6. Newman, R. L.: Improvement of head-up display standards. In: Head-Up Display Design Guide. Appendix, vol. 1. Crew Systems Consultants, Yellow Springs, OH, United States (1987)
7. Thomas, P., Biswas, P., Langdon, P.: State-of-the-art and future concepts for interaction in aircraft cockpits. In: Antona, M., Stephanidis, C. (eds.) UAHCI 2015. LNCS, vol. 9176, pp. 538–549. Springer, Cham (2015). https://doi.org/10.1007/978-3-319-20681-3_51
8. Comerford, D., Johnson, W.W.: Potential capabilities in a future, augmented cockpit. Ergon. Design **15**(1), 8–13 (2007)
9. Brandt, S.L., Lachter, J., Battiste, V., Johnson, W.: Pilot situation awareness and its implications for single pilot operations: analysis of a human-in-the-loop study. Procedia Manuf. **3**, 3017–3024 (2015)
10. Tran, T.H., Behrend, F., Fünning, N., Arango, A.: Single pilot operations with AR-glasses using Microsoft HoloLens. In: IEEE/AIAA 37th Digital Avionics Systems Conference, pp. 1–7. IEEE, London (2018)
11. Kharoufah, H., Murray, J., Baxter, G., Wild, G.: A review of human factors causations in commercial air transport accidents and incidents: from to 2000–2016. Prog. Aerosp. Sci. **99**, 1–13 (2018)
12. Australian Transport Safety Bureau: Loss of control and collision with terrain involving B200 King Air, VH-ZCR at Essendon Airport, Victoria on 21 February 2017 (Investigation No. AO-2017-024). ATSB, Canberra, Australia (2018)
13. Dismukes, R.K., Berman, B.: Checklists and monitoring in the cockpit: why crucial defenses sometimes fail (NASA/TM-2010-216396, TH-084, ARC-E-DAA-TN1902). NASA Ames Research Center, Moffett Field, CA, United States (2010)
14. Degani, A., Wiener, E.L.: Human factors of flight-deck checklists: the normal checklist (NCC2-377; RTOP 505-67-41). Ames Research Center, Moffett Field, CA, United States (1991)
15. Rouse, S., Rouse, W.: Computer-based manuals for procedural information. IEEE Trans. Syst. Man Cybern. **10**(8), 506–510 (1980)
16. Weiser, M.: The computer for the 21st century. Sci. Am. **265**(3), 94–104 (1991)
17. Ishii, H., Ullmer, B.: Tangible bits: towards seamless interfaces between people, bits and atoms. In: Proceedings of the ACM SIGCHI Conference on Human Factors in Computing Systems, pp. 234–241. ACM Press, New York (1997)
18. Kato, H., Billinghurst, M.: Marker tracking and HMD calibration for a video-based augmented reality conferencing system. In: Proceedings 2nd IEEE and ACM International Workshop on Augmented Reality, pp. 85–94. IEEE, London (1999)

19. Mine, M.R., Brooks, F.P., Jr., Sequin, C.H.: Moving objects in space: exploiting proprioception in virtual-environment interaction. In: Proceedings of the 24th Annual Conference on Computer Graphics and Interactive Techniques, pp. 19–26. ACM Press, New York (1997)
20. Dipietro, L., Sabatini, A.M., Dario, P.: A survey of glove-based systems and their applications. IEEE Trans. Syst. Man Cybern. Part C (Appl. Rev.) **38**(4), 461–482 (2008)
21. Erol, A., Bebis, G., Nicolescu, M., Boyle, R.D., Twombly, X.: Vision-based hand pose estimation: a review. Comput. Vis. Image Underst. **108**(1), 52–73 (2007)
22. Oberweger, M., Lepetit, V.: DeepPrior++: improving fast and accurate 3D hand pose estimation. In: IEEE International Conference on Computer Vision Workshops. IEEE, London (2017)
23. Stanton, N.A., Plant, K.L., Roberts, A.P., Allison, C.K.: Use of highways in the sky and a virtual pad for landing head up display symbology to enable improved helicopter pilots situation awareness and workload in degraded visual conditions. Ergonomics **62**(2), 255–267 (2019)

Human-in-the-Loop Evaluation
of a Manned-Unmanned System Approach
to Derive Operational Requirements
for Military Air Missions

Sebastian Lindner[(✉)] and Axel Schulte

Bundeswehr University Munich, Werner-Heisenberg-Weg 39,
85579 Neubiberg, Germany
{sebastian.lindner,axel.schulte}@unibw.de

Abstract. In recent years, a prototype was developed at the Institute of Flight Systems which enables the deployment of manned unmanned teaming (MUM-T) in a simulated military air mission. This article describes the design of this prototype with the required automation and presents the results of the human-in-the-loop experiment conducted with eight professional German Air Force pilots. For the experiment six realistic mission scenarios in three levels of difficulty were designed. We describe the success of the human integration in a MUM-T system by quantifying the human-in-the-loop experiments with interdependent indicators. Workload is – besides classic mission specific operational parameters – the main indicator of the efficiency of a human-machine system. The human's ability to collaborate with automation determine the efficiency of the overall system. The experimental data supports to derive operational requirements for the design of a MUM-T system.

Keywords: MUM-T · Future operating environment · Human-Autonomy-Teaming · Force composition · Human-in-the-loop · Unmanned systems

1 Introduction

The Future Combat Air System (FCAS) will encounter the challenges of future operating environments (FOE) for European Air Forces. One part of this system network is the Next Generation Weapon System (NGWS), the ability of which is to penetrate denied airspace. Due to the high risk associated with this task, it is envisioned to reduce the number of manned platforms using unmanned aerial vehicles. To investigate how this joint operation of manned and unmanned forces can be realized, we developed a laboratory prototype of cockpit and mission dynamics at the Institute of Flight Systems. Our approach is that the manned assets command the unmanned aerial vehicles, as well as their mission payloads. This approach is known under the term Manned-Unmanned Teaming (MUM-T). The term describes the interoperability of manned and unmanned assets to pursue a common mission objective. MUM-T requires to master the high work demands posed on the operator arising from the multi-platform mission management. We developed intelligent automation which supports and

© Springer Nature Switzerland AG 2020
D. Harris and W.-C. Li (Eds.): HCII 2020, LNAI 12187, pp. 341–356, 2020.
https://doi.org/10.1007/978-3-030-49183-3_27

cooperates with the pilot [1, 2]. This study describes an effort to evaluate our prototype within a human-machine experiment.

2 Background

This chapter details the made assumptions for the design of the MUM-T prototype, the hypothesis we address and the background on quantifying complex human-in-the-loop experiments.

2.1 Assumptions

Future Operating Environments
The FOE is the operationalization of possible military conflicts. It is an important objective for the capability development. From the guidelines of the FOE we generated realistic application scenarios with the involvement of military domain experts. The challenge resulting from these scenarios place requirements on the MUM-T prototype to be developed. A future weapon system must be capable of effective service in both permissive and contested air missions. For this reason, we must design automation approaches that are suitable for general use.

Human-Autonomy Teaming Technologies
The key aspect for a MUM-T system is to keep the pilot in the decision-making process without overtaxing him. All developed automation functions contribute to maintain the task load of the pilot in a manageable zone and facilitate the accomplishment of mission. For mission management and unmanned vehicle guidance we used a concept called task-based guidance. The pilot uses a generic task formulation to command unmanned vehicles [3]. The task assignment is supported by a mission planning instance interacting with the pilot, to find optimal mission plans in a mixed-initiative manner [4]. With increasing autonomy automation-induced errors arises [5]. The onboard assistant system supports the pilot in the decision-making process by analyzing his current activity [6] and his mental state [7] permanently. We decided to team the manned fighter with two types of unmanned system.

- Highly capable unmanned combat aerial vehicles (UCAV):
  It has a fighter jet like platform performance. They receive mission tasks from the pilot and are able to derive a course of action, including route planning, pattern calculation, sensor/effector management. Additionally, they incorporate intelligent cognitive automation for mutual support [8].
- Swarm UAV:
  It is a cheap disposable aerial vehicle which can be deployed in large numbers in enemy territory. They organize themselves in a decentralized manner and use different swarming algorithms dependent on the assigned task. Swarming promises a variety of operational advantages [9, 10].

All platforms must be integrated into a MUM-T system, and the human-machine interaction and hierarchies must clearly be defined. For this reason, the prototype design is a human-integration challenge. The description language for Human-Autonomy-Teaming [11] helps to visualize the present relations within our MUM-T system. Figure 1 shows a MUM-T system with the manned fighter jet guiding two UCAVs and one swarm network.

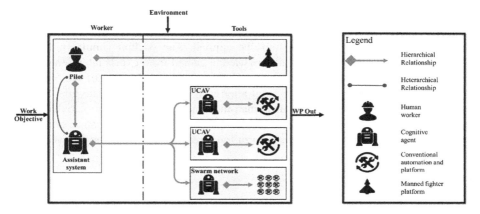

Fig. 1. Possible configuration of MUM-T system. The manned fighter jet hosts pilot, assistant system and platform. Both UCAVs comprise the cognitive agent and the platform. Represented by an avatar agent, the entities of the swarm are considered as a single team member.

Force Compositions

In this study, we consider the presented works on our Human-Autonomy Teaming technologies as the proposed technical solution. However, each mission scenario poses specific challenges and subsequently requires a specific composition of the MUM-T system. Thus, a significant challenge in composing valuable force compositions will be in identifying the combinations of parameters, from among the range of possibilities, that will be most relevant in the mission. The identification of these interdependent parameters are the operational requirements we can contribute to a future weapon system.

2.2   Hypothesis

Regarding the MUM-T prototype the following aspects are examined.

H-1: A pilot is able to guide a MUM-T system efficiently in a military air mission.

H-2: The human places trust in the automation (cognitive agents).

H-3: Keep the human in the decision-making process.

H-4: The force composition of the MUM-T system impacts the workload imposed on the pilot.

2.3   Quantifying a Human-in-the-Loop Experiment

Kantowitz [12] suggests that external validity for a complex human-machine experiment could be viewed as having three major issues; representativeness of subjects, of setting and of variables. Our professional military pilots meet the requirements as suitable subjects. Due to the complexity of military air missions, only experts can assess the system design and execute the missions. The setting representativeness refers to the coherence between the test situation in which research is performed and the target situation in which research must be applied. The cockpit simulator and the missions were developed with domain knowledge gained from expert interviews in the squadrons. The acceptance and realization of the mission is also part of the feedback questionnaire that the pilot had to fill out after each mission, to evaluate this. So, the remaining point for validation of our human-machine approach are the variables. For this, mission execution must be quantified using indicators for performance, efficiency and workload. Renger [13] was able to form four areas of indicators for the evaluation of human-machine systems.

- Goal achievement indicators
- Work rate indicators
- Operability indicators
- Knowledge indicators

We will base the discussion of the experimental results on this structure. The chosen variables relating to the individual domains are presented in Sect. 3.4.

3   HITL Experiment

The experiments have been conducted with eight active German Air Force pilots of different age, experience levels, trained platform types. Each participant was trained to our system for two days. Each pilot performed six full missions from take-off to landing to prevent incorrect result arising from a lack of immersion or decreased situational awareness.

3.1   Test Environment

Our MUM-T cockpit simulation consists of a generic fighter jet cockpit and a dome projection system as external view. In addition to throttle and stick, three multi-touch screens are available for input to the participant of the experiment. The central screen displays a tactical map and is mainly used for mission management, like tasking unmanned assets or threat assessment. Freely configurable additional information can be shown on all displays. A non-intrusive eye-tracking system is used for gaze estimation providing important context information for the assistant system to assess the pilot's activity [6] (Fig. 2).

Fig. 2. Generic fighter jet cockpit simulator of the Institute of Flight System.

3.2 Procedure

We defined missions in three levels of difficulty, from asymmetric conflict to a symmetric peer-level opponent. Within each difficulty level the threats, mission tasks, and timings are kept constant. Each difficulty level will be performed with two force configurations. The permutations are variables regarding i.e. the number of UCAVs and swarm networks, the payload, the authority/autonomy given to the UCAV. We want to verify the influence and possible operational advantages of different force compositions. Figure 3 shows the experimental design with the configurations that appeared most relevant for us. The faded areas depict potential possibilities in the design space.

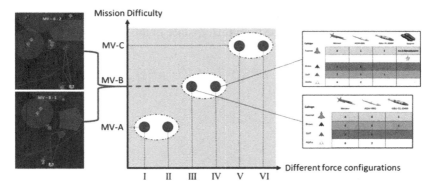

Fig. 3. Heuristic for selecting suitable scenarios and configuration. The dimension should be read as nominal scales. On the x-axis different composites of the MUM-T team are depicted, the y-axis shows the level of mission difficulty.

In total, six full mission were conducted with each pilot. Within these the MUM-T system had to cope with different kinds of tasks. A typical mission sequence is the penetration of enemy territory (Ingress), reaching the target area to achieve the desired effect and leaving enemy territory (Egress). Enemy Air defense (ground and air-based) had to be considered and dealt with. If the objective is the engagement of a ground target, a F2T2EA (find, fix, track, target, engage, assess) cycle had to be performed. Therefore, an imaging-capable platform of the MUM-T system and a suitable effector must be available at the desired location. In the following the missions and the main differences of the individual configurations are described.

MV-A (permissive): Find few unknown mobile targets with all enemy defense sites known.

- Configuration I: NGF with single-digit number of UCAVs.
- Configuration II: NGF with one UCAVs and a swarm network of around ten platforms.

MV-B (medium): Find a time-sensitive target within a medium sized target area (CAT 7) in partially known enemy territory.

- Configuration III: NGF carrying a swarm (around ten entities) with a single-digit number of UCAVs.
- Configuration IV: NGF with the same single-digit number of UCAVs.

MV-C (contested): Enable an Offensive Counter Air (OCA) mission by suppressing the belt of enemy air defenses during ingress and egress:

- Configuration V: NGF with a single digit number of UCAVs. Each UCAV could be tasked using an *Area of Responsibility*. Within this area each UCAV could operate autonomous by assigning targets fitting the task profile (i.e. SAM sites in a SEAD area).
- Configuration VI: NGF with the same single digit number of UCAVs and an air-launched decoy swarm (around ten entities) stimulating the enemy air defense.

These mission scenarios were designed to systematically analyze the MUM-T system. Thus, we must evaluate the team performance of this system in a quantitatively manner.

3.3 Test Persons

(See Table 1)

Table 1. Test persons for the HITL experiment

ID	Gender	Age [a]	Application - flight hours [h]	Total flight hours [h]	Operating hours [h]
P1	Male	35	Tornado - 700	1000	210
P2	Male	32	Tornado - 920	1200	200
P3	Male	39	Tornado - 1400	1500	120
P4	Male	35	WSO Tornado - 1000	1000	100
P5	Male	51	F-4F - 500 MiG-29 - 1000 Eurofighter - 2000	3500	–
P6	Male	38	F-4F - 500 Eurofighter - 200	1160	–
P7	Male	30	Eurofighter - 220	480	–
P8	Male	30	Eurofighter - 500	1000	50

3.4   Indicators of HITL-Experiment

Goal Achievement Indicators
contain the percentage of the achieved mission objectives and checks if the mission success criteria were met. All missions are underlain by rules (Rules of Engagement, ROE), compliance with which is also important.

Work Rate Indicators
comprise factors that specifically address the mission execution. In the experiment setting, two different types exist. The first measures system performance without considering the human explicitly. We will focus on the following parameters

- Time an enemy radar tracks a friendly force. The following list names the military abbreviations for different indications of the radar warning receiver (RWR) of the aircrafts. The resulting risk increases in the downward direction.
  - *DIRT*: RWR indication of surface threat in search mode.
  - *MUD*: RWR indication of surface threat in track mode.
  - *Singer*: RWR indication of a surface-air-missile (SAM) launch.
- Distance to threats (air or surface)
- Dislocation of own MUM-T system
- Average time for target identification

Within the scope of this article we focus on the tracking time of the MUM-T components. Besides these, there are the mental performance indicators. They describe the workload acting on a person. We decided to use the NASA-TLX questionnaire, which is a well-established tool and nowadays used far beyond its original application [14].

Operability Indicators
focus on the human user. Here it is evaluated which form of automation the pilot uses. Of interest are also measures that provide information about the task spectrum and activity of the pilot. In this way it is possible to trace down what a pilot does. For this

we use information provided by the eye-tracking system. The gaze measurements are real-time analyzed and evaluated with a specific task-model [6]. Beyond the scope considered here, an indicator is also system errors. Why and when did they become apparent during the mission and how to prevent them in further development?

Knowledge Acquisition Indicators
describe the effort that the test persons must put in to learn, understand and remember how to use the system. We did not evaluate those types of indicators qualitatively during the days of training. We assumed that the test persons will be in control of the system at the end of the test phase.

4   Results

This section contains the results of the human-in-the-loop experiments that will be used to validate our MUM-T approach. The first section provides the results of the performed missions. In the following section the subjective opinions gathered in questionnaires are presented.

4.1   Mission Results

The results are outlined according to the different indicators described in Sect. 3.3.

Goal Achievement Indicators
With all provided configuration, the pilots were able to carry out the missions successfully. With configuration I, one pilot was not able to fulfill the secondary task in MV-A. The rules of engagement were also violated twice, as the minimum safety distance to the enemy interceptors was not maintained. In configuration V, one pilot strayed away from other aircrafts which should be protected (Table 2).

Table 2. Goal achievement indicators for the different configurations.

Mission	Configuration	Primary Goals	Secondary Goals	Rules of Engagement
MV-A	I	100%	**87%**	**75%**
	II	100%	100%	100%
MV-B	III	100%	100%	100%
	IV	100%	100%	100%
MV-C	V	100%	100%	**87%**
	VI	100%	100%	100%

Work Rate Indicators
The results are split into two sets - the operational and the human related indicators.

Operational Work Rate Indicators
MV-A: This mission was a covert operation. In configuration I the pilots used a UCAV for the search and verification of the targets. In configuration II, this task was entrusted

to the swarm network. All pilots chose holding points outside the enemy's early warning radar. The assumption was made that the swarm platforms were not traceable due to their size. The enemy interceptors were alarmed when UCAVs entered the range of an early warning radar. The total time the configuration was DIRT is shown in Fig. 4 (top). The mean time of configuration I is 783 s and for configuration II it is 162 s.

MV-B: In this comparison the operational differences using a swarm network for time-critical missions are investigated. The UCAV needed for the search area (CAT 7 – coordinates) 225 s for a full scan. The swarm network using pheromone-based search algorithms [15] with around ten entities needed 45 s (97% coverage). Considering the overall workload for the pilot the missions comprised no difference. The time the system was *DIRT*, was reduced using the swarm network (configuration III) from 857 to 582 s. Thus, we had an increase in the *MUD* time for configuration III – 72 s (configuration IV – 17 s). Two pilots performing mission MV-B with configuration IV were even fired upon (SINGER).

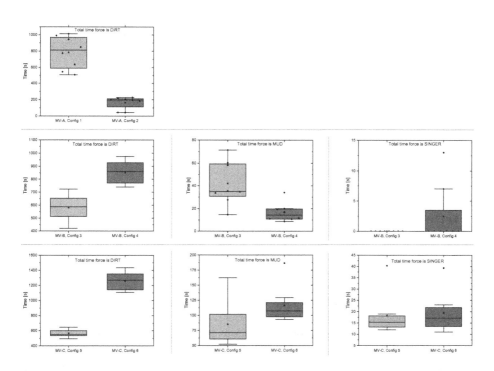

Fig. 4. DIRT, MUD, SINGER times for mission: MV-A (top), MV-B (center), MV-C (bottom).

MV-C: Within this mission we compared the impact of locally given autonomy for UCAVs to a situational awareness gained from decoy swarms [16]. Configuration 5 shows lower DIRT (565 s), MUD (85 s) and SINGER (18 s) times compared to configuration VI (1250 s, 117 s, 20 s). Also, the overall workload of the pilot Fig. 4 shows an increase of 7.2% (configuration V – 41.9%, configuration VI – 49.1%). Thus, MV-C with configuration VI has placed greater demands on both the system and the pilot.

Mental Work Rate Indicators
The workload of the pilots performing the missions with different force configurations is shown in Fig. 5. With the increase in mission difficulty (MV-A, MV-B, MV-C) an increase of the mean workload is discernible. Excluded is an outlier existing in MV-A with configuration II indicating higher workload for one pilot. For MV-A with configuration I the mean workload is 34.3%, for configuration 2 it is lower with 29.5%. The mean average of both configuration III & IV of MV-B shows the same workload of 36.5%. In MV-C the workload of configuration VI with 49.0% exceeds configuration V with 41.8%.

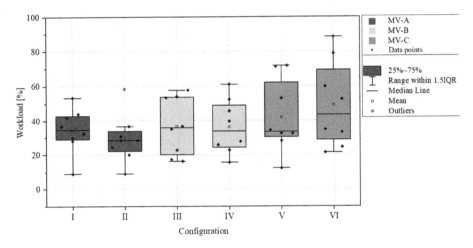

Fig. 5. Arising workload, measured with a NASA-TLX questionnaire, performing the different missions within the experiment.

Operability Indicator

This section focuses on how the human operate the system. Thus, we recorded the observations of the assistant system to gain insight into the pilot's activity. The task the pilot did, depended on two factors. The mission with its objectives, and the individual pilots. The chronological progression of the domains of occupation is shown in Fig. 6 for a single pilot with configuration I. Classic pilot tasks are aviate manually or with autopilot and navigate (red, light red and light green). Additional task load emerges with tactical assessment of the environment (blue), mission planning (green) and UAV management and monitoring (light orange). Analyzing the figure, one can deduce the phases of the mission. The time of the target engagement was (11.5 min after mission start). This pilot took over the managed aircraft and performed the attack manually. Before the engagement the pilot verified the target with a provided sensor picture (purple). Round about one minute after the effector was dropped the pilot confirmed the effectors impact.

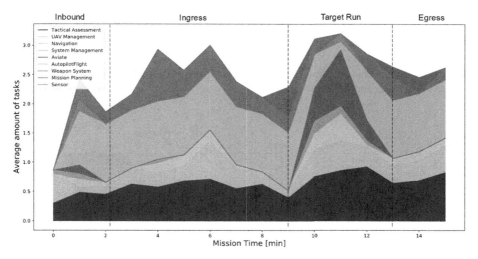

Fig. 6. Pilot activity determination for one pilot in MV-A and configuration I. (Color figure online)

Figure 6 points out the mission sequence for a single pilot. As mentioned, the activity history looks different for each mission and each pilot. To determine the differences of activity for all pilots, Fig. 7 shows the percentage of activity over the total mission time. The magnitude of the variation can be read off the Box Plot. The great variety of the quartiles for *Aviate* and *Autopilot Flight* can be attributed to the fact that they were exclusive. The system was flown either manually or by autopilot.

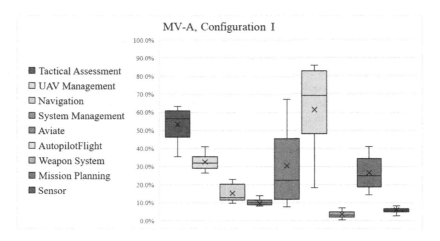

Fig. 7. Box plot of the percentage of activity over the total mission time for configuration I.

4.2   Questionnaire Results

The pilots conducted a questionnaire after each mission. An excerpt from the questionnaire is depicted in Fig. 8. Therefore, for each question are 48 data points available. The Likert-Scale was chosen to uncover subtleties of opinion understanding the received feedback and to improve the system.

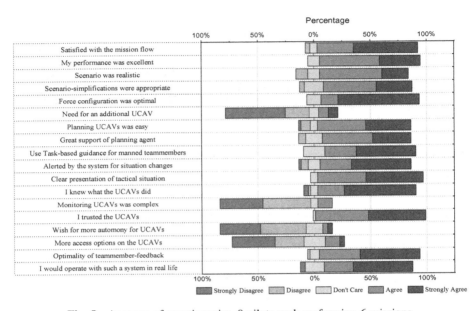

Fig. 8. Answers of questionnaire, 8 pilots each performing 6 missions.

The mission scenario design showed high acceptance. The chosen force configurations are remarkably compatible with a configuration desired by the pilots. The assistance system including the planning agent and the interface is predominantly very well rated. Trust was placed in the unmanned systems of both traits, UCAVs and the swarm network. Few would like to have more possibilities of intervention on the unmanned systems, same applies to more automation. The concept of task-based guidance was very well accepted and according to the pilot, it seems also suitable for delegating manned wingman. More than 50% could envisage conducting future military operations with the system design proposed here.

5 Discussion

We structured the discussion in accordance with the different indicators.

Goal Achievement

All pilots could efficiently operate the MUM-T system within various environmental settings. Thus, hypothesis H-1 is supported. In MV-A could be identified, that the use of a swarm network could positively influence the achievement of secondary goals and the compliance with restrictions. Same holds for the two configurations (V, VI) in MV-C.

Other advantages of configurations cannot be evaluated at this goal-based level.

Work Rate

Operative advantages incorporating swarming platforms are present in MV-A using configuration II. Due to the covert mission one must remain undetected by the enemy for as long as possible. Using swarm platforms in this mission contributes to a temporal resolution of the conflict with enemy aircrafts. This has direct impact on the arising workload affecting the pilot during the mission (supports hypothesis H-4).

In MV-B, the pilots also operated with a swarm network. Although the pilots must guide many vehicles, the necessary effort of delegation and monitoring stays the same. The pure number of platforms of configuration III and configuration IV more than doubles. This points in favor of our approach to integrate the swarm as an avatar into the system network. With equal workload, the target is found, identified and fought more quickly.

In MV-C with configuration 5 the pilots were able to give the UCAVs higher authority by allowing them to attack SAM sites within SEAD boxes on their own (*Area of Responsibility*). Thus, the UCAV was able to derive targets and actions as an autonomous, but locally restricted, system. This resulted in a reduction of the perceived workload (Fig. 5). In configuration 6, a swarm of cruise missile were used to stimulate the enemy air defense. Although most of the SAM systems were known, pilots experienced this configuration as more strenuous to fly. Objectively, the work index speaks for the higher automation, the pilots appreciate the operational advantages of the decoy swarm. In the debriefing 75% of the pilots in configuration 5 were no longer able to name the number and type of SAM systems that occurred. Reducing the workload by increasing the autonomy of the UCAVs inevitably yield a loss in transparency. Thus, the level of automation must suit the situation.

Operability

For the operability the activities of the pilot were observed. Classical pilot task like aviate and navigate are reduced using automation. In our case, these activities occupied round about 46 percent of the mission. One hundred percent would mean that the pilot is doing this task continuously. In a MUM-T system, the pilot no longer must deal only with his own aircraft, but with the operational planning of the unmanned aircraft. Thus, pilot tasks like mission planning and the monitoring which claim the pilot with 27 and 32 percent respectively. In parallel the pilots check the tactical situation for 53 percent of the mission execution time. Threat assessment can be count to the main responsibilities for a future MUM-T pilot.

General Assessment of the Pilots

The subjective rating of the pilots gave evidence for great acceptance of the overall system design. The degree of reality of the mission design was predominantly assessed as high to very high. The representativeness of setting is, as presented, one of main aspects contributing to the validity of human-in-the-loop evaluation, could be verified through the questionnaires. All missions could be performed within manageable work- and task load. In no situation did any of the test persons feel overwhelmed (supports hypothesis H-3). Thus, the trust in automation for the assistant system was high. All pilots relied on the unmanned systems to perform their tasks independently. This indicates support for the hypothesis H-2. Due to the high trust, the monitoring process has been kept to a minimum by the pilots. Operator responses to Likert-scale questionnaires as well as their verbal feedback during debrief sessions reinforced the finding that the task-based guidance concept is a sophisticated way of interacting with other teammates.

Operational Requirements

The operational requirements for a human-machine system can be derived from the mission scenarios, the concept of deployment and the automation. The missions define the need for specific platform parameters and abilities, each member needs to possess. We presented three different types of aerial vehicles, a manned fighter jet, highly capable UCAVs, and cheap disposable air-launched decoys. We used a teaming structure as the concept of deployment and integrated the UCAVs and the swarming UAVs into the team. To team with the swarming network we used an avatar representation which allows the network to be viewed as a single unit. Automation function must incorporate a concept for multi-platform guidance, intelligent agents onboard the unmanned systems and an assistant system supporting the pilot. Assuming the automation presented in this article, all pilots were able to conduct a military air operation together with unmanned system in a simulated environment.

6 Summary

The validation of modern military simulation relies heavily on the opinion of military experts, and it makes the validation task exhaustive and time-consuming. With our approach integrating the human in our system verification process, we receive additional subjective verification. The experts were able to contribute their knowledge through real-time interaction with the system. Their opinions therefore arose not only from pure observing a system. With the experiment, one can conclude that the design of a MUM-T system, as it was realized, enables a trained military fighter pilot to handle unmanned systems within a complex military air mission. The assistant system and the introduced automatic function for the cognitive agent onboard the UCAVs could reduce workload to maintain the human situational awareness. Even delegating a swarm network of around ten vehicles, additionally to UCAVs, can be made possible with the presented avatar. The human is adaptively kept in the decision-making process to form an efficient human-machine team. Concepts – like task-based guidance – can also be transferred to purely manned systems to improve cooperation. We were thus able to provide a first impression of how a MUM-T system might look like. We identified that with concepts like scalable autonomy individual habits of the pilots can be satisfied. It should be considered that automation-induced errors can occur due to the multitude of automatic functions. This can be counteracted with an adaptive assistance system that provides support based on the situation, the current pilot's activity and his mental state.

References

1. Gangl, S., Lettl, B., Schulte, A.: Management of multiple unmanned combat aerial vehicles from a single-seat fighter cockpit in manned-unmanned fighter missions. In: AIAA Infotech@ Aerospace (I@A) Conference, p. 4899 (2013)
2. Reich, F., Heilemann, F., Mund, D., Schulte, A.: Self-scaling human-agent cooperation concept for joint fighter-UCAV operations. In: Savage-Knepshield, P., Chen, J. (eds.) Advances in Human Factors in Robots and Unmanned Systems. Advances in Intelligent Systems and Computing, vol. 499, pp. 225–237. Springer, Cham (2017). https://doi.org/10. 1007/978-3-319-41959-6_19
3. Lindner, S., Schwerd, S., Schulte, A.: Defining generic tasks to guide UAVs in a MUM-T aerial combat environment. In: Karwowski, W., Ahram, T. (eds.) IHSI 2019. AISC, vol. 903, pp. 777–782. Springer, Cham (2019). https://doi.org/10.1007/978-3-030-11051-2_118
4. Heilemann, F., Schulte, A.: Interaction concept for mixed-initiative mission planning on multiple delegation levels in multi-UCAV fighter missions. In: Karwowski, W., Ahram, T. (eds.) IHSI 2019. AISC, vol. 903, pp. 699–705. Springer, Cham (2019). https://doi.org/10. 1007/978-3-030-11051-2_106
5. Parasuraman, R., Riley, V.: Humans and automation: use, misuse, disuse, abuse. Hum. Factors $39(2)$, 230–253 (1997)
6. Mund, D., Schulte, A.: Model- and observation- based workload assessment and activity determination in manned-unmanned teaming missions. In: EAAP Conference European Association for Aviation Psychology (2018)
7. Schwerd, S., Schulte, A.: Mental State estimation to enable adaptive assistance in manned-unmanned Teaming. In: 8. Interdisziplinärer Workshop Kognitive Systeme (2019)
8. Dudek, M., Lindner, S., Schulte, A.: Implementation of teaming behavior in unmanned aerial vehicles. In: Ahram, T., Karwowski, W., Vergnano, A., Leali, F., Taiar, R. (eds.) IHSI 2020. AISC, vol. 1131, pp. 966–972. Springer, Cham (2020). https://doi.org/10.1007/978-3-030-39512-4_147
9. Segor, F., Bürkle, A., Kollmann, M., Schönbein, R.: Instantaneous autonomous aerial reconnaissance for civil applications. In: Proceedings of the Sixth International Conference on Systems, pp. 72–76 (2011)
10. Balbuena, D., et al.: UAV Swarm Attack: Protection System Alternatives for Destroyers. Naval Postgraduate School, Monterey (2012)
11. Schulte, A., Donath, D.: A design and description method for human-autonomy teaming systems. In: Karwowski, W., Ahram, T. (eds.) IHSI 2018. AISC, vol. 722, pp. 3–9. Springer, Cham (2018). https://doi.org/10.1007/978-3-319-73888-8_1
12. Kantowitz, B.H.: Selecting measures for human factors research. Hum. Factors $34(4)$, 387–398 (1992)
13. Rengger, R.: Indicators of usability based on performance. Human Aspects in Computing: Design and Use of Interactive Systems with Terminals, Bullinger, HJ (1991)

14. Hart, S.G.: Nasa-task load index (NASA-TLX); 20 years later. Proc. Hum. Factors Ergon. Soc. Annu. Meet. **50**(9), 904–908 (2006). https://doi.org/10.1177/154193120605000909
15. Sauter, J.A., Matthews, R., van Dyke Parunak, H., Brueckner, S.A. : Performance of digital pheromones for swarming vehicle control. In: Proceedings of the Fourth International Joint Conference on Autonomous Agents and Multiagent Systems, pp. 903–910 (2005)
16. Cevik, P., Kocaman, I., Akgul, A.S., Akca, B.: The small and silent force multiplier: a swarm UAV—electronic attack. J. Intell. Rob. Syst. **70**(1–4), 595–608 (2013). https://doi.org/10.1007/s10846-012-9698-1

Establishment of National Safety Performance Evaluation Indicator System

Min Luo[1,2(✉)], Yijie Sun[1,2], and Yanqiu Chen[1,2]

[1] China Academy of Civil Aviation Science and Technology,
Beijing 100028, China
{luomin, Sunyj, Chenyq}@mail.castc.org.cn
[2] Engineering and Technical Research Center of Civil Aviation Safety Analysis
and Prevention of Beijing, Beijing 100028, China

Abstract. In order to achieve safety intelligence based on the objective judgment of the safety situation in China civil aviation, the research studied the global safety priorities identified by the ICAO and compared it with the accident and incident information of China Civil Aviation for the last ten years, and analyzed China's civil aviation industry operation quality monitoring information, China flight standards oversight information and state safety profile information from ICAO. After comprehensive analysis and judgment of these data and their characteristics, the study final constructs a classified, objective and data-driven civil aviation industry safety performance evaluation indicator system. The establishment of national safety performance evaluation indicator system breaks the data barrier of each operation management system and makes the data used for decision-making more objective and diversified.

Keywords: Safety performance indicators (SPIs) · Controlled flight into terrain (CFIT) · Loss of control in-flight (LOC-I) · Runway excursion (RE)

1 Introduction

In the fourth edition of the Safety Management Manual (SMM) of the International Civil Aviation Organization (ICAO), the concept of "safety intelligence" was put forward, which provides a new perspective for the future improvement of safety management in the world civil aviation. Safety intelligence concerned with leveraging safety data and safety information to develop actionable insights which can be used by an organization's leadership to make data-driven decisions, including those related to the most effective and efficient use of resources.

Also, according to the SMM, each State should consider the acceptable level of safety performance (ALOSP). The ALOSP expresses the safety levels the State expects of its aviation system, including the targets that each sector needs to achieve and maintain in relation to safety, as well as measures to determine the effectiveness of their own activities and functions that impact safety. The responsibility for establishing the ALOSP rests with the State's aviation authorities, and will be expressed through the set of Safety Performance Indicators (SPIs) for the State, sectors and service providers under their authority.

D. Harris and W.-C. Li (Eds.): HCII 2020, LNAI 12187, pp. 357–367, 2020.
https://doi.org/10.1007/978-3-030-49183-3_28

But compared with service providers, the evaluation of the State's safety performance is more complicated, because a large amount of operational information data is distributed in different operating and management systems. What kinds of SPIs can be represented as a national safety level? How to obtain the raw data to support these SPIs? Are these data sources and channels stable and long-term? All these questions are needed to solve.

2   Available Representative Data and Their Implications

2.1   High Risk Categories (HRCs) of Occurrences from ICAO and China Civil Aviation

The selection of types of occurrences which are deemed HRCs are based on high fatality risk per accident or the number of accidents and incidents. Based on results from the analysis of safety data collected from proactive and reactive sources of information (e.g. accidents, incidents, events), as well as from ICAO and other non-governmental organizations, the following HRCs, in no particular order, have been identified for the 2017–2019 edition of the Global Aviation Safety Plan (GASP) [1]: Runway safety (RS) related events, controlled flight into terrain (CFIT); and loss of control in-flight (LOC-I).

ICAO uses these HRCs as a baseline in its safety analysis. Figure 1 shows that in 2018, the three categories represented 96% of all fatalities, 73% of fatal accidents, 54% of the total number of accidents and 80% of the accidents that destroyed or caused substantial damage to aircraft [2].

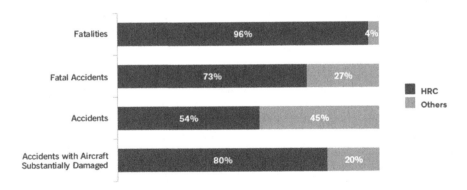

Fig. 1. High-Risk Category accident distribution

Figure 2 shows a breakdown of the three HRCs in 2018 and the respective distribution of accidents, fatal accidents, fatalities and accidents in which aircraft were destroyed or substantially damaged.

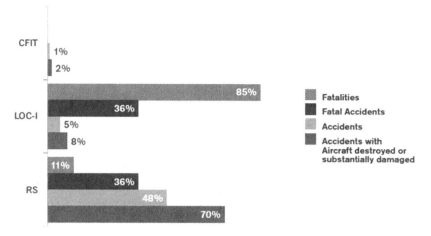

Fig. 2. High-Risk Category accident overview

Accidents related to runway safety (RS) accounted for nearly half of all accidents in 2018 (48%, compared with 53% in 2017), and included 4 fatal accidents with 54 fatalities. Loss of Control In-Flight (LOC-I) represented 36% of fatal accidents (up from 20% in 2017) with total 438 fatalities. There were no fatal accidents related to controlled flight into terrain (CFIT) in 2018.

According to ICAO, runway safety related events include the following ICAO accident occurrence categories: abnormal runway contacts, runway excursion, runway incursion, loss of control on ground, ground collision, collision with obstacles, undershoot/overshoot. But according to the event types of Chinese civil aviation, runway safety mainly involves heavy landing, touching the ground except for landing gear wheels, bird strike, runway excursion, runway incursion, landing on the ground outside the runway, and ground collision with obstacles. In order to further identify the major concerns of China Civil Aviation, this study need to combine the data analysis of the past decade in China.

According to the statistics of flight accidents from 2008 to 2017 from the Aviation Safety Information System (ASIS) of China Civil Aviation, as shown in Fig. 3, the statistical results show that CFIT, LOC-I and RS related events (runway excursion) are the types with high frequency of occurrence in China in the past decade.

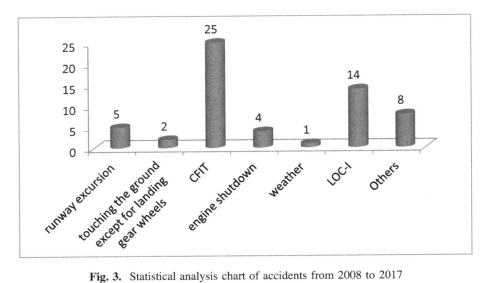

Fig. 3. Statistical analysis chart of accidents from 2008 to 2017

Therefore, combined with global safety priorities and China's civil aviation safety information, it can be set to CFIT, LOC-I and runway excursion(RE) as major concerns of China civil aviation. These are also seen as outcome indicator of the operational risk SPIs in national safety performance evaluation indicator system, and it can be provided intuitive data form the aviation safety information network such as the numbers of accidents, incident, general event, or specific types of events such as CFIT, LOC-I and RE.

2.2 Flight Operation Quality Monitoring Information of Civil Aviation Administration of China

In 2013, Civil Aviation Administration of China (CAAC) approved the establishment of CAAC Flight Operations Quality Assurance (FOQA) Station. In 2017, the China Civil Aviation Flight Quality Monitoring Service Platform (FQMSP) was launched, and by the end of 2019, the FOQA station could real time monitor 3700 aircraft from 54 CAAC transport airlines. Since 2018, the analysis has been focused on the red events which are exceed established standards monitored by the base station, and includes CFIT, LOC-I, and RE risk and related monitoring parameters.

According to the statistical analysis report on FOQA of CAAC on 2017 [3], the FOQA monitoring items with the highest influence degree on CFIT risk in the A320 series are respectively: GPWS Warning, Glide slope deviation, High approach speed, Localizer deviation, Roll high in landing, and in the B737 series are respectively: High IVV, Glide slope deviation, High approach speed, Localizer deviation and Roll high in approach.

The FOQA monitoring items with the highest influence degree on LOC-I risk in the A320 series are respectively: Pitch platform, Double side lever Input, and in the B737 series are respectively: Pitch high at takeoff, Pitch low in landing, Roll high in approach and Stick shaker.

The FOQA monitoring items with the highest influence degree on RE risk in the A320 series are respectively: High landing speed, unstable landing glide direction, Glide slope deviation. But in the B737 series are respectively: unstable takeoff or landing glide direction, ILS glide slope deviation, High approach speed, ILS localizer deviation, High landing speed and late landing flaps setting.

FQMSP can directly display the fusion value of the three risks and the actual value of the corresponding monitoring items. Take the risk value of LOC-I of CAAC in May 2018 as an example and the corresponding "Roll high in approaching" of one of the monitoring items, as shown in Fig. 4 and Fig. 5.

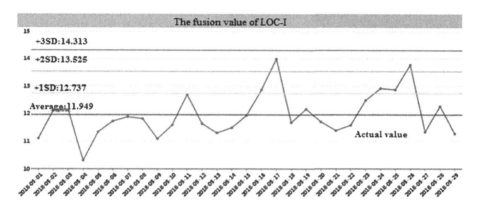

Fig. 4. The daily risk of LOC-I in May 2018

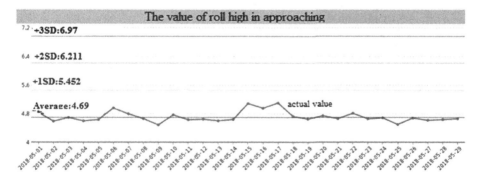

Fig. 5. The daily risk of roll high in approaching in May 2018

Also, the CAAC FQMSP can further show the number and incidence of different over-limit events in the A320 series and B737 series.

Therefore, through the civil aviation flight quality monitoring information research, the CFIT, LOC-I and RE risks of China's civil aviation, can be further decomposed into corresponding FOQA monitoring items as process indicators of the operational risk SPIs, and the flight quality monitoring platform is able to provide sustained, stable and real data for these indexes.

2.3   Flight Standards Oversight Information of CAAC

Flight standards oversight is one of the important methods for civil aviation regulatory departments to carry out safety management for airlines. Through years of efforts, CAAC has gradually set up a flight standards oversight program (FSOP). Based on the flight standards rules and regulations, the system is used for flight standards department of the civil aviation administration, regional administration and supervision bureau. In 2013, CAAC promoted the implementation of FSOP in the industry. At present, some data related to industry safety performance can be obtained continuously from FSOP system.

The source of data comes two parts. One is basic operating data that includes aircraft number, flights time, pilots (captains and copilots) number, fatigue index, effective flight attendants of each transport airlines, and these data can be collected and calculated monthly. The other is oversight data checked and found by the regulatory inspectors. The FSOP system can display the number of problems found by all inspectors in a certain period of time, as shown in Table 1.

Table 1. Number of problems identified in regulatory supervision from January to May, 2018

Checklist	Finding
Total	939
8.2.1 Aircraft Surveillance	246
8.1.5 Apron Surveillance	148
8.1.3 Apron Surveillance (operators outside the jurisdiction)	63
3.2.1 Dispatch/Flight Release	28
7.2.1 Aviation health assurance	28
3.1.4 Operational Control	22
2.1.3 Distribution (Manuals)	20
1.3.10 Parts/Material Control/SUP	20
2.1.1 Manuals updata	18
8.1.2 Apron Surveillance (Maintenance and ground service)	18
…	…

Meanwhile, the system can display the distribution diagram of the number of findings classification, such as procedures, controls, tools, manuals, personnel.

As a result, the FSOP system can provide some reliable data for safety management and foundation indicators of the operational risk SPIs, such as problem rate found by regulatory supervision, the problem rate found by different classification, as well as fatigue index and pilot-aircraft ratio.

2.4   State Safety Profile Information from ICAO

The integrated Safety Trend Analysis and Reporting System (ISTARS) is a web-based system on the ICAO USOAP audit consequence. ISTARS provides a quick and convenient interface to a collection of safety and efficiency datasets and web applications to make safety, efficiency and risk analyses. "State Safety Briefing" is a module of the system, which extracts the aviation safety profile of each State and gives a brief description of the 13 indicators from both target and completion values through the Dashboard, as shown in Fig. 6.

Indicator	Target	Value	Achieved
USOAP EI <small>USOAP overall EI(%)</small>	60%	86.78%	Yes
Significant Safety Concerns (SSCs) <small>Number of SSCs</small>	0	0	Yes
Fatal Accidents <small>Number of fatal accidents in last 5 years</small>		2	⚠
Aerodrome Certification <small>Validated status of USOAP Protocol Questions (PQ) 8.091, 8.083 and 8.085</small>	Satisfactory	Satisfactory	Yes
State Safety Programme (SSP) Foundation <small>Percentage of SSP Foundation protocol questions (PQs) validated by USOAP or submitted as completed</small>	100%	95.57%	No
State Safety Programme (SSP) <small>Level of SSP implementation</small>	Level 2	Level 2	Yes
IOSA <small>Number of IOSA certified operators</small>	>0	44	Yes
FAA IASA <small>IASA categorisation</small>	Cat 1	Cat 1	Yes
EU Safety List <small>Number of operational restrictions</small>	Unrestricted	Unrestricted	Yes
PBN <small>Percentage of international instrument runways with PBN approaches</small>	100%	13.16%	No
Global Aviation Training Activities <small>Number of courses delivered or developed by TRAINAIR PLUS Members in the last 12 months</small>	>0	14	Yes
Corrective Action Plan Update <small>Number of updates in the last 12 months on the Online Framework (OLF)</small>	>0	0	No
High Safety Indexes <small>Number of areas (Operations, Air Navigation, Support) with a high Safety Index over 1</small>	3/3	2	No

Fig. 6. An overview of China's aviation safety profile in 2019

From the dashboard, ISTARS can provide some direct indictors as the process implementation SPIs, such as USOAP EI, significant safety concerns, SSP foundation, global Aviation training activities, and corrective action plan update.

2.5   Other Authorization Information

In addition to the stable data provided by the above systems, relevant information can also be collected according to the authorization to continuously improve the national safety performance indicators. For example, SMS maturity information of some enterprises can be collected through SMS auditing tool.

3 Design Principles of Indicator System

Based on the above-mentioned in-depth investigation of data and information related to civil aviation safety performance of CAAC, this study classifies the sources, functions and types of data and information, and proposes to establish a safety performance indicator system of civil aviation industry. In order to establish a more scientific and accurate national safety performance indicator system, the selection and design of indicators mainly follow several basic principles [5–7]:

1) Clarify safety objectives
   It is determined that the safety objectives is to control the three core risks of CFIT, LOC-I and RE, and the safety objectives of industry safety performance can be adjusted according to the change of international and domestic safety concerns.

2) Set index category
   Based on the safety principles such as accident cause theory and actual deviation theory as the design theoretical basis of indicators, referring to the ICAO guidance document (DOC9859) [4] and the concept of safety performance management of operators, a rich and multi-dimensional industry safety performance indicator system is established, and the operation risk category is set (which can be divided into safety result category, operation process category, safety management category and safety foundation category), as well as process implementation category, to realize comprehensive evaluation of industry safety status from process and result, supervision and operation, resources and guarantee.
   Operational risk SPIs mainly reflects the safety performance of service providers, which is used to reflect the overall operation level of the industry. Specifically divided into:

   • safety result category: to evaluate accidents, incidents and other events related to core risks of the industry.
   • operation process category: to assess the degree of operational deviation affecting the core risks of the industry.
   • safety management category: to evaluate the ability and effect of industry supervision and management on Enterprises.
   • safety foundation category: to assess the overall resource allocation of the industry to the enterprise.

   Process implementation SPIs mainly reflects the risks in the process of management and operation, which is used to reflect the management ability of the industry.

3) Ensure sustainable and effective access to monitoring data
   Under the premise of ensuring that the industry safety performance indicators are quantifiable and measurable, considering that the monitoring data corresponding to the indicators can be obtained continuously and effectively, the research considers that:

   • Aviation Safety Information System of CAAC (ASIS) can provide stable data sources for operational risk (safety result category) SPIs.

- China Civil Aviation Flight Quality Monitoring Service Platform (FQMSP) can provide reliable data for operational risk (operation process category) SPIs.
- Flight Standards Oversight Program of CAAC (FSOP) can provide reliable data for operational risk (operation process category and safety foundation category) SPIs.
- ICAO Integrated Safety Trend Analysis and Reporting System (ISTARS) can provide reliable data for process implementation SPIs.

4) Ensure sustainable and effective access to monitoring data
    Pareto's principle tells us that 80% of output comes from 20% of important input. For industry safety performance management, it is impossible to identify, measure and manage all indicators related to industry safety performance. And in order to save the cost of management and achieve the purpose of managing the safety status, it is necessary to develop 20% representative key SPIs. Through the management of these KPI, it will achieve the purpose of monitoring the overall safety status.

4 Framework and Examples of National Safety Performance Evaluation Indicator System

On the basis of following the design principle of index system, it designs the industry safety performance evaluation indicator system. The specific framework is as follows in Fig. 7, and the following Table 2 is an example of national safety performance evaluation indicator system.

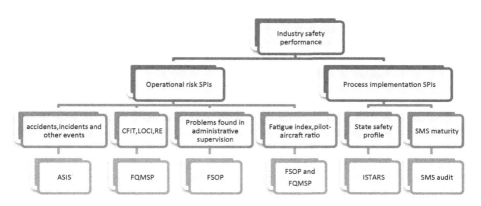

Fig. 7. Framework of national safety performance evaluation indicator system

Table 2. An example of national safety performance evaluation indicator system

Indicators	Required data	Data source	Metric	SPIs category
Air transport accident rate/incident rate	Number of accident or incident, Transport flight hours	ASIS	Ten thousand hour rate	Operational risk – safety result category
Ground Proximity Warning System (GPWS)	Number of QAR exceed standard events	FQMSP	Number	Operational risk - operation process category (CFIT)
	Number of effective legs	FQMSP	Hundred times rate	Operational risk - operation process category (CFIT)
	Transport flight hours	FQMSP	Ten thousand hour rate	Operational risk - operation process category (CFIT)
	Risk value	FQMSP	Risk = Severity* QAR exceed standard events	Operational risk - operation process category (CFIT)
Problem rate found in regulatory supervision	Numbers of problems found in regulatory supervision	FSOP	Number	Operational risk - safety management category
	Transport flight hours	FSOP\ FQMSP	Ten thousand hour rate	
Pilot-aircraft ration	Number of Captain	FSOP	Number	Operational risk - safety foundation category
	Number of aircraft on record	FSOP	Ratio	
State Safety Programmer (SSP) Foundation	Percentage of SSP foundation protocol questions (PQs) validated by USOAP or submitted as completed	ISTARS	Percentage	Process implementation

5   Prospect Application

The establishment of national safety performance evaluation indicator system breaks the data barrier of each operation management system to some extent and makes the data used for decision-making more objective and diversified. The study will continue to enrich indicators that can be used to evaluate the safety performance of the industry, and try to use mathematical models to evaluate and warn the comprehensive risks on the basis of these indicators, so that CAAC can conduct risk prevention and control of the industry safety trends in real time, and timely intervene to avoid serious consequences.

Reference

1. International Civil Aviation Organization: Global Aviation Safety Plan. DOC 10004, 2017–2019 Edition
2. International Civil Aviation Organization: State of Global Aviation Safety. ICAO Safety Report 2019 Edition
3. CAAC flight operation quality oversight statistical analysis report 2017. Civil Aviation Administration of China, China Academy of Civil Aviation Science and Technology (2017)
4. International Civil Aviation Organization, Doc: 9859 Safety Management Manual, 4th edn. International Civil Aviation Organization, Montreal (2018)
5. Rong, M., Luo, M., Chen, Y.: The research of airport operational risk alerting model. In: Duffy, V. (ed.) DHM 2016. LNCS, vol. 9745, pp. 586–595. Springer, Cham (2016). https://doi.org/10.1007/978-3-319-40247-5_59
6. Sun, Y., Luo, M., Chen, Y., Sun, C.: Safety performance evaluation model for airline flying fleets. In: Duffy, V. (ed.) DHM 2017. LNCS, vol. 10287, pp. 384–396. Springer, Cham (2017). https://doi.org/10.1007/978-3-319-58466-9_34
7. Chen, M., Luo, M., Sun, H., Chen, Y.: A comprehensive risk evaluation model for airport operation safety. In: Proceedings of the 12th International Conference on Reliability, Maintainability and Safety (ICRMS). IEEE (2018)

The Application of Safety II in Commercial Aviation – The Operational Learning Review (OLR)

Pete McCarthy[(✉)]

Cathay Pacific Airways/Cranfield University,
Cathay Pacific City, HKIA, Lantau, Hong Kong
pete_mccarthy@cathaypacific.com

Abstract. This pilot-study takes a concept (Safety II), and tests to see if the premise of the concept can be applied to a commercial flight operation. The aim being to enhance flight safety and operational effectiveness. The tool used to facilitate this application is the Operational Learning Review (OLR). The OLR is a prescribed interview technique which encourages the subject of a safety interview (review) to provide context and create narrative based upon event recall. 20 interviews were conducted using the OLR technique and this resulted in rich narrative which could then be analysed in order to create an influence map of the event. The influence map highlights performance variability and performance shaping factors – which in turn highlight resilient behaviours. The study demonstrated that extant statutory investigation requirements are met using this tool – in addition, system learning is greatly enhanced, allowing a shift to Safety II principles - learning, from positive work and behaviour.

Keywords: Safety II · Operational learning · Resilience · Performance variation · Systems thinking

1 Introduction

"Airlines are safe" - so safe in fact that our opportunity for learning how we might become even more safe is now greatly diminished! In the absence of accidents and serious incidents our current approach to learning from less significant events (deemed to compromise safety), relies heavily on the continued reporting of near misses and the use of evidence from flight data systems. This reality is the rationale underpinning the creation of the concept of Safety I and Safety II (Hollnagel 2014).

The traditional view of Safety which Professor Hollnagel refers to as Safety I, is built on the premise that as few things as possible go wrong. Safety is assured when risk to the operation is maintained at a level which is deemed As Low As Reasonably Practicable (ALARP) – this term (ALARP) first appeared with regard to safety and risk in UK law in the 1970s (Health and Safety at Work Act 1974). What this approach leads us to concentrate on however is the absence of safety (focus on when safety fails) rather than the presence of what it is that makes us safe! If we are focusing on events which demonstrate the absence of something (in this case, safety) and these events

© Springer Nature Switzerland AG 2020
D. Harris and W.-C. Li (Eds.): HCII 2020, LNAI 12187, pp. 368–383, 2020.
https://doi.org/10.1007/978-3-030-49183-3_29

happen rarely (because we are safe), we must surely look elsewhere to learn how we might improve our safety management going forward. Safety I is not to be dismissed however! This traditional approach and view has led us to the point we are at now, our dedication to leaving no stone unturned following accidents and serious incidents has helped shape the current Safety Management Systems (SMS), regulatory frameworks, international safety standards and quality and compliance frameworks which govern commercial aviation organisations.

The issue with Safety I is that it is reactive! We wait for something to fail, or we wait for an exceedance to manifest and be captured by our Flight Data Analysis Programme (FDAP) (ICAO 2008), we then focus our resource and attention on this anomaly. We track the trends with regard to unstable approaches, runway incursions, flight level busts and flight path deviations, and we do this as part of our quest for improving safety. These exceedances and events represent a tiny proportion of our daily activity in commercial aviation, possibly 1 or 2%, so what are we missing by only focusing on this! We are considered good and safe when these negative outcomes are not occurring, so why not also devote time, focus, energy and resource to understanding why they are not occurring, what does good look like? This is the Safety II approach.

Sidney Dekker talks about a new approach or new view in Safety Differently (2014). In taking this view, we begin to understand how our opportunities for learning from traditional safety metrics has plateaued. This new view moves us on from the linear causal logic/reactive approach (which served us so well as our aviation safety system matured), to a more "systems thinking" approach Hollnagel (1993), Perrow (2001), Rasmussen (2003), Reason (1990, 1997) and Woods et al. (1994). This approach takes in to account the socio-technically complex nature of a very different aviation system in 2020. This new view aligns with Safety II in many ways as it refocuses our safety effort to concentrating on the presence of safety rather than the absence of safety, it recognises the human influence and human input as a source of strength and resilience in the system, not as the weak link often portrayed in the past. This new view also encourages us to rightly approach the front line worker (in this case the pilots, engineers, cabin crew etc.) as being the experts in the field, an asset which can help us understand what really happens in the organisation day to day, a rich source of learning for the system. Safety II shines a light on the vast majority of activity occurring daily in our system which has successful outcomes often despite the intrusion of real life and real-world positive or negative influencing factors (see Fig. 1).

Background to the Introduction of the Operational Learning Review (OLR)

If we take a new view of safety, we conform to the following safety thinking:

- Being safe relies on the presence of safety, not the absence of safety (Dekker 2014).
- We need to understand work-as-done, not only work-as-imagined (Hollnagel 2014).
- System thinking for safety – Principle 1 (Eurocontrol 2014) The front-line workers are the field experts, Seddon (2005), we will learn what really happens day to day by engaging with them and giving them the respect, they deserve.
- The professionals we recruit, and train do not come to work to do a bad job or cause harm.

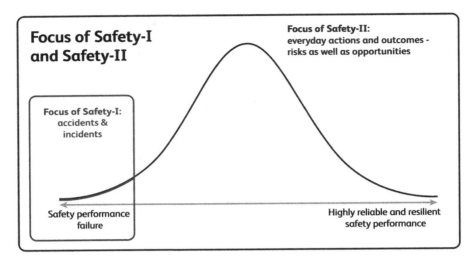

Focus of Safety-I and Safety-II

Focus of Safety-II: everyday actions and outcomes - risks as well as opportunities

Focus of Safety-I: accidents & incidents

Safety performance failure

Highly reliable and resilient safety performance

Fig. 1. Focus of Safety I and Safety II from Euro-Control

- Performance variability is a function of normal work - this is where the real learning lies in the new view of safety.
- With performance variability comes adaptability - this is a key component of resilience.
- We must avoid hindsight bias and ensure we approach understanding any event from a local rationale perspective.
- Normal and non-normal situations are opportunities for learning - there should be no jeopardy for the worker who helps us learn and improve the system.
- Accountability works both ways - both the worker and the system are accountable for safety and safety learning.
- Curiosity not judgement.

Safety is the presence of something not the absence of something. This concept is referred to in the introduction, it guides us to shift our focus and be cognisant of what is working well and providing the safety in our operation.

Work-as-done v work-as-imagined. There has been much literature addressing the difference between work as imagined and work as done. Some of the earliest references from a safety perspective were centred on a distinction between the system task description (work-as-imagined) and the cognitive tasks (work-as-done) (Hollnagel and Woods 1983), this distinction is now more broad and from an applied perspective work-as-imagined refers to work as seen from a management or organisation perspective (blunt end), it is work in strict adherence to the rules, regulations, guidance and procedures which direct that work. Work-as-done refers to the real work taking place at the sharp end. The individuals engaged in this activity are subject to a broad range of performance shaping influences, environmental, social and technical. The human operators have to adapt to these influences, shaping their performance in order to meet a range of sometimes competing goals. Tradeoffs are always occurring; this is described by Hollnagel when he outlines the "ETTO principle". ETTO refers to the Efficiency Thoroughness Trade Off we often see in action on the front line. Further to this, Safety is also at risk of being traded for efficiency or thoroughness if those competing goals are considered to be of more value than the safety goal!

If we want to understand work-as-done, then we must engage with those who do the work. These are the people making the tradeoffs, they find the work arounds when policy, procedure, guidance or regulation might not be fit for purpose or may not be workable due to other factors imposing limits on the task. These workers are varying their performance and are often providing resilience and adaptability, whilst ultimately getting the job done. Mostly this will be as safe as the system expects, sometimes they may even be safer – occasionally though we may be drifting toward failure (Dekker 2014).

To fully comprehend work-as-done, we must take a viewpoint which matches the local rationale of those engaged with the task. Rather than measure the performance only against the prescribed rules, regulations, guidance and procedures, we must consider why workers actions and decisions make sense to them at the time. Dekker invites us to get inside the tunnel with these front-line workers and understand what they did or didn't know when making decisions, what competing goals were they engaged with along the way.

Hindsight bias - passing judgement about performance once we already know the outcome will rarely prove to be valuable with regard to understanding work-as-done. Often guiding us to the obvious answer or solution, this approach bypasses the detail and context which is needed in order to understand why events happen, not simply how they happen or even more simplistic what has happened.

When events or occurrences present as an opportunity for learning, the worker involved should feel confident to engage in order to help improve the system. These individuals must be treated with respect and be given every opportunity to provide the narrative to frame the event or occurrence. They provide context and they describe the sense making that was key in shaping the outcome. This context is key to extracting learning not only from the event, but also in gaining insight into what the individual has learned from this experience, how they have reflected and how their behaviour may change because of the experience. The Operational Learning Review explores this narrative and aims to capture the learning in order to share this knowledge and experience across the wider system. Educating other workers, revising processes and procedures or designing technical or software solutions to make the system even more safe without necessarily compromising efficiency or thoroughness (tradeoffs which occur at all stages).

Trust is key to the Operational Learning Review; without it we lose the opportunity to understand the inner working of the system. Trust works both ways, as does accountability. The system is accountable to the worker and must provide training, tools, time and structure for completing the aviation related task undertaken by the worker, and the worker in turn should ensure they equip themselves for their role, making use of training and equipment provided.

1.1 The Operational Learning Review (OLR)

Designing the Framework

This framework based upon the Learning Review concept (Pupilidy 2015) was designed to support current occurrence review processes employed at a major airline. The airline already has a comprehensive and effective framework, policy and philosophy for dealing with occurrences and exceedances which come to light and need further understanding. The purpose therefore with regard to the initial implementation of the OLR was not to replace this extant process, but attempt to enhance it. The minimum acceptable measured output of the OLR therefore was the output already evident from current practice, the desired output would be the additional learning and understanding as described in the introduction section above – this learning would then be channeled back into the airlines Safety Management System (SMS), the goal being to further enhance both flight safety and efficient flight operations.

Current occurrence investigation processes employed across most of the high reliability transport sector is relatively person centred, Dekker (2014) refers to this when describing the old view of safety. This approach gives an indication as to what happened following an unwanted outcome or event, it may even point toward how it happened, it rarely gets to the why it happened. This old view has been practiced for many years across most organisations but doesn't necessarily fit with the modern socio-technical environment that commercial airlines now represent. Taking the old view, the trust and respect enjoyed by both the worker and the system can be somewhat compromised and there may be an expectation on behalf of the worker that punitive action may follow any event or occurrence they are involved with. Flight crew will not fully trust that airline managers will always fully listen to or understand their rationale following an occurrence therefore the bare minimum might be disclosed through Air Safety Reports (ASR) or communication with Flight Operations management.

1.2 Designing the OLR (Understanding Work as Done vs Work as Imagined)

The OLR is versatile and creative, it is specifically suited to uncovering sense making in complex systems. Complex systems, unlike simple or complicated systems, requires sensemaking to be applied across the system components in order to learn and develop - this sense making requires a different pathway and the characteristics of the method employed will be different. We can classify system types ranging from simple, complicated to complex (see Table 1) This classification helps us to understand the origins of the traditional thinking around safety investigation, it highlights why historically specific approaches were taken.

Table 1. Simple, complicated and complex systems - Pupilidy (2015)

System name	Components	Frame	Pathway	Characteristic
Complex	The parts are interconnected, interactive, diverse and adaptive (they adapt often predictably)	Organic - these systems cannot be broken down without losing the ability to understand the interactions	Sense making, improvisation and learning - developing adaptations in real time	Unlimited number of questions with an equally unlimited number of answers - requires sensemaking
Complicated	The parts are interconnected, interactive and diverse	Systemic - These systems are composed of nested sub-systems	Directional flow relationships - cause and effect connections exist with a limited set of outcomes	Each question has a limited number of discreet answers. Reacts well to analysis
Simple	The parts are interconnected and interactive	Mechanical	Cause and effect connections are strong - problems can be solved	Each question has one discreet answer. Reacts well to analysis

1.3   Designing the OLR (The Front-Line Workers Are the Field Experts)

Table 2. Comparison of expectations, novice to expert (adapted from Pupilidy (2015)).

We expect our novices to	We expect our experts to
Have knowledge of prescriptive policy	Apply rules to situations and adapt rules as needed
Comply with instruction	Know how to improvise to meet operational goals
Know basic rules, regulations, policy and procedure	Use complex adaptive problem solving or critical thinking skills to achieve results
Know and follow the plan	Use intuition to know when to change the plan
The basic goal is to control actions and limit decisions	The basic goal is to facilitate empowerment

Commercial aviation is highly regulated, and the operation is highly procedural, meaning that in respect of the expectations outlined in Table 2 the status of the workers is less clear. The qualified, current, competent pilot will be expected to comply with instructions (Air Traffic Control for example), know rules, regulations, policy and procedure (compliance with Civil Aviation Authorities across the world) - this brings an element of system control to the operation. Work-as-done will reflect this control, however the OLR will need to capture the adaptations and performance variability being demonstrated particularly when the pilot is improvising to meet operational goals, using complex adaptive problem solving or critical thinking skills to achieve results and using intuition (knowing when to amend or change the plan).

1.4   Designing the OLR (Performance Variability)

Pilots are constantly varying performance in order to meet the changes and fluctuations in the dynamic environment. By the time they meet with the rest of the crew at dispatch they will have already been subject to factors which may shape their performance as they undertake their duty. New factors, environmental (weather or the operating environment), social (crew dynamic, personal relationships), organisational (company or regulatory environment) for example will all have the potential to influence the task. These influences are keenly felt at the sharp end, with the sharp end operator making the necessary adaptations to cope with any disturbance to the planned operation. The blunt end (management or the regulator) will not normally be aware of the adaptations or performance variation unless an outcome falls close to, or outside of the parameters deemed safe for the operation - when the outcome is not as expected, an Air Safety Report (ASR) is filed or a Flight Data Analysis Programme (FDAP) exceedance is logged.

1.5   Research Question?

The resilient behaviours of the human (agent) operating in complex socio-technical systems are not clearly identified from a proactive safety perspective, therefore the relationship between the" human agents and the technical/environmental artefacts" (Stanton 2016) with regard to maintaining system safety within acceptable bounds are not obvious! Therfore:

- Can the Operational Learning Review approach identify operational (human) safety performance variability?
- Is the adaptive context of a socio-technical aviation flight operations system adequately captured by the Operational Learning Review process?
- Is trust and openness improved by taking the Operational Learning Review approach?

2   Method

This pilot study has considered the data gathered through conducting 20 Operational learning Reviews. This pilot study serves as a precursor to a much larger project planned for the organisation. A panel of experienced flight operations and flight safety specialists was tasked with developing the philosophy, framework and process for the introduction of the OLR. This panel consisted:

Human Factors Specialist (the author)
Aviation Risk Manager - Flight Operations - current pilot
Aviation Risk Manager - Group Risk
2 X type specific Risk Managers - line operations current pilots
Senior Flight Operations Managers and Training Managers - current pilots

The panel's first task was to agree and produce a philosophy document which would convey the intent of the OLR to the wider flight operations community, this guidance outlined the following:

OLR - background and rationale.
Commitment to learning.
Commitment to "Just Culture".
Human-centred approach.

A guidance document was produced which outlined how an OLR would be conducted, this document included detail around how the person conducting the OLR would engage with the front-line worker who had agreed to the review being conducted following an event. The guidance directs the person conducting the OLR to put the subject of the review at ease, ask open questions in order to gain understanding of the context of the event by hearing a free-flowing narrative. The next step is to discuss more directed elements of the narrative based upon this opening engagement, explore the sense-making which was happening at the time of the event, and that which has happened subsequently once the subject individual has had time to reflect on the occurrence. This same process was conducted with all individuals involved with the occurrences being reviewed - the aim then being to create an influence map consisting of those elements which had been shaping the performance of the individuals involved.

2.1 Design and Procedure

Two designs have been considered for this pilot study - interview to generate narrative and classification of factors to generate an influence map.

Participants were presented for interview having come to the attention of the OLR panel by:

- Self-reported concerns following an event or occurrence (Air Safety Report or informal communication to the flight operations team).
- An exceedance highlighted through the flight data programme.

Participants were welcomed to the review, thanked for their participation and giving a thorough brief on the purpose of the Operational Learning Review, this brief included the following:

- The sole purpose of the OLR being learning for the system and the individual involved in any event.

- No jeopardy for the individual engaged with the review - in line with extant Just Culture policy.
- The importance of their expert involvement with the process.
- An opportunity to take ownership of any personal development direction highlighted by the review, but also an opportunity to help shape the learning for the wider system.

The interview/review was conducted with a minimum of two interviewers/reviewers, designated number 1 and number 2.

Number 1 interviewer - The participant was informed that number 1 interviewer would lead the interview, and after building rapport would start the interview by asking an open question - often referred to using the pneumonic TED for Tell, Explain, Describe e.g.:

Tell me about the event ....
Explain your role .....
Describe the scene ....

This line of open questioning is to encourage the participant to start to recall the event or occurrence and provide a free-flowing narrative as they remember it. During this recall, number 1 interviewer will not interrupt the participant but will encourage the them to continue with their account if they begin to close down their communication. This is the first opportunity for the interviewer (number 1) to receive a download of data from the participant and it is important that they recall as much information as possible, even if they might consider it unimportant or irrelevant. Once this initial download is complete, the interviewer (number 1) will go back over the participant's account, using key phrases and notes taken during the recall. This is the first opportunity to understand the participants sense making. The participant will be asked to talk about what they were thinking and how they were feeling, during the event but also after the event once they had time to reflect upon the event and their actions. The number 1 interviewer uses a simple grid system for note taking and recall (see Fig. 2), this is to avoid interrupting the participant but also to maintain eye contact and open body language, thus encouraging dialogue. Once the line of questioning is complete for the number 1 interviewer, they will thank the participant and then hand over to number 2.

Number 2 interviewer - the initial role of the number 2 interviewer is to take detailed notes (working to the premise that participants may not give consent for recording). The number 2 interviewer will not interrupt the participant or the number 1 interviewer but will wait until the interview is handed over to them before asking any specific questions they may have regarding the event. This disciplined approach prevents the participants losing their flow or becoming confused during the interview. The detailed notes taken by the number 2 interviewer are crucial as it is these notes which will be used for thematic or categorical analysis once all the data has been collected. An influence map can then be generated. "Simple and complicated systems are governed by cause and effect relationships. Cause and effect relationships are the cornerstone for traditional investigations. Complex systems are governed by influence rather than cause" (Pupilidy 2015) (see Fig. 3).

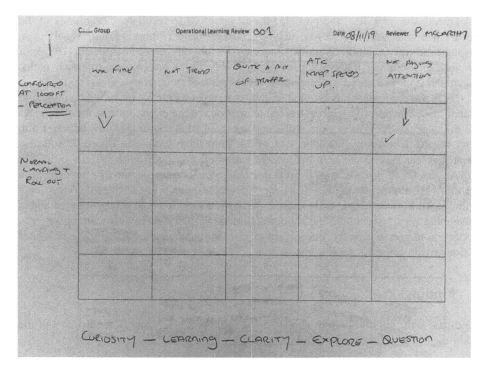

Fig. 2. Simple grid system for recording notes - interviewer 1

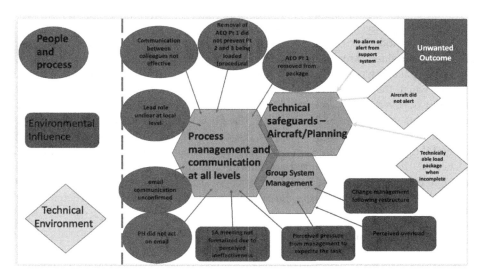

Fig. 3. Generic example of an influence map generated for display purpose only

During the interview, the participant will be asked to recall specific phases of the occurrence and the interviewer may encourage deeper thinking and recollection through the use of subtle cognitive interview techniques, Geiselman et al. (1986), or through encouraging the participant to draw key flight patterns or approach paths, annotated with perceived (or remembered) speeds and heights etc.

Once the participant has recalled all they can remember, they may then be invited to watch the animation (data reconstructed animation) of the event. One of the final tasks for the interviewers is to explore with the participant what they might now benefit from, with regard to learning (how the system can help them learn and improve, and also what they can now do to help the system learn and improve).

As the OLR process is still working alongside current occurrence investigation statutory requirements, there will be a perceived responsibility on the interview team with regard to maintaining and ensuring system safety - this is to be encouraged and is in keeping with "just culture". It is not the role of the interview/review team however to apportion blame or liability, but merely to gain an understanding of why the delegates actions made sense to them at the time.

3   Findings

Findings will be considered across 3 categories; these same categories will be addressed in the discussion section:

1. Participant - level of trust and engagement with the process (perceived).
2. System - increased understanding of context around an event.
3. System - understanding risk and meeting current statutory responsibilities.

Participant - Level of Trust and Engagement with the Process

The pilot study has relied on a perceived level of trust and engagement with the process, ascertained through direct communication on this topic with the participant. The participants attending the OLR's did so following a broad range of occurrences, some of which they may have felt were resolved by their actions, some of which they may have believed were exacerbated by their actions! The opening section of the OLR brief explains the purpose of the OLR, how the OLR will be conducted and importantly the view that the participant is the expert (they were there at the event) and the system is grateful that they have agreed to help with system learning following the occurrence.

Across the OLR's conducted to inform this pilot study, the interview panel encountered a broad range of perceived levels of trust (engagement will be discussed separately). Trust may have been an issue (positive or negative) for participants for many reasons:

Rank or position in the organisation.
Perceived level of accountability following a negative outcome.
Fear of punitive action following a perceived negative outcome.
Past experience of unfair treatment.
Vicarious feelings of being treated unfairly - due to others experience in the organisation.

Relationships with management unrelated to the occurrence or event.
Cultural influences.

These factors listed above must be considered during the opening section of the OLR, it is vitally important that the trust gained at this stage is then supported by the wider safety learning philosophy and "just culture" policy of the organisation. The OLR interviewers had to be prepared to answer difficult questions from the participants in direct response to any of the factors listed above - during the pilot study however, these factors did not prove to be challenging and the interviewers found that the thorough explanation of the process served to allay any fears and calm the participants ahead of the review.

System - Increased Understanding of the Context Around an Event

The OLR's conducted covered a wide range of performance (perceived positive or negative) across varying flight operations scenarios, the following generic occurrences are examples of the topics which could be addressed for deeper learning:

Taxiway incursion
Runway incursion
Unstable approach
Go-around
Crew Resource Management
Emergency procedures

The review team explored these topics with the participants involved and were able to very quickly ascertain in each instance what had actually happened. This "what" is important to the OLR in setting the scene (it is also important from a statutory viewpoint, which will be addressed in the discussion) and provides the start point for gaining further information to build context and an understanding of the sense-making.

Once the "what" element has been established, the OLR goes on to explore the "how and the why", but most importantly the local rationale "why did it make sense at the time". From these pilot (pilot study) OLR discussions a clearer understanding of the performance shaping factors (environmental, technical, social and system) was ascertained. In a bid to understand the context around the event, the participants were encouraged to speak freely and openly, they were not interrupted or questioned during the initial part of the review - this proved to be extremely important and was instrumental in setting the scene for broader understanding of the trade-off's which were occurring throughout the time period being discussed, and the time preceding this.

Once the context had been established, the narrative was then interrogated in detail - this serves different purposes;

Broader understanding of the context shaping performance.
Deeper analysis of the sense-making at the time of the event.
Deeper analysis of the sense-making since the event (reflection and reflective practice).
Understanding socio-technical shared and distributed Situational Awareness (SA) (Stanton 2016).

System - Understanding Risk and Meeting Current Statutory Responsibilities

At the end of the sessions, the participants are asked, what the system can do to help them learn following the occurrence, and what they can do to help the system learn? This is the whole point of conducting the OLR, it is therefore imperative that the loop is closed for the individual (provide them with assistance if required and accept their assistance if offered), and also to conduct deeper analysis of the individual accounts following an occurrence - also across the other occurrences considered for review.

There is as previously mentioned, the statutory safety requirement to ensure system safety. This element can be satisfied to the same level as was previously achieved through formal safety investigation methods. The data and evidence gained through the OLR can be analysed using extant analysis methods. For this pilot study a slightly amended version of the Accident Route Matrix (ARM) (see Fig. 4) was utilised to satisfy this statutory element.

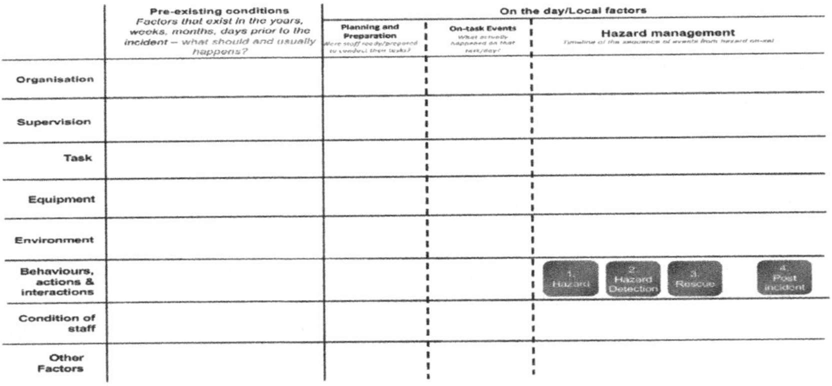

Fig. 4. Version of Accident Route Matrix model – derived from Harris (2011)

This analysis method (ARM) whilst reflecting cause and effect logic, does allow for the linking of factors with less direct obvious performance shaping affect, it therefore helps us to develop the influence map (Fig. 3) we are setting out to create through the OLR process.

4 Discussion

This pilot study has involved the creation and implemetation of a new philosophy and approach to learning from occurrences in a commercial aviation setting. The opportunity to employ the OLR method in a dynamic real-world flight operations environment, has provided the opportunity to apply a conceptual tool (the OLR interview methodology) and test whether or not it does provide for additional learning, but also meet current statutory requirements following an occurrence. The pilot study has demonstrated that this methodology does encourage and provide for wider learning and does equal or surpass current investigation methods in this environment.

The challenge throughout this pilot study has been to find ways to deploy the OLR methodology in order to not only understand normal work, adaptability and resilience in the event of an unwanted outcome being reported, but also in the event that nothing unwanted has occurred – this normal work without a negative outcome represents 98% plus of the operational activity undertaken by the organisation.

From the OLR's conducted to date, we have already identified factors and themes which may not have been uncovered using traditional methods of investigation (this refers to the low level incidents or occurrences addressed in this study to provide operational learning) - full safety investigation protocol following a serious incident or accident may uncover these elements, (those protocols would not be employed in these instances at present). It is of note that the traditional conceptual Threat and Error Management (TEM) approach may not have considered some of the factors uncovered in the OLR, therefore these elements would not necessarily have been brought to the conscious awareness of the crew even through exposure to the associated safety audit report! Through OLR we may uncover a trend demonstrating a crew's willingness to continue to land from an unstable approach in VMC conditions for example, maybe due to the (false) assurance provided by a visible runway! Using this as an example, the OLR would encourage the understanding of local rationale, and also probe as to what we might learn operationally from this dangerous condition that crews may unwittingly be subjecting the system to - how does the system protect itself from this and how might it quickly resolve the dynamic issue that has been uncovered?

Line Operations Safety Audit (LOSA) as described by Klinect et al. (2003) is a safety tool that gathers cockpit observations during normal flight operations - the key benefits being:

Provides a proactive snapshot of system safety and flight crew performance.

Identifies the strategies employed by crews in order to prevent or deal with undesired aircraft states.

Provides a diagnosis of operational performance strengths and weaknesses (without an unwanted event having occurred).

Provides additional insight to the airline regarding the "work-as-done" on the daily operation.

LOSA has proved to be a valuable tool for safety and will continue to add value from a safety perspective. The OLR in conjunction with LOSA will widen the net with regard to operational learning. LOSA gives us insight through understanding observable behaviours, the OLR will add additional insight by exploring the unobserved cognitive rationale and thinking that may be driving the observable behaviours and those not consciously observed by crewmembers in themselves or their team.

Going back to the opening statement:

"Airlines are safe" - so safe in fact that our opportunity for learning how we might become even more safe is now greatly diminished! In the absence of accidents and serious incidents our traditional approach to learning from less significant events deemed to compromise safety, relies heavily on the continued reporting of near misses and the use of data systems (Flight Data Recorders). This reality is the rationale underpinning the Safety I and Safety II approach described by Hollnagel (2014).

From a safety II perspective we want to understand what good looks like, we want to know what the resilient behaviours are that our crews are demonstrating almost all of the time in order to make the operation work. We want to understand the trade-offs between efficiency and safety, and we need to determine what the adaptive capacity looks like. Adaptive capacity and the ability to vary performance is essential for the operation, but we must bear in mind that our airlines have become safe through strict regulation and strict process and procedures developed to allow safe operation. The performance variation and adaptability therefore must happen within certain bounds of expected and predictable behaviour.

5   Further Research

Based upon this pilot study, the research will now be expanded to capture and analyse a much larger sample of flight operations data for the purpose of learning and the creation of influence maps to demonstrate the potential areas of interest to the operation. This analysis will be used in conjunction with the LOSA analysed data and it is predicted that this will give an enhanced view of proactive safety in the operation.

References

Dekker, S.: Safety Differently (2014). https://doi.org/10.1201/b17126

Eurocontrol: Systems thinking for safety, ten principles, a white paper. Moving toward Safety II (2014)

Geiselman, R.E., Fisher, R.P., MacKinnon, D.P., Holland, H.L.: Enhancement of eyewitness memory with the cognitive interview. Am. J. Psychol. (1986). https://doi.org/10.2307/1422492

Harris, S.: Human factors investigation methodology. In: 16th International Symposium on Aviation Psychology, pp. 517–522 (2011). https://corescholar.libraries.wright.edu/isap_2011/28

Hollnagel, E.: The phenotype of erroneous actions. Int. J. Man Mach. Stud. (1993). https://doi.org/10.1006/imms.1993.1051

Hollnagel, E.: Safety-I and safety-II: the past and future of safety management (2014). https://doi.org/10.1080/00140139.2015.1093290

International Commercial Air Transport (ICAO): Standards and recommended Practices, Annex 6, Pt 1, 3.3.5 (2008)

Klinect, J., Murray, P., Merritt, A., Helmreich, R.: Line operation safety audits (LOSA): definition and operating characteristics. In: 12th International Symposium on Aviation Psychology (2003)

Perrow, C.: Accidents, normal. In: International Encyclopedia of the Social & Behavioral Sciences (2001). https://doi.org/10.1016/b0-08-043076-7/04509-5

Pupilidy, I.: The Transformation of Accident Investigation: from finding cause to sensemaking (2015). https://pure.uvt.nl/ws/files/7737432/PupilidyTheTransformation01092015.pdf

Rasmussen, J.: The role of error in organizing behaviour. 1990. Qual. Saf. Health Care (2003). https://doi.org/10.1136/qhc.12.5.377

Reason, J.: Human Error. Cambridge University Press, University Printing House, Cambridge (1990, 1997)

Seddon, J.: Freedom from Command and Control, 2nd edn. Vanguard, Buckingham (2005)

Stanton, N.A.: Distributed situation awareness. Theor. Issues Ergon. Sci. **17**(1), 1–7 (2016). https://doi.org/10.1080/1463922X.2015.1106615

Woods, D.D., Johannesen, L; Cook, R., Sarter, N.: Behind Human Error: Cognitive Systems, Computers and Hindsight, Soar Cseriac 94-01, Dayton Ohio (1994)

Spatial Knowledge Acquisition for Cognitive Maps in Autonomous Vehicles

Yue Qin$^{(\boxtimes)}$ and Hassan A. Karimi

University of Pittsburgh, Pittsburgh, PA 15230, USA
yuq9@pitt.edu, hkarimi@pitt.edu

Abstract. Known as maplike representations of the environment, which humans build and store in mind overtime, cognitive maps are an essential element of spatial knowledge that benefit individuals from travel planning to wayfinding. Considering, on one hand, that active interaction with the environment leads to better spatial knowledge acquisition than passive exposure and, on the other, that fully autonomous vehicles will eliminate the need to driving cars, i.e., being only passengers and not drivers, it is of great importance to understand the impact of autonomous vehicles on human cognitive maps. In this paper, we conducted an online survey and analyzed responses from 204 participants to understand this impact. We found a significant interaction effect of the frequencies of driving and riding as passengers on the reported spatial knowledge. Further analysis indicated main effects of riding frequency for frequent drivers and driving frequency among non-frequent passengers. Variations in specific aspects of cognitive maps were also identified, all of which provided preliminary insights into the possible effect of autonomous vehicles on human spatial knowledge.

Keywords: Cognitive map · Autonomous vehicle · Spatial knowledge

1 Introduction

Cognitive maps are usually considered as maplike representations of large-scale environments that are stored in human minds. They play an important role in formulating human survey knowledge as opposed to route and graph knowledge in studies of spatial cognition. One of the most well-known evidence of cognitive maps is an individual's ability of finding novel shortcuts between two locations that have never been traveled between [3]. Beyond that, cognitive maps provide essential spatial knowledge about the environment for travel-planning and decision making. They are crucial in situations when navigation aids are not available, including when those systems fail (software crashes) or it is infeasible to rely on navigation apps (indoor when GPS signal is totally absent). Additionally, without the information in cognitive maps, potential travel routes and

D. Harris and W.-C. Li (Eds.): HCII 2020, LNAI 12187, pp. 384–397, 2020.
https://doi.org/10.1007/978-3-030-49183-3_30

destinations could not be utilized during planning and might be viewed as inaccessible.

Humans build and update cognitive maps through interactions with the environments, including the experiences of travel and navigation. Recent studies suggest that spatial knowledge differs within individuals choosing passive versus active travel modes [17]. However, with the evolution of driverless technologies and the promising future such automation will bring to human welfare and the environment, travel modes such as driving different levels of autonomous vehicles are yet to be explored. On the other hand, it is still unknown what effects will the shifting from zero automation to fully-autonomous vehicles bring to individuals as well as to the entire society in the long term. Researchers have agreed that active spatial learning contributes more to survey knowledge acquisition than passive exposure in a novel environment [7]. As human drivers are not required to actively engage in driving at Level 4 to 5 automation [21], the question arises: will the adoption of fully-automated vehicles impact people's acquisition of spatial knowledge for forming and retaining cognitive maps in the future?

In this paper, we aim to shed light on the possible consequences autonomous driving will bring to humans in terms of the spatial knowledge for cognitive maps by conducting an online survey. To the best of our knowledge, this is the first study that explores the relationships between the use of driverless vehicles and human cognitive maps. As drivers will become more like passengers in a highly or fully automated car [20], we grouped respondents by frequencies of driving as well as riding ground transportation as passengers. The self-report measures of spatial knowledge were leveraged based on Santa Barbara Sense of Direction Scale (SBSOD) [12], which has been considered highly reliable and well-correlated with tasks requiring survey knowledge. This approach allows us to get preliminary insights into the question with a large number of samples, before follow-up lab experiments are conducted, which will benefit from the general insights as well. In particular, we focus on addressing the following research questions:

- RQ1: What are the differences in spatial survey knowledge for cognitive maps among individuals with different frequencies of driving and riding as passengers?
- RQ2: What can we learn from these differences in regard to how autonomous vehicles will impact human cognitive maps?

The rest of this paper is structured as follows. We first outline the related work in the field of spatial cognition and automated systems. Then we discuss in detail about the method we used to formulate the questionnaire and conduct the survey. The results of the analysis are presented, followed by discussions on what we could learn from the study. In the end we conclude the paper with a brief summary and our plans for further research.

2   Related Work

2.1   Human Spatial Knowledge and Cognitive Maps

Cognitive maps are map-like, unified mental representations of the spatial environment. They are geometrically-consistent survey knowledge that brains store under a common coordinate system, sometimes known as "global metric embedding" [25]. Research interest in cognitive mapping originated from psychology, but later extended to geography and robotics as well. To build and update cognitive maps, humans acquire and process spatial knowledge about their environment through both direct and indirect experiences.

During spatial navigation, individuals rely on recalling and updating various forms of spatial knowledge besides survey knowledge. They include beacons and landmarks, route knowledge, and graph knowledge [30]. Survey knowledge, which is commonly regarded as the core component in forming cognitive maps, is "maplike" knowledge including metric distances and directions between locations. A person with such knowledge is capable of estimating spatial relations between two locations as well as placing them in a larger representation of the environment. Those abilities are widely deployed by researchers to evaluate an individual's cognitive map in previous studies.

Humans construct and update cognitive maps over time. This process of spatial learning usually involves the experience of travel and other resources, such as reading maps or having conversations [9]. A number of research has explored the varying performance in building spatial representations among individuals with similar learning experience. For example, [13] found significant differences in participants' abilities of forming accurate representations under the same phase of learning a new environment. The knowledge was gained through being driven around as passengers in vehicles. Researchers of another study in [23] let people learn actively by walking in a neighborhood, which also resulted in different performance during evaluation of the learned spatial representations. A detailed comparison between active and passive learning in acquiring spatial knowledge was further investigated by [7,8], where they concluded that both visual and podokinetic information contributed to survey knowledge, while cognitive decision making was the primary component of building graph knowledge, in the context of human spatial learning.

Previous studies showed that different travel experiences contributed to variations in cognitive maps. [17] demonstrated the finding that disparities in spatial knowledge could be partially explained by where and how people travel. They categorized driving and walking as "active" travel modes and compared them with "passive" modes such as public transit and being an auto passenger. Following the similar comparison of active and passive means of transportation, [16] found through user studies with London residents that car users had more complete cognitive maps of the city than people with other modes of transport. However, none of the existing studies focus specifically on the paradigm shift from driving a non-autonomous vehicle to riding inside driverless cars as a passenger. In this paper, we aim to provide indications with regard to the impact of self-driving vehicles.

2.2   Impact of Adopting Automated Systems

In general, the impact of reliance on automation has long been explored and discussed by researchers across multiple domains. With systems requiring less monitoring and intervention, humans exhibit decreased situation awareness, poor skill acquisition and maintenance, as well as delayed reaction to problems and emergencies [19]. It has been discovered that automated systems could hinder operators' abilities of dealing with new problems, as it is not necessary to understand how to manipulate them [22]. Another downside for automation is the reduced attention human pay to monitoring those systems, which can cause fatal accidents during system failures [10]. One widespread application of automation is automatic navigation, which has been suggested to correlate with degradation in human spatial knowledge. An empirical study conducted by [2] showed that pedestrians who use mobile navigation apps acquire poor spatial knowledge, while [5] provided preliminary evidence on the consequences of using vehicle navigation systems in terms of drivers' cognitive maps.

Similar issues have also been studied in research on self-driving vehicles. For example, according to an online survey conducted by [27], the introduction of autonomous cars could potentially cause driving skills degradation in the long term, if drivers fail to receive proper training in the first place. To address problems autonomous driving might cause, researchers proposed several approaches: [28] assessed a driver-vehicle interface of cooperative driving that can keep drivers in-the-loop, and [11] evaluated a proposed prototype implementing shared control between drivers and conditionally automated driving systems. In order to help better understand the effect on human spatial cognition, in our study, we explore the possible impact autonomous cars have on human spatial knowledge for cognitive maps.

3   Method

We developed an online questionnaire through Qualtrics survey system based on SBSOD and literature on spatial survey knowledge, aiming to provide general insights into the possible impact of utilizing self-driving vehicles on acquiring spatial knowledge for cognitive maps. The questionnaire contains 25 questions in total, and is divided into three parts: demographics, frequencies of driving and riding as passenger, and spatial knowledge for cognitive maps.

In the first part, participants were asked some general questions including their age, gender, driver's licence, information about their vehicles (whether they were equipped with semi-autonomous driving systems), main purpose of car use, and their experience with navigation apps. We took advantage of the skip logic during the design, so that participants could save time by not being asked certain questions based on their responses to the previous questions. For example, participants who indicated not having a valid driver's license were not asked questions on the year they obtained the license or information about their cars.

The second part was to group participants by their reported frequencies of driving and riding as passengers in ground transportation (ride-sharing, bus, shuttle service, light rail, etc.). As more driving tasks will be passed to the vehicles, at level-5 automation no one will be performing driving or monitoring tasks [21], making everyone passengers in fully self-driving cars. With this in mind, we designed the questionnaire to address different groups based on how often they drive and how often they are passengers. We were specifically interested in possible changes in the acquisition of spatial knowledge after adopting fully-automated driving, where individuals drive less and ride more as passengers. Ground transportation was addressed in these questions, since our major focus is on vehicles instead of other travel modes such as airplanes. We asked the number of times participants drive or ride as passengers per day during weekdays and weekends in separate questions.

The last part was consisted of 10 questions on participants' self-evaluated spatial survey knowledge about the neighborhoods around where they currently live. They were leveraged from SBSOD, a widely used and well-tested scale in the domain of spatial cognition, with the same 7-point Likert scale ranging from "strongly disagree" to "strongly agree". Some were reworded to closely match the measurements previous studies implemented to assess cognitive maps, such as "relative locations", "judging distances", and "point to where I live". We stated some questions positively and others negatively. A comprehensive list of questions could be found in Table 2. We also added a question on the time period respondents have been living in their current neighborhood.

The questionnaire was distributed on Amazon's Mechanical Turk (MTurk) from September 2019 to January 2020. Researchers have found that the quality of data acquired on MTurk is similar to data collected from traditional methods [4]. Participants were compensated US$0.01 for finishing the entire questionnaire, which estimated to take about 10 min.

4   Results

Overall, we received 217 completed responses out of 230 recorded questionnaires. Based on the findings from [6], we identified duplicate cases by examining multiple questions on demographics from the same IP address and removed them from our analysis. Respondents who indicated not having a driver's license but drove vehicles more than zero time a day were considered not paying close attention to the questionnaire and removed from the following analysis. As a result, a total of 204 responses was included in the final analysis.

Among the 204 participants, 74 were female (36.3%) and 130 were male (63.7%). Their ages range from 18 to 68 (M = 34.2, SD = 9.35). Most of the participants indicated having a valid driver's license (94.6%), and the majority of them reported their primary purpose of driving was commuting to work/school (79.6%), followed by 11% who mainly drove for a living (e.g., taxi drivers). Seven of the drivers had semi-autonomous driving systems equipped on their cars (3.6%), 6 of them were Adaptive Cruise Control and 1 was Tesla AutoPilot. For the experience with navigation systems during driving, more than half respondents stated using navigation sometimes or more than most of the time (55.1%), while only 2 never used the system (1%).

All respondents were grouped into frequent/infrequent drivers and frequent/infrequent passengers according to the calculated daily trips they made on average through driving as well as riding inside vehicles. According to [24], drivers in the US made an average of 2.24 trips per day in 2006, so we identified participants who drove 2 or more trips on average per day as frequent drivers. In regard to passengers, based on public transportation trips data from [1] in 2018 (including the transport mode of demand response), we estimated people in the US took public transportation around 1 trip per day on average. Therefore, respondents indicated riding 1 or more trips per day as passengers were considered as frequent. Table 1 summarizes the numbers of responses by group.

Table 1. Number of responses by group

	Frequent passengers	Infrequent passengers	Total
Frequent drivers	53	62	115
Infrequent drivers	23	66	89
Total	76	128	$N = 204$

We used IBM SPSS Statistics Version 25 to perform the statistical analysis on the data. Spearman correlation analysis was carried out for the questions in the last part of the questionnaire, showing significant positive correlations in all pairs of positively stated questions ($p < 0.05$) and significant negative correlations between all pairs consisting of one positively and one negatively stated questions ($p < 0.05$). Thus, it is likely that respondents were aware of the different phrasing of the questions and answered consistently with their perception of the spatial knowledge they had about the neighborhoods around where they live.

4.1 Single Factor Analysis

A one-way ANOVA was conducted for each item in the last part of the questionnaire to determine the effect of driving frequency on participants' spatial survey knowledge. Similar analysis was carried out on the same questions with the effect as the frequency of riding vehicles as well. The results are shown in Table 2 and Table 3, with lower values indicating more agreement with the description.

In total, we identified 115 frequent drivers (56.4%) and the rest as infrequent drivers (43.6%) among all respondents. The distribution of gender is 34.8% female in frequent drivers and 38.2% female in infrequent drivers. The mean age of the two groups is comparable: frequent drivers are on average 33.56 years, while the other group is 35.17 ($F(1, 202) = 1.49$, $p = 0.22$).

Table 2 shows a significant difference between frequent and infrequent drivers on the question about thinking of the environment in terms of cardinal directions ($F(1, 202) = 5.73$, $p < 0.05$). Respondents who drive more reported to have significantly higher tendency of using cardinal directions to mark their environment

Table 2. Mean and standard deviation of comparing frequent and infrequent drivers, lower value means more agreement with the statement. (*for significance $p < 0.05$, **for significance $p < 0.01$)

Statement	Frequent drivers	Infrequent drivers
"I am clear about the relative locations of the neighborhoods around where I live"	2.02 (0.86)	2.01(0.91)
"I am good at judging distances between locations in the neighborhoods around where I live"	2.22 (1.00)	2.41 (1.11)
"My "sense of direction" is very good whenever I am in the neighborhoods around where I live"	2.28 (1.11)	2.42 (1.23)
"I easily get lost in the neighborhoods around where I live"	5.32 (1.75)	5.51 (1.55)
"I remember routes very well while riding as a passenger in a car"	2.86 (1.59)	3.12 (1.52)
"It is important for me to know where I am at any time"	2.31 (1.21)	2.55 (1.25)
"I tend to think of my environment in terms of cardinal directions (N, S, W, E)"*	**3.53 (1.94)**	**4.21 (2.00)**
"It is hard for me to find the way ONLY using my own "mental map" of the neighborhoods around where I live"	4.59 (1.73)	4.75 (1.72)
"I could always find novel shortcuts successfully by myself without using navigation services in the neighborhoods around where I live"	3.26 (1.56)	3.39 (1.64)
"It is hard for me to point to where I live when I imagine myself standing at a location that is not near my home"	4.36 (1.80)	4.52 (1.76)

as north, south, west, east than those with less driving experience. We did not find significant difference in other questions between the two groups of drivers.

For the experience of riding as passengers, we grouped all participants into 76 frequent passengers (37.3%) and 128 infrequent passengers (62.7%). Both group has a similar gender distribution, with 32.9% of frequent passengers being female, and 38.3% female respondents in the other group. However, significant difference was found in the mean age of the two: frequent passengers share a mean age of 32.36, while infrequent riders have the mean of 35.39, which is significantly older than respondents who ride in vehicles more often (F(1, 202) = 5.13, $p < 0.05$).

Table 3. Mean and standard deviation of comparing frequent and infrequent passengers, lower value means more agreement with the statement. (*for significance $p <$ 0.05, **for significance $p < 0.01$)

Statement	Frequent passengers	Infrequent passengers
"I am clear about the relative locations of the neighborhoods around where I live"	2.13 (0.97)	1.95 (0.82)
"I am good at judging distances between locations in the neighborhoods around where I live"	2.30 (1.04)	2.31 (1.06)
"My "sense of direction" is very good whenever I am in the neighborhoods around where I live"	2.33 (1.14)	2.35 (1.19)
"I easily get lost in the neighborhoods around where I live" **	**4.56 (2.02)**	**5.92 (1.13)**
"I remember routes very well while riding as a passenger in a car" *	**2.62 (1.41)**	**3.19 (1.61)**
"It is important for me to know where I am at any time"	2.42 (1.12)	2.42 (1.30)
"I tend to think of my environment in terms of cardinal directions (N, S, W, E)" **	**3.12 (1.82)**	**4.25 (1.97)**
"It is hard for me to find the way ONLY using my own "mental map" of the neighborhoods around where I live" **	**4.00 (1.72)**	**5.07 (1.60)**
"I could always find novel shortcuts successfully by myself without using navigation services in the neighborhoods around where I live" *	**2.97 (1.32)**	**3.52 (1.71)**
"It is hard for me to point to where I live when I imagine myself standing at a location that is not near my home" *	**4.04 (1.74)**	**4.66 (1.77)**

From Table 3, we found that frequent and infrequent riders showed significantly different opinions towards most of the questions. Respondents who ride more indicated to get lost easier in the neighborhoods around where they live than those with less riding experience ($F(1, 202) = 33.43$, $p < 0.01$), while they significantly agreed more on that they remember routes very well when being passengers ($F(1, 202) = 6.65$, $p < 0.05$). In addition, frequent passengers expressed significantly more agreement to the tendency of thinking the environment in cardinal directions ($F(1, 202) = 17.42$, $p < 0.01$), and the ability of finding novel shortcuts without the help of navigation apps ($F(1, 202) = 5.31$, $p < 0.05$). On the contrary, frequent riders also indicated significant agreement to the statements on finding it hard to find the way using only their mental maps of the environment ($F(1, 202) = 17.65$, $p < 0.01$), and their difficulty of pointing to where they live when imagining themselves standing at a location that is not near their homes ($F(1, 202) = 4.75$, $p < 0.05$).

Besides frequencies of driving and riding, we also performed one-way ANOVA on the effects of gender, the time span participants live in the current neighborhood, and their previous experience with navigation apps on the spatial survey knowledge participants indicated in the questionnaire. Similar to the widely-reported sex differences of spatial abilities in navigation studies [18], we found females reported significantly lower sense of directions than male participants ($F(1, 202) = 4.604$, $p < 0.05$). There is no significant effect on the spatial knowledge in terms of the time period respondents have lived in the neighborhood ($F(3, 200) = 1.72$, $p = 0.16$). But a highly significant effect of navigation apps was found in our study ($F(4, 188) = 3.59$, $p < 0.01$), where the Tukey post hoc analysis suggests a significant difference between participants who "always" use navigation and those "sometimes" utilize the service while driving ($p < 0.05$).

4.2   Two Factors Analysis

A two-way ANOVA was conducted to determine the effect of driving frequency and being passengers on the self-reported spatial knowledge. We found a statistically significant interaction between the frequency of being drivers and riding as passengers on the levels of spatial knowledge ($F(1, 1) = 6.13$, $p < 0.05$). Table 4 provides an overview of the reported spatial knowledge among the four compared groups. As presented in the table, participants who drive frequently without much experience riding in vehicles reported to have the highest spatial survey knowledge, whereas frequent drivers and frequent passengers indicated having comparably poor spatial knowledge to the respondents that neither drive nor take ground transportation.

Table 4. Mean and standard deviation of self-reported spatial knowledge, lower value indicate better knowledge

	Frequent passengers	Infrequent passengers
Frequent drivers	3.02 (0.84)	2.65 (0.95)
Infrequent drivers	2.68 (1.07)	3.01 (0.88)

Simple main effects analysis shows that frequent passengers reported to have significantly worse spatial knowledge than infrequent riders when they are all identified as frequent drivers ($F(1, 113) = 4.64$, $p < 0.05$), but no significant differences when they do not drive as much ($F(1, 87) = 2.14$, $p = 0.15$). For infrequent passengers, there is a significant difference in terms of the reported spatial survey knowledge between frequent drivers and infrequent drivers ($F(1, 126) = 4.97$, $p < 0.05$), but no significant difference was found for participants belonging to frequent passengers ($F(1, 74) = 2.12$, $p = 0.15$).

5   Discussion

5.1   General Insights

Our results suggest that in general, the effect of driving frequency on the spatial survey knowledge is dependent on the individual's experience of riding as passengers. For people who drive often, their experience of being frequent passengers degrades their spatial survey knowledge about the environment, while among infrequent passengers, driving more significantly contributes to better survey knowledge for cognitive maps.

To answer RQ1, we found significant differences in certain aspects that account for spatial survey knowledge between frequent and non-frequent drivers, and among participants who differ in the frequency of riding inside vehicles. More specifically, frequent drivers have more tendency of thinking the environment in terms of cardinal directions than people who drive less often. A similar pattern was discovered by comparing frequent and non-frequent passengers, where the former are more likely to think the environment in north, south, west, and east. One possible explanation could be the variations in practice of wayfinding and navigation, where navigation tools present information in a north-up map [14]. Furthermore, frequent passengers stated their difficulty of finding their way relying solely on their mental map, and their likelihood of getting lost in the nearby neighborhoods is significantly higher than participants with less riding experience. This is consistent with the finding that it is harder for frequent riders to point to their homes at a far-away location, as their mental representation of the environment fails to provide adequate spatial information. Such information does not include route knowledge, as passengers reported to have higher ability of remembering routes when riding in vehicles. However, with poor mental maps, frequent riders could always find novel shortcuts without the aid of navigation apps. This could be due to a lack of relevant shortcutting experience, since passengers are usually passive in navigation and path planning. Thus, they may encounter significantly fewer situations that require finding novel shortcuts by themselves.

In the context of autonomous driving, our results provide a starting point to understand the possible consequences of adopting self-driving technologies in the long term. Our findings suggest that for people who drive frequently and do not to ride as passengers, they might experience a slight degradation in spatial survey knowledge after they ride with self-driving vehicles more as passengers and less as drivers. There are several explanations for this. One is the intuitive idea that passive exposure leads to poor spatial learning than active exploration [7]. As a result, passengers who passively interact with the environment are expected to receive less spatial knowledge if they instead drive and make navigation decisions by themselves. On the other hand, the impact of increased experience with becoming passengers in autonomous cars on human spatial knowledge for cognitive maps depends on individuals' previous driving experience, according to the interaction effect we discovered in the analysis. Therefore, to further explore the relationships between cognitive maps and the usage of autonomous driving, it is important to take people's previous experience of driving into account as well.

5.2   Importance of Cognitive Maps

Cognitive maps are considered as an individual's mental representation of the environment. Although they differ across individuals, the key features of cognitive maps including the relative locations of landmarks and distances between places are useful in both route planning and wayfinding tasks. Beyond spatial cognition, cognitive maps could also benefit designing pleasant spaces and city planning [16]. Recent work on transport demand prediction [15] outlines another potential of cognitive maps as a tool to predict human mobility and traffic planning.

In the future age of autonomous vehicles, humans still need to preserve and update cognitive maps under various situations. During trip planning, potential destinations could be easily considered unreachable without proper knowledge in cognitive maps of the environment. It is also possible to save time and increase efficiency if shortcuts between locations are known in advance. On the other hand, vehicles are not the only mode of travel in everyday life. Even with autonomous vehicles, humans will likely continue use walking, cycling, and other means of transportation that require some level of navigation without full automation. During this process, cognitive maps are extremely helpful in their capacity of taking efficient detours around obstacles and identifying useful shortcuts [26]. There are also situations where navigation assistance fails that could happen at anytime during self-navigation, for example, when GPS signals are absent indoor, or wayfinding apps may crash. With a more complete cognitive map, travelers can feel less lost and have a better chance of finding their way with minimum effort.

5.3   Limitations

Due to the nature of our approach that deploys online questionnaires, our data is completely based on participants' self-evaluation. Despite the effort of making the survey more understandable and attention checking through combining positively and negatively stated questions, it is possible that some participants did not fully understand the questions asked, or they failed to estimate their spatial knowledge in an objective manner.

Another limitation is considering the time and purpose of this study, we asked questions on scenarios where cognitive maps are applied, instead of actually testing the spatial survey knowledge of the participants using objective measures such as pointing or model-building tasks [29]. This can lead to participants overestimating their actual spatial knowledge, or underestimation could also happen. It is infeasible to request respondents performing specific tasks including pointing to a familiar location or drawing sketch maps, because of the diverse regions respondents of the online survey might live in. To further look into the question, we propose a controlled experiment using a driving simulator in the lab, which will be discussed in the next section.

6   Conclusion

In this paper, we investigate how the frequencies of driving and riding as vehicle passengers effect individuals' spatial survey knowledge for cognitive maps through an online survey. The findings of this research show a significant interaction effect of driving and riding frequency on the reported spatial knowledge, suggesting that in order to understand the relationships between cognitive maps and the adoption of autonomous vehicles, we need to consider the previous driving experience in addition to the increased role of passengers in self-driving cars. One interesting finding is the subtle decrease of spatial knowledge when comparing frequent drivers without experience as riders with frequent riders who drive less often. Variations in different aspects of cognitive maps were identified between levels of driving frequency and how often participants ride inside vehicles.

The main motivation of this study is to bring up the issue: what long-term impact will autonomous driving bring to human spatial cognition, especially with regard to cognitive maps? We argue that cognitive maps are important to carry out day-to-day activities. By understanding the possible consequences, we will be more prepared to deal with potential changes at an earlier stage, as well as providing valuable resources to designing the interaction with future vehicles. We hope to provide preliminary insights through an online questionnaire, and discuss new research questions on the topic with researchers from multiple domains.

To address some of the limitations of this study, we proposed a controlled experiment in the lab to further look into the question, and we are currently in the process of recruiting participants. We use a driving simulator in a virtual environment to simulate driving at both level 0 and level 5 automation, and evaluate participants' learned cognitive maps through pointing tasks, model building tasks, and map-sketching tasks. The purpose of the ongoing study is to provide empirical evidence on the differences in spatial survey knowledge individuals acquire of a novel environment after interactions with varying levels of driving automation. Future work include proposing driver-vehicle interfaces that assist with retaining the knowledge for cognitive maps in autonomous cars, and reimagining automobile-human interactions to increase spatial awareness of human passengers.

References

1. APTA public transportation fact book. https://www.apta.com/wp-content/uploads/Resources/resources/statistics/Documents/FactBook/2018-APTA-Fact-Book.pdf. Accessed 1 Jan 2020
2. Aslan, I., Schwalm, M., Baus, J., Krüger, A., Schwartz, T.: Acquisition of spatial knowledge in location aware mobile pedestrian navigation systems. In: Proceedings of the 8th Conference on Human-Computer Interaction with Mobile Devices and Services, pp. 105–108 (2006)
3. Bennett, A.T.: Do animals have cognitive maps? J. Exp. Biol. **199**(1), 219–224 (1996)
4. Buhrmester, M., Kwang, T., Gosling, S.D.: Amazon's mechanical turk: A new source of inexpensive, yet high-quality, data? Perspectives on Psychological Science (2011)
5. Burnett, G.E., Lee, K.: The effect of vehicle navigation systems on the formation of cognitive maps. In: International Conference of Traffic and Transport Psychology (2005)
6. Chandler, J., Mueller, P., Paolacci, G.: Nonnaïveté among Amazon Mechanical Turk workers: consequences and solutions for behavioral researchers. Behav. Res. Methods **46**(1), 112–130 (2014)
7. Chrastil, E.R., Warren, W.H.: Active and passive spatial learning in human navigation: acquisition of survey knowledge. J. Exp. Psychol. Learn. Memory Cogn. **39**(5), 1520 (2013)
8. Chrastil, E.R., Warren, W.H.: Active and passive spatial learning in human navigation: acquisition of graph knowledge. J. Exp. Psychol. Learn. Memory Cogn. **41**(4), 1162 (2015)
9. Downs, R.M., Stea, D.: Maps in Minds: Reflections on Cognitive Mapping. Harper-Collins Publishers, New York (1977)
10. Endsley, M.R., Kiris, E.O.: The out-of-the-loop performance problem and level of control in automation. Human Factors **37**(2), 381–394 (1995)
11. Forster, Y., Naujoks, F., Neukum, A.: Your turn or my turn? Design of a human-machine interface for conditional automation. In: Proceedings of the 8th International Conference on Automotive User Interfaces and Interactive Vehicular Applications, pp. 253–260 (2016)
12. Hegarty, M., Richardson, A.E., Montello, D.R., Lovelace, K., Subbiah, I.: Development of a self-report measure of environmental spatial ability. Intelligence **30**(5), 425–447 (2002)
13. Ishikawa, T., Montello, D.R.: Spatial knowledge acquisition from direct experience in the environment: individual differences in the development of metric knowledge and the integration of separately learned places. Cogn. Psychol. **52**(2), 93–129 (2006)
14. Ishikawa, T., Takahashi, K.: Relationships between methods for presenting information on navigation tools and users' wayfinding behavior. Cartographic Perspect. **75**, 17–28 (2013)
15. León, M., Bello, R., Vanhoof, K.: Cognitive maps in transport behavior. In: 2009 Eighth Mexican International Conference on Artificial Intelligence, pp. 179–184. IEEE (2009)
16. Minaei, N.: Do modes of transportation and gps affect cognitive maps of Londoners? Transp. Res. Part A Policy Pract. **70**, 162–180 (2014)

17. Mondschein, A., Blumenberg, E., Taylor, B.: Accessibility and cognition: the effect of transport mode on spatial knowledge. Urban Stud. **47**(4), 845–866 (2010)
18. Montello, D.R., Lovelace, K.L., Golledge, R.G., Self, C.M.: Sex-related differences and similarities in geographic and environmental spatial abilities. Ann. Assoc. Am. Geogr. **89**(3), 515–534 (1999)
19. Parush, A., Ahuvia, S., Erev, I.: Degradation in spatial knowledge acquisition when using automatic navigation systems. In: Winter, S., Duckham, M., Kulik, L., Kuipers, B. (eds.) COSIT 2007. LNCS, vol. 4736, pp. 238–254. Springer, Heidelberg (2007). https://doi.org/10.1007/978-3-540-74788-8_15
20. Pfleging, B., Rang, M., Broy, N.: Investigating user needs for non-driving-related activities during automated driving. In: Proceedings of the 15th International Conference on Mobile and Ubiquitous Multimedia, pp. 91–99 (2016)
21. SAE International: Taxonomy and definitions for terms related to on-road motor vehicle automated driving systems. https://www.sae.org/standards/content/j3016_201806/. Accessed 1 Jan 2020
22. Sarter, N.B., Woods, D.D., Billings, C.E., et al.: Automation surprises. In: Handbook of human Factors and Ergonomics, vol. 2, pp. 1926–1943 (1997)
23. Schinazi, V.R., Nardi, D., Newcombe, N.S., Shipley, T.F., Epstein, R.A.: Hippocampal size predicts rapid learning of a cognitive map in humans. Hippocampus **23**(6), 515–528 (2013)
24. Tefft, B.: American driving survey, 2015–2016 (2018)
25. Thrun, S.: Simultaneous localization and mapping. In: Jefferies, M.E., Yeap, W.K. (eds.) Robotics and Cognitive Approaches to Spatial Mapping, pp. 13–41. Springer, Heidelberg (2007). https://doi.org/10.1007/978-3-540-75388-9_3
26. Tolman, E.C.: Cognitive maps in rats and men. Psychol. Rev. **55**(4), 189 (1948)
27. Trösterer, S., et al.: You never forget how to drive: driver skilling and deskilling in the advent of autonomous vehicles. In: Proceedings of the 8th International Conference on Automotive User Interfaces and Interactive Vehicular Applications, pp. 209–216 (2016)
28. Walch, M., Sieber, T., Hock, P., Baumann, M., Weber, M.: Towards cooperative driving: involving the driver in an autonomous vehicle's decision making. In: Proceedings of the 8th International Conference on Automotive User Interfaces and Interactive Vehicular Applications, pp. 261–268 (2016)
29. Weisberg, S.M., Schinazi, V.R., Newcombe, N.S., Shipley, T.F., Epstein, R.A.: Variations in cognitive maps: understanding individual differences in navigation. J. Exp. Psychol. Learn. Memory Cogn. **40**(3), 669 (2014)
30. Wiener, J.M., Büchner, S.J., Hölscher, C.: Taxonomy of human wayfinding tasks: a knowledge-based approach. Spat. Cogn. Comput. **9**(2), 152–165 (2009)

Good Boy Here or Bad Boy Far Away?

Effects of Digital Nudging on Booking Decisions in Car Sharing

Tim Schrills[✉], Mourad Zoubir, Jacob Stahl, Katharina Drozniak,
and Thomas Franke

Universität Zu Lübeck, Ratzeburger Allee 160, 23562 Lübeck, Germany
{schrills,zoubir,stahl,franke}@imis.uni-luebeck.de

Abstract. The use of battery electric vehicles (BEVs) and car-sharing is one way to reduce local and (potentially) global transport emissions. In order to increase the use of electric vehicles in car-sharing, this work attempts to examine the effect of framing on car selection within the booking process users encounter in car-sharing. An online questionnaire ($N = 83$) with five different framing conditions (positive and negative goal framing, local or global focus of consequences) was used. For each of the different conditions, the individual, subjective utility of the BEV compared to a combustion vehicle was determined in a total of 80 trials. For this purpose, the participants were asked to make decisions either for the combustion engine vehicle (CV) or the BEV, whereby the prices and their relationship to each other were systematically varied. This study is based on behavioral economic paradigms. Ecological awareness was also assessed. It became clear that positive goal framing has an influence on decisions favoring BEVs in car-sharing. No significant effects could be found regarding the local vs global framing. The results show a main effect of the framing condition as well as for the ecological awareness. However, the interaction between framing (all conditions) and ecological awareness was not significant. The study also showed that the positive framing condition led to a higher subjective utility of the electric vehicle.

Keywords: Electric car-sharing · Framing · Prospect theory · Perception of environmental factors · Goal framing

1 Introduction

Human resource-related decision-making behavior has been researched for decades [1] showing that the majority of decisions are not purely rational, i.e. decisions based purely on objective values, but that there is always a subjective evaluation. Basically, the management of valuable resources like time, money, or energy becomes most salient in distinct situations where choices exist between different behavioral options that have to be decided upon, and where different effects on different resources need to be integrated. An integration of the factors to be considered can represent the subjective, expected utility.

© Springer Nature Switzerland AG 2020
D. Harris and W.-C. Li (Eds.): HCII 2020, LNAI 12187, pp. 398–411, 2020.
https://doi.org/10.1007/978-3-030-49183-3_31

Essentially, a decision refers to a situation in which a person has to choose between at least two options [2]. One option is selected and thus preferred to the others [2]. For example, in the case of car-sharing, a customer is faced with the choice between different available vehicles, sometimes involving the choice of different fundamental vehicle types (e.g. vehicle powertrains); this could be the decision between a battery electric vehicle (BEV) and a combustion engine vehicle.

A high utilization of electric vehicles in car-sharing (relative to normal combustion vehicles fueled by gasoline or diesel) is desirable from the perspective of environmental sustainability, given that BEVs have a considerably larger ecological footprint during production and thus gain their "environmental benefit" over their lifespan. Thus, the most sustainable way to utilize the mobility resources a BEV offers is to shift as many rides as possible from combustion to BEV. Consequently, to achieve the optimal utilization (i.e. km per day) of a BEV, it is inevitable to convince all car-sharing customers to decide in favor of electrical propulsion - i.e. for electric car-sharing.

Yet, a key question is how such an environmentally-conscious decision for BEVs (instead of CVs) can be achieved within a given car-sharing scheme with a mixed-powertrain vehicle fleet. Various hurdles (such as range anxiety or missing charging points) reinforce the necessity of the question: how can it be achieved, on the basis of a behavioral economics consideration, that users attribute a higher value to electric vehicles? In this study we ask how digital nudging can contribute to this.

Hence, the present study examines how non-monetary incentives - in this particular study: interface design modifications - can increase the probability of choosing an electric vehicle. Thus, the aim is to understand how the subjective expected utility of a decision option (i.e., vehicle type) can be changed in the context of car-sharing through the mere presentation of the decision alternatives/situation (i.e. framing).

Framing stands for changes in human decision-making behavior due to "minimal changes in the way information is conveyed" [3] framing emphasizes or highlights certain aspects or attributes of decision alternatives [4]. There are different types of framing: risky choice framing, attribute framing and goal framing [5]. In the given paper, we focus on the potential effects of goal framing in the given context of booking decisions in electric car-sharing. Goal framing is the framing of the consequences or goals of behavior [6]. For example, the consequence of the action "Share Car" could be framed positively: "Achieve demand-based and eco-friendly mobility" or - as a negative frame: "Avoid commitment and maintenance".

To investigate the potential effects of framing, an online questionnaire study was developed, in which the participants were asked to perform vehicle selection in an abstract depiction of a car-sharing booking process. In different conditions, two different types of framing - goal and spatial distance - were considered. The subjective utility, i.e. the perceived value, of a vehicle was used as an independent variable. For this purpose, the participants were asked to make several decisions between electric and combustion vehicles, while the displayed price of the two cars varied. With this approach the present research aims to consider which design of framing is most effective in the given context and how it can influence human decision behavior in the field of electric car-sharing.

2 Background

In the following section, the application context of car-sharing will be described in more detail before the application of prospect theory and the selection of appropriate framing approaches are explained.

2.1 Car-Sharing and Electric Car-Sharing

Many everyday rides are still made by people using a private vehicle in Germany. Car-sharing is a mobility option that could reduce this figure. This paper focuses on station-based car-sharing. Here the vehicles are parked at fixed, predetermined stations. A user can book a vehicle at a station and pick it up there. After the ride, the vehicle must be parked again by the driver at the same station [7]. Due to the possibility of reducing the burden on the environment and relieving cities through car-sharing, the concept is not only beneficial for the users but also for cities and the environment [8].

Electric Car-Sharing. Electric car-sharing refers to car-sharing with purely electric vehicles. This means that the vehicles used are exclusively electrically powered [9]. Electric vehicles are one way of reducing CO_2 emissions from road traffic. Often the increased purchase price is an argument against purchasing an electric vehicle yourself; another obstacle here is the short-range [10]. E-car-sharing is one way of increasing the share of electric vehicles and avoiding the described problem that the purchase price of the vehicle is too high for the individual consumer [10]. Range problems are also less significant: In car-sharing, vehicles are most often used for short to medium distance trips and for long-distance trips it is easy to use combustion shared cars. Furthermore, in station-based car-sharing, vehicles are located at stations where they can be charged at any time [10].

Electric vehicles are still used less than internal combustion vehicles [11]. Higher use of electric vehicles in car-sharing could therefore further reduce CO_2 emissions from road traffic and thus improve the environmental balance of car-sharing. Furthermore, higher utilization rates of electric vehicles would decisively improve their economic efficiency or achieve one at all. A better understanding of human decision making in the context of framing could help to improve the use of electric vehicles in car-sharing. When customers book a car-sharing vehicle through their provider, they can choose between different types of vehicles, including an electric vehicle. The choice of these is to be increased by way of framing. This mode of operation corresponds to nudging, of which framing is a part [12].

2.2 Application of the Prospect Theory

In the subsequent process, the mentally modified, i.e. evaluated, options are ranked. For this purpose, each option is assigned a value, the so-called subjective value [1]. The evaluation of the alternatives based on the reference point is one of the decisive statements of Prospect Theory. However, the environment of each individual, his motivational characteristics or his risk tendency can also modify this reference point [13] and therefore the expected, subjective value.

For example, the type of news source [14] or personal experience may also be a factor influencing the exact position of the reference point [15]. Hence, framing refers to the process of formulating or presenting alternatives and thereby triggering different decisions in an individual [16]. Again, in the context of electric car-sharing, for example, a situation could arise in which customers have the choice between two vehicles at their station: an electric vehicle and a combustion engine vehicle. According to the prospect theory, the two options are evaluated in terms of their value, based on a reference point.

2.3   Framing for Electric Car-Sharing

So, why is framing able to change the mental representation - and therefore the reference point - of a decision? The evaluation of options is on the one hand based on their mental representation, the decision frame [2]. This decision frame is - on the other hand - based on the perception and processing of information as well as on existing, activatable knowledge and one's values and characteristics [1]. Framing can work in different ways; both by creating new values in our memory, but also by reinforcing and activating existing views [16]. There are different types of framing, which have different levels of applicability for the context at hand.

In Risky Choice framing, different options are presented, each of which contains a risk. The level of risk is varied [17]. Risky choice framing is always characterized by a choice between two possible alternatives. In attribute framing, a single attribute or characteristic of an object is presented differently. This is intended to change the mental representation of it, which should ultimately result in a different evaluation [5]. A kind of framing of time was also investigated in the field of environment and climate change. There it was found that people tend to undervalue consequences in the distant future compared to consequences in the near future, e.g. [18]. Furthermore, the spatial distance of the consequences was also varied. In this framing of spatial distance, consequences are considered once for the immediate local environment and once for a large radius or even globally [19]. We have decided to aim for goal framing, as this is the most coherent research to date and both the attribute and risky choice framing are not suitable in terms of design.

While evaluating, which framing could be used to research framing in the context of E-car-sharing, goal framing was derived as applicable since the goal framing shows moderate effects and can be used for e-car sharing. The Risky-Choice framing is not suitable due to the non-variable level of risk. For the implementation of the attribute framing, there would have to be a characteristic that combines both positive and negative qualities. Since this is not given, this framing does not fit for this use.

2.4   Research Questions

So far, moderate effects have been found for goal framing, cf. [5]. If these decisions are perceived as risky, loss frames seemed to be more effective [20]. In a study by [21], loss frames performed better when deciding on a means of transport based upon the CO_2 values offered. Also generally, environmental communications have a better effect on loss frames [22]. Therefore, we expected that the negative formulation of goal framing is more effective in terms of raising the electric vehicles subjective value.

Q1: Is there an influence on the decision-making process through positive or negative goal framing?

Furthermore, we focused on the framing of spatial distance. In this context, studies have shown a consequence of behavior is not framed positively or negatively as in goal framing, but the consequence either related to a far-reaching or global space or related to participants in the local space surrounding the participants [23]. In each case, results found that local, spatial formulation was more effective than a control condition. However, [19] found no advantage of a framed, global messages versus a control message. For this work, this results in the assumption that local framing of the consequence is more effective than global framing.

Q2: Is there an influence on decision making by local or global framing?

In the previous section, research results on influences on the effectiveness of framing were explained. This showed that a framing statement is more effective if it is based on your convictions [24]. One can also assume that the personal attitude to an issue has a major influence on a decision [25]. The personal interest in a topic and the personal importance of this topic, therefore, also influences the effectiveness of framing [26]. In the present work, a scale for the measurement of ecological awareness, to assess the interest in and importance of the environment, is used [27].

Q3: Does the personal ecological awareness of a participant influence the decisions?

3   Method

3.1   Experimental Procedure

The experiment was run as an online survey. The survey was set up via Limesurvey. By creating several blocks of questions, the order of the tested conditions was randomized. All questions of the questionnaire were mandatory so that complete answers were guaranteed. Two scales were used in the questionnaire, both were created using 6-value Likert-scales (completely disagree - completely agree). At the beginning of the questionnaire, the demographic data of participants (Gender, age, and current student status) were assessed.

Table 1. Representation of the five conditions.*Travemünde is a coast location close to Lübeck.

Condition	Statement
negative-local	If you do not use E-CarSharing, you are not helping to reduce the CO_2 emissions caused by road traffic in Lübeck and thus mitigate the rise in sea level, not even here in Travemünde
negative-global	If you do not use E-CarSharing, you are not helping to reduce CO_2 emissions from road traffic and thus mitigate the global rise in sea level
positive-local	If you use E-CarSharing, you help to reduce the CO_2 emissions from road traffic in Lübeck and thus to reduce the rise in sea level even here in Travemünde
positive-global	By using E-CarSharing, you are helping to reduce CO_2 emissions from road traffic and thus mitigate the global rise in sea level
Control condition	You could use E-CarSharing

There were five conditions which were processed in random order by each participant. Consequently, each participant answered all conditions, only the order in which the conditions were presented, was different. The five conditions representing different decision frames were created by presenting different, highlighted sentences (see Table 1). The given decision frame was, therefore, either positive local, positive global, negative local or negative global. There was also a control condition. To capture the subjective value of the electric car in the different conditions, participants had to make 16 decisions between an electric vehicle and combustion vehicle - both vehicles represented the same type of car. A fictitious price per hour was assigned to the vehicles. In agreement with car-sharing experts, the price range depicted in Table 2 was defined as a range of realistic prices per hour for the use of a car-sharing vehicle. The price difference was determined at 0%, 10%, 20%, and 30%. The electric vehicle was always the same price or corresponded to a percentage price difference, more expensive than the combustion vehicle. Each price level was surveyed four times, with prices ranging from five to 15 euros: one decision per price difference in the price range between five and seven euros, one between seven and ten, one between ten and 12, and the last between 12 and 15 (see Table 2). This resulted in 16 decisions per framing condition. These were implemented in two blocks of eight decisions each. These two blocks per condition were not necessarily presented one after the other. The order of all blocks of all conditions was randomized as well as the order of the presented decisions. In total there were 80 decisions to be made. In other studies, which were based on subjective value or intertemporal choice, trailing numbers between nine and 29 were used [28, 29]. By aggregating the values of the decisions made, a percentage value could be given for each framing, reflecting the subjective added value. To measure the ecological awareness of the topic environment the questionnaire from [27] was used.

Table 2. Prices shown in Euro per condition.

Price difference 0%		Price difference 10%		Price difference 20%		Price difference 30%	
Electric	Combustion	Electric	Combustion	Electric	Combustion	Electric	Combustion
5.00	5.00	6.60	6.00	6.30	5.25	6.50	5.00
7.00	7.00	10.45	9.50	9.00	7.50	8.19	6.30
10.00	10.00	12.10	11.00	12.00	10.00	11.05	8.50
14.00	14.00	14.85	13.50	14.88	12.40	14.56	11.20

3.2   Participants

The survey was distributed to the entire student body of the University of Lübeck via the University's e-mail distribution list. Social networks were also used to acquire participants. Through a selection question, only people who already lived or still live in Lübeck were used. This was ensured so that the local formulation of the framing of the distance could be implemented. There were no further requirements for the participants. Thus the survey was based on a theoretical simulation, as not all participants had driving or car-sharing experience.

A total of $N = 86$ participants took part completely. Of these 86 participants, seven participants were excluded. This was due to the very short processing time of less than five minutes or due to very consistent, monotonously answered answers throughout the questionnaire, which indicated that the questionnaire was not processed seriously (more than 95% of answers identically). Thus the answers of 79 participants were included in the evaluation. Of these 79 participants, 43 were female (54.5%). The average age was 23.27 years ($M = 22$, $SD = 6.93$), with the oldest participant being 63 years old and the youngest participant 15 years old. 64 of the 79 participants stated that they were enrolled in a university course. The average driving experience in years was 5.59 years ($M = 5$, $SD = 6.29$) and the average number of kilometers per week driven was 125.06 ($M = 20$, $SD = 193.11$). In contrast, 8.9% of the participants had no driving experience at all. Here 72 of the participants stated extensive driving experience (more than 50 km as a driver) with a combustion engine vehicle. Only 9 participants (11.4%) stated extensive driving experience with an all-electric vehicle, whereas 8 participants (10.1%) stated extensive driving experience with a hybrid vehicle. Most participants had already heard the term car-sharing before the survey and knew what car-sharing is (74 participants). However, only 12 participants completed a ride with a car-sharing vehicle. Only 6 of the participants had completed a trip with an electric car-sharing vehicle at least once.

In the further course of the data cleansing, participants who always decided against the electric vehicle in all decisions were ignored. These decisions may be due to general uncertainty about electric vehicles. For example, some people feel less safe driving an electric vehicle or do not like the driving experience of an electric vehicle [30]. Moreover, some people possibly doubt the environmental performance of electric vehicles because of the production of the batteries for the vehicle or the generation of the electricity used for charging. These answers cannot be used to calculate the results. The goal of this study is to test whether framing the statements would make people more likely to test an electric vehicle in car-sharing. This study or the framing of the statements cannot overcome a general rejection of electric vehicles. As mentioned in the beginning, people with strong values or a clear opinion on a topic are more resilient to framing [24].

The significance level used for all evaluations was $\alpha = .05$ (two-tailed). The dependent variable, the subjective value, was tested for normal distribution using the Shapiro-Wilk test. The data were not normally distributed ($p < .001$). In general, an ANOVA is usually robust against violation of normal distribution, therefore no transformation of the data was applied [31]. According to the Mauchly-Test there was a violation of sphericity ($p < .001$), which is why the Greenhouse-Geisser Correction [32] was used for further evaluation.

4 Results

A two-factor mixed-design ANOVA was used to test the hypotheses. Here, the framing condition represented the within-factor and the Ecological Awareness scale, i.e. the personal interest, the between-factor. The dependent variable was the subjective value of each condition. A significant main effect of the condition could be shown ($p < .001$, see Table 3). Framing, therefore, seems to influence the decision between the vehicle types in the given study. Thus the overall statement "There is a difference in the decision based on the decision frame in car-sharing" can be confirmed. The effect size of $\eta^2_{part} = 0.134$ lies between 0.06 and 0.14 and can, therefore, be interpreted as a medium effect [33]. Furthermore, post-hoc t-tests for paired samples were conducted (Table 4). The given p-values are corrected according to Bonferroni-Holm in order to prevent an alpha error accumulation [34].

Table 3. Test results of ANOVA for the internal subject factor. Note: values corrected due to violation of sphericity.

Factor	df	F	p	η^2_{part}
Condition	2.734	10.696	<.001	0.134

Significant results of the pair comparisons are marked in Table 4. As shown, both positive framing conditions became significant compared to the control group ($p < .001$). Thus, on average, in the positive conditions, the participants were willing to pay more for an electric car than in the control condition. The difference in mean value was 1.61% between the positive-local group and the control group, and 1.81% between the positive-global group and the control group (see Table 4). It can also be seen that while comparing positive and negative framing conditions, a significant effect was found. Both the comparison between positive-local and negative-local ($p = .048$) as well as the comparison between positive-global and negative-local ($p < .001$) and negative-global ($p = .001$) were significant.

Table 4. Pairwise comparisons of the individual conditions, significant results are marked.

Pairwise comparison of the conditions		MΔ	t	df	p
Control group	positive-local	−1.61	−4.29	71	**<.001**
	positive-global	−1.81	−4.70	71	**<.001**
	negative-local	−0.45	−1.12	70	.538
	negative-global	−0.75	−2.03	70	.184
positive-local	positive-global	−0.31	−1.63	72	.327
	negative-local	1.05	2.75	71	**.048**
	negative-global	0.79	2.59	71	.060
positive-global	negative-local	1.37	3.76	71	**<.001**
	negative-global	1.11	3.49	71	**<.001**
negative-local	negative-global	−0.26	−1.11	71	.538

In general, the positive framings were more effective, i.e. the participants were more willing to accept a larger price difference. The average differences between positive-local and negative local were 1.05€ and between positive-global and negative-global 1.10€. The participants would have been on average willing to pay 10.33% more per hour to use an electric car; with the negative-local condition, however, this value was only 9.682% (see Table 5). A positive formulation would lead participants to accept a price difference of over one percent for the electric car.

Table 5. Means, median and standard deviation for the subjective value difference between BEV and combustion vehicle in % of each condition.

Condition	Mean	Median	SD
Framing positive-local (N = 73)	10.33	11.82	4.83
Framing positive-global (N = 73)	10.64	12.00	4.99
Framing negative-local (N = 72)	9.68	11.13	4.88
Framing negative-global (N = 72)	9.42	11.67	5.30
Control group (N = 72)	8.78	10.00	5.06

Thus, the hypothesis regarding Q1 "With negative framing, subjects are more likely to choose the electric vehicle than with a positive framing." cannot be confirmed. Rather, our results suggest the opposite: while deciding in a positive decision frame, subjects tended to decide for the electric vehicle, while the negative framing has no significant results, even when compared to the control group. The condition negative-local shows an average mean value difference compared to the control group of .45, but with a p = .538 does not become significant. The comparison between the condition negative-global and the control group shows a mean difference of .75, and was not significant either (p = .184). Based on this data, it can be concluded that the negative formulation compared to a neutral one has no effect on the subjective value of an electric car. With regard to Q2, the pairwise comparisons between positive-local and positive-global ($p = .327$) and between negative-local and negative-global ($p = .538$) were found to be insignificant in ANOVA. Because no significant effects have been found ($p > .050$), no systematic effect of Goal Framing on the decision of the participants can be shown.

Finally, to determine the impact of ecological awareness (Q3), the participants were divided into two groups. For this purpose the median ($M = 35$) divided the group into two groups. In the calculated ANOVA, the intermediate subject factor of ecological awareness was also defined as Main effect significant ($F = 10.120$, $p = 0.002$, $\eta^2_{part} = 0.128$). This means that Ecological Awareness has had an effect of medium effect size on the decision.

5 Discussion

5.1 Summary

This study examined the effect of goal framing on the selection of a vehicle in a car-sharing context. It considered how goal framing - taking into account ecological awareness - influences the subjective value of an electric vehicle compared to a combustion engine. In summary, the results show a main effect of the framing condition and ecological awareness, therefore affirmatively answering Q1 and Q3. However, the interaction between framing and ecological awareness did not show a significant effect, cf. Q2. It should be noted that the positive framing condition led to a higher subjective value of the electric vehicle. The positive framing conditions were always more effective than the control condition in direct comparison, while the negative framing conditions, when compared to the control and negative global conditions, were only weakly significant. An influence of spatial distance framing could not be shown. The influence of ecological awareness, i.e. the interest in the topic of environment and hence the importance of the choice of electric vehicles, was significant. Based on the assumption that personal values affect mental representation of a decision, it seems logical, that the actual decision is also influenced by this [2]. Therefore, If the topic of the environment is more important to someone, this was also part of their mental representation, and their decision may be in favour of the electric vehicle. [27] found that ecological awareness influences the perceived usefulness of an electric vehicle. This is probably a strong influence on the subjective value of using an electric vehicle, and the willingness to pay more for it.

5.2 Limitations and Implication

The participants were similarly distributed across gender. However, 81% of the participants still held student status (due to recruitment via university emails), therefore students are overrepresented in this study. In further research in this area, it would, therefore, make sense to select a sample that is more representative of the population and includes more age and education classes. This is particularly critical because students are not necessarily the primary target group of car-sharing. One way of doing this would be, for example, a neighborhood survey in the vicinity of a car-sharing station.

It is also conceivable that the young age average and the high proportion of students influence the effect of the chosen framing types. Framing of the spatial distance should create more personal relevance and thus personal importance in the local formulation. A sense of belonging to a place is created, for example, by memories of that place, cultural importance or possibilities of belonging [19]. Students with no particular connection to the city may, therefore, lack this connection. This would be an explanation for the absence of a difference between local and global framing. A supplement to the study would be, for example, a measurement of local connectivity.

Contrary to the hypothesis, however, there is no interaction between ecological awareness and the framing conditions. This suggests that framing in this study had affected all groups similarly. An effect between the importance of the environment and framing effects was often found in the literature [35].

[36] found that framing effects only occur when there is interest in the topic. In the given sample of participants, a high level of ecological awareness can be assumed. It is therefore conceivable that all participants, including those in the group with low ecological awareness, still show a high level of interest in the topic compared to the basic population. Young people may consider environmental and climate protection to be more important than other generations do Therefore, it is still possible that this interaction between ecological awareness and framing effects exists, yet it could not be found in the limited sample we had in our study. For both groups, participants' results were divided at the median. A division at the median can be influenced by the distribution of the data. Variance is also lost by converting the continuous variable into a dichotomous variable.

In principle, finding a framing effect is interesting for further research. The research situation in this area is uncertain, an influence of goal framing was not found in all studies [5]. The effect that occurred supports the theory behind goal framing and provides an approach to further investigate this also in the environmental field. However, an effect of framing the spatial distance could not be found. Here the exact breakdown of the influence of this framing was difficult, because it was always presented in combination with a goal framing. Some participants were not considered in the data evaluation because they decided against the electric vehicle in every decision. This may be due to uncertainty regarding electric vehicles [30]. Since value concepts and personal interests influence framing effects [16], a measurement of attitudes towards electric vehicles would also provide insight. In addition to attitudes towards the environment, the attitude towards electric vehicles can also change the effectiveness of framing.

Another possibility would be not to present this information before a ride and in a decision frame, but to use feedback after a completed ride to support the choice of electric vehicles in Car-Sharing. Thus, information after a ride is more likely to contribute to changing driving behavior or choice of means of transport than information before the start of the ride, as is the case with framing [37]. Based on this, one could test whether a message of the type "During this trip you have helped to prevent an increase of CO_2 emissions" after a completed trip with an electric vehicle, or accordingly "During this trip you have not helped not to prevent an increase of CO_2

emissions" after a completed trip with a combustion engine vehicle, could contribute to increasing the frequency of choice of electric vehicles in Car-Sharing compared to a control group that receives no feedback.

6 Conclusion

Finally, it can be concluded that in the given context of carsharing booking decisions - goal framing offers the possibility to influence a decision. However, the results so far have been very inconsistent. In principle, however, it is conceivable to change the choice between electric vehicles and internal combustion vehicles in car-sharing through an appropriate formulation of the consequences. The use of goal framing on websites and in a booking app of car-sharing could potentially encourage users to choose BEV.

References

1. Tversky, A., Kahneman, D.: Rational choice and the framing of decisions. J. Bus. **59**, 251–278 (1986)
2. Pfister, H.R., Jungermann, H., Fischer, K.: Entscheiden unter Unsicherheit. In: Die Psychologie der Entscheidung, pp. 169–224. Springer, Heidelberg (2017). https://doi.org/10.1007/978-3-662-53038-2_6
3. Stocke, V.: Framing und Rationalität: Die Bedeutung der Informationsdarstellung für das Entscheidungsverhalten. De Gruyter (2014)
4. Scheufele, B.: Framing-Effekte auf dem Prüfstand. Eine theoretische, methodische und empirische Auseinandersetzung mit der Wirkungsperspektive des Framing-Ansatzes. Medien Kommun. **52**, 30–55 (2004). https://doi.org/10.5771/1615-634x-2004-1-30
5. Levin, I.P., Schneider, S.L., Gaeth, G.J.: All frames are not created equal: a typology and critical analysis of framing effects. Organ. Behav. Hum. Decis. Process. **76**, 149–188 (1998). https://doi.org/10.1006/obhd.1998.2804
6. Krishnamurthy, P., Carter, P., Blair, E.: Attribute framing and goal framing effects in health decisions. Organ. Behav. Hum. Decis. Process. **85**, 382–399 (2001). https://doi.org/10.1006/obhd.2001.2962
7. Kagerbauer, M., Heilig, M., Mallig, N., Vortisch, P.: Carsharing - ein neues Verkehrssystem! In: Proff, H., Fojcik, T.M. (eds.) Nationale und internationale Trends in der Mobilität: Technische und betriebswirtschaftliche Aspekte, pp. 385–402. Springer, Wiesbaden (2016). https://doi.org/10.1007/978-3-658-14563-7_24
8. Riegler, S., et al.: CarSharing 2025 – Nische oder Mainstream? 66 (2025
9. Genikomsakis, K.N., Angulo Gutierrez, I., Thomas, D., Ioakimidis, C.S.: Simulation and design of fast charging infrastructure for a university-based e-carsharing system. IEEE Trans. Intell. Transp. Syst. **19**, 2923–2932 (2018). https://doi.org/10.1109/TITS.2017.2767779
10. Wappelhorst, S., Sauer, M., Hinkeldein, D., Bocherding, A., Glaß, T.: Potential of electric carsharing in urban and rural areas. Transp. Res. Procedia. **4**, 374–386 (2014). https://doi.org/10.1016/j.trpro.2014.11.028
11. Scherf, C., Steiner, J., Wolter, F.: E-Carsharing: Erfahrungen, Nutzerakzeptanz und Kundenwünsche. Int. Verkehrswesen. **65**, 42–44 (2013)

12. Ölander, F., Thøgersen, J.: Informing versus nudging in environmental policy. J. Consum. Policy. **37**, 341–356 (2014). https://doi.org/10.1007/s10603-014-9256-2

13. Bazerman, M.H.: The relevance of Kahneman and Tversky's concept of framing to organizational behavior. J. Manag. **10**, 333–343 (1984). https://doi.org/10.1177/014920638401000307

14. Ruth, J.A., York, A.: Framing information to enhance corporate reputation. J. Bus. Res. **57**, 14–20 (2004). https://doi.org/10.1016/S0148-2963(02)00270-9

15. Barkan, R., Busemeyer, J.R.: Modeling dynamic inconsistency with a changing reference point. J. Behav. Decis. Mak. **16**, 235–255 (2003). https://doi.org/10.1002/bdm.444

16. Chong, D., Druckman, J.N.: Framing Theory. Ann. Rev. Polit. Sci. **10**, 103–126 (2007). https://doi.org/10.1146/annurev.polisci.10.072805.103054

17. Piñon, A., Gambara, H.: A meta-analytic review of framing effect: risky, attribute and goal framing 7 (2005)

18. Chandran, S., Menon, G.: When a day means more than a year: effects of temporal framing on judgments of health risk. J. Consum. Res. **31**, 375–389 (2004). https://doi.org/10.1086/422116

19. Scannell, L., Gifford, R.: Personally relevant climate change: the role of place attachment and local versus global message framing in engagement. Environ. Behav. **45**(1), 60–85 (2013)

20. Lee, A.Y., Aaker, J.L.: Bringing the frame into focus: the influence of regulatory fit on processing fluency and persuasion. J. Pers. Soc. Psychol. **86**, 205–218 (2004). https://doi.org/10.1037/0022-3514.86.2.205

21. Avineri, E., Waygood, E.O.D.: Applying valence framing to enhance the effect of information on transport-related carbon dioxide emissions. Transp. Res. Part A Policy Pract. **48**, 31–38 (2013). https://doi.org/10.1016/j.tra.2012.10.003

22. Davis, J.J.: The effects of message framing on response to environmental communications. Journalism Mass Commun. Q. **72**(2), 285–299 (1995). https://doi.org/10.1177/107769909507200203

23. Leiserowitz, A.: Communicating the risks of global warming: American risk perceptions, affective images, and interpretive communities. In: Moser, S.C., Dilling, L. (eds.) Creating a Climate for Change, pp. 44–63. Cambridge University Press, Cambridge (2007). https://doi.org/10.1017/CBO9780511535871.005

24. Updegraff, J.A., Brick, C., Emanuel, A.S., Mintzer, R.E., Sherman, D.K.: Message framing for health: Moderation by perceived susceptibility and motivational orientation in a diverse sample of Americans. Health Psychol. **34**, 20–29 (2015). https://doi.org/10.1037/hea0000101

25. Kim, N.-Y.: The influence of message framing and issue involvement on promoting abandoned animals adoption behaviors. Procedia - Soc. Behav. Sci. **82**, 338–341 (2013). https://doi.org/10.1016/j.sbspro.2013.06.271

26. Lecheler, S., de Vreese, C., Slothuus, R.: Issue importance as a moderator of framing effects. Commun. Res. **36**, 400–425 (2009). https://doi.org/10.1177/0093650209333028

27. Schlüter, J., Weyer, J.: Car sharing as a means to raise acceptance of electric vehicles: an empirical study on regime change in automobility. Transp. Res. Part F Traffic Psychol. Behav. **60**, 185–201 (2019). https://doi.org/10.1016/j.trf.2018.09.005

28. Luhmann, C.C., Chun, M.M., Yi, D.-J., Lee, D., Wang, X.-J.: Neural dissociation of delay and uncertainty in intertemporal choice. J. Neurosci. **28**, 14459–14466 (2008). https://doi.org/10.1523/JNEUROSCI.5058-08.2008

29. Smith, C.L., Hantula, D.A.: Methodological considerations in the study of delay discounting in intertemporal choice: a comparison of tasks and modes. Behav. Res. Methods. **40**, 940–953 (2008). https://doi.org/10.3758/BRM.40.4.940

30. Graham-Rowe, E., et al.: Mainstream consumers driving plug-in battery-electric and plug-in hybrid electric cars: a qualitative analysis of responses and evaluations. Transp. Res. Part Policy Pract. **46**, 140–153 (2012). https://doi.org/10.1016/j.tra.2011.09.008

31. Glass, G.V., Peckham, P.D., Sanders, J.R.: Consequences of failure to meet assumptions underlying the fixed effects analyses of variance and covariance. Rev. Educ. Res. **42**, 237–288 (1972). https://doi.org/10.3102/00346543042003237

32. Greenhouse, S.W., Geisser, S.: On methods in the analysis of profile data. Psychometrika **24**, 95–112 (1959). https://doi.org/10.1007/BF02289823

33. Cohen, J.: Statistical Power Analysis for the Behavioral Sciences. L. Erlbaum Associates, Hillsdale (1988)

34. Holm, S.: A simple sequentially rejective multiple test procedure. Scand. J. Stat. **6**, 65–70 (1979)

35. Maheswaran, D., Meyers-Levy, J.: The influence of message framing and issue involvement. J. Mark. Res. **27**, 361–367 (1990)

36. Updegraff, J.A., Rothman, A.J.: Health message framing: moderators, mediators, and mysteries: health message framing. Soc. Personal. Psychol. Compass. **7**, 668–679 (2013). https://doi.org/10.1111/spc3.12056

37. Chorus, C.G., Molin, E.J.: Travel information as an instrument to change car-drivers' travel choices: a literature review. Eur. J. Transp. Infrastruct. Res. **31** (2006)

Experimental Validation of an Eye-Tracking-Based Computational Method for Continuous Situation Awareness Assessment in an Aircraft Cockpit

Simon Schwerd$^{(\boxtimes)}$ (ID) and Axel Schulte (ID)

Institute of Flight Systems (IFS), University of the German Bundeswehr
Munich (UniBwM), 85579 Neubiberg, Germany
{simon.schwerd,axel.schulte}@unibw.de

Abstract. We propose a continuous situation awareness (SA) assessment method based on eye-tracking and on-line display analysis. In our method, an explicit representation of the pilot's knowledge about the situation is constructed, which contains the pilot's perceived state of the system. To quantify SA for different information relevant to a task, the perceived state is compared to a ground truth to compute a metric of accordance between the pilot's situational picture and the system state. We evaluate this method in a fast jet cockpit simulator experiment with pilots, both professional and in training, from the German Air Force. The participant had to fly a demanding low-level route while reporting threats appearing at random times. We hypothesized, that low accordance between system state and pilot awareness predicts long response time in threat report, low performance in the flight altitude and low subjective SA. Results show, that pilot performance in the low-level flight was correlated to measured average accordance in the aircrafts altitude. Further, subjective SA ratings showed positive association to our measurement results. Response time did not correlate with the measured SA. Apart from that, our measurement approach identified grave decrements for individual participants in the perceptual level of SA, suited for assistance system interventions. We conclude, that the proposed measurement is a promising method to enable assistance systems adapting to the pilot's mental state.

Keywords: Applied cognitive psychology · Human error · Situation awareness · Eye-tracking · Operator state

1 Introduction

Pilot error is one major cause for aviation accidents. Improvements in safety procedures and training can reduce pilot fallibility but cannot eliminate it completely [1]. In this context, adaptive assistance systems could reduce the risk of accidents by removing possible sources of pilot errors.

One cause of pilot error is the loss of situation awareness (SA) [2]. When a pilot is not aware of relevant information due to perceptual errors or divergence in his mental

© Springer Nature Switzerland AG 2020
D. Harris and W.-C. Li (Eds.): HCII 2020, LNAI 12187, pp. 412–425, 2020.
https://doi.org/10.1007/978-3-030-49183-3_32

model, wrong decision-making may result in fatal consequences [3, 4]. With increasing complexity and automation in a cockpit, maintaining a high level of SA is an important aspects of a pilot's work process.

Pilot SA is model of situational cognition, which means that it is affected by the several factors of the situation. It does not result from a single factor, but is influenced by the state of the environment, automation, machine interface and pilot cognition. Therefore, a continuous measure of SA could be valuable input for assistance systems enabling them to adjust to the SA of the pilot. Conventionally, SA is measured for analytical purposes in simulation studies, where the goal is to evaluate operator performance or interface designs. In these cases, freeze-probe methods such as the Situation Awareness Global Assessment Technique (SAGAT) or online query measures such as the Situation Present Assessment Method (SPAM) are used to measure SA [5]. With freeze-probe measures, the simulation is halted at random times, all screens are blanked, and the participant is asked several questions referring to SA relevant information of the operation. On the contrary, online query measures require the participant to answer such queries without interruption of their task. Several reviews and meta-analysis [5–9] discuss the pros, cons and the validity of different measures. Apart from issues described in those studies, these methods cannot be used in an operational setting and therefore, it is not possible to use them as real-time input for adaptive assistant systems.

As an alternative to query methods, eye-tracking might be a way to measure SA in an operational environment [10]. It can be obtained continuously without intrusion and is a strong indicator of pilots' selective attention. Several studies used eye-tracking to correlate eye-tracking parameters (e.g. fixation frequency of relevant display elements) with task performance and query SA measures. In [11], fixation rates, dwell times, and entropy were used as indication for acquisition of information of air traffic controller. It was demonstrated, that controllers with high performance did focus their attention at important times and distributed attention when possible. The authors of [10] implemented an eye-tracking based measurement of SA for a simple monitoring task and compared it to SAGAT. In this case, task performance prediction by eye-tracking was superior to SAGAT. Their results also showed, that the participants attentional distribution depended on the dynamics and state of the task environment, hence SA is situated in the users work process. Based on these results, other studies explored the use of eye-tracking as input for assistant systems. The authors of [12] implemented a cockpit assistant system, which notified a pilot based on a comparison of scan patterns with a visual behavior database. However, evaluation showed mixed results with a lot of room for improvement. In [13], eye-tracking was used to continuously evaluate SA in the supervision of multiple UAVs. It could be demonstrated that this system enhances operator monitoring performance. In [14] and [15], eye-tracking was used to measure pilot workload as input for an adaptive assistance system for pilot helicopters, which showed promising results in operational use.

Most of the related research demonstrates the utility of eye-tracking in lab environments. However, there are three requirements for a measurement method used by an assistance system: First, a statistical approach to predict SA by analyzing eye-tracking data is not enough. While there are certainly meaningful correlations between SA and statistical gaze measures (e.g. fixation frequency on relevant areas), they possess an averaging nature. Therefore, rare situations of a pilot missing a relevant cue would be ignored when the overall statistical measure is good enough. Thus, statistical indices are missing important outliers, which are the most promising situations for an assistance system intervention. Second, an assistance system requires knowledge about context and the specific information, a pilot is missing. No meaningful information could be drawn from a single number quantifying SA. Third, the method must predict SA continuously and during operation to enable assistance. Most published methods rely on post-processing ([13–15] are one of the few exceptions).

In our contribution, we address these issues by a computational model which does not rely on statistical measures but holds an explicit representation of the information perceived by the pilot.

2 Computational Estimation of SA

The objective of the proposed system is to find potential sources of pilot errors related to the lack of SA. To measure this "lack", three questions are modeled by our approach: What information is relevant? What does the pilot know? What is the state of the system? In the following, we describe how our approach handles each of these questions.

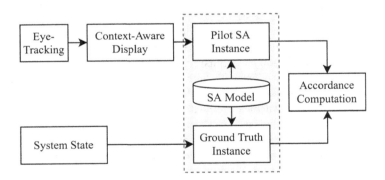

Fig. 1. Overview over the measurement chain

The measurement system is illustrated in Fig. 1. First, the pilot's gaze is measured by an eye-tracking system. The gaze position is used to analyze the fixated display elements in a context-aware interface. This interface application generates information about the display element, the pilot looked at. To infer SA, this information is input to a dynamic knowledge representation. This representation is instantiated from a SA model that associates displayed information to a domain model of SA. The pilot instance of this model is then compared to a similar model fed with the system's ground truth. This comparison is used to compute accordance and identify deviations. The modules are explained more detailed in the following subsections.

2.1 Eye-Tracking and Perception Analysis

The first module provides an estimate of the pilot's visual perception. For this, an eye-tracking system periodically determines the pilot's gaze position in the cockpit. In this stream of gaze positions, only fixated positions are used for further analysis, because they serve as a good indication of information intake [16]. To account for the imprecision of the eye-tracking system, we virtually add gaze samples in a small area around the measured gaze. In the following parts of the measuring chain, these virtual samples are analyzed in similar manner as the measured sample. This ensures that no display element is missed due to small eye-tracking imprecisions. All samples, both measured and virtual, are then passed to the display application.

2.2 Context-Aware Display

The objective of this module is to analyze a gaze sample for the information displayed at that position in the screen. For a given sample, the display application generates a specific observation which contains three types of information: semantic, content and identification. Semantic describes the meaning of the display element at the gaze position, which can be subsequently used to distinguish between all generated observations. The content describes the value of the information at the time of measurement. The identification indicates, which object the information is about.

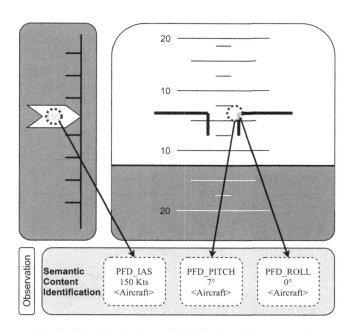

Fig. 2. Simplified primary flight display with two samples

As an example, Fig. 2 shows a simplified primary flight display (PFD) with air speed (left) and attitude (right) indicators: Two hypothetical samples are drawn on air speed indicator and attitude indicator. For the sample on the air speed indicator, the application generates the semantic *PFD_IAS* with a content of $c_{IAS} = 150[kts]$, displayed at measurement. The identification is set to the pilot's aircraft, which is the object, the speed information is about. The other sample on the attitude indicator encodes more than one information alone. It displays both roll and pitch angles of the aircraft by means of an artificial horizon. Therefore, the context-aware display generates two semantics, one for pitch and roll respectively. Both observations contain the value at the time of measurement and a reference to the pilot's aircraft.

2.3   SA Model

To use the continuous stream of observation data as a SA indication, a model is required to associate observations with meaningful information. What an observation *means* is dependent on the application, therefore is domain knowledge. The SA model needs to be flexible enough to capture situational information in different domains. For that purpose, we use a directed logical network. Every node in this network represents a SA-relevant information, subsequently denoted as SA node. The existing observations can be associated to these nodes, which means that a given observation carries the content for the associated SA node. When a gaze measurement generates this observation, the SA node is activated within the network. For example, the *PFD_IAS* from Fig. 2 is an indicator for the aircraft's speed.

As illustrated in Fig. 3, different SA nodes can be connected among each other to represent new aggregations, e.g. the distance between two objects on a map can be estimated by knowing the position of both. This is expressed by edges between SA nodes. These edges implement different logical functions, that define how an initial node activation propagates. However, in this contribution, we only use one type of edge that activates the child node if any parent node is active.

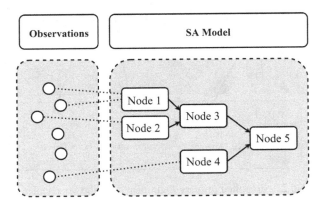

Fig. 3. Situation awareness model

During operation, the SA model is instantiated and fed with the stream of pilot observations. An observation activates every associated node in the model. To account for similar information related to different entities of the same kind, information nodes are uniquely instantiated for every *identification*. This is important, when two display elements represent the same semantic of information but are related to different objects in the environment; e.g. two buildings in a tactical map convey positional information, therefore two nodes are spawned for both buildings respectively. The node activation propagates through the network according to the logical functions of the edges.

A second instance of this model is used for the generation of a ground truth model. For this, we use the system state to generate all possible *observations* in the system containing correct values. These observations are used as input for the SA Model, which represents the ground truth during operation.

2.4   Accordance Computation

The last step is to evaluate the quality of the measured awareness. Thus, we compare the system state to the pilot's awareness. The content of both situational representations – ground truth and pilot's mental state – are used to compute accordance of the pilot's situational picture. In terms of information, a content can be numeric, text, states, times or an identification for another object. To compute the accordance of two values of the same semantic, a parameter c_{norm} is required. This parameter quantifies for every observation, what a desirable accordance between two contents is, by normalizing the difference of both. For example, it might be good enough to know the aircrafts altitude within 1000 ft. Note, that this parameter varies for different tasks, e.g. altitude in a low-level flight has a smaller normalizing parameter than a transit flight. For every observation, the accordance is computed as follows:

$$x_{acc} = \begin{cases} 1 - \frac{|c_{pilot} - c_{sys}|}{c_{norm}} & |c_{pilot} - c_{sys}| \leq c_{norm} \\ [3pt] \quad\quad 0 & otherwise \end{cases} \tag{1}$$

The terms c_{pilot} and c_{sys} denote the content of the pilot and system observation, respectively. The accordance for text, states and identifications is binary since there is no fuzzy area between two different information of such kind. For numeric values and times, there can be a continuous accordance normalized by c_{norm}. The result of this computational process is a model of the pilot's mental state describing the accordance with the actual ground truth. The accordance is specific to every information node in the system.

2.5   Limitations

For reasons of simplicity, we neglect three phenomena of cognition and perception which might affect SA measurement. First, there is no model for working memory of the pilot. An information which has been fixated upon by the pilot and generated an observation activates all associated nodes in the model. Assuming no change in the content, our model continuously predicts perfect SA without any notion of memory decay. Second, the perception is solely based on fixations, which are not a perfect measure of visual attention. While there is a high correlation between fixation position and information processing, our approach neglects look-but-failed-to-see phenomena [16]. Third, peripheral vision is neglected for the most part. As described earlier, a small area around a measured fixation is additionally analyzed but apart from that there is no way to observe what the pilot perceives in his peripheral vision.

3   Experimental Evaluation

To evaluate the SA measurement, we conducted a human-machine-experiment. For the experiment, we hypothesized that a low accordance measured by our assessment correlates with low performance as well as low subjective SA. Further, we expected to be able to identify situational errors, which in statistical analysis would be classified as outliers, but represent use-cases for an assistance system.

Fig. 4. Integrated gaze tracking system

Flight Simulator. We conducted the experiment in our fast jet research cockpit simulator (Fig. 4). The cockpit does not reflect an existing jet but is a custom research cockpit with three multi-touch-displays. Here, we implemented the measurement chain and fully integrated eye-tracking and the context-aware display to generate observations. For eye-tracking, we used SmartEye©-System connected to our simulator software. The gaze is measured with a sampling frequency of 60 Hz and covers three cockpit displays as well as the Head-Up Display (HUD).

Participants. The experiment was conducted with two groups of participants. The first group consisted of eight professional fighter pilots from the German Air Force with a mean age of 36.25 years (all male, $s_{pilots} = 6.8$). One pilot had to be excluded in the experiment due to data logging issues. The second group were nine pilot candidates from the University of the Bundeswehr Munich with a mean age of 22.6 years (all male, $s_{students} = 1.4$). All participants provided written informed consent.

Procedure. We conducted one experiment with each participant. The two groups received different training. The professional pilots got an extensive training on the simulator with a focus on other experiments. During that time, they did not encounter a version of the experimental task. They were required to perform the experiment without specific training for the experimental tasks. On the other hand, the pilot candidates were trained for two hours, but did encounter closely related tasks, e.g. low-level flying and threat reporting.

Right before each experiment, the eye-tracking system was calibrated for each participant. Nine-point calibration on every screen resulted in the mean precisions and accuracies given for each participant in Fig. 5. Mean tracking accuracy was $116.2[px]$ and mean standard deviation was $\bar{s}_{acc} = 63.5[px]$. Then, participants of both groups received a short briefing about the upcoming task.

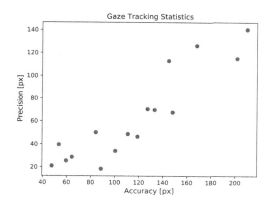

Fig. 5. Gaze tracking statistics

Experiment. In the experiment, the participants had to fly a demanding low-level route through a mountainous environment while keeping their radar altitude below 500 ft. Figure 9 shows an overview of this route. The altitude information was indicated in the HUD radar altitude read-out (marked red in Fig. 6). During the flight, air defenses appeared at random times. No audio cue was given as an indicator of threat. When the participant visually noticed a pop-up air defense either as a red symbol in their central display (Fig. 7) or as a radar warning indication in the HUD (Fig. 6), they had to report the type, their own position and mission time as quickly as possible.

Fig. 6. HUD   **Fig. 7.** Central cockpit display

As an indirect assessment of SA, we measured performance in two ways. First, we continuously measured if the pilot adheres to the altitude limit. Second, we measured time until the pilot reported his position. The latter can be interpreted as an adapted version of SPAM. The report is not explicitly requested by someone external but is required by an appearing threat. We assumed a quicker threat report to be related to a high pilot accordance in the aircraft position. For subjective SA measurement, the pilots answered a Situational Awareness Rating Technique (SART) questionnaire. For the experiment, we constructed a SA model that describes the relationship among all relevant information for the computational assessment process.

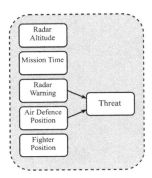

Fig. 8. Experimental model

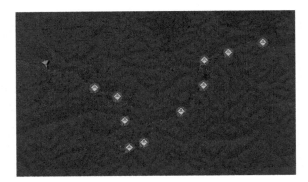

Fig. 9. Experimental scenario

SA Model. The constructed SA Model, illustrated in Fig. 8, reflects the simplistic nature of the task. The participant had to monitor their radar altitude and look out for a possible threat. The nodes *Radar Altitude* and *Threat* correspond to these tasks in the SA model. In the cockpit, there were two ways to identify a threat: Either in the radar warning display or in a tactical map. In both cases, the node *Threat* is activated for the air defense instance. Note, that a node is created for every new threat since the information relates to different logical instances of the same semantic, which means in this case different enemy air defenses all representing a threat to the pilot. The nodes *Mission Time* and *Fighter Position* are associated with the threat task, where this information must be reported.

Results. We correlated the accordance value of *Fighter Position* of the time right before the threat node was activated with the time duration until the fighter position was reported. We found no correlations between accordance in position and position report time.

Second measure of performance is the aircraft altitude. We assessed accordance of radar altitude to quantify, if low accordance is linked to a pilot violating the altitude limit. For that, we accumulated the time in four categories displayed in a confusion matrix in Table 1. Accordance was classified as high for $x_{acc} > 0.75$ and low otherwise. Note, that we selected a normalizing parameter $c_{norm} = 500$ ft, which means that a deviation of less than 125 ft was classified as high. Altitude was classified as wrong for $x_{alt} > 500$ ft and correct otherwise. The table contains the mean values and standard deviations of the percentage of time of the combination of two categories over all participants. There is a high percentage of true positives (correct altitude and high accordance), which means that pilot's flying under the limit also had a good knowledge of their altitude. In contrast, there is a great portion of false positives, where the pilots exceeded the altitude limit but, according to the model, were aware of their altitude within the limit. Percentage of mission time in wrong altitude differed strongly between participants with a mean of $\bar{e} = 0.118$ (± 0.118).

Table 1. Confusion matrix for accordance and altitude

	Correct altitude	Wrong altitude
High accordance	.842 ($\pm$.0.37)	.618 ($\pm$.122)
Low accordance	.128 ($\pm$.037)	.382 ($\pm$.122)

To study a general link between accordance and error, we computed the correlation between the average accordance of *Radar Altitude* and the time proportion violating the altitude limit. Figure 10 shows the percentage of time violating the altitude limit over the average accordance. Pearson's correlation coefficient is $r = -0.62$ with p < 0.02 (two-sided). We excluded one pilot from correlation computation because of his extraordinary bad performance leading to non-normal distributed data. Nevertheless, this outlier fits the trend of a linear regression.

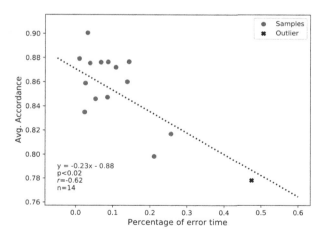

Fig. 10. Scatter plot of error time over average accordance

Further, Fig. 11 shows the average altitude accordance time over the normalized SART score. We computed a positive correlation of $r = 0.56$ with p < 0.04 (two-sided). Here, one student participant was excluded due to errors in their SART survey.

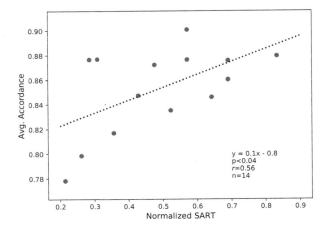

Fig. 11. Scatter plot of the normalized SART score over the average accordance

We could correctly classify the perception of an appearing threat in 73.8% of all samples (n = 16 participants * 10 threats = 160). A threat was classified as correct if the node *"Threat"* was activated and the participant reported within three seconds after activation. In 26.2% of all cases, the threat was not classified correctly due to three different reasons: The pilot reported incorrectly (n = 2), the threat node was inactive when the pilot reported the threat (n = 31) or the threat node was active, but the pilot did not report within three seconds after activation (n = 9).

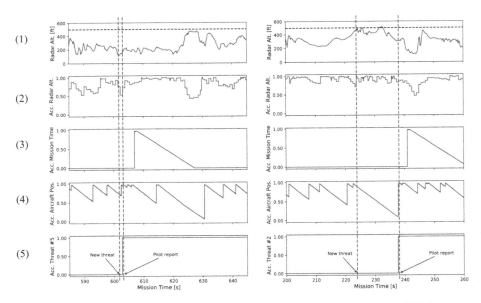

Fig. 12. Accordance for successful report (left) and unsuccessful report (right).

In three cases, a threat was missed for over six seconds by a participant. In these cases, the measurement identified the lack of SA as a deviation in an appearing *"Threat"* node. As an illustrative example, Fig. 12 shows characteristic measurements for both successful and unsuccessful report. The red lines indicate the time of an appearing threat and the time of pilot report, respectively. The data on the left shows, that the pilot quickly notices the threat ($t = 1.7s$), which is indicated in our system by a node activation of *"Threat #2"* (Fig. 12, (5), left) along with a peak in accordance which can be interpreted as the pilot's knowledge about this threat. After the participant starts to report the threat, he updates his knowledge about the mission time as part of the report, which is indicated by an accordance peak in the node *"Mission Time"* (Fig. 12, (3), left). In contrast to that, Fig. 12 on the right shows an extreme outlier of bad performance for the same participant. Here, the pilot misses the threat over a long period ($t = 13.1$ s), which is measured as a late peak in accordance of the threat node (Fig. 12, (5), right). The accordance values of *"Radar Alt"* (Fig. 12, (1), right) indicate, that the pilot was engaged in keeping his altitude below the limit. Nevertheless, the same pattern of updating his knowledge about mission time right after threat report can be observed.

4 Discussion

In this contribution, we sought to evaluate, if our proposed method can assess meaningful aspects of SA. Also, we tried to validate, if this approach can find causes of pilot errors. The results show, that measurement of aspects influencing pilot performance in the experimental tasks was possible. A strong negative correlation of average altitude accordance and error time shows a link between our computational model and performance in the task of low-level flight. Also, the SART results were correlated with the accordance in the flight task. As indicators of pilot errors, statistical outliers such as a pilot missing an enemy air threat were classified correctly. These results indicate, that our system has successfully measured perceptual aspects of SA, which were the dominant factor for performance in the experiment. The confusion matrix shows a high portion of false positives of accordance and error. This is not contradictory to our expectation, since SA can be high when a pilot notices his error. It means that in many cases, a pilot was aware of his altitude while committing an error, which suggests that the participants noticed their error but needed time to adjust. Thus, an adaptive assistance system should respect the pilot working on the solution of a problem.

However, there are also mixed results and limitations of the experimental design. In the threat report task, the response time showed no correlations with measured accordance in the aircrafts position. We assume that response time was not a good SA indicator in our experiment, since some participants were not always eager to answer quickly, and no participant bothered to update his position frequently to answer more quickly. Finally, statistical meaningfulness of the experiment is mitigated by a small number of participants, who were drawn from heterogenous groups (professional vs. unexperienced pilots).

Apart from experimental limitations, the model is based on simplifying assumptions and does not perfectly capture the pilot's perceptual process and mental model, which was obvious in the look-but-failed-to-see situations of threat report. Also, eye-tracking accuracy and precision differed strongly between participants which had a great influence on prediction quality. Finally, the model does not have a good mechanism to observe pilot intuition about the aircraft's altitude, yet. It is obvious, that spatial information such as altitude can be perceived not only by a numerical sensor indication in the HUD but also by the pilots "feeling" and peripheral vision of the course of the terrain.

5   Conclusion and Further Research

In general, our findings support the idea to assess SA based on eye-tracking and the correlations showed a successful operationalization of SA. Beyond conclusions from statistical inference, our system can provide detailed information about the situational context, which is valuable for an adaptive assistance system. In the proposed method, we addressed requirements for on-line SA measurement listed by [10]: we can measure what the pilot knows, what the system state is and merge this data in a SA model. With this model we can specify relevant information and quantify, how accurate the pilot's SA is.

However, the experiment mainly covered the perceptional level and the SA model was specifically designed for the experimental task. Also, results suffered from eye-tracking measurement errors. Therefore, further research will focus on two aspects: estimation of higher levels of SA by a more complex SA model and increasing measurement accuracy.

References

1. Reason, J.: Understanding adverse events: human factors. Qual. Health Care **4**, 80–89 (1995)
2. Endsley, M., Bolte, B., Jones, D.: Designing for Situation Awareness. CRC Press, Boca Raton (2016)
3. Kelly, D., Efthymiou, M.: An analysis of human factors in fifty controlled flight into terrain aviation accidents from 2007 to 2017. J. Safety Res. **69**, 155–165 (2019)
4. Silva, S.S., Hansman, R.J.: Divergence between flight crew mental model and aircraft system state in auto-throttle mode confusion accident and incident cases. J. Cogn. Eng. Decis. Making **9**, 312–328 (2015)
5. Endsley, M.R.: A systematic review and meta-analysis of direct objective measures of situation awareness: a comparison of SAGAT and SPAM. Hum. Factors J. Hum. Factors Ergon. Soc. (2019). https://doi.org/10.1177/0018720819875376
6. Nguyen, T., Lim, C.P., Nguyen, N.D., Gordon-Brown, L., Nahavandi, S.: A review of situation awareness assessment approaches in aviation environments. IEEE Syst. J. **13**, 3590–3603 (2019)
7. Bakdash, J.Z., Marusich, L.R., Cox, K., Geuss, M., Zaroukian, E.: The validity of situation awareness for performance: a meta-analysis. https://psyarxiv.com/kv7n3/. Accessed 24 Jan 2020

8. Kaber, D.B., Prinzel III, L.J., Carolina, N., Prinzel III, L.J., Carolina, N.: Adaptive and adaptable automation design: a critical review of the literature and recommendations for future research. Nasa/Tm-2006-214504 (2006)
9. Salmon, P., Stanton, N., Walker, G., Green, D.: Situation awareness measurement: a review of applicability for C4i environments. Appl. Ergon. **37**, 225–238 (2006)
10. de Winter, J.C.F., Eisma, Y.B., Cabrall, C.D.D., Hancock, P.A., Stanton, N.A.: Situation awareness based on eye movements in relation to the task environment. Cogn. Technol. Work **21**, 99–111 (2018). https://doi.org/10.1007/s10111-018-0527-6
11. van de Merwe, K., van Dijk, H., Zon, R.: Eye movements as an indicator of situation awareness in a flight simulator experiment. Int. J. Aviat. Psychol. **22**, 78–95 (2012)
12. Lounis, C., Peysakhovich, V., Causse, M.: Flight eye tracking assistant (FETA): proof of concept. In: Stanton, N. (ed.) AHFE 2019. AISC, vol. 964, pp. 739–751. Springer, Cham (2020). https://doi.org/10.1007/978-3-030-20503-4_66
13. Fortmann, F., Mengeringhausen, T.: Development and evaluation of an assistant system to aid monitoring behavior during multi-UAV supervisory control: experiences from the D3CoS project. In: ACM International Conference Proceedings Series, pp. 1–8 (2014)
14. Brand, Y., Schulte, A.: Design and evaluation of a workload-adaptive associate system for cockpit crews. In: Harris, D. (ed.) EPCE 2018. LNCS (LNAI), vol. 10906, pp. 3–18. Springer, Cham (2018). https://doi.org/10.1007/978-3-319-91122-9_1
15. Honecker, F., Schulte, A.: Automated online determination of pilot activity under uncertainty by using evidential reasoning. In: Harris, D. (ed.) EPCE 2017. LNCS (LNAI), vol. 10276, pp. 231–250. Springer, Cham (2017). https://doi.org/10.1007/978-3-319-58475-1_18
16. Newman, B.Y.: Inattentional blindness or looking without seeing. Optom.-J. Am. Optom. Assoc. **82**, 505 (2011)

Investigating the Effect of Conflicting Goals and Transparency on Trust and Collaboration in Multi-team Systems

Verena Vogelpohl[✉], Carmen Bruder, Jana Schadow,
and Dirk Schulze Kissing

Department of Aviation and Space Psychology, German Aerospace Center,
Sportallee 54, 22335 Hamburg, Germany
{verena.vogelpohl,carmen.bruder,jana.schadow,
dirk.schulze-kissing}@dlr.de

Abstract. In Air Traffic Management (ATM) multiple teams have to collaborate to achieve efficient and safe operation. Multiple-team operations rely on communication and information sharing between the team members. In this field, multi-team systems (MTSs) are the most common form of organization. The interface between the organizations involved (e.g. air traffic control, cockpit crews, airports) is of central importance. Apart from a common goal, different stakeholders may pursue individual goals governed by their own company culture or policies. Therefore, simply sharing all available information may not be enough to ensure safe and efficient operation. As part of the project ITC (Inter-Team Collaboration), an experimental study with 48 teams of three (n = 144) has just started to investigate the impact that conflicting goals have on communication and collaboration. Additionally, it examines whether and how transparency in roles, processes, and goals can affect performance, communication, and trust in multi-team systems. In the synthetic task environment (STE) ConCenT (Control Center Task Environment), teams of three have to collaborate to detect system failures in time, determine their causes, and decide on a solution in order to ensure successful production processes. Measurements of performance, perceived trust, communication, and gaze data will be analyzed to examine and compare different coordination and communication patterns on a group level. Results of the study will identify factors that may facilitate or hinder collaborative work processes in an MTS, thus enabling the validation of an approach to improve collaboration through transparency and mutual trust.

Keywords: Air traffic management · Collaboration · Communication · Multi-team system · Trust · Transparency

1 Introduction

1.1 Multi-team Systems in Aviation

With the constant change of working conditions and the rapid development of several technical and economic advances, the successful creation of flexible and adaptive organizational structures and processes is becoming more important than ever (Bell and

© Springer Nature Switzerland AG 2020
D. Harris and W.-C. Li (Eds.): HCII 2020, LNAI 12187, pp. 426–440, 2020.
https://doi.org/10.1007/978-3-030-49183-3_33

Kozlowski 2002). It is now commonplace that a great amount of information needs to be organized and distributed between human and technical actors in a sensible way. Especially regarding the fact that work processes are globalized in this day and age, there is the particular challenge of fostering successful collaboration among human actors from different organizations who pursue their respective goals and have their own perspectives on a system (Schulze Kissing et al. 2018). Particularly in aviation, teams from multiple organizations often work together across their organizational boundaries in what is referred to as a multi-team system (MTS). The tasks to be processed are highly dynamic and strongly linked, thus demanding the ability to respond quickly and flexibly to constantly changing conditions (Mathieu et al. 2004; Langan-Fox et al. 2009). Different stakeholders have to come together in short-term teams and collaborate in order to ensure safe and efficient air traffic operation, such as for example the coordination between a cockpit and a team of air traffic controllers on the ground, or like different stakeholders rescheduling the flight plan due to quickly changing conditions (e.g. strikes, thunderstorms) in airport management.

Considering the multiple potentially differing individual goals of each stakeholder, it is a meaningful challenge for the successful collaboration and cooperation of different operators in aviation not to lose sight of the common goal, namely to manage the current and future air traffic efficiently and safely (Keyton et al. 2012; Bienefeld and Grote 2014). In this area, conflicting goals between the parties involved quite often arise and can significantly affect the quality of communication and decision-making, as well as the development of mutual trust while working together. In order to promote efficient collaboration based on trust among operators in multi-team systems, two approaches are promising: providing system-wide information sharing methods and implementing interventions for improving the transparency of roles, processes, and goals.

1.2 Research Project ITC (Inter-Team Collaboration)

Within the European research program SESAR (Single European Sky Air Traffic Management Research), new operational concepts and technical solutions are being developed and implemented using the approach of "collaborative decision-making" (CDM) as a facilitator. These concepts and solutions rely on system-wide information sharing. But with respect to communication, it became apparent that sharing information alone is insufficient for optimizing the collaborative work processes in air traffic management (ATM). In such highly dynamic work environments, where short-term team members work together in a very interdependent manner under time pressure, it is essential to create an atmosphere where the respective roles, processes, and the individual goals of every agent can be made transparent. Goal conflicts and a lack of transparency in roles and decisions may engender distrust, which in turn has the potential to hinder or even prevent successful collaboration and cooperation within a multi-team system.

This study is part of the project ITC, which aims to provide system engineers with tools and concepts for human factors that enable systemic access to the social side of socio-technical systems. Collaborative work processes across organizational boundaries are investigated in order to develop guidelines on how to build up a more flexible and resilient multi-team system in the dynamic environment of ATM. In this context, efficient communication as well as the transparency of different roles, processes, and goals may be of critical importance. The experimental study presented here aims to investigate the impact that conflicting goals have on communication and collaboration. Additionally, it examines whether and how transparency in roles, processes, and goals affects the perception of trust, communication, and performance.

In the following section, relevant theoretical constructs that are linked to the topic of collaboration in multi-team systems will be defined and explained. Subsequently, an experimental study that is currently being conducted at the German Aerospace Center (DLR) will be presented. Following this, the current status of the study as well as further steps and potential implications for future collaboration in ATM will be described and discussed.

2 Background

2.1 Collaboration in Multi-team Systems

When several agents from different areas and organizations in aviation work together in order to plan and coordinate processes collaboratively or make joint decisions, they can also be conceptualized as a multi-team system. A multi-team system is defined as "two or more teams that interface directly and interdependently in response to environmental contingencies toward the accomplishment of collective goals. MTS boundaries are defined by virtue of the fact that all teams within the system, while pursuing different proximal goals, share at least one common distal goal; and in so doing exhibit input, process, and outcome interdependence with at least one other team in the system." (Mathieu et al. 2001). This implies that MTSs consist of outcome-interdependent teams, and that they are smaller than the organizations embedding them. In spite of belonging to different organizations, the team members still have to work together across their organizational boundaries. As a result, these systems often tend to share fewer common values and may have less motivation to work together than (intra-) teams that belong to a single organization (Zaccaro et al. 2012). These same potential problems need to be addressed in systemic human factors analyses in order to improve the current and future collaborative processes in air traffic management. This study focusses on the collaboration between short-term teams from different organizations who work together either remotely in different locations or together in a single control center environment.

Together with various other interpersonal factors (e.g. communication or group psychosocial traits), the collaboration between several stakeholders in order to fulfill a common task can essentially affect the outcomes of teamwork processes (Cohen and Bailey 1997). Effective collaboration and communication include, among other things, the accurate and timely exchange of information, regular performance monitoring, cooperative team orientation, adaptability, as well as trust and cohesion within a team (Owen et al. 2013; Wilson et al. 2007). But collaboration and decision-making processes are rarely ideal (e.g. Doyle and Paton 2017). They are mostly influenced by a variety of factors such as uncertain and dynamic working environments, time constraints, as well as poorly defined or competing goals among the different parties involved (e.g. Doyle and Johnston 2011; Klein 2008). Especially in aviation, multi-team systems often have to make important decisions under time pressure based on an initial subjective assessment of the situation.

In this field, the occurrence of goal conflicts has a great potential to contribute to the development of distrust. Likewise, the differentiation between in-groups and outgroups in multi teams can significantly impair the quality of information exchange, so that information is only shared with intra-team members rather than communicating it to all involved parties (Militello et al. 2007). The resulting lack of transparency in different goals, roles, processes, and decisions during the work can further increase the distrust and fundamentally impair the success of the collaboration and cooperation. On the other hand, trust in teams can have a positive impact on the intention to collaborate and share information between stakeholders (Doyle and Paton 2017). The formation of trust is therefore an essential factor for the successful collaboration of a team and has also been discussed in various studies as a predictor of traditional team effectiveness (for a review, see De Jong et al. 2016; Jahansoozi 2006). The investigation of trust in multi-team systems in particular represents a relatively new aspect of empirical (psychological) research. Since different actors interact and work in a very interdependent manner, the issue of trust within and between different teams becomes more complex (Jones and George 1998).

2.2   Trust and Transparency in Multi-team Systems

Trust is conceptualized as a multidimensional construct (McAllister et al. 2006) and contains a cognitive, an affective, and a behavioral component (Cummings and Bromiley 1996). Trust is important across multiple levels in organizations (Fulmer and Gelfand 2012). It can fundamentally shape the interactions within a team and is able to promote or to limit teamwork, influencing the cohesion, cooperation, coordination, and communication within a team (Holton 2001). Interpersonal trust can be defined as the "willingness of a party to be vulnerable to the actions of another party based on the expectation that the other will perform a particular action important to the trustor, irrespective of the ability to monitor or control that other party" (Mayer et al. 1995). It dynamically develops over time, depending on the attitudes, expectations, and behaviors of the people involved (Holton 2001; Mayer et al. 1995). In early stages of cooperation, trust is described as arising on the basis of cost-benefit analyses (calculus-stage). Later on, other components become more important, such as relying on the transfer of information (knowledge-based trust) or the emergence of trust through empathy and shared values among the team partners (identification-based trust, (Lewicki and Bunker 1996). According to Holton (2001), the individual perception of trustworthiness not only depends on the perception of another person's abilities, but also on the perception that the other will act according to the interests of the person who is allocating trust, as well as on the perception of integrity.

However, not only can trust arise in human-human interactions, but also in human-technology interactions (trust in technology, Bonini 2001). In aviation, trust in technology also plays a crucial role, but human actors are and also will in the future have to communicate with other human actors to coordinate the current and upcoming air traffic. In air traffic control, for example, a system of different agents (air traffic controllers, pilots, technology) works together to ensure safe and efficient air traffic. This can mainly be achieved by exchanging information as well as through the emergence of trust between the various parties. The development of trust in aviation, in turn, depends on the transparency of the different methods of operation as well as on the possibility of anticipating the behavior of the actors involved (Bonini 2001).

In order to generate trust when collaborating in multi-team systems, the establishment of a transparent working environment can be a promising approach. Transparency in work contexts can be understood either as a relationship characteristic or as an environmental condition for organizational processes (Jahansoozi 2006). Organizational transparency has the potential to increase trust and accountability in teams, as well as improve the quality of collaboration and cooperation (Cremer and Dewitte 2002). Jahansoozi (2006) assumed that when there is less trust, the need for transparency increases, which in turn has the potential to increase trust. Various studies found a close relationship between trust and transparency. For example, previous research on traditional teamwork showed that teams with little trust tended to share their information and ideas less frequently (Costa et al. 2001). Similarly, virtual teams tended to be less productive while working together with lower levels of trust (Jarvenpaa et al. 1998). Peters and Karren (2009) assume that virtual teams with a high level of trust, by cooperating and sharing more information with the other team members, were better able to deal with their generally lower shared understanding within the team.

However, the mere exchange of information is not sufficient for successful collaboration within teams or multi-teams. As Keyton et al. (2010) already stated: "Collaboration can only happen through communication." Communication is more than mere information exchange. Communication is multidimensional, highly dynamic, and interdependent. It occurs naturally in socio-technical systems. The method of communication and its dynamics always depend on the situation and the people involved. Different messages can be both explicitly and implicitly transmitted through verbal or non-verbal communication (Cooke and Gorman 2009; Keyton et al. 2010). In order to enable successful cooperation and collaboration between the members of a multi-team, it is necessary that team members have adequate knowledge of the situation, as well as of everyone's intentions, goals, and actions. This method of creating meaning can arise through fruitful communication (Klein et al. 2006; Lewis 2003). Taking into account the previous considerations, promoting trust through transparency and good communication during the collaboration could be a promising approach to building up an efficient, flexible, and resilient multi-team system, despite conflicting goals between the actors involved.

The approach of developing an intervention that is intended to promote a communicative exchange and trust between different team members has already been pursued by Peñarroja et al. (Peñarroja et al. 2015). In that study, it was shown that providing space for reflection and communicative exchange can, especially in early team phases, have a positive impact on the quality and frequency of interactions and on the perception of interpersonal trust. Here, virtual teams had to complete a problem-solving task where they had to collaborate and coordinate their behavior. After each session, the participants received feedback on their plans, their strategies for communication and information sharing, as well as on socio-emotional processes. In the process, each group discussed its strengths and weaknesses in order to develop strategies to improve their cooperation in future sessions. Through the joint elaboration and reflection phases, especially in teams with a higher degree of trust, positive effects on team learning and tasks processing were found. Likewise, Jarvenpaa et al. (1998) developed a training approach intended to increase the perception of trustworthiness in virtual teams by using exercises where information was shared concerning previous behavior and the team member's motives. Virtual teams that participated in these exercises significantly initiated more exchange and responded more often to the other team members. Furthermore, the subjective perception of the skills, integrity, and benevolence of the other team members increased. In another study, Prichard and Ashleigh (Prichard and Ashleigh 2007) found that team training in ad-hoc teams can significantly increase interpersonal trust across all dimensions (i.e. cognitive, affective, behavioral).

2.3   ITC Use Cases for Multi-team Systems in Aviation

The operational concepts and technical solutions of the European research program SESAR already aim to implement the approach of collaborative decision-making in ATM through system-wide information sharing. Various large-scale simulations with experienced operators have been conducted since 2019 in order to validate these methods. Furthermore, the methods presented here will be investigated in the context of three use-cases that have been developed as part of the DLR's contribution to SESAR. The three use cases are, firstly, the Airport Operation Control Center (APOC) for Airport Management, secondly the sector-less, time-based air traffic control, and thirdly the Multiple-Remote-Tower-Center.

In order to gain initial insight into the processes of collaboration in multi-team systems in aviation, APOC case studies were investigated at DLR in Brunswick, Germany (Papenfuß et al. 2017). Real-time simulations with operational experts were conducted (Piekert et al. 2019) for two purposes: on the one hand to test and to validate new technical support systems based on the concept of system-wide information sharing, and on the other hand to measure and analyze the interactions and behaviors of the human actors involved. In a control center environment, all relevant key players of an airport (i.e. stakeholders of an airport, airlines, ground handlers, air traffic controllers) came together to jointly derive and reschedule plans for the current and future air traffic. Here, close cooperation and coordination between the different stakeholders are of vital importance.

Following the simulations, expert workshops were held in order to discuss the experience gained in the APOC scenarios. The following items were jointly identified as important aspects and challenges regarding the processes of collaboration and coordination:

- It was observed that the processes and interactions were dynamically changing during collaboration. The specialized knowledge of each stakeholder was increasingly shared over time and the operators were increasingly able to integrate the existing knowledge of the entire multi-team.
- In the subsequent discussions, it became apparent that the operational experts developed trust in the other stakeholders over time, which was found to be helpful for the team cooperation processes.

- Good communication, knowledge of the different goals and needs of the operators, the opportunity to share and explain information and decision-making processes, as well as the opportunity to involve the other stakeholders in the ongoing processes were also perceived as beneficial.
- A guided debriefing, which took place between each planning session, also led to a subjective improvement in communication and coordination.
- On the other hand, missing or inaccurate information, difficulty understanding the actions of others, and developing trust despite competing goals were perceived as particular challenges for collaboration.

In conclusion, it can be derived that also in multi-team systems in operational practice, where stakeholders with different interests and goals come together and collaborate, the emergence of transparency, interpersonal trust, and good communication within a multi-team seems to be, in addition to the provision of information through technical support systems, of central importance. A promising approach could therefore be the development and implementation of interventions that are able to make various work processes more transparent and create a basis for trust between the operators involved in communication and collaboration.

2.4 Research Questions

Taking the practical conclusions from the investigation of the APOC use case and the theoretical and empirical knowledge and approaches from previous research into account, further exploration of the impact of goal conflicts on communication and collaboration in MTSs turns out to be of central importance in order to build up flexible and resilient multi-team systems in aviation.

Although there is already some research on the relationship between trust, transparency, and communication in both traditional and virtual teams (see Sect. 3.3), research on these processes in multi-teams, where actors with different individual goals need to collaborate, is still underrepresented. This study therefore aims to investigate these relationships during collaboration in short-term multi-team systems with competing goals. Based on the considerations above, it can be assumed that goal conflicts in MTSs could potentially contribute to the development of distrust. As a consequence, our research questions are:

- What effect do goal conflicts have on collaborative processes in Multi-Team Systems (Q1)?
- How do existing goal conflicts affect the development of interpersonal trust (Q2)?
- Based on previous considerations, an intervention promoting transparent and communicative information exchange could be a suitable method to improve the collaborative processes between the actors involved. This leads to the question of whether such an intervention can improve collaborative processes as well as performance and perceived trust in MTSs (Q3).
- In addition, suitable methods for quantifying and describing the processes of collaboration in MTSs need to be compiled and validated (Q4).

3   Method

An experimental study is currently being conducted to examine the influences of goal conflicts and transparency during the collaborative processes of multi-team systems on interpersonal trust, communication, and decision-making under controlled conditions. Together with the findings from the three use cases, the project aims to provide answers to the research questions above as well as to the question of how collaborative work processes in multi-team systems can be successfully designed, measured, and evaluated. The study is being conducted at the German Aerospace Center (DLR) in Hamburg, with a total of 144 participants who are all applicants for aviation professions and took part in selection processes at DLR Hamburg prior to their participation in the study.

3.1   Simulation Tool

The study makes use of a synthetic task environment of a control center, called ConCenT (Control Center Task Environment). It was developed and validated in order to investigate selected requirements for control room operators under controlled conditions (for further information: Bruder et al. 2019; Schulze Kissing and Eißfeldt 2015). ConCent simulates a control center where the production processes of several spatially distributed technical systems (i.e. factories) have to be monitored and controlled. In small groups of three, the participants have to monitor the operational processes and collaborate in order to detect and remedy system failures within a limited time frame. The causes of the system failures must be then determined collaboratively and the participants have to decide on one of two solutions in order to achieve the common goal of ensuring that the operation processes are successful. The specific tasks in ConCent are therefore (1) monitoring distributed operations collectively (monitoring task) with the aim of (2) detecting and reporting malfunctions (detection task), (3) determining their causes (diagnostic task), and (4) correcting the malfunctions by means of joint weighting (remedy task). An example depiction of the testing environment can be seen in Fig. 1.

Fig. 1. Depiction of the Control Center Task Environment (ConCenT)

3.2   Procedure

Three participants were tested in separated rooms or were separated by room dividers to prevent direct contact between the participants. After reading comprehensive instructions and completing several exercises for the ConCenT tasks, teams performed three subsequent test scenarios. Over the course of a scenario, a malfunction occurred at three different times during the monitoring task. Each malfunction had to be reported by every single team member within four seconds. If it was not reported by all members within the four-second interval, the system would automatically switch to the diagnosis task. Finally, they had to decide on their remedy (either to repair or exchange the affected technical system). In each test scenario, each participant is responsible for final decision once; the sequence in which the three participants are in charge differs in each test scenario. Figure 2 provides a schematic illustration of the basic design of the test scenarios.

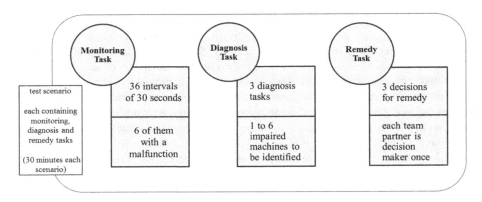

Fig. 2. Schematic illustration of the test scenarios

3.3   Study Design and Transparency Intervention

To examine the effect of conflicting goals, half of the groups work as teams of three and have no conflicting goals (control group), whereas the other half of the teams have to deal with conflicting goals (experimental group). Written instructions introduce the participants to their general roles, tasks, and responsibilities. These instructions differ between the control group and experimental group with regard to their role description and goals. In the control group, the participants are informed that they are part of a team that pursues the common goal of making the best possible decisions for the entire organization. In the experimental group, the three participants work in a multi-team system representing three different organizations and have to deal with a conflict between their own company's goals and the overall goal of the multi-team system in which they all have to work together. In consequence, the participants with conflicting goals have to both successfully handle the production processes and achieve the most beneficial result for their own company. The effect of goal conflict is further enhanced by a bonus system that gives the participants the opportunity to gain additional funds for egoistic or cooperative decisions. Finally, the participants are instructed to support their team (control group) versus their individual organization (experimental group) by detecting, diagnosing, and solving the emerging malfunctions as fast and efficiently as possible and to choose the cheapest solutions.

Derived from the previous findings and based on the experience with the simulation of the APOC use case (see Sect. 2.3), an intervention for a transparent and communicative information exchange was developed and will be validated in this study. It consists of both a moderated exchange of information between the team members and a systematic expansion on the information provided. This means that immediately after the first test scenario of the study, a ten to fifteen-minute, semi-standardized debriefing is conducted for one condition (transparency). Guided by a moderator, the team members are given the opportunity to exchange information and reflect on their respective roles, goals, and previous decision-making processes. In the process, the team members are able to share their role-specific knowledge and experience, to increase trust, and to talk openly about their common tasks, processes, and interactions in order to improve the processes of team collaboration and coordination. Table 1 provides an overview of the different experimental conditions.

Table 1. Overview of the experimental conditions.

Experimental condition	Goal conflicts	No goal conflicts
No transparency	Sample size (n) = 12 no intervention	n = 12 no intervention
Transparency	n = 12 debriefing and introduction of an information window after the first scenario	n = 12 debriefing and introduction of an information window after the first scenario

In order to further achieve greater transparency in the exchange of information, in this condition, a new information window is introduced after the first scenario. It contains additional information on the previous decisions and individual outcomes of the three team members and after each simulation round it appears periodically. In the other condition (no transparency), the participants neither receive an intervention nor additional information through the information window.

3.4 Measurements

In order to examine the various processes of collaboration, data on performance, eye gaze, and communication are being collected. Statistical comparisons between the different conditions (goal conflict, transparency) will be calculated. Table 2 provides an overview of the dependent variables and their measurements. From a multidimensional view, the data is gathered on both an individual and a group level and will be analyzed on a group level.

Table 2. Overview of the dependent variables and measurements.

Dependent variable	Measurement (per task and team)
Task performance	
Accuracy	Number of malfunctions detected Number of diagnoses performed correctly Remedy decisions made
Processing duration	Time needed to perform monitoring, diagnosis, and remedy tasks
Subjective ratings	
Personality	NEO-FFI (Costa Jr and McCrae 2008)
Interpersonal trust	Interpersonal trust scale (Costa and Anderson 2011)
Oral communication, i.a.	
Accuracy	Number of speech units containing false and correct information
Efficiency	Time needed for communication
Transparency	Number of shared intentions, decisions, and conclusions
Eye tracking data, i.a.	
Gaze pattern	Gaze recurrence quantification analysis (Zbilut 2007)

Performance measures include the number of correct and false actions, decisions made in the remedy task, and response times in seconds. The oral communication between the team members is recorded and timestamps for each speech unit are logged in the ConCenT file. Based in this, oral communication will be analyzed with respect to the accuracy, efficiency, and transparency when sharing intentions, conclusions, and decisions. In order to check potential confounding variables, personality is also collected using NEO-FFI. Interpersonal trust is assessed by means of the Interpersonal trust scale (Costa and Anderson 2011).

Eye gazes are recorded with the Eye Tracking System manufactured by LC Technologies, Inc. The raw data is managed using NYAN software. The system operates at 120 Hz and is combined with the simulation tool ConCenT to ensure that both systems use the same timestamp. Gaze data is collected at the individual level and will be analyzed on the group level. Analyzing the gaze patterns of teams under different conditions by means of recurrence quantification analysis is a promising approach to understanding the emergence of coordination in dyads, and even in small groups (see also Schulze Kissing and Bruder 2016). For this purpose, a method for analyzing eye-movement patterns in cooperating people is used (Recurrence Quantification Analysis, Zbilut 2007). This method was already tested in a previous DLR study designed to investigate collaboration and communication in teams (Schulze Kissing and Bruder 2017).

This enables the potential influences of transparency and trust during coordination and collaboration in multi-teams to be examined and compared from a multidimensional perspective.

4   Status Quo and Further Steps

At present, the study is being conducted at DLR Hamburg and expected to run until December 2020. Data concerning performance, communication, and eye gaze are being collected on an individual basis as well as on the group level. Following this, various statistical tests, correlations, and comparisons between the conditions will be carried out on a group level to examine the influence of goal conflicts on MTS communication and collaboration from a multidimensional view. Likewise, the effect that transparency regarding roles, processes, and goals has on communication, performance, and perceived trust will be analyzed. Moreover, the intervention that aims to promote communicative and transparent exchange of information while working as a team will be validated.

As the project ITC progresses, data from the large-scale simulations of other use cases involving operational experts – namely the Multiple-Remote-Tower center (Papenfuss and Friedrich 2016) and sector-less, time-based air traffic control (Capiot and Korn 2019) – will be analyzed and related to the findings of this study. These use cases have been developed as part of the DLR contribution to the European research program SESAR in order to support and optimize the processes of collaboration and decision-making in multi-team systems in aviation. Here, the interactions, as well as performance, communication, and eye gaze data have been gathered and will be analyzed. The integrated results of the various studies will then be discussed, with the aim of deriving appropriate guidelines and measures to improve MTS collaboration processes.

Not only despite, but also due to the constant development of technical systems in an increasingly globalized work environment, it is necessary to continue considering the social nature of the group processes involved in teamwork. Together with the findings from the real-time simulations with operational experts, this study will provide answers to the question of how collaborative MTS work processes can best be designed, measured, and evaluated. By combining the analysis of communication and gaze data, as well as performance measurements, this study will provide different methods to describe and quantify collaborative processes at a group level from a multidimensional viewpoint. Factors that have the potential to either promote or impair the collaborative MTS work processes can be identified and addressed.

Moreover, the study examines and validates an approach to improving MTS collaboration by enhancing transparency and mutual trust through communicative exchange. Based on the results, different behavioral norms and interventions can be developed and optimized to support the development of trust and collaborative decision-making in (short-term) multi-team systems. Appropriate interventions and methods can be pursued in order to further ensure efficient and safe coordination processes in current and future air traffic. As a result, existing obstacles arising from rivalries or conflicting goals during collaboration can be reduced or even prevented.

References

Bell, B.S., Kozlowski, S.W.: A typology of virtual teams: Implications for effective leadership. Group Organ. Manage. **27**(1), 14–49 (2002)

Bienefeld, N., Grote, G.: Speaking up in ad hoc multiteam systems: Individual-level effects of psychological safety, status, and leadership within and across teams. Eur. J. Work Organ. Psych. **23**(6), 930–945 (2014)

Bonini, D.: ATC do I trust thee?: referents of trust in air traffic control. In: CHI 2001 Extended Abstracts on Human Factors in Computing Systems, pp. 449–450. ACM (2001)

Bruder, C., Schadow, J., Schulze Kissing, D.: Oral communication as a performance indicator in control rooms. In: Proceedings of the 33rd Conference of the European Association for Aviation Psychology. European Association for Aviation Psychology, pp. 133–147 (2019)

Capiot, K., Korn, B.: Cognitive work analysis of the sectorless ATM concept with the Introduction of Teams. In: 38th Digital Avionics Systems Conference, DASC 2019 (2019)

Cohen, S.G., Bailey, D.E.: What makes teams work: group effectiveness research from the shop floor to the executive suite. J. Manage. **23**(3), 239–290 (1997)

Cooke, N.J., Gorman, J.C.: Interaction-based measures of cognitive systems. J. Cogn. Eng. Decis. Making **3**(1), 27–46 (2009)

Costa, A.C., Anderson, N.: Measuring trust in teams: Development and validation of a multifaceted measure of formative and reflective indicators of team trust. Eur. J. Work Organ. Psychol. **20**(1), 119–154 (2011)

Costa, A.C., Roe, R.A., Taillieu, T.: Trust within teams: the relation with performance effectiveness. Eur. J. Work Organ. Psychol. **10**(3), 225–244 (2001)

Costa Jr., P.T., McCrae, R.R.: The Revised NEO Personality Inventory (NEO-PI-R). Sage Publications, Inc., Thousand Oaks (2008)

Cremer, D., Dewitte, S.: Effect of trust and accountability in mixed-motive situations. J. Soc. Psychol. **142**(4), 541–543 (2002)

Cummings, L.L., Bromiley, P.: The organizational trust inventory (OTI). In: Trust in organizations: Frontiers of theory and research, vol. 302, no. 330, pp. 39–52 (1996)

De Jong, B.A., Dirks, K.T., Gillespie, N.: Trust and team performance: a meta-analysis of main effects, moderators, and covariates. J. Appl. Psychol. **101**(8), 1134 (2016)

Doyle, E.H., Johnston, D.: Science advice for critical decision-making. In: Charles, C. (ed.) Working in high risk environments: developing sustained resilience, pp. 69–92 (2011)

Doyle, Emma E.H., Paton, D.: Decision-making: preventing miscommunication and creating shared meaning between stakeholders. In: Fearnley, Carina J., Bird, Deanne K., Haynes, K., McGuire, William J., Jolly, G. (eds.) Observing the Volcano World. AV, pp. 549–570. Springer, Cham (2017). https://doi.org/10.1007/11157_2016_31

Fulmer, C.A., Gelfand, M.J.: At what level (and in whom) we trust: trust across multiple organizational levels. J. Manage. **38**(4), 1167–1230 (2012)

Holton, J.A.: Building trust and collaboration in a virtual team. Team Perform. Manage. Int. J. **7**(3/4), 36–47 (2001)

Jahansoozi, J.: Organization-stakeholder relationships: Exploring trust and transparency. J. Manage. Dev. **25**(10), 942–955 (2006)

Jarvenpaa, S.L., Knoll, K., Leidner, D.E.: Is anybody out there? Antecedents of trust in global virtual teams. J. Manage. Inf. Syst. **14**(4), 29–64 (1998)

Jones, G.R., George, J.M.: The experience and evolution of trust: implications for cooperation and teamwork. Acad. Manage. Rev. **23**(3), 531–546 (1998)

Keyton, J., Beck, S.J., Asbury, M.B.: Macrocognition: a communication perspective. Theor. Issues Ergon. Sci. **11**(4), 272–286 (2010)

Keyton, J., Ford, D.J., Smith, F.L.: Communication, collaboration, and identification as facilitators and constraints of multiteam systems. In: Multiteam Systems. Routledge, pp. 186–203 (2012)

Klein, G.: Naturalistic decision making. Hum. Factors **50**(3), 456–460 (2008)

Klein, G., Moon, B., Hoffman, R.R.: Making sense of sensemaking 2: A macrocognitive model. IEEE Intell. Syst. **21**(5), 88–92 (2006)

Langan-Fox, J., Canty, J.M., Sankey, M.J.: Human–automation teams and adaptable control for future air traffic management. Int. J. Ind. Ergon. **39**(5), 894–903 (2009)

Lewicki, R.J., Bunker, B.B.: Developing and maintaining trust in work relationships. In: Trust in Organizations: Frontiers of Theory and Research, vol. 114, 139 (1996)

Lewis, K.: Measuring transactive memory systems in the field: scale development and validation. J. Appl. Psychol. **88**(4), 587 (2003)

Mathieu, J., Marks, M.A., Zaccaro, S.J.: Multi-team systems. In: International Handbook of Work and Organizational Psychology, vol. 2, no. 2 (2001)

Mathieu, J.E., Cobb, M., Marks, M.A., Zaccaro, S.J., Marsh, S.: Multi-team ACES: A research platform for studying multi-team systems. Scaled worlds: Development, validation and applications, pp. 297–315 (2004)

Mayer, R.C., Davis, J.H., Schoorman, F.D.: An integrative model of organizational trust. Acad. Manage. Rev. **20**(3), 709–734 (1995)

McAllister, D.J., Lewicki, R.J., Chaturvedi, S.: Trust in developing relationships: from theory to measurement. In: Academy of Management Proceedings, vol. 1, pp. G1–G6. Academy of Management Briarcliff Manor, NY 10510 (2006)

Militello, L.G., Patterson, E.S., Bowman, L., Wears, R.: Information flow during crisis management: challenges to coordination in the emergency operations center. Cogn. Technol. Work **9**(1), 25–31 (2007)

Owen, C., Bearman, C., Brooks, B., Chapman, J., Paton, D., Hossain, L.: Developing a research framework for complex multi–team coordination in emergency management. Int. J. Emergency Manage. **9**(1), 1–17 (2013)

Papenfuß, A., Carstengerdes, N., Schier, S., Günther, Y.: What to say when: guidelines for decision making. an evaluation of a concept for cooperation in an APOC. In: Proceedings of the 12th USA/Europe Air Traffic Management Research and Development Seminar, ATM 2017 (2017)

Papenfuss, A., Friedrich, M.: Head up only—a design concept to enable multiple remote tower operations. In: IEEE/AIAA 35th Digital Avionics Systems Conference (DASC) 2016, pp. 1–10. IEEE (2016)

Peñarroja, V., Orengo, V., Zornoza, A., Sánchez, J., Ripoll, P.: How team feedback and team trust influence information processing and learning in virtual teams: a moderated mediation model. Comput. Hum. Behav. **48**, 9–16 (2015)

Peters, L., Karren, R.J.: An examination of the roles of trust and functional diversity on virtual team performance ratings. Group Organ. Manage. **34**(4), 479–504 (2009)

Piekert, F., Carstengerdes, N., Suikat, R.: Dealing with adverse weather conditions by enhanced collaborative secision making in a TAM APOC. In: 6th ENRI International Workshop on ATM/CNS. Tokyo, Japan, 29–31 September 2019

Prichard, J.S., Ashleigh, M.J.: The effects of team-skills training on transactive memory and performance. Small Group Res. **38**(6), 696–726 (2007)

Schulze Kissing, D., Bruder, C., Carstengerdes, N., Papenfuss, A.: Making multi-team systems more adaptable by enhancing transactive memory system structures – the case of CDM in APOC. In: Ahram, T., Karwowski, W., Taiar, R. (eds.) IHSED 2018. AISC, vol. 876, pp. 215–220. Springer, Cham (2018). https://doi.org/10.1007/978-3-030-02053-8_33

Schulze Kissing, D., Bruder, C.: Der Einsatz Synthetischer Aufgabenumgebungen zur Untersuchung kollaborativer Prozesse in Leitzentralen am Beispiel der" generic Control Center Task Environment" (ConCenT). Kognitive Systeme 2016 (2016)

Schulze Kissing, D., Bruder, C.: Interactive team cognition: do gaze data also tell the story? In: 19th International Symposium on Aviation Psychology, p. 512 (2017)

Schulze Kissing, D., Eißfeldt, H.: ConCenT: Eine Simulationsplattform zur Untersuchung kollaborativer Entscheidungsprozessse in Leitzentralen. DGLR-Bericht **01**, 157–170 (2015)

Wilson, K.A., Salas, E., Priest, H.A., Andrews, D.: Errors in the heat of battle: Taking a closer look at shared cognition breakdowns through teamwork. Hum. Factors **49**(2), 243–256 (2007)

Zaccaro, S.J., Marks, M.A., DeChurch, L.A.: Multiteam systems: an introduction. In: Multiteam Systems, pp. 18–47. Routledge (2012)

Zbilut, J.P.: Recurrence quantification analysis: Introduction and historical context. Int. J. Bifurcat. Chaos **17**(10), 3477–3481 (2007)

Usability Evaluation of Car Cockpit Based on Multiple Objective Measures

Chuanxiang Wei, Zhen Wang$^{(\boxtimes)}$, and Shan Fu

School of Electronic Information and Electrical Engineering,
Shanghai Jiao Tong University, Shanghai, People's Republic of China
b2wz@sjtu.edu.cn

Abstract. With the development of science and technology, many new human-machine interaction methods have appeared in cars. Therefore, how to improve the interaction efficiency in human-machine interaction has become one of the important research topics. Our research focuses on the interaction between car cockpit and driver. To make a usability evaluation of car cockpit, we designed multiple sets of comparative experiments with different concurrent tasks. In the experiment, we collected front scene binocular image and car speed to calculate driving performance, driver's heart rate and eye movement to represent driver's physiological state. Specifically, for front scene analysis, we simplified the feature point matching method and obtained quite accurate object distance estimation. Experimental data showed that car speed was closer to the required speed in speed control task than speed + direction control task or speed + temperature control task; distance was adjusted better in distance control task than distance + temperature control task; driver's heart rate was higher and has more fluctuation during the operation of secondary tasks; driver diverted their visual attention from the road to inside instruments more frequently during manual control than voice control. These results indicate when the task is more difficult or there is interference from secondary task, the driving performance would decrease and driver would be more stressed. And manual control task is more disruptive to driving performance than voice control task, but it takes more time. Finally, driving will be safer and more effective when using voice control instead of manual control.

Keywords: Usability · Stereo matching · Driving performance · Physiological state

1 Introduction

With the development of the times, the rapid innovation of technology in human life has prompted humans to seek to liberate themselves from the environment [2]. It also helps humans enhance the ability to adapt to the environment with the help of external devices. Therefore, various human-computer interaction technologies have emerged. Human-computer interaction technology occupies an important position in human society because it plays a channel of information exchange between humans and machines.

D. Harris and W.-C. Li (Eds.): HCII 2020, LNAI 12187, pp. 441–453, 2020.
https://doi.org/10.1007/978-3-030-49183-3_34

In human-machine systems, our goals include safety, efficiency, comfort, etc. [1] therefore, how to improve the interaction efficiency and reduce operational errors in human-machine interaction has become one of the important research topics. Ergonomics is just a science that studies the interaction between human, machine and environment and its reasonable combination. And its goal is to make the designed machine and environment system fit for people's physiological and psychological characteristics, in addition, improve efficiency, safety, health and comfort in production. In this paper, our research object is the cockpit of a car. The final purpose is to make a usability evaluation of the car cockpit and this evaluation can help companies produce more human-friendly car cockpits.

In order to realize the usability evaluation, we need to explore how does the driver's driving performance, behavioral response and physiological state change when he encounters different traffic conditions. The driving performance is evaluated by the binocular camera system. Behavioral response and physiological state of the driver are obtained by the heart rate and respiration rate measuring equipment and head-mounted eye tracking system.

The focus and innovation of our work are on image stereo matching whose result is used to obtain quite accurate object distance estimation under different task scenarios. Currently, image stereo matching algorithms are divided into two categories [3]: blocking matching algorithm [8] based on grayscale and feature point matching algorithm [5]. Compared with the two kinds of methods, the feature point matching algorithm has the advantages of small computation, good robustness, and insensitivity to image deformation [4], so in this paper, the method we used is just the feature point matching algorithm. Feature point matching algorithm mainly includes three steps: feature extraction, feature description and feature matching [9]. It first extracts the features of the image, regenerates them into feature descriptors, and finally matches the features of the two images according to the similarity of the descriptors [7].

2   Method

In order to realize the usability evaluation, we need to explore how does the driver's driving performance, behavioral response and physiological state change when he encounters different traffic conditions. After completing the experiment, in each group, we can get such experimental data: a group of images taken by a binocular camera during the experiment, drivers' heart rate, eye movement track characteristics, and the speed of the car from GPS. The processing of these data is shown as follow:

2.1   Image Stereo Calibration and Rectification

In the process of image measurement and machine vision applications, the process of solving parameters (internal parameters, external parameters) is called camera calibration. Through Zhang [10] we can get the relationship between the coordinates of a point in space in the world coordinate system and the coordinates in the pixel coordinate system are as follows:

$$s \begin{bmatrix} u \\ v \\ 1 \end{bmatrix} = K_{3 \times 4} \cdot \begin{bmatrix} R & T \\ O & 1 \end{bmatrix} \cdot \begin{bmatrix} X_w \\ Y_w \\ Z_w \\ 1 \end{bmatrix} \tag{1}$$

Where (u, v) is the coordinate in the pixel coordinate system, (X_w, Y_w, Z_w) is the coordinate in the world coordinate system, $K_{3 \times 4}$ is the internal parameter matrix, it has five internal parameters; $\begin{bmatrix} R & T \\ O & 1 \end{bmatrix}$ is the external parameter matrix, and $s = 1/Z_c$ is an unknown scale factor.

A perfectly aligned configuration is rare with a real stereo system, since the two cameras almost never have exactly coplanar, row-aligned imaging planes. And the goal of stereo rectification [16] is projecting the image planes of our two cameras so that they reside in the exact same plane, with image rows perfectly aligned into a frontal parallel configuration.

2.2 Disparity Calculation

We know that the object has obvious color changes at the boundary [13], so we choose the feature of gradient to select the feature point. First, calculate the gradient in the horizontal direction using the following formula:

$$grad(x, y) = Gray(x + 1, y) - Gray(x - 1, y) \tag{2}$$

After calculating the gradient values of all pixels in the image, a threshold value τ is set, and all points with gradient values greater than the threshold value are marked as feature points.

After obtaining the feature points of the left and right images, the next step is to match the feature points. According to the positional relationship between the two cameras, we know that the position of any spatial point in the left camera image is always to the right of the position in the right camera image [14]. The cost function that reflects the similarity of the two feature points contains two parts. One is the sum of the absolute values of the corresponding gradient differences in the $1 * 5$ pixel interval with the feature points as the center; the other is the sum of the absolute values of the corresponding gray level differences in the $1 * 5$ pixel interval with the feature points as the center. Formulated as:

$$C(i, i_l) = {}_{k=-2}^{2}\Sigma(\min(||I(i + k) - I'(i_l + k)||, \tau_1) + \min(||grad(i + k) - grad'(i_l + k)||, \tau_2)) \tag{3}$$

Where i refers to the position of the feature point on the left camera image, i_l refers to the position of the feature point on the right camera image with a relative disparity of l, τ_1 and τ_2 are two truncated data. When the cost function reaches the minimum the feature point is the matching point. After feature point matching, the disparity d of these feature point pairs can be obtained.

2.3   Point Cloud Generating and Refinement

According to the principle of small hole imaging:

$$\frac{f}{Z} = \frac{d}{T} = \frac{x}{X} = \frac{y}{Y} \tag{4}$$

Where f is the focal length, T is the distance between the two optical centers, and they can be obtained after Camera Calibration, d is the disparity, (x, y) is the feature point's coordinate in the left camera image coordinate system, (X, Y, Z) is the three-dimensional actual coordinate of the feature point in the camera coordinate system, and so you can get the actual coordinate as:

$$\begin{cases} X = \frac{T \cdot x}{d} \\ Y = \frac{T \cdot y}{d} \\ Z = \frac{T \cdot f}{d} \end{cases} \tag{5}$$

A sparse point cloud of feature points can be generated (see Fig. 1)

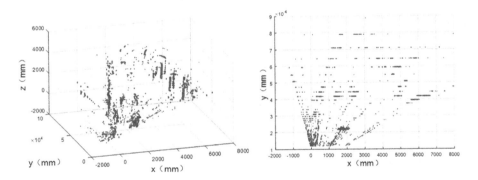

Fig. 1. Sparse point cloud of feature points (left image is a 3D view; right image is a top view)

From the point cloud, we can find two problems: the point cloud presents a distinct layered structure, and there are a lot of mismatches during the matching process.

The reason for point cloud layering is that the disparity value obtained by the above matching algorithm is the integer pixel accuracy. In order to obtain higher subpixel accuracy, further subpixel refinement of the disparity value is required.

Mismatches seriously affect target recognition [15], so we remove mismatches in three steps:

1. Filtering: we noticed that the point cloud distribution of the feature points on the target is often dense, and the mismatched feature points will be scattered to the unknown space area. Under this condition, we can remove the sparse feature point set based on the density of the point cloud.

2. Feature points enhancement: when the continuous feature point set is too dense, it will have a certain degree of impact on the subsequent matching results. Therefore, we can enhance a feature point set where the feature points are dense to a feature point.
3. Sorting feature points: feature point matching is to find the matching points of the feature points on the left image along the polar direction, and the feature points on the left image have the order of the coordinates. Therefore, the coordinates of the matching points in the right image obtained via the matching should also be ordered. With this condition, we can remove some matching points that do not meet the ordering.

2.4   Clustering

After removing the mismatch points on the point cloud, we can obtain relatively accurate sparse point cloud results. The next thing to do is to segment each target in the point cloud. As can be seen from the above point cloud, the points where the target is located is often concentrated, so the clustering algorithm can be used to complete the target detection and segmentation.

Commonly used clustering algorithms are K-means algorithm [18], DBSCAN algorithm [17], etc. The K-means algorithm requires knowing the number of data containing classes in advance, which obviously cannot be applied to our scenario. The DBSCAN Algorithm is a density-based clustering algorithm that fits well with the characteristics of our point cloud data and does not require the number of classes contained in the data to be known in advance. Therefore, we use the DBSCAN clustering algorithm. Figure 2 shows the clustering result.

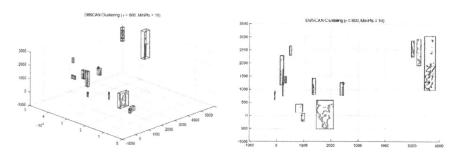

Fig. 2. The clustering result (left image is a 3D view, right image is a top view)

2.5   Timestamp Synchronization

In the experiment, we use distributed acquisition and timestamp synchronization technology. So we can configure flexibly and avoid system crash caused by single device failure. For the sampling timestamp got after clock synchronization, we should match the timestamp of each data file and combine them into one file. Based on a reasonable preset frequency f_p, perform downsampling on data with a frequency higher than f_p, and interpolation on data with a frequency lower than f_p.

3 Experiment

3.1 Experiment Design

In our comparative experiments, the driver should accomplish tasks on different experimental scenarios to induce different behaviors and state of drivers. We divide experimental tasks into primary tasks and secondary tasks. There are three sets of experiments. The primary task of experiment one is maintaining the same distance from the car in front (Distance Control), the primary task of experiment two is maintaining the same speed while driving on straight road (Speed Control), and the primary task of experiment three is maintaining the same speed while driving on winding road (Speed and Direction Control). Three experiments have the same secondary tasks, they are none, manual control of air-conditioning temperature and voice-control of air-conditioning temperature.

3.2 Participants and Apparatus

In this experiment, the main equipment we need includes one binocular camera for images collecting, some portable computers, one heart rate measuring equipment, one head-mounted eye tracking equipment and a car mounted GPS (see Fig. 3).

We invite three drivers to participate in this experiment. They all study or work at Shanghai Jiao Tong University. And they all have good vision and driver's licenses.

Fig. 3. Apparatus needed in this experiment

3.3 Procedure and Data Collection

The whole experiment procedure is as follows:

1. Equip all equipment: installing the binocular camera, GPS module, driving recorder; wearing the heart rate watch and eye tracker for driver.
2. Synchronize time: synchronize the system time of all computers to this time server via the local area network.
3. Start the data acquisition program: after the driver is informed of the experimental process and is ready, starting the acquisition programs of all devices.
4. Start experiment one: the primary task is maintaining distance from the car in front. Meanwhile, perform the following secondary tasks sequentially.
    a. None.
    b. Manually adjust the temperature of the air conditioner several times.
    c. Adjust the temperature of the air conditioner several times using voice.
5. Start experiment two: the primary task is maintaining speed while driving on a straight road at 20 km/h. Meanwhile, perform the following secondary tasks sequentially.
    a. None.
    b. Manually adjust the temperature of the air conditioner several times.
    c. Adjust the temperature of the air conditioner several times using voice.
6. Start experiment three: the primary task is maintaining speed while driving on a winding road at 20 km/h. Meanwhile, perform the following secondary tasks sequentially.
    a. None.
    b. Manually adjust the temperature of the air conditioner several times.
    c. Adjust the temperature of the air conditioner several times using voice.
7. Terminate the data acquisition program: terminate all data acquisition programs and place all data in a folder named after the driver's name and date.
8. Change driver: change the next driver and repeat the above steps.

4 Result

After completing the data processing according to the above method, in each group of experiments, we can get the driving performance via image processing and driving recorder. Plotting the heart and respiration rate curves over time can help us analyze drivers' psychology state. Eye movement tracker can record the track characteristics of human eye movement when processing visual information. After processing these data, we can get the following results:

Figure 4 shows a comparison of driving performance under different primary task conditions.

Figure 5 shows a comparison of drivers' psychology state under different primary task conditions.

Figure 6 and Fig. 7 shows a comparison of driving performance under different secondary task conditions.

Figure 8 and Fig. 9 shows how does the driving performance change in experiment one under secondary task conditions.

Figure 10 shows how car speed and eyes gazing area change over time in experiment two with manual control task.

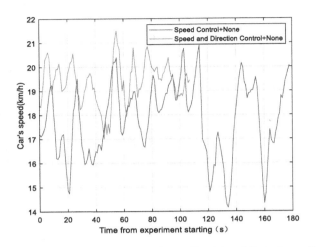

Fig. 4. Car's speed over time in Experiment Two(a) and Experiment Three(a)

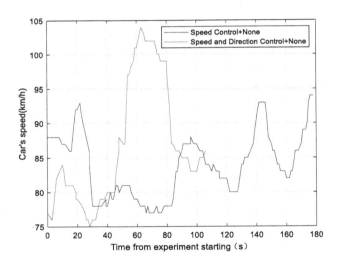

Fig. 5. Driver's heart rate over time in Experiment Two(a) and Experiment Three(a)

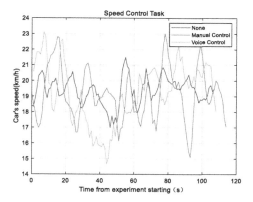

Fig. 6. Car's speed over time in speed control task

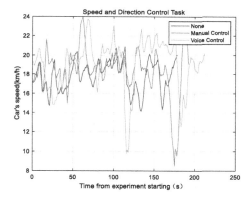

Fig. 7. Car's speed over time in speed and direction control task

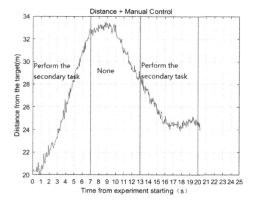

Fig. 8. Distance from the target over time in distance and manual control task

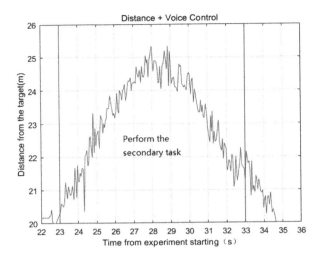

Fig. 9. Distance from the target over time in distance and voice control task

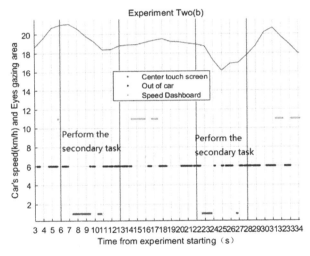

Fig. 10. Car's speed and eyes gazing area over time in speed and manual control

5   Discussion

As can be seen from Fig. 4, car speed in experiment 2 is closer to 20 km/h and it has less discrete. Calculation results show the average speed of the car in Experiment 2 is 19.4 km/h, and the standard deviation is 0.878; while the average speed of the car in Experiment 3 is 17.8 km/h, and the standard deviation is 1.527. Calculation results prove driving performance in experiment 2 is better, in other words, the driver's driving performance is better at lower task difficulty, this result conforms to common sense in our cognition.

As can be seen roughly from Fig. 5, driver's heart rate in experiment 2 is lower and smoother. Calculation results show the average heart rate of the driver in Experiment 2 is 83.9, and the standard deviation is 4.68; while the heart rate of the driver in Experiment 3 is 86.8, and the standard deviation is 9.02. Calculation results prove heart rate in experiment 2 is really lower and smoother, in other words, the driver is more relaxed at lower task difficulty, this result conforms to common sense in our cognition.

In Fig. 6 and Fig. 7, the secondary tasks of both experiment 2 and experiment 3 are none, manual control of airconditioning temperature and voice-control of air-conditioning temperature. Obviously, the driver needs to allocate more attention to complete the required tasks in experiment 2/3. We can think that these two sets of experiments were interrupted by secondary tasks. As can be seen from Fig. 6 and Fig. 7, car speed in experiment 2(a) with no secondary task is closer to 20 km/h and it has less discrete. Calculation results are shown in Table 1:

Table 1. Average speed and standard deviation in experiment 2/3

Primary task	Secondary task	Average speed (km/h)	Standard deviation
Speed control	None	19.4	0.878
	Manual control	19.1	1.675
	Voice control	19.2	1.905
Speed and direction control	None	17.8	1.526
	Manual control	18.4	2.409
	Voice control	19.1	2.616

Calculation results prove driving performance in experiment(a) is better than experiment(b), (c), and it is more obvious in experiment 2 than experiment 3. So we can get the conclusion that the driver's driving performance is better at no secondary tasks, but this comparison is less obvious when the primary task is more complicated. This result also conforms to common sense in our cognition.

In Fig. 8 and Fig. 9, the secondary tasks in experiment 1(b) and (c) are manual control of airconditioning temperature and voice-control of air-conditioning tempera-ture. And the car's distance from the target represents the drive performance. In Fig. 8, the secondary task is manual control, we can find that in the time period of 0–7 s in which the driver performs the manual control, the distance increases sharply from 20 m to 32.6 m; in the time period of 7–13 s with no secondary task, the distance decreases gradually; in the time period of 13–20 s with another manual control task, the distance decreases at the former period's descent rate. We can realize when performing the manual control, the driver's most attention is paid on completing the secondary task, so the drive performance would become extremely poor. In Fig. 9, the secondary task is voice-control, we can find in the performing period, the distance is constantly adjusted. Because when performing voice-control, driver doesn't need to look at the touchpad and have more attention to complete the primary task compared with performing manual control. This comparison shows it is safer and more effective using voice-control instead of manual control.

In Fig. 10, the secondary task is manual control of airconditioning temperature. In the time period of 6–12 s and 22–28 s, driver performs manual control. We can find from both periods that when the task begins, the driver's eyes gaze at the center touch screen to complete the manual control. And in the meanwhile, the car's speed decreases rapidly because driver's most attention is paid on secondary task. After finishing manual control, the car's speed is corrected again.

Another result in experiment is that the average time taken in manual control tasks is 14.91 s, and the average time taken in voice control tasks is 7.83 s. Obviously, using voice control takes less time.

6 Conclusion

From all experiment results, we can get conclusions as follow:

1. The higher the difficulty of the primary task, the lower the driving performance, and driver's emotions will be more intense.
2. When there is interference from secondary tasks, driving performance will also become lower.
3. Manual control tasks are more disruptive to driving performance than voice-control tasks.
4. Manual control tasks take more time than voice-control tasks.
5. While performing secondary tasks, driver's attention paid on primary task would be reduced, so the drive performance would be lower.

References

1. Patel, B.N., Rosenberg, L., Willcox, G., et al.: Human–machine partnership with artificial intelligence for chest radiograph diagnosis. NPJ Digit. Med. **2**(1), 1–10 (2019)
2. Zhang, S., Lu, Y., Fu, S.: Recognition of the cognitive state in the visual search task. In: Ayaz, H. (ed.) AHFE 2019. AISC, vol. 953, pp. 363–372. Springer, Cham (2020). https://doi.org/10.1007/978-3-030-20473-0_35
3. Scharstein, D., Szeliski, R.: A taxonomy and evaluation of dense two-frame stereo correspondence algorithms. Int. J. Comput. Vis. **47**, 7–42 (2002). https://doi.org/10.1023/A:1014573219977
4. Zhang, K., Fang, Y., Min, D., et al.: Cross-scale cost aggregation for stereo matching. In: Proceedings of the IEEE Conference on Computer Vision and Pattern Recognition, pp. 1590–1597. IEEE (2014)
5. Liu, C., Yuen, J., Torralba, A.: SIFT flow: dense correspondence across scenes and its applications. TPAMI **33**(5), 978–994 (2011)
6. Mei, X., Sun, X., Dong, W., Wang, H., Zhang, X.: Segment-tree based cost aggregation for stereo matching. In: CVPR, pp. 313–320. IEEE (2013)
7. Rhemann, C., Hosni, A., Bleyer, M., Rother, C., Gelautz, M.: Fast cost-volume filtering for visual correspondence and beyond. In: CVPR, pp. 504–511. IEEE (2011)

8. Wang, Z.-F., Zheng, Z.-G.: A region based stereo matching algorithm using cooperative optimization. In: CVPR, pp. 1–8. IEEE (2008)
9. Yang, Q., Wang, L., Yang, R., Stewénius, H., Nistér, D.: Stereo matching with color-weighted correlation, hierarchical belief propagation, and occlusion handling. TPAMI **31**(3), 492–504 (2008)
10. Zhang, Z.: A flexible new technique for camera calibration. TPAMI **22**(11), 1330–1334 (2000)
11. Ma, L., Li, J., Ma, J., et al.: A modified census transform based on the neighborhood information for stereo matching algorithm. In: 2013 Seventh International Conference on Image and Graphics. pp. 533–538. IEEE (2013)
12. Calonder, M., Lepetit, V., Strecha, C., Fua, P.: BRIEF: binary robust independent elementary features. In: Daniilidis, K., Maragos, P., Paragios, N. (eds.) ECCV 2010. LNCS, vol. 6314, pp. 778–792. Springer, Heidelberg (2010). https://doi.org/10.1007/978-3-642-15561-1_56
13. Hirschmuller, H., Scharstein, D.: Evaluation of cost functions for stereo matching. In: IEEE Conference on Computer Vision and Pattern Recognition, pp. 1–8. IEEE (2007)
14. Ok, S.-H., Shim, J.H., Moon, B.: Modified adaptive support weight and disparity search range estimation schemes for stereo matching processors. J. Supercomput. **74**(12), 6665–6690 (2017). https://doi.org/10.1007/s11227-017-2058-y
15. Choi, N., Jang, J., Paik, J.: Illuminant-invariant stereo matching using cost volume and confidence-based disparity refinement. JOSA A **36**(10), 1768–1776 (2019)
16. Kumar, S., Micheloni, C., Piciarelli, C., et al.: Stereo rectification of uncalibrated and heterogeneous images. Pattern Recogn. Lett. **31**(11), 1445–1452 (2010)
17. Tran, T.N., Drab, K., Daszykowski, M.: Revised DBSCAN algorithm to cluster data with dense adjacent clusters. Chemometr. Intell. Lab. Syst. **120**, 92–96 (2013)
18. Arunkumar, N., et al.: K-Means clustering and neural network for object detecting and identifying abnormality of brain tumor. Soft Comput. **23**(19), 9083–9096 (2018). https://doi.org/10.1007/s00500-018-3618-7

Design and Research of Civil Aircraft Flap/Flap Control Lever Based on Ergonomics

Fang Zhang[✉], Xianchao Ma[✉], Yinbo Zhang[✉],
and Ruijie Fan[✉]

COMAC Shanghai Aircraft Design and Research Institute, No. 5188 Jinke Road,
Pudong New Area, Shanghai, China
{zhangfang1,maxianchao,zhangyinbo,fanruijie}@comac.cc

Abstract. The Flap/Slat Control Lever is one of the important controls in the cockpit of a High Lift system. The design of the Flap/Slat Control Lever includes mechanical and electronic design, which needs to meet the requirements of functional interfaces, mechanical interfaces, electronic interfaces, ergonomics, airworthiness, safety, reliability and maintainability. The Flap/Slat Control Lever design is a complex process with multiple rounds of iteration and gradual progress. The overall shape, detent system design must conform to the pilot's control habits, have good control comfort and accessibility, the shape of the knob is smooth, easy to identify, simple, smooth and accurate operation. The gate design must satisfy the airworthiness regulations. The design process needs to integrate ergonomics, sample collection, evaluation methods, probability statistics and other factors for comprehensive design.

Keywords: Civil aircraft · Flap/Slat Control Lever · Ergonomics

1 Introduction

The Flight Control System mainly comprises Primary Flight Control System and High Lift System, wherein the Primary Flight Control System is mainly used for realizing roll, pitch and yaw control, trim control and air deceleration of an airplane in the air, lifting breaking-up control after the airplane is grounded; The High Lift System is mainly used to control the lift and drag of the aircraft during take-off and landing. The Flap/Slat Control Lever is one of the important control devices of the High Lift System in the cockpit, and the flap and slat surface are positioned at the command position according to the preset speed through the command of the Flap/Slat Control Lever. The design of Flap/Slat Control Lever includes mechanical and electronic design, which needs to satisfy the requirements of functional interface, mechanical interface, electronic interface, man-machine work efficiency, airworthiness, safety, reliability and maintainability.

The design of Flap/Slat Control Lever is a complicated process with multiple rounds of iteration and gradual progress. The overall appearance, detent system design shall conform to the pilot's control habits, with good control comfort and accessibility. The control lever shall be smooth in appearance, easy to identify, simple, stable and accurate to operate. The detent system design shall meet the requirements of airworthiness regulations. The design process needs to integrate ergonomics, sample

D. Harris and W.-C. Li (Eds.): HCII 2020, LNAI 12187, pp. 454–461, 2020.
https://doi.org/10.1007/978-3-030-49183-3_35

collection, evaluation methods, probability statistics and other factors for comprehensive design.

Based on ergonomics design theory and CATIA three-dimensional motion simulation, this paper analyzes the ergonomics characteristics of the Flap/Slat Control Lever of a civil aircraft, and makes a detailed analysis on the overall shape design, detent system design, control force and other details of the Flap/Slat Control Lever.

2 The Design of Flap/Slat Control Lever

The design of Flap/Slat Control Lever includes knob shape, detent system, lifting force and friction force design and so on. At each design stage, ergonomic evaluation needs to be performed in conjunction with pilot evaluation methods.

2.1 Design of the Knob's Shape

The general shape design of the Flap/Slat Control Lever should meet the following design requirements [1]:

a) The Flap/Slat Control Lever should satisfy the general shape shown in Fig. 1, but need not be designed to its exact size and specific proportions;
b) The shape of the Flap/Slat Control Lever should be designed so that mis-operation is unlikely to occur, and measures should be taken to prevent it from being mis-handled during flight.

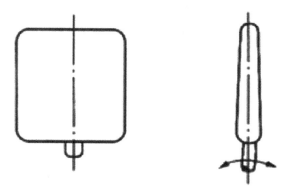

Fig. 1. Outline design requirements of Flap/Salt Control Lever

The main design contents of the Flap/Slat Control Lever include:

a) Movement axis point;
b) Flap/Slat Control Lever stroke;
c) Unlocking stroke of Flap/Slat Control Lever;

d) The distribution angle of the Flap/Slat Control Lever and the angle between two card slot;
e) Slope of Flap/Slat Control Lever's knob;
f) Weight and center of gravity position;
g) Height of Flap/Slat Control Lever;
h) Flap/Slat Control Lever knob's height, width and depth.

Figure 2 shows the outline of a typical Flap/Slat Control Lever.

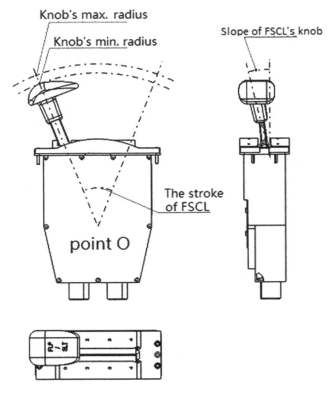

FSCL: Flap/Slat Control Lever

Fig. 2. Outline view of a typical Flap/Slat Control Lever

The shape design of the Flap/Slat Control Lever needs to be considered in combination with the unlocking method of the handle operating mechanism. At present, there are two main ways to unlock the Flap/Slat Control Lever of the civil aircraft in service:

a) Lift up the Flap/Slat Control Lever, as shown in Fig. 3;
b) Unlock the locking plate, as shown in Fig. 4.

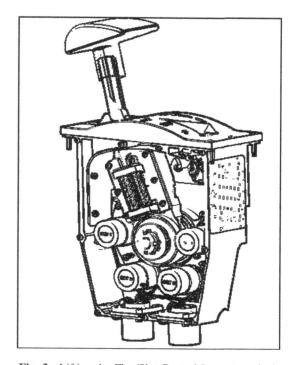

Fig. 3. Lifting the Flap/Slat Control Lever to unlock

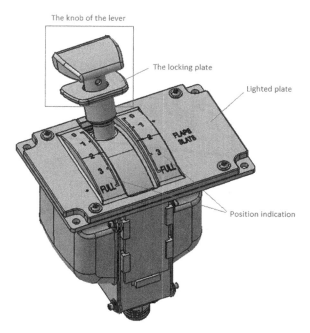

Fig. 4. Flap/Slat Control Lever with locking plate unlocking method

The shape of the handle selected by different aircraft manufacturers has its own characteristics. The shape of the handle directly determines the ergonomics. According to the experience of investigating pilots to operate the Flap/Slat Control Lever in multiple pilot evaluations, we can see that the designer cannot blindly follow the pilot's opinions to design, because different pilots have different opinions, which is related to their professional background, habits and preference, and the opinions of pilots are not the same all the time. Under different time and different physical conditions, their experience of using the knob is different. Therefore, the designer should consider the pilot's opinions and their own experience to consider the design.

2.2   The Design of Detent System

Figure 5 is a schematic diagram of a typical Flap/Slat Control Lever detent system design. The specific requirements of the detent system design of the Flap/Slat Control Lever are as follows:

a) The design of the detent system and gate should meet the configuration requirements of the flap and slat;

b) The design of the detent system should be clear, and ensure that the Flap/Slat Control Lever is released from any position, and the handle can automatically be drawn into the adjacent card slot without using external force;

c) The gate of the Flap/Slat Control Lever should ensure that the handle must have a distinctly different independent movement to move the device through the set position of the handle.

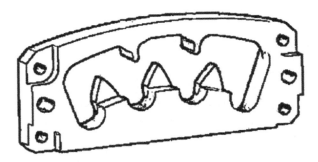

Fig. 5. Typical detent system design

The Flap/Slat Control Lever in Fig. 5 has 4 evenly divided card positions and 2 gate design. The design of the detent system should be designed in combination with the lifting force and the friction force, so that the handle cannot stay between the card positions. According to experience: If the pilot puts the handle near the card position, the handle should be automatically drawn into the adjacent card slot without using external force, instead of staying between the two card positions [2]. There should be a clear position indication on the Flap/Slat Control Lever lighted plate to remind the pilot where the handle is. The lighted plate provides monochromatic light through a light emitting diode (LED), and the brightness can be adjusted to meet the light requirements of different weather. The design of the gates in Fig. 5 are bio-directional gates. That is, when the Flap/Slat Control Lever is operated forward or backward at the position of the gate, it must be drawn into the corresponding slot to continue to manipulate the handle. A gate is a device that must have a distinctly different independent movement in order to move the lever through its set position. The purpose of the gate is to prevent the pilot from malfunctioning and make the lever of the lift device pass the gate [2]. The design of the detent system needs to meet the corresponding airworthiness regulations, which should be clear, specific and reasonable.

2.3   The Design of Feel Force

The feel force design of the Flap/Slat Control Lever should include the unlocking force and friction force of the handle. The design process needs to consider:

a)   The unlocking force of the handle is generally generated by a spring. It is unlocked by lifting the handle or compressing the unlocking plate of the handle, and it should remain unchanged during the entire handle movement. A typical flap/slat handle unlocking force mechanism is shown in Fig. 6;

b)   The friction of the handle is generally generated by the friction device. When the handle is not moving, the frictional force should keep the handle in the corresponding slot without shifting or shaking; when the handle is moving, the frictional force provides the pilot's feel force. A typical flap/slat handle friction mechanism is shown in Fig. 7;

c)   The operating force of the Flap/Slat Control Lever should be smooth without any impact or discomfort; under any displacement and amplitude of the Flap/Slat Control Lever, the minimum speed and frequency of the operating must be guaranteed;

d)   The unlocking force and friction force shall be in accordance with the ergonomic design and guaranteed to remain unchanged throughout the whole life cycle.

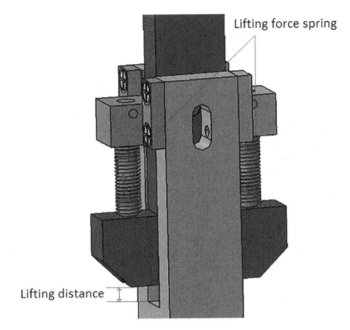

Fig. 6. Typical Flap/Slat Control Lever unlocking force mechanism [2]

Fig. 7. Typical Flap/Slat Control Lever friction mechanism

2.4   Other Design Requirements

The design of the Flap/Slat Control Lever also needs to meet the following requirements:

a) The number of sensors shall meet the system redundancy design requirements; The sensor of each position should meet the requirement of accuracy and keep the same in the whole life cycle. The type selection of the sensor should consider the electrical interface, durability, reliability and mechanical environment requirements;

b) The limited load on the Flap/Slat Control Lever shall meet the requirements of FAR25/JAR25/CCRA 25 parts, such as 25.305 and 25.405;

c) In order to ensure that the Flap/Slat Control Lever can be easily removed and replaced, the Flap/Slat Control Lever and the lighted plate on the lever can be used as the replaceable parts of the airline to reduce the maintenance cost of the airline and increase the competitiveness of the product;

d) The connectors shall be designed to avoid to the wrong installation of equipment;

e) The Flap/Slat Control Lever is installed on the central console of the cockpit, behind the throttle lever, aligned or deviated to the center line of the central console at least 254 mm behind the Landing Gear Control Device;

f) The Flap/Slat Control Lever shall be designed for easy disassembly and assembly, which can be completed without special openings designed on the central console;

g) Flap/Slat Control Lever shall meet the requirements of bonding, it is generally recommended to use surface bonding, and special bonding surfaces shall be reserved on the central control table to avoid direct bonding on the surface of the central control table, which the bonding area is too large to be easy for workers to operate, so it is difficult to meet the requirements of bonding. It is not recommended to use the fastener bonding mode, because the mounting force of the handle is too small and changed to meet the bonding requirements;

h) Commonality shall be considered to ensure the exchange of as many parts, small components or large components as possible.

3 Conclusion

This paper mainly introduces the design process of the Flap/Slat Control Lever of civil aircraft, including the shape design of the Flap/Slat Control Lever, the design of detent system, the design of feel force and sensor design. The design process of the Flap/Slat Control Lever of civil aircraft is a systematic process, which requires the system to consider the functional requirements, ergonomics, airworthiness and other requirements [2]. For the same aircraft manufacturer, it is necessary to consider the commonality of interfaces, electrical plugs, etc., so as to achieve the interchangeability of as many parts and components as possible between serial aircraft and between different series of aircraft, and even the interchangeability of handles, so as to provide its economy and competitiveness.

References

1. China Civil Aviation Regulations Part 25 R4. Airworthiness standards transport category airplanes. Civil Aviation Authority of China (CAAC), November 2011. (in Chinese)
2. Zhang, F.: The research of flap/slat control lever design process in civil aircraft. Sci. Technol. Innov. Guide **11**(24), 28–30 (2014)
3. Xue, Y., Zhang, C., et al.: Civilian aircraft control wheel design based on human factors. J. Aeronaut. **32**, 1–7 (2011)

Author Index

Printed in the United States
By Bookmasters